WILLIAM TEMPLE
ARCHBISHOP OF CANTERBURY

At Bishopthorpe, York

WILLIAM TEMPLE

ARCHBISHOP OF CANTERBURY

HIS LIFE AND LETTERS

By F. A. IREMONGER, *Frederic Athelwold* 1878-

SOMETIME CHAPLAIN TO THE KING AND HONORARY
CHAPLAIN TO ARCHBISHOP (TEMPLE) OF YORK
M.A. (OXON.) HON. D.D. (GLASGOW)
DEAN OF LICHFIELD

GEOFFREY CUMBERLEGE
OXFORD UNIVERSITY PRESS
LONDON NEW YORK TORONTO

Oxford University Press, Amen House, London E.C. 4

GLASGOW NEW YORK TORONTO MELBOURNE WELLINGTON
BOMBAY CALCUTTA MADRAS CAPE TOWN

Geoffrey Cumberlege, Publisher to the University

First published 1948
Second impression 1948

IN PIAM MEMORIAM

GULIELMI TEMPLE

VIRI DOCTI INTREPIDI HILARIS

CUM IN ECCLESIA TUM IN REPUBLICA

RES EXCELLENTIORES SECUTI

QUI AMICIS CARITATIS EXEMPLO

APOSTOLI DILECTI PRAECEPTA REPRAESENTAVIT

VITAE HUMILITATE BENEVOLENTIA PIETATE

MULTIS UBIQUE

CHRISTI IMAGINEM PRAESTITIT

PREFACE

WHEN the friends and disciples of William Temple knew that his wife had asked me to write some account of his career, their feelings were mixed; but the lack of one emotion was noticeably common to them all. As I first looked through their letters—it seems now a very long three years ago—I found not one which suggested that the writer was moved to envy; but they almost all expressed the gracious conviction that whoever undertook so formidable a task, if he were a man to be pitied, was also one to be helped. To the Archbishop's friends, therefore, I owe much of what may be of any value in these pages, and I offer more particular thanks to a few in the 'Acknowledgements' at the end of the book.

The larger part of my debt is due to Temple himself. Every man, he once wrote, 'is in a sense the author of his own biography'; and in the first annual lecture of the Book Council (delivered in the year before his death) he suggested the principle that should govern the biographer's choice of his material: 'The selection of events is that which helps us to see the life of the hero as a whole ... and so to understand the various parts of his life in relation to one another, with enough historical context to see how he fits into it or grows out of it.' I have done my best to act on this advice, but some stress must be laid on the perplexities with which the writer is faced who attempts to apply the method to a life so crammed with interests and incidents as Temple's. This book, it must be emphasized, is not for the specialist: it will satisfy neither the theologian, nor the sociologist, nor the historian— though I have tried to remember that, in dealing with the career of an Archbishop of Canterbury, the biographer cannot avoid making some contribution to Church history. I must risk raising doubts in the historian's mind whether 'enough historical context' is supplied, more especially in that section of the book which covers the years at Bishopthorpe and Lambeth; and a word is demanded, if not of apology, at least of explanation.

The difficulty of grouping actions and events, writings and speeches, principles and purposes, in that period is hardly to be imagined except by one who has struggled with it. Up to the end of the Manchester episcopate Temple's life pursues a direct and clearly defined course. After that the story becomes—to use one of his own favourite phrases—'quite immensely' complicated. In the effort to arrange the available material from 1929 onwards, again and again I found myself many years back in imagination—standing on the terrace at the Crystal Palace on a 'Brock's Benefit' night. A huge but harmless rocket is shot to what seems a vast height in the air; there is a moment of suspense, after which it bursts into a score of brilliantly coloured stars. Something like this happened, after the swift and straight flight of the early period, in the last fifteen years of Temple's life. Two of his friends wrote independently of the momentary 'poise' that they detected at the outset of his northern primacy before the stars began to coruscate and he flung himself with unsparing, and at times reckless, vigour into the active pursuit of his (and his friends') ideals. There seemed to be no other method of recording his innumerable activities than to follow, so to say, each star in its separate course, even if in doing so one played fast and loose with the strict order of events. Readers who like their chronology neatly tabulated—though they may find some of their requirements met by the Summary of Events—will perforce be disappointed. Thus Chapter XXIV, on the Oecumenical Movement, covers three decades; in the chapter portraying Temple as a Christian leader in War-time, the later Bishopthorpe and all the Lambeth years are telescoped; Chapter XXV contains Temple's views at several different periods of his life on a number of loosely connected problems of social living; and the estimate of his character, personality, and genius is placed (in Chapter XXVII) before the story of his rule at Lambeth. This last arrangement is deliberate, my hope being that the events of those two and a half years (including such incidents as the Albert Hall meeting in September 1942 and all that flowed from it) will be more intelligible if the reader has some mental picture of the man who was the central figure in them all, whose 'life as a whole' was not merely the successful career of an Anglican Primate, but was also the life of the greatest spiritual leader and the outstanding moral force in the Britain of his day—and, above all, of a prophet of God.

To whatever discontent with the shape or substance of the book the historian may be moved, the philosopher will, I hope, have little reason to share it. No biography, however slightly it might touch on Temple's thought, could be even adequately compiled without some account of this side of his learning; and such a contribution, to do justice both to him and the writer, had to be made by a philosopher for philosophers. To have produced such an essay myself would have been an impertinence, and the Professor of Philosophy in the University of Manchester has very kindly filled this gap. I am deeply grateful to Miss Dorothy Emmet both for the essay—in which her skill will have made Temple's thought intelligible not only to philosophers but to many less erudite readers as well—and also for her (somewhat reluctant) consent to dispense with footnotes to the text. (At the end of his brilliant study of Talleyrand, sixteen years ago, Mr. Duff Cooper gave more than enough reasons for eliminating these superfluous and disfiguring appendages, and thereby set a fashion which deserves to be widely followed.) But Professor Emmet's chapter provokes a further suggestion.

This is the third book on William Temple to be published since his death. Both Canon A. E. Baker's selections from Temple's writings (with a biographical sketch by the Bishop of Chichester) published under the title *William Temple and his Message*, and the composite volume *William Temple: An Estimate and an Appreciation* by six of his friends, have already helped many to some understanding of his character and genius. A fourth book remains to be produced. 'It would be of great interest', wrote Bishop Brilioth (in a letter from which a fuller passage is quoted on p. 605) 'if his philosophical ideas could be analysed in connexion with his sociological and devotional writings'. Here is a task ready to the hand of some fully equipped thinker and critic—to analyse and correlate the constituent parts of that complete system in which every branch of Temple's thought (alike in religion, philosophy, and sociology) was finally integrated. The work would not be easy. It demands a writer of patient industry, wide sympathy, and acute discernment. But it would be, not least for the benefit of future generations, worth all the labour entailed in its production.

It should be mentioned that, in reproducing Temple's letters, I have taken the easiest course. Except where there is an obvious mistake the punctuation, spelling, and capital letters are printed exactly as he wrote them, even though this may occasionally produce odd results: on the same page, for instance, the word 'judgement' may be found to be spelt in two different ways, the House Rules of the Oxford University Press demanding the insertion (as in the Book of Common Prayer) of a second 'e' which Temple (with the support of the Authorized Version of the Holy Bible) eschewed.

The rest of this prefatory note must be largely (but I hope not unduly) personal. More than once I have been tempted, in relating this or that incident in Temple's life, to point the moral; but always within reach of my arm there has lain the transcript of an address that sounds a cautionary note for the biographer who would turn propagandist. In November 1901 the late Lord Oxford and Asquith, out of his wide knowledge of literature and in that flowing and polished English of which he was a master— the *Hansard* of our day makes sad enough reading for those who can recall something of the culture that has passed from the speech of our public life—gave an address on 'Biography' at the Edinburgh Philosophical Institution. There is hardly a sentence in it which the humblest man of letters will not cherish, and to the biographer in particular this counsel is offered: 'The bias of kinship, the blindness of discipleship, are undeniable hindrances to just and even-handed judgment. *But the true biographer is not a judge.*' To discuss the words I have italicized, and to set against them in argument the considered opinions of no less learned dissentients, would be to go far beyond my present purpose. Let me be content to write that in the body of the book—loyal 'disciple' of Temple though I must confess to being—I have done my best to heed Lord Oxford's warning. It is therefore with a moderately clear conscience that I allow myself to pass one judgement and to draw one lesson for the Church, in this preface, from

Temple's life. In an article which appeared in the *Spectator* a week after the Archbishop's death, the Bishop of Southwell wrote:

But there is a warning, and we must not neglect it. Apart from his share in the high affairs of State, the Archbishop of Canterbury has to carry a crushing burden of administration and of sheer relentless routine work of which the public has simply no idea. He has nothing like an adequate secretariat and is asked to do the work of a Prime Minister with the apparatus of a headmaster. At the time of Dr. Temple's translation fears were felt that he might be overwhelmed by it, and find himself unable to continue what he had hitherto done so brilliantly. He refused to allow that to happen. He was everywhere, unspared and unsparing, constantly travelling up and down the country under the trying conditions of war-time, addressing audiences of every kind and touching the life of the nation at every point. He still persisted in putting into practice his own interpretation of his office and of national religious leadership. He did this not by shirking or neglecting the unrespiting official work of Lambeth—which is in itself more than a man can carry—or the pastoral care of his diocese, but by attempting to do this all at once. It killed him. Is the Church so rich in prophets that it can afford to squander the gifts of God? This lesson must be laid to heart. Some rearrangement has become imperative.

I would like to think that for the last three and a half years our bishops have been busy in planning and propagating such a rearrangement as that of which Dr. Barry wrote while the re-collection of Temple's life and death was still vivid: but human memories are notoriously short, and the Church still lacks its G.H.Q., that department devoted to planning and strategy—by whatever name it may be called—of which the need is constantly and continuously felt in the day-to-day work of our National Church. Nearly thirty years ago Charles Gore wrote to Temple: 'Episcopacy is only carrying on'—and the words have not lost their sting to-day. No matter whether thirty or three hundred bishops assemble at Lambeth this summer, there will be no halt in

Preface

the gradual disintegration from within with which the home Church is threatened until our whole method of strategy is—not reorganized because at present (as another bishop, Dr. Wilson of Chelmsford, has written) of strategy there is 'none'—but planned, prepared, and put into execution, with the help of the best and most imaginative brains, lay as well as clerical, that the Church can command. The growing intensity with which, during the forty-two years of my ministry, I have felt this conviction has been deepened by a succession of experiences, two of which are relevant to the production of this book. One was the last talk which I had with Temple in his study at Lambeth. As I looked across the hearthrug at that spent man with the tired eyes and ill-regulated engagement-book whom Christians of every name were trusting for leadership and inspiration in the post-war years, I could only ask, with shame and amazement, Dr. Barry's question: 'Is the Church so rich in prophets that it can afford to squander the gifts of God?' The second experience has been my study of the career which I have tried in these pages to portray; and, as I lay down the task, my last word is an appeal to the leaders of our National Church to undertake this 'imperative rearrangement'. If an excuse for the presumption of such a request in this context must be offered, let it be that I had planned, as my swan-song, a book on the subject which has now had to be abandoned; and I make no doubt whatever that my old friend would have been among the first to grant me the compensation of these few paragraphs, in which to point just one of the morals of his devoted life.

F. A. I.

Easter 1948

xii

CONTENTS

Contents

ILLUSTRATIONS

I

Home

Please don't waste the opportunity of writing a nice letter, by telling me
to do what I really like and not consider you, because whatever the
reasons may be, what I really like is to be at home.

W. T., letter to his mother, November 1899.

AMONG the letters and documents left by William Temple
is a sheet of linen-paper measuring about thirty inches by
twenty, on which is inscribed an elaborate genealogical tree, with
many branches and offshoots. It begins in the left-hand top
corner with Leofric Earl of Mercia, friend of Edward the Con-
fessor and husband of Lady Godiva, who died in 1057. The line
is continued through his son Ælfgar whose daughter Aldgyth
married the last of the Saxon Kings, and whose son assumed the
name of Temple, from the Manor of Temple near Hellesborough.
A 'de' appears before 'Temple' for many generations, after which
the head of the family becomes plain John, William, or Thomas
through the centuries that follow. How far this tree is accurate,
and what claim (if any) William Temple had to a place in it,
appears uncertain; probably he did not take it very seriously, but
in a letter to his brother in June 1926 on the subject he wrote:

> Of course Father used a coat of arms taken from the Duke
> of Buckingham's coat—and similarly the crest—so I suppose
> he convinced the College of Heralds of his right to do it.
> And his signature was the *fac simile* of that of the Sir William
> Temple who was a prominent statesman at the end of the 17th
> century.

A less distant retrospect discloses that William Temple's
great-grandfather was James Boswell's lifelong friend William
Johnson Temple, whom we know better (with his 'drab and
peevish wife and a pleasant grown-up family') since Wyndham Lewis wrote *The Hooded Hawk*; and that his grandfather,
Major Octavius Temple, after spending the early years of his

manhood out of England, returned home and lived at Axon, in Devonshire, on a farm which he bought and worked for a few years before taking up another appointment abroad as Governor of Sierra Leone. The thirteenth of Major Temple's fifteen children was Frederick Temple—Scholar and Fellow of Balliol, Headmaster of Rugby, Bishop of Exeter and of London, and Archbishop of Canterbury—of whom the full tale has been told in the two volumes of his biography.

William Temple was the younger of the Archbishop's two sons. He was born at the Palace, Exeter, during his father's tenure of the see, on 15 October 1881 (more than two years after his brother, now Colonel Frederick Charles Temple, C.I.E.), and was christened in Exeter Cathedral on 6 November, after the Second Lesson at Evensong. Before he was four years old his father had been translated to London; and the home of his boyhood, till he was fifteen, was Fulham Palace. Of the family life at Fulham, and later at Lambeth, much has already been written in the biography of Temple's father. At the heart of it was his mother, Beatrice Lascelles, whose letters to her friends, especially to Lady Frederick Cavendish, tell something of the happiness that began with her engagement, and grew in depth and range as sons were born to her and she came to accept the responsibilities of her position. For this she was eminently fitted by birth, breeding, and temperament. Born in 1845, she was the youngest of the nine children of the Rt. Hon. William Saunders Sebright Lascelles (a younger son of the Earl of Harewood) and Lady Caroline Howard, daughter of the sixth Earl of Carlisle. Most of her youth had been spent at Castle Howard and Naworth, and there were frequent visits to grandparents at Harewood, to Chatsworth, Holker, and Hagley. One of her husband's chaplains remembers Mrs. Temple telling him how as a child she had had the run of Bath House, Devonshire House, and Stafford House; and 'when first I got into the Lords', the old Archbishop used to say, 'I treated them all with respect; after I got married I treated them as cousins; and was generally right.'

But this distinction was of less importance inside the home circle than Mrs. Temple's more personal qualities, one of which

her son described in a letter to a Repton friend on her death in
1915:

> There was a spaciousness of mind about her and others of
> her generation which I don't think modern methods and girls'
> colleges tend to produce. She was never *taught* anything. She
> got rid of her governess when 11 years old; but she lived in
> houses where most of the leading folk assembled from time to
> time. No doubt Girton or Somerville is better than home for
> most. But to be about the place from childhood on, while
> Gladstone, Dizzy, Harcourt, Mat Arnold, Balfour, talked at
> large, must be better still.

The extent of his father's influence—in guiding, warning,
teaching, and stimulating—on Temple's life is beyond compute.
Much of it will appear in these pages; enough to say here that the
Archbishop won from his children their complete devotion, their
unaffected reverence, and a confidence that was absolute: 'Father
says so' clinched every argument. Contradiction would have
been sacrilege, and there was no appeal. 'Father will never tell
me his views', Temple once wrote from Balliol, 'because he knows
how much I am tempted to accept them without thinking.'

Two other personalities strongly affected Temple in his
nursery and schoolroom days. One of them was his old 'Nana',
Ellen Langdon, for whom he had a deep affection which lasted
till her death. Like himself she was a Devonian, the daughter of
a country station-master, who was a remarkable mechanic and
also something of an amateur astronomer. (He made several
photographic cameras, his own seven-inch equatorially mounted
reflecting telescope, and the observatory with a revolving roof in
which it was housed. The lenses and mirrors had all been ground
and polished with his own hand, after he had first made the
necessary tools. He was also responsible for a notable discovery
about Venus, which was accepted by the leading astronomers as
adding to their knowledge of the planet.) Ellen Langdon became,
as old Nanas of those days often did, an institution—perhaps too
much of an institution—in the household, and it was not until his
marriage that she suggested it was time for her to leave him. 'It

3

is just as horrid as anything can be', Temple wrote soon after his engagement to Frances Anson, 'but I am sure you are right . . . you know I can never say what I feel that I owe you, still less even properly thank you. But you won't want thanks.' She read all his books as they came out, but confessed that parts of *Mens Creatrix* and of the Gifford Lectures were beyond her; she died in a home for the blind at St. Albans, after bequeathing to him almost all her savings. The second influence was that of his governess, Edith Maskell, who was first called in to help in addressing the 1,700 invitations issued yearly to the Fulham Palace garden parties, held on three different days in June. Mrs. Temple then asked her whether she would care to teach William to read; and on 31 May 1886 the governess writes in her diary: 'Began to teach Freddy and William at Fulham Palace.' To her one of Temple's earliest extant letters was written during a holiday at Dolgelly:

> Thank you very much for your nice letter. I hope the hole which the Rat poked his head into was large enough for him to get out again: for it would be rather sad if he had to stay there all the rest of his days.

Is it fanciful to detect in the eight-year-old boy a promise of that reasoned precision of statement for which the Archbishop, half a century on, was to become noted, whose passion for lucidity already led him to mistrust the authority of an Early English Reader which declared that 'The Cat sat on the Mat', because (he complained) 'It does not say *which* cat'? Whatever prejudices he may have derived from the Reader, one of them was short-lived. In later life cats were among his favourite companions; a visitor to the Old Palace, Canterbury, was surprised one day to hear, on his way to the Archbishop's study (the door of which stood open), the familiar voice raised in re-buke: 'Now, it's no good your telling me that you are not winking at me, because I know you are.' The visitor was relieved to meet a duly chastened cat slinking from the room as he entered it.

Temple spoke often and gratefully of the thorough grounding his governess gave him. 'I never wrote to you', ran a letter from

Rugby in his last term, 'to congratulate you on my Balliol Exhibition; a great part of the credit certainly belongs to you'; and on her death he wrote to her sister that Edith Maskell was 'one of the most simply good and self-denying people that I have ever known . . . her death is the loss of a very real friend'.

The day at Fulham began with prayers in the Palace Chapel. For this there was a well-established ceremonial. The boys waited in the vestry, which was separated from the chapel by a stone-flagged passage. The butler also waited, with the Bishop's surplice over his arm, and passed the time cleaning his finger-nails for the day with a pocket-knife. Mrs. Temple and other ladies would come hurrying down the passage, followed by the Bishop. He never stopped, but kissed each of his sons as he walked on; and the butler put his surplice over the Bishop's arms extended backwards, and on to his shoulders. The boys fell in beside their father, who put his arms around them, looking (as was remarked) like a large angel with wings as he entered the chapel. He turned into his stall, and William stepped over his mother's feet to take his place on her left. Going out, the boys chased after their father, who dropped his surplice just outside the door, without looking round, into the hands of the pursuing butler, and again put his arms over the shoulders of his sons. The impression left on Temple's mind by these daily prayers never faded, and more than fifty years after he wrote to a friend:

> I am constantly thinking of the enormous difference that it must have made to you and me that from a date before we could clearly remember things, we heard some verses of the Bible read every day; probably three times out of five we did not directly attend to it; but it was flowing over our growing minds, even when attention wandered, and must have been producing a great effect in making natural and spontaneous that whole outlook upon life which the Bible expresses. Whereas one of our great troubles now is that the predominant outlook upon life is formed by scientific and not by religious categories. Causation is much more prominent in men's thoughts than purpose and judgment.

The morning was given up to lessons, and in these the two boys were joined by the children of the Vicar of Fulham, with one of whom much of Temple's time was passed. Every morning in his ninth year a small boy in a blue jersey would stand whistling under the windows of the vicarage, and Agnes Fisher would run out to join William and go back to the Palace for their lessons. In the afternoon—the garden was damp and lay very low, so that children could play in it only at the height of summer—they bowled their hoops together on Putney Common. There was then little danger for children in the streets of Fulham, which was still a country village. Fulham Palace Road ran between fields or large estates, and Fulham High Street, with a few quaint old shops on either side, connected the Fulham Road with Putney Bridge—the old wooden bridge which shook when any vehicle passed over it. On wet days the Palace was an ideal house for hide-and-seek which, next to sliding down the stairs on a tea-tray, was the favourite indoor game. William's most successful *cache* was under the writing-table between his father's legs, where not even Agnes Fisher had dared to look for him. The Bishop loved to have his boys round him whenever he was at home in the evenings (one of them sometimes sitting on his knee while he was writing) even though William once dragged the inkpot across the table and spilt its contents over his father's legs. 'It was a wonderful and beautiful family life', writes one who was his father's chaplain a few years later: 'the old Archbishop sitting in the evenings at a small card-table in the Lambeth drawing-room, writing his judgement on "Incense and Lights", and the boys in no way awed to silence.' Holidays always began—year after year without fail—at Woolbeding, the home of Mrs. Temple's Howard uncle, Lord Lanerton, and later of Colonel and Mrs. Henry Lascelles, Temple's uncle and aunt; usually a week or two were spent in the Lakes, with all the preliminary glamour of travelling in a saloon-coach and having lunch on the train. Sometimes they stayed at the Prince of Wales' Hotel, Grasmere, where the boys were once puzzled by the presence of another visitor, a widow who they were convinced was the Princess of Wales, because of the pictures they had seen of Queen Victoria

6

in her widow's weeds. Here William, who was then not quite four years old, had his first sight of the Lake country and his first climbs (though often he had to be carried on his father's back for the last mile or two)—joys which remained with him to the end. Occasionally, too, there were short visits to the seaside, during one of which, at Worthing, he had a slight sunstroke, which made him very susceptible to heat for the rest of his life. Here also, a circus one day failing to amuse, the thoughts of his elder brother turned to a much more satisfying entertainment at which he occasionally assisted, and suddenly Frederick's voice shrilled to the farthest corners of the tent: 'Boy wants to see Father shave!'

It is a commonplace of ecclesiastical biography that many a future priest and bishop has begun to rehearse his part in childhood. Some have built little shrines in a wood, some have indulged in premature mortification, others have collected their earliest congregation in the nursery. Of these last Temple was one. As a child he had his own robe-case, at the top of which was laid a carefully folded surplice and a diminutive mitre. Robed in these, he would give out a hymn—'Conquering kings' was then his favourite—and preach 'usually about conduct' to the nursery-maid, Patience Knight, and any others who might be interested. To one of his admirers the time soon came to say good-bye, for the Vicar of Fulham had accepted a country living. Agnes had not forgotten William's protecting care of her—especially once when, after she had glibly recited the answer to a question in the Catechism which the Bishop had put to her, he suddenly said, 'And what does that *mean*?', and William had seen the shame of her confusion and had answered for her. It must be presumed that he returned her affection, for at a very early age the two infants were solemnly united by William in some curious form of Marriage Service of his own composition. And, now that the sweet sorrow of parting had come, what could he do but offer some token of his attachment (the little greengrocer's shop, once fitted with baskets of coloured fruit and vegetables, survives to this day) and sob: 'I know what it will be, Agnes; when you get into the country, you will find another little boy you will like

7

better than me'? And what answer was possible but the passionate 'No, William, *never!*'?

Nursery and governess days ended before his tenth birthday, and his schooling began in the summer of 1891. A bunch of rather frightened small boys waited outside a class-room in a day-school that had recently been opened—it had started in Talgarth Road—by Mr. James Bewsher in the Hammersmith Road. It was their first term; the topic of conversation was their fathers' professions, and the others were duly impressed when one boy announced with pride that his father was Bishop of London. Among his school-fellows at Colet Court was the Rev. P. B. Clayton—who received the prize awarded to the top boy in the lowest class when Temple was head of the school—and it was from John Sankey, putting in a short time as an assistant master on his way to the Woolsack, that William Temple learned his Greek alphabet: 'He had a quick understanding', Sankey remembered, 'and picked up things easily and rapidly.' Letters written to his brother during the next six years suggest that he was happy and working reasonably hard, though an occasional lapse is recorded. To judge from the following—written before he had begun to grasp the mysteries of Greek accents—one at least of his many differences with an assistant master, and the consequent punishment, depressed him little:

Oct. 22.
Fulham Palace, S.W.

Keep the monogram on the envelope it's worth having.

Dear Old Gollumpus,

. . . a little while ago Botting, meaning to give me a long impot for fooling gave me the first three tenses of λυω to write out, I put

Date	Temple W.
Upper 2A.	

Long Imposition

λυειν, λυσειν, λυσαι

And he did get in such a wax. He thumped to me right and left (it was fine). He swore he'd report me to the Headmarster.

I told him he might. He told me to write out all the Active of λύω, I said 'How fine'. I did this wonderful Active of λύω, and as I was fooling the whole time, it took me ½ an hour. So next day I told him that the night before I had 'a pleasant 10 min*u*te minutes' doing the Active of λύω. So he told Jimmy, and Jimmy giggled. Goodbye.

Your loving underpaid servant
WILLIAM.

By the end of 1893 he was head of the school in classics and class-list, to which was added mathematics in his last term. No other boy was within fifty marks of his total for the final examinations, and on 25 July 1894 he records his crowning triumph: 'Yesterday I brought home my ninth and last prize from Colet Court.' But academic achievements hold a small place in the letters of his early boyhood. There are the usual family jokes and chaff, unintelligible outside a small circle—'How is your liver?' and 'If you are discovered you are lost' appear regularly for a few weeks—and he has already 'found a formula' in excuse for not giving his brother a birthday present: 'I cannot think of anything I can give you as it seems to me that anything that you want you have got! Or else it is too expensive as I am not very rich.' A note of patronage creeps into one letter, when he has heard that his older brother 'is learning to play'. He will probably find that the organ will suit him best, and he must not mind if his fingers are a good deal stiffer than his younger brother's; the drudgery will soon be over, but he should be careful not to let music interfere with his work. For himself, his music master recommends that he should not start on the organ till he has learned to play quite perfectly on the piano all the scales, major, minor, and 'cromatic'. After giving this rather sententious advice, he feels justified in signing himself 'Your loving brother, the musician of Fulham Palace (and Church music selector) William Temple'. Church choirs already fascinate him—what could be more splendid than Stainer's 'I saw the Lord' and Attwood's *Veni Creator* sung in S. Paul's Cathedral?—and he mentions the practice of an elaborate anthem at Fulham Parish Church for a

'Middlesex Volunteer Church Parade'. There is much excitement as the day for this grand service approaches, and he mischievously records that the Vicar was (pardonably, perhaps) 'in a wax' when 'the parade was found to consist of three men'.

Holidays had the particular joys that the London schoolboy of that decade well remembers: the Crystal Palace, Corney Grain, Penley in *Charley's Aunt*—'Nana laughed till she wept'—Saturday Pops. in St. James's Hall (Joachim is 'simply glorious'); Ada Rehan in *Twelfth Night*, 'whom most people think the best actress living'; and in the spring the Boat-race, watched from the roof of Fulham Palace. He managed also to get a good view of the opening of the Tower Bridge, where after the ceremony his father gave the Blessing 'with the guns firing a royal salute'. But there is an ominous sentence in one letter to his brother. Like other boys he was vaccinated, had occasional toothache, and 'soar throat', but on 11 May 1894 he writes of 'Gout in my big toe on my right foot'. The first attack had been when he was two years old: it was to be his bane for half a century.

Church-going he treated as a matter of course. He seems to have enjoyed it, and most of the sermons he hears are recorded as 'excellent'. In June 1894 he was confirmed, and made his first Communion a week later. He knew all the canons of S. Paul's, but resented a little the patronage they were inclined to offer him. Randall Davidson once said of him, 'The trouble with dear William is, he is so kind that he cannot say No'; Temple appears to have had no such difficulty when he was thirteen years old:

I went to S. Paul's this afternoon . . . and after the service the old Virger with the thin face came up to me to ask me to go to tea with Canon Browne, so I went inside the gates and waited for him. The first person to emerge from the Dean's vestry was the Reverend Canon H. Scott Holland. He ran down the steps pointing at me and said 'Here you are; come to tea', which offer I declined. The next person to come was the Very Reverend the Dean, who said 'Any of your people with you?' 'No.' 'Did you come up by yourself?' 'Yes.' 'Well done! Come to tea.' 'No thank you.' So then Canon Browne came down and said 'Coming?' so I said I thought mother would be expecting me; so I walked off and overtook the Dean who as it was raining gave me the scarcely necessary information that I should get wet!!!

In September Temple left London for his first term at a public school. He wrote no record of his arrival at Rugby, but the memory of Lionel Smith helps to fill the gap:

I have a very clear memory of being taken by my Mother as a new boy to the School House on Sept. 27th 1894. Just at the bottom of the steps up to the private entrance we passed, coming out, two men who seemed to me old and formidable— the Bishop of London, Frederick Temple, and the Headmaster, Dr. John Percival. One of them, who was two years later to be raised to the Archbishopric of Canterbury, was the father of my earliest friend.... It was on the evening of that day that I first met William Temple, and learnt that I was to share a study with him.

II

Rugby

If you are to develop in people a sense of public spirit, it can only be done by making them members of a community in which they have a real measure of responsibility, so that they know that the tradition of the community is entrusted to them.

W.T., at the Arnold Centenary celebrations, June 1942.

What is the principle of [our] traditional education? It is that real education comes not chiefly through instruction, but chiefly through membership in a society. We take our boys and throw them into a society of boys because that is the only kind of society in which they can realize membership to the full. Games immediately become the predominant interest. That is quite right, because it is in games that the boys can really manage their own concerns. . . . It is healthy and right that games should come first provided that this is only true of a stage through which they pass as they grow up. When therefore I praise the English traditional education, I am praising education by means of a corporate life, whose main expression is through organized games.

W.T., W.E.A. Presidential Address, October 1915.

I want you to know why some Rugbeians are so intolerably conceited about their school.

W. T., letter to his wife, July 1916.

FORTY-FIVE years before William Temple went to Rugby, the Trustees of the Rugby Charity had offered the Headmastership to his father. It was refused—the claims of Kneller Hall, then a training centre for workhouse schoolmasters, were too strong—but in 1857 the opportunity recurred, and for the next twelve years Frederick Temple fulfilled the hope expressed by Matthew Arnold that 'the union of piety, energy, and cheerfulness' in which he resembled Thomas Arnold would restore the school to the eminent position from which, for no particular reason except the weakness of a rather indeterminate conservatism, it had gradually fallen. From that day there was only one school for a Temple, and in no Rugbeian persisted a deeper filial piety than that which began with William's first term and ended only with his death, when he had been chairman of the

Governors for more than seven years: his father had held the post for ten. He has, fortunately, left on record some of the reasons for his enduring loyalty. In the middle years, not long after their marriage, he was separated from his wife for a few days which he was summoned to spend at Fulham Palace in a retreat-conference of the National Mission Council. There were several spare hours in the day. During one of these Temple was standing alone, staring out on the garden and apparently wrapped in deep thought, when a member of the party who had an urgent message for him apologized for interrupting his meditations—'It does not matter,' he replied, 'I am only trying to make out which of those large trees I found it so hard to climb when I was a small boy.' Another spare hour was spent in writing to his wife: the last part of this letter gives Temple's mature judgement of Rugby School, and explains his lifelong devotion to it. After mentioning several public schools, he draws these distinctions between three of them in particular:

Fulham Palace,
July 21, 1916.

Now I said I would write you a treatise on the greatness of Rugby, and I will . . . Winchester is the oldest, and in some sense the pattern School. Being small, it has kept itself intellectually select. Its intellectual standard through the School as a whole is far and away the highest; and as regards its top forms Rugby and, at times, Eton—no others—may equal it. Eton has the most distinct individuality. It alone has not followed the principles of Arnold's reformation. It draws from the families of great tradition and therefore far outdistances all Schools in the number of leading posts which its members secure (though of course from its superior numbers it will get more of these by following the usual proportion). It has a splendidly scholarly staff, so that a boy who wants to work probably gets better teaching than anywhere else. Its tradition of freedom encourages initiative; but also facilitates idleness. As the prevailing atmosphere is that of the homes of wealth and secured position, there is an air of elegant indolence. No boy is so pleasant as the good sort of Etonian, but he is usually without much moral energy. An able boy, coming from a home whose tradition will take him into public service, is the right boy for Eton. For brilliancy of achievement in scholarship or public life, no School ever comes near it. But there, as elsewhere, the brilliant are few; and for 'the rest' Eton does not supply the needed stimulus. The School is very self-contained and has had little influence on the growth of education.

Rugby is the exact opposite. One of my father's favourite maxims for School masters sums up a great deal of it: Justice for the stupid. It makes everyone work. Probably it is the most strenuous of Schools. There is very little free time, except for boys who by working quick can make it. (E.g. I had two hours' preparation on end for two consecutive hours in School: I could nearly always do this in $\frac{1}{2}$ an hour and so got an hour and a $\frac{1}{2}$ free. It was in time so made that I read the whole of 7 English poets before I left School. So free time can be got all right.) All work is in forms as in other Schools except Eton, which of course has a lot of private tuition. This means that the cleverer often have to wait for the stupid, who must never be left to stew. The great glory of Rugby is not the brilliancy of its results—it has few Cabinet Ministers and so on—but the incomparably high level of usefulness reached by its average products. Eton will produce, say, 2 or 3 Viceroys: Rugby will produce 20 or 30 first-class provincial administrators. But before all comes its influence on other Schools. Here it far surpasses any. First there is Arnold, who first clearly put character before brains as the aim of education, and made the senior boys his colleagues for securing it. Here every School, except Eton, has followed him. Whether it is true, as we were told Etonians say, that Rugby forces boys' moral development so that they cease growth later, I don't know: it wants enquiry. (Eton is liable, with its private tuition time, to do this to clever boys' brains.) But the Rugby plan can be followed with a little less intensity than at Rugby. With Arnold begins the process of founding Schools from Rugby. Harrow first became great under Vaughan, a pupil of Arnold. Cotton went from Rugby to start Marlborough. This process

Rugby
was at its height when Father was there. Marlborough reveres
Bradley as a second founder: he went there from my father's
staff at Rugby. When the Prince Consort founded Wellington,
he asked Father to nominate a Headmaster, and he sent Benson.
When Clifton was founded, he was asked to nominate, and sent
Percival. He also sent Arthur Butler to Haileybury, and Jex-
Blake to Cheltenham. Quite lately there have gone from Rugby
—Fletcher to Marlborough and then to Charterhouse; Wynne
Willson to Haileybury and then to Marlborough; David to
Clifton and back to Rugby; Waterfield to Cheltenham; Paton
to Manchester Grammar School; George Smith to Dulwich.
So Rugby has done a wonderful lot in training the men who
have guided the other Schools.

Well: that's all. . . . Oh yes: It was the first School (of the
Public School type) to have a Rifle Corps (now the O.T.C.),
or to teach science. Also of course it is the only one whose
game has become a national sport.

If it be true that Rugby was 'the most strenuous of schools',
Temple contributed much to perpetuate this tradition; few can
have wasted less time there than he did. He was placed for his
first term (September 1894) in Upper Middle I. In the summer of
the following year he was anxious to try for a scholarship, and
his father's advice was sought and given: let him thresh it all out
with his tutor—but might not the special preparation needed and
the time spent over it interrupt his regular work? He was by then
in the Lower Fifth; he decided to enter for the scholarship, and
was elected. Progress was thenceforward unchecked. He reached
the Sixth at the earliest allowable age ($15\frac{1}{2}$), and for two years and
a half he was in the Upper Bench till he left at the end of the
summer term in 1900. Through all these years he wrote faithfully to his mother (and heard from her) daily; to his father every
Sunday; and frequently to his brother—who has kept several
hundred letters written to him by 'the young 'un' from 1899 to
1944. Of the early letters to his brother the background is the
Boer War—at first dim and distant and of little relevance;
'People here', he writes, 'are ridiculously unhappy about Buller's

15

William Temple

retreat'—but later when his brother has volunteered the interest becomes keener, and in February 1900 he tells of the excitement roused by the Queen's letter and the news that Buller has again crossed the Tugela. In the foreground are such concerns as any boy with intellectual curiosity and a good idea of enjoying himself would choose to discuss with his family: books and games, concerts and plays he has heard and seen or has taken part in, chapel services and preachers, and a new bicycle—he must consult his father about a gear-case, and should the handle-bars be 'dropped, flat or raised?'—all of it interspersed with a collection of phrases such as Hall Arch, Jimmy Shout, Ends, Belows, and the rest, which presumably were intelligible to the two Rugbeians who received his schoolboy confidences.

The time-table exactly suited him (why it suited William Temple and disgusted R. G. Collingwood would make a good subject for an Upper Bench essay to-day). On his own initiative he had read during the preparation periods, before he left school, not only the seven English poets mentioned in the letter to his wife, but also the *Phaedo* and the whole of the *De Rerum Natura*: 'The philosophy', one of his teachers suggests, 'and rough magnificence of Lucretius appealed to him more than the subtler beauties of the Virgilian metre and language.' In his belief that all were as he was—how could any intelligent boy who was able to get through two hours' work in thirty minutes spend the remaining ninety except by adding to his store of knowledge?—he always contended that this opportunity for independent study and research should be given to every promising boy; and he followed the principle in teaching the Sixth Form when he was Headmaster of Repton.

Of the Rugby masters mentioned in his letters three are specially prominent. One was Godfrey Bradby—according to Whitelaw 'the last of the schoolmaster-poets'—who was his most intimate friend on the staff, both in term (as tutor of the School House) and during holidays on the Broads, where it was Temple's delight to scramble out of Bradby's yacht and to be towed behind in the dinghy, usually fast asleep. To Bradby his gratitude for many kindnesses was deep and lasting. Everything that 'G. F.'

16

1 *and* 2. *Boyhood*

3. *At the Rugby Club Camp,*
New Romney, August 1903

wrote he read and remembered, his favourite being *The Lanches-
ter Tradition*, which he regarded as the best school story (from
the masters' angle) ever written. Another was Robert Whitelaw:
'A first-rate teacher,' as Collingwood testified, 'a man who touched
nothing that he did not adorn . . . whose obviously sincere
assumption that you knew as much as he did stimulated his
pupils to incredible feats.' In Whitelaw's judgement of the
Classics, and in his exposition of S. Paul's Epistles, Temple came
to place the same decisive confidence that in all else was given to
his father—'Whitelaw says so'; that was enough. Dr. Pickard-
Cambridge (who was to be one of his tutors at Balliol) first met
Temple during the Christmas holidays of 1899, when he was
holding a small informal reading party at Lambeth for Frederick
Temple, already his pupil at Balliol, and one or two friends.
William occasionally joined them and, whenever there was a
difference of opinion on a particular passage in the *Republic*, gave
confidently the solution offered by Whitelaw. This faith, Dr.
Pickard-Cambridge recalls, 'was unshakable and generally justified'; and it was shared by his father who, when William had
reached the Upper Bench, wrote: 'Your scholarship was growing
fast under Whitelaw.'

The third of his teachers, and a lifelong friend, was F. (now
Sir Frank) Fletcher, of whom we get a first glimpse in a letter
from Temple to his brother:

> The other day Harry [Hardy] and I . . . came in 12 minutes
> late to Unseen. Harry, ὡς καὶ Δὴ νεώτερος ὤν, went to get the
> Unseen slips. Frank asked if I had condescended to come, and
> hearing that I had, sent me his compliments with a request to
> be more punctual in future. You see he is learning manners.

('Harry' comes frequently into the Rugby letters, and the context does not always make it clear whether the reference is to
Harry Hardy or Harry Tawney. With these two, and with
Lionel Smith, his intimacy deepened throughout the school and
Oxford days.) Sir Frank Fletcher saw and heard a good deal of
him—in the rackets-court, in the school debates, and at the meetings of the literary society called 'Eranos', of which Sir Frank was

c

president: he also taught him for two years in the Upper Bench, chiefly in classical subjects, in which—at least on the linguistic side—Temple never did himself full justice. The subject-matter of an author appealed to him more strongly than points of textual criticism and prosody, even of style or form; and grammatical niceties seemed comparatively trivial when the whole world of thought and action lay behind and before him. Neither his Latin prose nor verse was first-class, for lack of the narrow intensive study which such subjects demand of the student in the early stages; 'I remember', writes Lionel Smith, 'two hexameter lines of his which his composition teacher cannot have regarded as very hopeful. One was *Jamque cucurrit per fulgentem coelum Phoebus Apollo*—which shows a magnanimous disregard for the pedantries of grammar and metre. The other (a translation of "The stately homes of England") ran—*Tecta, domus, sedes, limenque laresque beati*, which at any rate shows that when his own inspiration could not get him up the slopes of Parnassus he had the practical good sense to see what Carey's *Gradus* could do.' But though he was never a pure scholar, Temple could hardly remember the time when he was not set on mastering the works of great thinkers. Between two and four on Sunday afternoons, when most boys were never indoors, he seldom left his study till the bell rang for chapel: and on holiday in the Lakes he would sit (at the age of seventeen) in a boat through a summer's afternoon, absorbed in Kant's *Critique of Pure Reason*, while his brother and his friends were fishing or rowing.

Yet from any priggishness in this passion for learning he was entirely free. He had been brought up in the close company of older men and women of whom many were addicted to thinking. Nearly all of them could talk, and talk well; and it was just as natural to him, while still a schoolboy, to ask his father whether he did not agree that the doctrine of the Communion of Saints was sadly neglected in the Church as it was to discuss with the Archbishop, for an hour at dinner and after it, the philosophy of Coleridge and Mill, or to go from his Kant to the same infallible authority with the question: 'Why do not philosophers rule the world, Father? Would it not be a good thing if they did?' His father's quick and emphatic answer—'They do rule it, silly, five hundred years after they are dead'—stirred his imagination, and from that day his attitude to all learning was fixed. It was not, then, to the tedious futility of word-splitting, nor yet to the hazardous solution of irrelevant and abstract problems, that the philosophers were dedicated. Their day would come: there was a conservation of intellectual and moral energy; and the accumulated wisdom of the ages would not be wasted. For one brief period, indeed, he had serious thoughts of testing his vocation as a philosopher; but gradually, still under the influence of his father's words and example and by the strong bent of his own inclinations, his concern with philosophy became centred on its practical significance for the conduct of life, and—when he grew conscious that there was a social problem—for the proper ordering of society.

This was a later development. As yet his business was to extract and absorb the learning of the wise on any subject that interested him—and few did not—and then to bring the results of his ceaseless, if sometimes superficial, cerebrations to the touchstone of the Archbishop's experience and erudition: so there poured into Lambeth a torrent of letters in which questions, criticisms, and conclusions were jumbled together and flung at his father to be disentangled. Very patiently and usually with gravity the Archbishop, snatching odd moments from his day's engagements, did his full share of the work and attempted to satisfy his son's untiring curiosity—on predestination and free will; on omnipotence and suffering; on the contrasting philosophies of Aeschylus and Euripides; on Descartes (whose *Cogito, ergo sum* Temple had found more convincing since he had been 'thinking a little about Brahminism'); on the scholastic philosophy, Butler's *Analogy*, and Bacon's *Advancement of Learning* (the author, Temple notes, has considerable 'felicity of illustrating by image and metaphors' but is 'too metaphysical'); on the book of Ezekiel (then his favourite among the Prophets), the Epistle to the Hebrews (does his father agree that Apollos is as likely to have written it as anyone?), and Ecclesiastes (eight closely written sheets on the alleged 'pessimism' of the author!); on a dozen other books, and above all on his father's Bampton Lectures, in which the Archbishop had presumed to criticize Kant, whose Categorical Imperative held his son under an early fascination. He even goes so far as to wonder whether 'Kant's system would not finally settle the question of the Real Presence, as it seems to solve all other metaphysical problems'. (This was the system which, six years later, he was to sum up in the one word 'bosh'!) The following are samples of the letters he wrote to his father during his last year at Rugby:

Dec: 8.

My dear Father,   S[chool] H[ouse] R[ugby].

I was rather interested this morning in a distinction which Gardiner draws between Dante and Milton. He says, 'To the Catholic Dante the complete submission of the individual human will to the Divine will is the final end and complete consummation of the Christian life, beyond which no work is conceivable as proceeding from the individual man. To the Puritan Milton the submission of the individual will to the Divine will was the beginning of the work.' It seems to me that the former is far nearer to the true conception of religion. When S. Augustine said 'Love God, and then do what you like', he meant, of course, that what such a man likes is to do what is right. But surely in this case we may consider the actions as necessitated, not by Fate but by Faith. If a man really believes in God, he cannot do wrong.

It seems to me, from the little I know of him, that in Dante there was a much greater harmony of intellect and spirit. It is quaint when he says that Satan was taller than three tall Germans, but does he say anything so incongruous as are Milton's remarks about Angels' digestive powers, when Adam asks Raphael to breakfast? Or even as the description of the very material battle in heaven? Milton's spiritual weakness and want of dignity is sufficiently shown in his *Eikonoklastes* and Pamphlets on Divorce. I get rather annoyed at the way in which some people set him up as a saint. I suspect Milton's submission to the Divine will was almost purely intellectual, and a matter of philosophical morality rather than genuine religion.

Oct. 16th.

My dear Father,   S. H. R.

I was given α and α- for two essays last week, the first on historical analogies, the second on *Studia abeunt in mores*. In the second I introduced Kant's statement that 'Imitation has no place in morals'. Against this was put this objection:— 'If you accept Kant, no human being is ever fully moral; no one really obeys the Categorical Imperative purely for its own sake.' But why should we be required to believe that anyone ever is fully moral? Kant says that religious hope is given to counteract our lusts, and then the conscience can be obeyed, so that he would never have asserted that any action was fully moral, because there is first the bias of this hope. But this hope does not come of itself, and it is the possession of it, and not the actions resultant from it, that is the fulfilment of the moral law. Nor can we say that no one obeys the law simply for itself. I should think it had been done over and over again, but even so, the man is only doing his duty: to be fully moral (in the negative sense) is all that we can attain to in God's eyes. For

> Merit is from man to man,
> And not from man, O Lord, to Thee.

There is a great advantage about Kant's system, which had not struck me before. If we consider that Time is a real object, of the nature of an eternal progress, and then say that God cannot change, as we must say, we shall very nearly destroy the Personality of our Idea; God will appear to us to be a fixed Law, capable of no modification, and if a Person at all—then a Person incapable of action; for action implies change of some sort, though not necessarily of character: and, which is far more important, we shall be unable to state with reason that prayers can have any effect. But if we abolish Time, God's Personality is just like ours; His real Essence is unaffected by Time; yet He is revealed to our sensibility by actions, representing in phenomena the Object of Deity. I think this argument is correct, and, if so, it is certainly one of the strongest I know in favour of Kant's system.

And so on—week after week, and term after term. In another letter he encloses two essays, in one of which 'I was told that I was too theological. I asked Cole how one could discuss "Ghosts" without being theological and he only said it was not what he wanted. He also said some people would object to my discussing S. Paul's vision and a banshee under one head, but I made him confess that that was because they do not think. He wanted an exposition of the ordinary individual's view; but I see no good in that.' Nor can he resist sending his mother a dissertation on his favourite character in all literature:

My dear Mother,

On Friday evening I was at supper with Bob Whitelaw. He had been quite captivated by Sarah Bernhardt's Hamlet. He said he neither missed the English nor the metre, which says a good deal for her power. But my prejudices are rather strengthened than otherwise by the following considerations. When Hamlet is told by Polonius that the actors are arrived and replies 'Buz buz', she introduces a bee and places it upon Polonius' nose! When he is asking Rosencrantz and Guildenstern to play upon the recorder, they come up to Hamlet keeping very close together; she (for *he* never did such a thing) puts her hands on their shoulders and then suddenly knocks their heads together! Hamlet could never have dreamt of doing such a thing. I can just excuse making Hamlet sad throughout, though it is a misrepresentation; he is sad, but not continually or morbidly so: he genuinely amuses himself with Polonius. In my essay on 'Was Hamlet mad?', which by the way was sent up, Cole put a ? against my statement that 'we *love* Hamlet as a madman cannot be loved'. If he does not love Hamlet he had better do nothing but read the play till he does, which will come some day: 'we needs must love the highest when we see it' and though Hamlet is not perfect he is one of the 'highest': he is nobler than Brutus, greater than Kent or Edgar, more deeply interesting than Romeo, tenderer than Coriolanus, more constant than Othello: these seem to me the most lovable characters in Shakespeare, and Hamlet has the advantage of them all. I am surprised to find how few people realize that a motive power in his mind equal to the Ghost's visit and sometimes stronger is his love of his mother. Only when his mother is dead and will not live to mourn for Claudius, and above all is to be avenged as well as his Father, does Hamlet rouse himself to kill Claudius. This is helped by the thought, which is only a secondary motive, that he has not long to live and must act now or never.

Most of his letters to his mother were on homelier and less controversial topics. It is humiliating, he admits, to find that so promising a philosopher as himself should be looked upon by the whole House as 'a sort of public buffoon', but 'perhaps it is a good thing to be able to amuse people'. There are frequent requests for jam (strawberry or blackberry, for choice), coffee cake, and guava jelly; and he tells her of a broken stylographic pen, 'which is the more unfortunate as I have been buying a good many books as well as eating ices. Comprennez-vous? If so, please tell Father.' When his father was appointed Archbishop of Canterbury—Lionel Smith was the first of his friends to hear the news as they were walking together on a Sunday afternoon— he wrote:

> We are very much excited. When do we begin to call him 'Your Grace'? We went and told some people this afternoon and Ginger said 'What a sell for Mrs. Peterborough! We shall have an ideal archbishopess, she'll be at home in the purple.'

Mrs. Creighton's retort, had she known of Ginger's sympathy, would have been worth hearing.

Of his two headmasters he was more attracted to his godfather Percival, for whom he had an affectionate veneration (which he expressed in the biography he wrote of him) than to James, whom he regarded with a respect tinged with amusement, though he was deeply moved by the letter he had from James on the eve of his ordination: 'Every day', his old headmaster wrote on 18 December 1908, 'I pray for every Rugby boy of my time who has taken or is meaning to take Holy Orders, so far as I know them: and it is getting a long list now, thank God.' These were not the days when James's life was divided, as it was by report of those under-graduates of S. John's who knew him in his last years as their President, between the stamp collection in his study and his stall in chapel, but while he was in the full vigour of a not unaggressive manhood, when he was capable of outspoken invective and rebuke —and also of sarcasm, which boys find it harder to forgive. None of his pupils enjoyed these outbursts more than Temple. He writes to his mother of a 'splendid scene':

> The Upper Bench has not been learning its lines very accurately this term, and James is getting annoyed. Yesterday when three people had had to be prompted he screamed out 'Why can't you learn your lines?' He said this louder and louder for some time and then screamed, 'I'm heartily sick and disgusted with it. Come in all of you this afternoon and say them, and write them out three times. Take your book.' Wherewith he hurled the book at the head of the fellow he had borrowed it from. Good old James—I do like a man who doesn't mind saying so when he loses his temper.

And this to his brother:

> James was splendid the other day. There were three constructions in one sentence and six consecutive people had not seen it. James was wild and roared with vast emphasis—'Well, I should have thought that any owl would have a—a—a—a— pricked up his nose at that.' Whereat we laughed, and he recovered his temper.

This kind of language lent itself well to imitation—there were few better mimics than Temple, and in the memory of friends some of his (and Bradby's) parodies still survive.

Attempts at the school prizes were taken as a matter of course. He won two Latin verse prizes in 1897, but in the spring of his last year the subjects were not congenial, either for the Latin or English verse:

> I am hoping shortly to write some Latin Hexameters about that rogue Agamemnon and his 'blameless wife', as he was wont to call her in this world: I expect they are scarcely on

speaking terms ἐκεῖ. When the time will come for me to say
Eructavit cor meum (perf. of rapidity, a point missed by the
A.V. or rather the P.B.V.) I cannot say . . . the English poem
Alfred I cannot attempt: that excellent monarch is as dull a
person as can be conceived. Knox told me in a letter the other
day that his character is disgustingly dull: he seems never to
have done a wrong thing—bar the burnt cakes—all his life.

In athletics Temple's achievements were limited. He was fairly
good at rackets, but he played without his glasses and had to
knock up for quite ten minutes before he began to focus the ball;
he used to say that he saw two balls at the far end of the court,
but knew where they would coalesce as they approached him.
For cricket he had neither taste nor talent—the only ground on
which he played regularly was the deck of the P. & O. S.S. *Marmora* in the Red Sea, many years later. But of his performances at
Rugby football legends abound; how his duty to the side was
merely to lean against the scrum which thereupon swept forward
with a fresh momentum; of the dread that possessed smaller boys
of being chosen to play against the School House, lest they might
be rolled on by Temple; and of the unique fame he won as the boy
who had never been known to fall down at football. Although he
played several times for the school in his last Easter term, he failed
to win his Colours; but he gained his Cap, and was not altogether
displeased with his own usefulness to the side. It is a pity, he
writes to his brother, that he has had his false teeth knocked out
'with the stumps', and will now have to wear a plate; but 'I am
11 stone 12 pounds in the scrum, if I am nothing else . . . I am
established thirteenth in the House XV; my report was "a slow
forward: can dribble, but lacks dash". The last, I suppose, is a
meiosis: however, I am pleased to find that yesterday the whole
side agreed that I had during the afternoon been once seen to
run!' (Rugby football enthusiasts of a generation and more ago,
who have not forgotten the name of Adrian Stoop, may note that
on 9 December 1899 a boy who had never even played on Big
Side was chosen for the School XV as a substitute at the last minute
and did not disgrace himself—'Stoop was admirable at half'.)

In the school debating society Temple was a frequent and fluent speaker. A glance through the back numbers of the *Meteor* shows that the subjects for debate were the same then as it may be presumed they have always been at public schools—classical *v.* modern, advantages *v.* disadvantages of civilization, brawn *v.* brains, and so on. Now and then a more topical subject crops up. In opposing the motion 'That this House, while viewing with regret the prospect of war with the Transvaal, does not regard the action of England in the matter in the light of either a blunder or a crime', Temple could carry only twenty-six votes, against one hundred and five in favour of the motion: but it need not be assumed that there was any more conviction behind his championship of this and other causes than is demanded from a schoolboy who is anxious to make his voice heard. In a letter, for instance, to his brother he tells how he had consented to oppose the Tsar's disarmament proposals in 1898, but later was asked to support them instead—'It will suit me just as well.' It did not, however, suit the House when he threw it into confusion by drafting— shadows of the Malvern Hills!—an amendment to a motion deploring the Guy Fawkes celebrations. Two accounts are extant of this incident. The first is Temple's own:

> I caused some havoc in a debate last night. As leader of the opposition, I spoke second, and in my speech proposed an amendment totally changing the motion, so that all the set speeches were thrown out, and certain people whom I had persuaded to support me were almost the only speakers. I hoped to produce some impromptu speeches, but only two were forthcoming. They were excellent.

The *Meteor* gives another version. The editor—or his contributor —was not too well pleased with Temple's first efforts at drafting: 'the House was in a state of bewilderment'; and some speakers found themselves called upon to oppose a motion not essentially different from the original one which they had undertaken to support.

From questions and statements scattered through his letters, some idea can be gathered of his literary taste and the development of his critical faculty. Matthew Arnold's *Essays in Criticism* is approved: Robert Louis Stevenson's letters are 'capital fun, with a very good paragraph or so of sermon occasionally thrown in'. Ophelia is 'unworthy, because she cannot sympathize with Hamlet's mental difficulties or strengthen his resolution'. Could *The Ancient Mariner* be interpreted as an allegory of Coleridge's own spiritual experiences? And should he read Ruskin? He is discouraged from doing so by seeing a remark of Ruskin's about the 'solid truth' in Byron: 'Byron seems to me to consist largely of rhetorical common-places, which cannot very easily fail to be "solid truth". Perhaps', he is just old enough to add, 'the fault lies in my slight knowledge of Byron.' For two other English poets his admiration is devout. (Although, probably incited by Whitelaw, he wrote an essay on *Abt Vogler*, and occasionally during holidays read his Browning with Mary Goodwin either on Grasmere Island or in the boat-house, he had not yet discovered the poet-thinker who was to fascinate and grip him a few years later.) Loyalty to his father suggested that anything written by Tennyson must be worth studying, and in his last year at Rugby he wrote a paper for the 'Eranos' Society on *Maud*, which offers a good example of his literary style at that period:

Mr. Tennyson has again laid the public under a very great obligation. We have not yet seen so daring a feat of genius as *Maud: A Monodrama*. He has taken all the great human emotions, and both of the two great occasions of emotion, as his theme: love and politics are intertwined in a poem which gives expression to the bitterness, the despair, the hope, the tenderness, the brightness, the gloom, the revolution of a single soul, whose marked individuality gives unity to the whole.

The paper ends:

All the great poetic qualities are to be found in their perfection in this masterpiece: dramatic insight, prophetic fire, lyrical exaltation—all are here. The form is a novelty, and yet needs no development, springing full-flown from Mr. Tennyson's genius as Athena sprang fully armed from the head of Zeus.

William Temple

More lasting was the impression of Shelley, on whom also he read a paper to the members of 'Eranos'. He did *The Cloud* into Latin verse for Whitelaw, and nearly half a century later, in the inaugural lecture of the Book Council delivered in the last year of his life, Temple quoted several verses of it—a poem, his father complained, which had not enough human interest and 'seems to be therefore rather concerned with what after all is not of the highest importance'. The Rugby essay ends:

> Perhaps in time Shelley would have added reason to his marvellous imagination; but it is futile to speculate upon what Shelley might have been. He is, as we have him, one of the greatest of modern prophets. All prophets bring some one message which, more than any other, they are bound to impart. Shelley's is a message which finds a proof by contrast in the discord of his life and of his soul. It is a message which appreciates that in his case at least the maxim is true that
>
> > Most wretched men
> > Are cradled into poetry by wrong:
> > They learn in suffering what they teach in song.
>
> We find it expressed with beautiful simplicity in *Julian and Maddalo* by the madman who represents Shelley himself:
>
> > There is one road
> > To Peace, and that is truth, which follow ye!

'I hope', he adds, 'I converted the froward Harry Tawney to a more favourable view of my prophet.'

All these activities of mind and body were interrupted in the Lent Term of 1899 by what the school doctor described as a dangerous illness—'characteristic influenza and pneumonia'. Many telegrams passed between Rugby and Lambeth, and a schoolfellow who was in the sanatorium at the same time as Temple remembers watching the leeches 'feeding on his (even then) ample form'. These gave considerable relief, and by the second week of March he was well enough to scribble a short letter in a shaky hand to his brother: 'I have been', he writes in describing his delirium, 'Edward I!—James wants to know what I thought of Edward II, but that did not come into it—

28

the room was transformed into a forest, with a waterfall in the grate'; his lucid moments were spent in composing a poem on S. Francis for the English Poem Prize. As soon as possible he was moved to Saltwood, and on the first Sunday 'went to church for morning prayer and returned thanks'. Of the organist he had little good to say—who has not heard her in the village church?

The organ was played by 'one' Miss ——, as Mr. Pownall would probably say, though it would be more odd if there were two. She thinks $f = presto$ and $p = adagio$. She also sees fit to play all emphasized chords as arpeggios, the school-girl-piano-system being particularly odious on the organ.

His musical appreciation was already keen and intelligent. Every year he and his brother were taken by their mother to hear *Messiah* in the Albert Hall, and to many good concerts. When he was fifteen the three of them attended a performance of the Bach Mass in B Minor at the Queen's Hall, and his mother laughed at the suggestion of a friend that such music was 'rather stiff for the boys'. On 31 May 1900—the day on which the school 'heard of the fall of Pretoria'—he comes straight from the chapel to write:

The Last Judgment was very beautiful, but the bass soloist ... had not enough power; he was quite nice, but the long air 'The Day of Wrath is near' requires a big voice. The beauty and tenderness of the chords struck me more than ever. I wonder if you remember the passage 'Then come, Lord Jesus'? It is like this: [an accurate transcription of the score follows]. The chord on 'come'—E♭, A♭, D♮, C♭, F♮—is as lovely a thing as I have heard. The passage is a quartet of eight parts. Spohr's trick of throwing in a minor sixth just before the common major chord at the end is very effective, as e.g. in 'Holy, Holy, Holy', where just before the final chord of E major, he puts in C♮.

Musicians to-day think rather differently of the Diminished Seventh from our ancestors, who revelled in this particular chord; but, when the state of music in the public schools half a century ago is remembered, Temple's musical taste would seem to have been considerably in advance of that of most of his contemporaries.

In the same year he writes of a school concert:

> Here is the programme of Leonard Borwick's recital. It was a wonderful performance. At the end of the song 'The Fairies' Lullaby' I quite lost my temper; the applause was tremendous because Miss Dale keeps a high chest note. The Beethoven Sonata, the *Largo* of which was as wonderful music as I ever heard, was received very coldly. However, the Schumann received a tremendous ovation, and so I recovered. The Chopin *Scherzo* is the piece with a kind of chorale whose lines are divided by rippling runs in the middle. We heard him play it once at a Saturday Pop. . . . The Rachmaninoff is the piece we heard R. himself play once at the Queen's Hall; Borwick's performance was far better.

Nor was he content to be merely a listener. Many years later, when he was Bishop of Manchester and was giving away the prizes at Stretford Grammar School, he examined the oboe which one of the boys in the school orchestra was playing. During his speech he referred to his own experiences with the instrument; '. . . but when I came in at the twenty-fifth bar instead of the twenty-ninth, I thought it best to resign'. There is more to be said than this of his orchestral ambitions and achievements. In a letter to his mother in the autumn of 1897, he writes:

Nov. 6th

My dear Mother, S. H. R.

Castle is awfully keen for me to be in the orchestra and so is Fred and so am I; they seem to have an awfully good time: so I had a consultation last night with Castle at my music lesson and he seems to think the French Horn would suit me best: it is a brass baritone instrument and as he can't play he proposes that we should both learn together: it would be awfully nice if we could and he is very keen to learn: so if Stebbing (the band master) can teach us what do you say to my learning? Of course it would include Christmas presents and tips for going up 8 places for half term and all sorts of things.

Castle will not learn if I don't. Please be quick and decide as Castle would like to start this term!

Your Importunate,

Wm. Temple.

It would seem that the balance-sheet—which bears comparison with the letters of J. M. Barrie's Primus to his uncle—did not appear in quite so favourable a light at Lambeth, and Temple had to look round for a less expensive instrument. He writes again to his father—'as you object [to the French Horn] I have practically decided to take up the oboe . . . hoping the oboe will suit your ideas better'. The merits of the instrument are then set out at length, but the usual difficulty is consigned to a diplomatic postscript:

> Castle thinks I had better do the oboe and if I may have lessons will lend me an old oboe of his to learn the notes on and then he thinks I shall be fit to use a good one. May I see about lessons and *shall I use Castle's instrument?*

Lessons were granted, and within a short time he is practising Haydn's 'With Verdure Clad', and—'I am to do Gounod's *Ave Maria* to which Bach was good enough to write the accompaniment'. After this, and the frequent mention of his progress on the organ, he is not very proud to record that in the school concert he has been chosen to play the cymbals. But the oboe he played in the school orchestra still survives as a treasured museum-piece in the choir-school at Canterbury.

He does not hesitate, at the age of sixteen, to direct his mother's musical taste:

> As regards Berlioz' *Faust,* I think you would understand it, as the quiet parts are very simple and the wild parts are only meant, I think, to represent confusion.

To the church music he has heard reference is frequent, and occasionally caustic. He rejoices that 'Prout in F' has been dethroned at Canterbury; but 'Stanford in B flat' is evidently too difficult for the cathedral choir, whose poor standard he constantly laments. After attending Westminster Abbey and S. Paul's

31

on the same Sunday, he sets down his impressions (which changed little as he grew up) of the two churches:

> Yesterday we went to S. Paul's in the morning: I agree with the desire for colour, but I hardly think Richmond's good enough. We went to Westminster Abbey in the evening. Father was preaching. The Abbey fascinates me more, but impresses me less, than S. Paul's. It is not a place I wish to pray in: I wish to wander about 'in vacant or in pensive mood', and to *feel* good and devout, and thankful, in all probability, that 'I am not as other men are'. A condition of mind, or rather of soul, which is not conducive to very practical prayer, or anything else befitting 'a finite intelligent'. It is partly the result of the 'dim religious light'. And now I must go and dress for dinner: all these bishops, Minnesota, Winchester, Oxford, etc., are rather a bore.

One other interest attracted his attention and helped to shape his career. It was a time when what used to be called 'social work among the poor' was the fashion, and many public schools had their Mission and clubs in the poorer parts of some great city. The Rugby Club was, and still is, in Notting Dale, and visits would be exchanged between the boys from the Mission and others who had the advantage of belonging to what Temple called in after years 'those large private institutions miscalled public schools'. One description of such a visit which he was fond of recalling was given by a character in a school novel by G. F. Bradby—'so we filled the little blighters up to the teeth, and then they hooked it back to their slums'. There was no greater favourite with the London boys than Temple, both at the New Romney Camp—washing-up after meals, shouting excerpts from Gilbert and Sullivan at the evening sing-song, accompanying hymns on his oboe at the Sunday evening service, or superintending the building of vast battlements of sand to defeat the incoming tide—and at their club in London, where he spent many noisy evenings, and extolled the virtues of chocolate cream as a staple article of diet.

As the last term draws to its end an occasional note of disap-

pointment creeps into his letters—had he, after all, done the best
that he might have done for the House? There is mention of a
'crusade' which he and his friends in the School House had
attempted, when some organized opposition was led by one boy
who was 'inclined to atheism'; and for all his efforts Temple
could think of 'no way of getting at him'. He discusses with his
brother the personalities who would or should be prominent in the
House the following year: 'After this term's clearance it will be
the objectionable who will try to assert themselves, while some
of those who ought to be leaders of fashion will remain in the
background unless they are developed now.' So he has a project for
bringing out some of the younger ones—why should not a few
(the party eventually numbered eight and was one of many such
gatherings of Rugbeians at Lambeth) come and stay with him for
the Rugby match at Lord's, so that he could see something more
of them than was possible at school, and give them some hints
on leadership for the next term? For himself, he is not sorry that
the Rugby days are over:

> It seems funny to think it is one's last term here: and after
> all it is quite time it came, as I have completely outlived my
> generation and am a little bit stranded. I suppose it was much
> the same with you and though it does not prevent one's having
> a capital good time it is just a bit lonely now and then; it has
> been more so than usual lately, as Harry [Hardy] only came
> back last night.

With him to Lambeth went his last report. His place for
Call-over was third of the twenty-two boys in the Upper Bench:
the two above him were G. A. F. M. Chatwin—now retired from
his Rugby mastership—and T. O. Hodges. He is not so thorough
as he might be in 'the higher grammar', but he is a good *viva voce*
translator because he appreciates his author: he has read a good
deal and is familiar with more ideas than most boys. Composition
is his weakest point, the style being 'rather bald and ineffective',
though he keeps a high level; in history he must cultivate accuracy;
his essays are good and thoughtful.

Temple left Rugby with a Major Leaving Exhibition, and a

D

medal awarded to 'a leader in the school'. (The award was not altogether a popular one, for his humane if injudicious preference for the rascals did not find favour with the more austere of his fellow-praepostors in the School House.) His one delinquency, it seems, had long been forgiven; but he himself never forgot how at house-prayers one evening the headmaster had noticed a movement in the swollen cheeks of one of his youngest boys, a movement apparently of suction as a large sweet was rolled from one side of the culprit's mouth to the other; and how the boy had wilted under the fierce rebuke delivered from a towering height in that broad Westmorland accent which Percival would assume when thoroughly roused—how dare Temple or any boy 'come gorging and guzzling into the presence of his Maker'? This was not allowed to count against him when the Chinese Ambassador visited the school and presented medals to the best classic, mathematician, cricketer, and so on. The Ambassador then asked for the best boy, to which James replied that public schools did not produce such things as 'best boys'; but His Excellency insisted that there must be some recipient of his last medal, and Temple was called forward. He was not altogether pleased; 'The medal', he wrote ruefully, 'is pewter or Britannia metal and I should think struck by the gross in Birmingham.'

In the memory of his schoolfellows an agreed picture of Temple remains. The same words are used again and again as they recall the stout vigorous boy with a striking and intelligent face; walking with a deliberate stride, a little uncertain what to do with his hands—but quite sure of himself in all else—with a straw hat set at such an angle that he has to throw his head back in order to look straight ahead of him; or with his hair flying in the wind as he dashes on an old-fashioned bicycle through the Lakeland villages or the Kentish lanes. Quick to absorb, ready to talk on all subjects and to laugh about most; with an insatiable thirst for knowledge, and an intense zest in life; enjoying keenly everything lovely and of good report, from cream buns to classical music. Very friendly to the smaller boys—'a kind of father and friend' as one of them remembers him—and to the Notting Dale boys an affectionate and resourceful big brother. Above all

34

unswervingly loyal to his father, his school, and his friends; already possessed by a sense of strenuous purpose, and with at least the outline of a philosophy of life.

'If you were told,' writes E. V. Knox, 'that there was a boy at an English public school of fourteen or fifteen years of age, who was destined to be, and himself intended to be, a headmaster, and perhaps an Archbishop, what would you have expected to find? A boy aloof from his fellows and leading an inner life, like Arthur in *Tom Brown's Schooldays?* Or one of those many earnest authoritative fellows who figure in the pages of Dean Farrar's romantic tales? A saint? A scholar? Or a prig? And what in the School House, Rugby (the date being 1895 or thereabouts), did you really find? A boy called Billy Temple, who was much more like Billy Bunter: and, for the sake of those who don't know, let me say that Billy Bunter is, or was, the rotund, good-natured, ridiculous boy of that popular school fairy-tale, *The Greyfriars Annual*, and its similar publications. Boys are not really like any of these people, and Billy Temple was Billy Bunter with plenty of idiosyncrasies. But he was stout; he was good-natured; he was "raggable"; he had that queer high laugh that went on so long and never left him: he was full of stories that he found at least as good as his hearers did. But from the start he had a sort of quiet purpose that was recognized. It earned some respect: grudging, I suppose; for boys admire prospective athletes and soldiers, not embryo theologians. *Si monumentum requiris circumspice*, said the Head of the House, alluding to his girth, but also perhaps paying tribute to a solidity of mind as well as physique, and it was soon discovered by those who wrote the end of term couplets for House Supper that *Templum* had a heaven-sent rhyme in *exemplum*. . . . It was his view then (I don't know how long he preserved it) that the proper refreshment for a hot afternoon was a strawberry ice sunk in a lemon squash, and I must have consumed more of these with him than I should ever have cared to do at any later time in my life. . . . I think of us in those days (or shall I say some of us?) as being rather super-cilious barbarians. No doubt these things have changed; but Temple could accept the rough and tumble, be a butt for mockers, give as good as he received, keep a fixed resolve and a simple faith, and interests in culture far outside the syllabus. . . . Masters, with probably more willing admiration than boys, knew well that he had an almost certain career before him. . . .'

Foremost among them was his headmaster, who closed Temple's last report with these words:

I find it hard to express how much I feel the inevitable good-bye. It has been something more than a pleasure to mark the extraordinary growth of his intellectual side in the last year or two; I think *anything* is possible to him and he has throughout been a pillar to the House—manly, transparently sincere, loyal, strong. I can only hope Balliol will gain all that we lose so far as the near future goes; for the rest my hopes are high, and their fulfilment, if God will, only a matter of time.

III

Balliol

... You will detect in this my habitual tendency to discover that everybody is quite right—but I was brought up by Caird, and I can never
get out of that habit.

W. T., letter to F. A. I., February 1944.

One of the great advantages of the college system at the Universities
is that it gathers together in very intimate social intercourse students
of different subjects. It would be impossible for me, for example, to
express what I owe to my intercourse with students of natural science
during my time at Balliol in Oxford. My own study of natural science
lasted for one term, during which I turned the age of thirteen ... but
I venture to say that I have acquired sufficient knowledge of how
scientists interpret the world to be of real service to me, and this I owe
almost entirely to being a member of a college which contained people
who studied natural science while I was studying classical languages,
ancient history, and philosophy.

W. T., Presidential Address to the Educational Science Section
of the British Association, September 1916.

'TAKE anything you can get at Balliol. Better at Balliol with
nothing than at Trinity with an Exhibition': so advised his
father before Temple entered for the Balliol scholarships. Two
of the papers seem to have suited him; he wrote to Harry Hardy:

Nov. 26.
The King's Mound,
Oxford.

My dear Harry,

... In the Greek Prose I think I rather distinguished myself,
at any rate I think 'all things being in a ferment' (reference to
French Revolution) is admirably rendered by πάντων, ὡς
εἰπεῖν, ἰλλιγγιώντων: tell Cole I got ἰλλιγγιάω in, it may amuse
him. I hope my other papers have been moderate, but my only
chance of success lies in the essay, where I was—I was going
to blaspheme and say 'lucky'. We had a choice of two subjects,
'The moral influence of war' and 'What poet has best and
most fully expressed the spirit of the nineteenth century?' I
wrote 15 pages, which as we have unlined paper would be

37

nearly 20 for Cole: it was nearly all quotations: I hope it may have impressed the authorities. I discussed Coleridge and Shelley at length; Wordsworth at less length; Browning at less still; Keats, Byron and Carlyle briefly; mentioned Rud; and finally accepted Tennyson with reasons.

Pray for me—I mean specially for my success.

Your loving
WM. TEMPLE.

Although, as he was frequently reminded by 'Jimmy' Palmer, a close and much-loved friend—then a Fellow of the College and later Bishop of Bombay—Temple's papers displayed the worst scholarship work the College had ever decorated, he was elected (on promise rather than performance) to an exhibition, and thereafter did exactly what was required and expected of him. He took reasonably good Firsts, put in much reading and writing and talking outside the official curriculum, discovered a new prophet or two, and filled every hour of the day to the last minute. Among his contemporaries at Balliol were E. A. Burroughs (later Bishop of Ripon), Stephen Hobhouse, G. M. Young, and Gaston de Vere, who came up with him from Rugby. Senior to him were F. S. Kelly (a noted musician, killed in the First World War), Archibald Main (later Moderator of the General Assembly of the Church of Scotland), F. de W. Batty (now Bishop of Newcastle, Australia), Professor Sir Maurice Powicke, and his Rugby friends R. H. Tawney and A. F. L. Smith (now retired from the Rectorship of Edinburgh Academy). Raymond Asquith and William (now Lord) Beveridge were in their fourth year.

It was an interesting period in the intellectual history of Oxford. In the country and the empire the teaching of T. H. Green was bearing its full fruit, as Professor Collingwood, in his Autobiography already quoted, has written:

The real strength of the movement was outside Oxford. The Greats school was not meant as a training for professional scholars and philosophers; it was meant as a training for public life in the Church, at the Bar, in the Civil Service, and in Parliament. The school of Green sent out into public life a stream of ex-pupils who carried with them the conviction that philosophy, and in particular the philosophy they had learnt at Oxford, was an important thing, and that their vocation was to put it into practice. This conviction was common to politicians so diverse in their creeds as Asquith and Milner, churchmen like Gore and Scott Holland, social reformers like Arnold Toynbee, and a host of other public men whose names it would be tedious to repeat. Through this effect on the minds of its pupils, the philosophy of Green's school might be found, from about 1880 to about 1910, penetrating and fertilizing every part of the national life.

But in the University itself, though his *Prolegomena* was still one of the text-books for Greats, Green's influence had noticeably waned. Two new stars had risen: inside Balliol Caird held the fort for idealism, but on Hegelian lines; and outside the College Cook Wilson was moving steadily towards a realist philosophy. Seven years before Temple went up there had been two candidates for the vacancy in the Mastership of Balliol caused by Jowett's death—Strachan-Davidson, who was already Fellow and Dean, and Edward Caird, Professor of Moral Philosophy in the University of Glasgow. Caird was elected; but most of the discipline and administration of the College remained in the strong hands of the Dean, and it was an ideal combination—as a contemporary jingle had it,

> 'Tis better to have Caird and Strachan
> Than never to have Caird at all.

To the new Master's genius Temple was drawn as by a magnet. He was never carried away by the attractiveness of Hegelian formulae, but the impact of Caird's mind and personality on his general philosophy of life was decisive and permanent. Not only did he learn to seek in all partial views and systems (however apparently antagonistic) some fragment that might contribute to an ultimate synthesis: the whole lay-out of his thoughts and convictions and their practical application were modelled on those of the Master:

Some folk thought that [he] made too much of system, and

39

was in fact wedded to system. The same critics said of his books that he went on repeating his system ... but why did he repeat himself? Because he had worked his way, not easily, to central convictions, and when a man has got central convictions I do not see very well how he can avoid repeating them in all their manifold applications. ... And why was he enamoured of system? Never for a moment ... because he allowed his system and his formulae to come between him and the realities of experience: no, but because he was not content with convictions however strongly held. ... Nothing could content him but to be a man of coherent convictions.

Again:

He gave us of his best unstintedly, says another witness, never making the mistake of 'talking down' to his audience, but rather seeking to stimulate his hearers by confidence in their powers. ... The effect thus produced ... was as if we were witnessing the creation of a new world. The dead-weight of custom and tradition was insensibly lifted, and we felt that for the first time we had begun to see things as they are.

These sentences were not written of Temple, but every word of them might have been. They are quoted from Professor MacCunn's 'Memorial Speech' in which Caird's genius was analysed and expounded with a rare and acute sympathy. Let any who must be content to take his Caird at second-hand read through this masterly oration, and he will find himself fitting one paragraph after another into the frame that holds his picture of the Archbishop—'The effect', for instance, 'was as if we were witnessing the creation of a new world.' It is a far cry from the Master's lecture-room at Balliol at the turn of the century to wireless receivers in the African desert or in the rest-billets of Cairo and northern France forty years on, but the impression conveyed is the same. There is no divergence of testimony here. Indifferent though all but a few of the fighting men might be to most broadcast religious services, they listened in numbers whenever Temple was on the air. Why was it? Their answer was ready: 'Now we understand for the first time'—the actual words recur in letters from the Forces—'what Christianity really is.' Stripped of all accretions and decorations, the Gospel sounded vivid and new. Like Caird's pupils, thousands of thoughtful men on active service, when Temple spoke, 'were witnessing the creation of a new world'. Or take the first quotation. Temple 'went on repeating . . .'. Undoubtedly he did. But who of all systematic thinkers does not repeat himself? His basic metaphysical convictions, once reached, were tenaciously maintained. There was little shifting of the premisses: could there be much variation in the conclusions? Temple's thought was completely architectural; and this was his excuse, if excuse were needed, for 'repeating his system'.

If the full flower of his idealistic philosophy was not to bloom till many years after, at least the seed was sown in Oxford. An eminent philosopher, when asked what it was he learned from Caird, replied: 'I do not know what I did not learn.' Temple would hardly have gone so far as that; but he proclaimed, to the end, the vast debt he owed to the greatest of all his teachers. Only once did he feel that Caird had done himself less than justice, when after dinner at Balliol Temple's father, who had come down to preach the University Sermon, had proposed *Domus,* and

> . . . the Master in replying told us solemnly that the College is 'always changing yet always remains the same', and looked surprised when we laughed. Really a man ought not to be allowed to be a philosopher unless he has a sense of humour.

The letter goes on:

> Young Picker [W. A. Pickard-Cambridge, his tutor's brother] proposed the guests rather cleverly, but was too long. The Warden of Merton replied, and was very amusing. So, by the way, is the last sentence of a letter I have had from G. F. B. [Bradby]: 'I am writing over the fire on a table that fidgets like a middle-schoolboy at fifth lesson: if I go on any longer, there will be what Stokes described in his last sermon as "almost involuntary ejaculations in a moment of distress which are not, strictly speaking, prayers".'

William Temple

The influence of the Master was more than academic. Caird never allowed his system to 'come between him and the realities of experience'. Long before he came south, he had been driven to contrast the material prosperity which marked the industrial progress of Glasgow with the horrible conditions under which thousands of the city's poor were forced to live; and his efforts for social reform were the natural outcome of his philosophic convictions. His share in the work of the Toynbee Hall Settlement in Glasgow; his constant advocacy of a fuller life for all who had nothing to occupy their leisure hours if these were to be enjoyed 'without orgies'; his pleas for improvement in the status of women in the factory, in the professions, and at the ballot-box; his quiet but pervasive energy in the cause of university reform—all these experiences were reflected in his teaching at Oxford and confirmed, as nothing else could have done, Temple's innate sympathy with the poor and the oppressed. They made another bond between teacher and pupil; and Temple never outgrew their effect on his life.

Many ways of showing that sympathy were then open to him, and he tried them all. He writes that he has 'sung quartets at a slum concert; a sort of penny-reading'. Was this some predecessor of the Balliol Boys' Club—a kind of noisy get-together in one of the less prosperous quarters of Oxford where altruistic undergraduates received a first breaking-in to social work, while their young victims rejoiced in the heartiness of the atmosphere and in the modicum of discipline and organization demanded by, or to be expected from, their patrons, most of whom were tasting the first sweets of emancipation from the strict rules and stricter customs of an English public school? Farther afield lay the Rugby Club, and the three University Settlements: Toynbee Hall in Whitechapel, the Oxford House in Bethnal Green, and the Oxford Medical Mission in Bermondsey. He sampled each of them. To Bermondsey he owed his introduction to a particularly vicious specimen of *Cimex lectuarius*: 'It is the only place', he wrote to his wife many years later, 'where I have found bugs of the large brown variety in my bed, so I have what the Archbishop of York [Lang] calls "sacred memories" of it.' Later still, he

42

described to a party of Bermondsey supporters some of his experiences at the Mission: 'At my lodgings there was a tin bed, rather rickety, and I lay on it with anxiety, for I always carried weight in every assembly. There was a tin wash-basin and a chair with three legs, upon which I read Bosanquet's *Logic*.'

One at least of the club boys saw his visits from a different angle:

There are many old Bermondsey boys in all parts of the Empire who will say, but for Bill Temple we would be godless and useless citizens. He shared in our worship, and in our pleasures. How often he would come with us from those dark drab streets of Bermondsey to the countryside in Essex and share with us for a few hours the pleasure of God's good sun. Those were the days of poverty and distress and starvation. But Bill Temple gave to us what God had given him. His thoughts were all for us who had never been given a chance, and lots more could be said of his work in Bermondsey. We could never think of him as the Lord Archbishop of Canterbury, but as just Bill Temple. Of course, as Lord Archbishop, we would gladly kneel at his feet. He was worth it because we owe him a lot; but still for all that we shall remember him as Bill Temple.

At the Oxford House he found a more secluded spot for his reading. The tradition persists of Temple squeezing himself through a skylight on to the roof and studying *Man and Superman* (just out) among the chimney-pots, with his head wrapped in a handkerchief knotted at the four corners, to keep the smuts from his hair; he also accepted an invitation to occupy the Christian Evidence stand in Victoria Park—'Where I am to demonstrate from an inverted tub that Christianity is essentially the only true religion'. He is a little critical of the club system he found established:

I have just come back from a stay at the Oxford House: splendid. But I want to abolish all men's clubs and to limit boys' clubs to 150 members each. Men's clubs break up families, and the energy devoted to them would be better spent in visiting. A big boys' club makes too much office work, and prevents the manager from getting good talks with the boys.

I found a dear boy from Luton in Bedfordshire in the London Hospital—aged 13 and reading Lubbock's book on Ants and Bees—son of a railway clerk and doomed to become one himself, but wishes to be a clergyman, for choice a missionary to China. I talked a lot to him and found to my surprise that I was giving a detailed exposition of S. John xiv ff. He seemed to like it. He had had a prize every year at his Sunday School, but complains that they have too much of the plagues of Egypt and wishes they would take up *Revelation*! (Poor teachers!) I wish I could help the brat—but he will be a blessing to the railway men who come near him. He said he liked books about boys, so I have sent him Tom Brown, and have promised to go and see him at Luton in the summer.

The hospitality of Bethnal Green was repaid every Whitsun Monday, when members of the men's and boys' clubs poured in a flood over Oxford. On one of these bank-holiday afternoons Temple spent three hours on the river punting to and fro a party of East Londoners, who were rewarded for their amiable acquiescence in the chosen recreation of their host by the kind of meat tea that only a Yorkshire farmhouse or an Oxford college could supply.

Each of the University Settlements had its annual meeting in some college hall or at the Union; and to these were brought down from London, as 'star' speakers, leading politicians or churchmen. The strongest impression on Temple was left by a Toynbee Hall meeting at which the success of the evening was a speech by Charles Masterman, whose *The Heart of the Empire* was (in Chesterton's words) to 'make the map of England crawl with life' and to present ' a really impressive vision of the moving millions of England'. The meeting had begun with 'The Right Honourable H. H. Asquith, K.C., M.P.' who spoke 'very badly'; but Masterman was 'excellent', and Temple had a luncheon party for him at Balliol on the following day. For a few years the two saw something of each other, and the friendship had its influence on Temple's political and social views. But he never called himself a Liberal; probably Edward Talbot's 'Conservative with a bad conscience' would have described him accurately enough at this period, when he also had a limited sympathy with the aims of the Tariff Reform League. An Oxford University branch of the League was formed; Temple joined it and for a time served on the committee, and in his third year he wrote to his brother:

So glad you are a Protectionist—for myself, so far as I understand the thing, I am pretty clear. I want protection for our home industries, and preference for the colonies—but I do not want retaliation. I hope that a wisely administered preferential scheme would make the Empire so powerful commercially that none of the devices would be needed.

Thirty years later he explained, in a letter to Bradby, the difference between his own views and those of the orthodox Protectionists of his youth:

Bishopthorpe,
York.
July 26, 1933.

My dear G. F.,
Yes—I know. Any adjustment made to suit existing mechanical development will be upset by the next invention. But part of the re-adjustment has surely got to be a re-distribution of work and leisure. We must (I think) get folk to see that an increase of leisure is inevitable, and also desirable.

On that basis I should agree with you about Protection. I have been a Protectionist since I first thought about it, and as an undergraduate joined in forming the Oxford Tariff Reform League. I was rather unpopular with that League because I always said Protection would make us poorer, not richer, but was worth it because it would enable us to organize our own economic life with a view to social welfare in shelter from the pressures of unmitigated competition. I believe that the *great* arguments for Free Trade, as developed in the '40s and '50s, now tell for Protection: because Cobden and Bright talked in terms of commercial exchange, with money as a pure medium of exchange. When the financiers found they could

45

make fortunes by treating money as a commodity, the bottom was knocked out of the Free Trade case. The financiers skimmed off the distinctive profits of Free Trade in the process of the exchange. Now Free Trade from Adam Smith to Mill is a repudiation of the Mercantilist theory which was based on the (then fallacious) identification of wealth with money; but the international financiers have made that theory a fact; as manipulated by them money *is* wealth, so we have got to go back and start from this which is now a fact, as it was not then. We must have *some* market (the larger the better) which is stable, and secure against the disasters arising from fluctuations in the currency. This can only be the home market. So we must pay for its security.

But there were problems other than political and economic to grapple with, and the variety of his intellectual interests is shown by the titles of the essays which Temple read to the many College Societies—'Keats and Shelley' to the Literary Society, 'The Progress of Science' to the Junior Scientific Society, 'The Atonement' to the Bible Reading Society, 'Abstract Speculation' to the Jowett Society; and 'Robert Browning'—in Temple's judgement 'the greatest product of the nineteenth century'. These essays have the same characteristics; they exhibit considerable knowledge, clarity of thought, a vivid imagination, something of the slap-dash of youth, and a facility in the writing of English that a more practised hand might envy. The last of them is of permanent value, and is probably the only one in which Temple would have made few changes had he revised it in later years. With no nineteenth-century writer had he a closer or more enduring affinity than with Robert Browning, who (apart from Shakespeare) was the fourth in order of the English poets as he then placed them. Shelley first; then Coleridge, whom the old Archbishop had taught him to revere as the great deliverer from the 'theological commercialism' of Paley and other unpleasant aridities and desolations, and among whose philosophical descendants he could not but number T. H. Green. Third came Spenser, though he cannot make up his mind 'how the *Faerie*

Queene is to be allegorized'. Milton's longer poems, he writes, 'bore me stiff'—a later confession runs: 'I am not worthy of Milton: I do not know if I ever shall be'. But Browning soars above them all. To his use of thought, as well as of emotion and action, for his material; to his doctrine of the earthly testing, the purposive growth, and the destiny of man; to his treatment of music and his conception of the functions of art (the Third Book of the *Republic* also comes in here); to his trumpeting of the vigour of youth and his reverent sympathy with the aged— Temple's whole personality responded with an almost devout alacrity. There was a completeness in Browning which he found nowhere else: his appetite was voracious, and it needed the immense span of Browning's thought, the depth of his art, and the wholeness of his vision, entirely to satisfy it. Shakespeare is magnificent (he writes in his essay) but it is a pagan magnificence; Browning's genius is fundamentally and thoroughly Christian; through his poems there rings the joy of work and worship; and 'to Browning the climax of history, the crown of philosophy, and the consummation of poetry, is unquestionably the Incarnation'. This aspect of Browning's philosophy and faith Temple pressed upon his not wholly sympathetic father. When in a quiet hour one evening at Lambeth he was trying to lead him to a keener appreciation of his prophet, he read aloud the climax of David's song before Saul. The Archbishop also had his favourites, and it was too late to change now. 'Yes', he admitted with a nod of his head, 'but you must leave me my Tennyson.' More whole-hearted support for his favourite came from 'a man called Cyril Bailey' who (he writes to his father in the autumn of 1902) has just been elected to a Balliol Fellowship. After a long walk with him Temple rejoices to report: 'he is a great scholar, so I was particularly pleased to find that he is as complete an admirer of Browning as I am'.

On the morning of the day on which he was to read his Browning essay, he wrote to his father:

. . . Jimmy Palmer's fertile brain has conceived the idea that we might employ Sunday mornings in discussing Browning's

47

poems that deal with or introduce religious ideas. This morning some of us discussed 'Cleon', and it was very interesting. The ablest person present—[now Lord] Beveridge—told us that the Categorical Imperative is really negative, and should be expressed, 'I must not do nothing' or 'I must not be useless', and proceeded to deny that there is any cause for any satisfaction after doing a good action, other than a relief from the horror of uselessness: the moral law, he said, derives its cogency from the eternal results of our actions on the human race, and if we were so conditioned that our actions had no results, they would neither be moral nor immoral. It was very interesting, and I think he made out his case very well; but I am more violently convinced that he is wrong than I was before I heard his excellent defence of his views.

The printing and circulation of this essay among a few friends had an interesting sequel. It came into the hands of a man of letters who was also one of the most fascinating personalities of his day, and few of the many tributes to her son were more worth the keeping to Mrs. Temple than this:

Saighton Grange,
Chester,
18 August 05.

Dear Mrs. Temple,

I have just read your son's essay on Browning with keen interest and close agreement. It is admirably done and every part of it was well worth doing. One cannot often say that of an essay.

For two years of my life, now eighteen years since, I saturated myself with Browning. I am very glad to know that others are doing so, because Browning told me of his delight at finding that the young read him in that way. He would have rejoiced or—rather—he does rejoice at your son's study and understanding.

He read aloud to me on several occasions and your son may care to hear that he read, by choice, most of the poems quoted in the essay and read them just as your son says they ought to be read. He seemed to set the greatest store by *Karshish* and

Balliol

A Death in the Desert. If it is at all permissible to speak of so great an artist's 'message'—a horrid phrase—his message is in those two poems.

In another category, he read with elation *Abt Vogler* and *The Last Ride Together*; in another, with perfect dramatic intonation, *Bishop Blougram's Apology*: and, lastly, *A Toccata of Galuppi's* and *Up at a Villa—Down in the City.* He always read—as your son has divined—dramatically but quietly; with an exact observation of punctuation and grammar; no sing-song; and always with a restrained, but lambent, humour playing over the deeps of philosophic pathos. He never liked going without reading the *Toccata* and *Up at a Villa.* In that he let himself go in dramatic impersonation, but with his humour present in every line. He was the Greek chorus to the Dramatic personalities of the speakers in each poem. But the chorus was of loving, pitying laughter, not of an inevitable clown; and with more happy laughter than pity. He revelled in the speaker's view of the contrast between the villa and the city.

The last time I saw him he dined with my mother and myself and no one else, and read to us till past one in the morning. He was affectionate in his kindness. Made me—most willingly and with awed delight—promise to stay with him in Venice. But he died that autumn.

So I know that he is immensely pleased with your son's essay.

Yours very truly,
GEORGE WYNDHAM.

Temple seems to have taken most of his reading in big doses. Now it was Jane Austen—*Emma* was his first love and remained his favourite—now it was Napoleon, about whom he confessed his father 'ragged' him a good deal. Was it then seriously wrong to admire Napoleon? 'Not in the least,' was the Archbishop's reply, 'provided you do not keep it up after you are thirty.' With George Eliot he was, at that time, entirely out of sympathy. In his first long vacation he writes of *Romola*:

E

49

The first necessity for a book is that its subject should be pleasant, for a great book it must also be edifying. Now the various stages of a soul's progress from the selfishness of a moment to the hell of eternity which is my idea of G. E.'s Tito is not a pleasant subject: I doubt whether it is edifying. Father compares *Romola* to a picture of a butcher's shop by a great painter: in every line you can see the master-hand; but the picture is unpleasant, it is even ugly. Besides this there is in G. E. a kind of pseudo-poetry which is odious to me. Last night Mother asked us whether there was a mis-print in a passage in *Middlemarch*. It was a description of some one sitting by a grave in a church-yard; 'and the shadows of the leaves flitted across the isles (query, aisles?) of sunlight, as though they knew they were in the presence of a grief'. The leaves would have fallen in just the same way anyhow; it is not true poetry to use a false image of that sort.

There were also the prophets of his own day behind each of whom his contemporaries were lining up according to their tastes and training. Though he found much to emulate in *A New Utopia* and used it later in his *Republic* lectures at Queen's, the cultural, historical, and philosophical approach of H. G. Wells to the problems and thought of the world was widely different in too many respects from his own for Temple to gain a great deal from the contact. With Chesterton, in every chapter of whose brilliant study of Browning he found delight, he was more nearly marching in step; but it was Shaw to whom he then looked as the outstanding social teacher of the modern world. The early fascination breaks out in more than one letter. 'Have you read', he asks his brother excitedly, 'any plays by Bernard Shaw, the socialist? They really are ripping. One of them, *Arms and the Man*, is as witty as anything I ever saw except possibly the *Importance of being Earnest*, by Oscar Wilde, which is very much the rage just now.' A little later he describes Shaw's plays as 'perfect', and promises to bring several of them for his brother to read while they are on holiday together. Rumours of this new-fangled learning reached the ear of his father, through ecclesiastical busybodies anxious for the orthodoxy of the Archbishop's son. The old man dug his mittened hand into the papers on his desk and dragged out a letter he had just received from Balliol: 'So long as he can write *that*', he replied to his chaplain with emphasis, 'there can't be much wrong with him.' The letter began with the words: 'I went to Holy Communion this morning.' Many of his letters from Rugby had opened with the same sentence, and there was little difference between the religion of Temple's boyhood and that of his youth. To his contemporaries his mind seemed in this respect almost full-grown. The internal conflicts and mental changes of the average undergraduate lay behind him—'I got over my intellectual measles at Rugby', he would say—and his spiritual crisis was yet to come. He writes to his father of one sermon that had particularly impressed him:

George Adam Smith was preaching at Mansfield this morning and I went to hear him: he was quite wonderfully good— on the character of Esau. Amongst other details, he wondered why in our Prayer Book the marriage of Isaac and Rebekah is spoken of as so particularly happy: and when one comes to think of it, it is very odd. He was particularly good on the words 'a profane person' (βέβηλος); the man whose heart is common property, round whose soul there is set no fence, into whose mind all thoughts may come. 'Surely', he said, 'that household of Isaac and Rebekah was a profane household if ever there was one.' All the common passions and petty vices ran riot there: the father cannot bless till he has fed well; one son with that strange common trick of exaggerating his own feelings, ('I am at the point to die' etc.) giving way to a greedy hunger; the other son thinking of no one's interests except his own; even the mother, who had herself set Esau the example of impatience and exaggeration (cf. her remarks on the daughters of Heth), deceiving her husband to support her younger son's selfishness. It was a very vivid picture that he drew, and his application of it was very powerful.

He is very striking in appearance, but only when he is roused; at first he looks commonplace. But his eyes really blaze when he is denouncing things. He has caught a good deal of the spirit of his beloved Prophets.

And this—on the contrast between Winnington Ingram and Lang:

> I am just back from a sermon by the Bishop of Stepney on 'Fervent in spirit, serving the Lord'. I think he is very great. Harry Hardy came with me, and having often heard me say that he impresses me more than the Bishop of London, was rather disappointed. But to me the difference is clear enough. When I hear the Bishop of London, I get very much excited— rather hysterical perhaps—and feel ready to do anything: all of which is done away by the next excitement, a concert or reading *The Critic*: and when I come on his text in the Bible, I remember that I was excited, and have a vague sort of conception why. But when I hear the Bishop of Stepney I am not moved at all: I have to listen for fear of losing the inevitable connexion of his points, and the pleasure is intellectual and not emotional: but when I come on his text afterwards I can remember all his points, just because their connexion is inevitable, and can then see whether I am following the precepts so obviously implied in the text. And for me there is no doubt that this is the more edifying by far.

He had need frequently to remind himself that there were Schools to be taken and routine work to be done. Few of his letters mention his reading for Honour Mods., but he writes that with the help of an alarm clock set at 5.30 a.m. he has read fifteen books of Homer in one week, and 'the *Aeneid* took ten days; last night it was to be finished, and I was rather alarmed to find that it was 9 o'clock before I started the twelfth book. However, the 950 lines were all done by 11.30, so I am happy again.' In March 1902 he writes: 'I am in the thick of Mods., without a conception whether I am doing well or not'; and, refusing an invitation when Schools were over, 'I really am not in a state to go anywhere, being very tired in the head, very easily tired in the body, and very uncertain of the control of my temper.' He got his First, and wrote to his father a few weeks later:

I have seen my marks for Mods, and was rather pleased to find that I had an α to spare: out of 14 subjects it was necessary to get 7 αs and I got 8 and one αβ. The subjects in which I got an α are Homer, Virgil, Cicero, Plato, Lucretius, Unseens, Greek Prose, and General Paper: on Logic I got αβ: on Demosthenes, Greek Plays, Latin Prose, and Latin Verse I got β: and on Greek Verse γ. I never could do Greek Verse. Some of my β papers were nearly α. I must ask about the Logic, as I was pretty sure I had done it quite well.

His work for Greats was more congenial: it was a relief to turn from the narrower field of classical scholarship to the achievements and speculations of the ancient world, especially to the *Republic*, which he read through eight times in his life, and on which his work was described by his tutor as 'uniformly good'. On the study of ancient history and literature he held that, so long as readers treated Latin and Greek in exactly the same way, many of the masterpieces of the ancient world would be spoiled for them. He re-stated and developed this view at some length many years later in an address to the Classical Association, when he contended that it was only a slight exaggeration to say that Latin literature should be studied mainly with a view to understanding Roman history, and Greek history with a view to understanding Greek literature: in other words, Latin literature should be subordinate to Roman history, Greek history to Greek literature. Great figures of statesmen and strategists stood out from the story of ancient Greece, but there was an odd lack of continuity about it all; it was disjointed, almost incoherent. Roman history, on the other hand, was a great and continuous movement—had it not laid the foundation of the whole modern political structure? —and the conspicuous personalities were seen as organs of something greater than themselves. 'I suppose', his Greats tutor, H. W. C. Davis, once said to him rather sadly, after he had listened to Temple reading an essay on some incident of Greek history, 'you take no interest whatever in this subject?' Temple could only plead guilty.

The tiredness of which he complained warned him that Oxford is not an easy place in which to keep physically fit,

especially for one of Temple's strenuous mental activity. He
played in the College XV, which he captained in his last year,
and there was some lawn tennis, which became rather desultory
after he had failed to secure the last place in the College VI. By
the middle of his second year he had worked out a definite plan
of exercise:

> I am rapidly coming to the conclusion that the really good
> thing in Oxford is to take real exercise one day in the week,
> wander about the river four days (from 2.15 to 3.45), not to go
> out at all two days, and loaf about on Sundays. This is what I
> have done this term, and certainly I have never been so fit both
> for work and other things.

Among the many 'other things' were music and the Union
debates. Soon after his twenty-first birthday he writes to his
mother:

Balliol,
Nov: 7.

> At my birthday time I was given several Lives of great
> musicians which I have been dipping into lately—it amuses
> me to try to classify them and compare them. But Mozart is
> such a puzzle—he stands in no relation to the others, that is to
> those others who are great enough to be compared to him.
> All of these express struggle of some kind: in Bach it is over—
> he is the musician of attainment; his atmosphere is that of S.
> John in his First Epistle; they are both in heaven—(or Paradise
> if you like). Beethoven is climbing the mount of Purgatory;
> he is as far from this world as Bach, but is undergoing purifica-
> tion 'so as by fire', and is still an individual—very much so—
> whereas Bach is already one with the saints and says
>
> > To me, that story—ay that Life and Death
> > Of which I wrote 'it was'—to me, it is;
> > Is, here and now: I apprehend nought else.

But Beethoven never says that. Nor does Handel; he is the
musician of victory in battles, but the campaign is not over;
he is altogether on earth, and the most human of them all,
with his floods of tears and triumphant shouts.

So far they all express some kind of spiritual struggle: but in Mozart there is none: he is the musician of innocence; he went laughing through life—that is as far as his music goes. He is a sort of musical Ariel. As great as any, because he is always perfect—and yet he seems out of place among those giants: he is like Sir Joshua's Cherubs—but why did he come on earth: and how did he keep that childlike innocence which is not the victory over temptation but the utter freedom from it? I don't know why I should send you this stuff . . .

The Sunday evening concerts in Balliol Hall, which had been introduced many years before by John Farmer, had become an established feature in the musical life of the University. They were arranged by a committee of the College Musical Society, with Dr. Ernest Walker as Musical Director. The detailed arrangements were carried out in practice by the chairman (Dr. A. W. Pickard-Cambridge) and an undergraduate secretary. Until Farmer's retirement it had been difficult to get much order into either the finances of the concerts or the seating of the audience; and among the musical enthusiasts of North Oxford were some who claimed an almost prescriptive right to certain seats in the Hall. It needed all the tact of the secretary to wean them from the idea that these concerts were given for their particular benefit. Temple, who was elected secretary during his second year, managed admirably, though impatience breaks out in his letters at the amount of work involved:

> I am now just beginning the agony of sending out tickets for the Eights Week concerts: it is a horrid bore. I have hopes that I may be able to cause a volcano to erupt in Oxford, as I am going to ask the committee to abolish the annual tickets at our Sunday concerts. The crowd that comes is intolerable, and keeps many 'Varsity men away. I should be rather unpopular in North Oxford if I succeeded.

At the Union Temple won the most pronounced of all his successes as an undergraduate. He was successively Secretary and Librarian in 1903, and President in the Lent Term of his last year; this was the only office he can be said to have coveted in his life. There was at that time a tradition that the Balliol influence predominated in the election of junior officers at the Union, and that it ought to be diminished; and every candidate from the College was by so much handicapped in the constituency. But there were one or two broad highways open to the President's chair—to speak often, to speak well, and to speak with a sympathetic understanding of an opponent's views—and in none of these approaches did Temple find his progress difficult. He spoke at least as often as any of his contemporaries during their first three years; he seems never to have failed; and the charity of judgement on which throughout his life even the most hostile of his critics could rely found its first expression in the Union debates. In his second year he spoke three times in one week; in New College on the Education Bill, at the Cambridge Union against a motion in favour of displacing the Government, and at the Oxford Union he moved 'that a revolution in Russia is both probable and desirable'. The comment of the *Oxford Magazine* on this speech was that Temple's argument was based on 'great and broad principles', and that it was interesting as an expression of the speaker's personality: his own verdicts on the three speeches were that he did 'rather well' on the first subject, 'decently' on the second, and 'really well (!)' on the last. A later speech on the Education Bill at the Oxford Union he regarded as his best: 'I made rather a hit on the Education Bill. The house was quite full, men standing in the gangways, and I knew the subject pretty well.' The only occasion on which he is remembered to have been embarrassed in the Union chair—and it was only for a moment—was near the time when he was due to deliver a much-advertised lecture on 'Isaiah and Imperialism'. In the middle of private business the house burst into a roar of laughter while he was making some merely formal remark. Noticing that all eyes were fixed on the gallery above his head which was invisible from the chair, he walked to the floor of the house and turned round, and laughed louder than any at seeing a large poster dangling from the gallery rails, inscribed 'Timothy and Teetotalism'. (The Bible was better known then than now, and among familiar and much-appreciated texts was the verse in which S. Paul advises Timothy to take 'a little wine for' his 'stomach's sake', and for his 'often infirmities'.)

On his outstanding talent as a speaker opinion was unanimous. 'He had already', his tutor notes, 'an unusual gift of ready and lucid speech', perhaps sometimes too ready, 'leading him at times to think that he had found a solution, when he had found a phrase.' (There was another disadvantage in the possession of this gift. Temple's father used to say of him as a boy that he was extremely difficult to teach, because he expressed himself so clearly as to give his teacher the impression of knowing more than he did.) Many years after, Dr. Pickard-Cambridge was in the congregation when the Archbishop of York came to preach on the thousandth anniversary of Rotherham Church, and after his sermon Temple asked his old tutor—'How's that? Beta minus?' One impression in particular remains on Dr. Pickard-Cambridge's mind:

> He was . . . already the man that he was later, and when I look over the list of my old pupils with whom I have still kept acquaintance, I can think of none who changed less in every essential . . . he was entirely void of priggishness and pretence.

Such was the judgement of Temple's tutor: there was also the verdict of his contemporaries. Nowhere is criticism more rife or more free than in the Junior Common Rooms of Oxford; and it was not to be expected that undergraduate opinion of Temple would be entirely favourable. All were agreed that he was completely honest with himself and the world; that, whatever career he adopted, nothing could keep him from the top of it; and that he was somehow unlike themselves—but how? He did ordinary things like ordinary people; he was as human as the rest of them; none enjoyed life more keenly or threw himself with greater zest into the usual activities, physical and mental, of a normal undergraduate. Yet—was it that he was a good deal more self-confident, even cocksure, than they were? A little more inclined than they could be to believe that wisdom would die with him? And more anxious, perhaps, to collect followers than to make friends? The candid critics described him at this period as 'bumptious', and there is a suggestion of this in the portrait of Temple as an 'Isis Idol'—to be so depicted in the weekly undergraduate paper was to reach the peak of Oxford publicity. Such criticisms were to be expected; and some of them may have been justified. In part at least they were due—the repetition must be risked—to the conditions of Temple's up-bringing, his constant intercourse with older people, and his conspicuously early development, so that he could not help standing out among those of his contemporaries who, at least in knowledge and experience, were by several years his juniors. His influence was, therefore, considerable; but he had more followers outside the College than in it. There were marked divisions at Balliol in his day; not merely into the usual social, athletic, and intellectual sets—the intellectuals themselves were rather sharply divided into believers and agnostics (both of a late Victorian type) or Platonists and Aristotelians. One of his most gifted contemporaries, G. M. Young, writes:

> In the introduction to W. T.'s Gifford Lectures, there is a passage which reminds me very forcibly of his manner of thinking, and expounding, in conversation or essays. He describes two ways of arriving at conclusions—one by con-sidering the evidence, the other by intuition, so that he found himself propounding as certain a proposition he had only just thought of. One heard so many of these propositions, *e.g.* 'Browning never wrote a line that was not poetry'. His exuberant self-confidence in action took, in thinking, the form of an equally exuberant certitude. And the Aristotelians ('Aristotle had the mind of a churchwarden') did not at all approve.

Neither of these two sets had much influence on the other—a report in the *Daily News* that Balliol had become one of the most 'churchy' colleges in Oxford evoked a protest from the Aristotelians—but 'Good Templars' were to be found in many colleges. A less restricted setting, a less rare atmosphere, were needed for the full exercise of Temple's powers, and a more open field for the testing of his leadership. The next few years would be critical; but how and where should they be spent? Not until Greats was behind him—'I think', he wrote to his brother, 'that heaven is just one continual evening of the day when Schools are over'—does Temple seem to have given much thought to his immediate future, or to have consulted others on what the next step should be. One of his counsellors—loved, revered, and trusted above all—had been taken; but not before he had paid a last visit to his old College and University. At the age of eighty the Archbishop had come down to Oxford, to preach on a Sunday evening to the undergraduates in the University Church. Unable —as he had been for some years—to see things on ground level, he groped his way down from the pulpit when the sermon was over. At the foot of the steps William Temple stood waiting; and the old Archbishop passed for the last time into the vestry of S. Mary's, leaning on the arm of his son.

IV

Queen's

Oxford ... would always desire to be judged not by the Oxford don, but by the Oxford man in any walk of life.

When ... I praise the English traditional education, I am praising education by means of a corporate life. ... Our intellectual training has often been very amateurish in method, and very feeble in result. We most undoubtedly need strengthening here. But you will observe at once that it is just here, and here alone, that German education has been strong; it has not aimed at the sub-conscious mind, as ours has done—moulding the whole personality by the silent appeal to imagination and sympathy which a common tradition embodied in a social life is alone able to make. That is the only way to train those elements in our nature which determine how we shall act in an emergency, when there is no time for reflection, or when ordinary standards are displaced. ... The product of our system ... is a body of men who, not always learned, and seldom able to formulate their principles of action, are undoubtedly the best colonial and imperial administrators of whom history holds record.

W. T., W.E.A. Presidential Address, 1915.

WHEN the Greats list was published, Temple was staying at Woolbeding. Several offers of work arrived by telegram, and two dozen more reached him within forty-eight hours. But the two which he considered most seriously had been made to him before his Class in the Final Honour School was known; neither of them was exactly what he wished, but one was nearer to his hopes than the other. During the winter of 1903, six months before he took Greats, he had gone down with a XV of Old Rugbeians to play the school, and he confessed to have been 'rather flustered' when the headmaster suddenly said to him: 'If you want to be a master here, you have only to let me know.' There were several reasons for declining the proposal: some were to appear later; others pressed upon him with more immediate argument, not least his eagerness to increase the sum of his learning and widen his social interests and sympathies—objects difficult to attain in the crowded time-table of a public school curriculum. He did not put aside the possibility altogether. But he still hoped for a Fellowship; if none were offered, then he would remember James's offer.

He was never seriously thought of for a Balliol Fellowship. This would have had to be in philosophy, and there was no room for more than Caird and J. A. Smith, nor was money then available for a Research Fellowship. It appears, however, that immediately after he had taken Greats and an offer had come to him from another college, A. L. Smith approached him privately with the warning that he would be unwise to accept it at once. 'He asked me', Temple wrote to his brother in August, 'to postpone the decision for six weeks, saying "I have a particular reason for this which I cannot tell you yet". Of course I cannot pay attention to reasons I know nothing about, and said so. The Queen's people want my answer by the end of this month, as they must let their second string know early in September.' A fortnight later he accepted the firm offer, and was busy choosing carpets and chair-coverings for his new rooms: they were at the top of the quadrangle arm that runs along Queen's Lane, at the end of it that looks over the High Street. To his mother the decision came with something of relief—at any rate, he would be living in Oxford—though she did not conceal her slight disappointment. Writing to Lady Mary Glyn in November, she makes the best of it:

8, Keble Road.

Thank you for all you say about Wm. He is very happy in his new work and life, and has most delightful rooms at Queen's; he comes to breakfast here every day and often at other times, but he lives *there*, and I felt somewhat bereaved at first: but I am very glad he has got this work to do, with time for his own studies and lots of keen, eager, quick-witted fellow-dons. It is somewhat of regret that it was not Balliol, for keeping the dear name there as a Fellow, but he must always remain a Balliol man.

Queen's, then, it was to be; and so began in some respects the happiest, certainly the most formative and decisive years, of Temple's career. Once, when asked how he had managed to amass his rich store of learning in a life throughout which every

61

moment that could be spared from administrative and pastoral duties appeared to be absorbed in causes and committees, he replied that during his most receptive years he had enjoyed the inestimable privilege of leisure for 'taking in', for accumulating the knowledge he was passionately eager to acquire; and a still greater gift was his power of assimilating a generous and varied diet with what one of his colleagues at Queen's exactly described as 'the perfect digestive organism of his mind'. His leisure was now ample. He was to lecture for three hours a week in one term of the year on Plato's *Republic*; for one hour a week in a second term on other subjects—among these were 'A Theory of Society', 'A Theory of Knowledge', and 'The Nature of Personality'—and for the third term he was to be free from lectures altogether. Further, in the first year of his Fellowship his time was entirely his own; and, though later the audience at his Plato lectures was fairly large, he never had more than a dozen pupils. He seldom used notes when lecturing, but walked up and down the room with his hands in his pockets, making his points with a delivery that was both fluent and incisive; and his exposition was already marked by the exceptional lucidity that was to characterize all his teaching to the end. But his notes were always carefully and fully written out, and all the Oxford Greats lectures survive—on his death they were given to Queen's by his wife with Watson Nichol's portrait of Temple as a young man and 200 of the philosophical books from his library. Two verdicts have been passed on them; one by a philosopher who has 'sampled' them, and writes:

As might be expected, they are vigorous, lively, fresh, and ingenious. They are very clear and must, I am sure, have been valuable to the young men who heard them. As is inevitable from the lapse of time, they are by now very obviously dated: views are taken for granted which would now have to be defended by careful argument; and the tone is more edifying than is fashionable nowadays. The lectures seem to me to have some of the defects of youth, as well as its merits. They indulge rather lightly, though always interestingly, in generalizations and analogies; and although they are scholarly, the scholarship—no doubt largely because of the lecturer's youth—does not strike one as very profound. The author is in some ways more interested in his own ideas than in those of Plato; and, although this adds to the liveliness of the lectures, it diminishes their permanent value.

Another opinion of them is given by one who heard them delivered, and whose conception of philosophy and its functions was completely altered by the experience: 'Without in the least sacrificing academic standards, he managed to make philosophy seem to be not a remote pursuit for recondite truth, but a study with a real bearing on life. He plainly wanted us to get good Classes ... but I think that even more he wanted us to be good—and, if possible, Christian—servants of man.'

Socially, both duty and pleasure urged him in the same direction. The relations between dons and undergraduates varied much in the colleges; at Balliol there had been a freedom of intercourse which Temple was determined to foster between himself and his new pupils, and the pastoral duties—for as such he regarded them—of a Fellow's life weighed so strongly with him that no later development in the University saddened him more than the failure, as he saw it, to maintain the tradition he had helped to establish. Queen's at that time, owing to the example of T. H. Grose and A. C. Clark, probably resembled Balliol more closely than any other college did; but by some undergraduates this informal friendliness between members of the Senior and Junior Common Rooms was resented. Was it within their tradition that a Fellow should be constantly looking for an undergraduate to take him for a walk, that he should invade his pupils' rooms between 10.0 and 11.0 at night and talk for an hour over the cocoa cups; that one of them, after pounding out Rachmaninoff's Prelude in C sharp minor on his piano, should be greeted on the stairs with 'Do you really like that Prelude?' by a don to whom he had never spoken; or that the first letter one received from a Fellow of the College should begin with 'It's time you dropped calling me "Mr."'? But it was noticed that these questions were asked only by undergraduates who did not receive Temple's attentions or accompany him on his walks. The more personally favoured appreciated the sheer friendliness of the new Fellow's bid for confidence and affection; and, if defence were needed to the charge often brought against Temple that he was interested in problems but not in persons, it could be given almost entirely in words of his pupils at Queen's, who still bear grateful testimony to the joy and profit of this simple and natural intercourse. For the more intimate of his undergraduate friends there would also be walking parties in the Lakes, at Buttermere or Grasmere, and reading parties at Church Stretton; the day usually ending with uproarious games that did not make too severe a demand upon the intelligence or the memory of those who had no more card-sense than their host. In these ways he gathered round him a circle of friends—it was never a large one, but it was drawn from all types of undergraduate. The tenure of his Fellowship was too short, and his interests were too widely spread, for him to play a part in the life of the College comparable with that of some of his colleagues. But the loyalty of his pupils endured, and not one of them lost for the Church reformer or the Archbishop the affectionate regard they once had for the young Fellow of Queen's.

By most of the older Fellows this type of don, forty years ago, was likely to be regarded with a measure of suspicion, nor was Temple's avowed socialism the best passport to the sedate and settled fellowship of an Oxford Senior Common Room. But he combined with his youthfulness of spirit an intellectual maturity that placed him at once on a level with his seniors, a position which a more diffident or a more assertive man would not have found easy to acquire or to keep. He took his place among them in the daily ten-minute walk up and down the cloisters which then followed the chapel service before breakfast, and the sound of his laughter would rise to the bedrooms of those who were still sleeping or dressing. The effect of this laugh— none of his family or friends can remember the time when he was without it—was not always favourable. One of his contemporaries, with whom Temple was dining at the Merton High

Fellow of Queen's College, Oxford (1904–10)

Table, was approached after dinner by an elderly colleague with a request that full notice should be given if Temple were ever invited to dine again, 'so that I can take my name off Hall—that laugh is fatal to my digestion'. 'Unlike my elderly colleague,' his host adds, 'I always fished for that laugh. It made me feel manlier and cleaner.' The same effect was produced on an undergraduate who has since achieved international fame. 'It was laughter', writes Dr. Julian Huxley, 'in the grand manner and on the largest scale, earth-shaking laughter that shook the laugher too. While it infected everybody who heard it with cheerfulness, it was a potent disinfectant against all meanness, prurience, and petty-mindedness. It was the intensely valuable complement of Temple's deep seriousness.'

Much of the happiness of those years was found in his mother's home. After the old Archbishop's death his widow was uncertain where to live. One thing she specially desired was to be near her sons; the elder was living in a remote Welsh valley, and the hope that Temple would gain a Fellowship was among the inducements that led her to make her home in Oxford. Temple rejoiced at the decision. His complete devotion to her was marked by all who saw them together either at home or walking in the streets; a flash from an undergraduate's memory records: 'He wore a schoolboy sort of cap with a wild straggling tie and clothes of an amazing cut. I give him full marks for walking round Oxford arm in arm with his mother in her Victorian bonnet. That needed some doing in those days.' After unsuccessful negotiations for two other houses, Mrs. Temple settled at 8 Keble Road, and while she was moving in Temple decided to keep out of the way. He wrote from Misterton Rectory, Lutterworth, on 7 July:

My dear Mother,

. . . I hope you were satisfied with the progress of affairs at No. 8: you will, I am afraid, be having rather a rush and bother now for a bit; I wish I were there to help, but I really must work so I am better away: and before long 'We two will live like birds in a cage', as William Shakespeare expresses it—only you must do the chirruping, because I am not very good at that: I will gnaw the lumps of sugar, if Nana gives us any.

I should think that is enough of sheer nonsense for one
attempt, so I will conclude
        'Wishing thee wholly where Zeus lives the most
        Within the eventual element of calm'—
which is better than Tennyson's line about 'beyond these
voices', because 'These voices' to a great extent produce the
'Calm' and the 'Peace', and there is no 'Beyond' in that sense;
Tennyson in his enthusiasm for evolution and its goal in the
future always forgot that 'The Kingdom of Heaven'—and
consequently all its citizens—'is within you' or 'amongst you'
whichever it ought to be: and that is a splendid fact:—
        The wonderful Dead who have passed through the body
                and gone
        [Are] back once more to breathe in an old world worth their
                new;
only one has to be so good if one is to *know* that!
                                        Your loving
                                        WM. TEMPLE.

Temple's own troubles began when he had to arrange his
books in the room that had been set apart for his study:

I revolved for some days like a colossal tee-to-tummy in
the centre of a vast pile of grimy volumes—a process that
induced giddiness, irregular pulse, torpid liver, and an aggravated
state of melancholia! All the Vol. IIs I have now close to the
Vol. Is of identical title and all are arranged by subjects: e.g.
the works of Shakespeare stand next their sole rival for the
foremost place in European fiction—the Statutes of Oxford
University. This example of true insight will suffice to assure
you of the admirable quality of the work. The house is really
delightful . . . my room is so splendid that I cannot work for
admiration of it.

Here, for six years, his mother held her court—it was almost that
—and to her tea-parties would come dons and undergraduates
attracted alike by her patrician dignity and the sense of humour
which was one of her unfailing charms. 'You probably passed a
curate or two on the stairs' she would say half-apologetically to a

visitor, at a time when one of Temple's activities involved some gathering of clergy in his mother's house. She would laughingly excuse his perpetual cerebrations—'William propounds the wildest plans at breakfast, but he has generally forgotten them by lunch time'—and more than once she would end some discussion with a shake of the head and twinkle of the eye: 'Ah, William, you know so much more than I do, but I know so much better.' She looked forward every day to breakfast, for then she usually had him to herself; but on Sunday afternoon her rooms would be full, though no guests, however important or numerous, would keep Temple in Keble Road beyond a quarter to six, so that he might take his place in the College Chapel for Evensong. Here— as in the College Musical Society—he took a lively and leading part. Evensong was sung daily by boys, the other parts being taken by members of the College. He could read music accurately; the clefs in the old music books had no terrors for him; he never tired of Byrd and Tallis and Orlando Gibbons, and an under- graduate who sang tenor at his side in the choir remembers the 'devotion with which he sang the Bach chorales'. One curious antipathy marked his musical taste. Many years later, at Bishop- thorpe, when the conversation had turned one evening on a certain plainsong melody, he remained unusually silent—for he enjoyed talking of few subjects more than of music—until one of the guests appealed to him for his opinion and was shocked to receive the curt reply: 'I detest plainsong'.

His musical activities were not confined to the College. He was a member of the Bach Choir under Sir Hugh Allen at a time when it performed the Beethoven Mass in D, the Bach Mass in B Minor, the *S. Matthew Passion*, and Brahms's *Requiem*; and he was one of those who sang the *Requiem* at the Queen's Hall in 1907, when the London and Oxford Bach Choirs combined in the memorial concert to Joachim. But it was for Wagner that he had at that time his greatest musical passion. On four days in one week he took the train to London in the afternoon, went to Covent Garden for *The Ring*, and came down by the last train from Paddington, appearing punctually in chapel at 8.0 o'clock the next morning. Of his devotion to Wagner, and his desire that others should share it, the Rev. W. M. Howitt (one of his pupils) has vivid memories:

A casual remark to the effect that I didn't care for Wagner's music—a remark prompted, of course, by pure ignorance— must have set him thinking. Anyhow, one evening after Evensong while we were waiting for the bugle notes which summoned us to Hall, he suddenly said: 'You are coming with me next Wednesday to Covent Garden, where we shall hear *Die Walküre*, and then you will tell me if you still dislike Wagner. I pay', he added, as if guarding against the only possible ground for refusal. . . . But for such an enterprise the mind must be prepared. So round and round the Quad we walked that evening, while he unfolded the whole story of the Ring, explaining Wagner's philosophy, the structure of the music dramas, singing out loud the *Leitmotive*, so that if I failed to appreciate the work, it would not be through ignorance of its devices. He must have been in those days a Wagner enthusiast, and he certainly made me one; and after our evening at Covent Garden we used often to go through on the piano, he singing, the manageable bits of the operas. *Die Walküre* was his favourite, especially the first Act, though *Tristan* was a close rival in his affections. . . . After his Oxford days he tended to leave Wagner out, though I don't think he ever ceased to admire him; what was remarkable was his appreciation of the many sides of Wagner's genius, not merely of his music. . . . Besides this, there was his private music-making. He played the piano at odd free times: occasionally he would bring out his oboe, if he happened to have a reed that would work; then the solos in *Messiah* were laid under contribution; mostly it was singing. He had a strong rhythmic and dramatic sense, a preference for the sublime and boldly imaginative, and his big vocal compass put a wide range of musical literature within his grasp. Among other things he sang a good deal of Schumann, notably the song-cycle *Dichter-liebe*—where *Die Rose, die Lilie* sometimes became a race between singer and player—some Richard Strauss and Hugo

Wolf, many of the songs of Schubert and of Brahms, whose *Vier ernste Gesänge* especially fascinated him, and some rather unusual English songs. He liked singing Arthur Somervell's *Maud* cycle, why I never quite understood, as Tennyson was not his poet, and he was as critical of words as of music.

In his first two years at Queen's Temple enjoyed a glorious liberty of mind and body. He wrote no book, he made no public speech till late in 1906, and the first crisis in his life had not to be faced till February in that year. But all the while he was deliberately educating himself, and his freedom from lecturing in his first year as a don, followed by two terms' leave of absence granted by the College, suggested to him an opportunity that was not likely to occur again of sitting under the noted philosophers and theologians who were then filling the lecture halls of the Continent. There was also a more immediate motive —the need to find some quiet place where he could write his thesis for the Ellerton Theological Essay Prize (though he did not gain it, he was honourably mentioned). Early in 1905 he took German lessons in Oxford, and after a short stay with his uncle, Sir Frank Lascelles, at the British Embassy in Berlin, he arrived towards the end of October at Jena, returning a year later to complete some work with one of the professors. For part of the time R. H. Tawney joined him; his other companions were Americans, among them the Rev. Dr. B. R. Brundage, a young Presbyterian minister from Indiana, who was spending his honeymoon in Europe. Jena—the 'Athens of Germany'—was then at the height of its reputation. Hilgenfeld and Ernst Haeckel were near the end of their careers; Rudolph Eucken was wearing the laurels of the Nobel Prize in Literature; Hans Heinrich Wendt (with his understudy Weinel) was at the peak of his fame. The Carl Zeiss laboratory glass and scientific lenses were renowned the world over, and to Jena travelled students from every land, pressing to be in the van of scientific and philosophic learning.

Temple had a comfortable home in a large two-story building, presided over by Frau Dr. Braun, the widow of a professor. Her school had once been patronized by the daughters of the more

hochgeboren English families who were being 'finished' on the
Continent; but advancing age compelled Frau Braun to give up her
teaching, and she now took paying-guests into her home. To be
accepted as a resident, or to be invited to an evening party, at
Steiger 1 was to enter the circle of the elect. Here Temple was
warmly received and, with his American friend, put in many
hours daily of solid work. His knowledge of German was still
slight, and to improve it he helped Dr. Brundage in his spare time
with the first English translation of Wendt's *Die Lehre Jesu*,
a task which the author had assigned to the young minister.
Of recreation there was little—the visit of a Zither Glee Club, at
which Temple's sense of humour got the better of him, was long
remembered—so that lectures and the Wendt translation, supple-
mented by private tuition and talks in the professors' rooms,
occupied a full day. In letters to John Stocks, Temple gives some
impressions of the professors and their teaching:

> These lectures are very odd. Wendt, a theologian, is the
> oddest. When he propounds a problem with the precise object
> of stating his solution, he assumes a despairing tone of voice,
> and says—*Wie kann es sein? Wie kann es sein?* Then, with a
> great *Ja*, he rushes at the solution he had up his sleeve the
> whole time. All the lectures are very rhetorical, not read, but
> delivered as orations with great animation and vehement
> gestures. Eucken, for instance, says materialism breaks down,
> and then shouts at the top of his voice—flinging a hand to a
> very dirty ceiling—*Freiheit! Einheit der Seele!* It is stimulating,
> and helps one to feel that the dry bones of philosophy are
> really the skeletons of the living world; but it makes progress
> very slow, because what in Oxford is one sentence is here a
> long and flowery paragraph.

Some months later he writes from the British Embassy, after
he had been working in close touch with Wendt for seven or
eight weeks:

> Jena was delightful. I do not think I heard any lecture that
> was, for me, worth hearing for its substance, except Eucken's
> 'Leading Ideas of the Time'. He never reached those important

articles, but his sketch of the history of thought down to the present was most suggestive. The lectures are all (or were *there*; I have not begun here yet) very rhetorical and 'popular'. Close work is done in the Seminar; I went to Eucken's Seminar—one has to be invited as it is *privatissime* always— where Kant's Critique (Pure R.) was taken section by section. I wish I could get into the habit of regarding Kant historically: I have a whole-hearted admiration for Descartes, though his system is bosh as a system—or would be if proposed now. But I fail to admire Kant properly, because his system is, from our point of view, bosh.

I got to know Wendt pretty well; we took walks and argued. He is a keen individualist in morals and thinks S. Paul was too; so we argued the question and fought for the body of the Apostle. The chief hint I got for myself was the possibility of making at least great chunks of one's lecture very general indeed and trying to stimulate interest even in the dull man— and then polish up people for essay work. I feel sure that most Oxford lectures are too dreary . . .

I arrived here on Sunday evening; on Monday was trussed up with red tape at the university. The next day paid fees, and to-day (in the middle of this letter) had my first lecture here, Simmel on Philosophy from Fichte to Nietzsche—to-day rather illuminating on Hegel's conception of 'Geist'. I had hoped to hear Harnack on 'Introduction to the New Testament', but he has now knocked it off, and only gives his other lecture—on 'Church History in the Middle Ages'—and I cannot bother about that. I must go and hear him once or twice, just to see him do it; ditto with Pfleiderer. At Jena I read some theology, including Moberly's *Atonement and Personality* (read it) and also had a go at Spinoza; I read all the Latin parts of him; he is the greatest of all of them—there! But if you play with him, have a look at Duff's book on him. Also Schopenhauer, Hegel's *Propädeutik*, and some odds and ends of Plato. When I have finished copying out my Ellerton, I start on Aristotle's *Metaphysics*. I hope I have cleared the reproach of not telling you about myself.

In another letter he writes that his study of Spinoza gives him 'the impression of being in the presence of a colossal mind more than anything I ever read'.

The Jena days were never forgotten. For Temple they were care-free and utterly happy, providing all that he then needed, an opportunity for strenuous work and a limited social circle of spirits kindred to his own. To his American and German friends they meant contact with one who, as they said, brought with him everything of himself—the rare atmosphere of his upbringing, his already considerable erudition, and his unaffected friendship. One of them still opens his old diary now and then and turns to the only page not covered with the notes and accounts and daily jottings of forty years ago. This page is blank except for the words: 'William Temple went away to-day.'

But there was one art which, for all his education, neither Rugby nor Balliol had taught him. It was to be a gala night at Steiger 1. Lena, the efficient maid, should serve the dinner as it had never been served before; at the heart of it there would be roast goose 'and', added Frau Braun in announcing her arrangements for the feast, 'Herr Temple shall have the honour to carve the roast goose'. Now, of the 'workers with hand or brain' there is little doubt to which section Temple belonged; but he was never one to shrink from an experiment. The moment for action came. Vaguely, but with a certain native force, he slashed here and there at the bird's unyielding body until he was stopped by an agonized cry from his hostess—'Ach! Herr Temple, you may no longer continue to carve. You are spoiling a 9-mark goose.' . . . But then, as Miss Deborah Jenkyns once sighed, 'From *some* mundane failings who is altogether free?'

V

Emancipation

It must be from the aspiration of the common people that the salvation
of the people comes. Nothing that is really good can be imposed upon
people by well-wishing superiors. In education, as in everything that
concerns the spirit, freedom is the one condition of progress.... There
is nothing that so much hinders the effective freedom of our people as
the fact that they are left without facilities for the whole development
of their faculties.

W. T., Presidential Address to the Educational Science Section
of the British Association, September 1916.

TEMPLE'S emancipation came just in time. A few more
years, and the life of cultured ease for which his upbringing
and academic training had fitted him would have claimed and
kept him—till he had devoted all his gifts and achievements to
the pursuit of a career from which, despite its obvious fascina-
tions, he was beginning to shrink: 'I do not want', he wrote, 'to
be just a lecturer in the morning and a member of the Senior
Common Room in the evening.' It could never have been quite
that. Progress would anyhow have been almost automatic; a
short spell as a Fellow—and then the headmastership of a school,
or the headship of a college, perhaps a mitre, would have fallen
to him as they had to many others of his antecedents and abilities;
and he would have adorned the highest office with a felicitous
grace. But he would not have been the William Temple who had
begun to lead the Church out of the wilderness, and whose words
were heard and heeded in five continents. Still less would he have
been the man whose name as President of the Workers' Educational Association was placed, to his own vast amusement, on
a list of dangerous—or was it merely 'suspicious'?—persons prepared during the first World War by the C.I.D.

The immediate cause of his emancipation was something which
began as an interest and became (it is not too much to say) a lifelong passion—the cause of education. On his return from Germany he was thrown into several movements concerned with it.

73

The most important of these came first. In 1905—partly at the suggestion of R. H. Tawney, and partly moved by the fact that the chair was to be taken by his old headmaster, Percival—Temple attended the first National Conference of the W.E.A. in Oxford. The story of this remarkable Movement has been well told by T. W. Price; but it exercised so strong and lasting an influence on Temple's life, and received so much of his close attention and supervision, that a short introduction is demanded.

For some years before the W.E.A. was founded, various attempts had been made to provide higher education for those workers who were ready—and able through geographical and other advantages—to profit by it; and the educational aspirations of pioneers so different as William Lovett and Frederick Denison Maurice had unconsciously prepared the way for the University Extension Movement. The intention of this Movement was excellent—to approach the members through their already established organizations—but in this, for all the devotion of its workers, it was hardly successful. It did excellent work for people of leisure, but considerably less for those on whose behalf it had been founded: and most of the Trade Union leaders of that time were more concerned with improving economic conditions than with widening the intellectual and cultural interests of Union members. It was, therefore, chiefly with the co-operative societies that contacts were established; and one of those contacts led to the founding of the Workers' Educational Association. Among the employees of the Co-operative Wholesale Society was Albert Mansbridge, a man to whose vision, energy, and perseverance the W.E.A. came to owe its existence and much of its eventual success. Through all the early hostility and discouragement he never flagged or lost faith; and he was not long in discerning a truth the earlier founders had missed, which was to change the face of adult education in Britain. The University Extension Movement had been imposed from above; its lecturers decided the subjects they would teach and their treatment of them. Was it possible to bring about a complete co-operation of artisans and university teachers, and so to make them equal partners in the great enterprise? Could the handworkers be given an opportunity of self-expression which

74

was denied to them as mere listeners to an extension lecture?
R. H. Tawney has given the reply:

Not the least noteworthy of the developments to strike the
future historian of the early twentieth century will be . . . the
emergence, among the rank and file of the working-class world,
of the conviction that education may be used as an instrument
of social emancipation, and a determination to build up, both
through and in addition to the ordinary machinery of public
education, an educational movement which is stamped with
their own ideals, and the expression of their own experience.
The time when English education could be described as a discipline imposed from above on an apathetic, if acquiescent,
population has at last ended. . . . What is significant in the
recent development of adult education . . . is the recognition
by ever wider sections of the working-class movement that if
it is to solve its own problems, mobilise its own forces, and
create a social order more in conformity with its own ideals, it
must attend to the education of its members with the same
deliberation and persistence which it has brought to the
improvement of their economic position.

Once convinced that this was right and possible—that the only
way to throw a bridge over the chasm that separated the handworkers from the intellectuals was to begin building from both
sides at once—Dr. Mansbridge turned his whole energy to working out the practical details. There were many lions in the path.
On both sides suspicion was rife. Several dons in Oxford, notably
Sidney Ball and A. L. Smith, were convinced, apart from any
considerations of policy, that justice demanded a fair hearing for
Dr. Mansbridge's plea: but the majority of them—like the member
of a Senior Common Room who voted for a colleague's proposal
to grant £50 towards the work of tutorial classes, on the ground
that it might be wise to 'placate the brigands'—were either nervous
or indifferent. Nor were most of the workers more enthusiastic.
The leaders of the Trade Unions had brought their members to
the point of feeling industrially, in some areas politically, conscious.
The men had trodden every inch of the rough way to power by

themselves; could they trust the hand that once pressed them under and was now held out to feed them? And what need was there of the only kind of book-learning, consisting largely of garbled history and reactionary economics, that was ever likely to come out of Oxford?

To a generation that has known two wars and the mixing of the nation's manhood in a struggle for survival, and is now carrying out a great and agreed scheme of educational reform, such words may sound wild and whirling enough; at that time they were spoken in deadly earnest—often with all the bitterness of the dispossessed—in the mines, the docks, the shipyards, and the factories of Britain. But it took more than this to daunt Dr. Mansbridge. With a definite goal before him, he swept aside one obstacle after another; his adaptability was amazing. He could thrill an audience of trade unionists with the glowing fervour of his own enthusiasm; half an hour later, to a company of dons in a College Common Room he would be (as Temple said) 'purring like any Common Room cat' and saying precisely the same things —but most certainly not in the same way. His triumph came when in 1907, at the Extension Summer Meeting, a resolution was passed approving the formation of a joint committee of fourteen, seven to be appointed by the Vice-Chancellor and seven by the W.E.A. Executive; and this was followed by united official action on the part of other universities, which resulted in the formation of a body known as the Central Joint Advisory Committee. Temple's words, spoken on the occasion of Dr. Mansbridge's retirement, were profoundly true:

I wonder if nowadays it is realised how great an achievement was the founding of this Central Joint Advisory Committee. The Board of Education had been struggling for years to persuade the universities and university colleges of England to come together in one body for any purpose that could be devised. If only they would unite on something—but it had been all in vain. Then Mansbridge persuaded the first Oxford Joint Committee to invite the other universities and the university colleges to join in forming the C.J.A.C. The thing

was immediately done. As far as I know there was no hesitation in any quarter; what had been impossible to the concentrated efforts of the British State was immediately achieved
when Mansbridge flourished his wand.

So much it has been necessary to say if the importance of the
W.E.A. among the manifold activities of Temple's life is to be
understood. In addition to all the other inventions with which
Dr. Mansbridge enriched the work and enlarged the scope of the
Association, Temple once said, 'As a merely personal matter . . .
he invented *me*', and his presidential address of 1909 opened with
these words:

> My friends, you conferred upon me last year what, in view of
> the place this Association is going to hold in the progress of
> the country, is likely to remain—is bound, I think, to remain—
> the greatest honour of my life.

It was not until 1924 that he felt he must lay down the presidency, which was indeed no sinecure; and he was also Joint
Secretary with Dr. Mansbridge of the Tutorial Classes Committee until he was appointed Headmaster of Repton. The
minutes of the first meeting of that committee, held at Balliol in
November 1908, were written by Temple himself on spare pages
of an old note-book. 'The writing', according to the Master of
Balliol, 'is both vigorous and boyish,' and he adds: 'If the adult
education movement has gone on being alive as I think it has
through all these years, it owes a great deal to the continued youth
of some of those who first inspired it, and particularly to William
Temple.'

But these are dry bones. Can we make them live with the
spirit of the man who, through the best years of his life, served the
Association with a single-minded devotion, and from first to last
regarded his work for it as among the most worth-while efforts
of his career? Fortunately there survive more of Temple's pronouncements on adult education than on almost any other single
subject. In his presidential addresses year after year, in the articles
he wrote for *Highway*, in the numerous meetings he addressed on
behalf of the Association—and these continued after he had

resigned the presidency—he set out the principles that lay behind the demand for a fuller intellectual life, the spirit by which learner and teacher alike and together should be inspired, and the pitfalls awaiting those who approached the great task of education with sectarian or sectional prejudices, with the calculating brain, the tabloid mind, or the cold heart. Principles (as always with him) came first and among them, essentially and pre-eminently, two stood out—the principles of Liberty and Justice. For several years he had studied the concepts that were implicit in these words; the day had now come when he was to discover how far as a fact they were explicit in the state of contemporary society and in the system by which that society was developing the personality of its members. The search was not encouraging. But the less of these two principles he discovered in the British educational system, the more sacred he regarded his duty to urge, with all the force at his command, their relevance to the training of the nation's citizens, and to the moral duty of the State. Temple's line of argument is worth studying, and can best be expressed in his own words:

The more thoughtful minds in the Labour movement have become increasingly convinced that the real root of social problems is spiritual. . . . What Labour is resenting is not so much poverty, short of destitution, but rather the insult to the personality of the poor man. It is the sense that the man who cannot buy recognition of his rights is treated as if he had no human rights, no other rights than those for which he has contracted. He contracts for a certain wage, and he is paid the wage for which he contracted; and beyond that he is liable to be treated as if he had no claim upon sympathy or respect, still less upon affection.

Until education has done far more work than it has yet had an opportunity of doing, you cannot have society organized on the basis of justice; for this reason, that there will always be that strain of which we have spoken between what is due to a man in view of his humanity with all his powers and capacities, and what is due to him at the moment as a member of society, with all his faculties still undeveloped, with many of his tastes warped, and with his powers largely crushed. There is always that strain. Are you going to treat a man as what he is, or as what he might be? Morality requires, I think, that you should treat him as what he might be, as what he has it in him to become; and business requires that you should treat him as what he is; and you cannot get rid of that strain except by raising what he is to the level of what he might be. That is the whole work of education. Give him the full development of his powers; and there will no longer be that conflict between the claim of the man as he is and the claim of the man as he might become. And so you can have no justice at the basis of your social life until education has done its full work.

And then again, you can have no real freedom, because until a man's whole personality has developed he cannot be free in his own life; he will not be capable of forming the ideal to satisfy his whole nature, and then setting himself steadily in the pursuit of it, following that ideal whatever other impulses or desires may arise from time to time cutting across his path; he will not be able to do this unless his various faculties have all received full development. Perhaps this means that none of us can do it. Very well; but, in any case, the further a man is from receiving the full development of his powers, the further is he from the possibility of really living his own life.

And you cannot have political freedom any more than you can have moral freedom until people's powers are developed, for the simple reason that over and over again we find that men with a cause which is either just, or at least contains much justice, are unable to state it in the way which might enable it to prevail. The cause on the other side, which also may be partly just, is stated with more facility and with more plausibility, and carries the day; and therefore you cannot have real political freedom until people's powers are so developed that they are able to give full force to the justice of their contentions; and until that time you will have what the Bishop of Oxford speaks about—you will have ignorance trodden under the foot of knowledge. . . . There exists a mental form of

79

slavery quite as real as any economic form. We are pledged to destroy it. . . . If you want human liberty you must have educated people.

These were the principles on which Temple would have the republic of the mind founded and raised. From them sprang always the substance of his appeal; yet with skilful artistry, by illustration and anecdote, and by a rare mastery of prose idiom and literary form, he so varied it from one audience and one occasion to another, that the listener was never left with the impression that he was hearing nothing but what he had heard before. Still less that the speaker was not entirely sincere: 'One hardly ever met Temple', writes one of his W.E.A. colleagues, 'without the meeting leaving a memory of some notable remark; and yet one never had the least feeling that he was speaking for effect'; and the Principal of Westfield College, Mrs. J. L. Stocks, recalls a meeting in the Sheffield City Hall, when he gave a lecture—'a real lecture'—on the philosophic conception of liberty . . . 'and the astonishing thing was that this vast audience followed his reasoning and responded to it, thinking along with him as he went'. On any who will trouble to read through at a sitting—or several sittings—the articles in *Highway* and Temple's W.E.A. presidential addresses, two impressions must remain; the consistency of his convictions and appeals, and the art by which he was able to present them year by year in some perpetually fresh guise.

No less important in his estimate of the work to which the W.E.A. had set its hand was the spirit of its members. He gave the word 'brotherhood' a new life, as he told of the sanctity of their calling. The W.E.A. was a sacrament—a sacrament of a passion for knowledge and for brotherhood in the pursuit of knowledge—and in every branch and all sections of their organization they were to ensure that this passion was continually expressed. 'Devotion, even to heroism' must be their motto. Their vocation was that of missionaries; only with utter self-denial and sacrifice could they hope to win converts; the moment self-satisfaction appeared, either at their headquarters or in the branches, the spiritual efficacy of their mission was doomed. Nor were they concerned only with the intellect: the sympathies and affections needed training and guiding no less than the mind; the whole personality, as they were to see the ideal, must be integrated in the pursuit of learning.

On the subject-matter of its studies Temple gave the W.E.A. a guidance much needed in its early years. Contrary, perhaps, to what might have been expected, few students in W.E.A. classes suffered from the temptation to use them as a ladder to personal advancement and success. The large majority regarded education as a powerful instrument of social emancipation; but they were well aware that a knowledge of history or economics or literature is not among the qualifications which enable individuals to 'get on' and 'rise in life'. Indeed, the fact that the Association did not appeal to economic motives, but provided a humane education for those whose opportunities of obtaining it had been slight, was the secret of its power. Temple shared that point of view, and drove it home continually with lucidity and vigour; he did not disguise his conviction that a predominantly utilitarian conception of education was a parody of all that the word implied. Seldom can he have laughed more boisterously than when he was told the tale of a nine-year-old boy in a Bethnal Green school, who handed to his teacher one morning an untidy piece of blue paper torn from a sugar-bag, on which had been scrawled with a blunt pencil—'DON'T teach my boy poitry he's going to be a GROCER'. Whether (as he intended) or not he ever quoted the story to a W.E.A. audience, the moral of it was frequently pressed home: there were treasures of learning yet to be revealed to the workers which could be of no conceivable use to them in their struggle for material contentment. Temple knew that a revolutionary movement will not at first be inclined to 'respect the stored wisdom of the ages', and he warned his audiences that to cultivate this disrespect would be by so much to forgo their spiritual birthright. The aim of education was to train men and women to understand the world they live in. Their standards and ideals must therefore be raised on the firmest possible foundations of wide knowledge and experience, if they

G

were to be qualified to assist or resist the ruling tendencies of their time.

But—and this was no mere academic question for one who was Fellow of an Oxford college and about to be headmaster of a public school—how were they to decide the respective merits of the two predominant types of education that had figured in British history, the traditional and the modern? Each had its claims to press. The traditional, seen most clearly in our public schools and older universities, was corporate; it had tended to be aristocratic, and had educated persons through influence rather than instruction. Chief among the instruments of this type of education had been the literature of Greece and Rome (it is to be remembered that Temple was strongly in favour of the abolition of compulsory Greek at Oxford and Cambridge); its aim had been to put the student's mind in touch with great minds of the past, so that he could judge the trends of the moment in the light of the best human experience. For all its strength the traditional type had its faults: 'I regret to say that it is perfectly possible', Temple once said, 'to obtain a Double First in Oxford without a sympathetic understanding of what a trade union is: and that seems to me, so far as it goes, a flaw in that system.' The modern type of education, on the other hand, was predominantly individual rather than corporate, intellectual rather than spiritual, democratic rather than aristocratic. It supplied students with knowledge of facts rather than standards of judgement; it called in aid intelligence and memory more often than sympathy and imagination. This type had its own weaknesses: it tended to assume that the significance of past events did not persist; in so far as it aimed at helping people to give of their best by pitting them one against another, it trusted to competition. Was it worth while to get the best work out of a student at the cost of teaching him that he was to make the effort in his own interest?

There was hardly a greater need in the whole field of education, Temple held, than that of drawing together these two types and tendencies: and, while uniting them, of leaving the whole strength of both unimpaired. He realized and regretted that the traditional form had become stereotyped and lifeless through lack of

contact with vital problems, and that the modern and progressive
type had become commercial and unspiritual through lack of contact with the thought and knowledge of the past. But he had no
doubt which type should predominate. In 1912 the W.E.A.
Summer School was held at Oxford, and in the presidential
address he delivered at Balliol in October of the same year he said:

Now I wish to express a purely personal conviction with
regard to these two types of teaching, and it is this: while we
have got to incorporate all, or at any rate nearly all, that the
more modern type of education has given us, it has got to be
used in such a way as to leave the great marks of the traditional
type predominant. Education, I hold, should remain primarily
corporate rather than individual, primarily spiritual (that is,
effective through influence, and through an appeal to sympathy
and imagination), rather than primarily intellectual (that is,
effective through an appeal to intelligence and memory),
primarily concerned with giving people the power to pronounce
judgment on any facts with which they may come in contact
rather than supplying them simply with the facts. It should be
primarily co-operative and not primarily competitive. To
some extent, it is precisely the work of the W.E.A. that has
shown one the need that the old traditional type should predominate. For it is the W.E.A. which has understood more
definitely than any other body I am aware of, that what it finds
of supreme value in the great centres of education is the spirit
of the place rather than the instruction: and those of us who
have received, or have been in a position to receive, the best
that Oxford can give, and those who have had just a taste of
her treasures at the Summer School, will agree that Oxford
does more for us than any lectures do. But while we say that,
we need also to insist on a greater energy and efficiency, a
greater and more living contact with the world of to-day in
some, at least, of the centres of the old traditional type. Yet it
is the traditional type that must control, because the traditional
type on the whole stands for spirit against machinery. I have
no doubt it is true that the old schools and universities are

amateurish in method: and I have no doubt that we ought to organize ourselves more efficiently. There is a good deal of waste that may be saved: but I shall regret the day when we become efficient at the cost of our spirit.

One Sunday evening, during the Oxford Summer School to which Temple here refers, has remained in the memory of all who shared the experience. He had already preached at the University Church in the morning, and it was suggested that he might be willing after dinner to take the chair at an informal discussion on religious questions and difficulties, with members of the School. He gladly assented, and the meeting was held in Balliol Hall. The attitude of most members towards religion and the Church was critical if not actually hostile: and Temple knew it. But for nearly four hours he dominated the gathering, leading the debate, answering some questions and inviting others, shirking no difficulty, and showing the utmost sympathy with the doubts and denials expressed. It was not the only occasion on which one flash of insight followed another as he stated far better than the critic the question that was asked, and then answered it with a dignity and directness enlivened by touches of humour that won the hearts, if not the minds, of them all. 'Well on to midnight', Dr. Mansbridge recalls, 'Temple, driven by the opposition, rose to great heights. I have never myself seen him so radiant and convincing elsewhere. Opposition inspires him'; and there were few in the hall whose conception of religion and whose attitude to the Church were not affected by that Sunday evening debate in Oxford.

Such an opportunity Temple grasped all the more eagerly since debates on religion were banned at W.E.A. meetings, and it was unusual to throw the columns of *Highway* open to religious discussion. (This deficiency, inevitable in a body so constituted as the W.E.A., made him the keener in his support of the Church Tutorial Classes Association which was founded in 1915, with Dr. H. M. Burge as its first president. Its methods were modelled on those of the W.E.A., and during his time at Manchester Temple took an active and personal interest in the Movement, preaching and speaking for it in his diocese.) Occasionally, however, the ban in *Highway* seems to have been lifted. In its issue of December 1910, a writer had suggested some causes for 'the decay of the power of religion'. Temple seized the opportunity to answer him. His article began with—'I wish to maintain that such decay cannot be accounted for because it does not exist', and ended thus:

> Mr. Gill gives an outline account of what Christianity is. I do not recognize it. It is, in the first place, infected with the error of his whole conception of religion, which, he tells us, 'is the discovery of a rhyme and reason in things'. Religion may include this: but in its essence it is an experience—the experience of a presence and power which we can only understand if we call it the presence and power of God. Guided by this experience, men make theories of life, and seek for 'a rhyme and reason in things'. The result of their search is not religion, but theology, which is the science of religion and of life as illuminated by religion. But Mr. Gill thinks that Christian theology maintains that 'God created the world for His Pleasure, and man to glorify the Creator'. This is the view which, as he holds, modern knowledge has made incredible. But it is not the Christian position, which is that God is love; love needs that to which it may give itself; and the universe is created as the object of the infinite love of God. Whether or not this is true, it is at least well able to defend itself; and, among many others, I should maintain that it is the only view capable of affording intellectual satisfaction.
>
> I will conclude by repeating that neither this theory nor any other theory is the essence of the Christian religion, any more than the scientific laws concerning electricity are the essence of a flash of lightning or of an electric shock. That essence is an experience of the power of the love of God in Christ changing our hopes and desires. And this power, in those who recognize its source and in those who do not, is greater to-day than it has ever been.

It is now time to ask whether the work and the sacrifice of these sixteen years were justified by their results. There are several question-marks that must remain after a study of Temple's

William Temple

career, but here the answer cannot be challenged. The results were far-reaching and permanent. By the leaders of the nation, watching the trend of working-class opinion and policy, it was recognized that many official calculations and assumptions had been upset: it could, for instance, no longer be maintained by any informed person that there was no demand for higher education among the workers. The sympathy of the Board of Education was assured: 'All power to your elbow with the W.E.A.', wrote H. A. L. Fisher to Temple, who had sent him a note of congratulation on his appointment as President of the Board; 'I shall want to help you in any way possible.'

On the members of the Association its effect became each year more obvious. A new force had come into their lives. Their intellectual growth was stimulated, their abilities were directed into channels of fresh interest and inquiry, and their paper-work reached a level that surprised those who read it: the verdict of A. L. Smith has been frequently quoted, that out of a bundle of W.E.A. essays taken haphazard 25 per cent. reached a standard of a First Class in the Modern History School at Oxford. But more striking was the result on the general social outlook and the home life of the members—of a west-country miner, for instance, who had a hunger for knowledge that nothing had satisfied until he heard of the W.E.A. Most of his day was spent lying on his back in the pit; on Sunday he read the Bible and attended public worship. This was his whole life till he had saved shillings enough to enable him to be present at a summer meeting at Oxford, where he heard lectures that suggested how his craving might be allayed. Back at Bristol, he started on a new course of reading with any neighbours who cared to take part in it; it was not long before a small bookshelf was fixed above the mangle in his wash-house, and on the backs of the books were the names of Ruskin, Carlyle, Seeley, Newman, Kingsley, Tennyson, and Browning. No less striking is the testimony of the Rev. C. J. Stephen, now Vicar of Silvertown:

While Dr. Temple was headmaster of Repton he gave the inaugural lectures at the formation of the local W.E.A. in the

86

Town Hall in Burton-on-Trent, just before the last war. My
dear father, a machine-minder at a local printing works, attended
those lectures. At the final lecture, Temple ended with these
words: 'The great tragedy is, that men should "go out" not
knowing these things.' His personality, his lectures, and these
words altered the whole course of my father's life. He became
the first member of the local W.E.A. and has seldom missed a
lecture these 40 years; and, though a working man, his general
education is far in advance of many men with better advantages.
His love of learning, started by Temple, bore fruit in his
children, three boys. He led us to the way of good books, and
the conversation in our working-class home was always of a
very high order—of Greece and Rome, of Drama and
Literature.

As we grew older and started to work he encouraged us in
the ways of reading, marking, learning and inwardly digesting.
He was earning 28/- a week when I was 14 and started work in
Burton-on-Trent as a joiner's apprentice. I attended Church
and Sunday School and saved my money and am now a parson.
My youngest brother was ordained at Lichfield three years ago
and is now on the staff, teaching, at Nottingham High School.
My second brother is studying to be a handicraft instructor. I
am convinced that the influence of Temple on my dear father
changed not only the course of his own life, but of his three
sons also, of whom I have the honour to be the eldest.

But in none was a greater or more lasting change effected than
in Temple himself. One disability, a direct result of his W.E.A.
contacts, clung to him for a few years: he was too apt to identify
the great body of workers with the members of the Association,
and this for a time coloured his whole conception of working-
class mentality. Except for the butler at Fulham and Lambeth
and his scouts at Balliol and Queen's, he had hardly spoken to an
adult handworker till he joined the W.E.A. Unlike his predecessor at Lambeth he lacked familiarity with the homely talks, the
ceaseless tasks and troubles, of the housewife which the parish
priest may encounter on every day of his ministry; and in his

early years he unconsciously assumed in his hearers a higher
degree of intelligence than many of them could claim. It was one
thing to address a big audience of workers who had come together
for the deliberate purpose of having their reason stimulated and
their wits sharpened by contact with a finer mind than their own:
it was altogether another to enliven the torpor and dispel the
petty worries of a congregation of simple people, mostly too tired
to assimilate any spiritual truths beyond those with an immediate
impact on their daily round. This weakness was overcome partly
through Temple's work for the National Mission, and the First
World War—which provided many contacts he would not have
made in more normal times—and it was overcome, not by the
easy way of cutting the heart out of his message and descending
to thoughtless chatter, but by the sterner discipline of learning
how to express the greatest truths in words that the least sophis-
ticated could not misinterpret. All his early connexions had been
with the very small world of the public schools and universities,
an even more restricted section of the nation forty years ago than
now: and, when he began to learn what the social system looked
like when seen from below, his natural sympathy reinforced the
conclusions to which his reason had been leading him. R. H.
Tawney has well written:

> The 'We and They' complex, which is so marked even among
> the most virtuous members of the privileged classes, might
> have clung to him as a habit, even though he knew it to be
> damnable in principle. It could not survive continuous
> co-operation with colleagues whose educational interests he
> shared, but whose experience of life was quite different from
> his own.

Such, and so wrought, was the emancipation of William Temple.
It would be too much to attribute the appointment of the Royal
Commission on the Universities in 1921 to the work and influence
of the W.E.A.; but the Association was one of several movements
which, fourteen years earlier, were disturbing the peace of the
University. Taken together, they were largely responsible for
the 'Six Tutors' Campaign' (though there were seven) in which

Temple played a part, and which led directly to the Royal Commission. At Oxford, in the first decade of the century, reform was in the air. Ruskin Hall, as it was called till 1907, was firmly established; at Pusey House John Carter, with a violence all his own, was proclaiming a Christian social gospel which Liddon would have shuddered to hear propagated within the four walls of the House that had in several respects so gravely disappointed him; the Fabian Society meetings were attracting some of the more brilliant undergraduates; and the only organization that seemed unaffected—it had been left to its own will and pleasure since the early eighties—was the University itself.

Even here changes were inevitable. A few of the younger dons, who would be said nowadays to have a 'leftish slant', agreed that a survey of the position from their point of view might be helpful, and formed themselves into the 'Catiline Club'. This small but notable company included W. H. (now Sir William) Fyfe, R. W. (now Sir Richard) Livingstone, J. L. (now Sir John) Myres, A. E. (now Sir Alfred) Zimmern, and Temple. They met weekly at what was called the 'Unholy Lunch', to distinguish it from the 'Holy Lunch' of the collaborators in *Foundations*; and one of them has not forgotten how, when pipes were lit after luncheon, Temple—much the same in appearance as he was in later years, 'perhaps a little more chubby and a little less large'—made up for his abstention from tobacco by finishing the pudding, especially if it happened to be a sweet one. Sir John Myres, who was the senior member by some years, was leader of the group; R. H. Tawney, though not a member, wrote trenchantly and effectively in the *Westminster Gazette*; and the conspiracy culminated in a series of articles in *The Times* (April 1907) under the general heading of 'Oxford and the Nation'. Temple's special help was given in two ways. He drafted the resolutions and recommendations of the Group—a feat in which he was already showing more than common skill—and he persuaded Gore (then Bishop of Birmingham) to raise the subject of University Reform in the House of Lords a few months later. This debate had a marked effect on public opinion in and beyond academic circles, not least (by his own confession) on Curzon, who was then Chancellor of the University. Of his own talk with the Chancellor, who paid a visit to Oxford to take some soundings, Temple wrote to his mother:

> I had a full hour with the Chancellor yesterday—he was very friendly and very intelligent! He has a great power of following intricate threads. Altogether he was very sympathetic to our schemes—and asked me to write to him on any points I was not sure of having made clear, and I have just composed a letter of eleven pages to him. Zimmern had had an hour on Friday, and also found him very friendly. I think he means business. He wants to find points on which a working majority may be hoped for.

Too much has since happened at Oxford and Cambridge—in the development and adjustment of their functions, in their administration, their teaching, and the general outlook of their leaders—to make even an outline of the reforms then suggested of any living interest to-day: enough to say that Curzon claimed that he had had 'an opportunity of hearing the views of almost every section of opinion in the University', and published in 1909 his 'Principles and Methods of University Reform' in *A Letter addressed to the University of Oxford*. Certain minor changes were made, but were largely ineffective. When it came to details, the senior members of the reform party were hopelessly divided; their opponents were skilful tacticians; and over much of the University danced the spirit of Hippocleides. After one of many divisions, as Strachan-Davidson and A. L. Smith left the Congregation House together, one of the two was heard to mutter to his colleague: 'Well, I think we can run the University under this management as well as under any other.'

At the other end of the educational scale, one of the fiercest conflicts in the history of Parliament was being fought out at Westminster. By an overwhelming majority the Liberals had been returned in 1906, at an election that marked the peak of the political power of religious nonconformity. The number of English nonconformist M.P.s (157) in the new House was exactly that of the whole Conservative opposition; and Birrell, whom Campbell-Bannerman had appointed President of the Board of Education, produced a Bill calculated to satisfy their pressing demands. Details of the unpleasant and bitter struggle which ended only a few days before Christmas, when the Lords decided by a large majority to 'insist on their amendments' and the Bill was dropped, can be found in the columns of Hansard and the records of the National Society. Temple's part in the year's disputations shocked the church party in Parliament and distressed many of the bishops who were prepared to hope great things of him. He showed his hand first in the Lent term of 1906, when he made an impressive speech at the Union on Birrell's projected Bill, and on the principle of undenominationalism. At the beginning of the summer term he developed his argument in the *Oxford Magazine*, where he crossed swords with another young don, each contributing two articles. Sir Walter Moberly writes:

> In this little tournament we were both *epigoni*, each espousing a cause which had been his father's, and indeed each using mainly his father's armour. At that time Temple's position was distinctly Erastian as compared with his maturer views ... the articles represent a stage in the evolution of his thought. Later we both modified our views substantially, and in recent years were entirely at one on educational policy. Indeed if there had been any nuance of difference, I suspect we should have crossed over, and Temple would have been slightly the more militant defender of specifically 'Church' interests.

What, then, were Temple's earliest formulated convictions on the policy and the duty of the Church in the education of the nation's children? Of their twofold origin there can be no doubt. They derived in part, as Sir Walter Moberly suggests, from the memory of his father's views. In one of the *Oxford Magazine* articles he quotes a statement made fifty years earlier by the Archbishop—it was an exaggeration, his father had said, to contend that religious teaching imperatively demanded a denominational system: that system might be the best way of securing religious teaching, but it was not the only way; and there was a point beyond which it ceased to be so much a security for religious teaching as for doctrinal teaching; and to lay so much stress on the doctrinal teaching of children in elementary schools was 'a mere mistake'. The other decisive influence was Temple's reverence for Thomas Arnold: and he brought the two together, adding a third plea, when he made his first public speech on 4 October 1906, during the Church Congress at Barrow-in-Furness. By that time, as he remarked in his opening sentence, the great mass of churchpeople had already made up their minds on the Birrell Bill, so that it could do comparatively little harm for him to lay down some of the principles which should have guided them to a decision. This freedom from responsibility—and it must be remembered that in 1906 Temple, in the eyes of church leaders, was merely a young lay Fellow (however brilliant in promise) of an Oxford college—enabled him to make his points vigorously and fearlessly, with no circumlocutions and few reservations. The first was that the teaching they were discussing was to be given to children; therefore the concern of those responsible for imparting it must be with child psychology; and modern psychology had done nothing but confirm the theory put forward about 380 B.C. It was not only useless but positively harmful, Plato had insisted, to appeal to the logical understanding of a child while that understanding was still undeveloped. Instruction should be emotional and imaginative, and given through parable and precept—'the logical element in religion must be developed out of the emotional element, and not before it, because it would stifle inquiry and paralyse imagination'. His second appeal was to the example of Christ, whose teaching—by parable and precept—it was not irreverent to describe as 'undenominational'; and, if it were contended that it was the Lord's personality which gave authority to the teaching, he would reply that, as doctrine could never fill that place, the only hope was to secure that the teacher believes what he teaches, and reveres the Person in whose name the teaching is given. He went on:

> The centre of the whole position is the training colleges, and we must secure that the training colleges are full of religious influence. Let us press the Government hard to the conclusion

of their own measure. They are trying to establish undenominational religion in the schools. Let them also establish religious undenominationalism in the training colleges. Surely if religion is undenominational, at least the undenominationalism had better be religious!

It was probably at the conclusion of this passage, which had been interrupted with frequent cries of 'No!', that one of the most vigorous Anglo-Catholic leaders was seen to show acute distress: 'I managed', Temple wrote in describing the scene thirty-five years later, 'to create a good deal of flutter, and I thought old Lord Halifax would shake to pieces in his rage at what I said.'

His third point was pressed most vehemently of all. He held at that time the strong conviction that Thomas Arnold was the greatest Englishman of the nineteenth century, and from his teaching Temple had drawn a conception of the Church and the State which was for many years to dominate his thought. The Church of England was a national Church: national denominationalism was a contradiction in terms. As a national Church, we were responsible for the education of all English children. If that were granted, where lay the injustice of asking churchpeople to pay for the religious instruction of nonconformist children? In a Christian nation the State exists in the interest of godly living: so, in a Christian nation, does the Church: the Church and the State are therefore indistinguishable. The Church is the organ of the Christian nation's specifically religious life, and the State is the organ of the Christian nation's civil life. If therefore, as was often urged, religious teaching ought to be associated with some definite society, that society is the Christian nation. If, further, the Church is national, we must forgo the 'particular joys of denominationalism'; and, as for the word 'Catholic', his ideal was not perhaps Catholic in externals, but it would be Catholic 'with the catholicity of devotion to the Person of Christ'.

All this falls strangely on our ears to-day, and Arnold was not the only pilot of Temple's early life to be dropped. It was altogether another State and a very different Church that emerged years later, in *Citizen and Churchman*.

At the end of his speech Temple explained—to a slightly less unsympathetic audience—the reason why there was no religious life in England: there had been no national life. The real England, he said, had just come to the birth with the return of a 'strong' Labour party to Parliament (37 out of 670) at the recent election. He had by this time run up his political colours, and grasped with eagerness such opportunities as occurred for pleading the cause of Labour. As a lay member (nominated by the Bishop) of the Oxford Diocesan Conference, he moved in the following year a resolution 'That the Church is called to set forth, both in teaching and in practice, the relation of Christian Faith and Life to the Labour Movement in this country'. The motion was carried without a dissentient—as well it might be—but not before Temple had warned the conference that the condescension with which a section of the Church had hitherto treated the Labour Movement was no less unchristian than the violent opposition which the Movement had encountered from other quarters of it. But it was at the Pan-Anglican Conference of 1908 that Temple offered the first reasoned statement of his social and economic faith to an audience of any importance:

This is not an economic question. It is a question touching the nature of human personality. It asks what are the deepest and most potent motives in the human soul. The question is not economic—to the Christian it is religious. . . .

If Christianity is to be applied to the economic system, an organization which rests primarily on the principle of competition must give way to one which rests primarily on co-operation. . . .

The question of the competitive principle is driven down into the Labour market, so that men compete against each other for the right to work which is the right to live. Go and see it at work in the London Docks. If one man is to secure the means of feeding himself and his family, he must be depriving another. Is that an exhibition of Brotherhood? Such a system embodies no principle but selfishness and mutual antagonism. . . .

94

As citizens we are guilty of a whole system of oppression: it is there: we tolerate it, and so become responsible for its results. There is nothing inevitable in it: it is all the result of human choices. I do not mean that anyone deliberately put it there; it is the greatest fluke in creation. But it is the net result of innumerable human choices, and by human choices it can be modified. Here lies our duty—and our guilt.

In the year of this speech Temple was a Deacon in Holy Orders, but it might have been the voice of the Archbishop of Canterbury, a generation on, that was heard in the Albert Hall on that day.

As time passed, each succeeding term brought its fresh list of engagements and responsibilities. There were occasional holidays, but these were few and short. Temple was already wanted everywhere and by everybody; his help was sought by Societies, Councils, Conferences, and propagandists of every kind, and their initials—W.E.A., Y.M.C.A., C.S.U., S.C.M., C.E.M.S., C.E.T.S., and the rest—sprawled over the pages of his engagement-book. His activity was immense, his strength apparently inexhaustible. 'It all seemed very breathless,' wrote one of his colleagues, 'but he was never out of breath.'

VI

Suspense

I have been determined to be ordained longer than I can remember, and I had very likely got quite used to the idea before really knowing what it meant.

W. T., letter to H. Hardy, September 1900.

IN the printed form which Randall Davidson required to be filled in by candidates for Holy Orders, one of the twenty-one questions was: 'How long have you been looking forward to the Ministry as the work of your life?' Temple's answer ran: 'As long as I can remember having any views on the subject, with one brief interval.' When this interval occurred cannot even be guessed, for in no extant letters to those whom he knew to be interested (not even to his father or brother) does he mention the subject until the year 1906, except to two lay friends younger than himself. We know that in the nursery he had decided to be an archbishop; but from that day there is complete silence about any such vocation or ambition until the year which was marked by the beginning of his correspondence with John Stocks. This is not easy to determine, for in those days Temple never wrote the year at the top of his writing-paper; and the first letters in which he refers to the ministry may have been written at any time between 1901 and 1905. For their exact dates internal evidence is inconclusive; but some of them seem to have been written before he went to Queen's, and the earliest while he was still at Balliol.

Of Temple's lay friends R. H. Tawney, Harry Hardy, and John Stocks were now the closest; they had all been with him at Rugby. To his intense grief, Stocks died at the height of his powers when he was Vice-Chancellor of Liverpool University, and the loss was a severe one. Temple's affection for Stocks was that of an elder brother; to no one did he write so frequently, so vividly, or so intimately; and it was in letters to him that he first opened his heart and mind on the Church and the clergy, and also on the possibility of Holy Orders being sought—by John Stocks.

96

This was to be expected. It was easier at first, and entirely natural, to set out the demand that the priesthood would make, and the obligations it would impose, on a friend rather than on himself; and these letters are among the most revealing he ever wrote. They were of a kind for which he had neither time nor taste in later life, but they throw a flood of light on the direction of his thoughts and desires at a critical period of his career. Here is the first:

Beech Farm, Ludham, Nr. Gt. Yarmouth. Aug. 4th.

Here I am, rather sleepy, having been kept awake most of last night by the midges that swarmed in our cabin: so why I should write to you I do not know, but as I am at it, it seems that this too was to be done, as Carlyle wd. say, whose French Revolution I am now reading with enormous joy.... But really do think—now that you are provided for as to the next four years of your so inexplicable existence—about taking orders. You are wanted in that sphere of life quite desperately—if only by me. You looked incredulous when I was talking about so-called Christians who would be just as good if they were called anything else. You see a man may be affected by religion in any of three ways: (1) only by the atmosphere of it round about him: (2) by occasional efforts of his own to raise his mind to spiritual things: (3) by the constant—if unconscious—reference of his conduct to a perfect standard—made easier for us by the personification of that standard in Christ. There are too many of (1): there are hardly any of (3). The only way to alter this is to force people to think about their religion: if it is taken as a pill, they expect it to work as a pill—which it will not do. If they are to think about it we must have an intellectual clergy— and a practical clergy. No more wild speculation about the state of sinners—but the application of Christian principles to everyday life, whereby the Housing Problem, etc. will solve themselves: but now most 'Christians' do not trouble to find out what their Master's principles really are. And I emphatically say that a man who has no serious purpose as the backbone of his life cannot be a Christian, no matter what creed he says: he is really unaffected—'Is it nothing to you, all ye that pass

H

by?' 'In as much as ye did it not. . . .' So I think, not without prayer.

Stocks's answer has not survived, but it provoked this retort:

> Old Palace, Canterbury. Sept. 22.

O John L. Stocks, for evermore never talk about 'entering the Church': seeing that you are in it already—at least in profession—and such careless expressions unconsciously form wrong ideas. I probably used the phrase myself—but that has nothing to do with it. Your letter contains an enigmatic pronouncement in these terms: 'Disappointment might prove disastrous, and the lowest place not quite so attractive'. . . . You misunderstand me: I do not ask you to take orders with me because I think that we two are such paragons of holiness that our mere presence in the ranks of the ministry will raise the average of the whole. I mean that the Church—and consequently the nation—is in a very critical state: I mean that it is doing very nearly as much harm as good—and perhaps more. And this because of its narrow spirit. There is a fearful complaint that the intellectual average of those who take orders is steadily sinking: this is far more serious than the diminution of numbers. You will hear economic reasons given: e.g. the clergy are so poor that they cannot send their sons to the 'Varsity. But the real reason is that the Church is about a century behind the times: she is driven to adopt the results of criticism—no one would object to *Essays and Reviews* now—but she will not adopt the spirit. We are still worshipping forms (which you observe is the essence of idolatry, εἰδώλων λατρεία); we have made Christ Himself into an idol. Our religion becomes more and more sensuous; preachers try to stir the emotions, not to direct the will. In short, anything more hostile to the New Testament than our modern English religion is hard to conceive.

Well, I believe that the only thing that can save us is a vigorous attack from within the Church on the existing conceptions of religion. While the Church is as it is, very few men of intellect *can* take orders: and until they do things cannot be much better. We shall not have a specially pleasant time in

98

wounding our best friends' highest feelings: do you think no *good* men were horrified when Luther said that the Papal indulgence was only a paper rag, combustible like other paper —which also he proved by means of a bonfire? It is because there is a true devotion to the existing idiocy that that idiocy must be cleared away. The prophets in Israel arose—that is the ones who wrote—when 'Jehovah had no rival', but was falsely thought of.

As a matter of practical politics—what is our so-called Christianity doing? Men are still rather encouraged to get drunk than otherwise; the poor are not housed, nor the naked clothed nor the hungry fed. And yet nearly everyone in England professes to believe that one at least of the sentences of final condemnation is 'I was a stranger and ye took me not in, etc.' Take another instance: it is a certain fact that in rich parishes the people who go to church most are the most selfish. And yet our Lord said 'Not everyone that saith unto *me*, Lord, Lord, shall enter into the kingdom of heaven: but he that *doeth* the will of my *Father*'—i.e. his duty to his neighbour. I might give instances for ever: but to put it shortly, the Church forgets that Christianity is not an attitude of mind, but a type of life: a man's spirit is known not by his opinion (creeds etc.) but by his actions and general conduct.

The ideal would be that about half a dozen or a dozen of us should by some contrivance become college chaplains in Oxford and both in sermons and in ordinary conversation do something to alter the existing state of things. I do not mind saying that in 20 years the difference in examinations for orders would be quite perceptible. Of course we shall not see the establishment of a Christian Imperialism: but we can prepare the way for it—and if you do not feel equal to it, read the first chapter of Jeremiah. Our motto might be 'Shew thy servants thy work and their children thy glory': but I for one would rather do the work than see the glory.

I have bored you long enough now: come to Lambeth for lunch some day and we will have it out in the afternoon. I know I am right in this, though I may exaggerate the evil: I don't

think so however—and if I lived 700 years before Christ I should call it the word of the Lord. I don't know whether Amos actually saw things—probably not: but his vision is mine—'I saw the Lord standing above the altar' (His own altar it was) 'and He said unto me, SMITE!'
R.S.V.P.

In the same vein he had written earlier to Harry Hardy:

Balliol.
May 15, 1901.

You said something about when you would be a 'poor curate'—did you mean it? I hope so: I am getting more and more convinced that an intellectual priesthood is at this time absolutely necessary—so much so that I can call up precious little interest in anything at present except the interpretation of the Bible (and lawn-tennis!) which may make me rather a bore. But there are times when it seems to me that there is now need and opportunity for the greatest work since the Reformation, perhaps since the age of the Apostles. The Church has been roused—by Wesley and others—to a new spiritual devotion: and to a new sense of beauty as an expression of this devotion by Newman: so we have got the devotion and its formal expression: the most important part still remains—namely to put that behind all actions whatever, and identify religion with life. For this intellect is needed—and of course spirit too: it is not that we now need a different and a lower faculty—but that we need the old spiritual zeal with intellect as well to direct it. And apart from the greatness of such a work in itself, if it can be done the Housing Problem, the Temperance Question, the differences between employer and employed will solve themselves, and the British Empire will become an instrument of real justice (not legal codes) and real education—not the doctrine of practical success. 'The Lord will hasten it in its time.' It can be done now, but the opportunity may pass: 'The harvest truly is plenteous but the labourers are few.'

Yours affly
WM. TEMPLE.

Stocks had evidently answered the letter of 22 September, for less than a fortnight later Temple writes again:

Lambeth Palace, S.E.

Dear John,   Oct: 3.

... Never shrink from being violent to me: I don't dislike it, and it does me good. Now first as to Elijah: there were left seven thousand in Israel who had 'not bowed the knee to Baal' —was there left anyone else who had 'been very jealous for Jehovah, God of hosts', beside Elijah? Jeremiah (ch. v) denies that there is a single righteous soul in all Jerusalem: no doubt he exaggerated, but there was a truth behind his denunciation. I have said conceited things to you before, and I will say some more: we are like Antigone and Ismene, and you say 'Not to attempt the impossible is best': but I *must* attempt the impossible, yes, and even deny that it is impossible at any moment when I honestly 'believe in God the Father Almighty'. At most times I do not believe in Him, but occasionally I do, and I always try to do so.

You say the reasons why candidates fall off are obvious, and enumerate various manifestations of the progress of mankind: these are not really to blame, for these are necessary: what is to blame is the conservative temper of the Church, who has not increased the attractions to her ministry at the same pace. It is right that these attractions should be intellectual and spiritual— not pecuniary, though the utter poverty of the clergy at present is a disgrace to the nation. By spiritual attractions I mean opportunity for doing good, not only by distributing doles, but by practically and really leading one's parishioners. By intellectual attractions I mean leisure for reading and thinking. The clergy now do not read—for they have no time: but the reading is more important than the saying of 'services', and some at least should be secured, even if the visiting suffers. 'Priesthood is an intellectual trust.'

You say that I mention evils that are deplored in every pulpit: but none the less they are rampant. The gloomy fact is that in a country that calls itself Christian, Government after

Government shelves the Housing Problem, and coldwaters the Temperance reformers, and refuses even to discuss religious education: and the Government represents the people, so that this is just a sign of unspirituality in the nation: and spirituality —or the Spirit, as S. Paul would more correctly say,—is that part of the nation for which the Church is directly responsible. You practically say that the Church is doing all it can: but it is not—and this because its ministers are not sufficiently intellectual. The gulf between the religious truth and its practical application can only be bridged over by the intellect. But worse than this—the 'religious truth' itself is unsound. The prevailing ideas about Christ are as unwarrantable by scripture as they are controvertible by reason. The doctrine of the Incarnation, permanently present in its true purity to Browning, is hopelessly mauled by nearly every clergyman who touches it, and certainly the notions in the minds of some of the people I have talked to are simply amazing. So it is too with the Atonement. Of course our redemption is achieved, not by contemplation of the Crucifixion, but by assimilation of its spirit. Our crucifixion may be metaphorical: it may be a ceaseless struggle against a life-long disappointment.

You have probably heard of the row that accompanied *Essays and Reviews*, and the very vigorous effort that was made to prevent Father's consecration as Bishop of Exeter; because he had written 'The Education of the World'. It is time to go further now, and to wound more deeply: for we have to tell people not only that their views on inspiration are absurd, but that their most cherished beliefs and their brightest hopes have no foundation: we have to teach S. James's doctrine—so spoilt in our Version—that 'Pure *worship* and undefiled before God and the Father is this—etc.' The reason why clerical complaints about the lack of everyday Christianity are ineffectual, is that they do not state the truth that where there is this lack there is no Christianity at all, and any one who is not interested in 'good works' is *pro tanto* Anti-Christ. The Christ men believe in and worship is to a great extent a myth and an idol—very different from Him who lived and died 'to bear

witness to the truth', and Whose Spirit lived and spoke in
Socrates and Buddha and Mahomet as it did also in Hosea and
Luther and Browning. Men do not realize that Christ requires
a good life and not church-going, and knowledge of God more
than communicating: just as long ago God said by Hosea, 'I
will have mercy (leal-love) and not sacrifice and the knowledge
of God more than burnt offering': men do not realize this, and
no attempt is being made—at least in any way that could possibly succeed—to make them realize it. This is the source of
all our troubles—and if one thing is more certain than another,
it is that no reform can be introduced unless the prevalent ideas
are condemned. *All* the early prophets condemned ritual and
ceremonial worship without qualification: and so we must, not
because they are bad in themselves but because, through abuse,
they have come to do more harm than good: we must treat
ritual (I don't mean ritualism, but church-going) as the prophets
did, and as Plato treated Homer. Of course we must employ
different methods—encouraging people to come to church, as
long as they try to live in a Christian spirit: but the principles
must be the same. For no doubt attendance at church without
Christian deeds, or ceremonial reverence for the Bible without
obedience to its precepts, is a worship of forms (εἰδώλων
λατρεία), and idolatry, and inevitably does more harm than
good.

Call me a fool and a bigot if you think me so, and try to
convert me: but do not dismiss the subject from your thoughts.
It is certainly worth consideration. Yours ever
WM. TEMPLE.

You needn't think me as conceited as this may sound: I know
I don't even try to live by my own principles, but that does not
affect their truth.

The correspondence on the subject ends with this, written
probably more than a year later:

British Embassy, Berlin.
Dear Johnnie,   Oct. 26.
... A friend of Father's once said to him 'My cook has gone.'

103

'Oh, what had you done to her?' 'Nothing: I spoke to her like a father—I called her a fool.' . . . I am about to do ditto, without the last part. Do try to see as much of —— as you can manage just now. . . . You will naturally be casting about a bit for views as to the future, and, if you will excuse my cheek in saying so, I am sure he has a point of view about it which I don't think is very strongly represented in Oxford; also I think he is older than the other people you are really intimate with, so my advice is good Aristotelianism. You know what is in the back of my mind—that if you come to think it right that you should take orders I should jump for joy, even though I come to the other conclusion about myself: for I do believe strongly in the Church as the great means of good in the country, and I want her to have the service of all the ability she can get, even though I may feel (I don't think I shall, but I may) that my own association with her formulae would be so deceptive as to be impossible. And consequently I do want the influences on that side to have their chance with you; for I suspect the Oxford ones are mainly the other way. I know you are fairly capable of making up your own mind, but one can only make it up about what is before it. This is d—d fatherly, but never mind.

These letters are so unlike any others Temple wrote that some attempt must be made to understand and account for them. What (it may be asked) has happened to the lecturer in philosophy whom some of his critics charged even then, as others did long after, with emotional poverty, summing up his personality in the unworthy sneer, *Mens et praeterea nihil* ? Why does he, usually restrained almost to a fault, break out into this diatribe on the failures and futilities of the contemporary Church? What is this sudden note of urgency—almost of passion—struck, for instance, at the end of the second letter to Stocks? Temple was no mere phrase-maker, nor was he emotionally stirred by sensational or ephemeral incidents; still less did he ever write a single word for mere effect. It may be suggested, for one thing, that he seems at this time to have discovered the Church of England. Not in its mystical sense—his appreciation of that was always lively, and his friendship and spiritual intimacy with von Hügel helped in after years to confirm it. Nor so much in its historical aspect—though he does allude to the place and function of the Anglican Communion in Christendom. The Church of England he discovered was the Church at work in England; not, again, the Church he had known all his life, the Church of Canterbury Cathedral and S. Paul's, of school and college chapels, of carved masonry and dark oak, and singing-boys and men; but the organization which alone in England had a foot in 16,000 parishes, with its unique opportunity, its cumbrous machinery, its crippling anachronisms, its complacent worldliness, and its representatives commissioned for their work with the highest spiritual authority they could receive. But commissioned for what? Apparently for the delivery of a Gospel the elements of which they had not been trained to understand, and for the teaching of a philosophy of life that they were entirely unqualified to expound.

This discovery—and other evidence is not wanting of the shock with which it came to him—set Temple thinking out the root causes of the Church's impotence; and he found the most conspicuous fault in the intellectual poverty of its ministers. (The conviction never left him, though it was naturally impressed upon him with peculiar force at a moment when he himself was facing the intellectual difficulties that threatened to come between him and the fulfilment of his highest hopes.) Here, then, lay the clear duty and the timely opportunity—to urge the most intelligent of his friends to throw in their lot, without counting the cost, with the Church that so desperately needed the help which they, and others with like qualifications, alone could give.

But was not he himself of their band? That is the question he is asking in these and other letters of the same period. The internal conflict was a severe one; and whether he writes of John Stocks or of Harry Hardy or of anybody else or of himself—whether it is 'you' or 'we' or 'myself' whom he mentions in the letters—it is the struggle in his own soul that he is all the time laying bare to his friends. This he confesses when particular issues begin to emerge. The following letter to Stocks was written probably a few months before he approached the Bishop of Oxford on the possibility of his being ordained.

Steiger 1
Jena.
Dear Johnnie,   Nov. 17.

. . . Of course I entirely agree with what you say—all of it. There are people who need not bother about the doctrinal side of things, but we must. Also I am very painfully aware of the desire to hear my own voice as a potent influence: Bernard Shaw's *Candida* revealed that to me. But to be at one with the Church in fundamentals is vital.

On the other hand (without qualifying that), it is not quite easy to settle what are fundamentals, and it is certain that the Church allows, and indeed invites, divergence on other points. It is the great wisdom of our Church that it was not founded to support any particular doctrines, as the Protestant bodies were: it stands as a historic Church, which broke with Rome because Rome encouraged definite abuses at that time. But freedom in doctrine is the life-breath of the Church of England. . . . Historically the thing is as clear as daylight—in the 19th century you have Gorham (Low), *Essays and Reviews*, and Denison (High) all prosecuted and all declared to be within the Law. For earlier history the whole thing is admirably put by Matthew Arnold in 'Puritanism and the Church' and 'Modern Dissent' in the *S. Paul and Protestantism* volume.

Perhaps all this is more suitable for me than you. What I have been taught to regard as the fundamentals do seem to me strictly continuous with my philosophy. I do honestly wish, though of course I don't do it, to 'confess Jesus Christ as Lord', and I believe that I am capable of, and definitely experience, what is called 'communion' with Him. I am inclined, I think honestly, to assent to the Virgin Birth, though I am pretty clear that it ought not to be in the creed, because it fastens attention on the wrong point. But it is hard to be really honest! One could cut the knot and say that if one is not sure one is honest one had better leave it all alone—but to me that

would be a plain dereliction of duty. I am quite clear that I
ought to be in orders, if it can be honestly done.

... I hope you don't hate these lucubrations. I am trying to
find my own way through, and it helps to talk it over, and
perhaps σύν τε δύ' ἐρχομένω.

Your loving
W. T.

Several other Oxford friends were in his confidence. One of
them remembers walking one evening with Temple round New
College garden and discussing the pros and cons of his being
ordained. 'I let him out', writes Sir Alfred Zimmern, 'by the
heavy garden door which opens on to Queen's Lane, and I can
still hear the door clanging, and the sense of decision that that left
with me.' In January 1906 the decision was taken.

VII

Ordination

As you know, the matter has given me some qualms both of mind and conscience: but it is a joy to have it settled in the way that I had become convinced was right, from my own point of view, and I hope the Church may not have any ground to regret the decision. In times when new categories are being freely applied to the whole field of thought it is difficult to avoid blunders in exposition; but I feel sure that it is better, with whatever friction, to try to bring forth 'things new and old' than to keep exclusively to the old; and I hope I may be able to take a small share in helping the Church to do this great thing. That is the hope which determined me to reopen the question; and I am thankful that the opportunity at least is offered.

W. T., letter to the Archbishop of Canterbury, May 1908.

AS a Fellow of an Oxford college, Temple would have been doing nothing unusual if he had sought his Orders at the hands of the Archbishop of Canterbury rather than of his diocesan bishop; but he was unwilling even to appear to be taking a course that some might regard as underhand, and it was to the Bishop of Oxford (Paget) that he first wrote. It is more than tantalizing that this letter has not been kept, though from Paget's reply it is fairly obvious in which directions Temple's uncertainties lay. (Whether his letter was a definite request for ordination, or merely a 'feeler' put out to elicit Paget's reaction to the idea of ordaining a man who held such views as Temple's, seems less clear. A sentence from a letter which Randall Davidson wrote to Temple in 1911 suggests one answer: 'So far as there was any refusal by the Bishop of Oxford, it was to the best of my recollection based upon a tentative letter from Germany which did not bring the matter to a definite issue, but was rather hypothetical in tone.') The Bishop of Oxford replied:

3 February 1906.
Cuddesdon
Oxford.

My dear Temple,

I have studied as carefully as I can the Statement which you sent me, with the further help of your subsequent letters. I am

108

grateful to you for having written to me thus freely and fully: nothing could seem more likely to lead in the end to a right issue than such thoroughness.

Some parts of what you have written to me I can but imperfectly understand: the thought they tell may be the thought and belief of my own mind read out into another form, a truer, worthier form perhaps than I have ever been able to give to it: but I cannot follow you closely and certainly enough to judge. If the burden of my decision rested on those parts of your letter I should have to get the help of some stronger and subtler mind than my own to make me sure. But I have found myself coming back to the first part of your letter, together with what you wrote on Jan. 21st, and feeling fairly clear of a grave difference between what is expressed there (so far as I can judge) and the ground on which we must stand if we are to teach others in the name of the Church of England, as witnesses to its Creed and Ministers of its Sacraments. You say, with regard to 'Points of History'—'I am inclined, very tentatively, to accept the doctrine of the Virgin Birth, and, with rather more confidence, that of the Bodily Resurrection of our Lord': and I have to read these words in the light of what you afterwards wrote to me: 'I am very conscious that my opinions are still subject to considerable change. In the statements I sent I stated definitely conclusions to which I am led by very slight preponderance of argument in some cases.' Weighing these words I have to say, with all respect, and with sorrow, and anxiety lest I may be judging amiss, that I could not take the responsibility of ordaining to the Ministry of the Church of England, and sending forth as a teacher in its Name, one who, in regard to those two main points of history which I believe to be essential to, inextricable from our Creed, stands on such uncertain, precarious, unsteady ground.

It goes to my heart thus to write: and I write the more sadly because I feel the ring of a true calling when you say 'I do believe that the helping men to reach the living Presence of Christ is the noblest work in the world.' I long to see that work given to you: and I deeply trust that, by better guidance than I have skill or power to give, or by closer contact than you have, perhaps, yet had with the plain, crying needs of simple, poor, suffering folk, you may come to stand as I think a man ought to stand to do that work. But I fear that I might be misleading you, I know that I should be misrepresenting my own mind, if I were to say that I think your words show that you so stand now.

I have not shown your letter to the Bishop of Southwark: I have had no chance of doing so: and had I had the chance I should have doubted somewhat whether it was right. But I hope, in view of what you tell me of your talk with him, that you will feel quite free to show or send him this, if in any way you wish to do so.

I know you will forgive me the pain I cause you: indeed I wish I could have refrained from causing it, or made it less. You will not doubt my entrance into the desire of your heart. May God grant you, when and as He wills, the fulfilment of it.

Believe me, dear Temple,

Always very sincerely yours,

F. OXON.

I ought to beg your pardon for not having written sooner: but you know something of the hindrances: and they have been, of late, especially heavy.

On receiving this answer, Temple wrote at once to the Dean of Westminster and John Stocks and, later, to his brother. His letters to the Dean (Armitage Robinson) suggest that the request he made to Paget was more definite than Randall Davidson seems to have concluded:

British Embassy,

Berlin.

Feb. 6.

Dear Mr. Dean,

You have only your own kindness to blame for this letter, for it prompts me to write. I think you know that I hoped to be ordained. I decided that it would be right to lay before the Bishop my chief divergencies from current orthodoxy—otherwise I felt I should be cheating him. I sent a statement of these to the Bishop of Oxford a few days ago, and he has now replied, in a most sympathetic letter, that he finds himself unable to ordain me. The chief, though I think not the only, obstacle is my inability to give more than a very tentative assent to the doctrines of the Virgin Birth and of the Bodily Resurrection of our Lord. I do not question the rightness of his decision though it is a great disappointment to me. I fear it is a greater blow to my mother than to myself as I was more prepared for it.

However, as a teacher I can be doing a form of pastoral work, and help in that way the building up of the 'One Perfect Man'—an ideal which, in that form, I owe chiefly to you.

To the same on February 10:

I am most grateful to you for your letter, and shall be very glad to talk matters over with you. I fear this cannot be before the end of the summer term, but there may be gain in waiting as my ideas may then be less chaotic. I will only say now that my chief object in writing to the Bishop as I did was to make it quite clear that I think that it is, for me, a primary duty to keep my mind open on some points of the creed—or at least of currently accepted Christian belief—to which I am at present prepared to give a tentative assent. As long as my business is to teach philosophy I must refuse to close, for the practical purposes of my life, questions which are theoretically open; for the practical purpose of my life is, at present, to be theoretical. I thought I could make this clearer in writing, as my desire to shew myself fit for ordination, and the natural response to his very great sympathy, might make me obscure this main point in a conversation with the Bishop. Perhaps it was unwise, but it was not done without deliberation, and the Bishop's reply leads me to think that he understood me perfectly.

As to the future I will at present say nothing. The fact that so scholarly and sympathetic a man as the Bishop of Oxford has taken this line has cast a new and not encouraging light on the question whether my position as a clergyman might not be a false one. I must think over this quietly, and shall be most glad of your help when I begin to be able to re-form my views of the situation.

Yours very sincerely,
W. TEMPLE.

To John Stocks:

British Embassy,
Berlin.

Dear Johnnie,   Feb. 7.

... I have just heard from the Bishop of Oxford that he cannot take the responsibility of ordaining me with my present views —particularly in view of my inability to give more than a tentative assent to the Doctrine of the Virgin Birth and the Bodily Resurrection of our Lord. So as long as I remain in Oxford it will be as a layman. I know of at least one Bp. who would ordain me, if I decided to take up parochial work in the future. I do not question the rightness of this decision, and perhaps it will be a real gain to me in mental freedom—but it is a most tremendous disappointment I confess. I fear my mother feels it even more than I do, as she had looked forward greatly to my ordination, and was less prepared for a refusal than I was. There are nasty elements in my disappointment— including the annoyance of a frustrated ambition to hear my sermons praised! Which shews that there were nasty elements in my desire to be ordained. But I had hoped to do useful work as a parson, and thought my gifts (!) peculiarly suited to that kind of work. However, new ways can be found πολυμερῶς καὶ πολυτρόπως. I expect you will really think it a good thing, and very likely you are right. But you will sympathize with a temperamental castle-builder who finds his castle was not only in the air but made of it.

Mention this discreetly, if at all.

Your loving
W. T.

To his brother:

British Embassy, Berlin.

Dear old 'un,   Feb. 22.

... You will have heard from Mother about the Bishop of

Oxford. I felt bound to send him a statement of my views before asking him to ordain me, that he might not act under a false impression, for to come forward without so doing would have implied complete orthodoxy. He refuses. He hit on the fact that I assent only tentatively to the doctrines of the Virgin Birth and Bodily Resurrection. I am forced, at present at any rate, to emphasize 'tentatively' more than 'assent', for as my practical aim in life is to be theoretical, I cannot close a theoretically open question for practical purposes. I think the Bishop right, for no doubt the Briton gets a contempt for all Church injunctions from the slackness of interpretation of the act of subscription. I still hope to take orders, but I confess I think it immensely improbable. The Church must be purged, I think, from without; for if I take orders and then exhort, it will be lawful for a hearer to 'interpret' my exhortation as I 'interpret' the charter of the society in whose name I exhort. But we must wait and see. I am however convinced that the Church needs very radical reform, and may perhaps help on that better outside. If I remain an Oxford philosopher, the spectacle of a philosopher trying to improve the Church as being the only means of grace, and that now a corrupt one, may be impressive!

Yr loving
W. T.

To the same, a few days later:

British Embassy, Berlin.

Dear old 'un, Feb. 27.

... I have told some episcopal friends of the Bishop of Oxford's action. They all urge me not to regard it as final. It is all rather distracting. Interesting to notice one change—that while I am agitated to find out what is the right course, the notion of being *pained* at disagreeing with the Church seems so remote as to be ridiculous—and I don't know anyone at all of our generation who would feel pain on such grounds. I am clear that this is a gain, for it means that we shall come nearer to co-operating for Christian work while leaving opinions quite free—which is no doubt the way to make them true. Hitherto

I 113

it has been impossible to give *complete* freedom of thought without hampering devotion to work. The two ideals are falling now into their proper places, and therefore are ceasing to be incompatible. But whether the change is or will be rapid enough to allow me to work as an official of the Church, I don't know—and of course the matter is only of a purely personal and individual interest.

Your loving
W. T.

And this, during the next summer:

. . . As to people's anxiety not to have my views discussed—I think their chief reason is that they expect me to return to the fold, if I don't now commit myself. Of course that is possible, but I see no sign of it. More and more I come to regard 'Churchiness' as a survival of the useless: it was necessary once; without the Dogmatism and ecclesiasticism of the early mediaeval church the whole of Christianity would have gone into smoke. But the walls built to protect now only confine and cramp, and should be pulled down. It seems to have been a pure fluke that S. Francis was kept within the Church, or that Luther was turned out; and probably it is better not to try a movement outside the Church, but inside it. If the Church turns one out one must go on outside.

Temple wrote truly that the blow would fall most severely on his mother; but she replies to a letter from W. J. Conybeare, who had been one of her husband's chaplains, with her usual placid courage—the chaplain is right, it would be unfair to describe Paget as 'narrow' for what he had done or refused to do, and she would try her hardest to think that the Bishop could not have done otherwise. She remembers the old Archbishop, and hopes that a 'young strong oak' may yet grow 'from the memory, example, and love of the parent strong oak'; but it will be better to say nothing more to her son about it at present—she will just hope and wait. She waited for two years. There was another who also was waiting—and watching, with the keen shrewd eye of a wide experience, and an affectionate regard for his old friend's and predecessor's son. There is no evidence that, after Paget's refusal, Temple saw the Archbishop; but in an undated letter—evidently about the middle of March 1908—he wrote to Randall Davidson that he was anxious to have a talk with him if the Archbishop could spare the time. Consent was readily given. Within a few days Temple had called at Lambeth and had spent a long time alone with the Archbishop, whom he described in a letter to his mother the next day as 'the essence of kindness and sanity—without a glimmer of inspiration. But I think he wants me to be ordained—certainly he does in the light of what I told him yesterday, and that was the worst!' But Randall Davidson asked him to say nothing to the Bishop of Oxford until the two had had an opportunity of talking the matter over. The Archbishop then wrote to Paget—the letter is in his own hand—

Lambeth Palace, S.E.

My dear Bishop,   22 March 1908.

... Quite a different matter. William Temple was staying here last week, and I had a great deal of talk with him about the question of his Ordination. It was *he* who raised it, not I.

I gather that he now feels that he put his difficulties or doubts before you in a very crude and curt and 'undergraduate' shape when he wrote to you two (?) years ago, and that while he still shrinks—as so many metaphysicians somewhat irritatingly do —from expressing himself categorically about things which rather need categorical expression, he is in a far more orthodox *spirit* than he was in those days. What is perhaps even more important, he says with an earnestness wh. touched me greatly that his *Xtianity* in the larger and deeper sense is a far more genuine and absorbing thing than it was two years ago. His experiences with 'Student Volunteer Movement', and his South London Settlement residence, have evidently touched a far deeper vein in his being, and I thank God for it with all my heart.

Upon the two specific points—of the Virgin Birth and the actual Resurrection—I had a gt. deal of talk with him.

To put the matter shortly—while he is anxious not to

represent himself as freed from perplexity, he told me quite definitely that with regard to the first, he accepts the position as stated by the Dean of Westminster in his booklet *Some Thoughts on the Incarnation*, and I should not myself regard that position as a dangerous one. With regard to the second (the Resurrection problem) he assured me repeatedly that while he declines to be dogmatically certain as to the mode of the mystery, he could explain neither Christianity nor European History if he did not firmly believe that our Lord was in visible tangible personal contact with the Disciples as Teacher and Guide after His Death and Resurrection, and he regards the evidence in favour of what you and I believe true, as being in his judgment far stronger than the difficulties which beset it. I myself regard him as being, *in all essential particulars*, an orthodox believer both in the Virgin Birth of Our Blessed Lord and in His Resurrection. I do not say that he expresses himself respecting either truth with the distinctness (at least as to detail) which has been usual in Orthodox Theology. But I can see no adequate reason why he shd. not now be ordained—and it is his distinct wish now to seek Holy Orders if allowed to do so.

All this being so, what wd. be *your* wish? Shall he reopen the question with you, and offer himself for your acceptance as a candidate? Or should you prefer that he offered himself to *me*, and that thus you did not have again to go into the details of his position?

I think I ought to say frankly that so far as my talk with him has carried me—and we talked it out pretty thoroughly— I shd. not feel justified in refusing him Ordination—but should on the contrary accept him thankfully and with profound hope and belief as to the service wh. he wd. render.

Whether you wd. fully share my feelings about it I do not know, though I am inclined to hope so. But I should, of all things, dislike to run counter to your wish in a matter so grave, and it occurs to me as just possible that, with a view to obviating any risk of that, you might prefer his making application to *me*, now, rather than renewing it to yourself. I do distinctly believe that his attitude now is a more sober and religious one as well as a more orthodox one than it was two years ago—and this it is which makes me feel that if I now accepted him for Ordination I shd. not thereby be necessarily running counter in any way to a decision which you came to *when the circumstances were different*. I have never known exactly what the then circumstances were. But I have a very deep respect for your judgment in such a matter, and I believe that you then weighed the whole matter most carefully.

I am not prepared to say that you and I would necessarily see eye to eye with regard to a man who was near the border line of acceptance or refusal. To *me*, Temple seems *now* to be quite clearly within the line of acceptance. I *think* you wd. agree, but I am not absolutely sure—and this it is which leads me to ask whether, if you feel anxieties on the point, you would prefer that the approach should now, in the changed circumstances, be made straight to myself. Please tell me.

I ought to add that nothing cd. have been more loyal and respectful than the manner in wh. Temple spoke of your own kindness to him.

I am
Ever affectionately yours
RANDALL CANTUAR.

P.S. Of course nothing could in itself be more natural than that a son of Archbishop Temple's should come to Lambeth for Ordination under the roof of his former home, and, as you know, Fellows of Colleges have all through the years been ordained most frequently here.

Paget replied at once:

Cuddesdon,
Wheatley S.O.,
Oxon.

Feast of the Annunciation 1908.
My dear Lord Archbishop,

Please, let me first thank you with true gratitude for your letter about William Temple. In my gratitude I am not thinking only of its kindness, nor only of its treatment of deep things (of that it would be unbecoming for me to speak). My chief gratitude is for a lasting example of the way in which the utmost stress and burden of work can be kept from hindering the true care for others.

Certainly your Grace's letter leaves on my mind the impression that I might rightly and happily receive Temple as a Candidate for Ordination. I do not know (or, at all events, cannot recall) the Dean of Westminster's book; and so at one point I cannot at present tell the full meaning of your words. But the whole tenor of what you have gathered from your talk with Temple, and the definite words which you use as expressing his firm belief concerning the Risen Lord, lead me to expect that I should feel safe in receiving him.

But I have to recognize two elements of insecurity about this course. First, it is possible (though not, I think, likely) that if he were to apply to me, and we were to talk over again what we discussed before, some fresh point of hesitation might incidentally emerge, or we might somehow fail to understand one another. Secondly, in the Examination, my Examining Chaplains might come on some difficulty which might lead to the Archdeacon's being unwilling to present Temple to me for Ordination: and this unwillingness might be impossible to overcome. (It is right—is it not?—to regard that presenting as a real act, involving a share in the responsibility for the Ordination.) I do not think that either of these two hindrances is likely to arise: but there is a possibility of them which ought to be considered.

In view of this possibility, and the feeling that there would be a special happiness in your Grace's ordaining Archbishop Temple's son, I should be inclined to advise his making application to you, were it not for one thing. It (quite naturally) became known in Oxford (not through me, for I do not think that I spoke to any one of it) that I had in effect refused to receive him—at least one person wrote to expostulate with me. I am afraid that if your Grace receives him it may be thought that he has sought and you have granted Ordination under the same conditions of belief and doubt as those under which I refused it: and this, I venture to suggest, would not be just either to your Grace or to him: it might somewhat seriously mislead the minds of those who knew of the former refusal.

This is the only reason which stays me from saying at once that I think his applying to your Grace would be the safer course. It is a reason which should, I think, be weighed—though it well may be outweighed.

Believe me to be,
Obediently and affectionately yours,
F. Oxon.

Temple again saw Randall Davidson, and the Archbishop wrote to the Bishop of Oxford:

Old Palace,
Canterbury.
Easter Sunday
19 April 1908.

My dear Bishop of Oxford,

In pursuance of what passed in our recent conversation I have had further prolonged talks with William Temple who has been staying with us here. He is now clear that he wishes to be a candidate for Ordination, and further, in view of the sacred associations which link him to Lambeth and Canterbury, he would specially like to be one of our ordinands *here* and to be ordained in Canterbury Cathedral.

I have told him that I knew from yourself your appreciation of this wish, and that I was quite sure that you wd. not deem it inappropriate if, in all the circumstances, he thus sought Holy Orders at my hands. There remains the 'question' (if we can call it a 'question'!) arising out of the fact that he was in communication with you, two years ago, on the subject of Ordination, and that you then thought it wd. be best that he should postpone his definite candidature, and give further consideration to certain theological points which emerged from your correspondence with him. From what Temple tells me it is perfectly clear that his position with regard to matters of Faith is different now from what it was two years ago. Were this not so I should feel great hesitation in accepting him as a candidate, lest I should appear to be over-riding a decision of yours, or implying that you had, in my judgment, dealt mistakenly with the matter.

But during the time which has elapsed since then, Temple has, as you know, not merely been thinking and reading—and, I am sure, *growing*—but he has been definitely sharing in Christian and Evangelistic work (both in connexion with the 'Student Christian Movement' and otherwise) and he has shown me, beyond question, that his whole attitude towards the Faith has undergone a change or a 'deepening', and that *credal* things possess now a reality for him which they did not, to anything like the same degree, possess before. Whatever the cause of this, the fact is certain—he admits it fully—and the situation is thus materially changed. I have been immensely impressed by his accounts of the Prayer Meetings, and the quiet, direct, Christian work in which he has been taking a keen and happy part. The Spirit of God has, I am persuaded, 'come in' upon his soul.

With regard to the two specific points upon which he put his difficulties before you—in, I gather, a rather crude and 'youthful' and ill-considered way—two years ago (I mean the Articles of the Creed relating to the Virgin Birth of Our Blessed Lord, and His Resurrection) I have had full conversation with him, and have gone into each article carefully. I do not think that on either point Temple's present attitude is such as ought reasonably to cause anxiety to a Bishop in accepting him for Ordination. I do not know *exactly* what he wrote to you on those articles, but I gather clearly from him that he expressed himself otherwise than as he wd. now write upon those solemn subjects. I think I can best express my clear apprehension of his position by saying that I can find no practical difference between his attitude and that taken by Dr. Sanday in his *Outlines of the Life of Christ*, pp. 170–186, and by the present Dean of Westminster in his *Thoughts on the Incarnation*. I have re-read with him some of the important passages so as to make sure of this.

I cannot think that, as matters now stand, any difficulty can rightly arise. I myself feel none whatever, and I am therefore prepared to let him go forward with a view to my ordaining him Deacon next Advent.

I have written thus fully, for two reasons.

First, because Temple (*who has listened to and approved those parts of this letter which give my description of his religious position*) is as anxious as I am that it should not seem as though I were running counter to your own attitude and decision in a matter of such importance, and still less, if possible, as though he were asking me to do so! The simple fact—a fact for which I am profoundly thankful—is that the situation is not what it was two years ago. The delay has been to Temple's great good.

And secondly I have written fully because it is right that you should have the facts on record, and that you should be able—if need arose—to show this letter privately to anyone who is legitimately concerned in the matter, or to any (appropriate) person who might be likely to misunderstand my action in its relation to your own. Temple does not think that what passed between you and himself two years ago is known to more than a few people. And he is strongly of opinion that nobody who now knows him and the work (evangelistic and other) in which he has been taking part during the last year will be surprised at his now seeking Ordination. You, I know, appreciate the naturalness and appropriateness of his seeking it here. I, on the other hand, appreciate most highly your considerate kindness in the whole matter and your confidence—which assuredly is not misplaced—in my own complete and fraternal loyalty to yourself.

I am

Yours affectionately,

RANDALL CANTUAR.

I have written this letter while the matter is fresh in my mind. (Temple has been here till now.) But it can await your return.

Paget wrote a reply with his usual grace, full of charity and good wishes for Temple's life in the ministry, and expressing complete trust in the Archbishop's judgement. Temple's joy and thankfulness were expressed in his final letter to the Archbishop:

'I do not know', he wrote, 'how to thank you for your letter, and all the other kindness that you have shewn me. To be ordained by you, and at Canterbury, will be a great thing, if it is God's will to allow it. I will give all the time that I possibly can between now and then to the reading and thought and prayer that may make me more ready.' Nor did the Archbishop forget to let Mrs. Temple know the good news at once. Her reply, like her son's, told of deep gratitude; she felt sure, moreover, that ordination would strengthen and settle his determination to serve in the sacred ministry to the utmost of his powers.

In November the three persons whose names Temple had given as references—the Provost of Queen's (Magrath), the Rev. E. M. Walker (one of Temple's colleagues in the Queen's Senior Common Room), and the Rev. H. H. Gibbon (Chaplain of Balliol)—wrote their commendatory letters to the Archbishop. Temple sat for his Deacon's Examination—'The exam. papers', he wrote to his brother, 'were very intelligent, and I quite enjoyed doing them. As Storr is one of the examiners,' he adds mischievously, 'I was able to let fly a bit in the papers he was looking over!' He was made Deacon in Canterbury Cathedral on 20 December 1908.

Only one incident of note occurred in the next twelve months before Temple was ordained Priest. During November and December, 1909, he delivered a series of addresses at the invitation of the Student Christian Movement in London, which were published in the year following with the title *The Faith and Modern Thought*. Before he delivered them, he sent a copy of the lectures to Randall Davidson, who passed them on to his trusted adviser, Vernon Storr, for an opinion. Storr wrote a careful reply, pointing out a few words and sentences which in his judgement might be modified or omitted; but otherwise his opinion of the lectures was almost enthusiastically favourable. He writes of their freshness and power, of the grasp of Christian doctrine they show, and of Temple's gift for getting at the kernel of living truth in formulae expressed in old forms of speech; 'I have enjoyed reading them very much', the letter ends, 'and I wish I could produce the like.' No less generous was the tribute paid

in a letter to Temple's mother by Sir Michael Sadler, who wrote
an introduction to the lectures when they were published in book
form:

Eastwood,
Bridgewater Road,
Weybridge.

Dear Mrs. Temple,   Nov. 25. 09.

I feel that I should like to write to you while the impression
made by your son's lecture this evening is still vivid in my
mind. I was much moved by it and am thankful to have heard
it. It was very brave and profound, but wonderfully simple
and natural. One felt that one was being taught by a teacher
of deep experience and insight and yet young. I have never
had the same feelings. Those who have known great painters
or poets in their youth must have felt the same. He filled one
with confidence, and all the time brought such unfolded
promise for the future.

Please do not bother to answer this.

Yours very sincerely,
M. E. SADLER.

Temple was ordained Priest in Canterbury Cathedral on
19 December 1909.

How is the gap of more than two years to be filled between the
approach to Paget and Temple's request for a hearing from
Randall Davidson? By what route or what stages did he become
'in all essential particulars an orthodox believer' in truths which
once had eluded him? The answer must be that no single cause
can be assigned; the confirming influences were many and
diverse. One of them can be found in the advice he would frequently offer in later years to those who were passing through
times of intellectual uncertainty: 'Get about among Christian
believers as much as ever you can.' To the introvert, the diffident,
or the self-conscious, such purposeful contacts can be disastrous;
but Temple had no scrap of any of these weaknesses, and recognized to the full the benefit to be gained through close spiritual
association with convinced Christians. Foremost among these

was Dr. Stansfeld, Warden of the Oxford and Bermondsey
Medical Mission, where Temple frequently made short stays
during the vacation, and underwent his first deliberate experi-
ments in 'practical' Christianity. 'Stansfeld', he testified when he
delivered the Beckly (Social Service) Lecture in the year before
he died, 'was one of the greatest men and truest Christians whom
I have known'—and he went on to recall an early memory of how
the Doctor worked:

> The Doctor's own methods were highly individual. The
> first time I visited the Club was during my second year at
> Oxford. I was taken into a basement room, where a crowd of
> some twenty people sat on benches round the wall; one corner
> was screened off. The Doctor stood in the middle with myself
> just behind him, and preached with great directness for about
> five minutes. Then he turned abruptly and dived into the
> corner behind the screen, beckoning me to follow. We found
> a rickety table and three uninviting chairs. I sat on an end one
> and was given a pencil and writing tablet; the Doctor sat in
> the middle; on the other chair sat the patients, one after another.
> With each a conversation took place on the following lines.
> 'Put out your tongue. . . . Where did you go to church last
> Sunday? . . . Open your mouth. . . . Why not? . . . Say ninety-
> nine. . . . Well, I'll give you some medicine, but mind you say
> your prayers and go to church in future.' The gaps represent
> inarticulate replies, the patient being in an attitude prohibitive
> of speech; but the Doctor knew the answers without hearing.
> Then after I had sat there taking notes for him at his dictation
> after each had left, he suddenly said: 'We must have finished
> the first lot by now and there will be another crowd; go out
> and speak the Word to them for a few minutes.' It was a
> Monday evening, so I recited what I could remember of a ser-
> mon preached in S. Paul's Cathedral by the Canon-in-Residence
> —Newbolt, I think—the day before. I cannot think what they
> made of it; but the Doctor seemed satisfied.

In the Student Christian Movement he came within a wider
circle. When Canon Tatlow, whose constructive work in the

early days of the S.C.M. was among the most noteworthy religious efforts of the time, first met Temple at a 'Dons and Beaks' meeting in 1907, he found him interested and prophesied a great place for him in the Movement when he was 'entirely won'. In July of that year a notable conference was held at Conishead Priory, and two days after it was over Temple wrote to his mother:

80, Dunchurch Road,
Rugby.
July 28, 1907.

My dear Mother,

. . . It has been a most interesting week: there is a great sense of seriousness about the whole thing, though people are very jolly and lively in the times 'off'. On the whole the most impressive meetings were two. One a description of the World Student Christian Conference held last year in Tokio, and followed by a missionary campaign in which the delegates—fellows about 25–30—took part: they spoke very simply, with a great deal of feeling, though with restraint; and clearly had, while out there, experienced something which they believed to be the upholding power of the prayers of the students who had sent them. The other was a meeting for Indian missions, where an Indian called Datta spoke quite wonderfully. Yet the thing that really lives with me is Scott Holland's extraordinary oration on the power of Christ to regenerate society here or anywhere else. . . . There was a lot of talk about forgiveness and so on to which I was unable to attach a particle of meaning. To be habitually working on philosophy does undoubtedly very much reduce the number of the expressions and phrases that really move one—that is I suppose the cost of this particular treasure. But the mere fact of 800 students all in deadly earnest about the things that really matter, and many of them pledged to devote part of their lives to foreign missions—coming from all denominations (except R.C.) and never finding need to disagree—is itself very inspiring. I hope the man who was chairman [A. W. Davies, now Dean of Worcester] this year—a Univ. man, one year senior to me I think—may be coming to us at Keble Road for the day or two before term. Don't have visitors between Oct. 7 and 11, if you can help it.

Your loving
W. T.

So began a lifelong interest. A few months after his ordination as Deacon Temple attended the Matlock Conference, which he always regarded as an important event in the history of the S.C.M., and a direct forerunner of the Copec Conference of 1924; and he was amply to repay his debt to the Movement in the days when no S.C.M. Conference seemed complete unless Temple were among the leaders or speakers.

There were also the personal help and counsel of his senior friends; of two in particular. From B. H. Streeter, with whom he was in closer spiritual contact than with any other member of the University, Temple acquired most of his views on New Testament criticism; and it was he who in the judgement of the retired Provost of Queen's (R. H. Hodgkin)—a colleague of them both —led Temple to take a 'reasonable view' of the declaration required from ordinands. No less persuasive was the influence of Henry Scott Holland; in one direction indeed Holland did him the greatest service of all by guiding him to the conviction that the Catholic Faith does not consist of a number of separate articles or formulae, but is a coherent whole. It is one structure. Therefore, Holland would urge, if there were several articles of the Christian Creed which an inquirer knew by his own experience to be true, he might feel sure that the intervening ones also (between the points where his experience left him in no doubt) could be accepted, even taken for granted, just because they belong to the integrity of the whole. Had Temple been asked whether his intellectual position underwent any important change between 1906 and 1908, he would probably have replied 'Very little'; but he would have been the first to confess that his approach to an integrated understanding of the Christian Faith had undergone a development that proved decisive.

Among the imponderables were the memory of his father, the hopes and prayers of his mother, and above all a sense of vocation, reinforced by what one of his pupils called his 'tremendous conscience' and persisting, except for a few brief intervals of disappointment, till it was satisfied at his ordination. Temple was convinced that God had given him some new thing to say to the men of his generation; and 'Woe is me if I preach not the Gospel' —the text cast on the 'Great Paul' bell which he had often heard ring out over the City of London—was sounding perpetually in his ears. But it would be a blunder to conclude that he desired no more than to be a preacher, to be merely the Amos of his letter to John Stocks. Deep down in his heart, though he said little of it, there was another longing—for the dedication, the irrevocable setting apart, the sacred and age-long functions, of the priesthood that might be his. *Sacerdos in aeternum!* In all that the words can mean was laid up the treasure of his young life's hoarding. And there his heart was also.

VIII

Repton

Yes—the Hall has had a fearful crop of failures. I expect Fisher will
be better than I was in these ways. I have always flattered myself that
I was rather good for boys of maturer mind or character . . . but I was
not good with the general ruck.

W.T., letter to D. C. Somervell, March 1915.

I envy you the right to preach habitually to boys.

W.T., letter to the Rev. C. K. Williams, September 1912.

I doubt if headmastering is really my line.

W. T., letter to his brother, October 1910.

TEMPLE spent the last part of the Long Vacation of 1910 in a
tour of Australia. He wrote in January that Dr. J. R. Mott,
who had visited the country and knew its universities, was trying
to arrange an itinerary that would be worth Temple's while, and
to secure a welcome for him. The three universities (Adelaide,
Melbourne, and Sydney) which had been founded at a time when
it was widely held that the days of Christianity were numbered,
had at first been definitely hostile to any intrusion of its propagandists; at one of them Mott had already been refused permission to address the students. But opinion was beginning to change;
the Australian Student Christian Movement was making headway, though slowly; and Mott's shrewd eye saw that a moment
of great opportunity had come, of which a man of Temple's
calibre could take full advantage. Temple felt bound to accept
the invitation; at all the universities he found an eagerness to hear
about the Christian Faith, to learn something of its meaning and
of its relation to the practical problems of the day; and he never
regretted having had a glimpse of Australia and its young men.
To such an extent had the work of the Christian Union affected
the whole life and outlook of the universities, that on his return
Temple went so far as to say that of all the marvels he had seen
in Australia 'the greatest marvel of all is the Australian S.C.M.'
His most useful work was done at Brisbane (though he could

stay there for only two days) where a new university was to be founded early in the following year, and the Christian Union wished to be assured that its activities would be welcomed by the authorities. Of the undergraduates he wrote:

> Australian undergraduates are very like English ones: more like grammar school boys than public school boys, perhaps altogether more like Manchester undergraduates than Oxford ones (but there is not much difference except in social ease). They know the ways of the world more than most public school boys, and they read a good deal less. It was hard work in the six weeks, all but two days, that I was there. I made ninety-one speeches of one sort or another. The worst day was in Sydney, where I began at breakfast and wound up with an after-dinner speech, having cut the dinner to deliver a lecture, getting through six speeches in all—two of them an hour long.

The outstanding achievement of his tour is mentioned in the following letter—the last he wrote from Australia:

> Bishopscourt,
> Melbourne E.
>
> My dear Mother,　　　　Beginning Thursday, Aug. 25.
>
> Though you will not get this till after you have got me, I have decided to go on writing just to complete the record of the trip. To-day I lectured on 'Materialism and Agnosticism' at the University at 1.20; had interviews from 3.30–4.30; spoke about Edinburgh at 4.45; lectured on the Atonement at 7.30.
>
> *Friday.* This morning an address to the Church of England Grammar School. Tea with the Labour Prime Minister of Australia—quite a good fellow. Lecture at 8.0—Education and Democracy.
>
> *Saturday.* This morning I went to the first part of the funeral service of the Dean, who died on Thursday. Then I was driven to a pretty place on the Yarra by some of the Christian Union folk; there we had a picnic tea. Then back to dinner with the Master of Ormond to meet some Professors.

K

Very pleasant. I moved to-day from Bishopscourt to Trinity College.

Sunday. Three sermons in the cathedral to-day. Morning—a large congregation. Evening—a huge crowd. Afternoon—service for university men and women: procession round the cathedral outside and all up the nave, with lots of men and women in gowns—and hoods if graduates—the Vice-Chancellor all in red: pretty good for a secular and (as regards the Professors) predominantly agnostic University. We had a lesson read by a Presbyterian (the V-C.); the Greek priest joined in the procession. A Brahms anthem: Stanford services: and the Hallelujah Chorus to wind up. Their music is capital —as good as the Abbey. So I have been the occasion of bringing to Church members of the University *as such* in each of the three University towns. It is symbolic, I am told, of a great change, for twenty years ago it would have been wildly impossible. I had a jolly supper with some of the men in Trinity College, where I am now staying.

Monday. Lectures to-day at 1.20 and at 7.30. Also innumerable interviews. Rather tired, for the first time since landing.

Tuesday. Breakfast with Presbyterian ministers at 9.0. Interviews 11—12. Speak Scotch College 12.0. Dean of Ballarat at Lunch 1.15. Interviews 3—4.30. Executive Ctee 4.30—6.15. Dinner 6.30. Speak Trinity Coll. 7.0. Lecture 8.0. Prayer meeting 9.0.

Tomorrow. Celebration 7.0. Breakfast Social Ctee of Synod 8.0. Interviews till lunch. Lecture 1.20. Train 4.30.

Your loving
W. TEMPLE.

The voyage home was broken by a day with Alec Fraser, then Principal of Trinity College, Kandy:

S.S. *Morea*,
Arabian Sea,
Sept. 16.

My dear Mother,

I am writing one more letter that you will only get after my

arrival. We reached Colombo early on Wednesday morning.
Alec and Mrs. Fraser had come down, and after breakfast we
motored out to Kandy—72 miles of lovely country. They also
brought a recent Reptonian, Greswell, who was anxious to see
me and form an opinion.

We arrived about 1.15; had lunch; went round the College,
had some tea, then went to a meeting of the Social Workers in
the school. Some of the older boys do a kind of C.O.S. work
in the Kandy slums, and have established a club house for rick-
shaw coolies. I talked to them for about 20 minutes when they
had done their business. Then we went to the cricket ground,
then to the great Buddhist Temple of the Tooth. Then back
to dinner, when some of the masters came in. It was a glorious
cool moonlit night, and we sat out a long while talking and
looking at the mountains.

Thursday morning we got up at 6.30. Early tea—7.0.
Prayers at 8.0, after which I talked to the upper half of the
school for about an hour,—on Materialism, etc., working
round to the demand of Christ on our lives. Then I saw some
classes; then prospected the site of the new cricket ground;
then went to a Buddhist service; then back to breakfast in Hall
at 11.0, after which we all motored back to Colombo to catch
the steamer.

It was the most interesting event of the whole trip. Alec is
very well and in far better spirits. He was pleased at your
writing to him.

On getting back to the ship I found all your letters. So glad
to have them!

Your loving
W. T.

During the voyage out Temple had to make an important
decision. He had known for some time that efforts would soon be
made to take him away from Queen's, and that in all probability
he would be offered the headmastership of a public school.
Towards the end of 1909 there had been a chance of his being
elected to take Dr. David's place at Clifton, and Gore had urged

William Temple

him to accept the offer, should it come to him. There is no doubt that, if he was to be a headmaster, this would have been the ideal school for him. It owed much to Rugby; a large industrial city with its own university, giving ample scope for his social and educational interests, would have been at his door; Percival backed him strongly; most of the staff would have given him a warm welcome; and he wrote to Percival to say that he would take Clifton if they 'threw it' at him. But it was not to be. 'There are some odd things I will tell you one day', he writes to his brother, 'about the Clifton election, but as I am not supposed to know I won't put them on paper now . . . but the masters wanted me, which is satisfying.' It may be doubted, however, whether he was entirely convinced that it was his vocation to be a headmaster—which makes it hard to understand why he felt a definite call to Repton less than a year later. Did he hope—as he seems to hint in a letter that follows—that he could take the lead in some attempt to reform the public schools, and that after a time he would gain influence enough to make his views prevail with the Headmasters' Conference? Did he feel a special vocation for the spiritual and intellectual care of adolescents, which he could discharge in entirely favourable conditions with sixth-form public school boys? Or was he prompted by that ever present 'daemon', the memory of his father—is it possible that he had an almost superstitious reverence not only for the Archbishop's character and example, but even for the sequence of stages in his father's career? The suggestion is thrown out by D. C. Somervell, who derived this impression from his many talks with Temple at Repton; and it is justified by a remark Temple once made to a friend that he was 'glad to have the chance of doing as his father had done'. Whatever the motives, he was at least prepared to consider the possibility of standing as a candidate for Repton, when Ford resigned to become Headmaster of Harrow. He consulted his friends, and to Frank Fletcher he confessed that his own inclination was against competing. He did not want to undertake any work of the kind for five years; yet it could not be denied that the proposition attracted him—'they want, confessedly, an intellectual revival'. A day or two before the

132

Governors met he went to look at Repton, and on the eve of sailing for Australia he wrote to Ford:

Queen's College,
Oxford,
June 15.

My dear Ford,

You will know that I am not saying what I say in this letter light-heartedly. Repton quite charmed me. And the welcome I should have had was a very strong inducement. But looking now at the question from a little distance I can see, I think, that my previous decision was right. I really believe I am 'called' to the work I am doing, for some time to come. If I meant to go to any school—other than Rugby which is a magnet to me, but where I daresay I ought not ever to go either—I would not choose any before Repton now that I have seen it. But I believe I am where I ought to be. I can talk to undergraduates so that they will listen: whether or not I could do so to schoolboys no one knows. And there is immense opportunity in the Universities.

All but one of those whom I have consulted say that I ought to stay here, and move, if anywhere, to an East End Parish. I think they are right. I remember that Tait wanted my father to succeed him at Rugby; but my father said he was devoted for the time to the new work centred at Kneller Hall and refused. So here. I should like to come; but I am sure I am meant to go on for a time as at present.

Many thanks for your great kindness.

Yours v. sincerely,
W. TEMPLE.

I have not yet heard from Gore or Sadler. If they say anything to make me waver I will write again. But I must ask you not to bring my name before the Governors to-morrow.

He had got no farther than Marseilles when he heard that the selection committee had recommended him to the Governors, and at Aden a cablegram was waiting to say that the Governors had elected him. A letter to Frank Fletcher explains why he finally decided to accept the offer.

William Temple

P. &. O. S.S. *Marmora.* June 27.

My dear Frank,   Port Said.

About the time this reaches you, you may have seen the appointment of the new Headmaster of Repton. In case they have taken me, I wish to say that I refused the invitation of the Masters to stand as their candidate, and asked Ford not to bring up my name; others brought it up however and they decided to ask me whether I would accept it if offered. The combination of staff and Governors was very strong, and after three days deliberation I wrote and told them my views and hopes concerning English Education; adding that only the hope of support in furthering these would induce me to leave my present work just now; but that if with this letter before them they chose to elect me, I would go.

I can't trace the considerations that led to this in a letter; but one was a belief, engendered by you, that the Headmasters' Conference is becoming amenable to reason, which makes me want to be on it!

Try not to think me a fool; I was never so sure that I had done right.

Yours ever,
W. TEMPLE.

Among the 'considerations' was one of which he allowed few to know till, more than twenty years later, he was conducting a Mission in Oxford. He seldom spoke of his own deeper spiritual experiences, but for the undergraduates in S. Mary's Church that night he recalled this moment of his life in moving words which went straight to the hearts of them all:

I had once to make a choice which I found very difficult. I was much interested in the work I was doing, believing it to be of some value. I was asked to take up another post which certainly was more conspicuous in the eyes of the world. I tried to avoid it. I asked all the friends of whom I could think, and they all said that I had better stay where I was. I had to make a decision in time to write a letter by a certain post, and having weighed up the question as carefully as I could—and

134

we must always do that—and having come to no conclusion at all, I began at eight o'clock in the evening to say my prayers, and for three hours, without a pause, I tried to concentrate all my desires on knowing clearly what was God's Will for me. I do not know how those three hours went; they did not seem very long; but when eleven o'clock struck I knew perfectly well what I had got to do, and that was to accept; and I have never had a shadow of doubt since that it was right. . . . Each man has to find his own vocation. Every man is able to find that out if, quite sincerely, he will seek to do, not his own will, but God's.

As Temple was known to be out of England, most of the congratulations were sent to his mother. Among them were letters from the Archbishop of Canterbury, the Provost of Queen's (Magrath), the Headmaster of Rugby (David), his own headmaster (James), Whitelaw, and John Stocks. Ford telegraphed, immediately after the Governors' meeting, 'William elected—so glad—*magnificat anima mea*', and Michael Sadler wrote: 'He is a very great power, with growing force in the national life. Hundreds of thousands of young men will watch his work and be helped by his courage and plainness of mind, and by his moral force. . . . His influence is wonderful, and the most varied characters and the most critical minds respond to it.'

Repton School had a history of several centuries behind it. Temple, in telling his brother the news, chaffingly reminded him that (in its present foundation) Repton is ten years older than Rugby, and that even in 1557 it was only refounded on a new basis. It appears once to have been a public school not only in name, for among the first twenty-five names in the register are those of five gentlemen, four husbandmen, nine yeomen, two websters or weavers, a carpenter, and a tanner. Under Lionel Ford it had prospered. The school was well equipped, the organization moved smoothly, numbers were well up, it was served by a competent staff, and the prefects carried out conscientiously their considerable share of maintaining the school discipline. Ford was serious, warm-hearted, and pious (with a piety which masters and boys were apt to call either puritanical or ecclesiastical according to their predilections) and he had raised the tone of the school from the rather low level to which it had recently sunk. But one thing was lacking. It needed a new infusion of vitality—with a commonplace headmaster the school might have done little more than remain in its own groove—intellectual vitality in particular, for in scholarship (though this had begun to improve) its record did not stand high. Who, asked the optimists, was better qualified to supply this deficiency than the talented and ebullient young Fellow of Queen's?

Temple, on the high seas, had escaped (as his mother wrote to Randall Davidson) a good deal of the preliminary nuisance of moving house—'It was a good thing', she added, 'that his poor old mother and Langdon were there' to get things straight for him in the Hall before he returned to England—and, it may be added, to give one more proof of her constant and devoted thought for her son and his welfare. No one is better qualified to tell of her personality and her influence during the Repton years than S. S. Jenkyns, who writes:

I was his house tutor throughout his time, living in his house, and therefore saw the domestic side both of him and of that shrewd and lovable, though often alarming old lady, his mother. . . . To come at an advanced age, the widow of an Archbishop, accustomed to the pomp and dignity of a palace, to supervise the running of a Headmaster's house containing 80 boys—not to mention the constant stream of guests of all kinds—assisted only by W.'s old nurse, was a fairly big undertaking. But her love for him and her interest in his career enabled her to be of enormous help to him. I know that she often felt anxious lest he should allow his gift of speech to run away with him and he should become something of a windbag; her wise criticisms carried great weight with him, and no one could have had a greater love and respect for her advice than he. She was a witty old lady and, though her rather sharp tongue frightened some of the Repton ladies, she was really kindness itself. The dinner parties, with the gold casket con-

taining the Freedom of somewhere or other in the middle of
the table, were apt to be somewhat formal and alarming; until
W.'s resounding laugh, following one of the stories from his
apparently endless hoard, set the guests at their ease. More
domestic is the picture familiar to many at Repton of Mrs. T.
seated before a table containing the pieces of an enormous
jigsaw puzzle; William comes in, kisses his mother, rapidly
places some quite featureless pieces of sky in their correct
positions, and retires to grapple with even more puzzling
school problems.

The masters had been warned not to expect his arrival at
the beginning of term; and on 1 October 1910 the boys (in
the middle of their breakfast) were assembled by the Head of the
Hall to give their new Headmaster a rousing welcome as his car
drove up: 'I wonder', he said to one of them a few years later,
'whether you all knew what a blue funk I was in?' On the same
day he met the staff; the following morning he spoke quite
simply to the school—Here am I, newest of all newcomers:
pray for me—and it was no small encouragement to him to be
shown the following letter, after his first Sunday at the school:

The Priory,
Repton,
Burton-on-Trent.
Oct. 3, 1910.
Dear Mrs. Temple,
I am sure that you will be proud to hear that the 6th Form
were enormously impressed with the Headmaster's first lectures
to them and that everyone—boys and masters—thought his
sermon last night one of the very best that we have ever heard
in our Chapel.
Yours sincerely,
HARRY VASSALL.

By the end of his first year Temple's personality had impressed
itself upon the place. 'Buoyant sunshine', 'radiant vitality'—
these, with their many synonyms, are words that recur throughout the reminiscences of his staff and pupils when they try to
convey something of the atmosphere which, from the day of his

arrival, Temple diffused over masters and boys alike. The vitality was noticed especially where he would most gladly have had it felt, in the school chapel, though he made no important alterations in the services: the tradition had been 'central', and Temple did not disturb it. He had become accustomed to seeing his father stand on the north side of the altar when celebrating the Holy Communion; but he writes to reassure Ford that he will not change the custom prevailing at Repton; he is convinced by the argument put to him by Harry Vassall (the Bursar, and trusted adviser of many Repton headmasters)—that to continue a tradition is not a 'party' move, to make alterations is—and he cannot be too thankful for the work Ford had done in 'fostering a real sense of the Church and getting the protestantism out of the evangelicalism of the place'. One custom which Ford had started was kept up in the daily chapel services, at which the Bible was read: every morning Temple gave a two-minute comment on the passage for the day before reading it, which stimulated the imagination of the boys and helped to secure their attention, as the Book came to life for them under the touch of a master-hand.

There were two other openings for religious teaching in the school time-table. One was the Sixth Form Divinity Lesson; and here Temple drew the distinction, not too carefully marked forty years ago, between teaching boys about (or the history of) religion and teaching them religion: the weakness of too much of the instruction then given in the public schools lay for him in the irrelevance of the books and lessons inflicted on the boys to the imparting of a personal faith in Christ as the Incarnate and living Lord, and to the abiding fellowship of the Christian Church. This distinction he made clear many years later in a letter to the Headmaster of Rugby, who had written for his advice on three books that had been recommended for use in the higher forms of public schools:

As from
Bishopthorpe,
York.
July 16, 1934.

My dear Headmaster,

I have read these three volumes with great personal interest

138

and profit, but with great doubt about what I should say of their use for a school. While actually reading them I am not conscious of objection, but when I get away from them I find them curiously and (I am bound to say) dismayingly tendencious. As regards the effect they would produce, an almost infinite amount depends on what may be in the boys' minds before they start on them, and an uncomfortably large amount on the extent to which the teacher will so supplement the text as in effect to correct the tendency.

To take the former point first. If the boys begin with a conviction that what happened in B.C. 6—A.D. 30 or 33 was a specific act of God for the salvation of the world—as S. Mark no less than SS. Paul and John believed—then they will here learn a great deal about the progressive apprehension and exposition of that act by Christians. But if they do not start with that conviction, these books will not lead them to form it, nor will they lead them to realize that this is what the Apostles, and the Christian Church after them, believed and believe.

The tendency represented is that of late Victorian and Edwardian Liberalism. The books give an account of opinions held about God and Christ—not an account of the 'power of God unto salvation'. To that extent I think personally that they are misleading; and also—though this is unimportant—I think them out of date. The whole movement connected with the name of Barth might never have happened. I am not a Barthian. But among the views referred to this should be included. It is far the most alive of movements at the present time.

What I personally miss throughout is all sense of a great historical movement characterized by a sense of divine mission. This begins with Abraham (whether that name represents an individual or a tribe), is the distinctive characteristic of the consciousness of Israel, is deepened by the Prophets, is reconstituted by and in Jesus the Messiah, and continues from then as the Christian Church. Binns gives a good outline of Jewish history, but no reason why we should be interested in it. Hunkin is (to my mind) most misleading about the outlook of the Apostles just before Pentecost. He suggests that the gloom of Good Friday endured till then, and allows nothing for the effect of the Resurrection (actual or supposed) though he lets it appear (somewhat grudgingly) that the Resurrection was the theme of the first Apostolic teaching. Bethune-Baker I found (to my surprise) the least unsatisfactory, though his 'tendency' appears in many places, as e.g. (p. 95) the total omission of any reference to the Lucan (or Johannine) 'words' from the Cross, so that a strong suggestion is left that the 'Eloi, Eloi' was the last utterance. It *may* have been; but there is in the N.T. a different suggestion.

In the upshot—there is nothing Numinous in the whole picture. The books do not correspond to their title. They do not set out 'The Christian *Religion*—Its Origin and Progress'. They set out 'The Growth of *Opinions* held concerning God and Christ by adherents of the Jewish and Christian Religions'. Everything is discussed as a belief or aspiration of men—nothing as an act of God.

Of course my comment is as 'tendencious' as the books. I only claim that my 'tendency' is that of the Old and New Testaments themselves. It is legitimate in general, and perhaps for Christians, to write books with an inverse 'tendency'. But it is not legitimate to write about the Old and New Testaments without explaining that these present themselves, not primarily as a record of men's thoughts about God, but of God's acts in dealing with men. . . .

Yours sincerely,

WILLIAM EBOR.

(The three books he recommends in place of those mentioned in the letter are: *The Study of the Gospels*, by Armitage Robinson; 'a book that may be out of print, and has a horrible title: *The Shining Mystery of Jesus*' [since republished as *Jesus, the Gospel Portrait*]; and 'Edwyn Bevan's most admirable volume on *Christianity* in the Home University Library'.)

The second opportunity was given by his Sunday sermons, which were looked forward to by masters and boys alike. Most of these were printed soon after they were delivered, and to read them through now in the volume of *Repton School Sermons* is to wonder that they were not too strong meat for all except the most intelligent of the older boys. This was deliberate. Temple had no doubt of the target to aim at, in speaking to public school boys —preach, he would say, to the sixth and fifth forms: the younger boys are not likely anyhow to understand what you say, even if they attend to it: they may perhaps pick up a stray crumb or two as you go along, but you must not expect more. The difficulty, even with the clever boys, was to concentrate for the first eight or ten minutes of Temple's sermons: there was a sense of the preacher climbing higher and higher—and the boys finding the going harder and harder—with every word till the peak was reached: then he would, as it were, ask his hearers to 'turn round and look at the view'; they would see some new thing of God and their duty that was worth all the climbing; and Temple would come rushing downhill to the end, with a vigorous appeal to the will and an unmistakably clear application of his words to the leading of a Christian life or the making of a Christian nation. On the last Sunday in the Christmas Term of 1910, Harry Vassall wrote again to Mrs. Temple:

> I am very glad to hear that you were well enough to be up again, but as you were not able to come to Chapel tonight you will like to hear that the Headmaster preached us another sermon of even more thrilling eloquence than the previous ones. Every one was very much impressed with it, and the boys even stopped coughing—the highest tribute they ever offer!

With most boys there were three stages in their relations with the Headmaster. At the age of fourteen they felt vaguely that in all Olympus none could hold a candle to 'The Boss', and his sermons—particularly a breathless two-minute shout of joy and thanksgiving one Easter Day—left them with the stunned sense of something terrific. The testimony of J. D. Harford, 'as a very small boy in the Headmaster's House' from 1912 to 1914, would be endorsed by a hundred others of his age:

> I write with fidelity of recollection and impression, as of one

141

living and not of the legendary dead. The indelible impression is of vigour, vitality, exuberance, joyousness, friendliness, faith. A unique and unchallengeable gusto. An unchanging constancy of Christian attitude, a superb equipoise of one supremely at home in the spiritual and temporal worlds. The terms may not be properly fitting; I speak only of the impression on the juvenile mind. The sturdy, erect, quick-moving figure; that imperturbable countenance, rich voice, ready smile, and tremendous, joyful, inimitable laugh; that effortless, unfaltering, oracular delivery from pulpit or platform—all took the young mind by storm and remained in lasting possession. It was a boy of 13 or 14 who scrambled in spellbound exaltation to his feet after the ending of a sermon with the two verses of Blake's 'Bring me my bow of burning gold' declaimed with a wholly transcendent fire, conviction, and lilt which have kept the very accents alive over three decades of memory.

Yet remembrance on these lines would, one can feel sure, make William Temple impatient. For me as for so many others, as we look back, the memory he would consider natural would be of the simple, joyous, affectionate, unsentimental relationship of man and boy. That dazzling embodiment of superhuman excellence was 'Billy' to the youngest boy admitted to his special friendship. That was the essence of the matter.

When boys had reached the age of sixteen, relations were not too easy to establish, and at Confirmation interviews there might be as much silence, an embarrassed and painful silence, on both sides as speech—if only he could always address individual parents or boys as if they were a public meeting, he once confessed to a colleague, how much more comfortable he would feel! But on reaching the Sixth the boys discovered their Headmaster, and with him the new world of thought and beauty which he opened to them. The words are deliberately chosen—for it was a quite 'tough' member of the Sixth who wrote to his mother on Temple's teaching of S. John's Gospel: 'Billy has opened up a New Heaven and a New Earth to me.' D. C. Somervell has thus described the subjects and the methods of his teaching:

Temple's early Divinity lessons to the Sixth Form aroused in many boys a degree of enthusiasm that those who entertain conventional ideas about public schools would barely credit. The 'Fordian' type, trained to an intense seriousness as regards the importance of such subjects, without having received any strong intellectual stimulus in relation to them, would naturally be responsive. . . . Apart from Divinity his most important undertakings were the reading of Greek and Latin texts with the Upper Sixth, mostly in the spirit of Greats rather than of Mods. Plato, Longinus' *On the Sublime*, Cicero's *De Finibus*, Aeschylus' *Agamemnon*, indicate the range of his interests. His work here was wholly admirable for the best—better value, I should guess, than any other schoolboys were getting anywhere else in England—and highly stimulating to the verge of bewilderment for the weaker brother. I remember hearing of a deputation asking him to expound the mysteries of the *Phaedo* 'again and not quite so quickly'. Temple himself described to me how he used to chant the choruses of the *Agamemnon* to tunes of his own composition, while the boys looked down and 'blushed for very shame at witnessing so intemperate a performance'. Those who knew him can supply from memory the immense laugh with which this relation must have concluded. He was rather fond of attempting this sort of thing. I remember once when we were on a holiday together he sat down at a piano and sang the last verse of Browning's *Abt Vogler* in recitative, accompanying himself with chords which carried out the musical directions contained in the text. He had very considerable musical ability, of which he would doubtless have made much more in a life of comparative leisure. He wrote a good tune for Kipling's *Recessional*, which we used in Chapel.

English poetry, too, he read with his boys, especially Browning, and Shakespeare's tragedies. To every boy who reached the Upper Sixth he gave a complete Browning as a present. His favourite poems were the more philosophical ones, 'The Pope' [from *The Ring and the Book*] and *A Death in the Desert* for example. . . . In the great Shakespeare tragedies he took the title role himself, assigning the other parts to suitable boys. His favourite play was *Lear*; but he specially fancied himself in the part of Hamlet on the ground that Hamlet was, like himself (in 1911) aged thirty, also 'fat and scant of breath', and given to talking too much. I remember carrying the parallel further and telling him that, if the ghost of his father told him to murder his uncle, he would make a sad mess of it; to which he did not demur. But he would have been much kinder than his prototype to poor little Ophelia.

As a teacher Temple was lucid and cogent, and he avoided two weaknesses to which schoolmasters have been known to succumb —he was careful not to parade his learning, and he never talked down to his pupils. They were treated as his intellectual equals, which pleased and stimulated the more intelligent of them to be worthy of the compliment. He had, too, a fund of humour on which to draw, and a lightness of touch even when the subject was one in which the depth and range of his learning were inevitably displayed. If one example is to be quoted of this treatment, let it be the paper he read on 'Scientific Ideas among the Ancient Greeks', which was an astonishing feat for one who made no pretence of scientific knowledge. The lecture begins with an apology for daring to speak on the subject at all:

. . . for my ignorance of all things scientific is so immense as to be distinguished. I did, when at school myself, rub glass rods on fur mats and then hold them over a bottle in which two gold leaves were hanging; but when, or if, the leaves moved I always secretly attributed the fact to a draught.

One after another the thinkers of ancient Greece, from Thales to Aristotle, come under review. Two samples of his lighter comments must suffice, this first on Heraclitus:

We may remember Shelley's expression of his feelings with regard to the mutability of things, and his sorrow as he reflected that 'Nought may endure but mutability'. That phrase is the summary of Heraclitus' view of things. But perhaps his melancholy was due not solely to his scientific interests. He found himself at variance with his fellow-citizens, whom he tersely described in the phrase 'They fill their bellies like cattle', adding that 'Ten thousand do not turn the scale against a single man of worth', he himself being the man of worth. His final advice to his fellow-citizens was as follows: 'The Ephesians would do well to hang themselves man by man. . . .' It is to be feared that his disposition was not genial.

And this of Pythagoras:

Into the theory of mystical numbers I will not lead you; but I must confess to a lurking sympathy with it—partly, perhaps, because numbers are to me of all things the most elusive. My own method of finding the sum of a series of numbers, for instance, in doing my accounts, may be poetically described in this way: I add them up, and then I add them down, and then I split the difference between the numbers so reached. . . .

The theories of Pythagoras come to us for the most part through Plato, who alternatively adopts and ridicules them. First I will give an instance of the latter treatment. He finds in the *Republic* that there are five leading types of human life— the Rational, the Military, the Mercenary, the Licentious, and the Bestial. He says that if we take the first to the third, that is three; and if we multiply these together, that is 9; but we want a well-established and solid result, so we must cube it, which gives us 729; and this is very nearly 730, which is twice 365, the number of days in a year. Hence the ideally good life is happier every day and every night of the year than the ideally bad life. He counts one of his stages twice over; he multiplies when he ought to add; he cubes the product for no reason at all; the result is very nearly but not quite a figure to which a perfectly fantastic meaning might be given. Obviously the whole thing is a satire on the mystic numbers of Pythagoras; but I need hardly say that the solemn German editors are sorely exercised to find the rationale of the philosopher's procedure.

It must not be thought that Temple was only interested in intelligent boys. He loved them all, the clever and the stupid, the good and the bad; not because it was his Christian duty to do so, but because his affectionate nature allowed him no other approach to them. Least of all did he regard them as persons to be disciplined; and herein lay the weakness of one of his virtues. He made no secret of it: 'The better one likes the purely personal relation with the boys', he wrote to his brother about a year after he left Repton, 'the more one shrinks from the disciplinary.' He was considered no mean adept with the rod (though not so expert as his predecessor) but there was something in his nature—some have not hesitated to call it a weakness—which shrank from inflicting pain or misery on any human being, however unruly or vicious. Nor could he adopt the constricted and local view that is essential for the good disciplinarian; his idea of a cosmos was something considerably wider than the average headmaster's, and that studied sense of proportion which was later to revolutionize the conviction of thousands about the essentials of Christian faith and life was little suited to the small-town politics of a public school. Was Temple deliberately passing judgement on himself— even 'pulling his own leg'—when he said that 'the "stars" can well supply the luxuries of education, but those capable of supplying its luxuries are often temperamentally ill-fitted to supply its necessities'?

One incident was long remembered. For some time and on a large scale goods had been missing from the school shop, and there was no doubt that among the Repton boys there were thieves. Temple spoke a word to the school about it between the giving out of two quite formal notices. Some of the older boys imagined what Ford would have said; of the result of his talk they felt sure—few in the school would have heard it without a sense of shame and disgust. But Temple dismissed the matter in a couple of sentences—I need hardly remind you that such occurrences reflect on the honour of every member of the School, and I shall trust to that sense of honour which is in each one of you to ensure that such cases of petty pilfering shall cease. 'Petty' enough, true—when compared with the enclosure of the English Commons or the rape of Poland (and for an adult audience)— but the word did not sound impressive in the ears of boys who were disgracing the tradition and poisoning the life of the whole small world they knew and, for a time, 'petty pilfering' became a catchword in the school. It is more difficult to account for the moral condition of his own house; and here too perhaps little can be said except that a virtue became a source of weakness. Temple must surely have been the only headmaster to choose Browning's *Now* for reading aloud to his older pupils, and his own innocence and chastity were so exceptional that the sexual malpractices of schoolboys lay outside the general scheme of things which had his immediate and sympathetic interest. It can hardly be said that he turned a blind eye to them. Probably the safest conjecture is that he was too far removed from them to be able to see what was required by way of discipline to limit their incidence and the atmosphere that encouraged them, or to understand the treatment which would correct them. 'I have never met anyone else', writes one of his colleagues, 'who gave at once the impression of being entirely "unspotted by the world". Of such are saints made, but not headmasters.'

But there was one question which Temple's critics were justified in asking. Where, after all, was the revolutionary that he had hoped and promised to be? In his first letter to Ford, after he had decided to let his name go forward to the Governors, Temple had written quite candidly of his intentions:

> 8, Keble Road,
> Oxford.
> June 20.

My dear Ford,

The deed is done so far as I am concerned. I have said I will come if the Governors still wish it after reading my letter; in that I mention my work for the Student Movement and Workers' Education, and say that I shall hope still to do for those two as much as full consideration of the School's welfare makes possible.

Secondly I said that the Public Schools seemed to me to reproduce our class-divisions in accentuated form, and that I should hope, after learning the ropes, to find ways of moving towards a system which would tend to diminish them. If they take me, knowing this, I come.

> Yours very sincerely,
> W. TEMPLE.

Rumours of his purpose had gone before him. High expectations had been roused; developments were awaited with less anxiety than might have been expected; and questions began to be asked—what form would the revolution take, and what would be the first moves? Soon after Temple's arrival a music master left the school (it was suspected that he had been removed) but two of the staff whose fate was regarded as sealed unaccountably stayed on. Perhaps, it was suggested, the new headmaster was reluctant to make drastic changes in a hurry; they would all come in good time. But the conviction grew that, if the axe did not fall on these two heads, there was little hope (or fear) of any large-scale reform. Sunday afternoon piano recitals were introduced, new hymns were sung at the chapel services, and there was a marked improvement in the general level of the school music. Temple also made an attempt to introduce the house-tutor system, but the masters opposed the idea and it was dropped. And, as term followed term with no rocking of the foundations, it began to be suspected that there was to be no revolution after all. The suspicion proved to be well founded, the revolution never came; Temple's experience had led him to change his mind. D. C. Somervell supplies the clue, from a note recorded at the time:

> I remember Temple telling me, near the end of his last term, that when he wrote the revolutionary letter, his ideas of public school policy were of the vaguest: a mixture of boyhood recollections and W.E.A. Utopianism. As he said to me on that occasion—'If there is one thing my time here has taught me, it is that institutions must be run on their own lines or else scrapped. You cannot turn an old institution into a wholly new direction and expect to be able to utilize its running powers as before.'

This was neither more nor less than he had said privately to many friends; and as early as June 1911 he writes to his brother, 'Things are going very well here: I have nothing to do except jog the show along.' No doubt time was a determining factor. One essential for a headmaster who hopes to bring about a revolution is a revolutionary staff, and this takes many years to collect. Another—if his principles of reform are to spread beyond his own school—is that he shall be able to urge his views with vigour and persistence on other headmasters. Temple was fully aware of this. In his letter to the Governors he had made it plain on what terms he would come; and he also felt a call to do a little troubling of the waters at the Headmasters' Conference. In fact, though he was elected in spite of his youth to the Committee of the Conference, he did not contribute much of importance to its deliberations; in a few more years his influence would undoubtedly have grown—but could these years be rightly spared to Repton? This question could not but recur during Temple's last year at the school. Had he gone to Clifton the problem would have been less acute: James Wilson wrote of his own headmastership there: 'I was compelled to take active interest in many things outside Clifton. I always felt that the school gained and did not lose by my multifarious interests. I think the contagion of a happy activity is an important element in a schoolmaster. In an indefinable way activity and interest in one thing stirs activity generally.' But Wilson had only to walk down Park Street to be in the thick of his 'multifarious interests' in Bristol: his school was not placed in a remote village in the Midlands, from which long train journeys were needed to bring the headmaster to the scene of his many extraneous activities. More and more exacting became the claims from outside the school on Temple's time and energy, more frequent were his absences from Repton; and none too soon he was convinced that either he must give up all his hopes of moulding a public school nearer to the shape of his own ideals, or else be released from most of his central work. As he weighed the alternatives, Temple became sure in which direction the more obvious duty lay; and in December 1912 there seemed to sound a clear call to new work. 'Can you keep a *dead* secret?' he scribbled in pencil on a torn scrap of paper which he passed to Vaughan at a conference they were both attending: 'I have been offered S. Margaret's, Westminster, with the Canonry at the Abbey. The Archbishop is *very* keen that I should go. I have been at Repton 2 yrs. & 3 mths! Have you a view?'

This church, as the Prime Minister pointed out in his letter to Temple, was one of great central importance. Its connexion with the House of Commons gave the Rector a unique sphere of influence in Church and State, and the preaching of Henson (who had accepted the Deanery of Durham) had attracted a large and intelligent congregation. No church could have been more suited to one of Temple's gifts and hopes; an added attraction was the Canonry at the Abbey to which the living was attached; and 'the Archbishop came near to ordering it'. There was, therefore, little surprise among his colleagues when they heard during the Christmas holidays that Temple had accepted the offer. The surprise came when, as congratulations and good wishes were pouring in, the Dean of Westminster discovered that Temple was not qualified to hold a Canon's stall as he had not yet been six years in Priest's Orders; and the offer was withdrawn. It was the kind of contretemps for which nobody, or everybody, is to blame. The Dean gracefully apologized for his share in the 'inadvertence'. Asquith apologized for his advisers. Randall Davidson apologized for Asquith, the Law Officers of the Crown, the Dean of Westminster, and himself. The only person entirely unperturbed was Temple, who appeared with the usual 'glorious morning face' at Repton on the first day of the Lent Term—for all the world (it was remarked) 'like a runaway wife who had missed her train'.

But everyone at Repton knew that this would be the first of many offers, and the end came when, in May 1914, the Lord Chancellor offered Temple the vacant Rectory of S. James's, Piccadilly. This living is in the gift of the Bishop of London (two turns) and the Lord Chancellor (one turn); and when he had made sure that this was one of the Lord Chancellor's turns, Temple accepted the offer. A day or two after he met Dick Sheppard (who was then in charge of the Grosvenor Chapel and Chaplain to the Cavendish Club) and told him of Haldane's offer, adding that he hoped they would be able to work together in the Piccadilly area. He thought that Sheppard looked at him rather strangely, and a little later Sheppard wrote: 'I hope you did not think me very un-welcoming when you told me about S. James's. Of course I would love to work in with you when you are there; but, you see, I was rather startled by your news, because the Bishop of London had just offered the living to *me!*'

The following extract from a circular letter to his staff expresses well what both he and they knew:

> . . . The reason that has chiefly weighed with me is this: during the last year I have been drawn more and more into the current of general Church politics and have felt wholly unable to resist; I have been made a member of three new Committees whose work is of central and urgent importance. But my work here has prevented my doing for those Committees the work which was really called for, while the interest of the problems with which they are concerned has drawn my attention somewhat seriously away from school and its needs. I trust that the school has not yet suffered from this, but it would suffer before long. I have therefore felt bound to accept the offer of a position where I can respond to the claims made upon me without feeling that my primary duty is being neglected. Of the feelings to which this decision gives rise in myself I will not now attempt to speak.

Headmasters, in common talk, fall into three categories, the 'great', the 'good'—and the others. Of the great there have been few: Arnold of Rugby, Thring of Uppingham, Sanderson of Oundle—besides them, how many? The good are less easy to specify or select, because goodness as applied to headmasters is a word of several connotations. There have been good administrators, good teachers, good disciplinarians, and good men; which particular goodness, and how much of it, entitles a headmaster to a place among the good? A simpler test is to ask whether Repton School stood in a strong position when Temple left it, in the view of masters, educationists, parents, and public opinion. One of his colleagues answers the question by declaring that Temple put Repton 'on the map'. In many respects it was there already. All that Ford did for Repton—and his contribution was a considerable one—can be found set out in Dr. Alington's memoir; but there was (one of his old boys writes) a 'streak of prosiness' in him which prevented him from being an inspiring teacher, either in the pulpit or the classroom. Temple brought with him a distinction in learning, in breadth of interest, in preaching, and in teaching, which left an indelible mark on Repton, and an intellectual and spiritual vitality of which the infection spread through the whole life of the place. 'He made the school think' was one of the greatest tributes paid to him; and the point was brought out in the first paragraph of the school *Terminal Record* of June 1914: 'Both by his great gift for preaching and by his magnetic personal influence he has infused new life into us all.'

But, as always, Temple's greatest gift was himself—his simplicity, his humour, his modesty, and the unaffected friendliness he showed both to the boys and to those members of the school staff who might least have expected it. He met them all on equal terms, never overwhelming even the cleverest with the sense of his intellectual greatness, and always leaving the humblest with the sense of complete social equality. The perpetual salutes of the village police sergeant were among his minor trials. Coming into lunch one day with less than his usual cheerfulness, he expressed his irritation in some such words as these: Sergeant Pett salutes me because he thinks I am a superior being to him just because I am a headmaster. Really, so long as he is a good police sergeant and I am (for the sake of argument) an equally good headmaster, there is nothing socially, or there should be nothing, to choose between us. I cannot bear this cap-touching. In the first place, returning his salute has made my arm ache. In the second place, it would be much healthier for Sergeant Pett's immortal soul if he thought less about himself as my inferior than about both of us as sons of God and princes of the universe. True, if he really thought of himself as one of the sons of God, he might, like them, spend much of his time 'shouting for joy'; and that, I confess, might interfere with the peace of the village and the execution of his duties.

The war fell upon him with heavy blows, as the news of the Rugby and Repton casualties came in; first Ronald Poulton—of whom he wrote 'I think I liked him as much as or more than anyone else in the world'—and then John Howell, perhaps his greatest friend among the Repton boys. He lost touch with few of those whom he had known at all well. His affection followed them out into the world, and he was seldom happier than when in their company—at S. James's Rectory, where he welcomed them in war-time at any hour of the day or night, at the theatre, at Oxford (where twelve of them sat down to dinner with him and his wife one summer evening at the Mitre), and even at a restaurant-bar in Jermyn Street where the habitués, lolling on *vieux-rose* plush settees, stared open-mouthed while Temple, entirely unconscious of their astonishment as he swallowed his soft drinks, made the restaurant ring with the laugh which his old boys were apt on such occasions deliberately to provoke. He took immense pains to advance their interests, and was more amused than discouraged by one unusual incident.

Soon after he left Repton, the following letter, received at the India Office with other testimonials from an applicant for a post, reached the new headmaster with a request for a record of the boy's career at school:

Repton College,
Derbyshire.
23. 7. 13.

My dear Mr. ——

On this the last day of the term I am writing you a brief letter as to-morrow you will leave Repton for holidays and after that you will be launching out into the world—a schoolboy no longer.

My dear boy, all I need say to you is keep up the courage, straightforwardness and sportsmanship you have always displayed in school and at sports and your success in any branch of life is assured.

Your example here as a higher form boy prefect and later as head of the school has been of such a high character I wish every boy would try to emulate.

May you have a pleasant holiday and remember I shall always be happy to greet you whenever you care to come to the

old school again and when you do take up your career, never
lose sight of the old motto—*Respice Finem.*

Sincerest regards,
W. TEMPLE, D.D.,
Headmaster.

The literary style of the Headmaster of Repton was not then
so well known as the Archbishop's came to be through his books
and broadcasts; but the veriest tyro in Higher Criticism might
have been a little dubious about this testimonial. However, it
served a good purpose, causing great delight among the staff at
Repton where it was read aloud at a Masters' Meeting, as well as
to the wholly innocent 'author' when he received a copy of it from
his successor.

Temple had many regrets in leaving Repton, but he felt no
anxiety for the future of the school when the name of the new
headmaster was announced. He had written to Frank Fletcher,
setting out a list of the many gifts—especially spiritual gifts—
which he considered essential in a candidate. Fletcher replied
that he only knew one man to fulfil the rather exacting conditions
—'but Fisher is too young'. An excited postcard from Temple
came by return of post—'Fisher we must have.' His successor
at Repton was also to follow him, thirty years later, at Lambeth.

IX

'Foundations'

The whole of my theology is an attempt to understand and verify the words: 'He that hath seen Me hath seen the Father.'

W. T., letter to R. A. Knox, October 1913.

BEFORE he left Repton, Temple had made his first important contribution to the theological thought of his time. Till then there had been much uncertainty about his standpoint, both among Church leaders whose suspicions of his unorthodoxy had not been altogether allayed by his ordination, and among the younger generation of students who were hoping that a new prophet had risen among them to talk to them in their own language, and to expound the relevance of the Christian creed to their lives: so far there had been nothing either deep or systematic enough in his casual writings to reassure the anxieties of the one or to justify fully the hopes of the other. Temple's intimacy with Streeter and his admiration for Rashdall—and the wisp of a white tie which he affected rather than the clerical collar—seemed to point in the direction of 'Broad Church'; but there was also his close personal association with Holland and Gore to suggest an influence drawing him nearer to the centre.

Foundations was published in 1912, with the sub-title—which sufficiently explains its intention—*A Statement of Christian Belief in Terms of Modern Thought.* The purpose of the book was explained in the Introduction. Christianity, and its traditional theology, it was stated, had come down to us from a very different age from our own: 'an age when the sun and stars moved round the earth, when the meaning of natural law and evolution was only dimly apprehended, when the psychology of religion, the historical method, and the critical study of ancient documents were yet unborn.' The writers had set themselves to 'a careful re-examination, and if need be re-statement', of their belief in the light of these developments. The volume consisted of nine essays, written by seven (past or present) Oxford tutors mostly of

155

Temple's own generation, with B. H. Streeter (who was senior to the rest of them) as general editor, though the book did not owe its origin to him in the sense that *Lux Mundi* did to Gore. *Foundations* grew out of a plan proposed by a Cambridge Anglo-Catholic, the Rev. H. L. Pass, who towards the end of 1910 had projected a composite volume of essays to be written by men of his own theological and church outlook, and had asked Walter Moberly to contribute an essay on 'The Being of God', for which thirty pages would be allowed. Moberly hesitated—was not the space allotted entirely inadequate even for the sketchiest treatment of the subject, and would he be likely to feel at home in so pronouncedly Anglo-Catholic a company? While he was considering his reply, two friends—the Rev. R. Brook (Fellow of Merton, now Bishop of St. Edmundsbury and Ipswich) and the Rev. R. Parsons (Fellow of University, now Bishop of Hereford) —happened to come to his room. They sympathized with his doubt but, after consideration, suggested that for such a composite book there was no need to look to Cambridge: a few like-minded Oxford churchmen might combine to produce it, each being allowed ample space for the development of his particular theme. Streeter, who was next consulted, welcomed the proposal with enthusiasm, and it was agreed by them all that Temple should be one of the contributors. There were shades of difference in theological outlook among the seven eventually chosen, Streeter standing a little to the 'left', and Neville Talbot a little to the 'right', of the other five.

The contributors were already friends—they were all members of the 'Holy Lunch' party—and so were able to criticize one another's drafts, which were circulated between the group meetings, with complete frankness, and to be reasonably patient of one another's heresies. The result was a book which showed a common mind rather more clearly than most of such volumes. But there was one exception; none of his colleagues was prepared to sponsor Streeter's theory of our Lord's Resurrection, and he stated explicitly in his essay that their views were not his own. There was also a deliberate omission, on which the critics were quick to fasten. Some of the group were at that time hesitant about the Virgin Birth of our Lord; and they agreed, if seriously challenged, to reply that, whether or not they were of one mind on the historical mode of that Birth, they were unanimous in not regarding it as a 'Foundation' on which to build, and for that reason the theme had been omitted.

Temple wrote two of the essays and the Epilogue. He also acted as Chaplain to the group and led their corporate devotions with Forms of Prayer specially compiled for the purpose. This part of his contribution is specially remembered by Sir Walter Moberly:

> Two recollections of Temple stand out in my mind in connexion with our work on *Foundations*. The first illustrates his remarkable energy and facility. At our Boar's Hill meeting we had spent the whole morning discussing his Christological essay, and we were due to meet again at 3 o'clock for an intensive discussion of one of the others. We were exhausted, and after lunch the rest of us sallied out to get a little air and distraction, but William did not accompany us. When we returned we found him sitting at the table writing. He stopped and handed his typescript to Streeter, saying 'Here it is. I have incorporated all the alterations which seem desirable and it is now ready for the press.' He then proceeded to take part in the afternoon's discussions with undiminished vitality. My other recollection is of his leading our devotions and giving us short addresses in his oratory at Repton. It was then that I first realized the depth of that side of him.

In his original draft Temple had prefixed to the Epilogue the text 'And there came out this calf' (Exodus, xxxii. 24)—words which at first attracted his colleagues as expressing appropriately their sense of humility and of dissatisfaction with their final achievement. But on maturer judgement they rejected it: it offered too easy a mark for any—and such critics were not wanting—who 'sat in the seat of the scornful'.

The subjects of his two essays were 'The Divinity of Christ' and 'The Church'. (The second was not part of the original scheme, but was required later to fill an obvious gap.) The evolution of the longer essay was characteristic. At the time he wrote it Temple was Headmaster of Repton, with all his routine duties at the school and his engagement book already over-full; and it was painfully obvious to his colleagues that the draft which he had circulated was a hurried piece of work, worthy neither of the subject nor of himself. The essay seemed to them hopelessly inadequate and thin—it covered no more than twelve quarto pages of typescript—and the contrast between it and Streeter's masterly chapter (which arrived at the same time) encouraged them to express, without any mincing of words, their grave disappointment. What followed shows illuminatingly Temple's ability and readiness to profit by the criticism of others, which never failed to stimulate his own thinking. With complete good humour and modesty he took the essay back, and re-wrote it in three parts. The second part, which summarizes the history of the classical attempts to work out a doctrine of our Lord's Person in the age of the Fathers, was wholly new; the third section was expanded and enriched. His colleagues were as deeply impressed by the revised version as they had been distressed by the original draft, and their judgement was endorsed by competent critics when the essays were published. Among the serious criticisms of the book as a whole was one offered, a few years later, by von Hügel in the course of conversation with one of the contributors; those parts of it which dealt with the Church he judged to be 'quite satisfactory', those dealing with Christology 'fairly satisfactory', while the section that dealt with the Being of God seemed to him 'wholly unsatisfactory'. A lighter touch marked a satiric poem, after the manner of Dryden, by the Rev. (now the Right Reverend Monsignor) Ronald Knox, then Chaplain of Trinity and a close friend of several of the contributors. The title of the poem was *Absolute and Abitofhell*, and the lines referring to Temple were as follows:

> First, from the Public Schools—*Lernaean Bog*—
> No paltry Bulwark, stood the Form of *OG*.
> A man so broad, to some he seem'd to be
> Not one, but all Mankind in Effigy:

Who, brisk in Term, a Whirlwind in the Long,
Did everything by turns, and nothing wrong,
Bill'd at each Lecture-hall from Thames to Tyne
As Thinker, Usher, Statesman, or Divine.
Born in the Purple, swift he chose the Light,
And Lambeth mark'd him for a Nazirite:
Discerning *Balliol* snatched him in his teens,
And mourn'd him, early forfeited to *Queen's*.
His name suffic'd to leave th' insidious tome
A household word in every English Home:
No academick Treatise, high and dry,
Canvass'd in Walks round Mesopotamy,
Or where in Common Room, when days are short,
Soulless Professors gulp disgusted Port.
'Not from the few, the learned, and the pale'
—So ran his Message—'we expect our Sale;
Man in the Street, our Publication con—
What matter, if the Street be Ashkelon?'

The final lines of the poem contained a satiric dedication to the
authors of *Foundations* from

an humble Friend,
Praying that Providence this Wind may use
To puff your Sales, and to confound your views.

Temple at once wrote on a postcard to Knox, 'Ta for Puff: OG'.

Our main concern with these essays must be to ask whether
they mark any important or noticeable stage in Temple's theological development. Clearly, they do not in all respects represent
his more mature convictions. There is much in them that dates,
or of which the emphasis was later to be shifted—the reliance on
Harnack, the championing of psychology against logic, of 'Will'
against 'Substance', of Antioch against Alexandria—and in
Christus Veritas (published in 1924) he modified certain phrases
and expressions and retracted others which he had come to
regard as open to justifiable criticism. But among the papers
he left was a copy of a letter that is of permanent interest to
the student of Temple's thought, for it sets out his personal

convictions on certain points at that period in his life as clearly and concisely as the subjects allow. The letter was written in answer to Ronald Knox's considered criticisms in *Some Loose Stones*—a book to which Temple was always ready to acknowledge his debt. Knox was then regarded as the protagonist, at least with his pen, of Anglo-Catholics in Oxford; and the whole tone of *Foundations* seemed to him the quintessence of that liberalism which he conceived to be undermining the faith of English Churchmen in the certainties of revealed truth. Here, in a few paragraphs, is his indictment of the tendency of 'modern thought' at Oxford in his day and of the disastrous encouragement he feared would be given to it by the authors of *Foundations*:

We are not concerned, now, to find how we can represent truth most adequately, but how we can represent it most palatably. We ask of a doctrine, not, 'Is it sound?', but, 'Couldn't we possibly manage to do without it?'; not, 'Is it true?', but, 'Can I induce Jones to see it in that light?' Jones is a banker in a provincial town; he has been at the University, and formed a taste for serious reading which he has not lost in the midst of worldly employments. His father was a colonel who went to church once a Sunday, to Communion three times a year, and never worried his head about books. His mother was a godly woman, vaguely affected by the Oxford Movement. As the result of a surfeit of Baasha at his public school, and an overdose of Hegel at College, his religious ideas have arrived at a stage quite beyond his power to express: a stage in which he never thinks much of going to church, except now and then to hear a brainy Minor Canon discoursing (with frequent reference to Browning) on the Problem of Pain. His local vicar, one or two old College friends, and a diocesan bishop who has formed the hazy impression that this is the sort of man we want to take orders, ask him out to luncheon at intervals, with the double idea that they are doing him good, and keeping themselves broadminded by cultivating the acquaintance of an intelligent agnostic. 'Such a good man', they all declare, '*anima naturaliter Christiana*, and all that.'

And the problem arises in each of their minds: How can we so dock and dove-tail the faith, so leave out of sight its unfortunate insistence on miracle, so reinterpret its crude statement of the Atonement, so retranslate its antiquated formularies, that Jones can honestly become a communicant? Jones is the hero of *Foundations*, all the way through. . . . Viewed from one angle, the whole book appears to be an attempt to reach, not a fixed deposit of truth, but an irreducible minimum of truth which will just be 'inclusive' of Jones.

Here was a challenge that had to be taken up. There was never any intention of writing, still less of publishing, a corporate reply, but Temple felt deeply some of the insinuations in this paragraph, especially in reference to the Atonement and belief in miracles, and he grasped the opportunity of making a personal confession. This included an exposition of his own general method of approach to the problems of religion, and a statement of his convictions on particular points of Christian belief. With marked courtesy, and with no lapse from his habitual good humour, he wrote the following reply [a few page-numbers are omitted in this transcription] to Ronald Knox and sent a copy of it to each of his colleagues:

The Hall,
Repton,
Burton-on-Trent.
Oct. 29, 1913.

My dear Ronnie,

Longman's have sent me *Some Loose Stones* and I have read it with very great delight. Some of it has given me furiously to think. But partly because of your over-kind remarks [about himself] and partly because of friendship, I hope you will manage to wade through this statement of my own position.

Probably I am (personally) in closer agreement with you in positive doctrine than any of the others, unless it be N.S.T. Probably also my methods are among those most repellent to you.

I was (and am) glad to be in this group—even to be associated with Streeter's discussion of our Lord's eschatology and of the

Resurrection—because I certainly believe his position to be tenable legitimately by a priest of the Church of England, and I know there are many who have through it been brought to reconsider their whole attitude of mind; in other words some Joneses are better Christians than they were even if not yet good ones in your sense. For I don't believe in the ideal of a Church with sharply defined boundaries; its unity (as I have heard Waggett express it) is like that of a ray of light—bright in the centre (? Rome) but ending none knows exactly where.

For your own understanding of my personal position I must state three propositions:

(1) I am not a spiritual doctor trying to see how much Jones can swallow and keep down; I am more respectable than that; *I am Jones himself asking what there is to eat.*

(2) . . . I can accept the paragraph on p. 34 as an exact statement of my position:

[The modern theologian is in the first instance inductive, applying fearlessly to the Bible the critical principles he would apply to any other book; examining doctrines from the standpoint of the modern mind; and then, as an afterthought, proves that his results are substantially identical with received doctrine. *R. K.*]

But that is my position as enquirer. I am ready, even eager, to insist that as enquirer I have not yet found all that the Church has found and in any divergence of judgment I bow to the Church for practical purposes (which include preaching) unless I think I can see plainly that the Church is wrong. As a matter of fact there is no point where I do see this. Hence my 'uncritical' attitude in preaching, for which J. M. Thompson attacked my published *Repton School Sermons* in the *Oxford Magazine*. But I do *feel* far more certain of doctrines which my own enquiries have established than of others: (S. John iv, 42); and therefore I act on these more consistently and preach them more forcibly. So I wish thus to verify all I can apart from 'presuppositions', but my belief is not limited to what I have verified.

(3) I try to think neither deductively nor inductively, but

(deliberately) in circles—or in pendulum-swings. I approach a group of facts, they suggest a theory; in the light of the theory I get a fuller grasp of the facts; the fuller grasp suggests modifications of the theory—and so on—until we reach a systematic apprehension of the facts, where each fits into its place. As old Caird used to say, 'there is no harm in arguing in a circle if the circle is large enough'. It was once a poser to say, 'If the elephant stands on the tortoise, on what does the tortoise stand?' But the law of gravitation says, 'If the elephant stands on the tortoise, the tortoise stands on the elephant'. I believe induction and deduction are both methods not of thought but of debate.

So (e.g.) I am content to argue thus: The Church has the promise of the Spirit, and will therefore probably be right—(not 'certainly' because the treasure is in earthen vessels)—I enquire independently into its decisions and find that whenever I reach a conclusion at all it is that the Church was right; this confirms my belief that the Church is the Spirit-bearing body and therefore also my belief in the authority of Christ to make the promise.

Now for my positive beliefs.

(*a*) I have no presupposition against miracles, and I believe Christ walked on the water. I believe in the Virgin Birth, but I cannot in my own mind find any real theological significance in it; still, it wonderfully holds before the imagination the truth of our Lord's Deity and so I am glad that it is in the Creed. Similarly I believe in our Lord's Bodily Resurrection, but if it could (*per impossibile*) be disproved, I don't think it would affect my faith as a whole.

(*b*) The only thing in *Foundations* that really disquiets me is the extent to which Schweitzer has dominated Streeter and Rawlinson-Parsons. You are right when you say that I do not expect a catastrophic end of the world—(though of course I do not dream of denying its possibility)—but then I am quite convinced that our Lord Himself did not expect it. I interpret the discourses as referring partly to the Fall of Jerusalem, partly to His own Passion and all that should flow from it, partly to the eternal significance of any moral decision. (If you care for it, you will find my views in *The Kingdom of God*, pp. 7–39 and 131–144; but I think you are probably right about Mt. x. 23, and I should want now to add something to what I said there about the evidential use of miracle. I think it was often used to confirm disciples, but never, or rarely, to attract them in the first instance.) Anyhow I think our Lord definitely rejected the apocalyptic idea of Messiahship. And if I thought He expected an immediate catastrophe other than His own Death and Resurrection, I *think* I should have to renounce Christianity.

(c) The main issue so far as I am concerned: I do not think the pendulum-swings, referred to in proposition 3 above, have yet reached a systematic apprehension; nor do I think they ever will. Hence the position laid down in the short paragraph on p. 250.

['Distinct refusals to define', coupled with repeated efforts to retake and understand as far as may be, must be our method, not because definition is an evil thing nor because the fact is in its nature unintelligible, but because all our language and mental apparatus is constructed to deal with a different class of data. We have to go back to the old story, see God and Man there made manifest, and then reinterpret human history and human psychology in terms of Christ. *W. T.*]

I *know* my own attempt is not satisfactory. I said in advance that it would not be, and afterwards that it had not been; (cf. also the Epilogue, which I wrote). It breaks down in a way parallel to that in which Chalcedon breaks down; and it is equally 'bankrupt' with that. But I think it is genuinely preferable because it says all that it does say in terms of spirit, and the problem is spiritual. (N.B. It was not from Bergson, as you suggest, but from Hegel and his friends, that I learnt the superiority of Subject to Substance; and my interpretation of Subject as primarily Will is, historically, due to Royce.) Moreover I think our Lord is a human individual as well as an all-inclusive Personality: if you like, I think Antioch and Alexandria were both right, and my terminology will enable them to unite while the Greek terminology really would not. Anyhow you are surely heretical yourself on p. 153 if you deny that He became not only a Man, but Man. The doctrine of inclusive personality used to be one of my great difficulties in the orthodox scheme; and I do think the old ways of expressing it made nonsense of it. But the thing itself I now see to be vital: and I hope that I have shown its importance and what may be its mode.

The real difference between us is concerned with what you say at the bottom of your p. 151.

[It is true that a convinced Ulsterman can say that, so far as politics goes, his will is the will of Sir Edward Carson. He can also say that he is of the same mind, or even, that he is of one mind, with Sir Edward Carson, in this matter. But he does not mean that by some curious process of hypnotism or thought-transference Sir Edward Carson's will, as a subjective function, has insinuated itself into the grey matter of his (the Ulsterman's) brain. He means that the object of his will, the thing which he wills, is the same thing that Sir Edward Carson wills. It is not a case of one will, in strict language, but of two wills, which are willing the same thing. He is not really of one mind, even of the same mind, as Sir Edward Carson, but of a like, of a similar mind; it is not a case of one thinking mind, but of two thinking minds which resemble one another in respect of the thoughts which they think. *R. K.*]

I do believe that the Ulsterman becomes 'of one mind' with Carson in a very real sense. Thus: Form and content are inseparable; in content they are identical; in form then they must be affected by the identity of content, though I confess I cannot say in what way. And where the unity of content is complete the effect on the form must be all the greater. Cf. the analogy of Matter and Spirit on pp. 258, 259.

You say that on my basis—'To say that Jesus was Divine will be to say merely that Jesus was Jesus-like', but it will not be merely that; it will be to say 'God is Jesus-like'. And that is to me, and I believe always has been for the Church, the primary import of the Incarnation. . . .

I should like to add a good deal on other points, but it would

not be fair. There is a vast difference in our methods of approach
—so much so that I am glad to be (what you would hate)
associated with the rest of *Foundations*. But as regards myself
personally, I believe I reach a position very like your own.
And I believe there is room and work for both. You may be
right in saying that Jones really wants your way; but if so I
know of several Robinsons who want mine. And if both lead
to the foot of the Cross *de facto*, even if yours is the only one
that arrives *de jure* (which I should deny)—need we quarrel?
My attitude to your book is Philippians i. 18.

Meanwhile I am writing another book. Its aim is to show
that Epistemology, Aesthetic, Ethico-politics, and Philosophy
of Religion are moving on converging lines; at present they
have no unity; but the point on which they converge and
where they can find unity is the Dogma of the Incarnation. It
would clear my mind as regards your own attitude if you
would say plainly whether you think such an attempt in its
own nature unwarrantable.

I have obeyed the last words of your chapter XII for some
years—(from time to time);

[. . . I commend this book to the charity of all who read it, and
its author to their prayers. *R. K.*]

I hope I may think you do the same for one at least of the
Foundationers.

Yours affectionately,
W. TEMPLE.

This is not a complete *Credo*; but it is definite and detailed
enough to show the kind of gospel Temple was to preach from
the pulpit of a church at the heart of London in his one
parochial cure.

X

S. James's, Piccadilly

There is nothing in my work here so delightful as the best parts
of school work—i.e. dealing with those boys whom one has got to
know really well. But as a job, taken all round, it is far more in my
line, and on the whole I think I like it better. The church is one
that people get very fond of, and I am already really attached to it.

W. T., letter to his brother, Christmas Day 1914.

'I CAN hardly think it practicable to make a single room so
capacious, with pews and galleries, as to hold 2,000 persons,
and all to hear the service and see the preacher. I endeavoured to
effect this in building the parish church of St. James's, Westminster, which I presume is the most capacious, with those
qualifications, that hath yet been built.' So wrote Sir Christopher
Wren when he had carried out a commission to build a church
for the parish that in 1685 had been carved out of S. Martin-
in-the-Fields by Act of Parliament. Henry Jermyn, Earl of St.
Albans, had obtained, a few years earlier, a grant of a plot of
land then on the outskirts of London and, after building St. James's
Square and the surrounding streets, had set aside part of the area
for a church and churchyard on the south side of Portugal Street
(now Piccadilly). Wren's plans were approved; the superb carv-
ing of Grinling Gibbons on the reredos, the organ case, and the
font added beauty to the dignity of the design: and the late Lord
Oxford testified to the practical success of Wren's experiment
when he recalled that as a schoolboy he had once stood in the
gallery of S. James's, Piccadilly, and had heard Liddon preach
for nearly an hour and three-quarters 'without any sense of
weariness'. The church had numbered many famous men among
its rectors—Temple was the fourth of them to become Archbishop of Canterbury—and his predecessor McCormick (father
of Gough, Dean of Manchester, and Pat, Vicar of S. Martin-in-
the-Fields) was among the most noted evangelical preachers and
pastors of his day. The rectory, which had been rebuilt in 1845,

had every advantage except one—the ceaseless noise of Piccadilly made it almost impossible for most of the windows to be kept open during the day or night—and when Temple had spent £1,200 on improvements, and had installed an electric lift for his mother's convenience, neither of them could have asked for a home more suited to their tastes and their needs. On 14 October 1940 the house was destroyed by a bomb, and the church suffered serious damage. Fortunately the reredos and font had been amply protected by timber baulks and sandbags and remained intact; the damage to the case of the Renatus Harris organ was very slight; and other treasures, such as the silver-headed wands and old registers, had already been deposited at the bank. The forecourt where the open-air pulpit had stood was cleared of rubble and opened as a Garden of Remembrance by Queen Mary in 1946.

In his letter offering Temple the benefice, Haldane had written: 'I know no one in the Church who seems so likely to occupy the position with real power and success in leading men in the direction of high thinking in religion as yourself. It is for this reason that I venture to offer it to you . . . there is said to be little parochial work of the ordinary kind.' No words could better have described the kind of post which Temple and his friends knew to be exactly suited to his gifts. His was not the stuff of which parish priests are made. He lacked facility for small talk with strangers. He knew little of the keen joy in ordinary human contacts with all and sundry and the excitement of imagining what might be on the other side of the doors he knocked at, without which pastoral visits become a heart-breaking round of duty-calls endured for conscience' sake by the priest and suffered with patient, if sometimes dazed, amiability by the parishioners. He was not quick to notice the pictures on the walls, the ornaments on the mantelpiece, and the dozen distinct and characteristic details of every home, from which the more observant visitor can deduce something of the tastes and habits of the household and start the wheels of conversation turning. And the deep-lying, utterly sincere sympathy with which he brought new heart and hope to the suffering and the bereaved needed something more poignant to evoke it than the lesser, if often persistent and gnawing, difficulties and worries of daily living. All the more is it to be reckoned to Temple's credit that, though he shrank from some of his parochial duties, he never shirked them; and only those who knew him well could guess the penance it was to him to call in turn at all the houses in S. James's Place—not yet converted into offices—and leave his card on the (frequently surprised) residents. For the routine work of the parish he was able to rely on the loyal co-operation of his two curates, the Rev. J. E. T. Evitt and the Rev. V. J. K. Brook, and of Sister Margaret, the devoted parish worker.

In carrying out another of the parish priest's duties Temple was no less conscientious. He regarded his attendance at Sunday services as of primary obligation: 'power and success in leading men in the direction of high thinking in religion'—here was his strength, and his opportunity. He had not forgotten the stress his father used to lay on the pronoun in paraphrasing the injunction, *Macte tua virtute, puer*—'that virtue which is peculiarly your own, and in the exercise of which you can most forcibly express yourself'. Was it not exactly for this that he had been waiting, the chance of leading a congregation of intelligent persons along the road of his own mental progress and spiritual achievement? He was never a 'popular' preacher, but the church was well attended on Sundays, and those who came appreciated the direct, logical, and spiritual presentation of religious truth which they could hear in no other London church. His congregation came from all parts: several were men and women of standing in the national life; many were members of the clubs in which the neighbourhood abounds; a few elderly aristocrats—there were still some left a generation ago—walked across the road from Albany and the houses of Mayfair to hear him; and three ex-Lord Chancellors worshipped regularly at S. James's during his incumbency. One failure he placed on record, in a letter to his brother. No church meeting can be more dispiriting—unless there is something highly contentious on the agenda—than an Easter Vestry, and even Temple seems to have been unable to infuse life into his. In 1916 he writes of it: 'Such a farce! One curate and one pleasant old fellow came—took it in turns to move and second the various motions that had to be carried to put us in order for the year. However, if people don't come, I suppose it means they are satisfied.' They were at least happy enough in the new rector's ministrations to approve of one or two minor reforms which were the fruit of his desire to make S. James's more obviously hospitable and accessible to the people, both during and between the hours of public worship. Before his ministry the church had been locked except during those hours, and pews rented by members of the congregation remained empty, in their absence, till after the singing of the *Venite* at Mattins. Temple's churchwardens readily agreed to have the church kept open all day. A few of the seat-holders, who were among the oldest and most regular attendants, objected to any curtailment of their rights, and a compromise was reached by which no seats could be reserved, unless the owners were occupying them, after the entry of the choir. All who worked closely with him became personally attracted and attached to him, especially his churchwardens (Col. Richard Owen and Dr. Seymour Maynard, his own doctor), Edward Redman (the parish clerk), and the organist Sydney Toms, who rejoiced at the introduction of the *English Hymnal*. Some years later, when Temple was Bishop of Manchester, the organist wrote reminding him of 'the jolly days I knew before Life and Liberty—(or rather, the call which would not be denied) wrecked at S. James's both our lives and our liberties'.

By the end of the year Temple felt reasonably sure that he had been wise to come to London. There were periods when his work was interrupted by attacks of gout, but—as so often in later years—he thought he had found the right treatment at last, and in October he wrote to D. C. Somervell:

… I am going to a man who undertakes to make me reasonably thin and free from gout by a little massage and by teaching me to hold my body in the right position. I believe in him because, after looking at me for a moment, he said 'Of course every time you take a lot of exercise, you are making your stoutness worse'—which is quite true. My fattening periods have always been those when I took most exercise, which was one thing

that led me to consult ———. So if one day you behold a figure
which beneath the front of Zeus combines the grace of Hermes
with the majesty of Apollo, you will know that it is I or Me,
according to the pedantry of your mind at the moment. . . .
I drivel on because I have such a frantic heap of letters to write
and it is already late, and writing to you staves off the necessity
of starting them—which will make it worse when it comes.
My state of mind is therefore a factual disproof of the efficacy
of deterrents, which is a topic on which no schoolmaster may
loyally meditate. . . . I think my hand-writing has decayed:
which shews that nothing is impossible with God.

> Yours affectly,
> W. TEMPLE.

Had the times been normal, Temple would have gradually
filled his church and have made a name for himself as the leading
preacher in London. But—the country was at war. Here he
knew exactly where he stood. By temperament and conviction
entirely non-chauvinist and as unequivocally non-pacifist, he held
that it would have been impossible for Great Britain, consistently
with honouring her solemn obligations, to keep out of the war.
But he felt equally sure that only by the complete dedication of
Church and nation, by eliminating every unchristian word and
motive in judging its enemies or justifying itself, could the
country emerge from the conflict with its soul purged and
enlightened—and of all things that mattered most. With this
foreground he began his ministry at S. James's, and he had little
doubt of the first points of approach to the hearts and minds of
his people. Among much that was fine and noble in the nation's
life and effort he noted two disturbing tendencies: one of these
was the growing spirit of hatred of the Germans, their culture,
and their works. He notes, for instance, of certain members of
his congregation towards the end of 1914:

> They are prepared to believe any evil of the Germans with-
> out a particle of evidence. They are very angry with the Navy
> for letting German cruisers shell Scarborough, and still more so
> with me for pointing out that the Navy's chief business is to

keep the seas open, and not expose itself to destruction by submarines in order to make sure that no English seaside resort is made uncomfortable.

With another tendency, no less distressing, he was specially qualified to deal. The faith of many believing Christians had been shaken, and few of the Church's leaders seemed competent to grapple with the more serious of the questions that awaited a Christian answer. How, for instance, in the face of the horrors of war, could it be contended that God is Love? War, the clergy replied, is a judgement—the judgement of God on our evil generation. But what sort of god was it that was hurling his tortures at the heads of millions of innocent persons who had apparently done little to merit so savage an outburst? For too many preachers the reply was quite simple: the war was God's judgement on sin—on the sins of drunkenness and immorality that stained the nation's life—and the nation must pay the penalty by the sacrifice of its sons: one enthusiastic interventionist went so far as to proclaim in the Press that God had 'sent' the war to punish the nation for having allowed the Welsh Church to be disestablished. Temple had little patience with this kind of apologetic. He saw that at the root of much of the intellectual confusion lay the fact that the majority of churchgoers had little mental background except the maimed, or even false and unworthy, conception of God—'intervening' and 'sending' this or that—which was being preached from the pulpits in the parish churches of England. The comfortable platitudes which the clergy had been dealing out Sunday by Sunday to their congregations were now recoiling on their own heads—how could they reconcile their past teaching in the days of ease with the present agony of the world? And how could they confirm the waverers in their faith? Only, in Temple's judgement, by gaining and teaching a new and a true conception of God. It was the old warning given years before by the leader of a Bible class of miners in the West Country, who began their study of the Scriptures with the words—'Whatever we think or say, boys, *let us be sure we keep clear the character of God.*' To this task Temple applied himself, through the written and the spoken word. 'War sermons' he avoided—there was already danger enough, in 1914, of the clergy undertaking the work of the recruiting sergeant—and one man prominent in public life declared that his reason for attending S. James's Church was that Temple was 'the only preacher in London who can be trusted not to mention the war'. That was to simplify too much his intention and his message. Temple conceived it to be his first duty to 'keep clear the character of God', and then to apply his conception of God's will and working to the instant problems of his day. Twenty-five years later he found himself under a like obligation. The questions asked in the next war were the same, and the answers of the Archbishop of Canterbury were the same as those of the Rector of S. James's, Piccadilly, a generation earlier. Here is an extract from a sermon preached in February 1916, on 'The War and Judgment':

We are always liable to think of judgment human or divine, as consisting in the infliction of censure or suffering or both upon guilty persons: the deliberate bringing to bear of pain upon those who are morally guilty. And there tends to be in our ordinary thought about it very little relation between the suffering inflicted and the nature of the guilt. We inflict arbitrarily certain forms of pain or inconvenience upon those who break our laws simply in order to persuade them not to do it, or to persuade others not to do it. So one has heard people during this war speak about it as if God had deliberately caused the war in order to punish mankind for certain sins—there are some who have even suggested to us that they know what sins it is that we are being punished for—that God has deliberately brought into the world all the agony of the war to punish men, at any rate in this country, for certain conspicuous vices or failings, such as drunkenness or impurity or Sabbath-breaking. I venture to say that is sheer superstition. We can trace the actual causes of the war, and we know quite well that its causes were in human wills, and we are not at liberty to say that God intervened in the history of the world to inflict anguish and pain by means of the war as punishment for certain sins that have no relation to it. How could the war grow out of drunkenness? All the way through this Gospel of St. John we are taught that a judgment of God is not a deliberate act of His intervening in the world to make guilty people suffer, but an automatic product of His Presence and Revelation.

So we shall think of this war. It is, indeed, a judgment upon the world of sin, a judgment of the sin from which it arises—the sin of selfishness, individual and national, of which in various degrees all men and nations throughout the world are guilty. The sin which led immediately to the outbreak of war we may believe to be mainly in one nation, but the root is to be found among all peoples, and not only among those who are fighting, but neutral peoples just as much. The punishment for that sin comes through the moral order which God has set up in the world, an order which reacts upon those who break it. So that if a man persists in doing what is contrary to the will of God, in doing evil which he has himself recognized as such, the consequences of his sin will at last overtake him. God has no pleasure in the infliction of that penalty, the penalty is rather a warning against indulging in the evil course at all. The pleasure of God is in men's salvation; men's salvation is His purpose. The repudiation of the will of God finds its climax in men's repudiation of Christ Himself. That is their condemnation. What more can be done? What worse can happen to a man than that he has rejected the very source of life? That condition is shown in that terrible sentence in the Book of Revelation, 'He that is filthy let him be filthy still, and he that is unjust let him be unjust still.'

The following, on 'The God of Love', belongs to the same year:

In an age that has been singularly free upon the whole from pain and suffering until the last two years, and which had become exceedingly soft in its own attitude towards pain and suffering, we almost came to think pain the greatest evil in the world, and pleasure the only good. It was natural, therefore, to suppose that love would show itself in removing causes of pain, and in giving us all the pleasure that we might like to seek. Then the blow fell, and many were much shaken in their belief in any God of Love; and those who had never held any such belief asked how, in face of the events of these days, we could without hypocrisy maintain such a belief. It is because we had fashioned an image of divine love after the pattern of our own feeble love, which set out indeed to give to those whom we loved what we thought would be good for them. Only, what we thought would be good for them was mostly enjoyment. We have been recovering, to our great gain, through the suffering in which we are being purged, the sense that the real good for man is not enjoyment, but that he should be used, and used up, in the service of God and man. But, if so, love will be stern quite as often as it will be indulgent. It will be hard against our self-indulgence and against our desires for comfort and those things which please. With regard to one side of man's nature it may be fashioned into instruments worthy of being used by God in His service and the service of man.

We have been brought back to harder days than we had known, and we need the strong authority of the Judge of men. Mere good nature and amiability are not qualities which now we can attribute to God or His representative. We need One who shall give us a call greater than that which the nation has given—a call to dedicate everything to His service; one who shall claim in tones of authority that brooks no resistance and no compromise and no bargaining, such as the Christ of the New Testament, the Christ whom we had often forgotten, the Christ who rules whether we would have it or not. 'Behold He cometh with the clouds'—the powers of heaven are on His side—and every eye shall see Him, and we who pierce Him. We may reject if we like as Jerusalem rejected, but it does not stay the coming of His kingdom. The very rejection was made the means by which He put forth His power, and the Cross of shame to which they nailed Him is the throne of His glory. Through all the generations He reigns and rules whether we will have it or not. He is the God whose power no creature is able to resist.

These and many similar utterances had their special relevance to the crisis of the hour; but something more was needed to build up the devotional life of his congregation, and for this Temple turned to that book of the Bible which was to be his spiritual mainstay for a lifetime, the Gospel according to S. John. Gore once remarked that here he could not follow Temple all the way: he admitted to being almost puzzled by the Fourth Gospel, by its authorship, its philosophy, and its sequences: whenever (he went on) he examined the problems of its authorship, he ended by saying—'Hurrah! That's quite clear now'—but a month later it would be as bad as ever again; whereas the moment he turned to S. Paul, he felt just as if he had 'come home'. Temple, on the other hand, confessed, 'With St. John I am at home': he often quoted with approval a saying of Dr. Nairne's that 'St. John, like nature, seems monotonous, and proves inexhaustible'. Of all Browning's poems his favourite was *A Death in the Desert*, which he described as the best commentary on S. John, and the Fourth Gospel was a text-book that never failed him in his work of guiding the spirit of man. So to his congregation at S. James's on Sunday mornings, in later years to ordinands at Manchester, York, and Canterbury, as well as to devotional gatherings of clergy and laity, he passed on for thirty years the results of his own research and meditations; and at last he gave to the Christian world, in the two volumes of *Readings in St. John's Gospel*, the greatest devotional treatise written by an English Churchman since William Law's *A Serious Call to a Devout and Holy Life*. Reinhold Niebuhr—not the least exacting of critics—in a letter to Temple, after the book was published, describes exactly its outstanding merit:

> I have finished half of the *Readings in St. John* and find the book tremendously stimulating, more than anything of the kind I have ever read. I think it represents a new medium in its combination of devotional and scholarly treatment. You disavow scholarship in it, but of course the depth in which a task is done cannot be effaced.

For his Confirmation classes the lessons were prepared with the

utmost care. His teaching was founded on the Catechism, beginning with ' "What is your name?" ' This is just to remind us that
we must stand on our own feet—each has a conscience which he
must obey: I Cor. iv. 1–5 (R.V.): 2 Cor. v. 10'; and the notes
he compiled for his instructions were fuller than those he used for
most of his Sunday sermons. So also were his notes for the Three
Hours' Service, which in an abbreviated form were always printed
on the service papers used by the congregation on Good Friday.
On 2 April 1915, he took the Three Hours' Service, following the
printed notes in detail, giving no impression of the strain under
which he was preaching. His mother had died early in the morning, but he would not have the rectory blinds drawn down, nor
any but the members of his household told of it till after the
service: 'I did not want the people', he said afterwards, 'during
the Three Hours to be feeling pity for *me*.' This was the harder
to be borne of the two great inevitable separations of his life.
No mother could rejoice with keener pride in a wholly devoted
son than Beatrice Temple, and everything that had meant 'home'
for him during the twelve years since his father's death—in
Oxford, at Repton, and in London—had centred on her. He
could only describe himself as 'numbed' by the crushing blow
and, although his old nurse remained and lightened his burden
as none but she could have done, the year that followed was the
loneliest in Temple's life.

But there was work to be done; and a wider field than the parish
of S. James's in which to do it. The national temper was subject
to varying gusts in the early days of the war, and a small group
of Christian thinkers—from Anglican and other Churches—was
formed in the hope of steadying and enlightening public opinion
among the intelligent on the issues at stake, and for suggesting
the temper in which they should be faced. (A few of the original
group were pacifists, but these were not long in seceding, when
they founded the 'Fellowship of Reconciliation' and put out their
own literature.) This was the purpose of *Papers for War-time*.
The circulation of the pamphlets was never a large one; but the
names of the writers (among whom were Arthur Clutton Brock,
J. H. Oldham, B. H. Streeter, and J. Arthur Thomson) secured

their welcome among cultured Christians. One of the most interesting came from the pen of 'A Leader of Religion in Germany', but when the final proofs had been passed and copies were on the point of being printed, the author forbade publication. The pamphlet would have had a mixed reception from British readers —the writer had many causes of the war to adduce besides the triumph of militarism in his own country, and England was openly charged with the sin of 'national hypocrisy'—and it was written at a time when the screw was being tightened in Germany. A good deal of courage would have been required to let such a sentence as the following go out among English readers under the name of a German leader of religion: 'Many German Christians are striving with an ever-increasing earnestness to oppose the hatred against England which finds expression among our people, difficult as the task is at the present time. For many weeks I have preached every Sunday, and in every sermon I try to discourage hatred against England.' Temple was general editor of the series, and wrote the first pamphlet under the title 'Christianity and War', which was chiefly a statement of the problems to be discussed by later contributors: the pamphlets, he wrote to a friend, 'will annoy some folk and they will interest others: but it is a united effort, which is my main interest in it. . . . It involves hours of work'. The letter ends: 'Then I have a W.E.A. meeting on the opportunity of the war every Saturday night in some remote place—Manchester this week, Newcastle next, and so on—and two sermons here next day.'

His most vigorous utterance at this period was a sermon he preached in the early summer of 1915. He had just returned from America, where he had delivered the Bishop Paddock Lectures (afterwards published with the title *Church and Nation*), and had been stung by the contemptuous reference in some American newspapers to the insignificant contribution which England was said to be making to the common war effort, as compared with the sacrifices then being endured by the French people. The sermon was preached on the last Sunday in May 1915. It was a twofold appeal—to the Government, that if possible they would take over the whole wealth of the country, and give to every citizen 'a soldier's wage, a soldier's ration, and a soldier's discipline'. Failing that, let every man be put under rules and perform the exact service required of him. Total prohibition should be introduced at once—it was difficult to exaggerate the moral value of 'some definite and abrupt action of this kind', which would 'be out of all proportion greater than a carefully guarded and highly reasonable compromise'. For the individual no sacrifice could be too great—'I find', Temple said, 'everyone in England very anxious that someone else should be made to fight or work. But we must look first to ourselves.' Let every man and woman, therefore, follow the King's lead in giving up all alcoholic liquor till peace was declared. As to shares in a brewery company or distillery, to hold these had always seemed to him incompatible with Christianity—'to-day it is incompatible with patriotism'. The strength of the appeal was weakened by some practical advice—a little involved and, it must be admitted, not entirely logical—to conscientious holders of such shares; but the sermon was widely noticed and was published later under the title *Go Forward—Some Thoughts on the National Crisis*. It has been singled out here for special notice because it looked forward to the uncompromising tone that was to mark his public utterances during the second World War. They exasperated a few, and puzzled many: but to thousands of thoughtful persons who were looking for direction, with high spiritual authority behind it, on their personal and social duty at a time of crisis, they gave the courageous lead that men had ceased to expect from the National Church, and a new confidence that there was something of value in the Christian message for the healing of a distraught and stricken world.

XI

The Editor

The *Challenge* is a Church of England weekly newspaper, independent
in all party matters, whether in Church or State. The title indicates the
hope and intention to express more and more adequately the challenge
offered by the Cross of Christ to worldliness and indifference, both
within and without the Societies which claim to embody the Spirit of
the Master.

W. T., on the purpose of the *Challenge*, 1914.

IN July 1915 Temple accepted an invitation to edit the *Challenge*.
He resigned in the autumn of 1918, and wrote his farewell
message to its readers in the last issue of that year.

When the first number of the *Challenge* appeared in 1914, four
Church weeklies were already in the field, three of which bore
each a definite stamp. Foremost was the *Church Times*, which had
a circulation larger than that of all the others put together. It
was read with uncritical avidity by most Anglo-Catholics, by
the rest with just enough disagreement about the relative emphasis
to be laid on 'Anglo-' and '-Catholic' to ensure lively controversy
in its correspondence columns and to tax the ingenuity of its
editor, the Rev. Henry Palmer, in his effort to embrace and cater
for the interests of them all. He was shortly to be succeeded by
the Rev. Hermitage Day, an able writer and a skilled journalist,
under whose guidance the paper prospered and its circulation
steadily mounted. Its strength lay in the two impressions which
Day was clever enough to leave, week by week, on the reader's
mind: one, that Anglo-Catholics were fighting with their backs
to the wall, that they were a comparatively small (and often persecuted) minority who, in face of the disdainful frowns of the
Bench and the sneers of Erastians, were upholding the Catholic
tradition in the National Church and re-introducing the people
of England to the forgotten glory of their true heritage. The other
impression conveyed was that the future lay with them: Anglo-
Catholicism was being borne on a rising tide, and its ultimate

triumph was assured. Could not its apologists point to one parish after another in which church life had been dull, formal, and stagnant before the arrival of some human, warm-hearted parish priest of their own colour, who knew exactly why he had been ordained (for the conversion of England to the Catholic Faith), and exactly why he had come to the parish—to teach the parishioners certain definite truths about God, their Saviour, and their Church which their former pastors had neglected, and to gather round him a compact convinced body of believers who would regard themselves as builders—some might even be martyrs—of the Catholic Church of England that was to be? These two aspects of the Movement were balanced with great skill in the paper, and everything in its columns—leading articles, notes, book reviews, devotional appeals, news, and correspondence—was made to illustrate or emphasize one or the other of them. It was, above all, a readable paper. The technical culture of its more learned writers was lightened by the less thoughtful, but more immediately attractive, articles of descriptive columnists recording the successes or trials of Anglo-Catholicism, and by the rebukes—always caustic and sometimes not wholly free from venom—administered by the editor alike to stout opponents and half-hearted supporters. Its influence could not be disregarded. Bishops might dislike or suspect it but, except for the least conciliatory, with a nervous vigilance they read it; and the furnishings of a clergy-house were considered incomplete without its weekly copy of the *Church Times*.

At the other extreme was the *Record*, not then emancipated from the narrowest of Protestant outlooks. Its circulation was small and was unlikely, under the leadership of those days, to increase. However much alive the old Protestant prejudices might be in the country—and events were to show that they were not dead yet—they were fading slowly but inevitably out of the Church. The demand was growing for life, beauty, colour, even for drama, in the presentation of religious truth, and these were not provided by repeated appeals for strict adhesion to what the *Record* conceived to be the 'Reformation Settlement'. Nor was there anything attractive, either literary or devotional, in the paper to encourage the patronage of those who took no interest in its Church views.

The *Church Family Newspaper* was read chiefly—as its name would suggest—on the country-side, in the suburbs, and in the market towns. In the farm-house and the draper's parlour its unpleasing shape, its repellent typography and make-up—now, happily, changed for much the better in the *Church of England Newspaper*—were not regarded with disfavour by readers whose only standard in such matters was that of the local weekly. Its church position was vaguely central; its tone homely; and the village churchwarden found nothing in its columns to offend.

The fourth was the *Guardian*, which went far to prove the truth of Northcliffe's saying that, if a newspaper has ever been a good newspaper, it takes a lot of killing. Once it had numbered among its contributors the most cultured thinkers and the best writers in the Anglican Communion—the article by R. W. Church (Dean of S. Paul's) on *The Origin of Species* was one of the most notable reviews of the book in any journal of the time—and it was not so long since the *Guardian* had been the one news-paper read in many homes. Its editor was still struggling to hold fast the 'High Church and High Tory' tradition; but the High Church was beginning to find the *Church Times* more to its taste, and High Tories were less interested than their fathers in the National Church and its doings. The paper had an influence considerably greater than its circulation would suggest, and its book reviews—Randall Davidson once said that he seldom failed to read them every week—remained on a high level. But it was already living in, and on, the past; it lacked the vitality and incisiveness demanded by those whose palates were now being tickled by the succulent vivacity of the new dailies.

So the ground was fairly well covered—but not completely. There was no church weekly of a liberal tone in its theology, in its general intellectual outlook, and in church politics; none exhibited the new treasures as well as the old which were said to lie in the spiritual storehouse of the National Church; none stood for the new conception of foreign missionary work, the new aspirations after reunion, the new demand for thorough-going measures of church reform, and above all for the new social gospel. Was there any place, and would there be any demand, for a paper which sought to commend such matters as these to the mind and conscience of the Church of England? To some adventurous spirits the chance seemed worth taking: and early in 1914 Dr. G. E. Newsom (then lecturer at King's College, London, and afterwards Master of Selwyn College, Cambridge) gathered round him a band of twenty to thirty men and women, who met from time to time in the Senior Common Room at King's to discuss the general lines of the paper and work out practical details. The result was that '*The Challenge* Limited' was incorporated, Temple taking up a fairly large holding in the company's shares. Barclay Baron was appointed editor with a board to help him—he had had no experience of Fleet Street—and Douglas Eyre was the first chairman, to be succeeded after a few months by Tissington Tatlow.

The aim of the *Challenge* was set out in a leading article in its first issue, dated 1 May 1914. It would adopt 'the standpoint of the Church of England', and would be written in untechnical language, in the hope of interesting the average layman. An attempt would be made to interpret all religious, political, and international issues 'according to the true standard of Christian conduct', and attention would be given to 'the pressing need of a reconciliation between the historic faith of the Church and the fresh knowledge which to-day pours in on us from every side'. Finally, special consideration would be given 'to three questions of supreme importance at the present juncture—the position of the laity, who have yet to enter on their rightful heritage in the life and work of the Church; the urgent . . .'—the leader unfortunately appears to have had no ending, owing to some accident in the printing; but, later, the aim of the paper was given more succinctly in the paragraph printed at the head of this chapter. Details of policy were settled at the meetings of the 'Round Table', which was composed of a number of experts on various aspects of church life and work, who squeezed themselves once a week into a small sixth-floor room in Arundel Street. They included one Congregationalist minister (the Rev. Edward Shillito) and three women, Miss Ethel Barton (who rendered consistent and devoted service), Miss Maude Royden (now Dr. Maude Royden-Shaw), and Dr. Jane Walker. The Rev. C. B. Mortlock joined Barclay Baron as co-editor in the early months of 1914, and became sole editor when Baron took up work with the Y.M.C.A. James Benson, the sub-editor, was the only trained journalist on the staff; he served the paper with selfless loyalty, and he and Temple became fast friends.

By the summer of 1915, it was clear that all was not well with the paper. Money was scarce; public interest was centred almost exclusively on the war and its innumerable side-issues; the circulation was not rising at the rate its promoters had expected; and the more critical could observe a certain lack of continuity which suggested the need for a strong controlling hand. There was one hope—shared by every member of the Board—which was that Temple would take over the editorship. He consented: and from that day he had what he (or at least his friends) had longed for, a medium through which he could express himself and make a wider public more familiar with the substance of his appeal. Not that the *Challenge* was in any sense Temple's 'organ'—still less was it, as was commonly held later, the organ of the Life and Liberty Movement—but from the date of his assuming control there was clearer evidence of direction, and a sense of the paper being pulled together, so to say, each week by the leading article. This was written almost always by Temple, and written as no editor can have written his leaders before or since. Sometimes— quite frequently—it was composed during the Board meetings. While he was listening to the views of his colleagues, Temple would be writing quickly and continuously, and when the talking was over he would read to them the result of their discussions, in the form of a clear and well-balanced leading article almost ready for the press. At other times the articles would be written in railway-station waiting-rooms, or between midnight and 2 a.m. in a strange bedroom after some meeting he had been addressing in the provinces, or late at night in his study at home. On one point testimony is unanimous: not once did the leading article arrive late for press, and only very rarely did it show the slightest sign of having been written in a hurry. The 'Notes of the Week' were divided up between members of the Board, Temple taking his share; and here as always he dominated, without dictating to, the group. He made no attempt to hide his own limitations: once, when it was suggested that the first Note should always be 'devotional' or, in the narrower sense of the word, 'religious', Temple demurred: 'anyhow,' he said, 'it needs a flair for that sort of thing, and I haven't got it. Somebody like Leslie Hunter might be able to do it.'

During the period of Temple's editorship it was inevitable that the war, and the problems arising in and out of it, should fill many columns of the paper; and even when his contributions were unsigned (he generally printed book reviews over his initials) it was not difficult to detect his handiwork. Questions of belief and conscience, problems of ethical and social duty, spiritual ideals, international hopes and aspirations—all these were treated, as had been promised, 'according to the standard of Christian faith and conduct'. Foremost among them was the question being asked then as it was to be five and twenty years later—'Why does not God stop the war?' Temple had to return to this again and again in the paper; but perhaps the most lucid summary of his own conviction was given while he was editor in two letters to the Rev. C. H. S. Matthews, with whom he was having some correspondence about a book that had been sent to the *Challenge* for review:

I expect the difference between us would come down to something like this. On the whole I tend to think of God first as Power; then comes the Revelation, that this Power is the Power of Love; consequently it is natural to me to say about a great many things that God *could* do them but He will not. I think you tend to begin with Love rather than Power, and therefore it is natural to you to say that because He is Love He cannot do them. So far the difference would be merely verbal. But I think it gives a different inclination to a great deal of one's thinking on the subject, and there are people whose minds work like mine, to whom your language perpetually suggests that God would like to do things but owing to some limitation or incapacity is unable. That, for example, He would have liked to stop the war but could not. I believe that He could but will not; and the reason for His refusal is His respect for human freedom which is the corollary of His Love. I believe the result of mine is a richer because even more self-sacrificing idea of His Love.

. . . I quite agree that if Power = Love, then God cannot do what contradicts Love; but it seems to me immensely important to emphasize, every time one says this, that only His Love prevents Him. If you like to put it so, I do not think His power is only the power of Love, *i.e.* the Power that Love wins over men's hearts by revealing itself. I believe this is the climax so to speak of His Power; but I do not see how that kind of Power could make a Solar System. . . . As regards my trying to save Omnipotence, the point is this. I am quite sure that there is an Infinite, or if you would rather call it so, a Whole. Pluralism seems to me nonsense. Either then God is this Infinite, and the controlling power of the Whole, or else He is within it. For Wells He is definitely within it. This is explicitly stated. Thus in *Britling*—'God is within Nature and Necessity. Necessity is a thing beyond God, beyond God and wholly beyond Space and Time; a mystery everlastingly impenetrable!' Now that is pagan if you like, because it says that the secret of the world is, at the end of the day, wholly unknowable—just a brute fact which we are up against. I believe that what Wells calls Necessity is in fact the overruling will of One whose nature is Love. The operation of that will is of course directed by Love, and it therefore will not, or in your language cannot, do things contrary to Love. I very much hope that one day you will read the last chapter of *Mens Creatrix* and tell me how it strikes you. I cannot get it shorter than that, so it cannot very well be put in a letter.

As the war went on and popular feeling towards the Germans became more bitter, Temple had cause frequently to recur to the duty incumbent upon citizens who were also Christians. He wrote vigorously against the mounting spirit of hatred and the growing demand for reprisals against the enemy. One extravagant exhibition of this spirit appeared in an advertisement published in *The Times* during July 1917. 'We can all help', the appeal began, 'to punish the Huns by circulating the following.' Below this were the laurel wreath of victory and the words: 'A Solemn Oath. To mark our horror and disgust of the methods of Germany since July, 1914, we swear that we will not (*a*) knowingly purchase anything made in Germany, (*b*) transact business with or through a German for ten years after peace is declared. So help us God.' A space was left for signature and address. Temple wrote:

It is presumably vain to protest against this kind of thing because the kind of person who will respond to this appeal will certainly not heed our protest. . . . We shall certainly want (after the war) to sell things to Germany, and we cannot sell to them unless we buy from them. The plain truth is that this 'solemn oath' is a piece of sentimental humbug, at once more dangerous and more contemptible because the sentiment is one of malignity and not of generosity. People sometimes think that it is only the generous who are sentimental; but hatred is a sentiment quite as much as love, and even more easily makes people blind and leads them to ignore plain facts.

Temple made no less vigorous protests, and not only in the columns of the *Challenge*, against the popular abuse of conscientious objectors. By 1939 the public conscience was better instructed and its whole outlook on the subject was more enlightened; but too many of the tribunals set up during the First World War were open to criticism of their members, their methods, and their manners. To have the question 'Do you believe in a Supreme Being?' barked at one from behind a table by an elderly and not too intelligent colonel of the old army, and to be told roughly to 'answer the question' if one dared to express doubts of its relevance, was not an uncommon experience. 'The C.O. question', Temple wrote in a private letter, 'ought to be more manageable, but it has been messed from the beginning.

The Government never had any clear principle about what constituted "conscientious" objection . . . any definition would
have been better than none.' But most deeply he felt the affront
offered to the personality of the objectors by those responsible
for the methods of the worst tribunals—their 'contemptuous
approach', he wrote in the summer of 1916, 'remains a reproach
to our civilization'.

Among the most controversial issues then before the country,
none was more urgent than that of alcoholic liquor—it was
agreed on all sides that there was an excessive consumption
which, through loss of working hours and in other ways, was
hindering the total war effort: disagreement began with the search
for a remedy. Some held that drastic temperance reform (including a further shortening of the hours during which licensed
houses should be open) would meet the need: some advocated
prohibition for the duration of the war: others urged national
purchase of the whole liquor trade—it was known that the
Government were seriously considering this possibility—to be
followed at once by total prohibition till peace was declared. The
policy of the *Challenge* was (as it had always been) exactly that
advocated by Temple in the sermon preached on his return from
the States; but no government was strong enough to persuade the
country to 'down glasses' for the period of the war, and the No
Treating Order was a faint-hearted and largely ineffective measure,
though it was probably as much as the workers were likely to
tolerate at that time.

In most of its social policy the paper marched in step with the
Labour Movement. The demand for a living wage constantly
recurs, and sympathy is expressed with those of the skilled workers
who hesitated to accept diluted labour into their ranks. But criticism is frequently outspoken, especially of those unions and
individuals—the A.S.E. is singled out for notice—who by independent action were hindering the ordered and united advance of
British Labour.

At the end of 1916 H. A. L. Fisher was appointed to the Board
of Education. Temple was delighted: 'for the first time', he wrote,
'a real educationist has been summoned to preside over that

office'. He attacked vigorously all suggestions of public economy in the education grants; he would like to see all London 'join in execration of its County Council for the paltry war bonus' offered to its teachers; he noted the danger of the children's interests being sacrificed now to the administrative, as they had formerly been to the denominational, squabble; and gave a warm welcome to the Fisher Act when it reached the statute book.

In ecclesiastical affairs the *Challenge* stood, almost in detail, for Temple's own opinions. These will come under review later, as most of them were linked up with, some entirely dependent on, schemes of wholesale church reform, such as were set out in the Church and State Report and advocated more definitely during the National Mission and the Life and Liberty campaign. On one point opportunity was given for a definite pronouncement. Church opinion, then as now, was not unanimous on the Reservation of the Sacrament; and an *eirenicon* had been composed by two bishops, each of them with a strong following in the Church, the Bishop of Oxford (Gore) representing the Catholic, and the Bishop of Chelmsford (Watts-Ditchfield) the Protestant position. No two churchmen, it might be thought, would have been less likely to be able to put out an agreed statement on this particular matter of all others, yet a joint pronouncement had been published by them which exercised a reassuring and a unifying influence on church opinion, except on the extreme Anglo-Catholics. Temple wholeheartedly supported the bishops. He saw in their joint action a sign that there was growing in the Church a central block which was both truly catholic and truly evangelical, and in a leader which provoked a good deal of correspondence he wrote—the words bear a remarkable resemblance to Pusey's:

> With regard to the Blessed Sacrament . . . we most fully and absolutely believe in the real and objective presence of our Lord in the sacramental elements for the purpose of sustaining the souls of the faithful in Communion, but we have no warrant for believing any presence for any other purpose.

Of other convictions expressed, policies affirmed, interests challenged or championed, and abuses attacked in the paper, a list of quite inordinate length could be compiled and classified. Enough has been written to show the main lines along which Temple guided the *Challenge* in the years of his control; but it may be disputed whether the paper was of great enough value to Church and nation at that time to justify the amount of work he put into it. Canon Spencer Leeson, who served on the editorial board from the first until he was appointed to the Board of Education, makes this comment in a letter (to Mrs. Temple):

The paper was certainly not modernist; but it did reflect the kind of feeling earlier expressed in *Lux Mundi*—an uneasy consciousness that the expression of the Faith was not clear to the modern world, or framed in terms of modern philosophy or social thought; and we made a determined effort to remedy this. It was a somewhat amateurish affair . . . and we none of us knew anything about the technique of journalism. But we somehow plunged along. . . . It was symptomatic of a particular stage in English religious thought at that time, and the fact that your husband directed it shows how naturally even then men and women of our generation turned to him for leadership.

That was the entry to be made on one side of the reckoning; a movement of just the kind that would appeal to Temple most strongly was stirring within the Church, and nobody but he could effectively lead it. What was to be entered on the other side? This, for instance—from a letter to his brother (from S. James's Rectory) dated 25 October 1916, on his work for the National Mission:

Here are my activities of the last fortnight. Oct. 8, Two sermons here. 9, Speech at Tottenham. 10, To Southwell. 11, To Nottingham: Sermon and Speech. 12, To Manchester: two sermons. 13, Three sermons in Manchester. Back to London. 14, Demonstration in Hyde Park. 15, Two sermons here. 16, Variety of Committees. 17, Three Committees. 18, To Ludlow: two sermons. 19, To Bridgnorth: two addresses—then to Hereford, and three addresses there. 20, To London: visited Nana for tea. 21, Quiet Day for teachers:

3 sermons. 22, Sermon here in morning: at Christ's Hospital (Horsham) in evening. 23, Two committees . . . So life is rather a strain!

Nor was this an exceptionally heavy fortnight. And if to the above be added Temple's work for W.E.A., University Extension, the British Association (he was President of the Education Section in 1916), C.E.M.S., Y.M.C.A., C.E.T.S., and other societies; sermons in public-school chapels, and at missionary and other services; addresses to the troops; perpetual calls on his time as rector of an important parish; constant visits to Lambeth and the Church House; the demands made on him in guiding the work of National Mission Committees; and the time needed for preparation and consultation—surely he must sometimes have asked himself how long the pace could be kept up? It must be feared that he did not (though in 1915 he confesses, 'Having been used to holidays and vacs. three times a year, I rather feel the absence of them'), and it can be almost assumed that, if he had not edited the *Challenge*, he certainly would have spent the time so gained not in recreation but in some other strenuous effort: but would that effort have been of greater service to the Church? In other words, when Temple was editing a newspaper, was he doing the work that he could do best?

He never claimed that he was a good editor: for one thing, he knew that he had started too late in life. Most of the great journalists have served an early apprenticeship at their craft: Northcliffe, at the age of sixteen, edited with some success the parish magazine of the church he attended in Kilburn; and William Randolph Hearst, complete with long cigar and trestle-tables littered with the dazzling 'comics' of his contemporaries, was the working brain of the Harvard *Lampoon* while still an undergraduate. Temple began at the age of thirty-four, by which time he was too busy, even if he was not too old, to pick up many of the tricks of the trade which in the normal career of a journalist would by then have become second nature to him. One thing is certain—he was a much better editor than he believed himself to be. Three essentials of the successful editor of a weekly paper

were his. He could write leading articles that bore comparison
with the best in any contemporary: his style was lucid and forceful, every week he had something to say, and he never failed to
say it. Further, he knew good copy when he saw it. And,
thirdly, he could command much of the best writing—though
little of it was outstandingly good—to be procured from that
small company whose first loyalty was to the Church, and who
could therefore write of church affairs with both knowledge and
conviction. But several secrets of the journalist's craft were
hidden from him; among them this—that a newspaper full of
good things is not necessarily a good newspaper. Any churchman with a fair knowledge of the problems of Christian faith and
conduct that obtruded themselves in the First World War, who
is inquisitive enough to look through the bound volumes of the
Challenge for 1916 or 1917, will be surprised at the high level of
excellence reached in the articles, the 'Notes of the Week', and
the correspondence columns; and yet . . . what is it (for there is
something) that is missing? A sense of continuity? A particular
and well defined mission? A really homogeneous editorial
board? Or was the width of the paper's interests so all-embracing
that the treatment of too many of them was hardly proportionate
to their importance, and so failed to satisfy? However these
questions may be answered, it would be agreed that no man
burdened with the weight of responsibility that already lay on
Temple's shoulders could give particular and intimate attention
to an effort that he could not regard as having the first claim on
his time and energy; and without that attention—no matter how
brilliant the contributors—the paper could not be firmly established. He was already so much in the habit of taking things in
his gigantic stride that their relative importance might at times be
missed or slurred over; and the lack of trained experience and
technical support on the staff of the *Challenge* made it all the more
essential that its editor should possess the detailed knowledge
and experience required to make up consecutive and consistent
numbers of a weekly paper. Not that he was inaccessible, or ever
failed in his duties. Whenever he was in London on a Monday,
he attended the meeting of the editorial board; and he was always

ready to oblige with last-minute alterations or additions. One evening, during dinner at Dean's Yard, the telephone bell rang. Temple left the table—it was the night before the *Challenge* went to press—and after a few minutes he returned. His expression suggested an inquiry. 'It was the *Challenge*', he replied: 'they want another inch and three-quarters for the "Notes of the Week", and,' with a chuckle, 'I gave it them.' Whatever he had then dictated was almost certainly sound sense, accurately and vividly expressed; but a good paper is not to be edited—except by a genius—over the telephone with a foot-rule.

During his last year as editor, Temple was not the only clergyman to ask himself whether, in the work he was doing, he was making his full contribution to the national effort. In the early months of 1918, which saw the dangerous advance of the German Army on the Western Front, the Government was concerned to use to the utmost the whole man-power of the country, and resentment was felt in some quarters at the apparently large numbers of ministers of religion who were still left in their peace-time occupations. Parish priests in industrial areas were accosted by small boys who, thumb to nose, shouted at them with irritating repetition, as they went about their parochial business, 'Kitchener wants *you*'—the caption of a popular recruiting poster remembered long after Kitchener's death—and the Government had been in consultation with the Archbishops, who were willing enough to discuss any suggestion that took into account the spiritual needs of the nation at home as well as at the Front. Temple consulted the Archbishop of Canterbury, and asked Gore's advice in the following letter:

April 24.

My dear Bishop,   The Rectory, Liverpool.

You know what I am trying to do better than anyone else I can consult: 'Life and Liberty', 'Challenge', W.E.A., etc. Well: the Bishops' resolution or declaration on volunteering is in *The Times* this morning, also the Bishop of London's letter to his clergy. It is his licence that I hold, though my work is more outside London than in it. My present disposition is to write to the Archbishop saying that my intention is to go on at my present work unless he thinks right to bid me definitely give it up; that if he felt able to tell me I was right in this, it would to some extent ease my conscience and would be an answer to the gainsayers; but that if he bids me volunteer for non-combatant service, or take any other step in view of the present emergency, I am at his disposal. May I ask if this line of action commends itself to your judgment? Of course I could 'lie low and say nothing', but I hardly like to do that on my own responsibility.

Yours affectly.
W. T.

Gore's reply was the same as Randall Davidson's. The Archbishop was prepared to 'take all responsibility' for Temple remaining at his work.

The subsequent history of the *Challenge* and its end does not belong to these pages; its failure to survive was due to more causes than one, the most decisive of which is clearer now than it then was. It is true that the paper never had enough capital behind it (probably £35,000 was all it could ever command), that the war distracted the attention of potential subscribers and supporters just at the moment when their help would have been most valuable, and that the lack of trained journalists on the staff was a grave hindrance. But, in retrospect, it would be safe to suggest that the chief reason was a fact which came home to Temple when he had a diocese of his own, that there was not then to be found in the Church a large enough body of readers of the type he was trying to attract, to form the basis of a lucrative circulation and advertisement revenue. 'A newspaper', J. A. Spender once wrote, 'gathers up the popular voices, and gives them back as opinions.' But what if the voices are few and faint? A church paper is a trade paper; and no trade, no Church, is (in the jargon of to-day) less 'newspaper-conscious' than the Church of England: the circulation of all its weeklies put together is considerably less than 150,000 copies. At that time movements for reform both in Church and community had as yet made, in spite of the valiant efforts of the pioneers, little headway among the mass of church-people, and few were interested in the kind of message which the *Challenge* had made its own. Had it been launched with the active sympathy of the Archbishop of York and a trained technical staff twenty years later—by which time churchpeople had conceived a wider and deeper interpretation of the Christian message—the seed would have fallen on well-prepared ground. As it was, the soil was cumbered with every kind of competing growth, and the seed was choked before it could germinate.

Temple's farewell to the readers of the *Challenge* ended with these words:

... I wish to make it clear how little I have in fact been able to do for the paper for a considerable period, and therefore how small will be the change involved in my ceasing to be nominally its Editor. Any who have valued the *Challenge* in the past will still find in it exactly those features which have recommended it to them, while they will also find the great advantages that will be secured by placing the control fully in the hands of an Editor able to give more of his time and attention to the paper. I am, therefore, able to relinquish my office not only with high hopes for its future, but confident that those hopes will be realized alike in the continued and increased support of the paper, and in its influence for good both within the Church of England and outside it.

There was, of course, more to be said about it all than this. And he wrote with complete frankness to his wife:

October 17, 1918.

Your letter arrived at breakfast ... I will think it all over; but I don't think I shall miss the *Challenge* as a means of self-expression! In a way I should like to carry it on, but I doubt if what I want to stand for is what they (the Round Table) want to stand for, and my position has to be maintained with complete consistency to avoid appearing to compromise. I suppose I am about equally in sympathy with the Central Catholic group of the Mosley or Hepher (or Scott Holland) type and the Neo-Evangelicals of the Gough McCormick or the Bishop of Peterborough [Theodore Woods] type. I want to say all that they both say—and of course add to this full liberty of critical enquiry. But the result is that one is not in an attitude of either offence or defence towards one's own view. But on the R.T. there is no one on the really Catholic line at all, except Branson who seldom comes. . . . There are plenty of Neo-Evangelicals, and there are plenty of people of no tradition in particular. I don't mind this situation as long as I can control what goes on in the paper; but I am too busy to do that, and don't want to be tied to it when my L. & L. effort is over.

But it had all been worth while. The *Challenge* was a gallant effort, carried on against heavy and continually increasing odds: it had shown that there was a stirring of the spirit within the Church; it had brought into the open views which had been hidden in the minds and hearts of a few thousand church members for lack of any means of expressing them; and it had proved a rallying-ground for reformers in Church and State. For Temple himself and his development the experience had done much. It had supplied opportunities of leadership, of self-expression, and of crystallizing his views and convictions. Of these he had made the fullest use; and the future was to show clearly that his time had not been wasted.

XII

Marriage

It requires a poet of consummate genius, like Browning, to reveal the
beauty of the deep peaceful happiness of married love.
      W. T., *Essays in Christian Politics*, 1927.

IN the summer of 1916 the gap which his mother's death had
left in Temple's life was filled by his marriage with Frances
Anson. The two families were not unknown to each other.
When Temple's father was Bishop of Exeter, one of the most
devoted laymen of the diocese was Sir Thomas Dyke Acland of
Killerton, whose youngest daughter had married Frederick
Anson, son of a Canon of S. George's, Windsor. The Ansons
lived in London and, as soon as she heard that the Temples had
arrived, Mrs. Anson with her daughter Frances called at Prince's
Hotel, where Mrs. Temple was staying while the rectory was
being made ready. Temple and Miss Anson first met at a Christmas
party for German refugees given by Miss Lucy Gardner at the
house of the 'Collegium' in S. George's Square; and they were
brought together shortly after when Constance Smith asked Miss
Anson to become secretary of the Westminster branch of the
Christian Social Union of which Temple was chairman. The
new secretary found the Union more to her taste than Temple did
at that time. Before one of the branch meetings he wrote to her:

> I have nothing to add to the agenda. On every C.S.U.
> agendum I want to put—'How to make the C.S.U. either
> Christian or social or united', but a chimerical aspiration can't
> be called an agendum. I have not seen the letter from the
> Central: are they becoming captious? If the C.S.U. question is
> controversial, could you come for a few minutes early and post
> me up about it?

Closer contact was possible in the autumn of 1915, when Miss
Anson was giving some secretarial help to Miss Barton (Secretary

of the *Challenge*) and saw something of Temple on his frequent visits to the office of the paper—he was even tempted to invite her out to lunch one day but was checked by his respect for the conventions! In April 1916, however, he took the plunge, and wrote to Mrs. Anson:

> . . . There is one thing that I ought to say. I am a very busy person, and likely to remain so. Anyone who consents to share the life of such a creature is almost certain to have times of being rather alone. The journeys for speechifyings, with return by night trains, will inevitably involve that. And for some years this rush is likely to be the form my work will take. These things ought to be considered, even if the personal question could be answered as I am hoping. I feel bound to open up the question now. I am spending time in thinking about Frances which ought to be spent in thinking about the [National] Mission. At least, that is my excuse for not resisting my desires any longer. You will, at any rate, forgive my aspirations.

Mr. and Mrs. Anson welcomed warmly the idea of their daughter marrying the son of so old a friend of the Acland family. On 4 May 1916 William Temple and Frances Anson became engaged, and the same evening Temple gave her his first present —a copy of each of the books he had written! He cabled at once to his brother in India (whose wife also was called Frances), who replied: 'Hope your Frances will be as great a success as mine has been', and a few days later Temple wrote:

> You will have had the telegram telling you that I am to marry Frances Anson. . . . Her mother is sister of Sir Thomas Acland and daughter of father's old friend. Everyone who knows us both seems to think it ideal, e.g. the Bishop of Kensington who nearly blew up with joy when I told him. She came with her mother to call on mother (and me) soon after we were in the house here—I know that mother noticed how well we were hitting it off and hoped for this though she said nothing. I too thought that day that my fate had appeared. But in the rush of work one had no time to brood on it; and then mother's death

left one numb for a little while, and it was not till last Christmas that I really began to think about it again.

Nana is 'over the moon', as mother used to say. She is very fond of Frances, and Mrs. Anson is a real friend since Killerton and Exeter days. Of course you know what it feels like, so I need not tell you. I thought I should be excited, and of course I was before the final interview; but from that moment there has been simply a sense of floating on a quite calm sea of contentment and happiness—with the water deliciously warm so that one need never get out.

There had been one cloud in the sky. How would his faithful and beloved Nana take the news? He could not remember the day when he had not been dependent on her, and she was the one link left with his boyhood and youth. But, as he wrote to his brother, all was well. Nana at once realized that she would have to suffer the agony of leaving him (which she did in the following autumn), but she consoled herself with the thought that she alone, after seeing them together at their first meeting—at a tea-party and from a distance—had felt sure that something would come of it.

Miss Anson and her mother were close and devoted friends, and she was dreading the parting with her parents when Temple wrote:

I hope these days, which you did not like the look of in advance, are going fairly easily. Nothing is ever as bad as one expects it to be, and the good things are always better. Or is that only the experience of the adipose? Anyway, it's mine. And every day after next Saturday is going to be better than anyone is capable of expecting anything at all to be. Hurrah, or Hallelujah—according to taste.

Temple's friends vied with one another in their expressions of joy. None was more delighted than Randall Davidson, who snatched a moment before leaving England on a visit to the war-front to write a note to Miss Anson's father which ended, 'Strange that you and I should have this further link after our friendship of more than 50 years, infrequent but never broken'. A letter over a dozen signatures arrived from the headquarters of the W.E.A. Among his old Oxford friends, Streeter wrote that the news had been brought to him by his scout who, when Streeter asked him whether Miss Anson was related to the Warden of All Souls, replied: 'Very likely, Sir: it's spelt with an "A" and not with a "Haitch".' Scott Holland, in his own characteristic style, began a (for him) exceptionally legible note. 'It is quite splendid. And perfectly right. Nothing could be better.' Two letters are worth quoting in full—one from the Bishop of Winchester (Talbot) expressed with all his usual grace, and the other from G. F. Bradby, shot through with flashes of no more than his usual wit:

St. Ouen's Manor,
Jersey.

My dear W.T.,   May 13, '16.

I could not hear without emotion of the news of this great Entry into your life of the great things of Love and Marriage. You have seemed so strong and αὐτάρκης, one wondered whether you were independent of these things. But you have known so well, in love and thankfulness, what it is to be a Son, that you will I know open a large heart to the great things which are to flood upon you as a Husband with a Wife to whom you can give, and from whom you can receive, in the blessed happiness of union.

God bless you in it. He seems to call you now, and as we think in the days to come, to great tasks and opportunities. May this which is happening to you enrich and strengthen and deepen you for it all, and carry with it much help for others and the great Purpose.

Yours affectionately,
EDWARD WINTON.

1 Hillmorton Road,
Rugby.

My dear William,   May 21, '16.

My blessing is a bit belated (an accident to which my blessings are peculiarly liable) not from lack of good will, but from natural sloth and the difficulty of finding adequate expression. For how is one to say 'Bless you, my children' impressively when one only knows one of the children? But I am glad you are going to marry. I am always glad when anybody marries: for though it diminishes the number of the elect, it adds to the number of reasonable human beings. I am never proud of being a bachelor any more than I am proud of having one eye and false teeth. I regard it as a disability, a flaw in an otherwise singularly noble nature. If I could begin life over again, I should try to accustom myself to the idea of double harness and endeavour to persuade some tolerant lady to put on the blinkers beside me. I would even pay the insurance premiums against that inevitable breakfast when I should fling the teapot at her head. But it is all too late now by 15 years. None the less I rejoice to hear that *you* are not going to 'differ from the kindly race of men' and are going, I hope, to gain happiness by risking the loss of a rather selfish content. I'm afraid that is in rather a low key for a lover, but everything is in rather a low key just at present—except American Notes. Here's luck to you both! But she won't like me. They never do; and it really isn't altogether their fault . . . I shall expect a farewell bachelor visit.

Yrs ever,
G. F. B.

Characteristically enough, Temple sat late into the night before his wedding finishing off *Mens Creatrix*. The marriage was celebrated at S. James's on 24 June. In his address Randall Davidson recalled the memory of Temple's father—'that manliest of men'—whose life and work in the Church had given a father's leadership to many others besides his son. He spoke of 'the resourceful and self-forgetting love which shone with a simple glamour of its own at Oxford and Repton' and now at S. James's; of his own lifelong friendship with the bride's father; of the 'rich and varied equipment' they would both bring to the making of a new home; and of the field of opportunity, than which none could be nobler, that was now theirs for the fulfilment of a high and strenuous purpose. The note of joy and thanksgiving rang through the service, the bridegroom taking full part in the hymns, 'his shoulders opening and shutting'—according to the eye-witness report of an observant member of the household staff—as he joined with special vigour in 'The God of love my Shepherd is'.

Only ten days could be spared for the honeymoon, which began at Porch Cottage, Luccombe, just under Dunkery in the Porlock Valley. This was near Holnicote, a house often lent to members of the Acland family for their honeymoons but occupied at the time, and rooms had been taken in the cottage of a carter who worked on an adjacent farm. (Some years later the carter's wife expressed her regret to another visitor that in 1916 she had no Visitors' Book. She was advised to write to Temple and ask him, if ever he happened to be in the neighbourhood, to call at the cottage and sign his name in the book she had procured since his visit. One summer afternoon in 1932 she saw to her great delight the Archbishop, who was staying with relatives not far away, walking up the hill to her home. He had come to sign his name in her book—an act of thoughtful kindness she has never forgotten.) 'The place is heavenly', Temple wrote, 'and the rooms very comfortable.' In the evenings he read aloud his favourite Browning poems, and the relief and peace of this week were hardly to be described. But he had a sharp bout of lumbago; the house was directly opposite a hayfield in full flower, and this brought on an attack of hay fever (to which he was always prone); and he was a very tired man. On the first Sunday he and his wife had planned to walk to the evening service at Selworthy church, but he settled himself for a nap at 1.45 and woke at 5.15.

On the second Sunday after the wedding they were at Repton: there were many congratulations and much handshaking, a stroll through the studies (in several of which, to his wife's delight, Temple's photograph stood in the place of honour) and the class-rooms, and an evening sermon on the National Mission in the school chapel. A few days followed at Bishopstone near Seaford, on the Sussex Downs, and the next Sunday was spent with the Alingtons at Shrewsbury—here again he preached to the school. On their return to S. James's Rectory, Mrs. Temple had the happy responsibility of making the old home a new one, with no loss of anything associated in her husband's mind with the devoted care of his mother. Her own personality and good taste, here as in each of their successive houses, produced an atmosphere of ordered beauty and quiet which was wholly to satisfy one side of Temple's nature. But there were other sides—not least one which needed all the restraint that she could impose upon it. For two years he had preached the gospel of strenuous work to those who were outside the combatant ranks in the war as their essential contribution to the national effort, and none had taken the appeal more to heart than the preacher himself. Even though he had cancelled many of his engagements, the demands being made on his strength were such as would wear down the sturdiest and could not but cause intermittent anxiety to his wife; for he was now to concentrate all his energies on a great venture to which the Church of England stood committed—the National Mission of Repentance and Hope.

XIII

The National Mission

What is the Church to say to the country? One of the things which has quite steadily grown in the minds of the people who are working this movement is that the phrase 'National Mission' must be taken to mean (as certainly, by the Archbishop at all events, it was always intended it should mean) not so much a mission on a national scale as an effort directed to the national life itself: not at the lives of individual people, but . . . at the ordering of our national life—of those things which exist because, as citizens, we produce or tolerate them.

W. T., to Guy's Hospital Christian Union, December 1917.

WHEN the First World War broke out, the best days of the Church of England—as a National Church with 'a resident gentleman in every parish'—were already behind it. The turn of the century had seen the peak of the parochial system. There had always been bad patches here and there— parishes in which the parson was idle, indifferent, or domineering —and there was little strategy at the centre in the distribution of the parochial clergy, whose allotment to a particular diocese depended too much on the taste of the individual priest and the personality of the bishop. Winnington Ingram, with his enthusiasm and charm, had drawn into the service of a weak, mixed, and shifting population in East London a body of devoted and vigorous men who by their constant visiting, their interest and influence in local affairs, and their parochial clubs and organizations, were making a contribution that none could gainsay to the spiritual and social life of the people; while to the North and Midlands, where the strength and stability of English Labour was to be found, it was not easy to attract the best type of parish priest. On the whole, however, in town and country alike the parochial system had worked reasonably well. If the Church was nowhere in possession, it was never in despair.

By August 1914 its influence had in most places waned, and questions began to be asked covering a wider field of enquiry than the parish, the club, and the church altar. As the war went on, many hitherto accepted spiritual values underwent a change—the full process of which is not yet complete—that was at once a puzzle and a challenge. Incumbents might point to satisfactory membership of clubs and parochial guilds (though even here a decline had begun) but what was the relevance of it all to a world in arms, after nineteen centuries of the Gospel they had been commissioned to preach? What connexion was there between the tired parish priest in some industrial town sitting over an inadequate gas-fire in his study, poring doubtfully over a communicants' roll, or planning the means to provide a billiards table for the men's club, and the horrors that had fallen with catastrophic violence on the earth? And was it possible that he and other representatives of his creed could be held in any way responsible—as was being widely suggested—for the powerlessness of the whole Body of Christ to prevent the appeal to a weapon which Christ Himself had taught His followers to forswear? Such were the questions, such gradually became the indictment; and nobody put the case against organized Christianity at this time with more deadly accuracy than Henry Scott Holland:

If only the world had been Christian, it would not be at war. . . . It must be its [*sc.* Christianity's] representation by its accredited organs and institutions that has so piteously failed to make it effectual. It has been allowed to lose its grip on the real facts, so that the big affairs of the world go on their way as if it were not there. In the World of Diplomacy, of International Relationships, it does not count. In Trade and Industry it has hardly any place. Over the dominating motives and aims by which our enormous wealth is created, it has little or no control. In many departments of Business it is openly denied. It exercises no authority over the wealth, after it has been made. It establishes no over-ruling conscience, no paramount sense of responsibility. . . . So men are bitterly aware . . . and they trace the curse of Materialism on us within, as on those without. They do not see that we, churchmen, contribute an ideal element to solid affairs. Conscience and politics are not changed by our taking part in them. We take our colour from them, not they from us. In our Business and in our Political interests we are too often just as other men are. The world is not aware of any difference in its temper or habits because we take part in its doings. So men assert.

The contrast between the actual and the ideal has once more been made painfully manifest since those words were written; but a generation ago the clergy were too much dazed by the threat to their traditional means and methods to grasp all its implications or to understand the questionings of a new age. Moreover, in the autumn of 1914 parish priests could report crowded services of intercession, and some were even talking of a religious revival after the war, though their more far-sighted leaders, Gore in particular, earnestly and often besought all such optimists to take down the history books from their shelves and to read whether war had ever led to a permanent revival of true religion. The flicker of spiritual enthusiasm soon died down. The Church of England, men were forced to conclude, was not organized for crisis, nor for any such adjustment of spiritual values as the language of its few prophets seemed now to emphasize and demand.

It was indeed 'high time to awake out of sleep', and the first stirrings came from a group of laymen—a fact to which the Archbishop of Canterbury did not refer when he told the Convocation of Canterbury in February 1916 of the 'successive steps in an endeavour' he had made to meet the 'most righteous and appropriate cry' of the country for spiritual help and direction from the Church—and it was not till this group had made its urgent representations at Lambeth that the Archbishop conceived the possibility of inaugurating some special effort in which the whole Church of England should be involved. Nor was the suggestion received with any enthusiasm. 'Your Grace's first reply', it was once said to Randall Davidson, 'to any appeal to do something outside the ordinary routine of the Church, is always to raise objections': 'that', he replied, 'is one of the first duties of anyone in my position.' The expected objections to the laymen's proposal were fully stated: the Church was very short-handed;

many of the strongest clergy and laity were serving in the Forces; the attention of the country was preoccupied with the more direct and clamant issues of the war; on all sides men and women were suffering from the pressure of overwork and the anxiety of bereavement: after the war there would be opportunity for a forward spiritual move in which the National Church might rightly take the lead. The laymen replied by informing the Archbishop of the state of feeling in the country—as contrasted with that of the official circles in which his Grace so naturally and confidently moved—and in certain quarters of the Church. They assured him that widespread support would be forthcoming for any call to the Church to rise up and take part in some spiritual adventure commensurate with the need of the hour. Randall Davidson was partly persuaded and, while not committing himself or his colleagues on the Bench to any particular plan, promised that he would take some preliminary steps. He chose twelve men, on whom he laid the obligation to unite in prayer that wisdom might be granted to the Church to take the wisest course. After three months' prayer the twelve went into retreat at Beaconsfield and on the morning of the third day, just as they were about to break up an entirely inconclusive conference, a plan was proposed on which they felt sufficiently of one mind to recommend it to the Archbishop. Randall Davidson laid it before the whole Bench; and it was decided that there should be a 'National Mission of Repentance and Hope', to be begun in the autumn of 1916. The Archbishop then, again *more dominico*, appointed 'seventy others also' to form the Central Council of the Mission—the number being later increased to one hundred.

Among the twelve was Temple. In describing, at the end of 1917, the early stages of the National Mission, he said:

Outside critics thought the procedure very odd, and so it was. What the Bishops had done was to say that there was to be a National Mission of Repentance and Hope, and it was to take place in the autumn of 1916, and they appointed several people to decide what it was that was to be so called. Looked at from the outside, that was fairly ludicrous. But in fact this was the first stage in a course along which we were being guided, and it was no small thing to have this emphasis on Repentance and Hope from the outset. The Council met. . . . At the first meeting we were in absolute chaos. People all wanted different things, and they were all rather savage about the things which other people wanted. That meeting broke up with every promise of sheer confusion. We only arrived at one conclusion, and that was that before we tried to do any more business—having so conspicuously failed this time—we must go away and say our prayers.

More freely he wrote to his brother:

> St. James's Rectory,
> Piccadilly,
> London, W.
> Feb. 20, 1916.

Last Monday was held the Council of the proposed National Mission. We were very much at sea, but I think it will work out as we go along. I expect I am to be one of its secretaries: if I can get the colleagues I want, it may become rather important, though it will make less of a splash than some would wish. There are those who merely want to blow the ecclesiastical trumpet and expect the walls of Jericho to fall down thereat. But I expect Jericho, in the form of worldliness and commercialism, is founded too securely for that nowadays. I should sooner expect it to collapse if the Church bodily went into the middle of the Sahara and there prayed till it died of starvation. The plain fact is that $\frac{3}{4}$ of English folk don't want the sort of Gospel we have offered them. No doubt that's partly their fault; but it's also probably due to our presentation of things. However, I need not make you my National Mission speech.

The Abp. of C., Winton, Oxon, Sarum, Wigorn and some others are sound. Ebor, London, and a good lot more just want a few mass meetings in the Albert Hall. That hardly seems an adequate way of meeting the end of a world. Well, well!

There was no more than the truth in Temple's summary. It was altogether too much to expect that a body of men and women,

208

many of them complete strangers to and not free from suspicion of one another, would reach immediate agreement on an agenda which did not exist about a plan that had not been decided. Nor was it likely that members of the Council would shed their predilections at their first discussions with other members who they knew disagreed with them on what seemed to each group to be issues of the first importance. Any who remember the acute divisions of those days within the Church, and the eclectic spirit that animated them, will agree that the initial success of the Mission was not gained by anything that was said or done at the first meeting by members of the Council, but by the mere fact that they were there at all—to take counsel together for the future neither of the Islington Conference nor the Anglo-Catholic Congress, but of the whole Church and, through the Church, of the nation. An almost harder task was to overcome the amateurishness that seems ineradicable from much of the Church's work. It was held almost unanimously, for instance, that the Church was 'out of touch with the working man'; therefore a special effort must be made to satisfy his needs. The working man had the reputation of being a simple soul; therefore any literature designed for his study must be simple. Clearly a special leaflet was demanded, *to be written entirely in words of one syllable.* It was vain to point out that, if the working man was in the habit of saying 'Shut the door', it was also not beyond his powers of expression occasionally to say 'Open the window'. But the opposition was borne down; the task was, naturally, entrusted to a Cambridge don; and, be it added, very well he did it. Then there was Mr. Horatio Bottomley. It may seem odd that he should have come into the picture at all; but the Mission had to be advertised in the Press, and *John Bull*, with its regular article by Bottomley, had an enormous circulation and was more popular among the Forces than any other weekly. Two steps were taken to secure Bottomley's sympathetic support. With characteristic *naïveté* the Bishop of London invited him to tea— of all meals!—at London House (then one of the Bishop's London residences) in St. James's Square; and a confession of the Church's misdeeds and omissions was set out in a letter beginning

P

'Dear Brother' for publication in *John Bull*. Fortunately there were one or two parish priests on the Council who protested strongly that, whether or not Bottomley was the dear brother addressed, it would be the depth not of repentance but of degradation for the Church to confess its shortcomings in the columns of a paper at that time identified with a man of his (already) dubious reputation; and the letter went no further. But Bottomley made good capital out of his cup of tea with the Bishop and began his next article with a reference to it. He went on to ask in vigorous language—What need was there of national repentance? The men at the Front, for instance, were not sinners; they were 'saints and heroes'. Two answers were made to this. Studdert-Kennedy, one of the most forceful of popular speakers then living, went on to the platform at a mass meeting of soldiers behind the line in France, with a copy of the paper in his hand. 'I see', he began, 'that Mr. Bottomley describes you as "saints and heroes". We don't talk quite as much about heroes over here as they do back at home, but—"Saints"! Well, eyes right, and have a good look at the man next door to you'; and to take Bottomley seriously after the roars of laughter that followed was difficult.

Temple offered a more reasoned reply in defence of the title of the Mission:

> There are a lot of people who say—and Mr. Horatio Bottomley has, perhaps, succeeded in saying it loudest—that it is inappropriate to call upon people to repent when they are doing their best, and when that best, moreover, is singularly good, when the people are ready for any amount of endurance and sacrifice for a just cause. But that objection all comes of people supposing that repentance is a miserable kind of thing, of which the normal exhibition would be the cringing of some evil-doer before a judge, in the hope of getting off from the results of his ill deeds: or else that you can only repent when things are so bad that you cannot remedy them otherwise. Mr. Bottomley plainly holds that view, because he said that if there were an imminent chance of a German invasion it would be reasonable to repent.

Now, in the first place, repentance is not a miserable thing: it is essentially a happy thing: it is a change from what was bad to what is good, and you cannot have anything happier than that. And if it causes joy among the angels of God, I do not see why it should make us miserable here. . . . Again the motive in Christianity is always hope, and not fear. The Gospel does not say things are so intolerably bad we must repent and get them better. It says, things might be so splendidly good that we must bring those splendours true. 'The Kingdom of God is at hand: repent'. So repentance and hope are practically the same thing.

From the date of the first meeting of the Mission Council, there were few hours in the week for the rest of the year that Temple could call his own. The necessary machinery had to be set up. Seven committees were appointed for various purposes, and five secretaries (with a general secretary) were nominated by the Archbishops. Later a central panel of messengers was compiled, of men competent and ready to deliver the message of the Mission, though it was left to each diocese to formulate its own plan of campaign. Temple was one of the five secretaries—the others were the Rev. C. C. B. Bardsley (later Bishop of Peterborough), Prebendary F. Leith Boyd (Vicar of S. Paul's, Knightsbridge), Douglas Eyre (a well known social worker), and Miss M. C. Gollock, who had had wide experience of office work with the Church Missionary Society. A letter of goodwill was sent to the Archbishop signed by the President and Secretaries of the National Free Church Council; offers of help and co-operation were received from many societies and associations (including the Prophecy Investigation Society); contacts were made with chaplains serving in the Forces; and soon the organization became as complete as time had allowed. Temple was responsible for the work of the Literature Committee and edited a series of pamphlets dealing with the wider issues raised by the Mission: he wrote several of them himself, of which *The Call of the Kingdom* was most widely read. This contained three of his favourite illustrations, which were to be used extensively in the coming years—

the reply of Cavour to the question why, instead of aiming at the unity of Italy, he did not concentrate on something more practicable such as the reform of the Kingdom of Naples, 'I cannot get the reform of Naples because no one is ready to die for it: I can get the unity of Italy because thousands of Italians are ready to die for it'; the appeal of Garibaldi (which was the source of Mr. Churchill's famous broadcast in the Second World War), ' "I am going out from Rome. I offer neither quarters nor provision nor wages. I offer hunger, thirst, forced marches, battles, death. Let him who loves his country with his heart, not with his lips only, follow me", and they streamed out after him into the hills'; and the Grand Inquisitor fable from *The Brothers Karamazov*—the greatest novel, in Temple's judgement, ever written. He pleaded for a national recognition of the world-wide authority of Christ, and for a national dedication to the service of the Kingdom; he confessed to the 'wicked folly' of 'the foolish and superficial contentment and pleasure-hunt' that had not long since been the most characteristic feature of society, and contrasted the capacity for heroism in ordinary people which the war had revealed with the failure of the Church in recent years to evoke from its members any such readiness to share and serve.

The work of the Council ran more smoothly after its Retreat at Westfield College, and Temple was able to spend many days and nights travelling round the country to speak and preach. He used his blue pencil heavily on the commitments already entered in his engagement book: 'Having lasted till now', he writes in March 1916, 'I ought to survive, as I am reaching the time when I have cancelled former engagements for the sake of the Mission'. Wherever he went, his welcome was assured; and after a short time he had an ordered technique for his appeal, which relieved him of the need for constant preparation. Large meetings and services in industrial centres had the first claim on his available time—from Manchester he wrote to his wife: 'Church packed, mainly with business men; splendid to talk to'—and by way of refreshment he visited some of the larger public schools, about one of which he writes to his brother on 16 July 1916:

Not much to say since I last wrote. One pegs away at many things—mostly connected with the National Mission. Then last night we went down to Eton, where I preached this morning. I never had such a tussle with an audience. I was on the Mission, and very keen to get it home, and at the start the Eton listlessness lay on the chapel like a blight. But I fairly pumped out energy, and after 10 or 12 minutes had them listening like anything. Rather a triumph!

A week later he went into Retreat with the London clergy at Fulham—old memories were stirred: 'It was, I think, the first time I had slept there since we left . . . the place looked lovely'— and the meeting of the British Association in Newcastle made a welcome diversion in September, marred by an attack of lumbago caught through 'sitting endlessly in a cold room'. By October there is a note of hopefulness in his letters and memoranda; he can detect signs that the Mission is having some effect:

The Mission makes life a perfect whirl just now. Last week I was at Bournemouth on Wednesday; London (all day committees) Thursday; three committees in London and then a sermon in Ipswich on Friday; meeting in Norwich Saturday. Two sermons here (S. James's) yesterday. This week will be worse. But there is no doubt that an immense amount that is very hopeful has happened.

Of the last two months in the year the tale is the same, with committees in London, meetings in the provinces, and supervision of the official literature of the Mission. Pamphlets and leaflets followed one another in well-ordered succession; more than a million of these had been sold before the end of September, and the Mission poster was displayed on hoardings and in church porches through the country. The competition for the design of the poster had been keen. Eric H. Kennington's was eventually chosen, but not before a few lighter moments had been snatched from the more serious business of the Council, to examine the efforts of the other competitors. One of these in particular, as it was passed round, drew much noisy thigh-slapping and chuckling from Scott Holland, and a melancholy 'quite intolerable' from Gore, as he raised his spectacles to his forehead and took one agonized glance at a representation of fighting-ships of many sizes floating on a calm and most emphatically cobalt sea, with the figure of our Lord poised in the air above them in grotesque and uneasy detachment—the whole picture being encased in a multi-coloured border of what the conjurers call 'flags of all nations'.

By the end of the year it was possible to take some reckoning of the impression being made on Church and nation by the National Mission, and at the tenth meeting of the Council, on 7 December, Temple presented the Secretaries' Report. One great disappointment had to be recorded: it was clear that through-out the country the church services had as a rule been attended only by persons already attached to the normal church life of the parish. A dozen contributory causes could be offered for this, most of them being exactly the reasons why church attendance has been on the decline ever since; and each could fill an essay. But, whatever the reasons, there the truth was, and it was an unpalatable one to swallow—that, in spite of all that had been said and done, there were no signs of a renewed desire on the part of the people of England to identify themselves and their ideals with the fellowship and the worship of the National Church. This did not necessarily mean that only those who came to church had heard the message of the Mission. Meetings had been much better attended than church services, and at open-air demonstrations thousands had listened attentively to the appeal for a wider sense of personal and corporate responsibility. Within the Church, the picture was brighter. The barriers of spiritual isolation which separated one parish and one priest from another, and had taken the heart out of country priests and the life out of many parishes, had been broken down and had given way to a new fellowship. The parson was in closer touch with his people. There was evidence of a deeper spirit of prayer among church members, and of a new longing for reality both in life and worship. The urgent need of church reform and the spiritual relevance of social work were being realized more keenly than ever before in living memory, and many consciences had been stirred as men listened to the tale of abuses that cried for remedy both in Church and State. The Secretaries' Report ended on a note of hope and thanksgiving:

> Prayer has been abundantly answered, the love of the Father to His children has once more been revealed, new gifts through His Spirit have been bestowed, and the Church, more conscious than she has been before of her union with the Risen and Triumphant Lord, can advance to all that lies before her with humble gratitude and strengthened courage and hope.

Two further developments remain to be recorded—one of them ought to have been as important as any other effort made by the Council of the Mission. This was the preparation of the Reports due from the five committees appointed to deal with special topics that might become subjects for discussion and study circles at parochial and other gatherings during the coming year. They covered the Teaching Office of the Church—Temple's most important contribution was to this Report—Public Worship, Evangelistic Work, Church Reform, and the Relation of the Church to the Industrial Life of the Country. Many conferences were subsequently to issue other statements—of the making of Reports in the Church of England there is no end—and none was to prove of greater value than these; but the Church, like many other institutions, awaits the advent of the genius who, when noteworthy Reports have been written and presented, can ensure that they will find readers. These five Reports deserved much closer attention than any of them has since received; and considering that each member of these Committees of Enquiry had his or her strongly developed personal views, the unanimity reached was striking. There was one notable exception:

Hatfield House,
Hatfield,
Herts.

Dear Mr. Temple,   Jan. 7th, 1918.

I am afraid I cannot subscribe to the Report of the Committee of Enquiry No. 4, as I was not able to attend its meetings.

Moreover there is much in the Report that I do not agree with;
and it would be a laborious task to frame a criticism explaining
what I agree with and what I don't.

Everyone is mad just now, so I am afraid I waste words in
urging moderation. But of course nothing can do so much to
hinder our self-government plans as putting forward more or
less alarming schemes of reform which are to follow as soon as
we set up our self-government machinery. It would have been
far better not to formulate any scheme of reform until we had
got our Bill through Parliament. However, I am afraid that
the Hereford storm will wreck us, and land us either on the
shores of disestablishment or in a prolonged and disastrous
struggle over theological fundamentals which will destroy all
the prospects of Church Reform. But I am perhaps pessimistical.
I remain,
Yours sincerely,
Hugh Cecil.

Events were to prove the truth of the last sentence.

A Continuation Committee was also appointed—again, like
many other continuation committees, it expected more work than
fell to it—and here Temple pressed the Archbishop to make the
secretariat as representative as possible of all sections of Church
opinion. He was anxious to use to the fullest advantage what had
seemed to him one of the outstanding achievements of the
Mission—the growing sense of unity between the three main
schools of thought in the Church. That he himself took every
opportunity of fostering this spirit is evident from a letter on
1 November in which he tells his brother that 'everyone is working in with everyone else'. In accordance with this principle he
had preached at High Mass at S. Paul's, Knightsbridge—'I
rather enjoyed it'.

A few days later he wrote to the Archbishop:

Yesterday evening we had a meeting of the three people
whom you had intimated as possible Secretaries for the Continuation Committee. . . . There is, however, one point that I
should like to raise, and it is whether you have fully considered

the advisability of asking Boyd also to act as one of the Secretaries. The original Secretaries were chosen with a view to representing three main elements within the Church, and Boyd has been quite invaluable in connexion with the Mission. He has worked most loyally, and I am sure that it is largely due to him that one of the great achievements of the Mission has been accomplished, namely, that the isolation of the ultra-Catholic party has been in great measure broken down. Now the ultra-Catholics are disposed to regard me as a Protestant and something worse; Bardsley of course is regarded as thoroughly Protestant, and Miss Gollock much the same. In no case is the judgment a fair one, but it is the prevalent one in that quarter. Would it be well therefore to ask Boyd to continue as one of the Secretaries? . . . My real concern is our contact with the extreme High Church party.

The Archbishop gave his willing assent. Apart from his personal regard for and friendship with Boyd, Temple was convinced that only by showing a united front to the nation could the Church hope to influence it, and that matters in which church parties had hitherto been sharply divided would be found irrelevant to the major issues soon to be forced into the foreground. 'The advantage', he wrote in September 1917 in his printed address to the electors of the Lower House of the Convocation of Canterbury, 'of being able to appeal for support to one or other of the chief parties in the Church is denied to me. But perhaps the very reason why I have been asked to stand is that the outlook before the Church is rapidly changing, and one who is not closely associated with any of the familiar parties of the Church, but desires to work harmoniously with all parties, may therefore be preferred. To me at any rate it seems that many of the questions which we have debated in the past are no longer matters of primary concern.' The two chief parties were at that time so highly organized that the prospects of an independent candidate gaining a seat in the Lower House were not bright; but Temple was elected on a Life and Liberty programme by a majority of thirty-five (254 to 219) over his opponent, the Archdeaconry of Hampstead being the only one in which he polled a minority of the votes.

By the end of 1916 his letters display the optimistic belief, then shared by many, that the war was nearing its end. A sharp reminder came when he and his wife were wakened one night by a loud crash and the sound of broken glass. A bomb had fallen on the north-west corner of Piccadilly Circus, but Temple was unwilling to believe it—the story that he turned over in bed muttering 'I wish they would shut that door to stop it banging' is apocryphal—until the housemaid appeared and told him that many windows had been broken. He and his wife dressed and went across to Vine Street Police Station, to see whether they or their house could be of any use, but the injured were already being taken in ambulances to the hospital.

At the turn of the year, there was a prospect of Temple being able to disentangle himself from some of his outside engagements and to devote more time to reading and writing. *Mens Creatrix* appeared in January 1917, when the busiest year of his life had just ended. Throughout 1916, whatever spare time was left to him from his work for the National Mission and editing the *Challenge* he had spent, in spite of all his resolutions, in speaking and preaching where he felt he was needed, and all the while he kept a guiding hand on the W.E.A. 'On Friday', he wrote in November 1916, 'I sat from 2.30 to 8.45 and yesterday (Sat.) from 12 to 8.50 on W.E.A. Committees. But we did the work, so it was worth it'; and there were many days on which the pressure was no lighter. Yet during that year he produced what some competent judges regard as his best work, for which he received the D.Litt. degree of his old university. What might he not achieve, it was beginning to be asked, if his energies were less dissipated, if there were more frequent periods of ordered quiet in his life, and if he would be at pains to make closer and more personal touch with men of his own calibre among the leaders of thought and action in the State? There is mention in his diary of a luncheon with Haldane, and of another with Asquith, but engagements of this kind were few. He had now reached an age, and a position in the Church, which made it desirable that he should take as full a share as possible in the intellectual and social interests of those who carried weight in the national life, and the opportunity seemed to have arrived when such contacts might be extended and developed. But it was not to be. One day, as Dick Sheppard and he sat talking in the Rectory study, Sheppard said with explosive suddenness, 'Don't you think, William dear, that there ought to be a "ginger" group in the Church?' ... So began a Movement that played a prominent part in English Church history during the next few years, and William Temple was its chosen leader and apostle.

XIV

'Life and Liberty'

We demand liberty for the Church of England because we believe
that liberty is essential to fullness of life.

W. T., at the Queen's Hall, July 1917.

AMONG Sheppard's many gifts was the ability to recognize
and seize for spiritual profit the opportunity of the passing
hour. What H. G. Wells called 'gawdsakery'—'for Gawd's sake
do *something*'—was an impelling force in his life and work, and
that the Church should 'get a move on' his most passionate
desire: the particular form any movement might take, what and
whom it was likely to involve, and whither it would lead—these
were generally matters that would settle themselves as one went
along. Never was this gift more valuable than in the early months
of 1917. Here, he believed, was a veritable 'day of the Lord' such
as prophets had proclaimed, when no venture of faith would go
unrewarded, and when for those who felt the breath of the Spirit
stirring through the Church no triumph was too splendid to be
impossible. The National Mission had left the Church in a state
of chastened discontent with itself, combined with a sense of
frustration that baulked and halted all efforts towards a full
recovery; the atmosphere was one of confusion in thought and
purpose, and there was little to clear the air beyond a vague
feeling that something ought to be done about it. It was one of
those hours in which leaders emerge, who interpret the stam-
merings of the multitude, clear its head, give point to its purpose,
and turn its aspirations into achievement. Quite certainly there
was no definite plan in Sheppard's mind when he suggested to
Temple the need of a 'ginger' group within the Church. His was
merely the true instinct and, though he rightly believed that he
could collect round him a number of sympathetic men and
women whose influence was not negligible, he was also aware

that he was not the man to work out the details of a practical policy or direct single-handed a far-reaching spiritual adventure. He therefore set to work in his own best way. Men and women, one after another in a long succession, were invited to his study, which they left with a firm impression that each had something of value to contribute to this new uprising in the Church; and the time came when he was ready to bring them all together round his table, where he believed that some definite plan would emerge from their discussions. But two things were missing—a leader and a programme. No deep thinking was required by Sheppard, or by any whom he had consulted, in the choice of a leader. There was only one man who seemed to possess all the qualities needed. Temple's work for the National Mission had brought him into close touch with every type of church member; comparatively few priests—and they were almost exclusively extreme Anglo-Catholics or extreme Erastians—did not trust him; and he could bring to the Movement a strength of mind and spirit that no one else could contribute. If with Sheppard's flashes of intuition and lively imagination were combined Temple's intellectual power, his wide knowledge, his ability in debate, and his charity in controversy, a strong rallying-point would be provided for the most forward-looking elements in the Church. And the programme? That would emerge from their meeting.

On 29 March 1917 the first conference of this new group was held at S. Martin's Vicarage. As each member entered, it was noticed by the others that he (or she) counted for something in the life of the Church. Later, when the names of Council members were published, few of the larger lay professions were found to be unrepresented on it; but for the moment the group numbered about forty, and the first afternoon was spent in threshing out an agreed policy. Almost immediately it was clear that on one point opinion was unanimous; they must first concentrate on the Church's own abuses and shortcomings. The 'repentance whereby they *forsake* sin' was still lamentably incomplete and, before the Church could hope to catch the ear of the nation, it must set its own house in order. The anomalies of church patronage, the inexcusable disparity between clerical incomes which seemed to bear no relation to the work involved, the conditions of tenure and the lack of pensions for super-annuated clergymen—these and other abuses in the life and organization of the Church militated against its witness and stultified its message. No less than this, of course, had been said by the Church Reform League for many years, though few had listened to its appeal; all such matters had been lightly dismissed, by most churchpeople who had thought about them at all, as details of internal organization and adjustment of which the importance had been exaggerated by a few radical faddists. But the war and the National Mission had brought a change of out-look: a new moral sense was emerging, and these abuses were seen to involve ethical and spiritual principles that could not now be disregarded if the Church was to be qualified to preach of moral duty and responsibility to the nation. It could no longer, for instance, be considered a mere 'anomaly', whatever private arrangements might be made between bishop and incumbent to adjust it—it was something morally unjustifiable—that in one of two contiguous parishes the incumbent should receive an annual income of over £6,000 for ministering to 850 persons, while his neighbour, in a parish with a population of 19,000, should be paid £400 a year; or that the right to present a priest to a living—technically called an advowson—could be hawked round the property market like a farm or a suburban villa. The list could be extended, and few abuses in the Church were not mentioned on that afternoon.

Why not, then, set about these reforms at once? The answer was obvious, and it was the deciding factor in shaping the future of the Movement. One body blocked all progress, and made swift and decisive action impossible. Not a single reform worth troubling about could be effected without the consent of Parliament; and to hope that during, or even immediately after, the war a Parliament bewildered and overburdened with the vast problems arising out of it would spare the time—even if the goodwill were there—to discuss such apparent trivialities showed small acquaint-ance with the history of Church Bills. If in the less crowded days of peace it had taken as many as nine sessions of Parliament to settle the salary of the Archdeacon of Cornwall, what possible chance was there of passing through all their stages in both Houses of Parliament, with the urgency that would be demanded, a dozen or more Church Bills, many of them concerned with intricate details of organization and finance on which not one member in twenty of either House was qualified to pass an opinion?

Here, then, was the obvious first step—to go to Parliament and demand freedom for the Church. But how much freedom? On this the group was divided. Some were convinced that all the liberty needed could be secured with no changes in the Establishment. Others held no less strongly that most of the evils from which the Church suffered were incurable so long as the State connexion was maintained; parliamentary control over the spirituality in any form was obnoxious; sometimes it amounted almost to sacrilege. No freedom worth having could be gained without paying the highest price, and only a disestablished Church could be truly and entirely free; disendowment must be part of the price to be paid, but the State could be trusted to behave with a reasonable generosity; and such an act of sacrifice on the part of the Church would touch the imagination of the country and win if not the allegiance, at least the respect, of the English people. Neither Temple nor Sheppard was then prepared to go so far; and those who favoured disestablishment were confronted with the dilemma—to stay in and work for as full a measure of freedom as could be secured, or to leave the Movement and form a more radical group of their own? They decided to stay, and a sop was offered to them in the minute drawn up by Temple, describing the first resolution taken on policy: 'It was agreed that the first thing to press for is church self-government, and it was decided provisionally to express this in the form that church self-government must be secured, even at the cost, if it be necessary, of disestablishment.'

To some members of the group all this seemed utterly unheroic. At the first and subsequent meetings, and in personal correspondence, chaplains who had been working in the Army and the

Grand Fleet pleaded that nothing short of a crusade would find any widespread support among the men who were serving; and what sort of a crusade would it be that had 'Pensions for Parsons' as its slogan and quicker legislation as its end? Temple replied that it had never been imagined, at least by those responsible for initiating the Movement, that Church reform was to be the 'end' of their efforts. The end was that the Church should be able, through a cleansing of its life, to preach the Gospel to the nation with a clear conscience, which at present was impossible. Not until abuses had been swept away could fullness of life come to the Church; then, and then only, would it be qualified to witness loyally for its Head.

Before members of the Movement could be enrolled, a name had to be found for it. Many suggestions were offered; in the end that proposed by Dr. David, then Headmaster of Rugby, was adopted, and the following statement was printed on the first circulars:

> The Life and Liberty Movement aims at securing for the Church without delay Liberty in the sense of full power to control its own life and organization. It does this in the belief that a unique opportunity is before the Church, which existing conditions prevent it from claiming to the full. The rising tide of Life within the Church demands Liberty, because Liberty is indispensable to the fullness of Life and its practical expression. It must no longer be necessary to wait for the convenience of Parliament before adaptations can be made and reforms effected. The opportunity is now, when our whole civilization has to be rebuilt. The Church must be able effectively to reform its own abuses and perform its part in the National and Ecclesiastical spheres. It is the Body of Christ, and must be free to obey spontaneously the command of its Divine Head, so as to make its witness obvious to the People, and effective for the extension of the Kingdom of God.

Within a month of the first council meeting the Movement was well under way. An office was taken in Victoria Street, with Miss Gollock in charge; literature was sold as fast as it could be printed; and the membership grew rapidly as applications were received from all parts of the country. The combination of Temple and Sheppard was in itself a guarantee that there would be both wisdom and imagination behind every step that was taken. The only fear was that the Movement might become too respectable: 'no gaiters' had been Sheppard's slogan at the start; but it was found that many archdeacons (and even a bishop or two) were single-minded in their desire for reform, and after a keen debate it was decided (by no means unanimously) that any-body in Holy Orders except diocesan bishops was eligible for membership of the Movement; but from the Council 'gaiters' were excluded.

Those who were in the Movement from the beginning have found it difficult to describe the thrill of those early days. One conviction was common to them all. They could hold out a hope to be found in no human institution. They had an answer to the question 'Who will show us any good?' which was being put on every side, as a disillusioned people groped its apparently aimless way through a darkness unlit by any ray of hope except the shining courage of the fighting Services. Politicians were dis-credited, unpleasant tales were abroad of contractors, commis-sions, and profits; public and private morals had touched a 'new low' level; and the cold grip of fatalism was fastening on the mind and heart of the nation. Was not this the time, if ever, when the Church of the living God was summoned to cast off its worldliness and sloth, and rise up once more to lead and inspire? Here lay the hope—and the response was immediate. Defeatism was killed outright; the depression that had hung over the Church suddenly lifted, and gave place to a faith and fervour that mounted as the Movement spread and was carried forward with a momen-tum that surprised even its promoters. The office was inundated with enthusiastic congratulations, questions, and suggestions. One exciting challenge came from an old lady who pleaded with churchpeople to have the courage of their convictions and to advertise the Movement as openly as she did. Every morning, it appeared, she was wheeled up and down the sea-front at East-bourne in a bath-chair—the snapshot she enclosed irresistibly

Q

suggested Mrs. Skewton's progress at Leamington Spa, even to the 'wan page' who pushed the chair from behind—tinkling her way with a bicycle-bell attached to the steering-handle, and displaying an out-size poster inscribed 'Life and Liberty for the Church of England'.

But the critics were not silent. Some, of whom B. H. Streeter was the most notable, held that the Movement was beginning from the wrong end and was emphasizing the importance of the Church's body to the neglect of its soul: if attention were fastened on the spiritual and intellectual condition of the clergy and laity, they urged, the machinery would take care of itself, and assume its true proportion in the whole economy of the Church. Others, represented by the Dean of Durham, Dr. Hensley Henson, deplored as indecent the haste with which the Movement demanded reform; let a Royal Commission be appointed, which would be in a position to weigh fairly the issues, and to strike a better balance than any likely to be reached by a mixed collection of young men in a hurry and a few shell-shocked chaplains. Anglo-Catholics—though several were members of the Council—were inclined to be suspicious: the Church of England, in the view of many of them, was like Rebekah with two children struggling in her womb; and the struggle must continue till one or the other came first to the birth. Among Nonconformists opinion was divided: the more critical saw in the aims of the Life and Liberty Movement an attempt to retain all the privileges of the Establishment and at the same time to secure freedom from State control; but many of the leaders were neutral, and a few definitely sympathetic. Support came later from an unexpected quarter when, after the demand for an Enabling Bill had been formulated, Sidney Webb prefaced a paper he read to the Fabian Society with the confession that he found himself in sympathy—'an unusual thing for me'—with the Church of England in its demand for the Bill, which 'seems to me a beautiful example of devolution to a group'.

It was now time for the Movement to come out into the open and make a public statement of its aims. On 20 June 1917 the following letter was published in *The Times*:

MOVEMENT FOR REFORM

Sir,

Amid the ruins of the old world, the new world is already being born. In the ideas of reconstruction now being formed there is hope of a new and better era. The Church has felt, and to some extent imparted, the new impulse in the National Mission. It has in altogether new ways realised its responsibilities and its impotence at the present time to discharge them. . . . A vigorous forward movement just now may revive waning enthusiasm and hopes, retain for the service of the Church the eager souls who now doubtfully watch it, and, by combining these together, exert such pressure on the official bodies as may result in real reform.

But as soon as we consider the changes that are needed to make the Church a living force in the nation, we find ourselves hampered at every turn by an antiquated machinery which we are powerless to change except by a series of Acts of Parliament. Every one sees that the House of Commons is a highly unsuitable place for the settlement of questions affecting the Church's life and work; and even if it were suitable in its composition it has no time. Whatever else may be thought of the scheme suggested by the Archbishops' Committee on Church and State, it has at least this advantage, that under its provisions it would be necessary to find time to stop legislation for Church reform from taking effect, instead of its being necessary, as it is now, to find time to pass it.

If the Church is to have new life, even if it is to maintain the life which it has, it must have liberty. Those who are promoting this Movement are convinced that we must win for the Church full power to control its own life, even at the cost, if necessary, of disestablishment and of whatever consequences that may possibly involve.

It is proposed to hold a meeting at Queen's Hall on the evening of Monday, July 16, when these principles will be enforced and support for them enlisted. . . . We propose to do whatever can be done by constitutional channels; we wish to arouse the Church to a sense of its vital need, and to call on

227

all who love it to demand for it the liberty which is essential to its life. We believe that the leaders of the Church are ready to advance along the path of progress if they are assured of an earnest and widespread desire to go forward. But with them or without them we are constrained by love of our Church and country to raise the standard of advance and call to it those who share our anxiety and our hope.

Yours faithfully,

LOUISE CREIGHTON, A. A. DAVID, A. MANSBRIDGE, J. B. SEATON, A. L. SMITH; W. TEMPLE, Chairman; A. P. CHARLES, F. A. IREMONGER, H. R. L. SHEPPARD, Hon. Secretaries.

This letter marked a beginning of the duel between Hensley Henson and Temple, which went on intermittently for two years, at the end of which they were still close friends. As soon as he had read the Life and Liberty statement in *The Times*, Henson at once wrote two letters. One was to Temple, asking for a ticket for the Queen's Hall meeting, and adding: '. . . It hardly needs saying that I think you and your friends are on the wrong tack.' This was followed by a statement of the wide liberty to be found within the Church of England—'the home of the only liberty a Christian minister could seriously desire or rightly claim'—and the Dean ended: 'My prophecy that Gore will play in the Church of England the rôle that Chalmers played in the Church of Scotland—that of the great Wrecker—is likely to be fulfilled sooner than even I expected'.

The other letter was to the Editor of *The Times*:

THE NATION AND HASTY MEASURES

Sir,

If times were normal, and we were not immersed in the efforts and anxieties of the greatest and most momentous war that has ever wasted this earth, I should certainly desire to examine very closely the remarkable letter signed by Mrs. Creighton and others which appeared in your columns of June 20. I should have insisted on two indispensable definitions as preliminary to any reasonable or useful discussion of

228

'Liberty in the Church'. What precisely is meant by 'liberty'? What is the 'Church'? I suspect, nay, I am persuaded, that any serious attempt to define those terms would have disclosed in the signatories such pinched and limited senses of both that the whole plea of the letter would appear paradoxical. But the times are too grave for ecclesiastical discussion, and I will attempt none. Only, once more, I beg leave to enter an earnest protest against the haste, unfair, irrational, indecent, which marks the procedure of the 'Life and Liberty' Reformers, who are now launching a movement for Disestablishment from within.

It is but a few months since the Report of the Archbishops' Committee was issued. That Report is a highly controversial document; it has been already severely criticized; when the nature and effect of its proposals are realized it will be widely condemned. Their Graces have so far recognized the gravity of the issues at stake as to permit the Representative Church Council to postpone their consideration of the Report while the war is raging. This concession, so obviously reasonable and just, fills the new Reformers with an exasperation which hardly respects the bounds of politeness. '. . . The precious moments are rapidly passing by. Just now people are ready for big changes.' The new Reformers are quite conscious that all will be over with them and their projects, if once the nation shall have time to think and opportunity to decide.

Is this the way in which the National Church should be handled? Is the nation thus to be shut out from concern with the oldest and greatest of its historic institutions? Is the religious settlement, which was slowly hammered into shape in the course of 130 years (1529–1662), and which has stood the test of more than two and a half centuries since it reached completed form, to be hustled out of existence in a few months, during the desperate distractions of a great war, by a handful of enthusiasts, who really have little title beyond their enthusiasm to put hand to the task? It is unfair to the Church of England; it is outrageously unjust to the English people.

. . . If it be the case that the nation desires to reconsider the

ecclesiastical settlement, which has served it so long, but which
is now so violently decried, then, I beg to submit, the constitutional procedure should be followed. After the war a
Royal Commission should be appointed to review the relations
of Church and State, to examine the present application and
distribution of the ancient religious endowments, to ascertain
the wishes and grievances of the parishioners, and to formulate
recommendations which could be considered with the deliberation due to the importance of the national and ecclesiastical
interests at stake. But until the war is over, and we can address
ourselves to the work without that fearful distraction, it is
worse than frivolous to start movements of the kind indicated
in the letter to which I have referred.

I am, Sir,
Your obedient servant,
H. Hensley Henson.

To this vigorous letter, written with less than Henson's usual
accuracy, Temple found no difficulty in replying. In three
particulars, he pointed out in *The Times*, the Dean had blundered.
The aim of the Movement was not disestablishment, but self-
government. The 'handful of enthusiasts who really have little
title beyond their enthusiasm to put hand to the task' included
the Master of Balliol, the Headmaster of Rugby, the Principal of
Cuddesdon, four past or present Heads of Theological Colleges,
a Regius Professor of Divinity, members of cathedral bodies,
Fellows of Colleges, and many of the most experienced and
responsible parish priests in England. Finally, what the Movement was seeking was not liberty *in* the Church, but liberty *for*
the Church—'The two are plainly distinct; both are precious,
but they are not the same.'

On the evening of 16 July the inaugural meeting was held.
In the artistes' room at Queen's Hall, Henry Scott Holland led
the prayers of those who were to sit on the platform—saying the
Lord's Prayer faster than it can ever have been said before or
since—and from the moment they took their seats the leaders of
the Movement knew that they would receive their mandate to go

forward. It was a summer evening in war-time, the meeting had been called at short notice with practically no advance advertisement, still less any publicity campaign; yet the Hall was packed with an audience more obviously expectant and more quietly determined than any which the most hardened frequenter of religious meetings could remember. There was none of the fidgeting, the preliminary settling down, the rustling of papers, usually noticed in the first few moments of such gatherings: in absolute stillness the prayers were said by the Headmaster of Rugby, and when Temple—still suffering from a gout attack of the night before—began his opening speech from the chair none could have felt more keenly than himself the responsibility that lay on him. His task was not an easy one. It was essential that the precise objects of the Movement should be set out in the plainest language. The Dean of Durham was only one of several who had misrepresented or taken the wrong measure of its purpose, and throughout the Church men were waiting for a statement that would enable them to form a clear and sober judgement. But no statement of aims or exposition of a practical programme would of itself call forth the enthusiasm needed if the Movement was to go forward with a convinced and resolved body of churchpeople behind it. There must also be a call to action, an appeal for dedication and service that would touch the emotions and stir the will. Temple rose magnificently to both demands. He began with quiet confidence and, as the audience heard his clear exposition and his forceful and moving appeal, they knew they were listening to a leader of sure spiritual touch, whose fixity of purpose would remain unshaken by the fiercest opposition. Every intelligent criticism was met. Disestablishment, the Church and State Report, the particular moment which had been chosen for an appeal to the Church to win her freedom 'without delay', the need for some Movement to interest and rouse the vast number of churchpeople who remained entirely unimpressed by resolutions of Convocation or decisions of the episcopal Bench—of all these subjects his treatment was masterly, as he set out the convictions of the Life and Liberty Council and his own with an assurance that convinced the doubters and

William Temple

confirmed the faith of the converted. The appeal with which he closed his speech can have been forgotten by few who heard it:

> The Spirit is calling to the Church of England to-day and is saying: Richly blest, are your blessings become your snare? Is the Catholic tradition that you have received become an excuse for stagnation instead of a spur to redemptive energy? Is the national status given to you allowed to clog your action instead of enabling you more potently to call the nation to God's service? Privileges which are abused are forfeit. Throw off what hampers your service, even though it be venerable with the history of ages or consecrated by dear familiarity. Use these things as aids to service if you can: but if they are only clogs cut them off and cast them from you. The day is come that burns like fire, for Christ has cast His fire on the earth. Come out from your safety and comfort; come out from your habits and conventions. Listen for the voice of the wind as it sweeps over the world and stand where you may be caught in its onward rush. Not now in ecclesiastical debate; not now in the careful defence of established positions won long ago is the service of God's Kingdom to be rendered; but in the establishment of justice between nation and nation, between capital and labour, between men and women. Here is your task. Will you perform it? Or will you stay as you are, to flicker out, a lamp that gives no light, unmourned and even unnoticed? So the Spirit calls. And shall we be deaf to that call? We cannot heed it loyally and effectively unless we have such power of control over our own action as may enable us to become a united and compact striking force, knowing our goal and agreed about the way to reach it. We can only be worthy of our name—the Body of Christ—strong to do His will and supple to adapt our action to the needs of our day, when we have freedom to act as the Spirit guides us. We claim Liberty for the sake of Life!

The other speakers—Miss Maude Royden, the Rev. Walter Carey, R.N., the Rev. Harry Blackburne, A.C.G., and the Rev.

232

H. R. L. Sheppard—all kept the same high level, and the following resolution was put to the meeting:

> That whereas the present conditions under which the Church lives and works constitute an intolerable hindrance to its spiritual activity, this Meeting instructs the Council, as a first step, to approach the Archbishops, in order to urge upon them that they should ascertain without delay, and make known to the Church at large, whether and on what terms Parliament is prepared to give freedom to the Church in the sense of full power to manage its own life, that so it may the better fulfil its duty to God and to the nation and its mission to the world.

The resolution was carried with acclamation; the one member of the audience to raise his hand in dissent was the Dean of Durham. And here a *caveat* must be entered. In his *Life of Randall Davidson*—two comprehensive volumes indispensable to the student of church history for the years they cover—Dr. Bell mentions the Queen's Hall Meeting: 'an enthusiastic meeting was held . . .'; the wording of the resolution is then quoted, and that is all, except for a 'view of the meeting' offered to the Archbishops in a long letter from 'the one dissentient', the Dean of Durham. The enormous mass of material available for Randall Davidson's biography must have made Dr. Bell's task of selection extremely difficult; but the reader would have been left with a less inaccurate impression of what actually took place at the Queen's Hall, of the general atmosphere, of the speeches made and the reception given to them, had all comment been omitted. This would at least have made a more reliable contribution to church history than to select, as the one description of the meeting to survive in the most important ecclesiastical biography of half a century, an account written by the only person (of the two thousand present) who voted against the resolution—an account, moreover, marred by distortions and coloured by prejudice, and utterly at variance with every other contemporary record.

Temple's first duty after the meeting was to inform the Archbishop officially of the resolution and to ask him to receive a deputation from the Movement. The Archbishop consented, and on 1 August the resolution was presented at Lambeth, the spokesmen for the Movement being Temple, the Rev. Cyril Garbett (now Archbishop of York)—who had presided at the overflow meeting in the small Queen's Hall on 16 July—and Albert Mansbridge. Nothing new was said on either side. Randall Davidson repeated that he was glad to see Temple and his friends carrying on the necessary work of educating the Church and country, but that—in reference to the words 'without delay'—he was unwilling to take any further official steps till the Representative Church Council had met. He himself was in favour of the action proposed by the Church and State Committee, and was anxious to go forward with reasonable speed. The Archbishop of York, who had returned that morning from a visit to the troops in France, concurred; adding that he had been much impressed by the interest shown in the matter by chaplains and officers whom he had met in the Forces.

Randall Davidson's mention of the Representative Church Council and the Church and State Committee makes a digression necessary, if the sequence of events (especially the main cause of disagreement between the Archbishop and the Life and Liberty Movement) is to be understood. Early in the century the need was widely felt in the Church for a National Church Council of the Church of England on which bishops, clergy, and laity would sit together to take counsel for, and when necessary declare the common mind of, the Anglican Church. It is a long and involved story: but the outcome was that in 1903 a joint meeting was held of the Upper Houses of Convocation (representing the bishops), the Lower Houses of Convocation (representing the clergy), and the Houses of Laymen, in the two Provinces of Canterbury and York. To one important decision reached by this body return must be made later; the first and main resolution was that 'it is desirable to make provision for the calling together of a Representative Church Council consisting of clergy and laity of the Provinces of Canterbury and York'. This was the Representative Church Council referred to by the Archbishop in his reply to the deputation. In July 1913 this body of 700 persons had passed a resolution asking the Archbishops to appoint a Committee 'to

234

inquire what changes are advisable in order to secure in the relations of Church and State a fuller expression of the spiritual independence of the Church as well as of the national recognition of religion'. This was the Church and State Committee mentioned by the Archbishop: Selborne was its chairman, and it made its report in the summer of 1915. In outline, the Report suggested a method of legislating in church affairs which would avoid the protracted and cumbrous procedure of Parliamentary Bills; it was proposed, instead, that the Representative Church Council should be legally recognized as the body representing the National Church, and should be empowered to pass 'Measures'. These would be scrutinized by an Ecclesiastical Committee of the Privy Council: were the Committee's report unfavourable, a Measure should not be presented for the Royal Assent till both Houses of Parliament had so resolved; were the report favourable, the Measure should be presented for the Royal Assent unless either House of Parliament resolved to the contrary.

It should be noted that, at the time when the Life and Liberty deputation was received at Lambeth, the Report of the Church and State Committee had been published for more than a year. The bishops had given a general assent to the principles embodied in it; a Church Self-Government Association had been formed (with Temple on its committee) in February 1917, to rouse interest in the Report; yet no attempt had been made to summon the Representative Church Council, and it was the need of this Council's approval which the Archbishop emphasized, before he would take any further steps in the direction of self-government for the Church.

The more the Life and Liberty leaders considered their reception at Lambeth, the less hopeful it seemed for their purpose. The Archbishop had shown his customary courtesy in receiving them, and all his suavity and diplomatic skill in replying to their Resolution; he had also assured them that he wished to go forward with all reasonable speed. Here was the difficulty. They need have had little knowledge of Randall Davidson and his methods on the one side, and of the prevailing temper of the Life and Liberty Council on the other, to be sure that their notions of what was 'reasonable'—in speed or in anything else—and the Archbishop's were vastly different. The securing of self-government was going to be a longer process than they had once hoped, but they were determined to catch the tide while it flowed; and it might have begun to ebb before the Representative Church Council saw fit to arrive at a decision. On 1 October, therefore, the Life and Liberty Council went into Retreat and Conference to think out their programme for the coming year. The place chosen was the Theological College at Cuddesdon where, while the students were on vacation, thirty or more persons could be put up: the Principal of the College was a member of the Council. No choice, as it turned out, could have been more unfortunate, for an incident which was at once tragic and ridiculous occupied much of the Council's time on the first day, and the Conference was held under a cloud which overshadowed all its deliberations. Among the prominent members of the Life and Liberty Council was Miss Maude Royden, one of the strongest and most influential personalities of all the religious leaders and teachers of the day. For some weeks she had been preaching regularly at the City Temple, a historic stronghold of Nonconformity, and one Sunday she had there baptized three children. The Principal of Cuddesdon, J. B. Seaton (later Bishop of Wakefield), decided that in view of this he could not allow Miss Royden to sleep under the college roof, and wrote (a few days before the Conference) to tell her so. Miss Royden pointed out, in reply to the Principal, that as a member of the Council she had a definite right to attend and that, if she were prevented from doing so, its proceedings would be invalid. She wrote in the same sense to Temple as chairman, and this was the position when the Council held its first meeting. Many of the leaders of the Movement were in a state of suppressed fury which was not allayed when Seaton had finished his statement, even though he was prepared to make one concession in Miss Royden's favour: he would permit her to attend the Conference, but he must insist that she should sleep elsewhere. A pollution so oddly circumscribed, which apparently did not extend to counsel or board but involved bed only—Miss Royden was presumably to be driven backwards and forwards between an Oxford lodging-house and Cuddesdon each day, perhaps in a closed cab—struck most of the Council as ludicrous; but it was the utmost that Seaton would concede, and somebody had to be deputed to convey the Principal's views to Miss Royden. The angriest man in the room—after he had been allowed to state exactly how he would treat such a message if he were Miss Royden—consented to act, and found her giving a baby which was under her charge its bottle, in a room opposite the east end of Poplar parish church. With a grace which the messenger will always remember, she agreed to come down to Cuddesdon and meet the Council. Temple asked her to put her point of view to the meeting, which she did with dignity and courtesy, expressing at the same time her willingness to resign her membership of the Council if this was their desire. The Principal again made his offer, throwing out a hint that he might be prepared to think differently if Miss Royden had no intention of repeating her offence. Miss Royden was unwilling to concede the point and again asked leave to resign her place on the Council. A taxi was ordered; the tainted lady returned to Poplar; and the incident was closed—but it had left an extremely unpleasant taste in the mouths of the Council. Temple, as chairman, was not in an easy position. He could understand Seaton's difficulties: Cuddesdon was a college with a definite High Church tradition, and its Principal might consider himself bound to take into account the effect on its reputation—and on the influx of an adequate supply of ordinands—of what in the Cuddesdon view would be regarded as the ecclesiastical irregularities of Miss Royden. There was no doubt where Temple's personal sympathies lay, and he was much distressed to lose so valuable a member from the Council; but he could not help remembering that they were the guests of the Principal, and he was reluctant to exert a pressure on Seaton that could end only in the break-up of the Conference. To the more revolutionary members of the Council the whole incident gave a severe and perhaps salutary shock; for they learned at the Cuddesdon Conference how long was the row that had still to be hoed by reformers, and how far removed was the 'official' approach to church problems from the outlook which they had taken for granted in any who professed a working belief in 'Life' and in 'Liberty'.

Of all the arrangements made for the future of the Movement, one decision taken by Temple himself was by far the most important. Work at the London office had been steadily increasing; there was almost a danger of it getting out of hand. Demands for meetings and speeches were insistent, especially from the large towns in the provinces where only the best speakers would be welcomed; but the leaders had other work with the first claim on their time, to combine with what they could do for the Movement. Was there any hope that one of them would resign his permanent post and give himself wholly to be the apostle of Life and Liberty throughout the country? Only two were of the calibre for this, and Sheppard was doing a work at S. Martin's that depended much on his own personality and methods; nor was it at all certain that either his health or his temperament would stand up to the kind of programme the Council had in mind for its ambassador. Was it conceivable that Temple might be willing to give up his living at S. James's, and devote himself entirely to the Movement? At first the idea was put aside as not seeming to make the demand exactly suited to his great and particular gifts. But it recurred: and at last it was thought reasonable that he should be sounded. Three of his friends in the Movement called one morning at S. James's Rectory. The talk was to be quite unofficial—but Temple knew at once that he had come to a turning-point in his career.

Worldly prudence and ordinary human feeling pointed in the same direction. Temple was now thirty-six years old. He had a living of more than £2,000 a year; he was bound by close ties of affection to his parish, his church, and his staff; and his best work at S. James's was, almost certainly, to come. He was beginning to gather round him a thoughtful and sympathetic congregation, to whom he could speak from his pulpit with the freedom enjoyed only by a preacher who knows that he is both appreciated and understood. On the return of normal times he would have spare hours and days for his writing, and for helping the many societies and organizations that looked to him for guidance. He was

already at the centre of church affairs, frequently consulted by
the Archbishop, and able (since his election as a Proctor) to make
his voice heard in Convocation. The commission he was asked
to undertake for the Movement was a temporary one; at the end
of two years he might find himself with no definite work, and
longing for the post he had given up. Moreover, he had been
married for only fifteen months and his wife had made for him
the ordered home-life he loved and needed. Was he justified in
asking her, already, to start a new home—where, he had no idea
—on little more than a third of the income he was now receiving?
It was a strong case.

On the other side were the dire need of the Church and his own
wish to give himself, in complete surrender, to its service. The
sacrifice hourly offered by men in the Forces was not being
matched at home, least of all by the Church's leaders. But most of
these were elderly men, whose lives were set—and set hard. To
scarcely one of them was the 'incongruity of palaces and large
incomes' at this moment in their country's history so immediately
and distastefully obvious as it was to the men in the trenches and
on the high seas. But Temple was of the age of the fighting men
—he at least could see a picture of the Church through their eyes
—and he sat more loosely to the world. Did he think back to his
own constant appeals for sacrifice to those who had stayed at
home? To the sermon he had preached in his own church on his
return from America? And, above all, to that memorable night
at the Queen's Hall and the message of the Spirit to the Church
that he had then declared: 'Come out of your safety and comfort
. . . listen to the voice of the wind as it sweeps over the world,
and stand where you may be caught in its onward rush'?

Rain was falling as the three friends left S. James's Rectory.
Two of them put up their umbrellas—for nothing less violent
than a cloudburst would Sheppard have unrolled his—and this,
with the noise of traffic in Piccadilly, made conversation difficult
before each went his way. Not that there was very much to be
said. To discuss what Temple's answer to their appeal was likely
to be would have seemed almost indecent. He had shown, as he
stood on his study hearth-rug that morning, few outward signs of

distress; but there had been just enough—an occasional contraction of the eyelids which was not quite a wince, and a more than usually deliberate twiddling of his silver watch-chain with the two first fingers of his right hand—to suggest to them what they now knew to be true, that they had put one of the best men in England on the rack and left him there. The moment of decision was not long delayed; with Temple it seldom was. A week or so later, during the Council Retreat, Sheppard met Temple and his wife as they were crossing the churchyard at Cuddesdon and gave him the official invitation—'Who but Dick', Mrs. Temple laughingly remarked afterwards, 'would have chosen such a spot for it?'—and before the Retreat broke up Temple was ready with his answer.

In the judgement of worldly-wise prelates and by the trivial standards of scheming men the whole project was quixotic, if not preposterous. But—beyond question or dispute—*sub specie aeternitatis* there was no greater moment in Temple's life.

XV

The Two Leaders

The conception of our leaders that the function of a leader is primarily to keep us all together seems to me disastrous. Is the summons to real adventure to come from those to whom we are looking for guidance or not?

W. T., letter to the Press, December 1917.

TEMPLE began his new work cheered by just the kind of encouragement that meant most to him. Some of it came from those church leaders whom he knew to be heart and soul with him in the Movement. On 16 December Scott Holland wrote from Christ Church:

You will not imagine, from my silence, that I have not deeply felt your gallant and singlehearted offer of yourself to the Cause. You have done what we failed to do. You have gone over the top. It does everybody good, God bless you! I am too ill to want to take part in anything. I can best look on: and wait: and pray. Remember me most kindly to your wife.

'Just a line', wrote the Bishop of Lichfield (Kempthorne), 'to say—God bless you in your new venture. It *is* a venture, but if we are learning anything now it is to "launch out into the deep". *Dominus tecum*.'

Gore had already approved. At the end of a letter on other important subjects, he had given this advice to Temple:

. . . Now I come to the great question you ask me. It is very hard to recommend sacrifice of income to other people especially to married people, and still harder to recommend what might damage prospects. You would rightly refuse to consider this, but not your friends, I think. I greatly wish you to be made a bishop, but on the whole I am disposed to think that that would not be affected.

Now as to S. James's;—as far as I can estimate, that is proving itself not so much valuable in itself, but rather as a basis for going about: so that in itself the sacrifice of the position

R

241

from the point of view of the Church would not be so very great. On the other hand I think that the surrender of such a position by such a man as you in order to propagate L. & L. would be impressive and would catch the imagination, and that the work that you would do would be immensely valuable. So, though I do not venture to urge or even to recommend, I do say that if I heard it were done I should justify and approve, and indeed give thanks.

I can't say more than this, and I am not quite sure that it is not impertinent to say as much. I will pray for a right judgment for you.

Further approval came in letters and messages from his colleagues on the Council, who knew that a fresh inspiration would be given to Life and Liberty by Temple's decision. Members of the Movement and unknown correspondents from all parts of the country wrote to thank him for the value of his example to the Church; it had, as Gore had prophesied, caught the imagination of those who heard of it and had provided a partial answer to the Church's critics. But no word had yet come from Lambeth, and Temple's affection and admiration for the Archbishop—he had never forgotten the wise sympathy of Randall Davidson's guidance at the time of his ordination—were so strong that he longed for a clear word of approval and goodwill. On the first day of November the letter came:

You will know that I realize to the full the vast importance of what you have decided, and you will be yet more certain that I wish you from the bottom of my heart every possible blessing and guidance in the new work to which you have set your hand. I call it new, but it is not new to you, for you have already been hard at work. If you decide on putting out any kind of programme or announcement of what your campaign is going to be, and of what the Americans call its 'platform', I should like to see it at the earliest moment. Further, I should greatly desire full talk with you about it all. If we can possibly work absolutely together at this intensely important time, it will be worth a great deal to me, and I think probably to you also.

There was a lack of warmth in this benediction which few, Temple least of all, could fail to detect. Randall Davidson's affection for him was deep and sincere, and it might be thought that the decision to give up the living of S. James's and all that went with it would have moved the Archbishop to a more appreciative recognition of Temple's sacrifice. But there were two things in the way: first, in Randall Davidson's eyes such an adventure was freakish, if not abnormal—none could have had a greater distaste for abnormality than he—and, second, the plain truth stands out through all his dealings with the Life and Liberty Movement that, certainly till the end of this year, he just could not understand what all the bother was about. Could not—or would not? In a man of the Archbishop's age and antecedents there is little difference between the two. He had reached the time of life when adjustment to new ways is always difficult and usually unpleasant. He had had many difficulties to surmount, many troublesome corners to turn, since he began the work of his Primacy; and his adroit tact, his experience of church administration, and his power of dealing with awkward persons and situations were unrivalled. But the idea of a new *tempo*—this lay at the heart of the difference between himself and the reformers —was intolerable to him, most of all when countless problems arising directly out of the war claimed his constant attention, and when he was beginning already to feel the weight of his years. He had explained to the Life and Liberty deputation all the difficulties that would be involved in the carrying out of their resolution. He had told them the exact order in which he wanted things done. Why could he not be left to work it all out in his own way? The answer is partly given in a letter Temple wrote to his wife from the war-front, about fifteen months later:

The impression left by the Archbishop here was that he was a perfect dear and a master of debate, but that he was facing the wrong way. They wanted him (here at any rate) to say what he wanted to do and to call on them to support him; but he spent his time explaining, very forcibly, how difficult it is to do anything and appealing to them for patience: —— [the

Commander of an Army Corps] who is a great personal friend of his, said of him: 'If he were a General, we should say he was tired and send him home.' They loved him; but they were disappointed.

The Archbishop's best word to Temple was yet to come; but not before issue had been joined over the main point on which the two were at variance. It was now November 1917, and ever since the Council Retreat at Cuddesdon the leaders of Life and Liberty had been waiting anxiously for the meeting of the Representative Church Council which was to consider the Report of the Archbishops' Committee on Church and State. There were prospects of a clear majority in favour of the Report and, if this were given, there would be little excuse for any further delay in seeking church self-government from Parliament. The Archbishop had declined to go forward till the views of the Representative Church Council were known, and expectations ran high that the last barrier to an advance would be now removed. When, however, the Council met a straight vote was not taken; it was decided to do no more than appoint a Committee 'to consider . . .'—but the story is best told in the words of the letter which Temple sent to the Press on behalf of the Life and Liberty Council; it expresses accurately the exasperation felt at this fresh excuse for delay:

> The Council of the Life and Liberty Movement met on December 4, and after consideration of the recent meeting of the Representative Church Council it was decided to issue this letter.
> The Representative Church Council has decided to ask for the appointment of a committee to consider the whole subject raised by the Report of the Archbishops' Committee on Church and State, and, if it thinks well, to draft a scheme on which future action may be taken. The fact that it was empowered to do this proves that the result of the meeting was by no means a triumph for the reactionaries. Nevertheless, seeing that the Report has been before the Church for eighteen months and more, we can hardly think we were over-optimistic

in hoping that a straight vote might have been taken on the broad issue and an advance made in the light of it. We wish the Council had insisted on making its judgment known. But no judgment was expressed: there is to be further delay. Nothing in the way of actual reform is now likely to be set on foot for months and possibly even for years, and this in spite of the fact that an overwhelming majority of the Church's members in the Army and Navy are almost in despair because we will not adventure. All this is to impose a grievous strain on the loyalty of many who believe passionately in the Church, not as she now is, but as she has the power to become. . . . In this hour of the utmost peril not only to Churchmanship but to Christianity, is it the business of our leaders to accompany the majority down the path it elects to travel? Bishops did indeed deprecate delay until the return of peace. We know that in their own hopes they are in advance of the general body of the Church. In Convocation they have formally approved the general policy of the Report. Why, then, do they not test their power to rally Churchmen to the support of their forward policy?

We seem to be involved in a vicious circle. The leaders wait till the Church as a whole desires to follow: but the Church as a whole gives little heed to the matter because no call to advance is given. Those in high office have unique opportunities of knowing in what direction our failures lie, and what is at the root of our comparative inefficiency. They know which of our systems are unworkable, and which of our Church societies are useless, and need no longer be lashed into a mild activity. They know what the next move ought to be. If, for instance, self-government for the Church ought to be our immediate objective in order that large things may be achieved, is it necessary to summon us yet again to deliberate? May we not be called to fight for it now, and may we not be given an opportunity of playing our part and rallying around our leaders?

We have waited long enough. We have attempted to offend no one. To this end we have met together always to deliberate and never to act.

We are weary of perpetual deliberations. A disturbance would be better than a continuance of inactivity. Need we calculate much longer? We are clear that the Church just now has her greatest and possibly her last opportunity of vindicating her Catholic and national character. But this can only be achieved by a struggle fierce and sustained, by a purging thorough and sincere, and by a summons such as many had hoped might be issued during these days of war to dare anything, that the Will of God might be done, as in Heaven, so on earth.

We need hardly say that we do not consider that the millennium will be produced merely by better machinery; but we maintain that the new spirit needs new channels through which to express itself.

In conclusion, we consider it necessary to protest against the plea of the obstructionists that no forward move should be made during the war while so many Churchmen are serving their country at the Front. Is there any other section of our society which is acting on this principle? Thousands of Trade Unionists and many of the keenest supporters of the Labour Party are at this moment in the trenches: yet the Labour Party has already begun its work of reconstruction and has actually worked out an entirely new constitution. Many of the keenest and the most capable of the younger school-teachers and educationists are at the Front, yet their absence has not delayed the bringing in of an Education Bill which a few years ago would have seemed almost revolutionary.

In one field of social life after another reforms are being pressed forward with the utmost enthusiasm; and are we to be told that the one body which is to wait the advent of peace before setting its house in order is the Church of the Living God? That the Church is ready to follow a strong lead our Movement exists to show.

Signed on behalf of the Council,
W. TEMPLE, Chairman.

Temple had written to the Archbishop, warning him that a letter was on its way to the Press which might wound him, but adding that the Life and Liberty Council felt bound to make public its distress at the decision of the Representative Church Council. The disappointment was felt as acutely by Temple himself as by any of his colleagues in the Movement. The wording of the letter was, obviously, not entirely Temple's own—more than one hand had itched to have a share in it—but most of it was actually written by him, and for every word of it he was prepared to accept full responsibility. There was little more in the letter about the Lambeth conception of leadership than the Archbishop himself had admitted to the Life and Liberty deputation at the beginning of the year, and the last two paragraphs answered in advance the Archbishop's contention that the time was inappropriate for attempting to secure attention to Church matters. Randall Davidson's reply was sent as soon as the letter appeared in the Press:

I waited until to-day in order that I might read your letter in the Press before replying to what you have privately written to me. I had a letter also from Mrs. Creighton, who I think feels a little uncomfortable about the published letter, as of course will some others of your body: indeed some of them are communicating with me to that effect.

I am not I think apt to be over-sensitive or thin-skinned in matters of this sort, or to seek to evade a criticism which, however rough, may be most useful. But of course you are right when you say or imply in your private letter that by what is now published my own personal difficulties are greatly augmented. That is a comparatively small matter unless it hinders the cause which I, like you, have at heart. This I fear it may do, but I shall endeavour to prevent it as far as possible. There is nothing in the letter which could be called violent or rude. Pray feel quite relieved on that score.

I am looking forward keenly to the outcome of your missionary effort to awaken the sense of Churchmen generally to the need of changes. I am certain that in that policy you are right. It is what specially needs doing at present, and it is just what can at present be done. Where I think that you and

others are mistaken is in your belief that we could with advantage
to the cause of wise reform take steps at the present moment
for propounding schemes in Parliament or committing thoughtful people who care about the Church's life to a particular and
detailed policy. I am mixing for hours on most days in the
week with the men prominent in our public life on whose aid
we should have to rely if the changes we want were to be made,
and I do not literally know one of them who would share your
view as to the practicability of the forward push in an official
way at the present moment when every thought and every
ounce of energy is absorbed in England's struggle for its very
life. This makes me absolutely certain that I have been right in
advocating or insisting upon the necessity of our eschewing a
policy of hustle and push in matters ecclesiastical during these
months of daily and nightly strain upon the thoughts and time
of every public man who is worthy of the name. I should like
to talk this over with you soon, and I will try, telephonically or
otherwise, to fix with you some day and hour.

Would you, that I may privately have as much knowledge
as possible about the whole facts, tell me what was roughly the
number of people of your Council who advocated the publication of this letter as it stands?

If the publication of your letter has the effect of stiffening
convertible people into unconvertibleness by the irritation it
causes, I shall feel that the responsibility is not mine, and, as I
have told you, I shall try to prevent it. Of course it is a distress
to me that things should be said which will I think be the
reverse of helpful in the direction we all desire. I honestly fear
that it may have that effect, and that, after all, is what matters.

Nothing in his work for Life and Liberty distressed Temple
more than to be at variance with the Archbishop, but he had no
alternative; for the decision of the Representative Church Council
meant that, probably for a year, no further step would be taken at
Lambeth. At the same time he knew how much depended on his
success in rousing church feeling throughout the country on the
need of securing self-government 'without delay'; and at least he

could go forward with his own mission. 'When are you going to begin your campaign?' he was asked soon after the Council Retreat at Cuddesdon: 'I have begun already', he replied, 'I have bought a Bradshaw.' (This was one of his favourite books: ever since the Oxford days, when he took a peculiar interest in working out complicated cross-country journeys by which his friends could join him in the Lakes, he always found pleasure in hunting up trains and discovering unusual changes and connexions; and at Repton, instead of the usual copying of lines for an imposition, he would occasionally give the culprit several elaborate railway journeys to work out with a Bradshaw.) He was planning to spend most of each week in the provinces; but he tried to keep Mondays free for the *Challenge,* and there were a few other commitments which he felt had a just claim on his time. The most important of these was the W.E.A.; when its Council met in the early autumn of 1917 he found it hard work to persuade them to be at all enthusiastic in their support of H. A. L. Fisher: '. . . they are going to be rather like the Russian Soviet. But they will at any rate not oppose the Bill as the total abstainers opposed (and killed) Lord Aberdare's great Temperance Measure in the '90s. And that is the one thing that will be disastrous.'

During the last two months of the year Mrs. Temple had been house-hunting in London. While Temple was considering whether or not to leave S. James's she had been wisely neutral; cost what it might for both of them, she felt that the decision must be his. But, when his mind was made up, she faced bravely the inconveniences of moving house in war-time, and the continuous separations that his work was bound to involve. Eventually she found a small house (20, Melbury Road) in West Kensington: 'Now', Temple wrote, 'I can begin to picture our life in the future again, and it makes just all the difference.' When they had settled in he celebrated the Holy Communion each week at S. Mary Abbots, Kensington, where he rejoiced to find one of his old Queen's pupils, Cyril Hudson, on the staff. Here he adapted himself, as his custom was, to the ways of the church. He preferred not to wear vestments, but was always ready to do so if it was usual at any church where he officiated. Hudson and other

members of the staff gave him careful instructions how the vestments should be put on—which amused him a good deal—and
at every Anglo-Catholic church that he visited he did and wore
all the right things with an agreeable conformity.

So the New Year began; and before its first month was over
the letter which he had longed for came from Lambeth:

January 26, 1918.

. . . May I take this opportunity of saying a word or two about
the work that lies before you? I think it quite possible that you
may feel as though I had been a little lacking in warmth and
enthusiasm about your project and the self-devotion you have
shown in putting your hand to its plough. The fact is that I
have been chary of saying anything which could be taken as
meaning that, having thought it all over, I was clear that the
call of duty for you was the giving up of S. James's, and the
donning of new harness. I could not satisfy myself on that
point, chiefly because I honestly have not a clear enough vision
of what the new work is going to be to enable me to weigh it in
relative importance against the work which you are laying
down. Now, however, that the rubicon is crossed, and you are
in harness for the great enterprise of teaching the Church the
full meaning of life and liberty, I have no qualms about wishing
you, with all my heart, God speed. We have all asked that you
might be guided aright and it would be faithless to doubt that
our prayers have been answered. I am absolutely sure of the
importance, at this juncture in our Church's life, of men, who
possess true enthusiasm, and the power of enthusing others,
being relieved from the local bonds of parish work, and free to
move about with an easy conscience, and to make and use
opportunities in all sorts of centres up and down the land.
Whatever colour our actual message may take, it is, after all,
one and the same—it is the message of the Gospel of Jesus
Christ to the souls of men; a message delivered and received
and acted upon as part of our corporate life. That life must be
made to glow, and we must do it with the liberty wherewith
Christ has made us free.

It is thus that I understand the watchword of 'Life and Liberty'. God has endowed you with exceptional gifts for such a task. He will show us the opportunities as they arise, will help us to create new opportunities for ourselves and for those for whom He sends us. You take up this task at a moment of quite unique importance in the history of the Church and of the world. You do it just at that epoch in your own life when a man's powers should be at their very best. You have an equipment, both in varied experience and in varied powers, which justify our high hopes. God grant that you may utilize them all to the bettering of the Church's life, and, through the Church, of the world's life.

I shall be constantly anxious to hear how things shape themselves, and if you feel that counsel from me is wanting, or would be useful, you must not scruple to ask for it. On the other hand, I do not want you to feel hampered by an endeavour, which would be quite in vain, to look at the problems of to-day through the eyes of an old man like myself, rather than through your own eyes, as God shall enlighten them. None the less, I do believe that old men have a contribution to make to the solution of new problems, something which comes out of long experience, if it has been used with reasonable receptiveness. I hope I have never been unready to believe in the new light which new men receive when old men are encompassed by problems unfamiliar to them in former days. I shall want to help you in every way that I possibly can, both for the Church's sake, for your father's sake, and for your own.

I am, Ever yours affecly,
RANDALL CANTUAR.

Stormy days lay ahead, and the high regard in which the old and the young leader held each other was to be severely tested. But Temple's gratitude for this letter lost no degree of its warmth in the strenuous controversy that followed, nor did the Archbishop thereafter allow any passing difference of outlook or intention to loosen the sacred ties by which he was bound in closest intimacy to the son of his old and revered friend.

XVI

'Without Delay'

The Movement is really going very strong, and, whether or not we get exactly what we set out for, we shall have made a stir in the Church of a most salutary kind. In particular the unity between entirely different schools of thought has been a great feature of our Movement, and full of promise for the future if only representatives of the different schools can be brought together, as we bring them together, not to argue about their differences but to help forward a definite bit of work. Then they all find the need of one another, and how their differences are not antagonistic but complementary.

W. T., letter to his brother, August 1918.

DURING the first three months of 1918, workers at the Life and Liberty headquarters had ample evidence that the Movement was taking root in the Church; and they became at the same time increasingly conscious of a stirring of interest outside the ranks of those whom their message might be expected to reach. The impact being made on the clergy and the more active members of their congregations was obvious enough from the church and secular Press as Temple went from one centre to another and received an enthusiastic welcome from almost all his audiences, with full notice in the provincial newspapers. But in the early months of the year laymen of a new type became attracted to the Movement. Several had had business experiences during the war which left them more than a little uneasy about the general tone of public life and affairs, and were ready to take an active part in any corporate effort to emphasize the fundamental decencies of social and commercial life. Most of them held no very high doctrine of the Church or, at least on their first attachment to the Movement, of its divine mission; but they saw in it an institution which above all others should provide a rallying-point for men and women of 'an honest and good heart', with a certain traditional authority to proclaim the high principles from which the country seemed at that time to be falling. To link up this moral enthusiasm with the cause of church self-government was a slow process—it needed some imagination in the idealistic layman to deduce a conception of the Church as it might be from the all-too-clear picture of the Church as it was—but gradually a number of influential lay members were drawn in who subscribed generously to the funds of the Movement, served on its committees, persuaded their friends to join, and on the whole bore patiently with what they regarded as the singular enthusiasms of the more ecclesiastically minded members. Church 'parties' were to most of them either unintelligible or irrelevant. They could see nothing worthy either of surprise or congratulation in the fact that at a Council Conference Francis Underhill would celebrate the Holy Communion one morning robed in the eucharistic vestments, and on the next day Gough McCormick would take the same service dangling a black stole over his surplice: it was the general social policy of the Movement that attracted them and gave intelligible expression to some at least of their ideals. A difference of emphasis between certain sections of the Movement's supporters on the various items in the Life and Liberty programme was bound to emerge later, but in 1918 church self-government as the first vantage-point to be seized 'without delay' was accepted by the whole membership.

To give a complete account of Temple's campaign in the country would be merely to rewrite the same time-table several dozen times. The details varied little. There would be informal talks with church leaders in the area and with men of influence in local affairs whose sympathy it was desirable to win; usually a mass meeting in the evening, followed on the next morning by discussion with the clergy either in Ruridecanal Chapter or smaller groups; then more personal talks, and the train to the next centre —or back to London for a night to hold consultations at the office, or to preside over a meeting of the Council. In the first nine months of the year he had visited (among many other places) Manchester, Huddersfield, Great Yarmouth, Bradford, Walsall, Lichfield, Birmingham, Liverpool (where Chancellor Dowdall publicly signed the membership form before leaving the Chair), Grimsby, Louth, and Cambridge. The following are

typical of the accounts of his doings which he posted regularly
to his wife:

> 8 Park Terrace,
> Cambridge.
>
> February 10, 1918.

... I had a very comfortable journey, and then went round,
after leaving my bags here, to dine with Carpenter at Selwyn....
That was over about 8.0, and we talked in Combination Room
(what in the more modest and decent language of the parent
University is called Common Room) till about 9.15. All very
pleasant. ... Then I spent about ½ an hour with Carpenter in
his rooms, after which I started for home and got to work on
the sermon [a University Sermon] at 10.15, and finished it off
at 12.15. I got some splendid quotations from Traherne ...
and then bed. This morning I worked over what I had written
last night and polished the style here and there (it is not very
perfect still, I am afraid), and then set out for Carpenter's
church, where I was to preach at the 'Sung Mass' at 11.0. The
Churchwardens . . . were most enthusiastic about Life and
Liberty.

When I got back I found Archdeacon Cunningham awaiting
me. We had a jolly talk for about 40 minutes. He is very keen
on administrative reforms, but not keen for legislative ones.
What he chiefly wants is for every parish priest to have a very
large amount of liberty and the responsibility that goes with
it. I told him I agreed, except that I want him to have to consult his people, and that to get what *he* wants legislation is
necessary.

> The Vicarage,
> Huddersfield.
>
> February 27, 1918.

... It was quite a good journey. I got to bed, well filled with
cake and cocoa, at 11.30. This morning at breakfast there were
6 Non-Conformist Ministers; capital fellows; 2 of them are
going to the joint retreat of the Fellowship after Easter. At
10.30 we had the Rural Deanery Chapter. Lots of parsons;

and all I think rather keen. One said, 'We feel hopeless; we all want these things. But we can't do anything. Our leaders must move first; we are all behind them.' So of course I told him the leaders didn't know this and had to be told, and the way to tell them was to join L. & L. and get others to join.

Birch Rectory,
Manchester.

March 15, 1918.

. . . The meetings here have been good and useful; no attempt at a public splash, but a lot of really valuable people, and I think they will get under way. Peter Green was useful at the clergy meeting. In the evening the lay meeting led to no comments, except blessings from the Baptist leader here, who, however, took it for granted that in freeing itself the Church would also surrender all privilege belonging to its State connection.

But the best part of all was breakfast this morning, when C. P. Scott, the Editor of the *Manchester Guardian*, came in. He is really delightful. He thinks Disestablishment is the only real solution and that we must at last arrive there. But he thinks a period of Self-government and Parliamentary veto would be an excellent preparation, without which Disestablishment might involve disruption. I *think* he would be friendly!

The Palace,
Lichfield.

March 20, 1918.

. . . It looks horribly raid-like. I hope you are not being bothered.

I got to Rugby very comfortably. There I had 50 minutes to wait, so I had tea, and then ½ a *Challenge* Leader in the waiting room. The windows had never opened and the gas had leaked for at least 3 months. Also the temperature was about 86° Fahrenheit, so I dare say the article is rather paralytic. Then I got on by a slow train to Birmingham. Then again on to Walsall. There I found the Bishop [Kempthorne], and after supper we went to the meeting—decidedly good. The Bishop was strongly in our favour. We motored straight out here, arriving at 10.30. Coffee, buns, biscuits, and for the Bishop a pipe. At 11.15 we adjourned, and I finished the Leader (so that at least is done). It is now exactly midnight. I am going to try to do the headlines and marginalia of No. IV Committee, and then go to bed.

P.S. 1.40 a.m. But I did not go to bed. I wrote the *Sunday Chronicle* article! Rather a good day's work altogether.

A good day's work indeed! But not of the kind to be too often repeated: yet his letters show that it was not exceptional. Fortunately Temple could sleep at any time, and for any length of time, in the train, which eased the strain a little: but by the middle of the year his wife began to feel anxious, and she was backed up by her mother who wrote in July:

> I dreamt about William: I suppose because I have been so much wishing he would put his foot down and (as you said he had done in one case) refuse to be over-rushed. He won't do the Church any good if he goes and *really* over-works himself. Tell him so, with my love—and that he is *not* to be a martyr to Life and Liberty, but keep well to use the liberty when it comes.

But the chief responsibility rested with the Life and Liberty headquarters, and after a while he was able to write to his brother that he had handed over the making of his engagements to the office, where 'F. A. I. does not seem disposed to fill my time as full as I filled it myself!'

In London, meanwhile, things had been moving—but slowly. The Grand Committee of the Representative Church Council had met under the chairmanship of Dr. Ryle, Dean of Westminster, and on 3 October its Report was published. It now became a race between the dissolution of Parliament—which was sure to take place on the declaration of peace, and after which the Houses of Convocation would cease to exist till the new Parliament was elected—and the consideration of the Report by the Representative Church Council. The time seemed ripe for a second deputation from the Life and Liberty Movement—accompanied, this

time, by a deputation from the Church Self-Government Association—to wait on the Archbishops. Eighty members from the two
bodies faced the Primates in the dining-room at Lambeth and feeling ran high, at least on the side of the deputation. Unfortunately,
in the heat of the moment, one of the speakers blurted out: 'The
trouble with your Graces is, you're both Scotsmen.' How much
the (supposedly) national characteristic of caution had to do with
the extreme deliberation with which the Archbishops had been
acting was perhaps rather too personal a question to raise on such
an occasion; both of them were already feeling far from comfortable, and it may be doubted whether even Samuel Johnson would
have chosen that particular moment to remind them of the land of
their birth. At once the sympathy of many who were present
passed to the Archbishops: but they had both been impressed by
the strength of the deputation and at last Randall Davidson wrote
to Selborne, 'gladly reiterating' his own 'deliberate opinion' that
the proposals of the Church and State Committee were 'sound in
principle', and adding that he earnestly hoped that the Representative Church Council would give a 'marked support' to the scheme.

This Council was accordingly summoned to meet on the last
four days of February. Temple intervened twice in the debate,
his first speech being on a subject which roused his keenest feelings. He had written to his wife during the session of the Grand
Committee in 1918, lamenting that 'the Committee has adhered
to its vile decision about women', and this debate on the place of
women in the Councils of the Church was to be critical. Temple
and others were determined to win for them the right to sit in
the Church Assembly. On behalf of the Grand Committee the
Dean of Westminster moved that 'all representatives may be of
either sex, except in the case of the Assembly, in which they must
be of the male sex', and the Bishop of Lichfield (Kempthorne)
moved an amendment to delete all except the first seven words.
In seconding the amendment, Temple pleaded that the Council
should consider the psychological situation in which they found
themselves at that moment. He confessed he was one of those
who, in the judgement of Dr. Henson, had invested the whole
matter with 'a false urgency': decisive action taken now by the

Church might have far-reaching results, while the same action taken later might be found to have missed a great opportunity. Of nothing was this more true than of their attitude towards admitting women into the Church Assembly. Not only had the whole national outlook on the general position of women in public life undergone a revolutionary change: younger women were drifting away from the Church, largely (he contended) because so little responsibility attached to the few minor posts open to them. The spread of education had increased the desire of women to be admitted to positions of importance in public life, so that the matter was now one of real urgency. Whatever could be said against women sitting on a Synod was irrelevant, for elaborate pains had been taken, ever since the inception of the scheme, to emphasize the fact that the Church Assembly would not be a 'Synod' in any sense of the word. The point, rather, was whether the Church was going to recognize women as being in a full sense members of the laity. In many parishes women were the mainstay of the devotional life of the Church; decisions taken by the Assembly would greatly affect that life; and it was reasonable to demand that those who were to be governed should have a voice in making the laws. Moreover, he looked forward to the time when the Assembly should speak for the Church with moral authority, and in every moral issue—whether it were religious education, the relation of the sexes, or problems of industry—the advice of women was in the highest degree desirable, more particularly as regret was widespread that in some industries during the war women had not secured their full rights. Temple's speech greatly helped to convince the 'considerable majority' by which the amendment was accepted.

The other subject—a technical but important one—on which he spoke was the Church franchise. The constitution of the Church Assembly and the subordinate Councils involved the election of representatives to serve on them. An election implies a body of electors—and who should these be? What exact qualification should be laid down for church voters? For some time past this question had been discussed at church meetings and in the church Press. There were three possible answers.

Electors should be 'communicants' of the Church. In theory this may have been the true answer. If a churchman was so little interested in the worship of his Church, so neglectful of his own contribution to its spiritual life, as to refrain from partaking in the most solemn and fundamental act of Christian fellowship, could he reasonably claim a share in electing the members of the Church's Assemblies? But, in practice, some more precise definition would be needed; for what exactly constituted a communicant? The Book of Common Prayer lays down that every communicant shall receive the Holy Communion at least three times in the year; yet could not one who received the Communion once a year (on Easter Day, for instance) declare himself a communicant? The test was clearly a difficult one to apply; and there remained the qualification of Confirmation or Baptism. Those who favoured the Confirmation franchise argued that the privilege of voting should not be granted to any who, from lack of conviction or courage or from any other motive, declined to accept the pre-requisite for receiving Communion laid down in the Prayer Book rubric. On the other hand, Confirmation, in spite of its frequent misinterpretation by novelists—was not Arthur Kipps described as having been 'confirmed a member of the Church of England'? —has nothing to do with church membership. The answer to the second question in the Church Catechism leaves no doubt who are members of the Church; in short, the Baptismal franchise seemed to be the only one that stood the test both of theological truth and practical convenience in application.

The debate on the franchise in the Representative Church Council reached a high level. The proposal of the Church and State Committee had been that qualified electors (of either sex) must be of full age, and must either be actual communicants or have been baptized and confirmed and admissible to Holy Communion. Some of the most trusted leaders in the Church—including the Bishop of Oxford (Gore), Selborne, and Lord Hugh Cecil (now Lord Quickswood)—were in favour of a Confirmation franchise. Temple, when he was invited to speak by the Archbishop, felt bound to say a word about the views of the Life and Liberty Movement as well as his own. Both had been much misunderstood, and he began by insisting that none of his colleagues in the Movement was a 'protagonist' for any one franchise against the others. The Life and Liberty Council had, as a fact, adopted the Baptismal franchise by a large majority; but they had never made acquiescence in that decision a requirement for membership, and every member of the Movement was fully entitled to give public expression to his dissent. There were weighty arguments on the one side, but he ranged himself definitely with those who advocated the Baptismal franchise. Why, he asked, was a person who had been confirmed and failed to attend Communion more entitled to vote than one who had failed to be presented for Confirmation? Nor was Confirmation a test that operated evenly throughout the Church: in a public school it required a certain amount of courage to refuse to be confirmed; for a member of the working class it required a good deal of courage to come forward. Lastly, there was no denying the truth that all baptized persons were members of the Church and in those days, if persons were excluded from voting, they would feel excluded altogether from membership. The speech was carefully reasoned, and well received. The Baptismal franchise was accepted—to the great distress of several, among whom was Gore. In sending a letter to the Archbishop resigning the see of Oxford, he wrote that, though it was not his main motive in giving up the bishopric, 'the choice of the moment is partly due to the decision of the Representative Church Council about the franchise'. Temple was genuinely grieved at his difference of opinion from Gore, who— as he had said in his speech—had done more than anyone on the Council for the cause of church self-government.

In a mood of elation that will be readily understood Temple wrote, a few days later, to his brother:

> Cathedral Rectory,
> Birmingham.
> March 5, 1919.

I am here for three days of 'Dinner Hour Addresses' on Life and Liberty in the Cathedral. Also there is a Town Hall meeting to-morrow night.

Our whole scheme was adopted in precisely our form by the Representative Church Council last week. The Archbishop was quite splendid. He struck in on the first day with a statement of the difficulties of the existing situation and of his conviction that it was right to go ahead, which abolished any opposition that there may have been. His chairmanship was admirable. When we came to the final vote, only one hand was held up against the proposal—that was the Bishop of Hereford, Henson's. Now the Archbishop is, I believe, ready to introduce the Enabling Bill this summer. We had feared that this long session of the Council would not be enough for all the amendments, and that we should still have our scheme lacking the official endorsement of the Church. But it is all right— and a tremendous mercy.

I have (apparently) been elected Master of University College, Durham. I say 'apparently' because the official notification is not yet come. I do not at present think it could be right to go there: but it is jolly of them to wish it!

From the day that Temple made up his mind to leave Repton, he had received many offers of work. The one he came nearest to accepting was the first—the Principalship of S. John's College, Agra—and he had already decided to undertake it when he was stopped almost peremptorily by Randall Davidson: the Archbishop felt that Temple's contacts with the Labour Movement and the W.E.A. made it imperative that he should stay in England for the home Church to reap the benefits of his unique experience. In 1916 he was approached by the Bishop of Newcastle on the possibility of his becoming Vicar of Newcastle; but Gore's advice was so definitely against it that he decided to refuse. In the same year the Prime Minister offered him—during the time when he was engaged to be married—the Canonry of Westminster which had become vacant through the death of Archdeacon Wilberforce. Attached to this Canonry was the incumbency of S. John's, Westminster, a large and poor parish; Temple had no hesitation in refusing work for which he had had no training, and the only post he accepted during his time at S. James's was that of Honorary

Chaplain to the King. But when, early in 1919, he decided to give up his embassage for Life and Liberty at the end of July, the question of future work became pressing, and he was bound to consider seriously all opportunities which seemed in any degree suited to his experience and his gifts. The next step might settle his future career once and for all—in the main, the choice lay between Church and University. Two academic posts were offered to him in the first six months of the year; one was that mentioned in the letter to his brother. The Council of the Durham Colleges had to appoint a new Master of University College, and Professor Jevons was bidden to approach Temple. There were many attractive features in the proposal. The work would lie with young men; it would be in the North, where he could keep in close touch with the Labour leaders on the Tyne; and there would be leisure for reading and writing. The Archbishop was out of England at the time but, on his return, advised strongly against it. Hadow, the Vice-Chancellor, wrote to tell Temple how gladly he would welcome him, while admitting that acceptance would involve 'a change of aim and a small field'; and Gore gave his advice in a letter which reflected his pessimistic outlook in the early months of 1919:

> Cuddesdon,
> Wheatley,
> Oxon.
>
> Jan. 11. 19.
>
> My dear Temple,
>
> I do not think Univ. College Durham thrills me.
>
> I had much sooner see you Canon of Westminster. I wish that could be managed. But I am no use with the P.M. However it is worth trying. There is sure to be a longish delay, I dare say. No, I can't say Durham excites me. I only know vaguely about it. I don't say *no*. Only I don't rise. Mansbridge is coming tonight. I will venture to ask him.
>
> Now I want to ask you a question about myself. Should you think me wrong, if I were to resign this Bpric with a view to retiring probably to London or near it to read and write and preach? It may be vanity, but I greatly want to write a biggish book before I die about fundamentals. Also I am disheartened

as Episcopacy is only 'carrying on'. I have almost made up my mind to resign. It is partly that Broad and High and Low and Conservative are all against me. So I stick. Also I'd like to join the Labour Party.

Yr. affly.

C. OXON:

On 4 March Temple received the official intimation that he had been 'nominated to the Chancellor of the University for appointment by him as Master of University College, Durham'; 'no other name', it was added, 'will be placed before him at the same time.'

The other university post was even more attractive. In the early summer plans were discussed in the Balliol Senior Common Room for the appointment of a teacher in philosophy which might shortly have to be made—a precaution which the course of events proved to be unnecessary—and the college chaplaincy was also under consideration. An entry in the College Minute-book records that on 29 May 'The Master was asked to invite the Rev. William Temple to act as Temporary Chaplain for the year 1919–20'. Temple and his wife went to stay at Balliol for a weekend with the Master, and discussions ranged a good deal farther than the chaplaincy, in the hope that it might be possible to find for Temple some permanent work which would carry a Fellowship; but these talks were quite informal, and it was on the college chaplaincy alone that he had to make up his mind. He was much drawn to it, and it is at least possible that his career might have taken this academic turn, had there not been the prospect of a third opening—to which Gore had alluded in his letter. Canon Pearce had been elected to the see of Worcester, and every effort was being made to secure Temple as his successor. Lloyd George was in Paris, with little leisure to think about church appointments; the delay, as Gore had foretold, was likely to be a long one; but the Dean was doing his best, and wrote as early as 5 March:

My dear Will,

The position is most tantalizing. I have heard nothing of

a definite character during the last three or four weeks. I can only say that the Archbishop and Lord Stamfordham are in agreement on the subject, and I spoke to the latter only yesterday. He had, however, no intelligence to communicate. He had done what he could, but the matter seemed now to be out of his hands. There is a certain amount of risk of falling between the two proverbial stools. But I should prefer to think that it were possible for you to take the risk. It is not likely that the powers that be would allow you to be unemployed.

Yours affectionately,
HERBERT E. RYLE, Bp.

Temple took the risk. He decided to refuse both the Durham and (later) the Balliol offers—the college chaplaincy was accepted by Neville Talbot—and in June the Archbishop sent for him, to tell him that the Westminster Canonry could be his. When the Prime Minister's letter came, his wife was away from home. She was picking fruit in the garden of a friend in Gloucestershire when a telegram arrived—'Westminster, but it is a secret'—and the next morning she received this letter:

20 Melbury Road,
W. 14.
June 16, 1919.

. . . I do wish you had been here when this arrived. At first I thought of waiting till to-morrow evening before answering so that we could discuss it together. But then I thought we really had decided it on Saturday when the Archbishop talked to us. So I answered by the late post in the enclosed terms.

I do not feel any doubts. There will be temptations at W. that there would not have been at Oxford; but at Oxford it would have been hard to do much in the effort to master the great stream of classical theology, which I wish to make. I have enough philosophical equipment for the work of translating the doctrine of the Church into the ways that men think now; but I have not yet enough grip of the doctrine itself. At Balliol I should have had to give a lot of time to working up philosophy I once knew or never knew. It would have been good mental discipline: but in itself would have led to nothing. Above all W. gives what I think I most need after these three years of rushing about—and that is the opportunity and even duty to 'worship the Lord in the beauty of holiness'. I want (need) to renew depth in religious life, and the peace which goes with it, if I am to have anything to interpret to the world at all. And the Abbey will greatly help in that.

And so, more than anything, will you. Anyhow, I hope and believe this will give us more time together in some degree of peace than Oxford would have done—at least in term.

But there is a lot to pray about, and I had better begin.

XVII

Canon of Westminster—The Enabling Act

The Enabling Bill is through its Third Reading in the Commons and will now be an Act before Christmas. So the chief thing I have worked for since Christmas 1917 is coming off, and that at the time we set which all the wiseacres said was impossible. Of course the job of using it properly is much more difficult than the job of getting it. Still, in Neville Talbot's phrase, 'The Church is out of the ditch and on the road.' So now we can drive ahead.

W. T., letter to his brother, December 1919.

IN the course of his career Temple set up more than one record; the most striking was that he was offered three different canonries at Westminster Abbey within the space of six years. His reasons for accepting the third were obvious and cogent. But before he was to enjoy the peace and beauty of the Abbey and its surroundings he had to finish off his travelling for Life and Liberty, and the last six months of this work were as exacting as any that lay behind him. They included a visit to the Forces across the Channel, during which he held conferences of chaplains and officers, with occasional larger meetings; everywhere he found a keenness for so reorganizing the Church as to fit it for effective action—from one Headquarters he wrote: 'We roped in Major-Generals in shoals.' One of these suggested to a junior officer on his staff that he should join the Life and Liberty Fellowship: 'What's the pension, Sir?' asked the young man; 'Eternal life, stoopid' was the General's retort, as he smacked his head; and the young man signed on. But with all the keenness Temple found an almost complete ignorance of the present condition of the Church and of its organization which was no less pronounced among officers than among the rank and file. In one way this made his work easier; to know the worst—as his audiences did before he had finished with them—was the best incentive to join the reformers, and impatience could always be directed into a channel of purposeful action. The following are a few extracts from the letters he sent home to his wife:

Paris-Plage,
January 31, 1919.

Things are immensely interesting. Last night's meeting was in the 'Colonial and Continental' Church—about 100 people present: very good questions afterwards. . . . This morning we had a Celebration at 10.0, followed by a meeting of Chaplains: 23 turned up. . . . Then all of us lunched together. My night had been somewhat disturbed because (1) my room opened into one inhabited by 2 officers who conversed loudly; (2) a dear little mouse clattered about the oil cloth on the floor in an interminable game. What *would* you have done? After lunch John Macmillan arrived and drove me to Étaples. There we found the Bishop (Gwynne) taking a Confirmation. A huge tea-party occurred in the big Rest Hut of the Hospital, followed by a really admirable meeting. Lord Ardee was in the chair. Sir John Bradford (the big surgeon) in General's uniform was there too. They seemed most enthusiastic. The Bishop has formally joined the Fellowship.

Valenciennes,
February 1, 1919.

. . . It was a cold drive, powdery snow falling nearly all the time, sometimes slightly, sometimes heavily. Just before Arras we did a prodigious skid, our back wheels swinging right round till they struck the bank at the right of the road with the car facing the wrong way along the road. Until Arras we saw no sign of war except vast expanses like the sheds at Didcot or on Newbury race course. But the moment we reached Arras it began. Arras looked appalling—just because it is not 'badly damaged'; that is, the main fabric of most houses is standing, but with all windows and all floors (of course roofs) knocked in. It consists largely of what one ordinarily calls ruins. But when we came out on the East side, the devastation was total. Most of the poplars along the road-side are smashed to bits; at one point for over a mile in a close-planted avenue every single tree has been smashed off by shell-fire, about 5 ft. above the ground. The villages here do not look dreadful because they do not look anything; there is only

267

a little extra unevenness in the ground to show that there once were houses. But the zone of wasted country on that line is narrow. By the time we got to Douai, we had left it far behind. In these towns out here the suburbs have been knocked about by our bombardment, but the centres are intact. The house I lunched in at Douai was for 4 years the Headquarters of Prince Rupprecht of Bavaria, and he had provided himself with an astonishing bedroom 12 ft. underground, encased on every side with a foot of solid concrete.

After lunch I was taken by Percy Woollcombe to Le Forêt for an Officers' Conference. About 130 came, including 6 Generals. Great keenness. Then tea, and the drive on here. Dinner at a Mess, where I met a charming Marlburian. Then a meeting of specially invited officers, with Sir H. S. Horne, G.O.C. of the 1st Army, in the chair. Renewed keenness. Horne quite fierce that the laity have not been told 'these things' and asked to help straighten them out. We went on with questions till 11.30. Now to bed. It struck 12.0 3 minutes ago, so this is Sunday morning, and I shall be with you again this week!

Valenciennes,
February 3, 1919.

This morning we started soon after breakfast for Mons. . . . At the frontier there is a barrier and a customs office: on the way to Mons I had to show my permit. On the way back the Belgian and French soldiers again wanted to stop us: but a Tommy who was also there called out 'Ow! It's all right. Go on.' I gather this is rather typical of a calm assumption by which Tommy takes control of all foreigners in a genial, contemptuous, and completely effective way.

Lille,
February 4, 1919.

. . . A good day (though rather foul weather with a thaw setting in and a tendency to rain). Neville Talbot turned up at Valenciennes at about 10.30 and drove me here. We got my room at the officers' club—a palatial apartment in what was a swagger hotel. Then I lunched with him at his Mess—a less desirable one than any I have struck so far. They got on to treatment of German prisoners, on which subject a Presbyterian Chaplain expressed the most odious views. Neville says he always gives the show away. He is a 'regular'. An old General present said little, but what he did say was on the right side. After lunch we drove to Roubaix for an officers' conference. General de Lisle, the Corps Commander, took the chair, and joined at the end of the meeting. There seemed to be plenty of keenness. We had tea there and then went to Tourcoing for an open meeting. About 250 Tommies came and showed real enthusiasm. After this meeting I drove back with [later Sir Harry] Markham, an O.R. of Surtees' House who was in the VI with me, and was always rather a friend of mine. He is a capital fellow now.

On his return to London, Temple deposited at the office the batches of membership forms that had been filled in during his tour. Some of his critics were inclined to doubt whether he was as effective in securing new members as he was in moving an audience. The following letter is one of many that might be quoted in retort:

> The Vicarage,
> Monkwearmouth.
> April 2, 1919.

. . . A meeting at Bishop Auckland was decidedly good—about 300 people. Just before it I got a telegram from F. A. I. to ask if I could write 1200 words for the *Sunday Pictorial*, but telling me to wait for a letter before replying. And as the Thurlows had a crowd in after the meeting, I was glad not to write last night. . . . Then I went on to Jarrow. By this time F. A. I.'s letter had come, so I wrote about 400 words before supper. At the evening meeting Sir James Douglas presided. Very good. There were about 230 people present, and 115 joined! . . . Then I came on here, arriving at about 10.15. I had some supper and then set to work to finish the article. It is done and is fairly crisp: so I hope it will suit. But I decided that I would try to get in a more idealistic strain than the natural man who reads the *S.P.* is probably accustomed to!

During the first week in July he writes from Exeter: ' . . . I expect this is my last letter, and then there is only the little Brighton trip to carry me off so far as Life and Liberty and all its works are concerned. Hurrah!'

It was with feelings of intense relief and joy that he started on his duties at Westminster; but there were two drawbacks. One was temporary—he confessed to being 'dead tired and needing a holiday', and he longed to get away for a short respite; but his first month in residence as Canon was August and, after being installed on 14 July, he and his wife were lent some rooms in Savile Row till their house should be ready. The second was more serious: he had to give up the cottage at Ramsbury, in Wiltshire, where they had spent many peaceful holidays and his wife had given much time and care to the garden; but they could no longer afford it, in view of the expenses incidental to keeping up so large a house as 20 Dean's Yard. This was ready by October, and their happiness at once more having a settled home of their own was in no way marred by the legend that the house was haunted. A lady who had lived there previously had 'seen things', including a severed and bleeding hand which slithered up and down the handrail of the staircase, and a monk who passed through the passage under the next house to the cloister. Neither Temple nor his wife was troubled by these visions, nor did they even hear on the stone flags of the hall an echo of the footfall of Samuel Johnson, who frequently visited his life-long friend, Dr. Taylor, at the house which was then a prebendal residence. Four hundred years before Johnson it had formed part of the Cellarer's building of the monastery, with its visitors' room on the first floor: the stone front to Dean's Yard had been little altered, except for the addition of a third story and an eighteenth-century front door, and part of the vaulted ground floor had been made, about a generation before, into a singularly attractive dining-room. Here Temple and his wife entertained their guests, who would afterwards be shown the sixteenth-century mural paintings on the first floor—peacocks and curious monsters, with foliated columns and pedestals—and the shield of the Tudor Royal Arms, with sea-lions as supporters, above the fireplace. It was the most attractive house they had yet lived in, and they both responded to its charm and beauty.

And they were surrounded by friends. The Dean and Mrs. Ryle gave them a warm welcome; Dr. (later Sir) Sydney Nicholson, an old Rugbeian whom Temple knew fairly well, was delighted when the new Canon asked to be enrolled as a member of his Special Choir, at the rehearsals of which Temple was a regular and keen attendant; and all who were serving the Abbey looked forward to a period of advance and a relief from the tedium of merely marking time, which they had inevitably endured through more than four years of war. Ryle had done a notable work as Dean. He had started monthly meetings of the Chapter; he had been the peacemaker of a body in which disagreements had not been uncommon; and his preaching was of a thoughtful, evangelical type exactly suited to the congregation, especially at the Sunday evening service which he seldom missed; Temple said of Ryle's 'Gospel Sermons' that the language of them was not only perfectly simple, it was also simply perfect. Yet several changes and reforms in the services and equipment of the Abbey were desirable, and Temple arrived just at the moment when the Dean needed the help and counsel of a younger man. Ryle himself was little interested in ecclesiology; but the Sacrist, Jocelyn Perkins, was now able—partly through Temple's influence with the Dean—to enrich the furnishings of the church, and to-day visitors to the Abbey can see on all sides some of the results of their work. Temple spent little time in worrying about what some might regard as the mere trimmings of religion; his was the common-sense view that when it was possible—and obviously desirable in so lovely a building as the Abbey—to have the outward adornments of worship both beautiful and correct, it was a sheer wilfulness of taste or temper to be satisfied with having them ugly and wrong. He recognized that preaching was his main work inside the Abbey. From the first Sunday afternoon of his residence—when the Archbishop came across from Lambeth to hear him—the Abbey began to fill, and he was never without a large congregation during his short stay at Westminster. Under the title *Fellowship with God,* fourteen of the sermons he preached during the first year after his installation were published (with one or two occasional sermons) in 1920. The central thought of them all is the Incarnation, through which God entered into fellowship with men and has thereby enabled them to enjoy that fellowship with God which is 'the profoundest need and the highest blessing of men'.

But the duties of a Canon are what he likes to make them. Beyond keeping his month's residence when the turn for it comes round, he is free to be present or not at the Abbey services —'No Canon in Abbey!' was sadly recorded more than once in Ryle's diary—and the rest of his time is his own. To his many activities Temple now added the chairmanship of the Universities Relief Committee, which had been started as the result of a conference of Vice-Chancellors of all the British universities called by Lord Cecil, with the object of helping universities in war-stricken areas. With Miss Iredale, its indefatigable secretary, addressing meetings of students through the country, and Temple helping to build up its committees and to deal with difficult people, it had a pronounced success, and for a time raised between £20,000 and £30,000 a year. But the greater part of his time was still given to Life and Liberty, and all the energies of the reformers were now to be concentrated on the passage of the Enabling Bill through Parliament.

The procedure adopted had been carefully chosen. 'What is this "Enabling Bill" that you are all making such a fuss about?' was a question frequently put to the clergy by their lay friends— the title did not suggest to the uninitiated anything to do with the Church at all. It came from the form of the Act by which Parliament recognized the existence of the National Church Assembly (as the central representative council of the Church was to be called) and 'enabled' it to do its work. The machinery by which the consent of Parliament would be given to church legislation had somehow to be set up through this Bill. One way would have been to include the constitution of a National

Church Assembly and its suggested procedure in a schedule to the Bill. This, which would have involved a church constitution being settled by Parliament, was avoided because a considerable section of the Church would never have accepted as binding a constitution so legalized; also it would have been possible for Parliament to amend or delete clauses or sections in the constitution in a way that might upset its rather delicate balance. But the Convocations were bodies with a legal status. It was therefore decided that the constitution should be settled by the Representative Church Council; the Convocations would adopt it and present it as an Appendix to Addresses to the King. The Enabling Bill would then be brought in, giving the National Church Assembly (whose constitution was referred to in the title) the necessary powers. Parliament would thus not be responsible for the constitution, but would recognize it when set up. The conscience of no churchman would be offended, and the constitution would be safe from any parliamentary amendments. On 14 May Temple wrote to his brother:

> The Life and Liberty Movement is over its second stile. The scheme was adopted in both Convocations last week, only 12 votes being given against it in all the four Houses. The Archbishop has already moved in Parliament and the Bill was read a first time in the House of Lords yesterday. So we are really getting on with some business.

But the opponents of the Bill were active, and for some months the controversy occupied a large space in the correspondence columns of the church and secular newspapers. In this wrangle Temple was forced to take a prominent part, though he described the perpetual writing of controversial letters to *The Times* as a bore; but (he added) 'it is part of our whole "hustle" about Church self-government', and it was over his name that most of the Life and Liberty letters appeared in the Press. The spade-work had been done thoroughly during the previous two years; the Archbishop was at his best when he moved the Second Reading of the Bill in the Lords on 3 June; and after an amendment moved in a closely reasoned speech by Haldane had been rejected by nearly a hundred votes, the passage of the Bill was assured. In the Committee stage the Archbishop accepted an important amendment moved by Lord Finlay; the Third Reading was carried on 21 July; and all now depended on the verdict of the Lower House, where Lord Wolmer (now Lord Selborne) had been working with a quiet persistence that told its tale when the division on the Second Reading was taken. This was on 7 November, while a Congress of Life and Liberty members was in session. The Congress had originally planned to meet early in October, but the railway strike had made it impossible for most of them to travel to London, and it was by this chance that the Congress happened to be meeting on the day. From 12.30 to 5.0 o'clock the session was suspended, so that members could take part in a great act of united prayer at S. Martin's Church during the debate in the House of Commons. They were back again at the Church House in conference by the time the division was taken and, when Temple came hurrying into the room where they were meeting to announce that the Second Reading had been carried by 304 votes to 16, all rose to their feet and sang the Doxology. At the thanksgiving meeting held in the Hoare Memorial Hall, Temple recalled the prediction of the wiseacres and the pessimists about the date by which the Bill could be passed through all its stages, and claimed credit for the Movement that these prophecies had been falsified. Sheppard was in his gayest mood: 'As I was coming along to this meeting, I passed a policeman looking very depressed in Trafalgar Square and I said, "Cheer up, Robert, the Enabling Bill's through all right"; and all he replied was "What's that you say?".' The Bill received the Royal Assent two days before Christmas, and on 26 February 1920 a special Service of Prayer and Dedication was held in the Abbey, at which the preacher was—not, alas! the Primate of All England, but his brother of York. Lang summed up in a sentence the outstanding benefit that would accrue to the life of the Church by the passage of the Bill:

> For the first time, at least since almost primitive ages, the laity in every parish throughout the land are offered vote and

voice in the management of their Church; and this not merely as parishioners or as citizens of the nation, but as citizens of the Church; and not merely by the favour of this or that incumbent, but as a right conferred by the whole Church with the concurrence and recognition of the State. In a degree never before possible, every man or woman who professes allegiance to the Church is now invested with a personal responsibility for its welfare, for the success or failure of its Divine Mission. All depends upon the spirit, the motive, the purpose, the outlook with which churchpeople enter the new era, upon the character which is impressed upon it at its start.

In this last sentence Temple saw clearly outlined the future task of the Life and Liberty Movement—which was to create the kind of atmosphere in which the Enabling Act would be used not as a bludgeon for the layman to flourish at the head of the parson, still less as a stimulant to the more autocratic incumbents to emphasize the legal limitations within which the laity could 'interfere' in the management of their Church, but as a charter that laid down the sacred duty of co-operation between the clerical and lay members as partners in the work of the one Body. Hopes for the benefits to be derived and the spiritual advance to be secured through the Act varied in intensity and scope. 'I find a little difficulty', Randall Davidson had said when he introduced the Bill in the House of Lords, 'in making my own all the hopes and ambitions which have found eloquent expression in the fine body of men and women who have advocated it.' Others were more sanguine: 'I understand', ran a postcard received at the Life and Liberty office from a churchwarden ('Lt.-Col. R.A. retd.') in the South of England, 'that now the Enabling Bill is through we can get rid of our parson. Please send full particulars by return. I write as a member of the Fellowship.' Both the Primate's doubts and the Colonel's conception of fellowship had to be reckoned with; the centre of interest and action now shifted from Westminster to the churchpeople of England—that is, to the incumbent and the whole body of faithful laity in every parish. The difficulties were formidable. On the one hand were the parish priests who—except for a very few who had already set up 'voluntary' Church Councils—had been accustomed to wield an authority so far unchallenged. In many parishes changes had been made in forms of worship and administration with the consent of a large body of parishioners, and the autocracy had been a benevolent one; but in several the disasters of one-man rule had been only too manifest. On the other hand were the laity, many of them already giving themselves without stint to the work of the Church, but carrying that most intolerable of all burdens—the burden of responsibility without power—that can take the heart out of the strongest. The members of this small but devoted body were ready to assume new duties which would be made all the more worth while by the 'vote and voice' which the Archbishop of York had assured them were now theirs; but they were not typical of the Anglican laity. Most of these lived in rural areas, and among the strongest prejudices of the country-man used to be that against signing his name to anything; at best it seemed to hint at a subscription, at worst it suggested the danger of a permanently binding commitment. In the cheery and sometimes fiery fellowship of the beer-house, he might be induced to add his name to a dozen others, praying for the opening of some blocked-up right of way; but to ask his parish priest for a pink form headed 'National Assembly of the Church of England', and then to declare on it that he was (1) or (2) and that he was neither (3) nor (4), involved a more definite statement of his spiritual allegiance than he would care for anybody, least of all the parson, to scrutinize. Nor was the exact meaning of the words 'Electoral Roll' at once clear to the less enlightened. In many parishes, under the terms of some local benefactor's will, loaves of bread used to be distributed to the aged and deserving poor at the church door on Sunday morning, and more than one letter contained a request for fuller information about the 'electric rolls' which were now, it was understood, to be included in the bounty of Mother Church.

A more serious difficulty arose when the clergy began to make known their plans for working the Act in their parishes. Many Anglo-Catholic incumbents were determined that their small band of communicants should not be swamped at the Church Meeting by a large influx of voters who normally took little interest in their church, and they deliberately refrained from making any general appeal for signatures: other parish priests might be seen hurrying from house to house with a dispatch-case containing a bundle of enrolment forms and a fountain pen, and impressing upon even the vaguest 'C. of E.' adherents their duty to assume the full responsibility of church electors. Others, again, took no more than the most formal interest in the enrolment of voters; and a few old-fashioned incumbents who saw in the Enabling Act 'the thin end of the wedge' and dreaded the prospect of Church rule from Westminster dismissed the whole business, in the true Podsnap tradition, with a flourish of the arm —'I knew it from the first. Centralization. No. Never with my consent. Not English.'

In the large majority of parishes, however, serious efforts were made to carry out the intentions of the Act. Church bells were rung, services of intercession were held, the people came in good numbers to the first Church Meeting of electors—and from that moment everything turned on the ability and personality of the incumbent. The laity had been encouraged to believe that they were now to play a vital part in the future management of their Church; at last the time had come when their newly won privileges were to be explained to them in detail, and the incumbent would answer all their questions from the chair. These answers were clear enough. Could they now appoint their parson? No. Could they now recommend a particular man, when the living was vacant, to the patron? No. Could they now decide what forms of service would be the rule in their church? No. What then were these new functions and privileges of which they had heard so much? For the cynic this was the moment of a lifetime: You are bidden by the Constitution to which the Act refers to elect a vice-chairman, and after that to co-operate with me in the spiritual work of the Church both inside and outside the parish. That was about all—and the temperature dropped to zero. There were then, as there have been ever since, two outstanding points on which feeling among the laity ran high—the appointment of the incumbent and the type of church services—and in both these respects disappointment was widespread. And it continues. No compromise has yet been reached between the traditional system of private patronage combined with the parson's freehold and 'the rule of the rich cheesemonger which is the bane of Nonconformity'; nor has it been found possible—indeed no effort has been made—to give the laity any statutory right to a voice in the management of services in their parish church which would not infringe the deeply rooted authority of the clerical Order to decide on all forms of worship. The disappointment was at that time felt least in those parishes where the ground had been carefully laid by a tactful and vigorous incumbent. But, however gently the news might be broken, there was no altering the disturbing truth.

This was the background against which the Life and Liberty Movement had to make an important decision, either to close down or to inaugurate some big campaign to meet the new situation. There was much to be said for either course. The Church, then as now, was littered with moribund Societies that ought to have committed suicide gracefully years before, but were perpetually being whipped into a fictitious and frequently useless activity, either to satisfy the vanity of their committees or because some aged and faithful official who had served a Society, often for a shamefully low salary, for a generation could hardly continue to live without his pittance. Moreover, the success of the Life and Liberty Movement had been due largely to the fact that it had one primary and definite objective—to get a Bill through Parliament. This had been achieved: far better, it was suggested, to close the office door now and to start (if need be) a new Society with an entirely fresh programme than that the Movement should outlive its purpose and fade out ingloriously at some distant date. Against this course two considerations had to be weighed. It would have been a poor response to the generous enthusiasm of the laity who for two years had been looking forward to the day when a freed Church could start on the work of attempting to christianize the national life—to choose this moment for closing down would be little short of a betrayal of their hopes—and it was also essential that guidance should be given to the newly appointed Councils of the Church at the start of their work. A measure of liberty had been won, but only a Society acting independently of the official Church could breathe life into the dry bones of the Constitution. It was therefore decided to continue the Movement for at least two years, and Temple wrote the following message to the Fellowship:

The New Year brings a new era for our Movement and (as we hope) for the Church. Our first objective is won; the Enabling Bill is become an Act of Parliament. We have been given our chance; now we have to take it. Two tasks immediately arise as a result of the passing of the Act. The first is to complete the machine by providing its full complement of parts. We have to get the Electoral Rolls filled up and the Parochial Church Councils elected. Then we have also to play our part in supplying the steam to make the wheels go round. We have to secure the election on all Councils of the Church of men and women who have some real vision of the Church as it might be and a real determination to bring that vision true. . . . At Christmas, 1918, men laughed when we said that we hoped to see the Enabling Bill passed into law before Christmas, 1919. They who laughed were wrong; we who hoped were right. We now confront a tangle of problems and a mass of vested interests; we know the difficulties of villages and of towns. We know how torpid Church life has in some places become under the pressure of these difficulties. It might be reasonable to be anxious; but it would be ungrateful and unfaithful. 'The Lord hath done great things for us.' We enter the New Year with an unclouded Hope.

W. TEMPLE.

Two tasks lay before the Movement; to guide into fresh channels of service the new life in the Church which, it was hoped, would now be released as a result of its recovered liberty, and to help in educating the recently enfranchised laity. Public meetings were held, at one series of which selected 'challengers' were invited to indict the Church with entire frankness, and none took

279

greater advantage of this open platform, or used it to better
purpose, than the Labour leader who was then known as 'The
Dockers' K.C.', Mr. Ernest Bevin. But the more useful and more
lasting work was done in smaller groups or conferences. It was
not to be expected that after generations during which too many
of the laity had regarded church attendance as the only necessary
outward sign of their membership—though a few had also been
in a position to satisfy Monsignor Talbot's summary of the
layman's duty, 'to entertain, to hunt, to shoot, to give alms'—
large numbers would at once take up with alacrity their new and
still vague responsibilities. For several years, therefore, the Life
and Liberty Movement organized a summer conference for
Parochial Church Councillors at Swanwick, where—under the
friendly leadership of Canon E. S. Woods (now Bishop of
Lichfield)—Church Councillors pooled their experiences, discussed how to express and interpret their faith in terms of the
common life of a town or country parish, and how to make their
fellow-members more forward to serve on the official assemblies
of the Church. Any such educational work was bound to be a
slow process. In many parishes attempts (too often half-hearted)
to work the Enabling Act and the subsequent Powers Measure
failed as many other spiritual efforts in the same parishes had
failed—though this does not justify the extravagant statement of
the cloistered Editor of *Crockford* (Supplement 1942–4) that 'where
the Councils have any effective existence, it is to be feared that
they are largely the resort of busy-bodies, such as have seldom
failed to make their presence felt ever since S. Paul wrote to the
Churches of Thessalonica and Corinth'. This verdict is considerably less than just to the thousands of laity, both men and
women, who in every diocese have learned the joy and the privilege
of serving their Church through the Parochial Councils, who in
just those parishes which are mentioned have relieved the parson
of much work and worry, and have helped to create and foster a
new conception of the responsibilities attached to church
membership, for the younger generation to emulate and to
develop.

It lies outside our present purpose to review in detail the

results of the limited self-government secured for the Church by the Enabling Act. Generally, it may be said that at the outset there was a sharp and fateful struggle between two groups in the National Church Assembly who differed widely in their conception of its policy and its purpose and may be called, roughly, the legalists and the moralists. The struggle was a brief one. The legalists—of whom Sir Lewis Dibdin, the trusted adviser of Randall Davidson, will be remembered as the leader—were soon in control; the voice of the Assembly is now the voice of the administrator, not of the prophet; and so long as its constitution and time-table remain unrevised (so that, for instance, few of the laity outside the more or less leisured classes can spare the time to attend the sessions) its present tone and temper will persist. A case can be made out for the contention that the Assembly was never intended to provide a platform for the prophet—the question where exactly in the temple of the National Church a niche can be found for that sadly neglected but scripturally essential figure still awaits our answer—and if it be granted that the object of the Assembly is to reorganize the administration and finances of the Church, its members deserve credit for many useful reforms which it might have taken two generations to effect under the old system of passing church Bills through Parliament. The power in the Church remains exactly where it was before, but at least it has a constitutional sanction in the hands of the bishops, archdeacons, and 'elder statesmen', who now direct the procedure and control the policy of the National Assembly of the Church of England.

XVIII

Manchester

Somehow I have always felt that I should go to Manchester one day,
and certainly I have long thought that I should have a better chance of
doing some good there than anywhere else.

W. T., letter to his brother, December 1920.

SIXTEEN months after he had been installed in the Abbey,
Temple received the following letter:

> 10, Downing Street,
> Whitehall, S.W.1.
>
> Dear Canon Temple, 26th November, 1920.
>
> SEE OF MANCHESTER
>
> I shall be happy with your permission to submit your name
> to His Majesty for appointment to the above See which will be
> vacated next month by the resignation of Bishop Knox.
>
> The Diocese is one of great importance, situated as it is in
> the centre of a large business community and comprising a
> great industrial population. The opportunity which it would
> afford you of being able to devote your gifts to the service of
> the Church and to the social and religious life of the country
> in so large and important a sphere, is one which I hope will be
> welcome to you.
>
> As His Majesty's consent must be obtained before any
> announcement can be made, I shall be glad if you will treat this
> offer as confidential; and I shall be pleased to hear from you at
> your early convenience.
>
> I understand that the retiring Bishop will draw a pension of
> £1,400 per annum.
>
> Yours sincerely,
> D. LLOYD GEORGE.

As soon as they were alone together, Temple put the letter into
his wife's hand. They were both slightly dazed and, after some
talk, agreed that Temple should write to the Prime Minister asking

for a few days in which to think over his proposal: four persons in particular had to be consulted—the two Archbishops, Gore, and the Dean of Westminster. After dinner Temple rang up Randall Davidson, who was at Canterbury; the Archbishop came to the telephone himself and deprecated any delay in accepting the offer—could there be two opinions of Temple's duty? He had better reply to the Prime Minister at once; he could be assured that the Archbishop of York also knew and approved of the proposal. A restless night followed and, after the morning Service at the Abbey, Temple saw the Dean who had been told of the Prime Minister's intention and had no doubt of what the reply should be. Temple then telephoned to Gore who replied: 'I know. Go. And of course I'll come to supper.' By the time Gore had left Dean's Yard on Sunday night, Temple's course was clear and he at once wrote two letters:

To the Prime Minister:

November 27, 1920.
20, Dean's Yard,
Dear Mr. Lloyd George,   Westminster, S.W.1.

Yesterday afternoon I received your letter referring to the See of Manchester; I realize the honour you have done me, and I know the greatness of the opportunity you offer me. I only wish I had more capacity to make proper use of it.

I have had some conversation with the Archbishop of Canterbury and it seems so clear that I ought to accept your offer that I am writing without further delay both to thank you for the honour you have done me and to agree to your proposal to submit my name to His Majesty.   Yours sincerely,
W. TEMPLE.

To the Archbishop of York:

Nov. 27.
20, Dean's Yard,
My dear Lord Archbishop,   Westminster, S.W.1.

I have just had a letter from the Prime Minister saying that he wishes to submit my name to the King for the See of Manchester.

I know something of the importance of the work, and it makes one feel very small. But I suppose my training is such as to enable me to do some useful work there, and that I ought to accept unless there are objections of which I have not yet thought. But it would make a great difference to me if I might know how you regard the matter.

Please remember me in your prayers.

Yours affectly,

W. TEMPLE.

I need not say that it would be to me a great happiness to work as one of your suffragans.

Forty-eight hours later, the two Archbishops wrote:

29 Nov. 1920.

Old Palace,

Canterbury.

My dear William,

You need no assurance from me of your being at this moment ceaselessly in my thoughts and prayers.

The vacant post is one of the greatest in the Church of England or perhaps in the whole Church of Christ, alike in the possibilities and in the weight of its burden—May your strength abound, in accordance with the abounding need. You have great traditions to maintain. Fraser and Moorhouse were Titans in their popular powers, and Knox is a man of immense ability, whatever one may feel about the wisdom of his rule or the range of his sympathy. I have been anxious for the last fortnight, as things seemed to have hung fire and I feared some hitch. I have from the first desired that you should take up the burden, for I believe that you have the gifts which are needed there—though I am not going to imagine that all will be smooth or unobstructed. Such is not the way of Manchester! I wish you had, in these busy years, been less 'rushed' from post to post. But that has not been your fault, and now if God preserve you in health we may in quietness and hope look forward to a spell of continuous opportunity—opportunity which will grow in its possibilities as your experience of the city and its surroundings grows. I find it difficult to believe that Knox can have been right in deprecating the division of the Diocese, but I imagine that the problem *how* to divide it is one of the toughest which exists!

However, all these things are as nothing in comparison with the thought of the sacred greatness of the trust.

You will need the help of all our prayers—and you will not count upon it in vain.

For Frances too our thoughts and prayers go up. The vista which opens, as we peer forward into the years, is wonderful indeed.

I wish your dear Mother were yet here to join visibly in our hopes and prayers. Who knows what measure of actual fellowship there is across the sundering stream?

God be with you, my dear Son in Christ. I look forward to (somehow) seeing you very soon and talking things over.

Yours affecly,
RANDALL CANTUAR.

Bishopthorpe,
York.

My dear William,   29th November 1920.

I have been greatly cheered by a letter which I have received this morning from the Prime Minister's Secretary informing me that the Prime Minister has written to you offering to submit your name to His Majesty for appointment to the See of Manchester. I need not tell you that this proposal has my most heartfelt concurrence. I have long felt that you are the man of all others to enter into the great work of that great Diocese, and I hope with all my heart that you will be willing to accept the offer. I know how trying it must be both to you and Mrs. Temple to think of giving up your work and home at the Abbey after so short a time, but you have yourself to blame if you are marked out for posts of importance such as the Bishopric of Manchester, and in these days men must be willing to go where the need is greatest. There are of course, as always, some difficulties to be overcome. As you will have been informed, Bishop Knox is obliged to take a retiring pension;

William Temple

but the house, as compared with other episcopal residences, is not expensive. The Diocese will understand the limitations which the pension puts upon the resources of the Bishop; and I shall be surprised if the laity do not take some steps to make things easier for their Bishop. Moreover, there is the momentous question of the Division of the Diocese which will require both great energy and great care, and you would have to put to the test your views about the division of dioceses which you expressed at the National Assembly. Further, it is only right to say that there are few places in England where Churchmanship and Conservatism go more closely together than Manchester, and I have long felt that there was need of some one who would make a more effective appeal to the new power of Labour than has been made in the past; but I am sure that this will have to be combined with some wise and tactful considerateness for traditions which go very deep into the life and history of the Church in Manchester. ... I think you will feel that you cannot set aside this call, coming as it does from responsible authority with I know the approval of both Archbishops. I need not tell you what a joy and help it will be to have you among our Northern Bishops. May God guide and strengthen you.

Yours affectionately,

Cosmo Ebor.

One other person had hitherto shared all his hopes and plans, and a few weeks later Temple wrote to his brother:

... There could be no real doubt about accepting. But it is quite horrid to have to tear up our roots here so soon, and to leave our lovely house; also the financial situation is rather desperate. But we will work that somehow. ... As Frances has written, we were at Bishopscourt last week and saw it. It is too big, though, as Bishop's houses go, not *vast*. It will cost a lot to make decent; though we shall have to reduce our decorations etc. to what is really necessary. Everyone concerned has been extraordinarily kind. Both Archbishops were emphatic that I must accept—indeed they had strongly pressed the Prime Minister to offer it to me. And the Manchester folk

286

are delightful. The Dean is a great friend of ours; the two suffragans came to see us at Bishopscourt and were as nice as anyone could be. And of course old Canon Scott is delighted. So the atmosphere, morally, is pleasant!

Throughout the Church the appointment was received with acclamation. If one or two heads were shaken in the Manchester diocese, they were those of the older churchmen who were in complete sympathy with the ecclesiastical and political views of Temple's predecessor and felt that—whatever might be the gifts and graces of their new bishop—he was certainly cast in a different mould. It was a safe conjecture. Knox was, without a single qualification, a Protestant of Protestants and a Conservative of Conservatives; Temple was never a Protestant, and his inherited conservatism (uneasy from the first) did not outlast his undergraduate days. Knox was an autocrat who kept in his own hands the strings of every diocesan organization: to Temple this was a waste of time: 'When I have learned the ropes', he wrote to his brother soon after his consecration, 'I shall be able to settle which committees, etc. I mean to attend. Just now I must go to all of them to see what they do and how they do it. Knox attended them all and largely ran them. But that I won't do. Probably I shall be thought lazy, but there are plenty of other things to do.' Knox was known to be almost fiercely opposed to the division of the diocese: Temple believed that, in whatever activities a bishop might usefully spend himself, he could not fulfil the functions assigned to the episcopate by Catholic tradition and endorsed by the words of the commission every bishop receives at his consecration, in a diocese as large and geographically inconvenient as Manchester. Knox had administrative powers of a high order, and the diocese had accepted the regimentation imposed upon it by a bishop whose enthusiasm and efficiency were held to justify the rigour of his rule: Temple's organizing ability had yet to be tested. Here, then, were several sharp contrasts, and one question-mark. Yet, for all their differences, the two men were alike in one outstanding quality. Each was entirely sure of himself—and that goes a long way in Lancashire.

William Temple

Certain formalities have to be complied with before a bishop-designate of the Established Church can take up his diocesan duties. After nomination by the Sovereign, he is 'elected' by the Cathedral Chapter of the diocese to which he has been appointed. This election is a mere form: when the Sovereign sends the Dean and Chapter the *Congé d'élire*, it is accompanied by a Letter Missive in which is mentioned the name of the person whom the Sovereign wishes them to elect. The penalties for refusing to comply with the Royal wish are laid down by Blackstone: 'if such Dean and Chapter do not elect in the manner by this Act (23 Henry VIII, c. 20) appointed, they shall incur all the penalties of a *Praemunire*; that is, the loss of all civil rights, with forfeiture of lands, goods, and chattels, and imprisonment during the Royal pleasure.' These penalties have never been inflicted, as no Dean and Chapter has yet refused to elect the King's nominee, though on one or two occasions in the last century there was some opposition. (The storm-centre when Henson was nominated to the see of Hereford in 1917 was not the Cathedral Chapter.) One was when the Dean and Chapter of Exeter divided on the election of Temple's father and seven members of the Chapter voted against him, thirteen being in his favour. Another is to be remembered chiefly for Lord John Russell's retort to the Dean of Hereford in 1847 when the orthodoxy of the Crown's man was questioned, and the Dean had written personally that he could not give his vote for Dr. Hampden. The Prime Minister replied: 'Sir,—I have had the honour to receive your letter of the 22nd inst., in which you intimate to me your intention of violating the law—I have, etc. J. Russell.' This may have frightened the Chapter, or perhaps the Dean had less backing than he thought; in the end he could only find one supporter, fourteen voting for Dr. Hampden.

When his election has been confirmed the bishop-designate (unless he is already a bishop) is consecrated, and finally enthroned in his own cathedral. The Confirmation of Temple's election—it is an expensive and (one must suppose, to the antiquary) an interesting ceremony—took place in York Minster on 24 January 1921. The Proctor for the Cathedral Chapter of Manchester exhibited his proxy, the Registrar read the Letters Patent, and the Vicar-General was asked to proceed with the Confirmation 'in according to . . . the exigency of the Law'. Temple was then 'judicially produced' by the Proctor, the Vicar-General called for opposers and, as none was forthcoming, the Proctor proceeded to 'porrect a schedule', asking for summary procedure and the assignment of 'a term' to prove the schedule. The Vicar-General suggested that this might be done at once. After the taking of oaths and signing of declarations, the Proctor 'porrected a definitive sentence' and asked that a Public Instrument and Letters Testimonial should be 'made out of and concerning the premises'. The Vicar-General replied, 'We do decree as prayed' —and all seems to have been for the best. On the next day, with a ceremonial that was at once simple, dignified, and satisfying, Temple was consecrated bishop. The hymn 'S. Patrick's Breast-plate' was of his own choosing, as was also S. S. Wesley's anthem 'Thou wilt keep him in perfect peace'. The preacher was his close friend and colleague in the Life and Liberty Movement, H. R. L. Sheppard, who—in answer to the question of his text, 'Who is sufficient for these things?'—declared that none but 'a wise man with love in his heart' could hope to grapple with the present and imminent problems of Church and State and at the same time be a father-in-God to the clergy and laity in his own diocese. 'He helped us', Temple wrote in describing the service, 'to say our prayers. It was just what we wanted.' Nothing was lacking in the beauty of the music and its rendering. When Temple wrote, a day or two later, to express his 'deep appreciation' of it, Bairstow replied that, though he had been an organist for many years, he seldom received such letters, and he was there-fore all the more grateful for the Bishop's considerate thought for the Minster organist and choir.

For the final ceremony (of enthronement) on 15 February the cathedral was filled from end to end with representatives of every phase of the diocesan life: few towns in England can boast a stronger local patriotism than Manchester, and no trouble had been spared to ensure the co-operation of other civic authorities in the diocese. In the procession from the Town Hall to the cathedral the Lord Mayor, with the Recorder of the City and the Town Clerk, was followed by the mayors—wearing their furred gowns and chains of office—of thirty boroughs, and the town-clerks in wig and gown; the Judges of the Assize, the Hon. Mr. Justice Acton and Sir Alfred Tobin, K.C., were escorted by their javelin-men; Temple was attended by his chaplains and by his suffragans, the Bishops of Burnley and Whalley. His three knocks on the cathedral door and his request to be led to the Bishop's seat were answered by the Dean with the invitation to enter and to 'proceed forthwith to those solemn rites and ceremonies with which your enthronement shall be accomplished'. After the enthronement, McCormick addressed the Bishop personally in what he himself aptly described as 'words of human and homely welcome'. Speaking as Head of the Cathedral Chapter, the Dean stressed the joyous unanimity with which the Letters Missive of the Crown had been answered: 'The measure of our welcome may be gauged by this fact—that out of the whole orbit of the English Church we would freely have chosen you first to guide the destinies of this great diocese.' On behalf of the clergy, he pledged himself and them, 'so far as men may pledge themselves before an unknown future, to loyal obedience and comradely support' in any spiritual effort to which Temple might summon them: and the cordial welcome of the laity, he ended, could not have been more strikingly expressed than by the great and representative congregation which had assembled to greet their new bishop on that day. Nothing in the whole service was more moving than the unstudied simplicity of Temple's reply. After referring to Gough McCormick's father whom he succeeded in the Rectory of S. James's, Piccadilly, to his own close friendship with the Dean, and to his predecessors in the see—Fraser, Moor-house, and Knox—he went on:

Such servants of our common Lord as I have named are witnesses to the power of faith. They point beyond them-selves to One who is at once the pattern and the object of our faith, and bid us run the race that is set before us, looking unto Jesus. Those words I should wish to take as my motto to-day.

I come as a learner, with no policy to advocate, no plan already formed to follow. But I come with one burning desire; it is that in all our activities, sacred and secular, ecclesiastical and social, we should help each other to fix our eyes on Jesus, making Him our only guide . . . Pray for me, I ask you, not chiefly that I may be wise and strong, or any other such thing, though for these things I need your prayers. But pray for me chiefly that I may never let go of the unseen hand of the Lord Jesus and may live in daily fellowship with Him. It is so that you will most of all help me to help you. So shall we go forward together—not without stumbling, not without weariness—but always towards the loving welcome that awaits us in our Father's home, where the conflicts which now beset the earth will have vanished, where self-seeking cannot find entrance, where misery gives place to joy and quarrelling to peace, because self is either sacrificed or forgotten in the realization of the Love of God.

A week later Temple wrote to his brother:

It has been a great week. The enthronement was a wonderful ceremony and the crowds in the street astonishing . . . . I have taken two Confirmations and one Ordination. On Sunday evening I preached in the Cathedral, which was packed (i.e. about 2,600 people). On Monday there was a Free Trade Hall meeting and an overflow, on Fellowship in Industry. On Saturday we were received at the University by about 500 folk from the W.E.A. Tutorial Classes run by Manchester. The Vice-Chancellor was extraordinarily kind in his welcome.

The letter was written from Bishopthorpe, where he was staying with the Archbishop of York for his first meeting of the Upper House of York Convocation. Temple was by many years the youngest diocesan in the Northern Province, but the Bishops of Ripon (Strong), Carlisle (Williams), and Durham (Henson) were already his friends; he described the gathering as 'a very jolly party', and on 22 February he wrote to his wife:

. . . Tommy Strong is not coming till tomorrow. Our party is Durham, Wakefield, Sheffield, Liverpool, Chester, Bradford,

Carlisle. At dinner they got on to Ireland. Ebor fails to see any difference between our action there and the German in Belgium. Sheffield thinks extermination of Sinn Feiners the only hope. Durham very uneasy, but could not go against the Government because he has no alternative policy. I urged that the whole question be sent to the League of Nations and that we undertake to accept the decision; but Henson won't face independence, so he can't agree to that.

February 23. . . . An interesting day, and a very good one. Henson spoke many times! The last was a complaint of the 'hypochondriacal valetudinarianism' involved in tinkering at the Church's constitution by setting up Diocesan Synods. He refused to serve on the Committee about it, as he had refused to join other Committees before; whereupon his Grace the President observed—'My dear Bishop of Durham, if you think you can get out of doing the solid work of Committees merely by making fantastic speeches, we shall have to prove to you that you are mistaken.'

The official residence of the Bishop of Manchester (Bishopscourt, Higher Broughton), lies on the north side of the city opposite the house which was then the Deanery. A high brick wall separates the garden from the Bury New Road, and a lodge stands on each side of a large and rather formidable-looking gateway. Three acres of garden slope steeply down to the river Irwell, with a view across the river, the race-course, and the old golf-course to the distant line of the hill on which stand the Pendlebury Mills—to be seen at their best against a smoky sunset with a red glow behind the mosque-like outline of the mill buildings. The house itself is not beautiful—the contrast between Dean's Yard and the Bury New Road hardly bore thinking of at first—but in many ways it is convenient. None of the diocese outside Manchester itself lies to the south of it, the diocese of Chester beginning in the southern suburbs, and it is within easy reach of the railway stations. The drawback for Temple was that the house was several miles away from the University and those districts where many of the most helpful laymen in the diocese lived; friendships were made at meetings rather than over the dinner-table; and it was not easy (till they were presented with a car) for him and his wife to meet informally these laymen and the members of the university staff. Some weeks passed before they were able to move into their new home, and for part of the time they were the guests of Canon and Mrs. J. J. Scott. The Canon had been a close friend of Temple's father; he was something of a 'character', and a notable force in the life of the cathedral. Dinner-parties in Fallowfield were the talk of the town: an ascetic clergyman, in describing one of them, declared that 'Mrs. Scott almost shed tears into the ice pudding when I refused her eighth course.' Canon Scott had not worked happily with Knox; now that the son of his old friend had been appointed, his delight was unbounded, and he offered the Temples the hospitality of his home for as long as they pleased. The quiet and comfort he found here were just what Temple needed at the moment, and he succeeded in finishing a book that had been on his hands for some time, the *Life* of his revered headmaster, John Percival. In September he had written to his brother, from the Isle of Wight, where he was spending part of his summer holiday:

> I am working away at John Percival's Life. It is difficult to arrange, because he had his work at his own official posts, and side by side with that a general public career. This was in itself quite continuous and needs a separate story. But it re-acted on his work at the official posts and therefore has to be alluded to in accounts of his activities at these.

Every spare moment in the autumn had been given up to the book, and by the beginning of March the proofs were coming in. On 1 March he writes to his wife, who was in London arranging for the removal of their furniture:

> It is March and now, in a few days, you will arrive!
> Interviews to-day; but a slack afternoon. I have prepared the spare proofs to send out to the critics as I want to send them off as quick as possible.
> Fisher has asked me to be Chairman of a new Committee on Adult Education which he is setting up. I don't know at all!

... There is a lot to be said for trying to keep in touch with such things, and for the Church taking a lead with them. The Universities are all nominating their best men on to it. It is, of course, not administrative, like the Examinations Council, but will aim at promoting effective work of the W.E.A. type, advising both Universities and the Board with regard to this. I have asked for a few days of grace.

(On 21 April the Committee was set up and Temple was appointed Chairman. Its main purpose was to co-ordinate all national organizations for Adult Education and to help in establishing more local voluntary organizations in co-operation with the local Education Authorities. Temple resigned from the committee in the following summer.)

On 5 March, they moved across Manchester, to stay at the Deanery—it was a great convenience to be exactly opposite their own house while they were moving in, and Gough McCormick was one of Temple's closest friends. He already had a great reputation as a preacher, especially at the Sunday evening service in the cathedral, which was always full when the Dean was in the pulpit: but he was a sick man when he left London, and his death a few years later took from the Church one of its most notable and charming personalities. At last the move was completed. Both Temple and his wife were by this time beginning to feel the strain; it was essential for them to get away. Wiltshire always drew them like a magnet, and at the end of the month Temple was able to write to his brother from the Castle and Ball Hotel, Marlborough:

March 30, 1921.

By the time Easter came I felt I had been a bishop for years. Anyhow I was pretty tired, and Frances has had a fearful time. But we have got down here now for a week and should soon be full of beans. It is jolly to get back to the edge of our old haunts (Ramsbury is 5 miles away) and the country is looking lovely.

I begin to realize the difficulty of getting round a diocese. I have over 600 parishes, and have been in 24 churches in 6 weeks of especially hard going, with Confirmations apparently incessant.

A week! It was not a long holiday for two very tired people with the heaviest years of their life before them, during which Temple's powers were to be tested to the utmost by new and exacting tasks.

XIX

The Bishop at Work

This life is a wild kind of turmoil. But it is jolly to be in a place where so much happens and one is really up against the things that matter. It is in that way far the most invigorating job that I have had.

> W. T., letter to G. F. Bradby, April 1922.

We are in the midst of the National Assembly, and very dull it has been. There has been a cruel rush of London engagements lately. They make one's own work almost impossible. I was up a fortnight ago for two days, last week for four, this week for five, and next week I have to be in York for two, for Convocation. But one drives the ship along by these efforts, I suppose.

> W. T., letter to his brother, February 1922.

THE Form for the Consecration of Bishops which is printed with the Book of Common Prayer contains a number of questions that the bishop-elect is required to answer. They deal more with character than function, with spiritual ideals rather than particular duties, and the exhortation delivered by the consecrating archbishop lays down principles to be observed in the exercise of episcopal authority which are independent of all temporal fluctuations and ephemeral claims. But tradition suggests—and the needs of the Church demand—that certain functions come within the bounden duty of every bishop. It is required of him that he be an administrator, a pastor, and a teacher. The wheels of the diocesan machine must be kept moving, the souls of clergy and laity are committed to his direct and watchful care, and to his spiritual guardianship are entrusted the mysteries of the Christian Faith; the particular emphasis laid on each of these duties and the extent to which they should be delegated to others can be determined only by the diocesan himself. A further responsibility is laid upon the bishops of our day. The contrast between sacred and secular, which was one of the less profitable legacies of the Reformation, is now held to be false by all except a handful of Manichaeans; and over great areas of the national life, where conduct was once regulated by the whims or prejudices of individuals, and relations between persons and classes were settled largely by axioms long since discarded, the Gospel writ again runs; or should run, were it as easy to apply Christian principles to the baffling and particular complexities of modern living as it is merely to recite them in general terms. The wide and often specialized knowledge essential for realizing this ideal is lacking in most Christian congregations and their ministers —to whom should they look but to their bishop for leadership in Christian thinking and the relevance of their Faith to all the relationships of life? One exacting and more clearly definable duty remains. It is now taken for granted that, as Benson laid down many years ago, 'the office of a bishop in the Church of England is not a local one'. Decrees and pronouncements of binding force for the whole Bench are not issued from Lambeth or Bishopthorpe: the alternative method, of consultation and discussion and—since the passing of the Enabling Act—of legislation by consent, makes a heavy demand on the time of all diocesans, who are obliged at the beginning of each year to write off several weeks in their engagement book for the central work of the Church—for private meetings of the bishops, for Convocation, for the sessions of the Church Assembly, and for reading prayers in the House of Lords. It is easier, without (it is hoped) doing too much violence to the sequence of events, to look back over Temple's work at Manchester in these five aspects—though they will be seen to overlap at several points—than to attempt a strictly chronological record of his activities during the eight years of his episcopate.

His first and chief administrative task was to carry through the division of his diocese. In any list of obviously desirable reforms the creating of smaller sees was at that time agreed to hold a high place, and a Committee on New Sees and Provinces had already been set up by the Church Assembly with Temple as its chairman. Doubts were expressed about the wisdom of more than one scheme for the sub-division of the English dioceses which was then put out, but a strong case was presented when the claims of Manchester came to be considered. The population of the diocese was about $3\frac{1}{2}$ millions; it contained over 600 parishes; the city and cathedral were at its extreme southerly end; and the bishop had to give up a whole day in order to attend a meeting at Lancaster, for instance, or Blackpool which might last for no more than an hour. There was some opposition in principle outside the diocese, especially from old-fashioned churchmen who resented any increase at all in the number of sees. Of these Lord Long was typical, and when in January 1923 he wrote to *The Times* deprecating any proposals for sub-division—his particular reference was to Salisbury—Temple, as chairman of the New Sees Committee, took up the challenge, and set out the principles on which the growing demand for smaller dioceses was founded. The diocese, he urged, in the first place, is the inevitable unit of church administration, and it must be of a size to make it a convenient area of self-government, in which the burdens of finance and administration will be shouldered not only by a few leading laymen but by many others of the average type and social position. The people, moreover, desire to see the bishop occasionally in their own parishes—'his visits should be rare enough to remain something of an event, and frequent enough to let the people feel some real contact with him'—roughly, once in five years. It is unlikely that, with all his other engagements, the bishop can pay more than sixty such parochial visits in one year, which suggests 300 parishes as the maximum number. Of the clergy it could be contended that they had everything to gain from working in a small and compact diocese. If it was the duty of a bishop to foster their spiritual life, to be intimate enough with them to administer episcopal patronage with a wise impartiality, to advise other patrons who might appeal to him, and to know the individual difficulties and needs of his parish priests, this could be fulfilled only by a bishop who was not smothered in administrative detail; and the suggested alternative—that of providing a larger number of suffragans—was an inadequate substitute for the personal spiritual oversight that no bishop can delegate to others. Finally, perhaps the greatest drawback of all in over-large dioceses was felt by the bishop himself, who was in danger of losing spiritual vitality and of finding his own general direction of affairs out of sympathy with the clergy and people.

Inside the Manchester diocese opinion had been slowly moving in favour of division. It began to be expressed soon after the first World War, but loyalty to their bishop restrained many from taking active part in a project which was utterly distasteful to him. As soon as Temple arrived and it was known that he was in favour of immediate action, enthusiasm revived. In the spring of 1923, he wrote to his brother in India:

> It will be a supreme mercy when this diocese is divided. I hope that may happen in about 18 months from now. But it all depends on the pace at which money can be raised, and that depends on trade. India, of course, has let us down rather badly for some time past. And I expect you would not be popular if you started a crusade for the assistance of the trade of Lancashire, though as it would hasten the division of my diocese it would be a brotherly act!

The choice of the see city lay between Preston and Blackburn, and gave rise to no little contention. It was widely held that, if the diocese of Manchester was to be divided into two, Preston was the better centre. It was the town from which the civil local government of the whole county was administered; it was also one of the most ancient boroughs in England, which had always in fact been the capital of a great area of central Lancashire, and had learnt to combine traditions of dignity with modern standards of administrative efficiency. There was, however, a suggestion that there should be a third diocese in the northern part of the county with a see town at Lancaster. If this project were ever to become practicable, it was obviously better not to have another see town so close to Lancaster as Preston; and Blackburn had the advantage of being nine miles nearer than Preston to the industrial population of East Lancashire. The case was argued at a diocesan conference held on 16 June 1922, and it was decided, on a vote, that Blackburn should be the see town of the new diocese. When this had been settled, there was still much preliminary work—apart from the necessary legislation —to be done before the issue of the appeal: but Temple could now move with greater confidence; he took counsel with the clergy, consulted the influential laymen and women of the diocese, and addressed many public meetings. He wished his own contribution to involve some sacrifice, but the Committee had decided that none of the income of the see was to be transferred, so he sold stock to the value of £1,000. The example of his gift did not have the full effect he had hoped for on many of the richer churchmen of the diocese; but by the end of March 1926, £70,000 had come in, and the whole sum of £80,000 was raised within a year of launching the appeal. He still had the second largest diocese in England, with 2 million people and nearly 400 parishes; but the creation of the new see saved him the oversight of 1½ million people and 220 parishes, and no church in the diocese was now more than an hour's drive from his door.

On the last day of February 1927, Dr. Percy Mark Herbert, Bishop-Suffragan of Kingston-on-Thames, was enthroned by the Bishops of Manchester and Liverpool as Bishop of Blackburn in an episcopal chair set in the chancel of the parish church of S. Mary, which was now to be his cathedral. With a mallet of which the stone head was probably 3,000 years old (it had been found not long before in the bed of a stream at Whalley) and the haft had been cut from one of the oldest yew-trees growing on the site of Whalley Abbey Church, the Bishop knocked with vigour on the door of the cathedral—'Flint Mallet Dints Church Door' (*Blackburn Times*)—demanding admittance. Temple bade his farewell to the people of the new diocese, and after being enthroned the new Bishop preached his 'enthronistic' (*Burnley News*) sermon, and spoke of the greatness of the task and the opportunity that lay before his people and himself. After the service Dr. Herbert was officially welcomed by the Mayor at a lunch in the Town Hall. It had been a great day for Blackburn: tradesmen decorated their premises, crowds pavement-deep lined the road between the Town Hall and the Cathedral, Free Churchmen had cordially welcomed the new bishop, and the civic authorities had given every possible token of their goodwill. But for none was it a greater day than for the Bishop of Manchester, whose wise and vigorous leadership had set the churchpeople of Lancashire to their task, and carried it to its great conclusion.

His predecessor had already acknowledged the extent of Temple's achievements:

7/2/27.   18, Beckenham Grove,
My dear Bishop,   Shortlands, Kent.

Rowbotham has just sent me the new Directory, and I cannot refrain from sending you a word of very sincere congratulation on the extraordinary achievements of the early years of your episcopacy. Not only is the new diocese completed but when I look down the pages of the Directory I can hardly find one living under £300 and very few between 3 and 4 hundred. Remembering the financial straits of the last few years I am amazed, filled with joy, and at the same time with shame. You make me feel how lazy I must have been and I thought that I worked hard . . .

Yours affectionately,
E. A. KNOX, Bp.

Temple was well served by his assistants. Of the three suffragans in the undivided diocese there remained J. C. Hill, who had been appointed Bishop of Hulme in 1924—it was suggested by Canon Peter Green that Temple should choose the name of one of the poorest and dreariest districts of Manchester—and with him the Bishop probably had more in common than with any other of his clergy: he delighted in Hill's rather old-fashioned manner, and the flashes of wit that lit up his talk. In 1927 the first Bishop Suffragan of Middleton was consecrated. The title of the see was chosen partly because Middleton was an ancient parish—in its fine church is the oldest war-memorial window in the country (to the men of Middleton who had fought at Flodden in 1513) —which had given Cardinal Langley to Durham and Bishop Durnford to Chichester: partly because, owing to their rival claims, it was difficult to choose one of the larger Lancashire towns. Temple nominated Canon R. G. Parsons (now Bishop of Hereford) as Bishop Suffragan, an old friend from Oxford days and a collaborator in *Foundations*, who had been appointed Rector of Birch-in-Rusholme, Manchester, eighteen months before Knox resigned. He did not divide up the diocese, as is more usually done, into districts, nor were the suffragans entrusted with the administrative or pastoral oversight of parishes in any particular area. He and his two assistants roamed over the whole diocese for Confirmations, and either of the suffragans might be asked to perform some episcopal act or ceremony in any of the parishes. There was no regular meeting of the bishops at stated intervals, though Temple constantly asked their advice about matters in which he knew them to be interested or concerned, and each of them was made chairman of one or two important diocesan Councils or Boards. They were hardly ever consulted about parochial appointments.

So long as the diocese suffered from the 'financial straits' to which Knox alluded, it was not easy to apportion fairly and wisely the amount of money available. The incomes of the clergy were seldom out of Temple's mind; he regarded their claim on the diocesan funds as paramount, and the Board of Finance wholeheartedly supported him. There was less unanimity when Whalley Abbey came on the market. Temple was determined to procure it for the Church of England and, though some were critical of the price (£17,800) eventually agreed between a committee appointed by the Bishop for the purpose and the owner, his general policy has since been amply justified: the Abbey is now in constant use as a Retreat and Conference House by the diocese of Blackburn and many organizations outside it. On Temple's share in the general financial work of the diocese, Mr. S. Rowbotham, the Secretary of the Board of Finance, writes:

On general matters of routine diocesan administration, Dr. Temple always found time to keep himself fully informed, and he never took the chair at a meeting for which I was responsible, without first going through the agenda and getting a grip of all the questions to be considered. He was always ready to be consulted, to advise, and to support. So far as I was concerned, Dr. Temple was always in close contact with diocesan affairs, however great the claims from outside in the wider matters affecting the Church as a whole. He did not himself go deeply into the more intricate questions of finance, but he attended regularly the monthly meetings of the Board . . . and saw to it that responsible laymen and clergymen were in charge of affairs. By giving them his complete confidence, he secured wholehearted and competent service. In presiding over Diocesan Committees, Dr. Temple's method was to give full latitude of expression from all sections, and discussion was never stifled. Some may have said that he suffered fools too gladly, but the freedom he allowed was rarely exploited and seldom did a meeting go over the prescribed time. He had a quick intuition and sensed unerringly the moment when the matter in hand could be put to the vote. Whatever minor defects his method had, it possessed the supreme advantage of giving the feeling of free and unfettered discussion, and in Lancashire this meant much. He himself spoke little at meetings except to guide discussion and at the end to give a masterly summing up.

There is one feature of diocesan and parochial life which a bishop, in fulfilling his administrative duties, dare not (even if he would) neglect, and that is 'the Organizations'—the rather grim collective name by which are known the hardy and multifarious efforts to guide and guard the souls of church members from the kindergarten to the grave. Temple did his duty by them all, and was genuinely interested in most of them, though he was without the knack which enabled his brother bishop (for instance) of London almost to convince the leaders of each organization—in successive weeks—that theirs was the one effort in the diocese that lay next his heart. The 'Youth Organizations' made a special appeal to him. At the time of his arrival in Manchester the Church Lads' Brigade was down in the trough, because of its alleged 'militaristic tendencies'. Pacifism was then a rising force, and many C.L.B. leaders feared that their work might not have the approval of the new Bishop. After a visit to the parish of S. James's, Gorton, where the Brigade was to be seen at its best and strongest, Temple gave it his unqualified support. He took the salute at the annual review at Belle Vue, and a detachment from the Manchester C.L.B. was proud to form a guard of honour

outside the Minster for his enthronement at York. Of local and
more spectacular interest was the Whit Sunday procession of
Sunday School children through the streets of Manchester, his
first experience of which he described in a letter to his brother:

> Bishopscourt,
> Manchester.
> May 18, 1921.

A trifle of rest comes with the Whitsuntide holidays, which
are a tremendous function in these parts. But if the pressure
had gone on as it was from mid-April till a few days back, I
should have crocked up.

On Whitsunday there is a marvellous event here. Over
25,000 Sunday School children assemble in Albert Square,
which is just in front of the Town Hall, and set out on a
procession, which takes over three hours to pass any point.
As many as can crowd into the Cathedral; as soon as it is full
there is a Service—and on they go. I had to talk to them this
year. The girls all wear white, and most carry baskets of
flowers; there are swarms of banners and floral emblems, etc.,
so it is a great show.

Lancashire churchpeople have for many years been noted for
their missionary zeal. Every year Temple took the chair at the
great Church Missionary Society and S.P.G. Rallies in the Free
Trade Hall, and he missed no occasion for bringing home to his
diocese the world-wide mission of the Church. But if any of his
efforts is to be singled out for fuller treatment, it should be his
work for women, apart from his support of the established
organizations. The Moral Welfare work was re-organized with
his constant interest and support by Miss Meliscent Sheppard,
who has since served the same cause with a like devotion in India.
He described the Mothers' Union—though later, while he was at
York, his relations with its headquarters were not free from
occasional strain—as 'one of the main sources of strength to the
life of the Church'; and many hundred members of the Girls'
Friendly Society, of which his wife was the vigorous and devoted
Diocesan President, enjoyed the hospitality of Bishopscourt. But

Temple's work went deeper than this. Among the chapters in its history of which the National Church has no cause to be proud, that which tells of its treatment of women workers is one of the least creditable. The conditions of status and salary under which many of them then worked were to Temple intolerable. He championed the cause of women, not because they were women but because they were human beings whose personality was sacred in the sight of God, who were a section of the laity, of the people of God; it was this conviction that gave an urgency and a stability to the reforms he was determined to effect. And here he was fortunate in having the help and sympathy of his wife, whose spiritual zeal and practical work for the movement must be ranked high among the factors that made for its ultimate success. Outside the Church changes in women's work, especially in their education and vocational training, were then being made and planned which altered the whole popular conception of woman's position and functions in the community. Before Temple came to Manchester a few women had tried to interest the Women's Diocesan Council in these changes, and a deputation from the Council waited upon the Bishop soon after his arrival, asking him to inaugurate Women Messengers' work in the diocese. Temple listened with sympathy, expressed his willingness to employ Messengers, but insisted that women's church work in the diocese needed reviewing as a whole, and announced his intention to set up a Board of Women's Work which would consider all the aspects of that work, including the appointment of Women Messengers. Possibly those concerned only with Messenger work were disappointed at the delay, but others came away feeling that they had been given more than they would have asked: above all they saw in Temple a bishop who was prepared to devote to women's work the same consideration as that accorded to men's, and who looked to receive from women intelligent and responsible co-operation.

The Board of Women's Work came into being in January 1922. Such Boards already existed in a few dioceses, notably London and Southwark, and together they formed an Inter-diocesan Council which gave strength and cohesion to the diocesan organizations, and helped gradually to secure uniform action in matters of training, status, and salary. The idea was a new one in Manchester and its reception was not entirely cordial; but Temple quietly prepared the ground in a way which showed that he had a knowledge and understanding of the whole subject deeper than that of anyone else in the diocese, and before the end of his first year as Chairman of S. Hilda's Training House for Women Layworkers—a House which under Deaconess Amelia Bromley had laid good foundations and done excellent work but was in some ways out of touch with modern conditions—S. Hilda's had completely revised its constitution and had become, as the Bishop wished, a training centre for deaconesses. The members of the new Board included some of the ablest clergy and women of the diocese, among whom were Dr. Parsons, Dr. S. C. Carpenter (now Dean of Exeter), and Violet Hewit, who became the secretary and constant inspiration of the Board. The Bishop appointed Canon Hill, Rector of Bury, who has been mentioned as one of his suffragans, as chairman: it was an ideal choice, for not only did Dr. Hill share fully the Bishop's faith in the contribution women could make, he also showed a personal care for the spiritual and material welfare of the workers which brought happiness and courage to many isolated lives. The attention of the Board was first concentrated on the parochial workers, who were entirely unorganized and mostly untrained. Within the first year the Board had joined the Inter-diocesan Council for Women's Work, regulations for the licensing and authorization of the workers had been drawn up with the Bishop's sanction, a training scheme for S. Hilda's Training House was being prepared which was soon accepted by the I.D.C., and the House was recognized as an I.D.C. training centre: a little later a minimum salary was fixed and Women Messengers were started. In 1925 a Pensions Scheme—later to be merged in the inter-diocesan scheme—came into force and regulations were drawn up for women speaking in church. Along with these activities the Board was proving its value to the workers by arranging lectures and classes to help with training, retreats, and opportunities for social intercourse, by its readiness to help individual workers in any difficulty and, above all, by the annual cathedral service at which the Bishop licensed and authorized qualified workers. Always in his addresses Temple expressed his faith in and his respect for women's work and encouraged them to give of their best; and a marked change was to be noticed in the workers as they realized the value set on their efforts and became conscious of a growing fellowship. In November 1925 the 'Form and Manner for the Making of Deaconesses' was used for the first time in the diocese, and in 1927 the Bishop installed Margaret Wordsworth as Head Deaconess of the Diocesan Training House. With the advantage of her wide vision and wise guidance the students at the House reached a good standard in their studies (some of them taking university courses) and in devotional training; they were gaining experience in social work and learning the right use of leisure, and the House was well filled.

Temple's achievements in this part of his pastoral work cannot be summarized better than in the words of an address presented to him, with an attaché case which he used to the end of his life, when he left the diocese. It was signed by more than eighty women workers—and there is no more than the truth in any line of it.

Dear Lord Bishop,   November 22, 1928.

On the eve of your departure from the Diocese, we the women workers of the Diocese of Manchester (and of that part of the old Diocese which is now the Diocese of Blackburn) desire to express, though in but a small and inadequate way, our deep gratitude to you for your generous labours on behalf of Women's Church Work.

By your consistent advocacy in Convocation and elsewhere you have done great service in raising the whole conception of the Ministry of Women throughout the Church in England, and deaconesses and laywomen alike are grateful.

But most of all we desire to thank you for your sympathetic and fair treatment of your own workers. From your first coming into the diocese you have shewn equal respect and consideration for women's work as for men's. By your wise

William Temple

counsel and judgment; by your constant interest and understanding; by your steadfast belief in the need of the Church for our services; by the high standard of work you have expected from us; by your patient willingness to help at all times, and often to be troubled by small details and never to show you counted it a trouble, you have given us a new hope and courage and a new vision of what our work may be and ought to be.

You have given dignity and authority to our work by your Licences and Authorizations and by the beautiful Annual Service in the Cathedral. You have started a Pensions Scheme which will bring security for the future of an increasing number of workers, you have secured for us conditions of work and pay which we could not ourselves have asked and which by easing our difficulties will help us to do better work; you have provided for us opportunities and illuminated our understanding of the Christian Faith: and whereas seven years ago we were scattered units often lonely and isolated we know now the joy and strength of fellowship in building the City of God.

It is not only with great gratitude and respect but also with great affection that we now desire to say, Thank you.

We will ever watch with prayerful and affectionate interest your future in that high state of life and service to which it has pleased God to call you, and so we bid you fare-well and God-speed.

Your obedient affectionate servants.

It can be imagined how keen was the relief of Temple and his wife to get away sometimes from organizations and enjoy the warmhearted fellowship of churchpeople in the diocese—for nowhere is there a stronger social side to church life than in Lancashire. At six different centres they were invited to receptions held to greet them, and there was a friendly rivalry between the local efforts to give them a cordial welcome: after shaking hands with 800 people at Burnley, Temple was approached by one of his hosts who asked confidentially—'Did they give you as good a "do" at Accrington?' The Bishop returned this hospitality by having four 'At Homes' during his first year, at which the social

308

charm and grace of his wife ensured the success of the first, and all her other, diocesan parties. They also had their own close personal friends, among whom were John Stocks (who had been appointed Professor of Philosophy in the University) and his wife, and Sir Walter and Lady Moberly.

The generosity of churchpeople in the diocese was, again, typical of Lancashire. Temple was not a good beggar but, once they were convinced that an object was a sound one, the laity were ready not only to make their own contributions but to do the Bishop's begging for him and win the support of others. In 1928 this generosity took a specially pleasing form. The pension that Knox took out of the Bishop's income made careful economy essential at Bishopscourt, and for nearly four years Temple had done his travelling in trains and trams, hiring a taxi only when it was absolutely necessary. In 1925 Canon Dorrity, Rector of S. Ann's, Manchester, was asked by one of the leading laymen to be honorary secretary of a small company who hoped to raise a few hundred pounds with which to buy the Bishop a car. The sum needed was soon subscribed, and Temple and his wife both learned to drive the Austin 12 which was the model they had chosen. The Bishop was a painstaking, but never a good, driver, as he could see only out of his left eye and complained that he had to 'look round his nose' in order to reverse; nor could he claim any deep knowledge of the car's mechanical mysteries. A few weeks after the car arrived he wrote to his brother:

> I am a tolerably assured motorist now—provided nothing goes wrong with the engine! That has not happened yet, but whenever it does, I shall be done! Our car has taken to rattling a great deal. I hope some tightening of screws will remedy that, but I am rather wondering if we should not have done better after all to get a saloon.

To his great delight he found in the diocese many old Rugbeians, who, in May 1921, gave him a dinner at the Midland Hotel. Sir A. A. Haworth, Lord Kilbracken, J. L. Paton, and the Headmaster of Rugby were the speakers, but the hit of the evening was E. V. Knox's *Vive-la*:

Of famous Rugbeians the list never closes,
And Dr. Jex-Blake said the first one was Moses,[1]
And deep though your search into history dug be
You'll not find a school that's had masters like Rugby.
Time forbids me on all those great men to sing paeans
Whose lifted right hand left a mark on Rugbeians:
From Arnold, whom nothing could daunt or intimidate,
We will pass at a bound, if you please, to the 'Jimmy' date.
So much wisdom did James and his masters exhibit
That all other schools said 'We simply must crib it',
And telegrams kept coming faster and faster,
'Please send per return one James brand of headmaster.'
So the Masters at Rugby were soon made to shift on,
And Manchester seized one, and one went to Clifton.
And here Manchester showed what she'd always been great on,
Her sound common sense and how firm is her pate on:[2]
And not long by the Philistine armies enslavéd
To the School House once more came triumphantly David.
But meanwhile there arose and waxed stalwart and ruddy,
In quad, hall, and form-room, in choir and in study,
Our guest of this evening, most shining exemplum
Of Rugby's strong building, mirabile Templum.
Inspired by our long list of notable names,
And tutored by Paton and David and James,
He ate into Virgil and Plato and Thicksides,
He played up at Hobley's, he played up in Bigsides.
The son of that famous Headmaster and Primate,
The Close proved for him a most nourishing climate.
In knowledge and learning so stoutly he stepped on,
He was still but a babe when they snatched him to Repton.
But London grew anxious: with bells sounding shrilly,
'We must have this boy!' cried St. James, Piccadilly.
He paused there a moment, then breathlessly ran on
To be Westminster Abbey's most infantile canon.
Then Manchester thought, 'If we don't quickly borrow,
What London thinks now we'll be thinking to-morrow.'
So he broke through the scrum, speaker, preacher, and writer

Till His Majesty said, 'You may now wear your mitre.'
And Manchester greets him convinced that he 'll stir well,
Now he hangs his harp by them, the waters of Irwell.
Were there time I would sing how he 's introduced quite a
New motto for Churchmen, LIBERTAS ET VITA.
How he flung out a Challenge, made workers' life rosier,
And still walks a Pilgrim, though propped by a crozier.
But suffice it to say that we greet as spectators
The youngest thing yet in episcopal gaiters.
We are sure that that garb he most worthily fills,
Our Enabling and also our ablest of Bills.
And whatever the strain on the Church or the tug be
We can always rely on a Temple from Rugby.

¹ 'Moses, an excellent man and an old Rugbeian', Dr. Jex-Blake (according to tradition) in a sermon.
² J. L. Paton, High Master of Manchester Grammar School, 1903–24.

A long catalogue could be made of Temple's manifold interests, and of the number of points at which he touched the life of Manchester: a few of them call for special mention. Foremost among these was the University. He had his seat on the Council, but his connexion with the governing body was more personal and went far deeper than that of an official; when he was presented for an Honorary Doctorate by his venerable and loved friend Professor Alexander (who also paid a gracious tribute to Mrs. Temple) there was wide evidence of the respect and affection in which he was held in academic circles. His relations with Roman Catholics and Free Churchmen were entirely cordial; he was Chairman of the Council of Christian Congregations, a body composed of Anglicans and Free Churchmen for taking united social action, and Free Church ministers with their wives were always assured of a hospitable welcome at Bishopscourt. He took part in the Quadrennial Conference of the Student Christian Movement in 1925 and in the activities of Toc H, and gave lavishly of his time to the W.E.A. No chance was missed of speaking to bodies, of both employers and employed, responsible for the industrial life of the city—to the Manchester Engineering Council, to Works Committees, and to the Manchester Luncheon

Club, among whose members were representatives of the University, the Church, the professions, commerce, and industry. Here especially the Bishop was always welcome; he was in the chair on several occasions, the last being in 1942 just before he went to Canterbury, when he explained the 'Religion and Life' Movement in which he was then taking a leading part. His closest social contacts were naturally with churchmen, and it is the Old Rectory Club in Manchester that the Church regards as its social centre. On the ground floor of the building is the Holdsworth Hall, much used for meetings. Above it are the Bishop's rooms where clergy and laity can see him privately; and on the third floor is the Club, where the latest Church news is to be heard and clergy relax over their food and talk. Here Temple had frequent opportunities of talking over the finance and other business of the diocese with leading laymen such as Ernest Fletcher and R. C. Longridge, and he constantly lunched at the Club between meetings. Occasionally there would be a dinner to which members could bring guests, and whenever it was possible Temple was of the company; nor would he be allowed to leave before he had sung the 'Chancellor's Nightmare Song' from *Iolanthe*, which never failed of its applause.

Many attempts have been made by the parsons and laymen of Lancashire to record their impressions of Temple's episcopate. The tale is a consistent one; of ever increasing vitality, of spiritual advance—'I shall never forget', his old friend and teacher J. L. Paton had written on giving up the Highmastership of Manchester Grammar School in 1924, 'the stirring of the spirit on the day you came to Manchester'—of the Church's new social influence, of freedom in discussion and fellowship in the Faith: but one word stands out with a recurrence that witnesses to its truth— theirs was a *happy* diocese.

XX

The Pastor and Teacher

The great issue for religion in our day is not to be found in our differences about sacramental doctrine; it is not to be found in our disagreements about validity of ministries; it concerns faith in the living God. The first duty of the Church is to be sure that it knows how to present the truth of God so as to reveal its adequacy to the knowledge and the needs of to-day. That God is Himself both Ultimate Reality and Supreme Value we are well assured; but it is not enough that we should be assured; we must so present Him before men alike in our teaching, in our worship, in the enterprises to which we give our thought, in the choice of subjects on which we dispute with our fellow-Christians and in the very manner of our controversies, that others may find the assurance which means so much to us. We must do this in our teaching.

W. T., *Thoughts on some Problems of the Day*, 1931.

ONE of Knox's most important legacies to his successor was the Blackpool Mission. Knox was a keen evangelist and, on the principle that the Church should follow the people, took a band of missioners every year in August Bank Holiday week to the town which had become a traditional holiday resort for thousands of the people of Lancashire. A number of 'stands' were set up on the beach from South Shore to Fleetwood, and the missioners included the ablest preachers and evangelists in the diocese. To be chosen as one of these might not be an entirely pleasant experience. The Mission was conducted throughout on rather old-fashioned evangelical lines, and Knox had a habit of roaming round the 'stands' and listening to the closing words of an address: if the subject-matter was not approved, the missioner ran the risk of being told that his services were no longer required, and that he could leave by the next train. Temple's most valuable innovation was the appeal he made to the heads as well as the hearts of the people; he could only work, he would say, on his own lines. During his first year's Mission he gave mid-day addresses in church on S. John's Gospel, and their success encouraged him to treat the Book of The Revelation in the same way in 1922. One of the missioners recalls their apprehension when this project became known:

> Lunch-hour talks! In church! During August Bank Holiday week! In Blackpool! On The Revelation! Most of us felt that he was batting on a sticky wicket, and despite extensive postering not more than 40 or 50 people turned up. The next day there were over 200, and for the remaining days the church was packed, a queue outside stretching almost down to the Front, waiting to get in—a wonderful example of his judgment and an amazing testimony to his power of exposition!

By the end of the day the Bishop and his missioners were ready to relax. The Headmaster of Rossall allowed them to use the school buildings as their headquarters and dormitory, and every evening there was much 'merriment of parsons' in the Senior Common Room. Knox was a kindly man but his humour, even in his most jocular mood, suggested Dr. Grimstone rather than Father O'Flynn. Temple—not 'unbuttoned', for he was never buttoned up, but quite spontaneously—became the centre of all the fun and fellowship, and his laughter penetrated to the floor above where the Headmaster would have liked to be busy in his study. Of his many stories one was much appreciated—about the mourner who had taken rather too much pre-funeral sherry, and fell asleep in church during the burial service. He woke with a start as the words were read, 'As in Adam all die, even so in Christ shall all be made alive', and commented loudly with a nod of approval—'Quite right too: what could be fairer than *that*?' One of the missioners has summed up his impressions of the week in 1923:

> We have just returned from taking part once again in the Bishop's Mission at Blackpool. I think that every member of the staff has been more than ever impressed by the real greatness of Dr. Temple. His perfectly ordered and amazingly clever mind is a constant source of astonishment. Everything he does—he does well. The surprising thing is how he finds time to do it. At Rossall he is most friendly—just like a big brother to every man. His notoriously hearty laugh is a tonic,

but all the time you feel that he is reading you through and through, behind those veiled eyes. On Sunday night, after four crowded services, at each of which he had given a masterly address, I went into his room to find him busy editing the *Pilgrim*. He was still at it at eleven o'clock! In spite of the exceedingly strenuous week, he found time to read two volumes of French history and made notes of the same, and all this time he was suffering intense pain from a very bad attack of gout.

Temple's own impressions were recorded year by year in letters to his wife:

July 31, 1921.

... Just back from my 3 sermons. Over 1200 folk at each, and I think they went well. Everyone is commenting on the greater number of men at these functions, which is rather encouraging.

My foot was worse again this morning, and remained bad till lunch time, but then got a good deal better. Of course standing on it is bad, and it hurt a lot after each service. Now to bed.

August 6, 1923.

... To-day I was in S. John's—on the Apocalypse. There were about 700 people there—rather wonderful on a bank holiday. The staff is much intrigued by a hoarding on which may be read the following enticing advertisement:

DON'T MISS THE GREAT DIPPER   THE BISHOP ON THE SANDS.

I gather that the dipper is in fact a switchback with a peculiarly deep sheer drop; the hoarding is a narrow, long one, and the two notices are made to fit it, with the above result. ... I have done a sermon, and most of the magazine. And the Calendar for 1924. To-morrow I hope to do most of my part of the *Pilgrim*. Hugh Cecil's article has come and is very good.

August 7, 1923.

... This evening there were 900–1000 people in the church for 'The Sealed Book'. It is very striking that they should want to attend a 50 minutes' lecture on a bit of the Bible like that.

It is a very happy party. Peter Green is enjoying every

315

minute of every day.... Of course the 2 Archdeacons [Aspinall and Hornby, Temple's devoted friends] are darlings and Darbyshire [later Archbishop of Capetown] is an all-round success.

> August 8, 1923.

... This morning I was at Fleetwood for the children.... Then North Pier. After lunch—letters and *Pilgrim*. At tea time a letter came from Cosmo to say that if I would set out the whole case for a 3rd suffragan in a formal letter, he would forward it to the Crown with his support. So I wrote hard, and the Archdeacon of Lancaster typed each sheet as soon as it was written and we got it off by the 6 o'clock post. Then my 3rd lecture. Peter Green says my lectures have for the first time enabled him to 'see a shape' in the Book of Revelation.

> August 2, 1924.

... This is last night's letter, but I got so late reading *Back to Methuselah* that I went to bed without writing it.

> July 30, 1925.

... Everyone seems very happy and jolly. Peter is much pleased because in my Fleetwood discourse—having alluded to signs of penitence in dogs—I said that this never occurred in cats, but Canon Green would tell them that this was because a cat can do no wrong, and that I agreed with him.

> July 31, 1925.

... It has been a delicious day from morning to night. I had an easy time, as I was only speaking twice this morning (Central Pier and Tower) and had no fixtures after lunch. I have written 2,000 words more of the book [*Christian Religion and the Life of Fellowship*, the Bishop of London's Lent Book for 1926]—it is 23,000 now. Also, having in my rooms the *Encyclopædia Britannica*, I have set to on that article on France which David [Somervell] said was so excellent. So far I have got to the end of Louis XI. It will make a splendid skeleton to fit reading in the Island on to: and as I go on trams, I murmur the dates of Philip Augustus, Louis IX, Philip the Fair,

Charles VII and Louis XI—who seem to be the epoch-marking persons so far.

What a mercy about the coal strike! There can be no doubt Baldwin was right to buy it off, but it is a shocking precedent all the same.

August 5, 1925.

. . . I took a small and most delightful Confirmation at S. Stephen's—of 5 dancing girls at the Winter Gardens, who are shortly going to New York. Then my address in S. John's. . . . Then lunch with the rotary Group and a speech full of glittering wit and massive wisdom on 'Parties and Partisanship'.

August 2, 1926.

I think the mission is going well, but it is hard to get much comparison with other years: I suppose that really means that it is much the same as usual and nothing strikes one as special. But this itself probably means that it needs shaking up and I hope the new Bishop of Blackburn will be able to tackle it.

In the yearly round of his more settled pastoral work, Temple would plan to spend two or three days at a time in the northern part of the diocese, before it was divided, holding Confirmations and preaching, and seeing as much as he could of the clergy and laity in their parishes. While on one of these tours, he writes to his wife:

The Vicarage,
Carnforth.
May 26, 1922.

. . . 2 delightful services yesterday—13 candidates at Yealand and 63 at Warton (the mother parish of Carnforth), and 2 delightful Vicars. I shall have officiated in 8 churches in this Deanery, as well as 4 in Lancaster and one in Garstang, when I get home on Wednesday. I hope you are getting some peace and rest. I can hardly be said to be achieving that, but it is a rest in itself to be in the country; and a service in a country church is very refreshing.

When Dr. Guy Warman succeeded to the bishopric he found that none of Temple's ministrations was more keenly appreciated

317

than his Confirmation addresses. There were still occasions on which he misjudged the intellectual standard of his audience, one of which is recalled by Sir Walter Moberly, who was Vice-Chancellor of the University during the last three years of Temple's episcopate:

I am not in a position to speak of his more intimate work as diocesan bishop or of his pastoral relations with his clergy. . . . But I can say something of his general impact on the city. Of course he could not but be liked, respected, and admired. But somehow I do not think Manchester ever quite took him to its heart in the sense in which, according to tradition, it once took Bishop Fraser. Looking back I am rather puzzled to account for this. In view of his greatness, his warm humanity, and his entire absence of self-importance, one might have expected him to make an immense appeal to Manchester. But though he was successful there, I should not call him super-latively successful. He was welcome everywhere, as notably on the University Council. I fancy he was felt just a little too impersonal and intellectual for real warmth of intimacy. This is illustrated by a Sunday he spent in Manchester after he had already gone to York on the occasion of the 250th anniversary of the death of Hulme, the benefactor of Manchester and of Brasenose College. In the morning he preached to university students at Hulme Hall and 'took them between wind and water'. It was exactly right: no one could have been more effective. In the afternoon he preached to a large congregation in the Cathedral, a considerable section of which, contrary to his expectation, was composed of boys and girls from the various Hulme schools. He delivered a thoughtful, and to me deeply interesting, discourse on some of the fundamental changes in educational ideas which have occurred since Hulme's day. But, for all his lucidity, it was above the heads of the congregation. For the next few days nearly everyone I met said to me either—'Well, I suppose *you* understood the Arch-bishop?' or, 'Not even you can have understood what the Archbishop was driving at!'

No such mistake was made at Confirmations. Here he was the true pastor, expounding the Word of God, and driving it home with simple lessons of witness and service. But the greatest joy of his episcopate he found in the ordinations and the retreats which led up to them. These were always held at Bishopscourt, unless the numbers were too large, as they were when there were thirty candidates at Michaelmas 1923, when use was made of Hulme Hall. It is significant that, among the presentations made to him and his wife on their leaving the diocese, was a special gift (an arm-chair and a fender stool) from all those whom he had ordained; many of them recall those week-ends as among the most formative spiritual experiences of their lives, and every detail still stands out in their memory. There was the warm and unaffected welcome they received from the Bishop's wife (whose memory for faces and names helped to put the men at their ease, and whose friendly charm at once reassured the sensitive and loosened the stiffness of the embarrassed); and the countless *obiter dicta* of the Bishop were long remembered and quoted, such as this, on Christianity and War: 'At the beginning of the war I went to hear Dean Wace speak on this subject. I did not find him helpful. On my return I consulted the *Summa*. I thought that S. Thomas might be more illuminating than Dean Wace. . . . He was.' Inevitably the Bishop dominated the company, but it was not the domination that is felt to discourage freedom of expression and repress the natural impulses of social intercourse. No subject was too serious to discuss, and none too trivial for mention: 'What was it he wanted you to ask me?' Temple suddenly said to one of the candidates whose next-door neighbour, at supper on the evening of their arrival, had whispered something that almost reached the Bishop's ear. 'Oh! He was just wondering, my Lord, whether you would tell us what size your Lordship takes in collars': 'Only 17½', replied Temple, with just enough of apology for the fact in his tone of voice as to appear to justify the question—and after the laughter that followed every tongue was loosed: how could there be any tension, how could any of them feel ill at ease, in the home of so human a bishop? Yet he insisted on strict discipline during the retreat. He read aloud to the ordinands at breakfast—the books most often chosen were that inimitable collection of Anglican reminiscences, Scott Holland's *A Bundle of Memories*, and Dr. Alington's Shrewsbury and Eton *Fables*—and they were allowed to talk from lunch till 10 p.m., but after Compline the rule of silence was absolute: 'The only time I ever saw the Bishop near to anger', writes one of those whom he ordained, 'was when an ordinand broke the rule of silence after Compline.' In his private interviews with the men Temple encouraged them to confidences that few were not relieved to bestow; his gentleness and tolerance drew out the secrets of their souls. No heresy could shock, no immaturity could annoy: only with unabashed conceit was his impatience unmistakable. On the last evening came the climax of the retreat, when the Bishop sat in a chair before the altar in his chapel and expounded—almost always with the Fourth Gospel as a background—the relevance of the sacred ministry to the redemptive purpose of God: 'It was never the time for practical hints', recalls the Bishop of Bath and Wells: 'he shewed us the Lord, high and lifted up.' No word of his charge was written, and all noticed the absolute stillness of his body while he spoke—not as the scholar, the preacher, or even the Bishop, but as the man of God who knew his own insufficiency and unworthiness and yet was assured that the divine power could work miracles in the hearts and lives of those who believed that God had called them into the ministry of his Church. Nor did his interest in the men cease after their ordination. Sometimes he took one of the younger curates in his diocese with him to Oxford or Cambridge for the week in September set apart for the meeting of the Commission on Doctrine; and, if he were driving to some town of interest such as Shrewsbury or Carlisle, he would occasionally ask an incumbent to give his curate a day off and after lunch leave the young man to explore the place while the Bishop did his business. If it happened that for some reason he was not motoring back, he never forgot that curates have little money, and a railway ticket was his parting gift for the day.

The most severe criticism of Temple as a bishop has centred on his judgement of men. This will come under fuller review in a

At the Blackpool Mission

later chapter; it must here be admitted that, so far as his choice of ordinands is concerned, his examining chaplains had some difficult moments, when they and their bishop failed to agree about the fitness of certain candidates. They were not satisfied, for instance, when Temple pleaded on one man's behalf that, although after several attempts he had failed to pass either part of the General Ordination Examination, he had 'passed every paper in G.O.E. *at some time or another*'! The Bishop of Hereford, who was one of his suffragans, probably comes as near to the truth as possible in this short summary:

Certainly he made some rather surprising appointments, and admitted to Holy Orders a number of men of a type previously not often ordained. I am perhaps a prejudiced witness; but I don't think his criticized appointments by any means always turned out to be mistakes: nor did all his rough diamonds prove merely to be rough. He was, I believe, moved by his awareness of his own unusual abilities, to beware of testing others by the standards he would apply to himself and his intellectual peers. This may have led him to be unduly uncritical in some cases, and there was in him a very real humility, which played a part in this.

It has already been remarked that Temple shrank from inflicting pain and suffering even on those who least deserved his mercy. This weakness—if such it was—was shown in his occasional reluctance to have personal dealings with priests (especially the older of them) who had gone morally wrong: others, he pleaded, acting on his behalf would deal with them much better than he could. It was thought by many that he was too lenient with the backsliders—certainly he gave some of them more chances than most bishops would have thought wise—but no effort to reclaim them could fail so hopelessly as to make Temple believe that it must be the last. One particular lapse of a priest in his diocese he found it almost impossible to dismiss from his mind. He hardly ever lay awake at night, but the problem of how to deal with this delinquent haunted him, and after a wretched night of sleeplessness he wrote to his wife:

Y

. . . A comfy journey and a dull afternoon. An early dinner and a good meeting of S.S. teachers in the Central Hall. I was grateful for that, because having to speak at it did completely detach my mind for a time from its present obsession. However, I have had a talk with Cosmo and fixed up in principle what is to be done, so I am out of the distraction of doubt, though the stark misery of the thing is still there.

In Temple's conception of episcopal functions, the Teaching Office was almost a part of the Pastoral Office: to him it seemed at least as essential to guard and feed the minds of Christian people as to nourish their souls. Too many of the clergy, the official teachers of the Church, seemed blind to one important aspect of the Gospel, and it was this—the social message of Christianity—that he set himself to teach and propagate. One weapon lay ready to his hand: this was the *Pilgrim*, a monthly magazine with the sub-title 'A Review of Christian Politics and Religion'. In 1920, while he was still at Westminster, Temple was approached by R. G. Longman with the suggestion that he should edit a new periodical which might attempt to present a Christian view of the major problems of the day in politics and citizenship: the editor was to contribute one article to each issue, and the finance would be the responsibility of the publishers. The distinguishing feature of the *Pilgrim* was to be its balance— the combination of Politics and Religion in one periodical—'A religion which offers no solution to world-problems fails to satisfy; a scheme of reconstruction, apart from religion, strikes cold and academic. Our effort is to bring home to men the claim of Christ that He is the Way, the Truth, and the Life.' Criticism of such a venture was to be expected. Dr. Inge wrote an undated and characteristic note to Temple:

I think you must admit that 'Christian Politics', in the *Pilgrim* and elsewhere, are tinged with the roseate hues of early dawn. I should never call my brand of Whiggery Christian Politics, though they are the politics of one Christian.

When Temple went to Manchester he consented to remain as editor, though the time he could give to the *Pilgrim* was severely restricted. It had been welcomed with striking cordiality by the secular Press of all political shades, by members of the Roman Catholic as well as the Anglican Church, and by men prominent in affairs of state; yet the sales remained obstinately low. Longmans persevered gallantly from year to year, and it was hoped that Copec—a Movement to be described in the next chapter—would provide the fillip needed to establish the journal. But there was no appreciable rise in the circulation, and in 1927 the publishers had to surrender. Temple's last reference to it is in a letter of 18 May 1927 to his brother, about the Government's Trade Union Bill: 'I can't dissent from the objects of the Bill, but I doubt if it is calculated to attain them . . . the only consolation is that the *Pilgrim* died before its editor had to formulate views for publication on this subject!' The *Pilgrim* suffered the same fate as the old *Pilot* and the *Challenge*, and for the same reason—there were not enough church members interested in its message—but some of Temple's own articles survive in *Essays in Christian Politics*, a composite book of addresses published in the year before he left Manchester.

In the same volume are printed four of the six presidential addresses he delivered to the Diocesan Conference of the undivided diocese. These addresses are triumphs of educational oratory, and they made the Manchester Conference an event of exhilarating interest, almost of excitement, in the life of the diocese. Here was none of the ennui sometimes to be noticed at such gatherings, when members appear to be fulfilling some irksome duty with no excessive hope of spiritual profit, and have learned by experience exactly what to expect: the Bishop, first, with his Few Thoughts on Fortitude, or A Concise Commentary on Current Topics; then, in due succession, the secretaries of committees and societies with their depressing statistics, the meticulous bore, the effusive crank with his 'one thing' (were there not so many) guaranteed to 'save the Church of England', the grave jester, the raiser of the debate to a higher level—it is the half-yearly opportunity of them all, and kindly bishops in the chair are tolerant enough to remember this as they disregard the obvious desire of the meeting to be perpetually passing on to the next business. Under Temple's leadership and control an altogether different atmosphere pervaded the Holdsworth Hall on the day of the Conference. A thousand persons were crammed on the floor and in the galleries, and not one of them would be late lest he should miss even a few sentences of the Bishop's address. This lasted from forty minutes to an hour and invariably took the members far beyond the boundaries of their diocesan tasks and achievements, and brought them to grips with problems of outstanding spiritual interest and importance. Tradition and Modernism, The Obligation of Worship, The Ministry of Healing, were some of the subjects treated—and (perhaps the ablest address of all) The Vocation and Destiny of the Church of England. It may be doubted whether Temple ever spoke better from a platform than he did in his Manchester days—certainly he never had a more enthusiastic audience than that which packed the Holdsworth Hall year after year—and there was no suggestion of strain or effort in a single sentence. Each year the applause was spontaneous and prolonged, and a motion would be unanimously carried that the address be printed. The only corrections Temple ever made in the galley-proofs were 'literals' and, one year when the shorthand writer failed to appear, he dictated the address a week later walking up and down his room, without a single note: yet so perfectly trained was his memory that no reader of the address as it appeared in print suspected that it had not been taken down verbatim at the conference. On another occasion, after a particularly masterly address, the Bishop of Middleton asked him how he had found time to prepare it. 'Oh, I did it last night' was the reply: 'I knew', Dr. Parsons commented, 'that he had had other things to keep him busy that night.'

But the Conference was never a one-man affair. The purpose of a conference, Temple insisted, is to confer. No one was afraid to speak, so long as he was sincere and had something to say; and the meeting lost its chief value in Temple's eyes unless speakers said what they thought, and not what they thought they were expected to think. He welcomed criticism, even of his own proposals: sometimes if a nervous or halting speaker had failed to make his point, he would be surprised to hear Temple making it for him in his summary of the debate. He suffered bores gladly and, when asked how he managed to be so patient with them, replied: 'By prolonged bouts of deliberate inattention.' Only very occasionally was a speaker awed to silence: Temple, in the words of one of his clergy, 'had the punch, but no man ever used it so sparingly'. 'But your revered father said', insisted one speaker to whom the Bishop had already given considerable latitude—'I do not know whether my revered father said it or not,' Temple replied, 'but if he did I disagree entirely with what my revered father said.' The Conference applauded loudly, and the speaker gave way.

He used the same method at the Synod of his clergy, which he summoned to confer with him in March 1926—'a most impressive affair' he described it in a letter to his brother, 'with 850–900 clergy present'—but his Primary Visitation was more formal. The Charge (published in the autumn of 1924, the year in which it was delivered, with the title *Christ in His Church*) was given to assemblies of the clergy in eight centres. The theology of the addresses is that of *Christus Veritas*, which was published in the same year and (as he wrote to his brother some months later) had 'gone quite well'. The book is a sequel to *Mens Creatrix*, which had appeared in 1917. Temple himself described *Mens Creatrix* as being 'mainly philosophical in its aim', *Christus Veritas* as being 'mainly theological'. In effect, the two are companion volumes. *Christus Veritas* contains a good deal of philosophy, and *Mens Creatrix* a good deal of theology. In both works there is set forth a philosophical view of the world of which the Incarnation is the keystone and culmination. In both it is made abundantly clear to the reader that in Temple's view theology and philosophy mutually interpenetrate and imply one another; and that (as he wrote in the preface to *Christus Veritas*) 'what is needed', alike in the interests of philosophical truth and of a theology which has been fully thought out and has become aware of its own implications, is 'a Christo-centric metaphysics'. *Christus Veritas* is a difficult book to estimate. It is written with zest, and Temple is obviously doing much of his thinking as he goes along. He retracts or modifies at various points views and opinions previously set out in *Foundations* and elsewhere. He develops a specific doctrine of Value, involving the thesis that 'Value is, in the order of being, prior to existence', which he was well aware would appear to many philosophers a strange paradox; but he is at pains to point out that the greater part of his argument is 'independent of the particular doctrine of Value developed at the outset'. The book does not represent Temple's own final position as a philosophical thinker—this will be discussed in a later chapter—for the influences of Liberalism in theology and of the quasi-Hegelian idealism of Caird in philosophy are here more marked than in the later phases of his thought. Yet it is at once a powerful presentation of a Christian world-view and a highly characteristic expression of the author's mind—a mind sure of itself and amazingly able, provided (as it would seem) with a lucid and confident answer to all possible questions, and yet giving rise from time to time, by the very precision of its answers, to the suspicion that the truth must be somehow more complex and the problems more difficult than Temple's treatment of them would seem to suggest.

This was the theological background of his Charge, but the addresses were mainly concerned with immediate duties and problems. In the Introduction to the book Temple recounted some of the grave difficulties in the face of which the work of parish priests was being carried on, and told of his own duty and pleasure to offer whatever encouragement and stimulus he could: 'I wish to express', he wrote in the Preface, 'my profound and ever deepening admiration of their splendid devotion.' To the laity, in the section of the Charge delivered to the clergy of the Rural Deanery of Burnley, he pays a no less sincere tribute, for their generosity, their practical good sense, and their pertinacity in carrying through any task they had undertaken; but he detects a possible source of weakness in Lancashire churchmanship of which he does not hesitate to speak. 'Our people', he said,

love to be doing things. They are a little impatient of any effort from which they do not see some amount of real result.

But it always happens that when a disproportionate emphasis is laid on any side of human nature, the other will take its revenge somehow; so . . . I think you will always find that among those who tend to be a little hard in practical or business relationships there is a tendency for religion, and for interest in literature if any such thing exists, to shew a strongly sentimental tinge. For the emotions of human nature must have their outlet somewhere; and they will find it down some channel which leads to no kind of result and in a mere indulgence of feeling, unless they are allowed their place in the actual determination of conduct.

That is shrewd analysis. A successful employer of labour, who had the reputation of being 'an hard man' in his business dealings, once told a friend that his favourite hymn was 'There is a land of pure delight'—because, he argued, 'it is as different as possible from anything I have to think about on the other six days of the week'. It relieved him to find certain Lethean properties in

> The stream that waters paradise
> And makes the angels sing

and the business man forget some of his tougher Monday-to-Saturday moods and measures. This, Temple contended, is a dangerous dichotomy, for the full harmony of personality is not found in those who 'tend to exercise their emotions all in one field, and their practical activities in another'.

Forthright warnings of this kind did not lessen the warm regard in which he was held by the men and women of Lancashire as, through the written and the spoken word, he taught them 'the things pertaining to the Kingdom of God'. They were not long in taking the measure of their new bishop. When he spoke they listened and, whether they agreed or dissented, he won the affection of many and the respect of them all. But an even wider sphere than that of a great diocese was needed to display the fullness of Temple's powers. In the fourth year of his episcopate the opportunity came.

XXI

Copec—The Coal Stoppage

Many conferences have been held on the various subjects we are to consider, but these subjects have been usually considered in separation from each other. That makes possible a thoroughness of discussion which is impossible here; but it also involves a real falsification of the issues. The whole of human life is too completely one for consideration of any one aspect of it in isolation to be really satisfactory. Attention has often been concentrated, for example, on the problems of Industry; but such reforms as men have been led to advocate are often dependent for feasibility on parallel reforms in Education and improvement in International Relations, as well as in many other departments of life. There was a clear need, therefore, for such a survey of the whole field as is attempted in this Conference and in the Reports presented to it.

W. T., to Copec delegates, April 1924.

IN April 1924 a Conference was held at Birmingham on a scale never before attempted, which came to be known as Copec, a short title for 'Conference on Christian Politics, Economics, and Citizenship'. The gathering was not only remarkable in itself: it also centred to so striking a degree on Temple, both in its inception and achievements, that it deserves record in any attempt to consider the Bishop as a leader in social thought during the years of his Manchester episcopate.

Some of the influences that gave point and direction to his thinking on social and industrial issues have already been noticed; but one truth must be held to be axiomatic, in any attempt to trace the origin and growth of his social creed—Temple had always been on the side of the under-dog. None of his relatives or friends can remember a time when this was not so. In his seventh year he was staying with his parents for their holiday in the Lakes, and the hotel had provided roast chicken for lunch—a dish of which he was specially fond. Somehow, in the course of conversation, it was mentioned that the servants were not allowed chicken, whereupon Temple put down his knife and fork and burst into tears. It was not easy for his parents to understand this sudden breakdown, and their answer to his 'Why not?' has not survived. But the questions 'Why?' and 'Why not?' began to batter at the doors of his heart and brain—surely the eternal justice of things was being flouted if, while he was enjoying roast chicken in the dining-room, the servants below stairs were being fobbed off with a beef stew! It was no more than an incident—and grimmer experiences were to follow. Nearly twenty years later a Sweated Industries Exhibition was held at Oxford. Here Temple saw the results of a *laissez-faire* industrial system: match-boxes made at the rate of 2*d.* a gross, the worker having to find paste, hemp (for tying up), and firing to dry wet boxes, spending 2 hours a day in fetching and returning her work, and receiving 8*s.* a week for 10 hours' toil a day; trousers which were basted, machined, finished, and pressed at a net wage of 6*s.* a week for 12 hours' hard daily work; artificial flowers for the making of which the worker provided her own paste, and earned an average of 10*s.* a week for a 14-hour day: stall after stall decked with the produce of free enterprise, including one devoted to the wages and hours that prevailed in the industry of 'Bible-folding'. Temple, in co-operation with the Christian Social Union, was responsible for collecting the committee which organized the Exhibition, and in the handbook he wrote:

> It is the system which is foul and rotten. Producer, capitalist, consumer—all are entangled in the meshes of its net. While we prate about the spread of refinement; and while we pride ourselves on the spread of education; while we glory in an Empire whose Flag is said to stand for Justice—we are convicted by the facts at our own doors, of stupid coarseness, of ignorant insensibility, and of wanton oppression. We form Army Corps, we build 'Dreadnoughts'; we discuss endlessly what metaphysics are to be taught to children in our schools. But if we listen, there is still the desolate cry of the Son of Man: 'I am hungry and ye give me no meat.'

He was still thinking out the answer to his question when, in the following year, he wrote to his mother, who had complained of the difficulty of finding labour in the country districts:

9, Bute Gdns,
Hillhead,
Glasgow.

My dear Mother,   Sept. 12, 1908.

I can't answer your riddles. But in general the difficulty is due to two things; first, and chief, that working men are rather stupid about finding what work is going on, and (more important) have few means of finding out. We need a regular system of Labour Exchanges, where information of all the work offered may be obtained, so as to bring the advertising employer and the out of work man into touch. Second, there is the dullness of the country, consequent upon the rush to the towns. Both your cases are in the country. Men would rather take the risk of starving (with the chance of not starving) in a town than settle down to the living death of life in the country. Here we need two things—real agricultural education, which by making country work scientific may make it interesting, and the revival of all the festivities of village life which the Church kept going until the Reformation set a gulf between the Church and the everyday life of poor people—not the old festivities, which would seem childish to people who have submitted to compulsory education, but the means out of which new ones can grow, of which the chief is ease of movement from village to village, good roads, electric cars, etc. As it is, there are very few out-of-works in rural districts. In many places there is need for more men than can be got. But the men have learnt to love society—(and gas-flares, and pubs, and street rows, no doubt)—which is in itself a good thing, but makes the thought of country life under present conditions intolerable.

A problem. Your friend owns land and is willing to spend £52 a year on it on one man. All the men who might do that work want to work, but in towns; they want that £52 spent in a way that will employ them in towns. Why should the accident of possessing £52 a year beyond what is needed for life enable her to say 'You shall do the work *I* choose, or starve'? She is enabled to set her will against theirs on a matter vital to their whole lives. WHY? Now as far as I can see there will always be inequalities in wealth; and these will always give a certain amount of power to the richer over the lives of the poorer. But if capital is in the last resort under the control of bodies representing all classes, you will at least allow the workers to make their wishes felt otherwise than by dying on Dives' doorstep.

Your loving

W. T.

It was remarked by Dr. Inge some years ago that any young man who knew something of the miseries of the very poor must be hard-hearted if he did not become a socialist; but that, as he grew up, if he did not discard his socialist creed he must be very soft-headed. Of Temple this was certainly not true. With him head and heart never parted company. There was hardly a spiritual movement for social betterment with which he was not connected, and all the while he was studying and seeking an answer to his question, in his work for the W.E.A. and to a lesser extent (under Scott Holland's guidance) for the Christian Social Union. This was one of the pioneer societies of its kind in the Church. Its members were told by the scoffers that they took themselves rather too seriously, especially when they produced a 'White List' of London tailors who were known to pay fair wages; and West End tailors would raise supercilious eyebrows and cough discreetly when, before ordering a summer suit, dapper young curates from S. George's, Hanover Square, or Holy Trinity, Sloane Street, would ask them with a pathetic lack of confidence whether their firm was 'on the C.S.U. White List': or when members of the Union flung away their cups and saucers and allowed only leadless glaze on their tables and sideboards—but at least they were honest in their hope that by doing so they were helping to reduce the appalling number of deaths from lead poisoning in the potteries, an effort with which the name of Constance Smith, one of the C.S.U. pioneers and later H.M. Senior Lady Inspector of Factories, will always be honourably associated.

At last Temple discovered what he never ceased to believe was the true answer to his question. Why—why did there exist, side by side, extremes of misery and luxury, of sweated labour and wild extravagance, of squalor and the ordered comforts of a decent home? Could the answer be, merely because all but a few of his fellow countrymen were too ignorant, too idle, and too selfish to put an end to it—to a state of things which could have no place in any decent human order, still less in the divine order of eternal justice called the Kingdom of God—and to set up another in its place? There was nothing in the present system—or the lack of one—fixed unalterably by the laws of nature or economics, or sacrosanct by any law of God. Good will, good sense, and good work were all that was needed to change it. And what of the few who knew, and cared, and tried? At least he could throw in his lot with them, and share their task of destroying and rebuilding. In 1907, while still a layman, he describes to his mother a Sunday he spent in Leicester:

> . . . I then sped away to the other end of the town, to the Labour Church, where I took the chair and Mrs. Bruce Glasier (wife of the Editor of the *Labour Leader*) spoke very finely. Then tea with Wilford—one of the men Mansbridge brought to Oxford in August—and then again to the Labour Church. I had meant to repeat my Extension Lecture on 'Socialism and Education', but they had been getting a deal of abuse from some clergy at that end of the town, and were very keen for me to talk on 'Socialism and Christianity'. So I did; and began by exhorting them to set a Christian example to the church folk who abused them by not 'reviling again'. They are not all Christians (in metaphysics) at that Labour Church, but I have seldom felt so near the real presence of pure religion. To-night I talk to the Church Socialist League.

During the next ten years many factors served to strengthen Temple's sympathies with the Labour Movement—chief among them were the growing influence of Gore on his social thinking, the Industrial Report of the National Mission, and the new interest aroused in social reconstruction by the war—and early in 1918 he announced to the Lower House of Canterbury Convocation that he had joined the Labour Party. He had for some years questioned whether the clergy should attach themselves to any political group but that doubt was now resolved, and he was glad to make clear a week or two later (in an article in the *Daily News*) a distinction which he believed to be valid. After stating that there were two marks by which a 'truly spiritual movement' could be known, freedom and fellowship, he went on:

> Now the Labour Movement is essentially an effort to organize society on the basis of freedom and fellowship. As such it has a right to claim the sympathy of the Church. The Labour Party is a different thing: that is a political organization, and the Church as a whole must not be attached to any political party—not even to the Tory Party. But churchmen ought to consider very carefully the formulated programme of the Labour Party, and whether they should individually subscribe to it. Here is a party which has at least put forward an outline scheme of reconstruction in national and international life. It is a scheme based on moral ideals. We must not support it simply because we sympathize with the motives behind it: but if we believe that these motives are, on the whole, applied with wisdom, we have no right to stand aside. We must go in and help.

That was the point Temple had reached when the Copec Conference started. Its origins go back many years—he used to say that Copec was the direct result of a Student Christian Movement conference at Matlock of which he was chairman in 1909, when the subject for discussion had been 'Christianity and Social Problems'. Before that conference broke up, three conclusions had been unanimously reached—that multitudes of churchpeople, most notably the clergy, were almost entirely ignorant of the elements of the social problem; that education must precede conviction, since speech-making without instructed thought was a mere beating of the air; and that some organization was needed which would prepare text-books for social study of the same type as those already issued for examining the problems of the mission field. It was therefore decided, largely on the initiative of Malcolm Spencer, that a body should be formed whose members, drawn from many denominations, would share a common life of prayer and thought directed to the social problem, a few of them living together and others residing for varying periods and purposes. This was the origin of the 'Collegium', of which Lucy Gardner became secretary; Temple was its chairman; and a house was taken in St. George's Square where small or large gatherings could be held. Only one book, *Competition*, was published; but a habit and temper of discussion were formed which set the general lines to be followed, and the subjects to be reviewed, in any further conferences that might derive their inspiration from the 'Collegium' group. Of these the most ambitious was Copec, and for no conference can there have been more careful preparation. It was first mooted in 1919, while Temple was at Westminster, and officially launched at an Interdenominational Conference of Social Service Unions of which Gore was president. Its object was to seek the will and the purpose of God for men and women in every relationship of their lives—political, social, industrial, and the rest. Four years were allowed for study and campaigning; and a special impetus was given by the appeal for Christian Unity put out by the Lambeth Conference of 1920. Twelve commissions were set up; 200,000 questionnaires were dealt with at 75 centres, and the whole of 1923 was spent in studying the replies and producing the commissions' reports; Temple, as Chairman of the Movement (with Dr. Hugh Martin as Chairman of the Executive Committee, and Lucy Gardner and Dr. Charles Raven as joint-secretaries), was involved in much of the preparatory work, and early in 1924 he wrote to his wife:

> Lollards Tower,
> Lambeth Palace.
> February 15, 1924.

... Rather a day! But very useful. We sat at Copec from 11.0 till 4.20, except for lunch which we had all together, so of course we went on at Copec 'shop'. . . . Then I went on to Church House for a Committee at 5.0 on the continuation of Copec. I was afraid dear —— would fog the whole issue. But when he had talked about 25 minutes I cut in with a perfectly clear-cut proposal, which was accepted. I think what I thus

334

carried was what the rest of the Copec people wanted, but it seemed necessary to put out something quite definite if we were ever to get anywhere. Then I rushed off to the School of Economics where I dined with the C.U. Committee. Will Beveridge came to dinner and Harry Tawney joined us a short while. Then the debate, where W. B. made a great impression by sitting on the platform. The Director [of the London School of Economics] has never done such a thing before.

When the Conference opened, Temple looked down from the Chair on 1,500 delegates; eighty of these came from outside the British Isles; six European countries, and China and Japan, were represented; one and all were convinced that the only possible solution to the entrenched evils of their day lay in corporate Christian action; and they set out to integrate the Christian Faith with contemporary social responsibility. Messages were read from the King, from the Prime Minister (Ramsay MacDonald), and two ex-Prime Ministers (Baldwin and Asquith). Temple set the tone of the Conference by stressing its spiritual basis and aim:

> With the steadily growing sense that Machiavellian statecraft is bankrupt there is an increasing readiness to give heed to the claims of Jesus Christ that He is the Way, the Truth, and the Life. We represent here to-day the consequence of a spiritual movement in the Church prompted by loyalty and hope, and a spiritual movement in the world prompted by disillusion and despair. Our opportunity is overwhelmingly great; so also is our responsibility. . . . Our aim is to hear God speak. . . . Those who speak will speak as in God's presence; those who listen will listen in dependence on God.

The high level of the Conference never dropped, nor did the initial enthusiasm flag, throughout the week. Of its many fruits one calls for special mention, not only for its absolute value but also because of its relation to Temple's future work. The Copec Conference affected the whole Oecumenical Movement in the Churches, and gave to international Christian thinking and planning a sense of direction which was to prove of first-rate importance in the subsequent history of that Movement.

If before the Conference Temple had any spurs left to win as a master of assemblies, they were certainly his by the time it was over. His chairmanship was described as 'superb'. Not only was he fully equipped in every technical sense—in knowledge, in mastery of the agenda, and in the sense of proportion which enabled him to relate every section of it to the whole programme —he could also win and hold the respect and warm regard of every member of the Conference. He showed to a marked degree the indefinable power of keeping them all in a good temper and at their best, even when difficult and controversial issues (such as 'Christianity and War') were in debate; and this was set off by the tangle in which the Conference became involved during one session at which a substitute was in the chair. 'I shall always think of this', writes Professor W. F. Lofthouse, looking back on the Copec Conference, 'as one of Temple's greatest services to the Church and the Kingdom of God.'

After full debate the Reports of the Commissions were accepted, principles were agreed for the guidance of Christian conduct in all departments of human life, and the delegates dispersed to put them into practice in their communities, their professions, and their homes. The challenge of an opportunity was not long in coming, for there was need of acute thinking and clear leadership when in the spring of 1926 the stoppage in the coal industry led to the General Strike. The stoppage was the climax of seven years' ferment. Since the Armistice, trouble in the coal industry had been endemic. In 1919 a national strike of miners had been averted by the appointment of the Royal Commission presided over by Mr. Justice Sankey, and the unwillingness of the Government to act on his Report, which recommended that both coal and the collieries should be nationalized, had aroused widespread disappointment among the miners. Two years later the de-control of the coal industry on 31 March 1921 (five months earlier than the date first agreed upon by the Government with mine-owners and miners) had helped to throw the wage-arrangements of the industry into confusion. In 1925 a further breakdown had been averted only by the Government paying a temporary subsidy; and another Commission had been appointed which reported early in 1926. At the time when the stoppage of that year—described by the miners as a lock-out and by the employers as a strike—had led to the General Strike, Temple was abroad undergoing a cure for his gout. He was distressed to be out of England at such a crisis; but the Archbishop of Canterbury (whose part in the dispute has been described at length in Dr. Bell's *Life*) wrote to him on 10 May:

> I do not think there is anything to be gained by your coming home at present, so far at least as central affairs are concerned, though of course your presence as a counsellor would be very valuable. I will let you know at once if I see any real necessity which would necessitate your breaking off your cure in order to be in England. I see no light just now upon the situation, though there are a good many endeavours being made to-day. I am hourly interviewing men like members of the Cabinet, Ramsay MacDonald and his friends, Lord Henry Bentinck, Sir Henry Slesser and Bishop Gore. . . . I feel deeply for you in the necessity of being absent from England at such an hour.

Two days later the General Strike was over, but seven months were to elapse before work in the mines was resumed. Temple—who had not forgotten how Westcott (when Bishop of Durham) once succeeded in bringing coal-owners and miners together—had consented to join an *ad hoc* committee (convened by Prebendary P. T. R. Kirk, Director of the Industrial Christian Fellowship) which attempted to mediate between the contending groups; it was composed of Bishops and other Church of England leaders, Free Church leaders, laymen and women. Few incidents in his career attracted more notice or provoked stronger criticism than his share in the work of this committee—'We are abundantly criticized', he wrote to his brother, 'mainly for things we did not do'—but any considered judgement must be founded on a knowledge of the facts and on Temple's motive and purpose in acting as he did. Some of the facts are clearer now than on the day he arrived in London to take part in a deputation to the Prime Minister. Early in 1926 the Royal Commission on the Coalmining

z

Industry had issued its Report—a document, in Temple's words, 'prepared by men of independent judgment, great ability, and unquestioned integrity'. When, in the efforts being made to settle the dispute of 1926, it seemed that deadlock had been reached, and bitterness was increasing, the group of Anglicans and Free Churchmen convened by Prebendary Kirk invited both sides to meet them, and urged the adoption of the Report as a basis of settlement. The meetings took place. The representatives of the Coal-owners' Association made no positive suggestions, except to state that they were unable to adopt the Report. The miners' representatives expressed their willingness to drop their slogan ('Not a penny off the pay, not a minute on the day') and to put forward for the consideration of the Government certain proposals based on the Report. *This was all that the Churches' group knew when they took their deputation to the Prime Minister on 19 July.* But it turned out to be not the whole story. An independent group of three persons—B. Seebohm Rowntree, a noted authority and writer on the problems of industry, W. T. (now Lord) Layton, then editor of the *Economist*, and Frank Stuart—had been negotiating with A. J. Cook, the Secretary of the Miners' Federation, and on 3 July a draft basis of settlement was drawn up by the negotiators which Cook signed after adding these words: 'I am prepared, speaking for myself, on condition that the Government does not proceed with their Hours Bill, to recommend my officials and committee to consider these proposals as a basis for discussion.' The Government delayed the passing of the Hours Bill, but Cook did not place the draft proposals before his Federation. He cancelled an appointment which he made with the Rowntree Group on 13 July (at which they had intended to press him to bring the draft basis of settlement before his Executive Committee at the earliest possible date, as he had promised to do) because he had 'another important meeting'. This was with Prebendary Kirk and the Rev. Henry Carter, at which the conference between the Churches' group and the miners' representatives was fixed for 15 July.

At this point Temple takes up the story (in a letter to his wife):

Lollards Tower,
Lambeth Palace, S.E. 1.
July 19, 1926.

I think it was worth while to come, and anyhow I was chosen to be one of the speakers.

I drove straight to Fellowship House and found [Kempthorne, Bishop of] Lichfield and Kirk. I at once stated my misgivings, that we were acting as the spokesmen on one side only. Lichfield replied—quite fairly, I think—'Yes: but we have seen both parties and only one has made a proposal. That proposal is a real concession and gives evidence for the first time of *some* desire for a settlement by goodwill. We are here as agents of goodwill and it is as that that we go to the Prime Minister.' That satisfied me.

Then I was given the enclosed memorandum, prepared by Clement Edwards (a really big authority on Trade Union matters) and by Dick Reiss. This immensely increased my confidence, as they do know what they are talking about. You will see that it meets the P.M.'s refusal of a subsidy with a suggestion of a loan. They assured us that the Banks are ready to make the loan, if they are given statutory powers of collecting the sum annually due, and that the Miners would agree to it in place of the subsidy. This does seem to me a very fair proposition in principle.

The list of speakers was agreed to as follows: Lichfield, Dr. Gillie (on the subsidy or loan), Bp. of Winchester, Garvie (both on movements of public opinion) and W. M. on Hours as a source of added embitterment and need for rapid steps to arrest growth of this. Baldwin was very nice personally, but not disposed to budge. He attributes the perpetual trouble with coal to past readiness of Governments to intervene; he says the industry has been taught to expect public money whenever it howls and has determined to end that. The proposal of a loan he would not discuss much until its shape is more definite: he was very discouraging about it, but did not slam the door. As regards the report, he said: 'The Government adopted the whole of it that concerned them except purchase

339

of Royalties and municipal selling.' Other Ministers there were Bridgeman, Worthington-Evans, and Steel-Maitland: also Tom Jones and Ernest Gowers.

Plainly the Government wish that we would keep out of it, and are disposed to say that if we encourage the Miners we prolong the Strike. They expect a break fairly soon. But that is 'war attitude' and is, I am sure, not the most right.

My one fright came afterwards. We agreed to get their formal assent to the substitution of loan for subsidy—and then ditto with at least some owners. Then Kirk wanted us to say that, failing this, we would join the Miners in a fight on that basis. He got no support, though some thought it might come to that. But Lichfield agreed with me that while the Church, acting for goodwill, may pass on technical proposals tending to promote it, it is quite another thing for the Church to take the field saying that some technical proposal (e.g. a loan) is certainly the righteous line of action. Cook, of course, will call us rats if we do not fight; and perhaps will be right to do so: but we *must* stick to our own job.

The question at once arises—why did Cook not report to the Executive of the Federation that he had signed certain draft proposals and had agreed to recommend them as a basis for discussion? (One of the miners' leaders who saw the text of them later said: 'If this memorandum had come before our Federation, I feel sure the terms would have been acceptable and would have led to an early peace.') Some years afterwards B. S. Rowntree suggested an answer to the question in a letter to Temple:

There is no doubt at all that the memorandum would have been laid before the Federation, had it not been for the intervention of the Churches' committee. . . . What convinces me that the strike would have ended in July rather than in December but for the intervention of the Churches is that up to the date on which that intervention took place we were steadily succeeding in bringing the two parties closer together and everything pointed to the fact that we were rapidly approaching a successful issue of the effort in which we were engaged. *But from the moment that the Churches intervened the atmosphere changed completely.* The miners thought that they had the whole of the Christian Churches behind them, and they were no longer prepared to consider making any concessions beyond those which were contained in the terms they had offered to the Church delegation.

This is one answer; are others possible? The story of those months is one of great complexity, and there are still gaps which cannot (on the evidence yet available) be filled except as the inquirer's speculations or predilections may suggest. Many proposals for a settlement were coming before the miners' leaders. In deciding which to pursue further, it was necessary to consider not only the text of the proposals but also the credentials of the persons who submitted them and the ability of those persons (should the miners agree to them) to secure that they would be carried out by the owners; and Cook may have decided, at a certain point in the negotiations, that the Rowntree Group could not speak officially for the Mining Association and may have feared by further discussion to prejudice the miners' case when formal negotiations should eventually have started. Nor did the verdict of the miners' leader quoted above necessarily represent the policy of the Federation as a whole, which was a weak and loosely organized body. It was the County Associations that mattered most, and the problem was to secure a majority vote for a settlement from a miners' conference representing all the districts. (Cook, by the way, as the villain of the piece was largely the creation of the Press. The most formidable obstacle to a settlement on the miners' side was the President of the Federation, Herbert Smith, a determined and in some ways likeable personality—whose very much photographed cloth cap became an oriflamme of No Surrender—but almost impervious to argument.)

To assess the degree of responsibility for the continuance of the stoppage that can be rightly attributed to the Government, the owners, and the miners—not one of the three groups can be acquitted of its own particular blunders—is not here our concern;

but there is something more to be said of the part played by Temple himself. Looking back on it, sixteen years later, he drew certain conclusions and made some admissions. These were: that in his judgement the Churches' intervention had not been very skilfully conducted in detail; that he himself knew nothing of any negotiations between Cook and the Rowntree Group, nor therefore of the memorandum which Cook had signed; that, had he known of them, he would have been led to reconsider his own line of action. On 8 July 1942 he wrote to B. S. Rowntree:

> Whether we should have held off if we had known of your private negotiations, of course I cannot say; but for myself I think it would have altered the situation. But we did not and could not know that other people were at work.

He admitted also 'a tendency to try to make capital for the Church out of it by publicity when the thing ought, if done at all, to have been kept entirely private'. Lastly, the claim that the miners' leaders consented for the first time at the conference between Cook and the Churches' representatives to withdraw their slogan cannot be substantiated, as—to the disgust of Herbert Smith—Cook had made the same offer to the Rowntree Group a fortnight earlier. Temple, of course, did not know this when he wrote the letter to *The Times* quoted below. He acted throughout on such knowledge as he had—but it was not enough. Even so, can his action and that of the Churches' group be justified? He had always held that it was the duty of the Church to mediate between conflicting parties, but not to advance definite technical proposals for the settlement of an industrial dispute. 'I must repeat', he wrote in a letter to *The Times* on 19 August, in which he set out a history of the efforts for peace, 'that the only terms proposed by our side consisted of the Report itself. These proposals represented a method of bringing the Report into operation.' The words 'represented a method' were not, perhaps, quite the happiest Temple could have chosen, for he exposed himself to the question whether, in discussing the method by which the broad principles of the Report should be carried out, it was possible to evade technical issues in which specialist knowledge was essential.

For any who like to point a moral the whole incident affords material in plenty. . . . But let Temple have the last word. His letter to *The Times* ended:

> But if it is urged that such action as we took is improper in principle, we completely disagree with such a view. As Christians, and most of us as Christians charged with official responsibility, we saw two parties doing great injury to the community by a continued conflict which was bound to be ended by negotiation sooner or later; our religion and our office required of us that we should do anything which lay in our power to bring them, in the literal sense, to reason. We never imagined either that we could suggest satisfactory terms of our own or that economic facts can be modified by humane sentiments. But we felt a responsibility for trying to secure that the settlement should be not only economically sound in itself, but reached with the minimum of bitterness or resentment and the maximum of good will. Whether the particular steps which we took to discharge this responsibility were wise or foolish is another question, not for us to answer. I will only mention that, while the policy of the 'slogan' was bound to be withdrawn sooner or later, it was in fact at the conference with our group that the withdrawal took place. And if we be still accused of acting for the miners and not for the owners, we reply that this is only because the miners did, and the owners did not, reach proposals in conference with us based on the Report and showing a readiness to substitute reason for force as the arbiter of the dispute.

One result at least had been achieved by the Churches' group. Coming as it did immediately after the Archbishop's action in the General Strike, its intervention changed completely the miners' attitude to the Churches. By organized labour organized religion had hitherto been held to embody the reactionary spirit of a privileged caste and to be consistently opposed to the welfare and progress of the workers; notable leaders of the Churches had now come into the open with an independent and unprejudiced outlook. Whether the time chosen and the means employed for effecting such a transformation were right or wrong, wise or foolish, will continue to be discussed whenever the history of those disastrous seven months is remembered and reviewed.

XXII

The Prayer Book in Parliament

Those who were there say that the House developed the atmosphere
of a revivalist meeting, was impatient of argument, and only listened to
those who preached at it. So the one effective speaker on our side was
a Baptist minister! We shall make some explanatory changes, but no
substantial ones, and send it up again. Many who know the House
think it will pass next time. If it does not, some sort of Disestablishment is (I suppose) the necessary result.

W. T., letter to his brother, Christmas Day 1927.

ONE of the most interesting of the buildings which go to
make up Lambeth Palace—the London residence of the
Primate of All England and the headquarters of the Anglican
Communion—is the Lollards Tower. In a survey of Lambeth
Manor made in 1647 it is thus described:

Atte the Northend of the Courte is a greate Bricke buildinge,
with Windows opening towards the Thames, foure Storeys
high, covered with Lead, Behind which Buildinge, alonge by
the West end of the Chappell is a paire of Staires leading upp
into chambers five storeys high, over which is the Lollards
Tower all covered with Lead.

At what date the name began to be applied not only to Bishop
Chichele's dungeonless tower with its pleasant 'solar' and sleeping apartments but to the whole building, what the connexion is
between it and the larger and more infamous Lollards Tower at
S. Paul's (which perished in the Great Fire), and concerning the
prisoners committed to it, antiquaries still dispute. The certain
facts of its more recent history are that it was hit by incendiary
bombs in December 1940, and on 10 May in the following year
the two top floors were burnt out and the whole building made
uninhabitable through damage by fire and water. Several bishops
were thereby deprived of their London home, for Lollards Tower
had for some years been divided into comfortable flats, which the
Archbishop offered to four selected bishops as their private

apartments when they stayed in London. They shared a common dining-room, attended the palace chapel for their daily services, and were close at hand for consultation when the Archbishop needed their counsel. In 1923 Temple had the good fortune to be chosen by the Archbishop for this privilege: the bishops already installed were Winchester (Theodore Woods) and Chichester (Burrows); a little later they were joined by Lichfield (Kempthorne). He wrote on 19 November to his brother:

Nov. 19, 1923.

The Archbishop had offered us the rooms in the Lollards Tower which the Talbots are vacating. But an arrangement was made that they should remain in occupation till Easter. Now Ely has resigned; and we shall, in fact, take over their rooms—which are much nicer, the same ones which the Davidsons once had. But I fear all this will be no use to you, as the rooms are lent on the strict condition that only the bishop concerned and his wife use them.

Till May 1941 Temple used these rooms as his London headquarters; and there was a constant coming and going of young men whom he had known at public schools, or had met during his university Missions. Central engagements claimed much of his time: he was on the Central Advisory Council of Training for the Ministry, being specially concerned with the inspection of Theological Colleges and the Service Candidates; as well as being Chairman of the New Sees and Provinces Committee of the Church Assembly, he served on its Patronage Committee; from time to time he addressed large meetings for societies and movements in which he was interested, such as those held in the Queen's Hall by the Life and Liberty Movement; he spoke in the House of Lords, particularly on the lack of houses for the workers (which he declared to be one of the chief causes of industrial disaffection); and in 1926 he introduced both the Bishopric of Shrewsbury Measure and the Parish of Manchester Division Act 1850 (Amendment) Measure into the House and moved that they be presented for the Royal Assent. One of his few recreations was an occasional dinner as a member of 'Nobody's Friends', a club composed largely of clergy and lawyers, founded by William Stevens. 'Nobody' was the founder's *nom de plume*, and on his death 'Nobody's Club' became the club of 'Nobody's Friends'.

The weight of his London commitments was substantially increased when the Revised Prayer Book came before the House of Bishops of the Church Assembly: this was the most exacting central church work in which Temple was engaged during his episcopate. No attempt can be made here to examine in detail the Prayer Book controversy in its theological, liturgical, and historical aspects: our concern must be limited to the part played by Temple himself in the years during which the Church was hammering out the Book of 1928. In one of his most convincing pamphlets (published, unfortunately, too late to dispel popular prejudice) Temple wrote that, after the passing of the Enabling Act, there were three great reforms to which the Church was bound to address itself. These were: to secure that there was a law of public worship wide enough for modern needs, so that it was morally capable of enforcement; to secure Ecclesiastical Courts possessed of full moral as well as full constitutional authority; and to secure for the people of a parish an effective voice in determining the type of incumbent who should be appointed to the benefice—and it was a 'vital necessity' to start with the first. This was the relation of Prayer Book Revision to the whole scheme of church reform.

The subject has a prominent place in his engagement-book and in letters, from the date when the Revised Book began to be considered by the House of Bishops. He writes to his brother of successive weeks when he has to be in London for sessions of the House of Bishops, and of work piling up daily at home in his absence; and this to his wife from Lollards Tower on 20 October 1925:

... It has been rather an incessant sort of day. We discussed the division of the [Prayer Book] Measure into 2 and in connexion therewith all other topics under the sun for the whole morning. I spoke for about 10 or 12 minutes and was apparently approved. ... My regret is that I did not wait a little longer, as Barnes [Bishop of Birmingham] spoke, saying that adoration of the Reserved Sacrament was 'a recrudescence of fetish worship' and repeating his dogma that 'dead matter cannot be endowed with spiritual qualities'. I wish I could have answered him. I suggested to Carlisle as we came out that all Bishops who are ex-Greats-tutors should unite to issue a memorandum about this, to which he said: 'Well, something ought to be done; it is getting intolerable.' That session lasted till 1.40. At 2.0 the Patronage Committee met. Dibdin said my new motions are hysterical, so I promised to gesticulate freely in moving them. Wolmer will support them. At 2.30 the House resumed and we polished off the Prefaces, and reached the Calendar. . . . The House rose at 5.5, and at 5.30 the Committee on Grouping of Dioceses met.

Occasionally there are references to lighter moments in the Bishops' debates:

. . . The only moment of great hilarity was when Bradford moved for an alternative collect for Trinity Sunday, on the ground that the existing one is hard to understand, and Durham said, 'There really must be some limit set to this lust for intelligibility.'

Nothing came of the proposed composite answer to Dr. Barnes; but in 1927 his *An Open Letter to the Archbishop of Canterbury*, part of which dealt with sacramental teaching, drew from Randall Davidson one of the most telling and politely crushing letters he ever wrote, and Temple made his own reply when he spoke to a joint meeting of the Diocesan Conferences of Manchester and Blackburn on 29 April 1927. His words are worth quoting at length, as they express concisely his own sacramental faith:

There are those who draw a distinction which I am wholly unable to draw—though that does not much matter—between organic and inorganic matter. While they are ready to believe in the power of the Holy Spirit over bodies which are organic to spiritual life, they are absolutely not prepared to regard the

Holy Spirit's action as even possible on material things which are not in that way organic to spiritual life, but which are none the less deeply significant for spiritual beings. As I say, that is a distinction which I cannot follow. But it is said—at any rate, it is sometimes said—that 'you cannot endow dead matter with spiritual qualities'. I wish to say that that statement is irrelevant so far as it is true, and untrue so far as it is relevant. It is true in the sense that nothing can make a piece of dead matter into a piece of living matter. Nothing can make it, in technical language, a centre of consciousness except the creative act of God Himself, and thus no one supposes that the Consecrated Bread of the Eucharist becomes in that kind of way, so to speak, alive. That is not in question. On the other side, if it is meant that dead matter cannot be the vehicle of spiritual meaning and power, that is what I wish expressly to deny. That which is not in itself life can take on a spiritual meaning for life. A great many of our difficulties in the past have arisen because we have thought in accordance with the habit of mind of science to the exclusion of that which is induced by art. Religion is something that binds art, as meaning the outward expression of what is spiritual and emotionally vital, with science, as the impulse to ascertain truth. Both are there, and we must allow quite as much for all those apprehensions which come to us through the world of art as for those which come through the world of science. Where is the beauty of a piece of music? All that exists for science is certain undulations which are measurable and which strike upon the drums of our ears, and these, when they have passed, are gone. But, as we apprehend the beauty we none of us suppose we create it; we receive something from without, something that is conveyed to us by the physical means of musical instruments of one kind and another; yet the thing that we receive is a spiritual thing. Our experience quite apart from religion is already so rich in instances of the interpenetration of matter by spirit that I cannot see the smallest objection to believing that the Holy Spirit will use matter as part of His plan for the most sacred purposes of our spiritual life.

William Temple

As controversy increased in range and volume Temple found himself almost the chief apologist for the Revised Book, and the Archbishop depended on him to keep *The Times* well supplied with copy. On 16 March 1927 he wrote to his wife:

... The Archbishop wanted me to answer Saintsbury in to-day's *Times*, so I did; but I felt very keen to answer McNeill's letter too; so I wrote an answer and shewed it to His Grace, who wanted it to go in too. So that may appear tomorrow! After which I must lie low for a bit!! But McNeill asked the same question that Knox keeps asking and I wanted to answer Knox under cover of answering McNeill.

McNeill's plea was for 'an authoritative declaration as to what the doctrine of the Church actually is with regard to the two schools of thought' which, 'divested of the subtleties of theological metaphysics', he had defined as follows: 'The one school holds that the material elements remain after consecration in all respects the same as before: the other believes that they do not.' Temple replied that this was far from being 'simple language', for it concealed the ambiguity out of which a great part of the controversy had arisen. After a reference to the wisdom of the Church of England in refusing to give a dogmatic answer to this question, which he contended could not be made without pre-supposing one of two possible philosophical opinions, he ended:

Half of our difficulties come from the fact that each party supposes the other to mean by its assertions and denials something which, in fact, it does not mean, because it interprets the other party's statements by its own presuppositions. I can testify from my own experience that I have found in conversation with Anglo-Catholics and Evangelicals that they often mean the same thing when they think they are at variance, because each group misunderstands the other. The Church of England most wisely refrains from giving the 'authoritative declaration' for which Mr. McNeill asks. By its repudiation of transubstantiation it declares that the Bread when consecrated is still Bread; it refuses to determine the philosophical question whether, in virtue of its new significance as an 'effectual sign' (the phrase of the Articles) or 'instrumental cause' (the phrase of Hooker), it is to be regarded as in any way changed in itself or not. It is its significance which is of religious importance; and about its significance when received in Holy Communion (as distinct from the philosophic account to be given of that significance) there is very little dispute among members of the Church of England.

In his own diocese Temple had to reckon with strong opposition. There were probably more Protestants in his diocese than in any other who were convinced that the new Prayer Book sold the pass to Rome, and the flame of loyalty to their former bishop was fanned by the share that Knox took in working, writing, and speaking for its rejection. Temple was determined from the first that no word of his should increase the rising animosity between the contending groups; his plea was twofold—that all discussions and speeches should be kept on a high level of prayer and waiting upon God, and that all citizens (whether attached to the Church of England or not) should refuse to take their opinions from slogans, but should set themselves to understand the principles that lay behind the whole plan and pattern of revision. In 1926 the Book formed the subject of his presidential address to the Diocesan Conference, and a year later the vote of a conference of the two dioceses of Manchester and Blackburn was taken. Temple delivered his *A Plea for the New Prayer Book*—a masterly exposition of its history, its purpose, and its contents. He described the conference as 'rather a thrill': after he had spoken for 65 minutes, and the applause had lasted for nearly three,

> The Bishop of Blackburn spoke for about 20 minutes; very good, measured, balanced, weighty. Then we adjourned. At 1.30 I tried to answer a whole sheaf of written questions which were sent in. . . . The debate was poor. I called on the protestants pretty freely so that they might not complain of being stifled. Keeling made the only good speech until at 4.0 I called on Peter Green. He had an ovation, and very excellently pressed the point: 'Where shall we be if this Book is lost?'

Then we voted by papers, and for the undivided diocese [the result was]: For, 718: Against, 266.

It was one of Temple's greatest personal triumphs. But there was more than learning and authority to account for it: the tone and temper of all his utterances on the Prayer Book were so completely Christian that in a diocese where tradition was strong and old prejudices and antagonisms died hard, he succeeded in creating an atmosphere, if not of complete agreement, at least of tolerant forbearance and goodwill.

The Revised Prayer Book Measure was introduced in the House of Lords by the Archbishop of Canterbury. Temple, who had taken his seat in July 1925, described it as 'a great debate, and yet in one way a trifle hollow'. He went on:

> All speakers felt the impossibility of arguing in that House the points of intimate devotional concern which yet are the heart of the whole discussion. There was nothing to regret; it was all worthy so far as it went, and of great educational value. But one wondered how long either Church or Parliament will consent to the constitution which requires that a debate on such a theme should take place under those conditions.

On 15 December 1927 the House of Commons rejected the book. The Bishops decided to re-introduce the Measure, with certain modifications, in the Church Assembly and to present it again to Parliament, when it had received the assent of the Convocations. Temple summoned all his clergy to meet him in the cathedral. He sent a letter to every M.P. in his diocese, with a copy of his address to the Diocesan Conference, gave detailed instructions for constant prayer to be offered, issued a Pastoral Letter to be read in all churches in his diocese on 13 May, and published his reply to Joynson-Hicks. But he was not hopeful. He wrote to his brother that the situation grew 'more perplexing', and that it seemed as if 'the only sort of book which Parliament would accept is one which could not be administered'. Through the months of renewed deliberations in the House of Bishops, he kept his wife informed of their progress; of one incident he wrote:

Bishop of Manchester, 1921

March 6, 1928.

. . . We have gone slow to-day. Randall turned out to be desperately eager for a stiffening of one of the Reservation rubrics, to the extent of saying he could not go on if it were not done. Ultimately we got words which are (I think) free from objections, but it means that we have altered a rubric which both the other Houses have passed, which I regard as very serious in principle, though the alteration is fully within our declared intention. I voted for it, with a big majority, but I never gave a more unwilling vote. It won't do harm if people are really reasonable; but it will give excuse to the unreasonable. . . .

The House of Commons rejected the book for the second time on 13 June 1928. Temple was in the House for a part of the debate, and described it in two letters to his wife:

> Lollards Tower,
> Lambeth Palace,
> S.E. 1.
> June 13, 1928.

. . . After dinner I went to the House (the Lords have postponed that Temperance Bill) and got in as Greaves-Lord was speaking. He was rather disagreeable, but I fear was effective. The Duchess of Atholl was first rate; Macnaghten bored the House; Courthope was good but heavy; Rosslyn Mitchell was good in form and manner but failed to rouse them. Ammon was excellent, but most people left when R. M. sat down. R. M. had had a House of about 200. When I went in it was about 100 and grew till he began.

The noise of applause is against us but I *think* the numbers were with us, and Kenworthy whom I saw afterwards was emphatic that of the House sitting to-day we had a majority. But that is no indication. Our folk feel rather on their mettle and are working harder. In the gallery were Cantuar, Ebor, Southwark, Liverpool and I, and (part time) London. So far there is no excitement in the atmosphere at all. But that was bound to come (if at all) tomorrow. My own feeling is that it

A a

nearly all turns on the extent to which the P.M. can grip the House at the end.

June 14, 1928. . . . Your fears were just—as you have known, I expect, for some time as I write. I had come to expect it too, so there was no disappointment. But the situation is certainly most difficult. The Arch. will certainly be opposed to any more defiance than can be avoided: but I don't see how we can avoid, in one way or another, declaring our intention of administering the Deposited Book. Of course in one way the whole business is due to the over-long acquiescence of the Church in its legislative impotence from the Reform Bill to the Enabling Act. But that does not make it easier to see the wise course now.

I got into the House about 8.0, when it was nearly empty. No one then was good until Dunnico—but I gather Horne and Hugh Cecil had been very good earlier. Dunnico and Inskip were both good, though Inskip talked as if there had been a formal proposal to the Arch., of which the latter says that it was a casual suggestion in the middle of ordinary conversation.

[In Baldwin's speech] . . . there was a beautiful passage about the 2 streams in the Church of England which made a deep impression. But then he lost grip altogether. There was no excitement—but there was a great sense of tense feeling. All I heard of the debate was entirely honourable to the House. But there is plainly a very deep suspicion, not only in quarters where one expected it, but elsewhere also, of all that is faintly Catholic. The Arch. seemed tired but not at all knocked out.

The diocesan bishops were at once summoned to confer on the gravest crisis affecting the relations of Church and State since the Reformation. On two days of their deliberations Temple wrote:

June 27, 1928. . . . It was a good discussion to-day. Poor Henson is horribly worried because he mistook the time and only arrived at 5.0—and he feels he might have affected the course of events if he had been here earlier. Of course he wants heroics. And his pressure is good, as Cantuar's tendency is far too much towards trying to smooth it all out with no principles asserted at all. I hope that, if only to avert a tornado from H. H. H. [Bishop of Durham] in the Assembly, his own utterance will be fairly sturdy.

Lollards Tower,
Lambeth Palace,
S.E. 1.

June 28, 1928. . . . Not much to say. We have reached something like an agreement about what Cantuar should say on Monday. He suddenly prolonged the session and I forgot at the moment that Mr. Briggs, M.P. was coming here—so when I got here I found him asleep in an arm-chair. I am horribly vexed at this having happened, but I think he was quite happy. What he came to say was that there was talk among M.P.s to the effect that the Bishops mean to defy Parliament and he did not like to think what it would result in if they did. I was able to console him, for I fear there will be less defiance in the Abp's utterance than I should wish for.

In fact there was none. For a short time after the second rejection those who wished to see the Church entirely freed from State control were hoping that the challenge of Parliament would be taken up, especially as they knew that Temple expected 'some sort of disestablishment' to follow, and they looked to him as the man to lead such a movement. But as the weeks dragged on into months and they remembered the complete ascendancy of Randall Davidson over the Bench and the traditional reluctance of Lambeth to take decisive action, they came to see that their hopes were vain. In July 1929 the Bishops issued a statement which was, in brief, to the effect that they felt justified in recommending that under certain conditions the Book of 1928 might legally be used in the churches of any diocese whose bishop, exercising his rights as Ordinary, gave his permission. This recommendation was to remain in force 'during the present emergency and until further order be taken'. By this time nearly twelve months had passed, popular attention had shifted to other interests, to few outside the

Church did the statement seem worthy of more than a passing notice, and there was not a headline in it from the first word to the last. But among the more thoughtful laymen (including a number of churchmen) there was to be clearly detected an undercurrent of feeling that one of the few remaining canons of middle-class morality had been broken, and that the way out of the impasse taken by the bishops was 'not quite straight'. Opinion shaded off from the view that the chosen solution reached the height of ecclesiastical statesmanship to the conviction that it touched the depth of ignominy, but the lay verdict most frequently heard ran something like this: 'We can understand the Church saying to Parliament, "You have deliberately torn up and flung away the result of the twenty years' hard and intensive work which the best minds of the Church have given to a revision of its liturgy and worship. You have flouted the deliberately expressed opinion of more than four-fifths of the Church's duly elected representatives in its diocesan conferences. You have twice insisted that you cannot acquiesce in forms of worship which the Church declares that it needs for the spiritual welfare of its members. Therefore the State tie has become intolerable. We propose to ask you for our complete freedom from State control, and trust you to give us a fair deal." Or we can understand the Church saying to the State, "We bow to your verdict. We are deeply distressed at it, but we value the fact of the Establishment and all that it involves so highly that we will give way and withdraw the Book." Either of these would have been a course taken on some clear and honourable principle. But to say, "We accept your ruling, and we fully understand that the Book cannot be an official Book of Common Prayer. But the inconvenience caused by your decision is not insuperable, as any Bishop by the use of his *jus liturgicum* can give permission for one or all of its Services to be used in the churches of his diocese; and this is what we recommend"—No, not quite straight!' . . . So was a common conviction expressed, and there the matter rests. The controversy received its dignified and undramatic euthanasia by a time-honoured device. A clerical wit once remarked that, were Randall Davidson to be at Lambeth when the last trump sounds, he would be sure to nominate a representative committee to consider and report whether it was the last trump or the last but one. The tradition persists: in 1930 yet one more Commission was appointed 'to enquire into the present relations of Church and State'. The names of the Commissioners (with Lord Cecil of Chelwood as their chairman) carried great weight and the two results of their interim Report, which was published in 1935, may be summarized as follows. Action was taken on an initial—and surely, in its context, astonishing—recommendation that agreement should be sought between the various church 'parties' on subjects of controversy in connexion with the Holy Communion and Reservation: the Archbishop appointed a 'Round-Table Conference', which ended in a deadlock; its last meeting was to have been held in October 1939, but this was postponed and no subsequent meeting has been held. Second, there was an 'interim proposal' (which has been considered in Convocation and at Bishops' Meetings) that the Convocations should frame a Synodical Declaration on what is meant by 'lawful authority' in the Declaration of Assent made by every priest at his ordination. But the chief hope of many is centred on such a revision of the Canon Law as has been brought within the scope of practical politics by the Report of the Commission in 1947, and the declaration of church leaders that this revision is to have priority over all church reform.

Temple's attitude towards the Establishment and its final hardening were felt as a grievous blow by many of his followers. There was indeed some excuse for their bewilderment at the many phases of his thought and his successive pronouncements on the relations between Church and State. His championship of Arnold has already been mentioned. This was the first phase; but a theory that had so little regard for realism could not long survive, and by 1913 he was at the other extreme. When he was asked by the Archbishops to serve on the Church and State Committee to be set up as a result of the recommendation of the Representative Church Council, he expressed some doubt whether he ought to join it, since—to quote his own words—'I did not believe that there was any means of release from our difficulties

357

except by way of disestablishment'. The Archbishops, who were not blind to the advantages of making a poacher head-keeper, replied that they needed someone with precisely those views on the Committee, and Temple agreed to serve. The scheme proposed by the Committee seemed to Temple to provide a means of securing at least a measure of freedom, without having resort to what he now called the 'great calamity' of disestablishment. By 1925 his conversion was complete: 'The question [of disestablishment] is one', he declared in his Manchester Visitation Charge, 'in which the Church need take no interest at all. It is a question for the State only.' That is indeed a 'hard saying'. But there was a look-back to the Life and Liberty days when he proposed the appointment of the new Commission in the Church Assembly:

> It may be in the minds of some who were associated with us at the time that the first declaration of the Life and Liberty Movement was that effective self-government must be obtained for the Church even at the cost, if necessary, of disestablishment and whatever that might be found to involve. I merely mention this to show that I do not think there is any radical repudiation on my part of the policy which I previously adopted; but I wish to add that I have seen more reason since, than I saw then, for valuing what is called the Establishment. While I still consider that spiritual independence is so essential that the price of disestablishment would not be too great to pay if it really appears that there is no other means of securing that independence, yet we must search long and carefully before we decide that that price has got to be paid.

Eleven years later, in *Citizen and Churchman*, he was still protesting that 'there are features of the present "Establishment" in England which seem to me in the proper sense intolerable; the Church as a fellowship of worshippers ought to have absolute freedom to order its own worship without any restriction from persons and representatives of persons who may or may not be members of that fellowship'; but apparently it is exactly these persons—and not the representatives of churchpeople—who are to interest themselves in the precise moment at which this freedom shall be granted. However these statements may be reconciled, Temple made no attempt to disguise the complete *bouleversement* of his earlier convictions; in his later years he became more and more convinced of the advantages to be gained by the State from its connexion with the Church, and this dominated his thinking to the end. Some of his old colleagues in the Life and Liberty Movement look in vain for another of his calibre and authority to lead a Disestablishment movement from within the Church such as once appeared possible—and the Establishment is to be left to 'rust out'. The next step, if it is to be worth taking, will not be taken by the Church. Parliament killed the Revised Prayer Book and, if there is to be any more shooting, *que messieurs les assassins commencent!* But (be it not forgotten) the 'emergency' continues, though 'organized deadlock' would be a better name for it.

In July 1928 Randall Davidson resigned the Primacy—he chose 12 November, his golden wedding day, as the actual date of retirement—and in less than a week after he had seen Lord Baldwin on 26 July the appointments to Canterbury, York, and Manchester were all settled. Temple and his wife had arranged to spend a holiday in Brittany, and on 30 July they went up to London. When they arrived at Lollards Tower Temple found a note from Randall Davidson asking him and his wife to come to the Palace after dinner, as the Prime Minister wished to see him— 'You will know', the note ended, 'what that means.' Later in the evening they went through to the drawing-room, and Lord Baldwin took Temple with him to another room, while the Archbishop told his wife the news. He discussed with her all the projects for Temple's future, particularly the popular hope that he would be appointed to the see of London at the next vacancy, and in due course pass on to Canterbury. But there were several reasons why he was sure that Temple should accept the Northern Primacy. Apart from abundant evidence that he fitted in well with the Northerners and they with him, he would still be able to continue his work in the Universities, with the W.E.A. and

S.C.M., and perhaps to write; and Randall Davidson felt strongly that no other bishop would be able to work so happily or so easily as Temple with the new Archbishop of Canterbury. Meanwhile another conversation had begun in a room a little farther down the first-floor corridor of the Palace: 'I expect you know why I have asked you to come and see me': 'I have my suspicions': 'Well, what about it?'

In a letter to his brother Temple described the offer as 'gratifying', but he added: 'I wish that we could have stayed some years yet in Manchester'—twelve years, rather than eight, was what he had hoped—'but it is a plain duty to go.' The generous Mancunians knew that this was true, but it did not lessen their grief at his departure. They knew what they were losing—which was well summarized by the Editor of the *Bolton Evening News* in a leading article headed 'Godspeed to the Bishop':

> Every section of the community is in Dr. Temple's debt. In an extraordinary way he has impressed himself on the life of this county during his seven years among us. . . . Dr. Temple is a man of very rare mental and moral type. He is an intellectual giant—one of the first half-dozen minds in this country; a splendid expositor and interpreter of ideas; a great and sympathetic administrator; a first class philosopher and writer; a cogent and persuasive preacher; a tremendous worker; and finally a most humble and lovable man.

The wrench of parting was felt no less keenly by Mrs. Temple than by the Bishop. She had been active at the City Police Court as a Justice of the Peace, had led the Moral Welfare Work of the diocese, and had formed very close friendships in and beyond the city: and to move once more—again in the depth of winter—into a house so different from her Manchester home as Bishopthorpe was a grim prospect. In the last months there were farewell presentations, parties, speeches, and dinners, while letters poured in from young and old, clergy, laity, churchmen and non-conformists, all with their own memories and farewells. Among the letters that Temple specially valued was one from the Bishop of Hulme:

The Rectory,
Bury,
Lancashire.

My dear Bishop,   18 December, 1928.

Forty-one years ago today your Father made me a deacon in S. Paul's Cathedral—so, to a sentimental person like me, this would seem a fitting day on which to send you a word of written goodbye, to be added to what was spoken, or rather unspoken, on Saturday.

To have served under your leadership has been a delight passing words, and my heart is full of gratitude for everything that it has meant, both officially and personally. It is one of the great things that 'remain', even when the conditions are wholly changed.

May all happiness and blessing be yours and Mrs. Temple's 'all the days'.

Yours affectionately,
J. C. HULME.

Another was written six months later by one of Manchester's greatest citizens, the Editor of the *Manchester Guardian*:

The Firs,
Fallowfield,
Manchester.

My dear Temple,   July 18/29.

Your letter is most kind and I am grateful. You are greatly missed in Manchester. It only happens once in a lifetime that we get a Bishop of all denominations. That was Fraser's title and might be yours. I suppose it may happen that even quite soon we shall have to face the tremendous task of disestablishment and I should like it to happen while you are in control, just because you have such uncomfortably wide and various sympathies, or affiliations. Also there will be of course a big constructive work there to be done, for which you have already partly prepared in the Life and Liberty Movement. I realise what you say as to the great practical importance of the Church to the State, and that would prevent any serious attack from

361

without; the old active disestablishment movement of my early days is dead, but that from within has taken its place. I am taking a little holiday with my daughter Mrs. C. E. Montague, but habit is strong and I shall return in a few days to my accustomed place.

Yours very sincerely,

C. P. SCOTT.

Among the presentations were a portrait of the Bishop by T. C. Dugdale which now hangs in the Manchester Art Gallery, and another which was a personal gift to the Bishop and his wife 'from their friends and fellow-workers in the dioceses of Manchester and Blackburn'. A dinner was given by the civic authorities in the Town Hall—the Temples had been on the friendliest terms with E. D. (now Lord) Simon and Alderman (now Sir Frederick) West during their Lord Mayoralties, and with their wives—and another at the Old Rectory Club, where the members heard their Bishop sing the Chancellor's Song for the last time. One farewell gathering has not faded from the memory of those who took part in it. Over the first week-end in October Temple called many who had been associated with him in active diocesan work—the chairmen and secretaries of the various Boards and Societies, Sunday School and Moral Welfare workers, and others —to meet him at the Watermillock Retreat House. Here, in the dedicated peace of the chapel, he directed their worship and led their prayers, gave them his last message as their father-in-God, and later in the evening sang to them three of his favourite hymns—'King of Glory, King of Peace', 'O King enthroned on high', and 'Round me falls the night'. It was a fitting end to the Manchester years—'The setting sun, and music at the close'.

XXIII

Bishopthorpe—Between two Wars

I have just written to the P.M. to say I will go to York. It is a dreadful
responsibility, and that is exactly the reason why one should not refuse.
W. T., letter to F. A. I., August 1928.

ON 10 January 1929 William Temple was enthroned in York
Minster and received possession, from the Dean and Chapter,
of 'The Manor House at Bishopthorpe'. This has been the home
of the Northern Primates since early in the thirteenth century,
when Archbishop Walter Grey bought a parcel of land in the
village of Thorpe S. Andrew, four miles from York, and built the
chapel and the palace which were completed in 1241. He was
present when Magna Carta was signed at Runnymede and showed
some sense of the rapacity of monarchs, and of the dangerous ease
with which ecclesiastical estates could be alienated to the Crown,
when he made over the palace and chapel in trust to the Dean and
Chapter of York. Parts of the thirteenth-century palace, including
the chapel, remain; but it has suffered many transformations, the
most thorough being that effected in the late eighteenth century by
Archbishop Drummond, who was responsible for the 'Strawberry
Hill Gothic' front and completed the famous Clock Gateway,
some of the stones for its building being brought from another
primatial palace at Cawood, where Wolsey was arrested in 1533 on
the way to his enthronement at York. Every century has added
something to the history of the palace. Here Archbishop Scrope
was tried and condemned under his own roof for his part in the
rising of the North against Henry IV; here kings and queens have
been entertained, from James I to Queen Mary; in the grounds a
mob from York burned Archbishop Harcourt in effigy at the time
of the Reform Bill of 1832; and for a few years, if legend be true,
a grave servitor stood behind the Primate's chair in the dining-hall
or replenished the claret glasses of his Grace's guests, who was
to become a highwayman of repute and to be executed, as Dick
Turpin, in the city of York.

William Temple

Much had to be done before the Temples could move in. The old kitchens at the palace were given up, many rooms were redecorated, the electric light was installed, extensions to the telephone were carried out; and with floor-boards up all over the house, in an atmosphere of intense cold, dust, and general discomfort, their new life began. It cheered, though it saddened, them to say good-bye to seven hundred men and women, who had come in three special trains from Manchester and Rochdale to see their own bishop enthroned, and after the service Temple and his wife hurried down to York station in a storm of sleet to give them the send-off for which they had hoped. The brunt of the work of removal and reconstruction fell on Mrs. Temple; Temple allowed no interruptions to disturb his usual routine. Mrs. Dicker—who, as Miss Joan Hughes, was then his secretary, and was succeeded on her marriage by Miss Dorothy Howell-Thomas—recalls how

> with joiners hammering, plumbers and electricians testing wires and telephones, furniture being heaved about, and housemaids 'hoovering' busily he sat calmly in an armchair in a dust-sheeted room, an attaché case of momentous documents by the side of him, serenely dictating the day's letters. If he was asked to move to another room, he would break off in the middle of a sentence in a complicated letter with the utmost tranquillity and proceed ten minutes later from the exact point where he had left off, having in the meantime given his opinion on the placing of a chair or a picture, or assisted in the choice of colour for the kitchen walls.

He kept an appointment at an S.C.M. Conference almost on the eve of his enthronement, and spent his first week-end at Hull, where he made four engagements to preach or speak on the Sunday.

But both his wife and he knew that the arrival of the new Archbishop meant something more than a mere change in the tenancy of Bishopthorpe. In a word, the spacious days were over. It is doubtful whether Temple ever cast off a certain uneasiness—more will be written of this later—at the thought of the vast house and grounds that were now to be his home and his care; all that he had said and done and been at Manchester could hardly be made to fit into this new setting—so grand and yet so anomalous! His predecessor had felt no such qualms. Cosmo Lang was not the man to break a tradition of splendour. He loved to entertain his friends—members of the House of Lords, owners of large estates, officers of the Northern Command, and visitors from America—at Bishopthorpe, and his personal distinction of appearance and speech helped him to carry off the part he thought should be played by the Primate of England. This is not to suggest either that Lang's relations with the grandees of the Northern Province were merely social—his spiritual influence on the lives of many of them could not be gainsaid—or that his friendships were confined to those distinguished by place or purse. He loved Yorkshire and all its people—peers, landlords, and labourers—and there was no doubt of the sureness of his touch with the farmer-churchwardens and the people of the moor and dale villages in his diocese. (Of them he had a fund of good stories, with one special favourite— 'Ah've nothing but praise for our new vicar', a Yorkshire farmer said to his churchwarden friend: 'So I noticed when I handed you the plate on Easter morning', was the blunt retort.) But Lang's conception of what an Archbishop should do and avoid in maintaining the dignity of his office died with him: he prided himself on having never set foot inside a shop in York, and he warned Mrs. Temple that it would shock local feeling considerably to see her travelling in and out between Bishopthorpe and York in the common omnibus. At home Lang had been the perfect host; and never was he happier than when he was doing the honours of the palace, or displaying to his guests one of the most famous gardens in the north of England. Ten minutes' walk from the palace was the formal walled flower-garden, where the statistically minded visitor could count fourteen beds ablaze with wallflower and myosotis, polyanthus and tulip, and seventy-five yards of double herbaceous border, separated by a generous width of grass, in which delphiniums were 'nothing accounted of' if they were less than eight to ten feet in height; in the spring thousands of daffodils would be in flower along the lime avenue, and crocuses of many colours dotted the banks that sloped down to the river's edge.

Much of this had to go. In his first Diocesan Letter Temple wrote: 'I must not attempt to keep up the flower-garden in the splendid beauty which has made it so great a delight in recent years': but the gardens by the house and river were to remain 'much as they are with their singular beauty'; and here, whenever possible, he would walk after breakfast with his wife and 'Jock', their Scotch terrier. The day began with Mattins in the palace chapel, which Temple and the Vicar of Bishopthorpe, who acted as his chaplain, usually said together. Family prayers followed, attended by the staff and guests: the Archbishop introduced the Scripture reading with a very short and simple explanation of its context and meaning, and offered prayers for the everyday needs of the nation, the diocese, and the parishes which were remembered in rotation throughout the year. He opened his own letters in the dining-room while breakfast was being brought in; by ten o'clock (usually after a short walk in the garden) he was in the secretary's study, ready to deal with a pile of correspondence. His secretaries remember the almost aesthetic pleasure with which they took his dictation. Hardly ever did he hesitate for a word. Every letter previously sent or received, even on the most intricate subjects, was within his memory at the moment of replying; he never consulted a file unless it were thrust upon him, and only on the rarest occasions did his memory play him false. By eleven o'clock he was back in his study or he had left Bishopthorpe for work in the diocese, in the province, in London, or wherever he might have been summoned by the multifarious duties of an archbishop—except on Fridays which he tried, not altogether successfully, to keep free from outside engagements. That he was fully equipped, mentally and spiritually, to grapple with them all, none doubted less than his predecessor: 'I cannot tell you', Lang had written in his last Diocesan Letter, 'how thankful I am that the Bishop of Manchester is to be my successor. He is in the very prime of manhood. His great gifts of mind, of speech, of personality, are known to you all. I rejoice to think that I shall be able to leave the charge of the diocese in his strong and able hands. To me personally he

has been for years an intimate friend, almost a younger brother.'
It was not to be supposed that Temple could at once put behind
him all the memories of his old see, and he took the people of
Yorkshire into his confidence with the first Letter he wrote to
them:

> ... Luckily, York is very different from Manchester, and this
> makes me hope that it is possible to love both equally in differ-
> ent ways; for we have become so deeply attached to Manchester
> and its people that I should be bound to regard as an intolerable
> rival any at all similar place which made a claim upon our affec-
> tions. After all, Yorkshire and Lancashire are the only two
> Roses among the counties; and as an impenitent Devonian I
> feel a great pride in being associated with both the Red Rose
> and the White; moreover, my mother always claimed to be a
> Yorkshirewoman. ... No doubt I shall make many mistakes;
> when they come I hope you will be true to your county's repu-
> tation and tell me all about them with such additions about
> myself as you would like to add; and, even if I prove a slow
> learner, I promise to be a conscientious one.

The burden of new responsibility was not lightened by the
Archbishop of Canterbury's illness shortly after his appointment
to Canterbury. Lang could do little work for several months—
his illness was to recur in 1930 and 1931—so that Temple had to
undertake the duties of both Primates. These included the chairmanship of the Church Assembly and of Bishops' Meetings, and
several decisions on important matters of central church policy.
On 17 May 1929 he wrote to his brother:

> Of course I knew that on coming here I should have to pre-
> side over this Convocation—and felt faintly shy at the prospect.
> But as a result of Cosmo's illness I have, in the last fortnight,
> presided over the Church Assembly, the Bishops' Meeting, and
> the Convocation of York. I was a bit nervous the first day at
> the Church Assembly, and had at once to rule on a point of
> order for which no precedent existed; but it went all right, and
> I was quite comfy in the chair for the other four days.

It was also the time of King George V's illness, and on 1 April he writes again:

> I have missed a lot of mails lately. But on the top of Cosmo Cantuar's illness came a breakdown on the part of the Bishop of Hull, one of my own two suffragans. So I had to arrange for all his Confirmations, and also undertake a rather elaborate re-organization of diocesan work. So there has been lots to do.
>
> The last little addition was a rush to Bognor at short notice on Tuesday last to do homage. I found both the King and Cosmo really recovered, as far as I could judge, though of course the King will take a long while to get really strong again. But as he talked to me, there was nothing of any kind to show that he had been ill.

There is a further reference to the act of homage in the Archbishop's letter in the *Diocesan Gazette:*

> It is impossible not to feel some gratification that the first official act of the King, since his illness, was to receive the homage of the two Archbishops, and it was a surprise, as well as a delight, to notice how completely His Majesty had recovered, though naturally there is still need of the greatest care, and the public must not yet ask of him anything involving prolonged effort or strain. The Archbishop of Canterbury also seemed to be in genuinely good health again, though still under orders to avoid great exertion; there is every reason to believe that when he returns from the Mediterranean he will be completely ready for the burden of Lambeth. Incidentally, it is, perhaps, worth while to use the episode of our homage as a warning to the public against the vagaries of reporters. For some reason many newspapers have asserted that we wore copes and mitres on that occasion; some have even described these in detail—as for example one which says of us: 'They were glittering medieval figures in their scarlet and white robes, covered with gorgeous copes of wonderful embroidery in gold and silver thread and silks of many colours. They wore their mitres.' Of course we did not wear either mitres or copes, but ordinary Convocation robes. The paper just quoted adds that 'they

rendered their act of homage by kissing the King's hand'. As a matter of fact there is no kissing of hands in the ceremony of doing homage. It is well, sometimes, to remind the public that not all so-called news is true. I have the strongest personal reasons for gratitude to the gentlemen of the Press; but there are occasions when some protest also seems to be called for.

It was not the last of such protests that Temple felt obliged to make.

The Archbishop's first important pronouncement was made in his Visitation Charge of 1931. This was published under the title *Thoughts on Some Problems of the Day* and is the most revealing of all guides to his convictions (which changed little from that year to his death) on the theological, doctrinal, and social issues that seemed to him to stand out at the time. York, in contrast with Manchester, was largely rural; and this fact influenced him much in deciding which of the three opportunities open to a diocesan he should personally make use of when preparing his Visitation Charge: it was possible for a bishop, he wrote, to declare the mind of the Church on subjects of wide spiritual import, or to comment on the work of the Church in a diocese as set forth in the Visitation Returns, or to offer some contribution to the common stock of thought and knowledge which would help the clergy to carry their thinking further, and also to understand their bishop's own views on matters of contemporary interest or debate. In the third way, Temple suggested, he could best become known to his clergy in a large diocese, where personal contacts with every one of them were impossible. This was unduly modest; by the time he left York, he had visited all but thirty-three of the 457 parishes in his diocese once, several of them many times; and if he stayed away for a night it would usually be at the parsonage rather than with the squire. This is not to imply that he deliberately avoided the company of the landowners or that they were backward in offering him the hospitality of their homes. They mistrusted his social and economic convictions but were prepared to take him as they found him, and their personal relations with him were for the most part entirely friendly, sometimes cordial. 'I hope', he said to one county magnate who owned the advowson of a Yorkshire living, 'that you will soon be able to present to me the right man for that village.' 'I was just going to write to your Grace about it', was the reply: 'I've got a first-class fellow.' 'Oh! How did you find him?' 'Advertised for him in *Horse and Hound* —capital fellow!' A peal of laughter followed from the Archbishop—and he might have added that the appointment was not so far out of the Anglican tradition, for had not the Primate of All England, who during his tenure of the see of London had ministered to Charles I on the scaffold, once kept his own 'pack of good hounds [which] exceeded all other hounds in England for the pleasure and orderly hunting of them'? But this was a little off Temple's line of country; of horses and hounds—except for the succession of his own dogs—he knew nothing. At Garrowby, where he occasionally visited Lord Halifax, a round game was sometimes played which those with the widest general knowledge usually won, and Temple was always in the first flight till they discovered his Achilles' heel—he knew the names of no racehorses. From that day, under one roof and in one respect, he was a beaten man!

His own personal hospitality at Bishopthorpe was necessarily limited. When his own and his wife's time-tables allowed it, diocesan clergy and their wives, three or four couples at a time, were asked to spend a night at the palace; but conferences and gatherings, official and unofficial, followed hard one on another, and unallotted days and nights became fewer as these increased yearly in number and importance. Rural deans (several of whom would stay the night together), the suffragan bishops and archdeacons for their monthly staff conference, the northern group of the Doctrinal Commission, the S.C.M. Advisory Committee, members of the Indian Mission of Help, the provincial bishops' wives, W.E.A. leaders, Dr. Oldham and other collaborators in the Oecumenical Movement (among them Dr. Emil Brunner, Pastor Marc Boegner, Archbishop Germanos of Thyatira, and Pastor Merle d'Aubigné), the ordinands and examining chaplains each Embertide—one and all found at Bishopthorpe the ideal centre for work and talk and spiritual fellowship. Temple enjoyed particularly the visits of his Repton and Queen's pupils—the skill of one Old Reptonian, 'Bunny' Austin, on the lawn-tennis court was long remembered—and the company of Stanley Baldwin, for whose character he had a sincere admiration: 'I suppose', Temple wrote to him, when he laid down the Premiership, 'that there is no case in which you have caused bitterness, and you have healed a multitude of wounds.' One summer afternoon, as the Archbishop and the Prime Minister were sitting on the terrace at Bishopthorpe past which flows the Yorkshire Ouse, a barge came drifting by, and to the delight of them both the bargee took his pipe from his mouth and called out—'Keepin' better company to-day, I see!' 'I wonder', commented Baldwin, 'for which of us that pretty compliment was meant?'

And twice a year there would be a suggestion of the old palatial state. No part of the palace was more beautiful than the dining-room, its moulded ceiling dating back to the days of Archbishop Frewen, when the thirteenth-century dining-hall was restored in thanksgiving for the return of Charles II. Down the middle of it ran the old refectory table, blackened with age, at which twenty-two persons could be comfortably seated. It had been in use, with another table and two old benches, in the servants' hall till Lang bought them all from Maclagan for £10, and was offered £1,000 for the table a few years later: he preferred to bequeath them in perpetuity to his successors at Bishopthorpe. Here, during the sessions of the Upper House of Convocation, the northern bishops would sit at dinner in their purple, with the room almost in darkness except for the light thrown by black candles in silver candelabra on glass and plate, and the reflection of them in the sheen of the polished oak. But it was at Christmastide that the room looked its loveliest, when thirty or forty children of the clergy who lived within easy reach of Bishopthorpe had their party and Christmas tree. This was always followed by 'musical arms', the fathers being dragged out of the study where they had been talking and smoking to act as 'arms', and the small competitors each struggling to be 'last in' with the Archbishop. Temple was never shy with children, nor were they with him and, if it be true that highly placed ecclesiastics do not as a rule attract very young hero-worshippers, he

371

must have been an exception. It was a small boy in a Yorkshire village who was shown a flag flying from the church tower on 23 April and, on being asked 'Who is the patron saint of England?', replied—'Please, sir, Mr. Temple.' An older boy, in a school for young delinquents, chose as the subject of one of his compositions—'How Dr. Temple Rose to Power'. It was a painstaking effort in the best Samuel Smiles manner but, as the plot developed, the leading characters became a good deal confused, till in the end it turned out to be the writer himself who was depicted starting his career with a broom at a street-crossing and reaching, after an adventurous but faultless climb, the dizzy heights of a shop assistant in a white collar.

With Temple's new responsibilities as Primate came new and exacting commitments. In a letter written to his brother while he was still at Manchester, he had taken himself to task for not having kept enough days free for the frequent emergencies and unexpected duties that must interrupt the fixed appointments of every bishop. This need was now intensified, and to keep his engagement book in any sort of order became, from 1929 to the end, an intractable difficulty. An archbishop is still a diocesan; he has also an undefined spiritual oversight of the Province of which he is Metropolitan; he is expected to speak in the House of Lords, to assume a certain leadership in the State as well as the Church, and to be in constant touch with his brother archbishop for the taking of common counsel and action as need arises; further, if he is also an outstanding figure in the national life, his advice and support are begged or claimed by every 'uplifter', from the most sane of idealists to the craziest of bores and cranks. It is therefore the more remarkable that no suggestion was ever made that Temple neglected his diocese. There is little to be said of this part of his work that has not already been written of his Manchester episcopate: no bishop changed less in his pastoral ideals and administrative methods, and the tributes paid to his work by the clergy and laity of Yorkshire were in no degree or kind different from those he received in Manchester. Only the names change. Among his close friends in York was H. N. Bate, Dean of York, a man of wide culture and conversational charm, with whom

Temple once said he would rather spend an evening than with any other of his friends. There were the suffragan bishops—Frank Gurdon, Bishop of Hull, who brought to his work a humanity enriched by his parochial experiences in both East and West London, and who was succeeded by Bernard Heywood (a man loved not less as a bishop than as a priest) and later by Henry Vodden; Harry Woollcombe, to whom Temple was devoted, once Head of the Oxford House in Bethnal Green, who was suffragan first of Whitby and later, as his strength declined, of Selby; Carey Knyvett, who succeeded Woollcombe at Selby; and Harold Hubbard, whom Temple had brought from Cheltenham College to S. John's, Middlesbrough, and later made Bishop of Whitby in Woollcombe's place. But neither they nor the clergy of the diocese nor his examining chaplains have anything new to record of Temple that was not said of him at Manchester. One tells of his 'massive and all-pervading friendliness with the clergy'; another of his patience at interviews; another of the 'dignity, tenderness, and insight' of his ordination Charges, of his not always wise selection of ordinands, and of his reluctance to 'reject conscious vocation' to the ministry. Others remember the fellowship of the School for Clergy at Scarborough and of the diocesan conferences where none but he could have continued to give his clergy the 'strong meat' they had been used to receiving in Lang's presidential addresses; the synodal secretary, Chancellor F. Harrison, whose office brought him into the closest touch with the Archbishop, recalls how as President of the Northern Convocation— of which he had already been a member for seven years—he gave to Convocation by his friendliness and patient good humour a family life of its own; and the Vice-Chairman of the Diocesan Board of Finance, Mr. J. Louis Lawton, testifies to Temple's 'unique competence in presiding' over the meetings of the Board, while 'his grasp of accounts and knowledge of finance were unmistakable'. Mr. Lawton adds:

Although he had from time to time discussed with me his views on the immortality of Capital, which he regarded as wrong, he always showed appreciation of the attraction of an

investment for the Board which produced a safe income and
held a possibility of a rise in its market value.

But Temple was better at managing money than raising it.
Though he threw himself whole-heartedly into the 'Archbishop's
Appeal' for a quarter of a million pounds, the total sum raised (in
addition to a large legacy) was only £100,000: yet even this was
no mean feat at a time when the national financial crisis was acute,
when industrial unrest was causing widespread anxiety, and when
spiritual values were at a discount.

Outside his own diocese, but still in the Northern Province, the
most important local event during his primacy was the transfer of
the diocese of Southwell to the Province of York. For some years
there had been a growing desire among the churchpeople of Southwell to restore the assignment made by King Edgar 1,000 years
before, when the area covered by the present diocese was given
to the Northern Province, and to revoke the arrangement by
which for a century it had been included in the Province of
Canterbury. There was no opposition in the diocese or the
Church, the Archbishop of Canterbury wrote a formal letter
releasing Southwell from its allegiance to Canterbury, and at a
memorable service held in Southwell Minster on 26 October 1935
the Archbishop of York received the homage of his new suffragan.

A visit was also paid to the island diocese of his Province, of
which he wrote to Bradby:

> Bishopthorpe,
> York.
> July 26, 1933.

My dear G. F.,

I go to-morrow on a state visit to the Isle of Man. While
still engaged in putting my stomach right side in, I shall be
received by the Mayor who will present an address of welcome
—at the Pier. Half an hour later, fainting for hunger, after
giving my breakfast to the sea and my luncheon (untasted) to
the steward, I shall be received by the Governor who will present an address of welcome. Two hours later, when sleep is
become irresistible, I shall preach in St. George's, Douglas . . .

after the Bishop has delivered a brief address of welcome. Oh! Boy!!=οἶβοι. Or as Cassandra said, with suppression of the final consonant because she was a prophetess—Ἀᾶ.

Next Tuesday I leave that island early enough to escape addresses of farewell and travel without pause to Paris, where I confer on Faith and Order till Friday. On August 5 I get back to England, and then—then, we bury ourselves in a farm on the Quantocks in Somerset, and I shall sleep for 666 hours on end—or in other less apocalyptic words, like a hog.

Outside the Northern Province official engagements in London claimed much of the Archbishop's time. In 1934 he was present at the wedding of the Duke of Kent, and he assisted at the Coronation of King George VI in the Abbey where, thirty-five years before, he, his brother, and (now Sir) Eric Maclagan had been gentlemen-in-attendance on their respective fathers when Edward VII was crowned. In 1932, on his way to preach before the international Disarmament Conference at Geneva, he wrote to his wife:

> British Embassy, Paris.
> January 29, 1932.
> . . . I have had a most interesting talk with the Ambassador [Lord Tyrrell], about 2 hours. Now he has to go to an official dinner, and I dine with 2 of his staff—one of whom I knew before the war as a very young W.E.A. lecturer and a friend of Tawney's. The Ambassador says my speech in York Theatre last Sunday had a tremendous echo here. As he talked I had to tell him that my sermon is already written or he would think (if he saw it) that I was just repeating his conversation!

Two days earlier he had written to Bradby:

> To-morrow I start for Geneva to preach a sermon which is to be broadcast in Switzerland and England, and also (I believe) in Germany and Scandinavia. I suppose that no sermon preached to a crowd ever did much good. Some have had a great effect—one launched the First Crusade—but then I think it was a bad effect. Good spiritual work is done on one person or a dozen people at a time. Still, it is, I suppose, a greater

chance externally than was ever given before to one sermon—and it makes one feel a considerable mule. I shall have left Geneva before the conference meets in an atmosphere poisoned by my rhetoric!

But it is a silly world, isn't it? The direct cause of our poverty is the ease with which we produce wealth. And we are told to cure this by saving money we should like to spend so as to invest it in making the production of wealth easier still.

Towards the end of his sermon Temple delivered his soul about the War Guilt clause in the Treaty of Versailles. After stating that no treaty should be 'revised except by the authority recognized in international law as competent to revise it', he went on:

> One clause there is in the existing treaties which offends in principle the Christian conscience and for the deletion of which by proper authority the voice of Christendom must be raised. This is the clause *which affixes to one group of belligerents in the Great War the whole guilt for its occurrence.* . . . We have to ask not only who dropped the match but who strewed the ground with gunpowder.

Letters poured in to the office of *The Times* and the postbag at Bishopthorpe. The most influential of the Archbishop's critics was Sir Austen Chamberlain, who contended that, in denouncing the War Guilt clause, Temple was 'not really serving the cause of peace or making international morality a force in international affairs . . . it does no service to morality, it is not the enforcement of Christian faith but a denial of Christian morals, *to say that all nations were equally guilty*'. A comparison of the two sentences here italicized shows the length to which misinterpretation can be carried, even by a man of the high political stature and reputation of Sir Austen Chamberlain. Temple was quite impenitent. He answered his critics with vigour in a 'Prefatory Note' to his sermon which was published by the League of Nations Union; and on 29 March he wrote to his brother:

> You will have had the actual text of what I said at Geneva before now. I am sure it did more good than harm. If you fasten on a point like the War Guilt Clause a lot of people forget

(or never read) what you actually say, and attack you for something else. But if you only state principles, without any concrete application, no one knows that you have said anything at all.

Of all the worthwhile tasks undertaken outside his northern diocese, none bore more fruit than his Missions to the universities. The most notable of these was the Oxford Mission of 1931, in which he was helped by the Rev. Tom Pym, then Canon of Bristol. The prevailing spiritual atmosphere of the University was one of scepticism and indifference; a few religious societies had attracted like-minded undergraduates into small coteries, but these made little impression outside the circle of their own adherents, and there was no sense of the Christian Faith inspiring and sanctifying the academic and social life of Oxford. Some big forward move was demanded; and it was to Temple that the committee responsible for organizing a Mission to the University turned as the one man for whom a hearing could be assured, both from Christians (whether Anglican or Free Churchmen) and from many with no religious attachments. The preparations lasted for a whole year, and not even the most sanguine had hoped for the results that were achieved. What the Mission did for Oxford seemed to the Vicar of S. Mary's, the Rev. F. R. Barry (now Bishop of Southwell), to be 'beyond calculation':

It 'stopped the rot' in the Christian life of post-war Oxford. There are large numbers of men and women rendering influential Christian service all over the world to-day who owe all that is best in them to that week. It was, indeed, a decisive moment in the history of that generation, and the influence still endures and spreads. It was when the tide began to come in; and if we can to-day claim with truth that the intellectual initiative is now in the hands of Christian theology, that is due to a very large extent to what Temple then did in Oxford.

On the first night of the Mission the Vicar had arranged to meet the Vice-Chancellor at the door of S. Mary's, and pay the usual ceremonial courtesies. This turned out to be physically impossible. Every seat was taken; undergraduates were sitting on the

377

pulpit steps, even on the floor of the church, and the Vice-Chancellor had to push his way to his seat through a tightly packed mass of men who were preparing to stand throughout the service. Never was a missioner's appeal less directed to the emotions than when Temple, unfolding night after night the fundamental Christian world-view as a coherent philosophy of life, startled his hearers by his obvious and profound belief in truths which many of them (in so far as they had thought of them at all) had come to regard with contempt, and justified his convictions by rational appeal. He had none of the tricks of the professional missioner: only once did he take a risk—on the last night of the Mission. The moment for dedication and resolve had come. The hymn 'When I survey the wondrous Cross' was being 'roared out' when, before the last verse, Temple stopped the singing and said: 'I want you to read over this verse before you sing it. They are tremendous words. If you mean them with all your hearts, sing them as loud as you can. If you don't mean them at all, keep silent. If you mean them even a little, and want them to mean more, sing them very softly.' There was dead silence while every eye was fastened on the printed hymn-sheet, and then—to hear Isaac Watts's words

> Were the whole realm of nature mine,
> That were an offering far too small;
> Love so amazing, so divine,
> Demands my soul, my life, my all

whispered by the voices of 2,000 young men and women was (in the recollection of one of them) 'an experience never to be erased from my memory till the whole tablet is blotted'.

It was the same in other universities. In Cambridge, London, Leeds, Newcastle—wherever there were young men and women —they heard Temple gladly: one letter from Oxford, describing the interest aroused in the women's colleges, told how 'not even treacle pudding can stop them discussing the Holy Ghost at luncheon'. In Trinity College, Dublin, Canon Eric Abbott, who was Temple's assistant missioner, described the undergraduates as 'almost mesmerized' by the evening addresses—'the atmosphere was splendid; they listened like anything', Temple wrote to his wife—and he was equally sought after by the penitents to whom he gave absolution and the members of the Evangelical Union in whose prayer-meetings he joined. One pleasant feature of the Dublin Mission was an encounter between the Archbishop and an old janitor who had been in service at Lambeth Palace in the days of Frederick Temple and greeted his son with unfeigned delight— 'I have not seen you, Mister William, since you were a little boy at Lambeth.' 'I hope, Smith,' Temple asked, 'that I was a good little boy?' 'Well, Mister William, I don't think you have changed very much' was the extremely ingenuous reply.

Once only is Temple remembered to have failed with an audience of young people. At one of the many S.C.M. weeks at Swanwick a series of talks was given on 'Why I believe in God', and he was the chosen speaker on the Saturday evening. He had a great reception in the camp and everybody came to hear him, when to the astonished distress of those who had known for years his genius for approaching and holding the young, he seemed to hesitate, to fumble about for words and lose his grip, with the result that his address was described by one of the audience as 'almost a complete flop'. The next morning Mary Trevelyan (then Warden of the Student Movement House in Bloomsbury) was driving him to a church nearby at which he was to preach, and asked him what had been the matter: 'I don't know', he replied, 'why I shouldn't tell you. You see, *I have never known what it is to doubt the existence of God*, and I felt I had no right to be speaking to that audience of young people!' Yet at the Student Movement House he was the only speaker whom non-Christian students always came to hear, and he not only bore but invited their heckling in the discussions that followed. One evening a clever and most offensive Indian got up and said, almost threateningly, 'I suppose you'll think it blasphemy, but . . .' and he proceeded to give his views, which differed widely from those of the Archbishop. Temple waited patiently and, when the young man had exhausted himself, began his reply with the words, 'I cannot think why you should consider it blasphemy to disagree with *me* . . .' and then, when the laughter had subsided, gave a careful and reasoned reply to his critic. On his last visit to the House he spoke magnificently on the meaning of

Christian love, and walked to catch his bus to Lambeth with a Chinese and a Russian, one on each side of him, carrying his bags.

This unique influence over the young, of which Temple could not help being conscious, led him to accept an invitation to take part in the Conference of North American and Canadian Students at Indianapolis in December 1935. And there were other motives at work to take him across the Atlantic. In the United States he would be able to renew and strengthen his acquaintance with the American Episcopal Church—a Church without privileges but with a vivid and vigorous life of its own, and of much greater influence than its membership of 2 millions might suggest—and also to make personal contacts with many leaders in the Oecumenical Movement on their own ground. Four thousand persons attended the service at which he was welcomed in the Cathedral of S. John the Divine in New York, and on 8 December, forty-eight hours after he and his wife had landed from the North German Lloyd S.S. *Bremen*, he broadcast over the 'Church of the Air', and stressed the fact that he had come 'not chiefly as a representative of England, not of the English branch of the Catholic Church, but as a minister of the universal Gospel and of the Catholic Church itself'. He delivered lectures at the universities of Harvard and Chicago and to the College of Preachers at Washington (for their titles see p. 635), and wherever his time-table—which was as congested as only that of an American lecture tour can be—took him his reception was the same. There was little in common between his style and that of the platform speakers to whom American audiences were accustomed; but the combined weight and fluency of his words made a deep impression; his humility, his humour, and his 'reconciling mind', were singled out as his most notable characteristics; and in the universities, whenever he was able to take part in the small group-discussions that followed some of his lectures, the forthright and eager American students—many of them at that time convinced pacifists—responded with alacrity to the human friendliness of so unprelatical an archbishop. As the outstanding events of his tour he himself named the Conference at the College of Preachers in Washington, the meeting with leaders of five inter-Church world movements at Princeton, the Indianapolis Convention, and his lectures at the University of Chicago.

Few distinguished visitors can expect to come wholly unscathed through the attentions of the American Press. When Temple's predecessor at Bishopthorpe arrived in New York during the first World War, one newspaper—owing to an indiscreet conversation the Archbishop had held with a complete stranger on board S.S. *Philadelphia*—announced, within four hours of his landing, in a streamer-headline: FORMER PACIFIST NOW SAYS EYE FOR EYE AND TOOTH FOR TOOTH (whether the first or the second part of this announcement made him the more angry, Lang found it difficult to decide); and eighteen years later Temple had to submit to the attacks of the Hearst Press which, in many of the largest cities in the States, protested editorially that 'Bungling and mischievous visitors of the Temple type should stay at home—and if necessary, *be kept in confinement*'. As a set-off against this he could place the almost exaggerated reverence of a small child who —having been warned by her mother, 'When you speak to the Archbishop don't forget to say "Your Grace" '—stood with drooping head and crossed hands in front of Temple and whispered: 'For what I am about to receive, dear Lord, make me thankful'; her faith must have been strengthened when Temple was human enough to stoop down and kiss her. In summing up the results of the tour Bishop Manning of New York spoke for the whole Episcopal Church when he declared that Temple's visit had been 'a great help to us in our own Church, in our relations with Christians of other Churches looking towards Christian reunion, and in our work for social progress, truer international friendship, and world peace'.

Other efforts were made to entice him abroad: from time to time the suggestion was repeated that he should visit China, especially its universities: but the only other purpose for which he left the country, except for those detailed in the next chapter, was for the consecration of the new cathedral at Cairo. After a flying visit to Venice he and his wife spent a few days in Athens—where he preached on Easter Day at the invitation of the Bishop of Gibraltar—and on S. Mark's Day, 1938, to the joy of his old

friend Gwynne (Anglican Bishop in Egypt) and with the congratulations of all the Christian communions in Cairo, the Church
of S. George was consecrated as the centre of Anglican worship
in Egypt. On his return he was able to land for a short time at
Malta; from Marseilles he went to The Hague, and thence to
Utrecht for an inter-Church meeting of critical importance.

During the years between the two wars, Temple's letters to his
brother became less and less cheerful, with their frequent allusions
to economic difficulties at home and the threat of another World
War. None strove harder for peace through these years than he
did. One appeal followed another, on the platform and in the
Press, and as early as 1932 he had taken part in a deputation to the
Prime Minister on disarmament. On 20 October he wrote to his
wife:

> . . . The deputation went off pretty well, I think. A few of us
> were taken into 10 Downing Street first, where the P.M. and
> Simon discoursed on difficulties. Then we went on to the
> Foreign Office where there was a fair crowd of us—about 100.
> . . . Cosmo was good, I thought; Scott Lidgett very useful; and
> I was by way of underlining chief points. I instanced the Note
> to Germany as the sort of thing that had troubled us, with its
> apparent subordination of the moral claim to the legal situation,
> because only on that basis of law can public affairs be justly
> ordered. The P.M. in his reply adopted the old dodge of saying
> he 'was sure I would admit' what I had in fact clearly stated: as
> he ended one paragraph with the words 'I am sure His Grace
> would admit *that*' and a look at me, I interjected 'I said it';
> whereupon he chuckled very engagingly and said, 'Well, I
> thought it just as well to repeat it.'

There was still one hope—that the moral authority of the League
would be strong enough to direct the policy of the member States,
and to preclude that isolated action in international affairs which
it had been instituted to supersede. But this hope was dashed
when, early in 1933, the British Government decided to ignore
the decision of the League on the embargo of arms in the Sino-
Japanese war. There was no doubt which State was the aggressor,

and the League resolved to advise member States to impose an embargo on the export of arms and munitions of war to Japan. The British thereupon decided to impose the embargo on export to both belligerents. To Temple this policy seemed disastrous. On 25 March 1933 he wrote one of his most trenchant and effective letters to *The Times*, which was printed in 9-point type on the middle page. What, he asked, were the principles that were now governing our international policy?

... My submission is that our primary principle should be that of acting not so much with as through the League of Nations. Let me take an illustration from the problem presented by the embargo on the export of arms, in relation to which our Government took the only quite indefensible course.

If we had imposed an embargo on the export of arms to both China and Japan while the dispute was under consideration at Geneva and methods of conciliation were being attempted, there would have been much to say in defence of such a course. What we did was to wait until the League had discriminated and then take a non-discriminating action. What would, or at least might, have been right in the earlier stage was certainly wrong at that stage. . . . When the judgment has been given the primary need is to uphold it. What we did was to ignore it.

Among the many letters he received was one from Siegfried Sassoon, who deplored Temple's suggestion that a resort to force might be justified in support of the League:

As you say, the League is our only safeguard; but it has the powers of darkness working against it all the time. The Church exists to defeat the powers of darkness. Cannot the Church make some gesture which is above 'practical politics'? ... Can you not speak for the poets, who, after all, are something more permanent than the politicians?

There was an attractive other-worldliness about the suggestion —yet 'practical politics' went on their wicked course, and no gesture on behalf of the poets would have emptied Hitler's concentration camps. But at least a protest was possible. Temple collected all the reliable evidence he could about the camps, had it examined by a Judge of the High Court, and wrote a personal appeal to the German Chancellor, which was signed also by (among others) Gilbert Murray, G. M. Trevelyan, A. D. Lindsay, Michael Sadler, and Keynes. What was the chance of it ever reaching Hitler's hands? Two emissaries went over to Berlin on Temple's behalf to spy out the ground. They saw the Chancellor—taking coffee one evening a few tables' distance from them in the lounge of their hotel—but returned only to report that he had by now refused to hear or read a single word about concentration camps. Eventually, in December 1934, the letter was sent to Ribbentrop, who formally acknowledged it and suggested that, when next he was in London, 'an exchange of views' between himself and the Archbishop 'might be very useful'. The two never met.

As the years passed Temple became convinced that our foreign policy was being less and less guided by the directive force of any strong and consistent moral principle. We had failed to take effective action on the Lytton report after the invasion of Manchuria; in the war between Italy and Abyssinia sanctions had been held up just at the time when they might have begun to prove effective; and the situation in Spain and in China was a warning of the horror that might at any moment break over Central Europe. In July 1938 he issued, with the support of leading Anglican churchmen, a statement protesting against this policy of drift and opportunism, and pleading for a return to a recognition of International Law:

. . . There is a real moral case for a repudiation of the use of armed force altogether; but our country has not been persuaded that it is sound. There is no moral case for building and maintaining armaments without clear moral principles to direct their use. We are anxious lest the recent trend of events should develop into a drift away from all moral principles and result in an acceptance of sheer expediency as the guide of our action.

We recognize the paramount obligation of avoiding general war, if that can be done without gross betrayal of principle; but we contend that an even greater evil is involved in international anarchy, which would, moreover, almost inevitably lead to general war.

384

We desire, therefore, to reiterate our conviction that the maintenance of international law must, on moral grounds, take precedence of any national interest in the direction of foreign policy and should be its supreme goal.

With the same object Temple made, immediately after the Munich agreement, a strong plea for the calling of a Congress of Europe; but by the end of the year a growing fatalism had fastened on the country—a mood occasionally interrupted by outbursts of protest against the racial persecution which was increasing month by month in Germany. The most striking of these was a meeting in the Albert Hall at which Temple, supported by Cardinal Hinsley, the Chief Rabbi, and Mr. Herbert Morrison, gave an impressive warning of 'the real and great danger that the world will sink into moral numbness and lethargy'.

By the time Temple had returned from Cairo the shadows had deepened, and the world was nearing the abyss. In August 1939 he and his wife were among the guests at Chatsworth for the coming-of-age of his cousin William Hartington. The house was full of young people, and the celebrations were on a magnificent scale, with the usual presentations, speeches, and fireworks; but behind all the rejoicings lurked the fear of what was coming and the thought of the grim work to which these young men might soon be called to set their hands. The Temples went to the Quantocks to finish their short holiday, but on 1 September they hurried back to York, on hearing over the air the plans for evacuating children from the danger areas. The whole day before, except when they were listening to the wireless bulletins, they had sat out in the garden at Weacombe where Temple read aloud *Alice through the Looking-glass*. On Sunday, 3 September, the Archbishop announced from his throne in the Minster that the country was at war, and that night the first sirens wailed over the city of York.

Changes were inevitable at Bishopthorpe, and were smoothly made. Towards the end of their time the Archbishop and his wife took to living almost entirely in the north wing of the palace; a pleasant bedroom facing south and west did duty for Temple's study, and a small room near the kitchen, looking out on the garden, for their dining-room. Mrs. Temple and her invaluable secretary, Miss Sinker, became adept at improvising floor (and bed) space at the shortest notice; a dozen evacuees, including some children, occupied rooms at the end of the north wing and a flat over the garage; members of the Women's Institute made jam in the old kitchen; for a few months the drawing-room was used for A.R.P. lectures, whist-drives, and dances; the Home Guard had a rifle-range for practice in the walled garden; and the local N.F.S. did not disguise their amusement when Temple took part in a rehearsal and lay flat on his front directing the nozzle of a stirrup-pump at an imaginary incendiary bomb. An important local achievement was the institution of the York Council for War-time Service, which co-ordinated the work of all the canteens and clubs for the troops organized by many agencies; the voluntary helpers at one of the largest of these centres were organized by Mrs. Temple and Miss Sinker who, on several nights in the week, drove nine miles to the I.T.C. at Strensall; sometimes the Archbishop, who was Chairman of the Council, came out to the canteen to talk with the men or to hold an occasional service for them in the canteen. Yorkshire had its full share of attacks from the air; there were two devastating raids on Hull, and one on the city of York; but it was not until they reached Canterbury that the Archbishop and his wife were to know the horrors of an air-raid at first hand.

And now the scene changes. The war must recede for a while into the background and personalities must give place to causes, to three especially from which Temple at the height of his powers withheld no possible effort—the cause of the world-wide Church, the cause of social righteousness, and the cause of Christian unity at home.

XXIV

The Oecumenical Movement

Our period of history is marked by two contrasted tendencies—one in the secular, one in the Christian realm. The secular world has lost all experience of unity and can do no more than play with the aspiration towards it. The Christian world is moving steadily and rapidly towards deeper unity, and has an actual experience of Christian fellowship across all secular divisions which is full of hope for the future of Christendom and through it for mankind.

W. T., Prologue to Is Christ Divided?, 1943.

As though in preparation for such a time as this, God has been building up a Christian fellowship which now extends into every nation, and binds citizens of them all together in true unity and mutual love. . . . Almost incidentally the great world-fellowship has arisen; it is the great new fact of our era; it makes itself apparent from time to time in World Conferences such as in the last twenty years have been held at Stockholm, Lausanne, Jerusalem, Oxford, Madras, Amsterdam.

W. T., on his enthronement in Canterbury Cathedral, April 1942.

I believe in the Holy Catholic Church, and sincerely regret that it does not at present exist.

W. T., Addresses on Church Unity, passim.

WE read that, when the Laird of Monkbarns was spinning for William Lovel's benefit some yarn of his great-great-great-grandfather, he interrupted his own story to remark: 'It's a shame to the English language that we have not a less clumsy way of expressing a relationship of which we have occasion to think and speak so frequently.' What, we may wonder, would our antiquary have thought of 'Oecumenical Movement'? No student of the last forty years of Church history can avoid 'thinking and speaking frequently' of it, and the fact that the dictionary defines the word 'oecumenical' as 'belonging to or representing the whole [Christian] world, or the Universal Church' might have moved its godfathers to adopt some 'less clumsy way of expressing', and some more inspiring title for commending, an adventure with no bounds on the habitable earth. Yet there the word is—and perhaps the founders of the movement, if such there were,

387

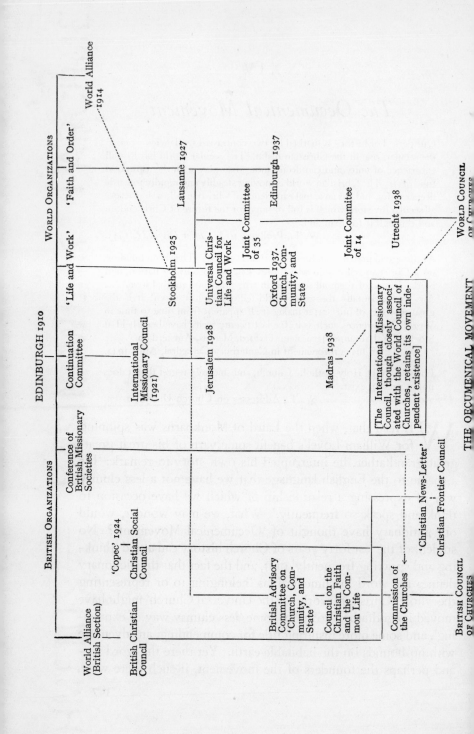

THE OECUMENICAL MOVEMENT

had less faith than was needed in the year 1910 to foresee the almost countless organizations, societies, and conferences that were to spring from the parent stem. Indeed it must have been difficult, even for those most familiar with its ramifications, to avoid the danger of being lost at times in a tangle of parallel and (it almost seems) competing organizations—the graph printed on the opposite page, for instance, makes no claim to be complete—and the less expert explorer who would cut his way through the jungle of trees, suckers, shrubs, and creepers can only mutter 'This is the forest primeval' and sharpen his stoutest axe. But the plunge must be taken. And first it may be worth while to stand outside and have a view of the wood, before penetrating farther to examine some of the finer and more fruitful trees.

The inspiration of the Movement is beyond dispute. It can be found in what Temple described as 'perhaps the most sacred passage even in the four Gospels—the record of the Lord's prayer of self-dedication as it lived in the memory and imagination of His most intimate friend'. This is the seventeenth chapter of S. John, of which the eleventh verse runs: 'Holy Father, keep them in thy name which thou hast given me, *that they may be one, even as we are.*' There is little to be gained from reciting here the tedious catalogue of the divisions and differences which have split the Christian Church for 1,900 years; what the Church has lost through them is set out in Temple's comments on this passage:

> The unity of the Church is something much more than unity of ecclesiastical structure, though it cannot be complete without this. . . . The unity which the Lord prays His disciples may enjoy is that which is eternally characteristic of the Triune God. It is therefore something more than a means to any end, even though that end be the evangelization of the world; it is itself the one worthy end of all human aspiration; it is the life of heaven . . . Before the loftiness of that hope and calling our little experience of unity and fellowship is humbled to the dust. Our friendships, our reconciliations, our unity of spirit in Church gatherings or in missionary conferences—beautiful as they are, and sometimes even wonderful in comparison with

389

our habitual life of sectional rivalries and tensions, yet how poor and petty they appear in the light of the Lord's longing. Let all of us who are concerned in Peace Movements or Faith and Order Movements or 'Conversations' with fellow-Christians of other denominations, take note of the judgment under which we stand by virtue of the gulf separating the level of our highest attainment and noblest enterprise, from 'the prize of the call upwards which God gives in Christ Jesus'—*that they may be one as we.*

For forty years the Churches of the world (the Roman Catholic Church standing aloof) have been striving to wipe away the reproach of this disunion and to come nearer—in faith, in worship, and in works—to the unity of his followers for which our Lord prayed, and which was to be a convincing proof to the world that His mission was from God. Three separate approaches to unity have been made—in the work of Evangelism among non-Christian peoples, in 'Faith and Order', and in 'Life and Work'. The story of each attempt demands its own telling.

I. EVANGELISM
Edinburgh, 1910: Jerusalem, 1928: Madras, 1938

Nowhere were the disastrous results of Christian disunion more patent than in the mission field, and nowhere did its origins seem less relevant: 'Fathers and Brothers,' cried Dr. Azariah, Bishop of Dornakal, at Lausanne—his eyes fixed on the millions of 'untouchables' in his vast Indian diocese—'be patient with us if we cannot very whole-heartedly enter into the controversies either of the sixth or sixteenth centuries.' The modern quest for unity along this road began with the International Missionary Conference held at Edinburgh in 1910, when the Church (not for the first time) was to learn the lessons of its own missionary enterprise. The Chairman of the Conference was Dr. John R. Mott, an American layman then chiefly known for his pioneer work in building up the fellowship of the World Student Christian Federation. Mott's double connexion with students and missions is symbolic, for it was from this twofold origin—the friendships made and kept by student leaders were invaluable—that the Oecumenical Movement sprang. He combined evangelistic fervour with an almost unrivalled knowledge of Churches, men, and affairs both in his own country and throughout the continent of Europe; he was trusted by statesmen and governments as fully as he was esteemed alike by young students and by those who had given the best of their lives to the missionary cause. The Conference was attended by 1,200 persons representing the Churches of Asia, Africa, North America, Great Britain, and the continent of Europe; its general purpose was to discover by consultation how the Churches could help, instead of hampering or competing with, one another, and to pool whatever knowledge and experience each had gained in its own particular sphere of work. Such gatherings are usually of more value for what precedes and follows them than for the actual discussions that take place at the time, and this was specially true of the Edinburgh Conference. Several Commissions were appointed at an early stage, whose reports in eight volumes formed the basis of the deliberations; and a successful attempt was made to bring into membership of the Conference some who were inclined to regard it with suspicion. Among these were the Anglican High Churchmen. The Society for the Propagation of the Gospel had hitherto taken no part in any missionary conference which included representatives of other Churches than the Church of England; but at Edinburgh the basis of the Conference—that 'questions of doctrine and Church polity in regard to which those participating in the Conference differed among themselves' were excluded from its purview—made it possible for the S.P.G. to take part. Edward Talbot, Walter Frere, Henry Scott Holland, and Charles Gore had a share in the work of the preparatory Commissions, and the official seal of the English Church was set on the Conference by the presence of the Archbishop of Canterbury, who made a special journey to Edinburgh in order to address it.

Temple was twenty-eight years old, and his part in the Conference was a small one. He was a member of the preparatory Commission on Missionary Education, and attended not as a delegate but as a guest—and also as a steward, for the S.C.M. had been given the task of appointing the stewards, and among those chosen were Temple, Neville Talbot, and Walter Moberly. Though he was present at most of the sessions, Temple had to leave before the Conference was over, in order to keep his engagement with the S.C.M. to visit the Australian universities; but he often testified that his first acquaintance with the world-problems of the Church was made in 1910, in the Assembly Hall of the Church of Scotland.

The most important sequel to the Conference was the appointment of a Continuation Committee. At no previous conference of the kind had any steps been taken to develop its work and to see that its resolutions were carried out; this mistake was not made at Edinburgh. The Continuation Committee was supplied with a secretariat; and it was the choice of Dr. J. H. Oldham which made it effective and led to the formation, eleven years after, of the International Missionary Council, which Temple later described as 'now quite an indispensable part of the machinery for carrying the Gospel throughout the world'. The Committee's progress was signalized by the next Oecumenical Missionary Conference, which was held at Jerusalem in 1928, when not only were more representatives present than before of the younger Churches, but also their delegates were chosen not, as hitherto, by the missionaries and the missionary societies but by the Christian communities and Churches throughout the world. Temple played an important part in the Conference. His wife had stayed at home in Manchester, and to her he wrote his impressions of the Conference—and of the Holy Land. He joined the *Naldera* at Marseilles, and from that point the story can be best told in his own words. It begins on Sunday, 16 March, when after the Bishop of Salisbury (Donaldson) had celebrated the Holy Communion and the ship's captain had taken the morning service, Temple was asked to preach in the evening. He wrote to his wife:

P. & O. S.S. *Naldera,* March 19, 1928. . . . I started on my article for the Institute of Philosophical Studies. I did not hurry and it took 2 hours. . . . We went through the Straits of Messina yesterday during dinner, and mercifully found it quite flat on this side. There was a large congregation—about 300—

at the evening service, and the Chief Engineer, who appears to look after the Seamen's Charities, said afterwards, 'Well, you knocked the Captain's collection silly.' Yesterday afternoon Sarum and I talked to Ormsby Gore [now Lord Harlech] and [Sir Harold] Kittermaster, who are both on board, the whole afternoon, from lunch to tea, without once moving.

Tuesday, March 20: Yesterday I finished *Wintersmoon*—it is immensely interesting. As far as it has a moral, it is in favour of the old-fashioned virtues; but I suppose the author would hate the notion that he had one at all. I have enjoyed it enormously.

Tabagha. Friday, March 23: We breakfasted at 8.0 and then went up to the top of the hill behind Nazareth; quite wonderful views, with the snowy tops of Hermon dominating everything. . . . Nazareth is strangely like Assisi: Esdraelon is very like the great plain below Subasio; the city is very white, on a dry hillside; the chief buildings are Italian, and the most frequent trees are cypresses. But it is higher above the plain, has more of a level space to sit on, and is much nearer the top of its own mountain. . . . The first place we passed on our drive was Gath-Hepher, the birth-place of Jonah. Then Cana of Galilee, where we went to the Greek Church. . . . Thompy [an old Queen's pupil, the Rev. O. H. Thompson] told the priest who I was, and he said Sarum had passed through yesterday but had not come to the church (I don't know how he knew). Then he took us through the Eikonostasis, lit a candle on the altar, slipped a broad Greek stole over my head, and asked me to pray for the unity of the Church. . . . Very soon we came to the edge of the last drop and the Lake was in full view. It was deep blue, with the hills beyond and to the left a reddish brown with green patches (plough and wheat), to the right deep bare slopes of limestone, above the Northern ones to the left Hermon was still supreme. We soon reached sea level and ran on to Tiberias, 682 ft. below it. From there we came by a road along the Lake, a little above it at first, and then nearly level with it, across the Plain of Gennesaret. It is almost like a vast water-meadow, very lush, full of dandelions and kingcups. . . .

At 1.0 we arrived here at Tabagha, a hospice of S. Vincent de Paul; it must be one of the loveliest spots in the world. It looks down the Lake obliquely from N.W. to S.E. The Lake laps on a stone beach, with a little harbour formed by 2 piers of loosely set stones. We have had lunch and Thompy has been resting while I wrote this much.

Later: At that point we had tea on the lovely terrace here, and then walked to Capernaum—a short two miles each way.... I have been wondering how much of one's feeling for the Lake is due to association. But it is anyhow most beautiful, and full of a delicious peace. When the sunset light fell on the Eastern hills, the steep sides were much greener than I had seen before, though the rock comes through a great deal. The red in the Northern parts became glorious....

Jerusalem, March 25, 1928. . . . Our camp is on the Northern part of the Mt. of Olives, and there is a considerable dip between us and the summit, which is the traditional site of the Ascension, and which has below it Gethsemane and opposite it the entrance that leads straight to the Temple Court. I am surprised to find how completely Jerusalem is in a hollow. . . . The only text which corresponds with what I have so far seen is 'The hills stand round about Jerusalem'. We look down upon it from far above. On the other side we look out over very desolate hills, with two or three stretches of the Dead Sea between them. . . .

Our huts are in three long buildings with a corridor right through the middle, and doors along it into compartments five yards long and three yards wide. The furniture is, a small but comfortable bedstead, and a table carrying basin, jug, etc. There is no sort of cupboard or drawer. We are partitioned to the roof on the corridor side but only as high as the angle of the outside wall and roof between the compartments. The whole thing is made of board, so sounds travel. Consequently I knew all about the unfortunate man in the same row who had violent sick attacks at 1.0, 3.0, and 5.0 a.m.!! The Conference doctor went in to try and help him, so I was not called on for ministrations.

The Bishop sent his car for us at 6.45 and we had a very nice quiet service in the Cathedral. Sarum was very good (as Mott also had been last night) at a service this morning. Then I had a stroll with Oliver Quick. . . . After lunch to-day I attended a small Committee, because I am to be Joint-Chairman, with Speer (U.S.A.), of the Section on the Christian Message in relation to other religions. The method is not that of Lausanne. Here we shall have two mornings on that subject in full conference, and two afternoons on it in groups—Hinduism, Buddhism, Islam, Confucianism, Secularism. Then a Committee made of the Chairmen and Secretaries of those groups, with Speer and myself, will settle down to draft 'findings', to report to the full Conference, and go on till we have done. The other subjects will be tackled in the same way.

March 26. To-day we have opened up the main subject. I think discussion has been extremely good, but the most impressive people (I think) have been Oliver Quick this morning, and Harry Tawney this afternoon. Harry is very much impressed, especially by the Orientals.

March 26, 1928. . . . I had my fling at the Conference this morning, summing up the discussion on 'The Christian Message and non-Christian Systems'. It seems to have gone rather well.

March 27, 1928. I celebrated at our daily Communion to-day —it has to be at 6.45—as breakfast is at 7.30. We use the end of one of the galleries of the Chapel. The roof of the Chapel has three great mosaic pictures: in the apse is the Ascension: in the centre is the Alpha and Omega: West of that is the Kaiser enthroned, to whom the Grand Duchess who founded this place is presenting the building!

March 27, 1928. . . . At the evening session I fired off my discourse on the Church. They were certainly interested: Sarum is much pleased; but the intensely nationalist Easterns were (I think) quite largely in disagreement. I urged that of two extreme alternatives it was better for China to have many denominations, all international, than a united Chinese Church which was national only. Dr. Wey was talking to Tawney and me afterwards and Wey virtually said they must have national unity, whether they had international connexions or not; to which Tawney said 'All you Orientals seem determined to go the European way to Hell'. It is horribly true.

April 3, 1928. I was drafting all the morning, and seemed to be regarded as having done rather conspicuously my parlour trick of fitting everybody's pet point into a coherent document when they thought they were contradicting one another.

This afternoon the whole Conference went to the Temple area. The American Colony had persuaded the Grand Mufti to give us leave to go out of hours. As Sarum had already seen the dome, we prowled about generally and then walked along the Via Dolorosa to the Church of the Holy Sepulchre which contains the traditional sites both of Calvary and of the Tomb. . . .

This evening we had before us a very good report on Industrial conditions in the Mission field, largely of Tawney's drafting. I think it will get through all right, but the old stagers may have been gasping too much to speak this evening.

There is a draught in the hut this evening for some reason so my own candle is hopeless on the table. I have had to put it on the floor and write lying on the boards on my tummy.

April 4, 1928. . . . After tea I presented our report on the Message. There was keen anticipation and even anxiety about it, as it is felt to be the main business of our gathering. When I had read it they were quiet for some while, then an American urged that there be no detailed discussion of it for fear of spoiling it: whereupon Garfield Williams proposed that it be accepted *in toto*. But it was felt that this would be unfair to the non-English speaking members, so the matter was adjourned for the reading of it and G. W.'s motion will be taken to-morrow. But I seem to have written what opens the doors for the progressives while perfectly satisfying the conservatives. As a matter of fact the *writing* was quite easy. We got the various sections so to state their own views that they were compatible with one another; and then it was only a matter of putting the bits together in the right order. I hope their night's perusal of it will not awaken suspicions of it in the breasts of the old stagers.

April 5. Our 'Message' was unanimously accepted this morning by a standing vote, followed by silent prayer and thanksgiving. There is great jubilation, as it is thought to be good in itself, and there was apparently great anxiety that we should not be able to agree on anything substantial at all.

Sarum and I went to the Bishop for lunch and also for baths —the first since we left the P. & O. at Port Said. Then there were more sessions. We nearly all went down to Christ Church for 7.0 o'clock when the Bishop always takes an Evening Communion there on Maundy Thursday. I did not receive, having done so at our own morning service. Afterwards the Bishop leads the congregation from the Church . . . along the Via Dolorosa, out at St. Stephen's Gate, across the Kedron and into Gethsemane. This time he did not go to the Garden, because of the numbers, but went to a place on the hill-side where he took a series of meditations, with hymns. There were arrangements for another service, without hymns, in the Garden, near the Russian Church. I went with the latter company, but inside the Garden got away to myself and had a rather wonderful time in the brilliant moonlight. Then I went into the Russian Church and said some prayers there. But it is not their Holy Week, so it was scarcely lit. Then I went down to the Franciscan Church, lit only, but beautifully, by candles round the walls. There I was favoured, as there were at first many praying silently round the rocks which they believe to be the actual site of the Agony. But soon the peace was broken, because the Crown Prince of Italy (who is leading a pilgrimage here) had finished his prayers and came out. At once a subdued hubbub began, so I came out and walked slowly up the hill. As I did so a violent storm got up, which is now howling—and I felt a few rain drops, the first since we landed at Port Said.

I shall not forget the 20 minutes or so that I spent all alone in Gethsemane, looking across at the dome in the Temple area. It is the one thing that has given me 'feelings' in Jerusalem.

The 'Garden' is a steep hill-side, with some paths and a good many cypresses. No doubt it is all altered. But it is still a peaceful place at the foot of the Mt. of Olives, and just across Kedron from the Temple court on its hill. opposite.

April 7, 1928. . . . The Report on Religious Education has now become a very fine document and was accepted this morning. We have now got really good pronouncements on that, on Race, on Industry, and (I hope) on the Christian Message.

At 3.0 I am to preach at an annual Easter Eve commemoration held here in the British Cemetery. At 4.15 the Council re-assembles, and has to pass five more reports before it breaks up to-night. At whatever hour that is, Sarum and I go down to the Bishop to spend these two nights there. So I shall not be sleeping again in my hut. It has done very well, but I am not sorry to have done with it! And it makes me feel that I am starting for home. . . .

Easter Day, April 8, 1928. . . . The service in the Cemetery was quite an impressive little ceremony yesterday. It ended just before 4.0, and at 4.15 we began our last session. It went on till 6.15, when we adjourned for dinner. After dinner the session began again (at 8.0) and went on till past 12.0. Sarum and I came with the Bishop to his house where I am now writing. We had finished the business of the Conference, and the last two hours were occupied with the very difficult question of the line to be taken about the Protection of missionaries. This morning I assisted in the Cathedral at 8.0 (when Sarum celebrated) and preached at Christ Church at 10.0, after which I celebrated there. . . . Then back here to lunch. Then to the Conference again for a meeting of thanksgiving and prayer. I had to leave that at 6.0 to get to the Cathedral for the 6.30 service at which I preached.

Now to bed—and to-morrow we start for Cairo.

The 'Messages and Recommendations' of the Conference were set out in *The World Mission of Christianity*, and it is not too much to say that the fellowship of these leaders of the Christian forces in fifty countries, which deepened as they spent their Passiontide in prayer and counsel on the Mount of Olives within sight of Calvary, marked the beginning of a new missionary outlook in many Churches: 'An atmosphere was generated', wrote Dr. Mott, 'in which serious difficulties and conflicting views, while never ignored but frankly expressed, were transcended': misunderstandings were removed, the way to even closer co-operation was opened, and the younger Churches experienced the stimulus of being treated not as pupils on whom the teachers of the Western world were seeking to impose the stamp of fixed ecclesiastical forms and practices, but as partners in a great enterprise for the Kingdom of God to which they could contribute something of their own genius and their own racial culture. The presence of a much larger proportion of delegates from the younger Churches when the next missionary conference was held ten years later at Tambaram, near Madras, shows that this confidence in them was not misplaced.

II. 'FAITH AND ORDER'
Lausanne, 1927: Edinburgh, 1937

The first advance toward unity had been made—but, so far, on a very narrow front. Strategically they seem to have been justified whose first desire was to bring the representatives of the Churches together in order to secure a basis of practical co-operation; but at the root of this decision lay the old fallacy that 'practical' activities could be completely divorced from doctrinal issues. Among those who diagnosed this weakness was Charles Brent, Bishop of the Philippines and later Bishop of Western New York, a leader of wide vision and untiring energy, who was convinced that, so far from the discussion of doctrinal differences being out of place at an oecumenical conference, it ought to be attempted, even if in another context; only so could the Churches discover exactly where they held divergent views, and take common counsel how to heal their divisions. The dangers were obvious. 'The Apostle of Christianity', Trollope once wrote, 'and the infidel can meet without the chance of a quarrel; but it is never safe to bring together two men who differ about a saint or a surplice.' But Brent was not to be daunted and, on his return to America, he consulted other bishops and brought before his Church Convention in 1910 a proposal that another movement

should be launched which would be concerned with the 'Faith
and Order' of the Church. The Convention supported him and
an invitation was issued to all Churches to take part in the new
adventure. At Lambeth it was received courteously but with
caution. The Archbishops were unwilling to appoint a representative committee, as the American Church had asked them to
do, but they appointed a 'co-operating committee' which was
instructed to keep a watching Anglican eye on the Movement.
A preliminary gathering was held at Geneva, at which Gore and
Canon Tatlow were present. While it was in session the unity
movement received a fresh impetus by the publication of the
Appeal to all Christian People issued by the Lambeth Conference
of 1920; and by the time the first World Conference on Faith and
Order met at Lausanne in 1927 the National Church Assembly
was ready to agree that the Church of England should be officially
represented and asked the Archbishops to appoint a delegation on
its behalf. Temple, who was then Bishop of Manchester, was one
of the nominees. The leadership of the Conference still remained
largely with the older men—Brent, Söderblom, Deissmann,
Garvie, and (from the Church of England) Headlam and Gore—
but several eyes were turned in Temple's direction as the debates
went on, and many more before they were over. He was deputy-
chairman of the section that dealt with 'The Nature of the Church',
and it was soon noticed that the veteran William Adams Brown
had come to place great confidence in his deputy. Fifteen years
later Temple told his diocesan conference at Canterbury of one
incident which he was fond of recalling with a chastened delight:

> The Conference was, I need hardly say, of quite extra-
> ordinary interest. The interest appeared quite as much in the
> discovery that we were agreed when we thought we were dis-
> agreed as in any exploration of the differences, and in the
> discovery, alas, sometimes that we disagreed when we were
> apparently agreed. The most astonishing instance of the latter
> —at least the most astonishing I met—was in the section on
> 'The Nature of the Church', when the Lutherans and the
> Orthodox combined in a demand that we must at all costs state

concerning the Church that it is both visible and invisible. Now, there are not very many things that the Lutherans and the Orthodox hold in common concerning the Church, so we were delighted, of course, to fall in with this and nobody wished to dispute it. Then we had to add a footnote because, quite accidentally, it became apparent that according to the Lutherans the Church is visible indeed but only in its activities —preaching the Word and administering the Sacraments. In respect of its membership it is quite invisible; nobody knows who are members of the Church, except God; they are the elect. . . . But the Orthodox, of course, did not mean that at all. By the Visible Church they meant the Orthodox Church and its members and by the Invisible Church they meant the deceased members of the same, and none of the rest of us were in it at all! So, having first discovered this complete and enthusiastic verbal agreement between the Lutherans and the Orthodox we then, as I say, regretfully added a footnote to say that they meant not only different but diametrically opposite things by it.

The two main points on which the Conference was agreed were that the Faith of the Church is that to which the Apostles' and Nicene Creeds bear witness and that, if unity of Order is to be achieved, it must rest on the basis of the historic episcopate. There was also a statement of the Gospel (drafted by a group led by Dr. Deissmann) which was adopted by the whole of the Conference and has become one of the classical documents of the Oecumenical Movement. Temple considered these results 'very great'; his own part in helping to bring them about was described in a speech by Pastor Merle d'Aubigné, when he was publicly thanked for his 'tact and consideration, which had built up' in one section of the work, 'with all the contrasting traditions it represented, a genuine Christian unity'. On his return home Temple wrote to his brother:

Aug. 28, 1927.

We had an extraordinarily interesting time at Lausanne, but also very exhausting. I think the Conference did as much good as it was possible to hope for. Certainly we got further than I had expected. The main thing after all was to ascertain exactly what are the principles of the various divisions of Christendom, and why people cling to them. In this we got a long way.

The increasing confidence felt throughout the Churches in Temple's powers as a leader was shown when, in August 1929, a chairman had to be appointed of the Lausanne Continuation Committee, and no other name than his was suggested. Eight years later the second World Conference on Faith and Order met in Edinburgh, and it fell to Dr. Garvie (the only Vice-President of the Lausanne Conference in the gathering) to move the appointment of a chairman. After referring to many of the old leaders who had passed away, he proposed that Temple be called to the chair, describing him as 'a Saul among the people, whose devotion to the cause of reunion has been fully proved'. In nothing had this devotion been more obvious than in the sacrifice of his time, and of his energy of mind and body, during the years between the two Conferences. He did not fail once to preside over the Continuation Committee, which almost always met on the Continent; between November 1932 and February 1937, he took the chair at seven meetings (four of them abroad) of the Executive Committee, at which most of the important preparatory work was done; and between the meetings he was in constant touch with the Secretary, Professor Leonard Hodgson, to whose patient determination and conspicuous ability he more than once paid tribute. Whenever these committees sat on the Continent, he wrote regularly to his wife; the first of the following letters was written soon after Professor Hodgson's appointment as Secretary:

> Belfast Hotel, 10 Avenue Carnot,
> Paris.
> August 3, 1933.

. . . Yesterday we sat in Committee from 11.0–1.0, 2.30–4.30, 5.15–6.45, and did a lot of work. Our company is W. E., [Headlam, Bishop of] Gloucester, Garvie, Merle d'Aubigné, Hodgson, Miss Croot (his secretary), William Adams Brown, MacCracken, Merrill, Leiper, Boegner. Sasse is coming tomorrow. . . . Altogether it has been the best Faith and Order meeting that I remember, and we are all very much encouraged by the prospect of our new Secretary. He rather bullies us, but no one shews signs of resenting this: on the contrary, they are pleased to have a Secretary who really formulates proposals; and he is perfectly good about accepting and working decisions of the Committee.

> Schlosshotel, Hertenstein.
> September 3, 1934.

... This is a place of the most superb beauty. We are on a wooded promontory and look across the Lake to another such which runs steeply up to about 1,000 ft., while other tops shew over this from behind. . . . I had a long talk with Sasse, after luncheon—very interesting. Among other things he said—'I gave a lecture lately on the religion of Hitler; but I did not call it that; I called it the religion of Robespierre.' . . . All goes happily but, as always at the beginning, we have moved very slowly. The Germans can never discuss what to do to-morrow without shewing how their view depends on the divine purpose in creation—the existence of which must therefore be first established. None the less, we do get on.

> Hindsgavl, Middelfart, Fyn, Denmark.
> August 4, 1935.

... This morning a car called at 8.45 to take me and Dr. Deissmann to Odense to my sermon in the Cathedral. Several had gone in already. I have never heard greater sincerity than in the 'No, No' with which the Bp. of Gloucester last night answered the question whether he wished to breakfast early in order to go to Odense to hear me preach!

The service was ante-Communion—very like ours, taken by a minister vested in a pre-Reformation chasuble with a crucifix embroidered on the back. There were 5 (no less) hymns of the chorale type. At the beginning, to make me feel at home, the organist played a Prelude on the tune of 'The Church's One Foundation'—even here! Then we went to luncheon in a private room at a hotel. The table was loaded with dishes, and each person's plate was replenished from some other as soon as his last mouthful of the last was off it. I got off light with bits of smoked salmon, lobster, chicken and assorted vegetables—mercifully small portions of each. Then came a great dish with several kinds of cheese and several sorts of salad. There is a lovely instrument like a fish-slice with a bent down flange in it which cuts shavings of cheese with delightful ease.

We got over knotty points in the Agenda till tea-time.

August 6, 1935. . . . We have settled Edinburgh as the place for the World Conference of 1937, the dates August 3–18 (Ugh!), but there is no help for it. And if the Doctrinal Commission is over and I can postpone that Ordination by a fortnight, we will get a good spell clear.

Temple steered the Continuation Committee and its Executive safely through many dangerous shoals in the years before the Edinburgh Conference. One of the immediately pressing difficulties was how to make a selection of delegates to Edinburgh from the German Churches which should be both just and realist. The German Evangelical Church was rent with dissension from 1934 onwards, as its official machinery had been captured by a pro-Nazi group anxious to keep on good terms with the Hitler movement. Both this official Church and the protest it had called forth in the Confessional Church were represented at Düsseldorf, and sooner or later a decision had to be taken whether one of these Churches (and, if so, which one) or both should be entitled to nominate delegates. Professor Hodgson recalls the skill with which Temple solved the problem:

Our task for the moment was to keep in friendly contact with all and avoid admitting the claim of any to an exclusive right to nominate the German delegates to the World Conference. Throughout dinner Temple kept the conversation to purely theological questions. By the time that the live issues of ecclesiastical politics were raised he had so won the confidence of all by the ability and sincerity of his theological discussion that they were prepared to accept with good humour his explanation of why the Faith and Order Movement must wait to see how events developed in Germany before deciding to whom invitations to appoint delegates should be sent.

In the taxi on the way back to our hotel the Archbishop remarked to me that one of those present had said to him, 'Why should you object to Hitler doing for our Church what Henry VIII did for yours?' 'Of course', he went on, 'if a man in the twentieth century claims to be judged by the standards of the sixteenth, there's nothing more to be said; but I couldn't very well say that to his face at a dinner party.'

Another issue that could not be avoided was of more far-reaching import and required the utmost sympathy and skill in its handling. There can hardly have been a single gathering of the adherents of many Churches in recent years at which the problem of intercommunion among its members has not arisen; and at a conference summoned to further the unity of Christendom the question is asked with peculiar force: If the Sacrament of the Lord's Supper is the greatest symbol of our unity in Christ, how can those who acknowledge him as Saviour and Lord—who have worked together, prayed together, and taken counsel together in his name—show more significantly their common allegiance and their longing for union than by partaking together of the Sacrament of Unity? The argument appealed with a compelling force to most members of the Continuation Committee and of the Edinburgh Conference who were not of the Anglican Communion, and nothing saddened Temple more than to take the opposite view. For two reasons he felt bound to do so. To him—whatever exceptions he might occasionally admit—intercommunion was the sign and the assurance that full unity had been reached, rather than a step in, and a help towards, its achievement; nor could he forget that he took part in and led the Conference not only as a delegate of the Anglican Church but also as its Archbishop. He now represented all sections of thought within his own Church, and he could not regard it as his duty to take a step which would cause the utmost distress among a large number of its members and involve dissension and strife throughout the Anglican Communion. But he had never intended that the issue should be shirked at Edinburgh. This was the chief fear of many non-Anglican members—that the Conference would devote itself almost entirely to matters of Faith and neglect, perhaps deliberately, the no less pressing question of Order. A few days before the Conference Dean Sperry—an American Congregationalist with whom Temple formed a close and enduring friendship—hurried from Oxford to Bishopthorpe to express these fears to the Archbishop. Temple came in at the end of a long day, tired and ill with a heavy cold, but with patience and sympathy he heard Dr. Sperry out, and then assured him that he intended both to have the matter discussed at the Conference and also to make a quite definite statement in his opening sermon. He then outlined what he intended to say, and Dr. Sperry replied that this would clear the air and dispel all doubts either of the policy of the Anglican representatives or of Temple's own candour and charity.

It was entirely fitting that the opening sermon should be preached in the Cathedral Church of S. Giles in Edinburgh where, twenty-seven years earlier, Brent had seen his vision of what a World Conference on Faith and Order might stand for and achieve. Temple set out, in words of prophetic devotion, their reasonable grounds for faith and hope. But, he added, there was one 'matter for deep penitence':

> I speak as a member of one of those Churches which still maintain barriers against completeness of union at the Table of the Lord. I believe from my heart that we of that tradition are trustees for an element of truth concerning the nature of the Church which requires that exclusiveness as a general rule, until this element of truth be incorporated with others into a fuller and worthier conception of the Church than any of us hold to-day. But I know that our division at this point is the greatest of all scandals in the face of the world; I know that we can only consent to it or maintain it, without the guilt of unfaithfulness to the unity of the Gospel and of God Himself, if it is to us a source of spiritual pain, and if we are striving to the utmost to remove the occasions which now bind us, as we

think, to that perpetuation of disunion. It should be horrible to us to speak of and to think of any fellow-Christians as 'not in communion with us'. God grant that we may feel the pain of it, and under that impulsion strive the more earnestly to remove all that now hinders us from receiving together the One Body of the One Lord, that in Him we may become One Body—the organ and the vehicle of the One Spirit.

The subject had yet to be discussed at the Conference, and it was unfortunate that the terms in which intercommunion should be referred to in the Conference Report were one of the last matters debated in the whole fortnight. Towards midnight on 17 August an obviously tired and impatient gathering listened to a number of suggestions, but none of them commended itself to the whole body of delegates, and there was a danger that the harmony of the Conference might be broken in the last hour of its deliberations. Temple was noticed to be quietly writing, while never ceasing to follow the quick interchange of opinion on the floor of the House; he allowed the debate to go on till every member was hoping and praying for its end, and then he rose and suggested this wording:

> We feel moved to say in this connexion that neither those who press for intercommunion nor those who feel obliged to oppose it should condemn the other, but should in all ways respect one another's consciences: but all Christians should be saddened by every hindrance to the fellowship of full communion with all sincere disciples of our Lord.

The words were at once accepted, and they stand as part of the Conference Report. The closing service was held in S. Giles's Cathedral. When the Affirmation of Unity (see Appendix at the end of this chapter) had been read to the Conference during their discussions, most of the delegates had become so involved in debating minor points that little or no sense of inspiration had come from their hearing of the words. It was a sign of Temple's spiritual awareness that he should have read the Affirmation again from the cathedral pulpit at the closing service. This, with his own reading of John xv which immediately followed, left, if not a sense of achievement, at least a conviction of their spiritual unity among the 400 delegates from 122 Churches who had taken part in a Conference that has left its indelible mark on the pages of Church history.

III. 'LIFE AND WORK'

Stockholm, 1925: Oxford, 1937: Utrecht, 1938

But the Christian Church does not exist *in vacuo*. All this might be dismissed by the cynic as just ordinary domestic tidying-up—for how did it help the Church to fulfil the terms of its all-embracing charter? A Church does not become either the salt of the earth or its light, nor does it leaven the hard lumps of the world, merely because its ministers can produce certificates of their authentic apostolic succession. Whatever it might decide in the first half of the twentieth century about its own Faith and Order, the Church had still to reckon with the order of the society in which it was set—a society which was little interested in the diplomatic manœuvres of Christian sectaries and for several generations had been guided by no dominant philosophy of life in its casual direction of the practical activities of living, social, political, and economic. And if it had ever been imagined that this direction was 'near-Christian', who would any longer hold that assumption now that the first World War, and the chaos and disillusionment that followed it, had thrown into almost frightening relief the contrast between the way of the world and the Way of Christ? Among the Christian leaders who saw the danger of a pietistic isolation was Nathan Söderblom, Archbishop of Upsala, a man of vivid imagination and tireless energy, who became convinced that there should be some means of expressing the mind and conscience of Christendom on the problems of social, industrial, and national life, and some organization through which that expression could be made representative of all the Churches and so reach the ears of men in all countries. If the Churches could attain some measure of unity on matters of their own Faith and Order, could they not set out to discover the true relevance of the Christian Faith to the social and international order, and unite to make some agreed impact on a world that

needed the very guidance they had been commissioned to give?
For six years preparations were made for a World Conference on
Christian Life and Work, and in 1925 more than 500 representatives of the greater number of Christian Communions from
thirty-seven countries met at Stockholm,

> to concentrate the mind of Christendom on the mind of Christ
> as revealed in the Gospels towards those great social, industrial,
> and international questions which are so acutely urgent in our
> civilization.

Temple was not at Stockholm, but he kept in close touch with
the Universal Christian Council for Life and Work (formed to
carry on the work of the Conference) on which the leading Anglicans were the Bishops of Winchester (Theodore Woods) and
Chichester (Bell). Twelve years passed before the Oxford Conference was held, and they were years in which the issues between
the Church and the world became luminously clear. To none
were they more obvious than to Dr. Oldham, whose study of the
Report of the Jerusalem Conference of 1928 led him to the conviction that the most serious danger to the Christian Faith lay, not
in the propaganda of rival religions, but in the secularism which
was clearly defined by the trend of political organization and
social thinking in the years between the two wars. From the
earlier and casual theories there had now emerged two definite
dogmas—totalitarianism and 'scientific' humanism—which constituted the dominant creeds in State and Community. Here were
two weapons pointed straight at the heart of the Christian Faith
and the Christian Way of Life, and Dr. Oldham (helped by his
wide experience of the mission field) set himself to make contacts with Christian leaders in all parts of the world who realized
the growing menace of this secularism, and to further a vast programme of international study and research, with groups in the
countries of two hemispheres. Among these were the leaders of
the Life and Work Movement; and one of the few in the Churches of
Britain who had any real understanding of the urgency and range
of the problem was William Temple. After long preparation
—hampered by difficulties and intricate details of organization

that need only be mentioned here—a Conference was held at Oxford in the summer of 1937, with the general title of 'Church, Community, and State'. Lang, then Archbishop of Canterbury, who was one of the six Presidents representing different countries and Churches, presided at the opening meeting of the Conference, but he left the chairing of the sessions to Dr. Mott.

Temple was to preside at the Edinburgh Conference a week or two later, and therefore he held no office at Oxford nor did he take a prominent part in the discussions. These ranged over the whole social and political life of a Christian community. Education, health, leisure, economics, international relationships, the respective claims of God and the State to the Christian's loyalty, the standards to be set by the Churches side by side with those of the State, were among the subjects reviewed by the Conference. Temple was a member of one of the Commissions and of a sub-Commission appointed to consider 'The Church and War'. The sequel to this came later: the immediate importance of its findings lay in the admission that pacifism was a legitimate position for a Christian to adopt when his country was at war. It also fell to him to draft the Message of the Conference—on 21 July he writes to his wife: 'I was writing till 1.15 last night; I wrote continuously for $4\frac{1}{2}$ hours, and so finished a draft of the Message'—and he was kept busy with private talks and soundings on the steps that might be taken by both Conferences to strengthen the whole Oecumenical Movement. The more far-seeing leaders in all countries knew that the moment had now come when the seal might be set on all the preparatory work of the last thirty years. From every point of view—whether of efficiency, expense, practical convenience, or the concentration of spiritual strength—it was desirable that a single body should be set up in which all the organizations working for Church unity could be merged, and so present to the world a united front of Christian thought and effort. 'Overlapping', Temple declared, 'and even collision are increasing.' The Life and Work Movement, for instance, found itself bound to appoint a theological commission, with instructions that it should inquire into the nature of the Church—thus trespassing on the ground already being covered by 'Faith and

Order'—and the more inclusive fellowship that had grown out of the various efforts towards unity needed a new focus and a wider setting for its full expression. But would the separate bodies, of which the two chief were 'Faith and Order' and 'Life and Work', be willing to lose their identity for the sake of the larger unity and added power to be found in a single organization? It was no secret that some of the older representatives of 'Faith and Order', of whom the most influential was Headlam (Bishop of Gloucester), were anxious to maintain the independence of their body.

The answer was forthcoming in the summer of 1937, and it was decisive. Both at Oxford and Edinburgh resolutions approving the union were passed by overwhelming majorities—though the opposition at Edinburgh was stronger than the voting suggested —and after many difficult corners had been turned and Temple had done an immense amount of work in preparing the Agenda, a meeting, at which representatives of seventy Churches were present, was held at Utrecht in May 1938, which set out the draft constitution, the doctrinal basis, and the scheme of membership of the World Council of Churches that was to be—for all these proposals had to be presented to the Churches and approved by them before the World Council of Churches could come into effective being. Temple was appointed Chairman of the Provisional Committee, with Visser 't Hooft as its General Secretary, and William Paton (in London) and Henry Smith Leiper (in New York) as Associate Secretaries. In presiding over the Utrecht Conference, Temple was at his best. Church assemblies are no more immune than others from the kind of lobbying that is almost inevitable when two organizations are to be merged—and some of their officials thereby become redundant. The Good and the Great took part in this scramble with no less zeal than the smaller fry, but through it all Temple pursued his way—quite unperturbed, entirely competent, and fully aware of what was going on; yet charitable to men's foibles, doing his best to spare the susceptibilities of the older men who would drop out of the offices they previously held, pressing the claims of 't Hooft against the objection that he was too young for the responsible post of Secretary, and solicitous (as always) for the rights even of the smallest minority Churches. Day by day his friendship grew with the delegates—one of whom, Pastor Boegner, when he came to England after the liberation of France, remarked that all through the occupation of his country by the Germans he had lived for the moment when he would see Temple again.

During 1938–9 the plan for the World Council was submitted to the Churches represented at Oxford and Edinburgh. Before the war broke out forty Churches had asked for membership of the Council, and since the war began more than sixty others have sent a favourable reply. In England the going was not altogether easy. Many Anglo-Catholics regarded the project with suspicion; the primary need, as they saw it, was for the development and strengthening of a church-consciousness rather than an oecumenical one. The Bishop of Gloucester remained firm in his objections—'You are practically destroying the Faith and Order Movement', he wrote, with his own blunt frankness, to Temple, 'and very probably destroying a great deal of the Re-union Movement'—and an unsuccessful attempt was also made to organize opposition in the Church Assembly. But after a preliminary debate in 1938 the Assembly passed a resolution proposed by Temple, on 11 June 1940, 'That this Assembly welcomes the establishment of the World Council of Churches constituted in accordance with the scheme submitted to the Assembly and accepts the invitation to be represented'. In February 1939 Temple wrote to the Cardinal Secretary of State at the Vatican, to inform the Holy See that the World Council was being established, expressing the hope that it might be possible 'to exchange information with agencies of the Church of Rome on matters of common interest' and that the Council 'should have the help from time to time of unofficial consultation with Roman Catholic theologians and scholars'. Several months passed before an answer was received through the Apostolic Delegate in London, to the effect that His Eminence saw no obstacles in the way of carrying out Temple's proposals.

The World Council was still only 'in process of formation', as it is to-day; it has existed structurally as a provisional committee

—the meeting at which it will be formally constituted is to be held in the summer of 1948—but its use as a rallying-point for unity has already been proved. It is assured of the co-operation of the International Missionary Council, and also of the Christian Youth Movement, the vitality of which was shown at a great Youth Conference held at Amsterdam in 1939, when 1,500 delegates of youth organizations met in a fellowship that was to be interrupted, but not broken, by the Second World War: 'It was a wonderful gathering', Temple wrote to his brother, 'with 72 nations represented.' During the war, moreover, up to the time when Switzerland was sealed off by the German occupation of Europe, contact was maintained with the German Churches by the Geneva office of the World Council of Churches. As late as 1942 Temple received through this channel an assurance which he valued very highly; it was that his broadcast addresses and several of his printed pronouncements had not only been welcomed by leaders of the Churches in occupied countries and neutral territories but had been studied with great care by the leaders of the German Confessional Church, who found themselves in substantial agreement with him. This was more than a personal tribute, for he was conscious of speaking not only as the head of the Anglican Communion but as the Chairman of the emergent World Council of Churches, and it meant that the unity underlying the organization held firm, in spite of the immense strains of war.

The story of the formation of the British Council of Churches —the British 'arm' of the World Council—is long and involved, and to recount the difficulties that had to be overcome would be to do little more than repeat the tale of the earlier struggle. The same doubts were expressed, the same suspicions had to be allayed, the same critics pacified or outvoted; but Temple won through and, on 23 September 1942, at a great Service of Inauguration in S. Paul's Cathedral, he outlined his convictions and his hopes:

. . . To-day we inaugurate the British Council of Churches, the counterpart in our country of the World Council, combining in a single organization the chief agencies of the interdenominational co-operation which has marked the last five years. . . . These departmental agencies, two of them hampered by very cumbrous names, could never catch the public imagination. The newly formed British Council of Churches may very likely do this, and so become the channel of new influences upon our common life.

There is no compromise of our distinctive principles in our coming together. But there is a choice involved between two different directions of attention, two different points of emphasis. In days when Christianity itself in its fundamental principles is unchallenged, it may seem natural to lay most emphasis on the points which distinguish one communion from another. But in days like these, when the basic principles of Christianity are widely challenged and in many quarters expressly repudiated, the primary need is for clear and united testimony to Christianity itself. The difference between Catholic and Protestant is very small as compared with the difference between Christian and non-Christian, between those who do and those who do not believe that in Jesus Christ God 'hath visited and redeemed his people'.

Our differences remain: we shall not pretend that they are already resolved into unity or harmony. But we take our stand on the common faith of Christendom, faith in God, Creator, Redeemer, and Sanctifier; and so standing together we invite men to share that faith and call on all to conform their lives to the principles derived from it. . . . We owe united witness as a duty to our nation and to the hope of Christian civilization. But we owe it still more to our Lord Himself. While we show ourselves to the world only as divided, we alienate men from Him. Only as we unite to present Him to men as the one Lord of life, our life and theirs, can we be true witnesses to Him.

This was a brave challenge, thrown out while the nations of the world were locked in their fateful struggle for freedom and, under the guidance of Temple, Paton—whose wide knowledge and indomitable strength and patience had been invaluable from the inception of the Oecumenical Movement—and Dr. A. Craig, the British Council promised to become an effective body. Little more than two years were to pass before Temple and Paton were both taken, but not before Temple had brought in Dr. Fisher (then Bishop of London) to be chairman of the Council's Executive Committee. On Temple's death Dr. Fisher took his place as President.

A hundred large volumes could be filled with the history of the search for Christian unity in the twentieth century. No more has been here attempted than to mark the stages by which the first objective—the creation of a World Council of Churches—was gained, with particular reference to the contribution made to the achievement by William Temple. It remains to account for the unchecked growth of his unique influence in that mixed company of Christians representing the Anglican, Orthodox, Lutheran, Methodist, Baptist, and Congregationalist traditions, as well as the younger Churches of Africa and the East; and for the inevitability with which three times (in 1929, 1938, and 1942) he was called to lead a new advance, and no one else was even nominated by any member of the electing body. If the answer could be summarized in a sentence, it would be that all with whom Temple was associated knew that they could trust him as a thinker, as a chairman, and as a friend. He was well grounded in the history of social, theological, and philosophic thought and, while remaining exactly sure of his own position, seemed to understand almost instinctively the traditions and tenets of other Churches and other men, into whose thoughts and—which was no less important at oecumenical gatherings—whose ways of thinking he could enter with effortless sympathy. He had a foot firmly planted in each camp, being equally concerned for fundamental theology and for the practical problems confronting the Christian citizen and the Christian Church in the modern State: and it was because not even his most hostile critics could believe that he would ever relegate theology or Church Order to a secondary place that the waverers came to his side when Headlam prophesied disaster and ruin for the cause of 'Faith and Order', should it ever become merged with 'Life and Work'.

As a chairman he was without a rival. Besides being unswervingly impartial and a master of procedure, he was able to rely on
an almost infallible memory which was particularly accurate about
decisions already reached and resolutions passed that might be
relevant to any subject under debate. He was not a lax chairman,
nor was he a hustler. He not only allowed, he encouraged, every
one to have his say. His attention never wandered, no failure of
courtesy or patience could ever be scored against him; some
indeed thought him almost too considerate to the cranks and the
bores. How many who have sat under Temple, at meetings where
discussion was free and open, have not wondered more than once
whether too much licence was not being allowed to speakers who
wandered from the point, and whether the time had not come to
apply the closure? Yet the moment always arrived when he would
rise and say, 'I wonder whether something like this represents
the sense of the meeting?', and his summing-up would be so
comprehensive of all the speeches that there was nothing more
to be said. Of his resourcefulness in overcoming difficulties and
reconciling divergent views something has already been written:
this 'parlour trick', as he modestly called it, was never used to
better purpose than at oecumenical gatherings, where differences
of language, national and ecclesiastical tradition, and social and
philosophic outlook intensified the difficulty of doing justice, in
a few unmistakably clear sentences, to the convictions of all the
members. The story is told of a committee meeting at which
disagreement had been so acute that it seemed humanly impossible
to reconcile the conflicting views. But Temple was in the chair
and the familiar question was at last asked—'How will this do?'
He started to read from a sheet of paper on which for a minute or
two he had been writing, and when he had finished there was an
almost awed silence, broken after a few moments by two voices;
one conveying the grave congratulations of an English theologian, the other in the crisper phrasing of the New World
from an American delegate who sat opposite Temple at the
table—'Archbishop, you tickle me pink!' It should be added
that nowhere was Temple's contribution to the Oecumenical
Movement more widely recognized and appreciated than in the

416

Churches of America. Preaching in S. Paul's Cathedral on the first Sunday after Temple's death, Dr. G. A. Oldham (Bishop of Albany, U.S.A.) said: 'It was perhaps the cause closest to his heart, and certainly it is the one for which he is best known and esteemed in the United States by Christians of every name.'

But not even all these gifts together could have raised Temple to the place he filled in the Oecumenical Movement had the personal graces been lacking. Whatever might be the pressure of the moment, his great humanity remained. His friendliness towards the members of a conference and his interest in each of them were simple and unaffected. One of his most valued assistants (the Rev. Eric Fenn, whose patient and selfless work—but not his deep concern—for the Movement ceased when he joined the staff of the B.B.C. in 1939) well remembers Temple's personal care at Utrecht even for the least conspicuous of his fellow-workers: he needed to be assured, for instance, that the stenographers and translators were comfortably housed, and that they had proper intervals for rest and recreation; and no matter how trivial or tiresome a man or his business might be (and what conference has ever lacked one or two such men?) Temple attended to him with a sympathetic courtesy that made him the man's friend for ever. Of the source of these many graces Professor Hodgson has written the true word:

> I am convinced that his courtesy and his patience both had their roots in his devotion, in that inner communion with the Lord through which it became second nature for him to see in the least of men 'one of these, my brethren', and to care intensely for truth and justice. Occasionally the veil was lifted and the hidden source revealed. I remember an occasion when we met in Switzerland in the summer of 1936. It was to be the last meeting of the full Continuation Committee before the Edinburgh Conference next year. It was in some ways a difficult and stormy meeting. . . . Right up to the end feelings ran high and found expression in debate. Then, when at last under Temple's guidance we had arrived at decisions in which all acquiesced, he led us into the chapel of the school where we

were meeting for our closing devotions. As he opened his Bible and began to read from Isaiah xl and S. John xv the whole atmosphere changed. There was no mistaking the fact that in heart and soul we were being lifted up into the realm where he habitually dwelt. We knew then whence came the courtesy, the patience, the love of justice, and the calm strength with which he had led us into order out of the chaos of our controversies.

The Professor's judgement is worth our weighing, in making any assessment of Temple's work for Christian unity. A few bishops, since the days of the Apostles, have risen as swiftly to place and power as he did—of how many is the record stained with the blotches of worldly ambition and ecclesiastical intrigue? There was nothing of these to mar the spiritual progress of the young Oxford don who in 1910 showed the members of the Edinburgh Conference to their seats in the Assembly Hall of the Church of Scotland, and thirty years later stood out pre-eminently —among Christians not owing obedience to Rome—as the greatest force in 'the Holy Church throughout all the world' and the dominant spiritual figure among 350 million Christians.

Roman and Orthodox Churches

From these continued efforts for Christian unity one branch— and that the largest—of the Church stood officially aloof, and the setting may be an appropriate one in which to mention Temple's views on, and his associations with, the Church of Rome. His earliest reactions were described at some length while he was still at Balliol, after 'the re-condemnation of Dreyfus', in a letter to Harry Hardy which was written with all the vigour of an undergraduate who has a strong case. There are references to 'the chief officers of the Roman Church', 'angels of Satan', 'premeditated turpitude of heart', and the 'need of some Sheridan to thunder':

> If the judges are honest men, then the French administration of justice is such as seems to demand the obliteration of such a people by the hand of the Ruler of the world Himself.

With the passing of years, his inclinations leaned less and less towards polemics of this kind; but, as he considered the places held in Christendom by the Roman and Anglican Churches, his conviction grew that 'the whole ethos of the two Communions' was 'radically different'. This was written to a parish priest in 1933, and the letter goes on:

Broadly speaking, I am not afraid of giving ammunition to Rome, because I think that the people who are drawn to Rome are mostly people who would not be very valuable to the Church of England, nor would succeed in gaining from it the points of strength in which I believe it to be superior to Rome. Some day, no doubt, in a very remote future, the question of union with Rome will become practical. At present I regard it as almost infinitely remote, and do not believe that we gain greatly by retaining in our body those who are capable of being much attracted by the other.

It can be believed, from Temple's lifelong devotion to the cause of freedom, that here lay the focal point of his distaste for the Roman ethos. He writes to a chaplain to the Forces in August 1943:

I think it is quite clear that the late Pope had no kind of sympathy with Fascism and the record of the Vatican throughout his period was beyond reproach, but I also think it is true that an authoritarian organisation of religion is always bound to find itself lined up on the whole with authoritarian politics. I think the Church of Rome will always stand in its support of democracy in politics for emphasis on the rightful power of the majority, without which no doubt there is no democracy, but will make very little of the moral rights of the minority, without which democracy cannot be wholesome.

Their whole attitude to freedom of thought is, to my mind, quite unsatisfactory. They acknowledge that compulsory faith is a contradiction and useless; but they also take the view that if, as in Italy or Spain, only the Roman Church exists on any substantial scale, they are entitled to use the arm of the State to prevent propagation of any other form of belief. The faith of the people in those countries is, therefore, not compulsory; it is just what they have grown up in and their wills consent to it; but neither is it a deliberate choice because alternatives have been shut away from them. In other words, the Roman Catholics treat grown-up people permanently as children and that is a frame of mind which inevitably overflows into politics. I think this is really the source of the trouble.

I believe that all the doctrinal errors of Rome come from the direct identification of the Church as an organised Institution, taking its part in the process of history, with the Kingdom of God. This is just as bad, theologically, as the view which regards the Church as a mere instrument in preparation for the Kingdom of God. The only wholesome view is one which regards it as being constituted as the Church by the powers of the Kingdom of God within it and yet as being always composed of people still citizens of this world, so that those powers manifest themselves partially and fitfully, and the historical Church is a mixed body.

But nothing in this divergence of opinion was allowed to hinder or interrupt co-operation between representatives of the two Churches on social and international affairs, within the limits imposed by fundamental differences of doctrine, or to impede any act of courtesy and friendliness that Temple could personally render. Thus in 1938 he gave a lecture to the Thomas More Society, which is composed almost entirely of Roman Catholic lawyers, on Medieval Philosophic Thought. The lecture, writes Mr. Justice Vaisey—one of the three non-Roman members of the Society—'was thought too difficult for many of his audience, but was regarded as a notable incident in the history of the Society'. It was a more critical audience, including some learned English Dominican theologians, that faced him in the Caxton Hall on 19 October 1943 when he accepted an invitation of the London Aquinas Society to give an address on 'Thomism and Modern Needs'. As usual Temple spoke from a few headings written on half a sheet of notepaper, but the substance of the lecture was printed in the next number of *Blackfriars*, with a critical comment by Fr. Victor White, O.P. A former President of the Aquinas Society wrote in the same issue that the address

> may be said in a sense to mark the confluence and reunion of the Anglican and the Catholic philosophical tradition; and to reflect the prevailing spirit of collaboration among Christians and of co-operation in all charity;

and the tribute paid to Temple on his death by the Cardinal Archbishop of Westminster ended with these words:

> Only a few months ago he addressed the Aquinas Society, and showed how real and thorough was his appreciation of the great philosophy of St. Thomas. He was breaking new ground in giving us this lecture, and he liked breaking new ground with his eager and adventurous mind and that warm charity which drew new friends to him all through his life.

The same charity moved him on two occasions to send personal messages to the Pope, through the Apostolic Delegate in England, Archbishop Godfrey. The first is dated 11 October 1943:

> My dear Archbishop,
>
> I have read with great sorrow the accounts in the Press which seem to indicate that His Holiness the Pope is being subjected to grievous restrictions upon his freedom of action and utterance by those who pose as his protectors. I should like if it were possible to express to His Holiness my own profound sympathy and that of multitudes of Englishmen who are not of his Obedience. If you think fit and have opportunity to inform His Holiness of this expression of feeling I should be deeply obliged.
>
> Yours very sincerely,
WILLIAM CANTUAR:

On 18 January 1944 the following reply was received from the Apostolic Delegate:

> 54, Parkside,
London S.W. 19.
>
> Your Grace,
>
> The slowness of letter communication with the Holy See has not made it possible for me to receive before now the

acknowledgement of your kind message of sympathy to His Holiness in his present difficulties and anxieties.

The Cardinal Secretary of State has instructed me to thank you on behalf of the Pope for your message, which His Holiness was most pleased to receive.

I gladly take the opportunity of offering you my most sincere greetings and wishes for the year that lies before us, assuring Your Grace of the expression of my high regard.

Yours most sincerely,
WILLIAM GODFREY.

The second was written on Good Friday in the following year:

My dear Lord Archbishop,

On this day, when all Christians are united at the foot of the Cross in adoration, penitence, and thankfulness, I should like, if it is possible, to send through you to His Holiness the Pope, a message of deep sympathy with the painful and sorrowful position in which he and the city of Rome are placed by the developments and occurrences of the war.

May God in His great mercy grant an early restoration of peace on a foundation of justice, and may the whole fellowship of Christ's disciples be so guided by the Holy Spirit that we may together declare the Christian principles for the ordering of human life and recall our suffering world to that obedience to God's will in which alone can be found deliverance from the evils which afflict mankind.

Yours very sincerely,
WILLIAM CANTUAR:

The Apostolic Delegate replied:

Apostolic Delegation,
London.
18th April, 1944.

My dear Lord Archbishop,

Your letter written on Good Friday has now been received and I wish to tell you how deeply I appreciate the words which you were moved to write to me on the day which is so sacred and held in such grateful remembrance by all who love and follow Our Lord and Saviour Jesus Christ.

I shall not fail to make known to His Holiness the Pope the message which you wish to convey to him through me.

We pray that God our Father may grant us His peace which cannot be made save on the foundation of His law, in justice and in love, through the guidance of the Holy Spirit and in the fellowship of His divine Son.

In such a peace, and in that alone, is there hope that we may find deliverance from the evils which lie so heavily on mankind.

Yours very sincerely,
WILLIAM GODFREY.
Archbishop of Cius.

An important movement was made towards fuller co-operation between the Churches when a joint statement was issued by the (Anglican and Free Church) Religion and Life Movement—an activity of the Commission of the Churches for International Friendship and Social Responsibility—and the (Roman Catholic) organization, The Sword of the Spirit. A joint committee of the two bodies was set up to unite informed and convinced Christians in common action on broad lines of social and international policy: intellectually this involved an exposition and defence of the Natural Law as it had always been honoured in the true Christian tradition; practically it involved the application of moral theology to the complex problems that were to vex increasingly the mind and conscience of the community. Press comments were uniformly favourable; meetings were held in several large centres of population; and Dr. Fisher (then Bishop of London), who was chairman of the joint standing committee, described the co-operation contemplated by the leaders of the movement as 'a measure of joint action such as has not happened in this country since the Reformation'.

Temple never disguised his belief that the differences between the Roman and Anglican Churches cut deep into the intellectual and spiritual life of both Communions, but this separation did

423

nothing to impair his friendship with Cardinal Hinsley—there was a notable sympathy between the two men, and each had a warm regard for the other—and he had begun to work happily with Hinsley's successor Cardinal Griffin, who declared that he was 'looking forward', at the time of the Archbishop's death, 'to many years of fruitful association' in their 'common tasks'. Temple also had plans, towards the end of his life, for making a more personal approach to the Vatican, in the hope that Roman and Anglican theologians might be encouraged to undertake some joint study of the Natural Law as the basis of Christian living, but for more than one reason he decided to abandon the project.

With the leaders of many of the Orthodox Churches Temple kept up as intimate an association as was possible in war-time, largely through his contacts with them in the Oecumenical Movement. Strictly speaking, the Orthodox Church—though some of its constituent local Churches accept Anglican Orders as possessing the same validity as those of the Roman, Old Catholic, and Armenian Churches—does not recognize as valid without qualification any Orders except its own, nor does it practise intercommunion with other Churches. But, by the exercise of what is known as 'economy', Anglicans have been and are admitted to Orthodox Sacraments in several parts of the world where they are unable to receive the ministrations of their own clergy. Official relations between the Anglican and Eastern Churches have become increasingly cordial during the last half-century, and a strong Orthodox delegation attended the Lambeth Conference in 1930. Owing to the war little advance was made during Temple's short time at Canterbury, but there was an outstanding official event when a delegation from the Church of England, headed by the Archbishop of York, paid a visit to the Russian Orthodox Church in 1943. With the preparations for this visit Temple was intimately concerned, and he wrote a personal greeting to the Patriarch Sergius of Moscow which was delivered by the Archbishop of York. He also took part in the preliminary arrangements made for the return visit of a Russian delegation to England, but he died before this took place in 1945.

It was chiefly through his personal intercourse with the Orthodox leaders that Temple rendered his special service in drawing the two Churches together. None of these leaders ever left a conference or a meeting at which they had sat with him, often under his chairmanship, without a more sincere respect for the Church he represented and a deeper admiration for its leader. They recognized that with his instinctive sagacity he understood the Eastern approach to the problems of Christian union, that he knew the history of their Churches and nations, and that he had never failed to raise his voice, when he believed that protest was called for, on behalf of their lost or threatened liberties. The practical sympathy of his efforts was stressed at the Mnemosynon (memorial service) for Temple which was held at the Greek Cathedral of S. Sophia, Bayswater. No record is known of such a service being held in an Orthodox Church to the memory of a non-Orthodox prelate, and in the eulogy of Temple which was read after the Mnemosynon these words occur:

> In particular the tragic circumstances amid which both clergy and laity of the Orthodox Church were smitten, the suffering and martyrdom to which so many of them were condemned, the anguish and privation of their peoples, called forth the spontaneous expression of the feelings of Christian love and goodwill that abounded in his heart.... To whose inspiration, if not to his, do we owe the formation of a special committee, entrusted with the task of promoting the rebuilding of churches and religious institutions including the Orthodox, which the savage fury of war has not spared in the enslaved countries of Europe?

The speaker was Archbishop Germanos of Thyatira, Temple's closest friend among Orthodox leaders, for whom he had an affectionate regard, and who was the first recipient of the Lambeth Cross. This decoration—inscribed *Hoc signum amicitiae et benedictionis d.d. Archiepiscopus Cantuarensis*—was instituted by Lang, to be conferred on representatives of European Churches who had 'rendered exceptional service to the cause of Christian unity, and specially to strengthen the relation between these Churches and the Anglican Communion'. Lang himself had made no award. The second was also made by Temple—to Bishop Brilioth, another close friend, representing the Protestant Churches on the continent of Europe (with whose leaders, especially Pastor Marc Boegner, he was on terms of personal intimacy). He found great satisfaction in choosing these two men for the honour, standing as they did for two widely differing traditions of faith and worship, each of which had its own particular contribution to make to the cause of Christian unity.

APPENDIX

AFFIRMATION

of union in allegiance to our Lord Jesus Christ, adopted by the Edinburgh Conference by a standing vote on 18 August 1937, *nemine contradicente*:

The Second World Conference on Faith and Order, held in Edinburgh in August 1937, brought together four hundred and fourteen delegates from one hundred and twenty-two Christian communions in forty-three different countries. The delegates assembled to discuss together the causes that keep Christian communions apart, and the things that unite them in Christian fellowship. The Conference approved the following statement *nemine contradicente*:

We are one in faith in our Lord Jesus Christ, the incarnate Word of God. We are one in allegiance to Him as Head of the Church, and as King of kings and Lord of lords. We are one in acknowledging that this allegiance takes precedence of any other allegiance that may make claims upon us.

This unity does not consist in the agreement of our minds or the consent of our wills. It is founded in Jesus Christ Himself, Who lived, died and rose again to bring us to the Father, and Who through the Holy Spirit dwells in His Church. We are one because we are all the objects of the love and grace of God, and called by Him to witness in all the world to His glorious gospel.

Our unity is of heart and spirit. We are divided in the outward forms of our life in Christ, because we understand differently His will for His Church. We believe, however, that a deeper understanding will lead us towards a united apprehension of the truth as it is in Jesus.

We humbly acknowledge that our divisions are contrary to the will

426

of Christ, and we pray God in His mercy to shorten the days of our separation and to guide us by His Spirit into fulness of unity.

We are thankful that during recent years we have been drawn together; prejudices have been overcome, misunderstandings removed, and real, if limited, progress has been made towards our goal of a common mind.

In this Conference we may gratefully claim that the Spirit of God has made us willing to learn from one another, and has given us a fuller vision of the truth and enriched our spiritual experience.

We have lifted up our hearts together in prayer; we have sung the same hymns; together we have read the same Holy Scriptures. We recognize in one another, across the barriers of our separation, a common Christian outlook and a common standard of values. We are therefore assured of a unity deeper than our divisions.

We are convinced that our unity of spirit and aim must be embodied in a way that will make it manifest to the world, though we do not yet clearly see what outward form it should take.

We believe that every sincere attempt to co-operate in the concerns of the kingdom of God draws the severed communions together in increased mutual understanding and goodwill. We call upon our fellow-Christians of all communions to practise such co-operation; to consider patiently occasions of disunion that they may be overcome; to be ready to learn from those who differ from them; to seek to remove those obstacles to the furtherance of the gospel in the non-Christian world which arise from our divisions; and constantly to pray for that unity which we believe to be our Lord's will for His Church.

We desire also to declare to all men everywhere our assurance that Christ is the one hope of unity for the world in face of the distractions and dissensions of this present time. We know that our witness is weakened by our divisions. Yet we are one in Christ and in the fellowship of His Spirit. We pray that everywhere, in a world divided and perplexed, men may turn to Jesus Christ our Lord, Who makes us one in spite of our divisions; that He may bind in one those who by many worldly claims are set at variance; and that the world may at last find peace and unity in Him; to Whom be glory for ever.

XXV

The Malvern Conference—Social Order

The first half of the twentieth century is likely to be regarded by those
who have lived through it and survive to a later period as the Age of
Conferences. The new means of transport have made possible the
gathering together of people in a way hitherto impracticable; consequently a fashion has grown up of convening conferences on almost
all topics of human interest. These are, broadly speaking, of two kinds.
Some are conferences held for the exploration of new fields of thought.
In such the results reached are of value in proportion to the thoroughness of discussion taking place within the conference itself. Others are
held for the ascertainment and registration of the amount of agreement
reached among a number of people who have given thought, perhaps
for many years, to the themes discussed. In this case the value of the
results is largely independent of the course of discussion in the conference, except so far as this elicits and makes evident a body of agreement
already in existence when the conference meets, though at that stage
the several members may be still unaware how far other members
agree with them. The conference of Anglicans which lately met at
Malvern College was of this second type.

W. T., in the *Spectator*, January 1941.

THE war had hardly broken out when the question what was
to be done at the end of it began to be widely asked. The
word 'reconstruction' recurred, with prominence, in the speeches
of politicians, the sermons of preachers, and the agenda papers of
societies and committees. Men in the Services—some of whom
had not forgotten the promised 'homes for heroes' of twenty years
before—were assured that there was to be no repetition of the
aftermath of the First World War, no mass unemployment, no
tedious misery of the dole; and conferences were held to draw
up schemes, pledges, and manifestoes for the encouragement of the
fighting men and the welfare of the country to which they hoped
to return.

Among churchpeople there was no general desire to escape this
epidemic. The first suggestion that an Anglican conference on
reconstruction should be held came from Prebendary P. T. R.
Kirk, General Director of the Industrial Christian Fellowship.

For some years he had been leading a gallant effort to propagate the social message of the Gospel among employers and employed, and had gained the support of many large industrial firms and prominent trade unionists. Such a movement by its nature invites criticism and even opposition, for the comprehensiveness which to the more impartial seems its most attractive feature is held by extremists in both sections of industry to be the best excuse for regarding it with suspicion. Thanks, however, to the courage of its General Director and to the determined, but always uphill, work of its lay agents in the bigger industrial centres, the Fellowship has become an established feature in the evangelizing work of the Church, and 'Industrial Sunday' is now observed annually in many churches.

But it was not to be expected that great importance would attach to a conference convened by the I.C.F. unless some notable personality could be persuaded to preside over it, and when in the early summer of 1940 Prebendary Kirk had received the promise of the Archbishop of York to be chairman and convener, he knew that he would be able to secure the active support of many who could contribute to its success. The Conference was 'by invitation', and its objects were set out in a letter from Temple to all who were invited. These were:

> to consider from the Anglican point of view what are the fundamental facts which are directly relevant to the ordering of the new society that is quite evidently emerging, and how Christian thought can be shaped to play a leading part in the reconstruction after the war is over.

This kind of phrasing had by then become common form, and probably three out of four of those who accepted the invitation were troubled by no questionings about the purpose of the Conference. William Temple was to preside—that was what mattered —and at least they would find refreshment of mind and soul and a sorely needed opportunity for renewing their spiritual strength, possibly also a brief rest for the body, much worn by fire-watching and the exacting duties of the Home Guard. But there were some who would have welcomed a clearer prospect of the Conference.

Obviously there was to be some theology in it—'the Anglican point of view' and the 'shaping' of 'Christian thought' suggested this—some sociology too, for a 'new society' was expected to emerge in the post-war 'reconstruction'. But who, if anybody, was to do the thinking? Was the Conference to consist of a group of expert theologians and sociologists who really would both think and confer, or were the windows to be brilliantly dressed with findings and resolutions that might or might not impress the outside world, but would at least provide the already lavishly equipped parson with even further material—perhaps for one of those 'study circles' which he understood had been so strikingly successful in parishes where (he made no doubt) they could be more conveniently inaugurated and sustained than in his own? These questions were answered when the Conference settled down to work. The magnet had attracted some of the finest steel—here were Mr. Middleton Murry, Mr. T. S. Eliot, and Miss Dorothy Sayers; Sir Richard Acland and Mr. Kenneth Ingram; Mr. D. M. MacKinnon and Professor Hodges; Dr. V. A. Demant and the Rev. W. G. Peck—Mr. Maurice Reckitt was prevented by illness from attending, and Temple read his paper for him—with thirteen diocesan and two suffragan bishops and nearly 400 of the clergy and laity to listen to them. . . . And to confer? This was the great weakness of the Malvern gathering: whatever else it was or achieved, it certainly was not a conference. A glance at the names given above is enough to show that the programme was heavily overloaded. It lasted less than three days. Every one of these speakers, in a paper which took three-quarters of an hour to read —and some of them were read very quickly—gave the Conference enough to think about for at least a whole day. Many of the papers were not free from jargon, most of them were unsuitable for a large conference, and only a small minority of the listeners understood even what the issues were in the sociological and theological fields. These might have emerged if the members had really conferred; that is, had split up into small groups with capable leaders and threshed out their own findings. As it was, Sir Richard Acland dominated the proceedings with his claim that 'common owner-ship' is a matter of fundamental Christian principle, and the wide issues raised by Dr. Demant, Mr. MacKinnon, and Mr. Middleton Murry were almost entirely shelved. As the more and more dazed and exhausted Four Hundred came to the third day of the Conference many were asking whether anything could be salvaged from the wreck, but the shrewder members comforted one another with the hope that, so long as ink and paper were available, Temple would somehow save them—and the miracle happened. Without a trace of flurry—though he made the admission (an unusual one for him) in a letter to his brother that the Conference had been 'very exacting'—he sat down on the last night and wrote a series of 'conclusions' which, he informed an astonished Conference on the next morning, expressed its 'common mind'. This was indeed news to the members, but never was news more welcome. They had done little in the way of conferring, but they could go home happy in the thought that they had taken part in what one of them called 'a series of meetings with resolutions imposed from above'.

Of one resolution, however, this was not quite true. The subject of private ownership had filled much of the time-table, and there was some weight of opinion for stressing its evils. Temple's draft was too emphatic to ensure general approval, and a few chosen members were asked to withdraw and to come back with something that would express less definitely the 'common mind' of the Conference. The result was a section which was adopted without a dissentient vote. There were certain features of our social life which 'act as stumbling-blocks, making it harder for men to live Christian lives'. Among these,

> we believe that the maintenance of that part of the structure of our society, by which the ultimate ownership of the principal industrial resources of the community can be vested in the hands of private owners, may be such a stumbling-block.

This was not the first conference at which an effective salve has been applied to tender consciences by substituting 'may be' for 'is', and the Malvern Four Hundred were content—at whatever cost of disappointment to Sir Richard Acland—to place private ownership in the same category of potential social dangers as beer, tobacco, and sixpenny bridge. Temple deprecated the 'woolliness' of 'may be' which (he wrote after the Conference to Sir Richard) 'drew the sting of anything that' the resolution 'might contain': he would have preferred 'is', but on the condition, as he wrote to another correspondent, that 'immense stress' was laid on the word 'ultimate' in the same sentence. In his letter to Sir Richard, Temple added—

> ... the question whether in the circumstances you describe in your letter, you are rightly described as the 'ultimate' owner of your own estates, is I think rather an academic one. Obviously the ownership is in fact limited in some ways but beyond those limitations is unfettered. My own view of that matter would be that you are not the ultimate owner because the King is (which is certainly sound Common Law) but that in practice you are treated much more as an ultimate owner than is desirable. . . . I cannot tell you of any at all recent summary of the traditional Christian doctrine of property. Of course you can dig it out of St. Thomas or get anybody acquainted with him to do it for you. . . . The heart of it is a full recognition of private property combined with an insistence that it must always carry responsibility. The property without the function is the thing that is condemned. Now this condemns a very large amount of the property that exists to-day: to some extent in land, to an enormous extent in stocks and shares . . .

—and so on for several weeks, during which Temple appears almost to have enjoyed his correspondence with the critics. To one who had questioned the 'moral or intellectual right' of the Conference to 'publish conclusions' he replied:

> I cannot in the smallest degree accept your view that generally agreed findings are a denial of intellectual integrity. Incidentally I feel that view would necessarily abolish all forms of democratic government and land us in government by experts, which is probably the worst in the world. Of course the agreement was not the work of the Conference. It was brought about by the thought of many members in the past decade or so and the general currents of thought and feeling which are moving among Christians. But it was really possible, I think, to

disentangle points on which that body of people was in fact generally agreed, and if they were so agreed, it was important both to discover this and let it be known. In no circumstances can a conference, summoned by invitation and consisting of people of very various degrees of intellectual equipment for the work, have more than a trifling authority. *The value of registering such agreement as is found is that it may be used not to require assent but to challenge thought and so carry forward the general process that went on in the Conference.*

In the words here italicized lies the value—and the paradox—of 'Malvern 1940'. As a conference, it could hardly have been less skilfully arranged: in all that it provoked and produced, it is difficult to see how it could have been more effective. The findings were quoted and discussed widely in the British and American Press: they afforded a certain satisfaction to that vast but elusive body of persons who are said to be 'looking for a lead from the Church'—let us be thankful that the word 'wistfully' has been dropped from this formula—the I.C.F. set itself to 'carry forward' through the country the 'general process that went on in the Conference', and the climax was reached at the Albert Hall in September 1942 (page 578).

Temple knew how much depended on the 'follow-up' of the Conference, and to Prebendary Kirk and others he repeated his anxiety lest the Movement should pass entirely into the hands of Anglo-Catholics (at that time the most vigorous church group on behalf of social reform) or into the hands of the 'political left'. Many church leaders, he wrote, had more sympathy with the left than with the larger part of the right political wing, but 'we must be very careful that we do not give the impression that the Church is an agency for supporting left wing politics which are often based on presuppositions entirely un-Christian'. He wrote in the same sense to Canon Tatlow in February 1941:

Christianity has something quite specific of its own to say about these things, and it seems to me immensely important that we should say it and challenge consciences with it rather than look round for that proposal in the political field which we

F f

think at the moment most likely to help in the right direction. This latter has got to be done but it is the job of the Christian politician rather than of the Church or its agencies themselves, and there is a great deal of course in the Left wing movement which is no more Christian than that of the die-hard Right.

Temple's other hope, that the Conference would 'challenge thought', was realized at several gatherings of Christian economists who met under his chairmanship at Lambeth and also when Mr. Maurice Reckitt produced in May 1945, on behalf of the 'Christendom group'—with which Temple always had closer affinities than with Sir Richard Acland and Kenneth Ingram—*Prospect for Christendom*. Members of this group had been granted a large share both in producing the syllabus which was the basis of the Malvern Conference and in presenting the selected themes; and they returned home in dismay, not that they had been opposed, but that they had not been understood. For this the Conference was not wholly to blame, for—many and outstanding as are their gifts—not even their best friends can credit the members of this group with the knack of being able to say what they want to say in succinct and popular form. They did realize, however, that the failure of comprehension which, as it seemed to them, the Malvern gathering evinced, constituted a challenge to present in constructive form a theological and sociological view which had emerged from twenty years of corporate thinking; and this background has been widely held to give the book the considerable significance conceded to it. The movement for which it spoke 'sought rather in Christian doctrine and tradition than in the ethical idealism of the age the sanction and the clue for the recovery of a Christian sociology'. The sixteen contributors claimed 'that the steps which we advocate in the essays in this book are in all respects applicable to the conditions of this century and this country. They are therefore "practical" in the primary sense of that word. They are not to be dismissed as utopian. . . . They indicate a way of approach to the problems of the age which could become effectively constructive just in proportion as Christian opinion was rallied to the support of it . . . for it is not utopian to believe that obedience to God's laws in the purposes which men set before themselves will give them a healthy society or that the Christendom of former days provides us with clues for the recovery of one.'

The book was thus not far out of line with Temple's own convictions, and these were expressed in his widely read 'Penguin Special', *Christianity and Social Order*, which was published in 1942. It was snatched at by an avid public, till 139,000 copies of it had been sold, and in the last two years of his life he would probably have retracted none of the main contentions nor modified a single one of the fundamental claims put forward in these seven very important and highly condensed chapters. It will strike the reader who has attempted to trace the development of Temple's social appeal that his method of approach to the problem set by the title of the book differs here from that of his earlier writings. The principles enunciated are identical; but the emphasis has shifted, and the exposition is now aimed at a wider and, in some respects, more critical public. So long as the leaders of social thought in the Church had perforce to expend their energy in pleading with a mass of indifferent churchpeople to 'take an interest'—as the old phrase had it—'in the social question', the impact of the Church upon the world was bound to be negligible; it was the merest sniping of unorganized levies against a well protected and deeply entrenched opponent. Copec marked the beginning of the change; teachers and leaders in the Church were brought to see how meagre had been their conception of the Christian Gospel, and some started to preach its fuller content to a Church whose heart had been touched by the Copec reports and its will stirred by an awakening social conscience. But the more effective—largely owing to Temple's leadership—the impact became, the larger grew his audience and the more marked was the opposition he aroused. It can almost be said that in his earlier years Temple spoke (on this matter) in the first place to the Church, and towards the close of his life more directly to the nation—especially to two sets of persons. There were many who lacked convictions about the duty and place of the Church in the social life of the people, but were ready to listen to a case that might be put up for the 'interference' of the Church in the secular order; there was also a notable volume of opinion which vehemently denied that social and industrial problems came at all into the Church's legitimate scope of thought and action. At these two bodies, primarily, the 'Penguin' was aimed: it is significant that more than a third of the book is taken up with a defence of the Church's right to 'interfere', considered from two aspects—the commission laid upon the Church as the agent of God's purpose, and the history of Christian action in this particular field.

The argument begins with Temple's conception of Natural Law, with its two great regulative principles of Love and Justice. In common talk to-day 'Natural Law' has a meaning so different from that in which he used the words that Temple's definition must be borne in mind:

> In earlier times, Christian thinkers made great use of the notion of Natural Law. They did not mean by this a generalization from a large number of observed phenomena, which is what a modern scientist means; they meant the proper function of a human activity as apprehended by a consideration of its own nature. In practice, the Natural Order or Natural Law is discovered partly by observing the generally accepted standards of judgment and partly by consideration of the proper functions of whatever is the subject of enquiry. This is a task for human reason; but so far as reason enables us to reach the truth about anything in its own essence and in its relationships, it enables us to see it as it is in the mind of God. Thus it is a Natural, not a Supernatural Order with which we are concerned; but as God is the Creator, this Natural Order is His order and its law is His law.

He goes on:

> It is wholesome to go back to the old conception of Natural Law because it holds together two aspects of truth which it is not easy to hold in combination—the ideal and the practical. We tend to follow one or other of two lines: either we start from a purely ideal conception, and then we bleat fatuously about love; or else we start from the world as it is with the

436

hope of remedying an abuse here or there, and then we have no general direction or criterion of progress. The conception of Natural Law will help us to frame a conception of the right or ideal relation between the various activities of men and of the men engaged in them. For consideration of the status of an activity in the light of its social function keeps both the ideal and the practical full in view.

Of these 'various activities'—to take an instance from the economic field—none is more important than those of consumer and producer:

> Production by its own natural law exists for consumption. If, then, a system comes into being in which production is regulated more by the profit obtainable for the producer than by the needs of the consumer, that system is defying the Natural Law or Natural Order.

It is possible, Temple admitted, to isolate the economic process —and a system which is not true to the Natural Order may still, at and for certain periods, provide a reasonably high standard of living for a good part of the community—but to do so is to commit a breach of the Natural Law, according to which every human activity must be considered in relation to its context in the whole economy of life. To isolate man's economic activity and to judge it by its own 'laws' alone makes the economic process an end in itself, which it is not: for 'it and all its parts are primarily a means to something more than economic—the life of man'. It is here that the Church comes into the picture:

> If what has true value as a means to an end beyond itself is in fact being sought as an end in itself, the Church must rebuke this dislocation of the structure of life and if possible point out the way to recovery. It is bound to 'interfere' because it is by vocation the agent of God's purpose, outside the scope of which no human interest or activity can fall.

The word 'interfere', of course, begs the question. If the dictionary definition—'to meddle with; to interpose in something without having the right to do so'—be correct, the first answer to the critic is that the Church has, and has always claimed, such

437

a right. This Temple established by a double appeal. The first was to the nature and mission of the Church, which is called the Body of Christ because 'it is to be the instrument or organ of His will, as His fleshly Body was in the days of His earthly ministry'— it has received its commission to fulfil the purpose of God. But he was equally concerned to show that the assumption that the Church should exercise no influence in the sphere of politics and economics could be disproved by a study of history. Thus on the first page of his 'Penguin' he writes:

> Few people read much history. In an age when it is tacitly assumed that the Church is concerned with another world than this, and in this with nothing but individual conduct as bearing on prospects in that world, hardly any one reads the history of the Church in its exercise of political influence. It is assumed that the Church exercises little influence and ought to exercise none; it is further assumed that this assumption is self-evident and has always been made by reasonable men. As a matter of fact it is entirely modern and extremely questionable.

In this contention he was supported by J. M. (later Lord) Keynes, to whom he had sent the proof-sheets of his book. One passage in Keynes's reply was as follows:

Treasury Chambers,
Whitehall, S.W.
3rd December 1941.

My dear Archbishop,

. . . The main points which have occurred to me are the following:

I should have thought that in Chapter I you understated your case. Along one line of origin at least, economics more properly called political economy is a side of ethics. Marshall used always to insist that it was through ethics he arrived at political economy and I would claim myself in this, as in other respects, to be a pupil of his. I should have thought that nearly all English economists in the tradition, apart from Ricardo, reached economics that way. There are practically no issues of policy as distinct from technique which do not involve ethical considerations. If this is emphasized, the right of the Church to interfere in what is essentially a branch of ethics becomes even more obvious.

I should have thought again that you were understating your case in the third chapter, where you consider the past record of the Church in these matters. I should have supposed that it was a very recent heresy indeed to cut these matters out of its province. Are you not going too far in suggesting that in the XVIII Century the Church accepted this limitation? I should have thought decidedly not. Leaving out the Scots, such as Hume and Adam Smith, and foreign residents in London, such as Mandeville and Cantillon, I can think of no one important in the development of politico-economic ideas, apart from Bentham, who was not a clergyman and in most cases a high dignitary of the Church. For example, Dean Swift interested himself in these matters. Bishop Fleetwood wrote the first scientific treatise on price and the theory of index numbers. Bishop Berkeley wrote some of the shrewdest essays on these subjects available in his time. Bishop Butler, although primarily of ethical importance, is not to be neglected in this field. Archdeacon Paley is of fundamental importance. The Reverend T. R. Malthus was the greatest economist writing in the XVIII Century after Adam Smith. I agree that unless one includes Laud there are not many Archbishops before yourself entitled to be included in the list. But Archbishop Sumner's early work was on economics.

The book ends with a statement of six objectives which Christians should call on the Government to pursue—concerning family life, education, income, labour's share in the management of industry, leisure, and liberty—and an appendix containing 'A Suggested Programme'. Temple felt some doubt whether it was wise to include this and consulted Keynes and R. H. Tawney: both recommended that it should be inserted, and for exactly the same reason; 'it will add reality to the book', Keynes pleaded, and R. H. Tawney wrote that it 'adds a note of realism'. But Temple was careful to insist that the programme was set out less for adoption than to invite criticism, and he ended:

439

Let no one quote this as my conception of the political programme which Christians ought to support. There neither is nor can be any such programme. I do offer it as *a* Christian social programme, in the sense of being one which seeks to embody Christian principles; but there is no suggestion that if you are a Christian you ought to think these steps wise or expedient.

So much for theory—and in Britain between the two wars there had been no lack of material on which to test it in practice. The gravest symptom of the country's social disease was the fact of unemployment, which was ruining the health and eating out the heart of some of the finest of the nation's manhood; and for twenty years Temple's mind and affections were continuously exercised on this intractable problem. His diagnosis of it—and here we must go back a few years—was given in a letter to *The Times* in the autumn of 1934, when he commended the generous enterprise initiated by the High Sheriff of Surrey for the 'adoption' of Jarrow, one of the areas most severely affected:

It cannot be too strongly emphasized that the help for the unemployed which has proved really redemptive and recreative of character is that which has enabled them to realize themselves and fulfil their function as members of the community, of whom the community has need. The gravest evil and bitterest injury of their state is not the animal grievance of hunger or discomfort, nor even the mental grievance of vacuity and boredom; it is the spiritual grievance of being allowed no opportunity of contributing to the general life and welfare of the community. All efforts for their assistance should therefore look towards the provision of that opportunity.

Earlier in the year, Temple had made a strong appeal, through *The Times*, to his fellow Christians. He contended that, if there were to be any surplus in the national budget for the coming year, the unemployed had the first claim on it, and suggested that those who agreed with him should write to their M.P. and urge that the restoration of 'cuts' to the unemployed should take precedence over any other form of tax remission. This roused the Chancellor of the Exchequer. Of all forms of 'interference' Neville Chamberlain liked priestly interference least and lost no time in saying so. Temple replied with unruffled good humour. Was it, after all, a great offence to ask a body of persons who thought as he did to say to the Government—'Please don't put us first'? This was a type of pressure so seldom exerted on His Majesty's Ministers of State that he would have expected the Chancellor to be grateful rather than annoyed; he made no apology for his suggestion, for —'if we can sometimes introduce into our political life some specific note such as a group of people forgoing a claim which they could have made, I believe it must be for the general good'.

But this did nothing to reduce the volume of unemployment: its intention was merely to make the lot of the victims less intolerable. Temple's approach to the whole subject underwent what he confessed to be a salutary change during his years at Bishopthorpe. At first his attention was concentrated on the actual misery of the unemployed, and on possible means for alleviating it; with the encouragement of the National Council of Social Service he had pleaded and worked for the opening of clubs, where at least the interminable days of idleness could be passed less unpleasantly than at the corner of the street. But merely to promote the right use of leisure barely scratched the surface—the need was pressing for an enquiry that would go to the root of the problem and survey it in all its aspects and relations. In 1933 Temple had called together and consulted a group of friends, all of whom were agreed that there was need for a more thorough and scientific investigation than had yet been made. At the same time the Pilgrim Trustees, for whose generous help the promoters of many good causes have reason to be thankful, were also anxious that an enquiry into unemployment should be undertaken. The Pilgrim Trust therefore agreed, in 1936, to finance the investigation; and Temple's committee, with the addition of one or two members nominated by the Trust, was to be responsible for carrying it out. The members of it were the Bishop of Chichester, the Master of Balliol, Sir Walter Moberly, Dr. J. H. Oldham, and Sir Edward Peacock, with Temple as chairman. The secretary of the committee was Miss Eleanora Iredale, described by the Archbishop as 'the initiator of all its activities', whose indomitable vigour and clear sense of direction were invaluable throughout the enquiry. The Committee were able to rely on the help of a strong body of investigators, who made a detailed study of the problem in six districts—Blackburn, Deptford, Durham, Leicester, Liverpool, and Rhondda U.D. The enquiry was limited to long-term unemployment (i.e. lasting for more than a year) and it included a survey of the industrial and social background, the causes of various forms of unemployment, and the different categories of the unemployed, with sample investigations of personal cases, and an examination of the principal forms of social action (particularly those undertaken by voluntary bodies) for the welfare of the workless. Among practical achievements was the effective organization of occupational centres, with craft-work, lectures (many of them organized by the W.E.A.), and instruction classes: so successful were these that between January 1938 and September 1939 no fewer than 1,500 occupational centres were started, the largest number being in S. Wales and other special areas; many of the centres are now Workers' Clubs or Community Halls. The task to which the committee had set their hands took a long time to complete, but when their Report was published in 1938, in a book of 450 pages with the title *Men Without Work*, it received the warmest praise. On all sides it was hailed as a work of scientific and human investigation of a high order. Temple's practical ability and his competence were admitted by thousands who had hitherto been sceptical, and 'his stock'—in Sir Ronald Davison's words— 'certainly rose in Whitehall as a result of the Report'. Those who had worked with him on this enquiry not only looked forward to an important 'follow-up' of the Report; they were also conscious of the development that was taking place in Temple's own mind. Among those was W. F. Oakeshott (now Headmaster of Winchester) who writes:

I am inclined to think that the enquiry did represent what would have been a new departure in method for him—though the immediate threat of war prevented this from being at all widely employed—viz. the creation of small groups of men to think out the relations of this, that, or the other social problem. To some extent Oldham's *Christian News-Letter* developed out of the enquiry . . . .

In this context it is convenient to group together a number of other problems affecting the social life of the community about which, as opportunity offered, Temple was able to express his own convictions and to guide Christian opinion. On two of them he gave evidence that was afterwards published. One was the Penal Code, with special reference to capital punishment, on which he appeared before a Select Committee of the House of Commons. As a trustee of the Clarke Hall Fellowship—founded to perpetuate the memory of a metropolitan magistrate whose work as President of the Juvenile Courts had been, in the words of Lord Samuel (one of Temple's co-trustees), 'a landmark in the history of the treatment of the juvenile offender' —Temple gave the first annual lecture instituted by the Fellowship, on *The Ethics of Penal Action*. He also wrote and spoke for the Howard League for Penal Reform and the National Council for the Abolition of the Death Penalty. Here, as on every aspect of penology, he took his stand firmly on certain Christian principles, the first and greatest of which was the sacredness of personality and the value of every human life in the sight of God. On the third of the generally admitted elements in punishment— the reformative, the retributive, and the deterrent—he wrote:

Now, so far as punishment is deterrent only, it is treating the criminal as a means to an end, and though the law which condemned him may aim at preserving him from the crime, the actual infliction of the punishment is mainly concerned with other people. So far as this is true, it is non-moral; and if there were no other element in any instance of punishment, it would be immoral, for it is always immoral to treat a person only as a means to some end other than his own well-being. No form of punishment is so purely deterrent as the Death Penalty. It has, indeed, been argued by T. H. Green for example, that the sentence of death may be the one shock needed to call the criminal to a sense of his guilt and so to stimulate repentance. Perhaps sometimes it is so. But there does not seem to be much evidence that in practice sentence of death has this tendency. Of course it is only on the hypothesis of immortality that the death penalty can be regarded as reformative at all; and it is doubtful whether many of those who incur it have a sufficiently vivid faith in a future life to accept the sentence of death as a temporary discipline.

Preaching the John Howard Anniversary Sermon at S. Martin's-in-the-Fields in 1930, he again emphasized that any form of excessive punishment defeated its own end because it 'encouraged a callousness in people by the very violence of the suffering inflicted', and that when the State takes life, even when it does so in return for a life already taken, its example 'does more to lower the value of human life in the minds of its citizens' than the deterrent influence of the death penalty can do to protect those lives; the popular feeling worked up on behalf of a criminal awaiting execution results in the sympathy that ought to be with the upholding of the majesty of the law being arrayed against it. He made the same plea before the Select Committee in July 1930:

The Chairman. What would you reply to the argument that the life taken by the murderer was sacred, and that the sanctity of life was still further emphasized by the community taking the life of the murderer?

W. T. The effect of the State so respecting life as to refuse to take it would undoubtedly be greater than the effect of its so condemning murder as to take the life of the murderer. The reaction of the individual to the behaviour of the community as a whole is so largely imitative, rather than argumentative, that the effect of the State taking life tends to lower the general conception of the sanctity of life.

It was not, therefore, the duty of the Christian (who believed that physical death was not the end) to oppose capital punishment on the ground that it puts the criminal out of existence:

The Death Penalty must be opposed on the ground that it renders impossible the effective maintenance of the standard which the law demands of the Christian; and in this way to those who in the past have upheld and enforced this penalty because they believed that it engendered a reverence for human life, we can claim that we are not destroying but fulfilling their law.

The same line of argument was applied to the more complex problems of betting and gambling. Here Temple was concerned to insist that it was impossible to arrive at reasonable conclusions unless reason had been used in forming them: 'plenty of people feel', he wrote, 'and feel strongly; very few seem to think. . . . Phrases of moral description or classification are regarded as an index of feeling, of approbation or disapprobation, rather than of any clear judgment. This makes moral discussion almost futile.' What was needed was a consideration of principles and (again, as always) of personality:

The moral value, positive or negative, lies always in personality—that of the agent and that of anyone affected by his act—but it must be tested by three things: the character expressed in the act, the principle involved in the act, and the consequences resulting from the act.

He examined these three things, when applied to betting and gambling, in an article which he wrote for the *Pilgrim* while he was Bishop of Manchester, and gave his conclusion on each of them. Gambling is not necessarily a practice springing from an evil *character*—'I think it is possible', he said in evidence before the Royal Commission of 1932 on Lotteries and Betting, 'for people, simply through failure to perceive the bearing of the principle, to bet without any degradation of character at all; I seem to know many people of whom that is true.' And he was careful always to dissociate himself from those who used extravagant language about the 'sin' of gambling. At the same time, it was wrong—and therefore sinful in *principle*—however small might be the amount of evil involved in 'moderate and self-controlled gambling'. For this reason he appealed to his clergy to have no lotteries or raffles at their church bazaars and, in answer to a question from the Chairman of the Royal Commission, he said:

If I am asked, as I am from time to time in my position, to

give my name as patron to a bazaar for a hospital, I always make it a strict condition that no raffles or lotteries form any part of the programme, and I have been able to get these items excluded from some programmes and my name excluded from certain other programmes by that method; they have to choose which they will have.

On the third point—the *consequences* resulting from the act—there was little need for Temple to argue; few students of the social life of Britain, and fewer expert welfare-workers, could be found to contend that excessive gambling was not a serious cause of harm to the individual character and to social well-being. This was the point he stressed when, on 17 November 1932, he carried a resolution in the Church Assembly, 'That this House views with grave anxiety the great evils caused by betting and gambling . . .': he asked the Assembly to note that he was inviting it not to give its assent to any declaration on betting or gambling, but to the fact of their harmful consequences.

On another grave social problem—the relations between the sexes—Temple was frequently called upon for direction or advice. He had a grateful admiration for the two well-established Church organizations, the Mothers' Union and the Girls' Friendly Society, but he was alive to the weakness of all institutions bound by rigid rules in which movements of social life and the corporate Christian conscience may later suggest some relaxation. In 1936 a change was made in the third Central Rule of the G.F.S., which had laid down that 'all those who join the Society must have borne a virtuous character'. The new Rule, adopted by a decisive majority at a poll of the whole membership, ran—'All who join the Society pledge themselves, God helping them, to uphold the Christian standard of purity in heart and life'. Nothing helped more to secure this change than a letter Temple wrote in the Society's *Review* for October 1935:

I have been asked how I can hold that the proposed change of the Central Rule could avoid a 'lowering of the standard'. My answer is that wherever the spiritual foundation of the Society is at all real, it will in fact bring a raising of the standard.

446

For the essence of purity is positive, not negative—spiritual, not physical. It is, as I said in the Jubilee Sermon, 'a passionate aspiration towards the holiness of God'. Where that aspiration exists it guarantees bodily purity; but it cannot be said that the maintenance of bodily purity is always a sign that this aspiration exists. On the contrary, the maintenance of bodily purity is compatible in some natures with an almost total lack of spiritual quality, being rooted in nothing better than a cold and self-regarding prudence.

A girl with such a character can do a great deal of harm to the purity, both spiritual and physical, of those with whom she associates. She lowers the whole moral temperature; the effect of her influence may easily be to foster the feeling that self-control is not a matter of spiritual character, but only of social propriety—a view pernicious in itself and liable to lead to complete disaster if violent temptation arises.

On the other hand, nothing but good could come from the influence of a girl who, though in the past she has yielded to temptation, has been truly penitent, and, after a time sufficient to show the steadfastness of her purpose, is admitted or re-admitted to membership. There may be in her an aspiration towards holiness which is all the stronger and more constant because of what she has passed through.

The conservatism of the Mothers' Union was more deeply rooted. In 1939 a branch of the Union had been disbanded by the Central Office because its members, while not proposing that divorced persons should be admitted to the Union, refused to pass judgement on those outside its ranks by affirming that divorce is in no circumstances allowable. This action seemed to Temple to go beyond the powers and legitimate decrees of the Union, as it expressed 'a particular view concerning the law which the State should make for all its citizens, including those who make no profession of Christianity'. With unwearying patience he argued and pleaded with the Central Office, and eventually wrote a memorandum which led to 'a period of quiescence in the controversy', and he looked forward to the day when he would be able to suggest some healing of the division between the old and the new outlooks 'that will really give general satisfaction'.

Any suspicion that Temple was lax in his views on marriage would have been groundless. One of his most telling leaflets was on *Christian Marriage*, which was published in the form of 'a letter from the Archbishop of Canterbury to those who desire to be married in Church', and combined impressively a statement of the principles of Christian wedlock with practical suggestions and warnings for the daily living together of husband and wife. But the frankest and most concise expression of his basic convictions about sex relationships is to be found in an address to the C.E.M.S. in July 1943, when he lifted up the whole subject to the height from which he surveyed every department of human life and where two thoughts were dominant—the sacredness of personality and the fact of God. After speaking of the respect due from all men for one another's personality, he went on:

It is just the same with sex relationships. To use that function of our nature as an opportunity of passing amusement always involves treating another person as a plaything or a toy. That is destructive of the freedom we are fighting to maintain, for the heart of that freedom is the dignity of personality. But here, even more than in the other case, the religious background makes all the difference in the world. There is nothing nasty about sex as God has made it; there is no reason why it should not be spoken of in a natural and matter-of-fact way; but it must be treated with respect and even with reverence, because it is the means by which men and women are enabled to act on behalf of God in the creation of His children, which is why parents are said to procreate. The reason for not joking about sex is exactly the same as for not joking about the Holy Communion. It is not that the subject is nasty, but that it is sacred, and to joke about it is profanity. Moreover it is the point at which the spiritual and the physical come into closest interplay, and this no doubt is why moralists normally take it as the example of the moral struggle. Sexual sin is not the only sort of sin nor the worst kind of sin; the supreme sin and the fountain-head of all the others is pride, not lust. But if we let this function be used for our pleasure and amusement we are spoiling one of the most splendid things in the world.

It was for this reason that he felt alarmed at the growth of divorce. He looked in vain for some principle at the root of the increasing laxity and found only the fulfilment of personal desire at the will of each individual, which he regarded as 'disastrous for public policy'. A similar weakness seemed to mark the action of the Government in the treatment of venereal disease. This was a highly controversial matter in which Temple, by no intention of his own, became personally involved. In June 1942 the Minister of Health invited him to become President of the Central Council for Health Education. Ernest Brown mentioned in his letter that the Council had just taken over the educational work on venereal diseases which had previously been done by the British Social Hygiene Council, and wrote of the 'great stimulus' that would be given to the work if Temple were President. The offer was accepted; but a few months later Regulation 33B (on the 'compulsory treatment of venereal disease') was promulgated by Order in Council. With this regulation Temple disagreed and wrote at once to the Minister resigning the post of President, partly to clear his own conscience, partly because he had no desire to use the vantage-point of an office the Minister had invited him to hold from which to criticize one of the Minister's Regulations. The confidence felt in Temple's character and leadership was shown when Ernest Brown asked him to remain in office, with complete freedom to criticize the Regulation. Of this permission Temple took full advantage, and on more than one occasion he outlined his case against what he conceived to be the wrong approach to the problem. Briefly, this was that the Government were giving a false priority of emphasis to certain aspects of the question. They were treating a moral problem as if it were primarily a medical one, whereas he was bound to hold that 'where spiritual, moral, social, and medical aspects are all discoverable in one fact and tendency, they should receive attention in that order'. Further, the instructions given to army recruits in the use of prophylactics 'suggested that the authorities expected a considerable number to practise fornication'. At an address to a conference convened by the Central Council for Health Education, Temple said:

> Far more potent than any teaching, any exhortation, any attempted compulsion, is the suggestion afforded by habits of practice and conversation and by the attitude adopted by authority. It really is time that this elementary psychological principle should be universally accepted and acted upon: if teaching and suggestion are in conflict, suggestion will win every time. Therefore the first question we have to ask about any proposed action in this field is 'What suggestion is it offering?'—not 'What result does it aim at?' nor 'What inducements or penalties does it provide?' but 'What suggestion will it make?'

He remained President till his death, and the Minutes of the Council record the sorrow of its members at the loss of 'a man of such uncommon brilliance and charm as the Archbishop, whose name gave standing to the Council and added enormous weight to its deliberations. . . . He was not only a great figure, but a great man'.

When Temple was asked for guidance on the use of contraceptives by married persons, he took his stand on the Lambeth Report of 1930. He deprecated the wording of the 1920 Conference (of which he was not a member) which admitted the use of contraceptives in 'abnormal cases'—what, he asked, constitutes 'abnormality'? In 1930 the Report and Resolutions of the Lambeth Conference were more carefully thought out, and Temple was ready to explain and justify them. He stressed the emphatic statement of the bishops that procreation is the primary object of sexual intercourse—to which they had added that intercourse has also ' "a secondary end within the sacrament of marriage", i.e. as an expression or bond of married love':

> It was argued [by some bishops] that we should say that (when further parenthood must be avoided) the way of total abstinence is the higher, but that in certain circumstances a lower way could be tolerated. This simply won't do. Any decent ethic, but

450

above all the Christian ethic, must point each conscience to the highest way and to none other. But there is no such thing as a highest way in general; there can only be a highest way for each pair in their own circumstances.

It had also been argued by some bishops at the Conference that the higher way should be chosen on the ground that it is the harder. Of this Temple writes:

The way of Christ is the way of the Cross: but that is not a way of hardness chosen for its own sake. The question of hardness has as little as possible to do with the question of right or wrong, and the Christian duty is to follow right, whether it be easy or hard, and to be ready for any degree of hardness as he does so. The forms of self-sacrifice to which Christians are called are very various. A man who feels called to abstinence within marriage—a most difficult vocation—must not suppose that another who uses contraceptives is shirking the Cross. He may be bearing it equally in some other way and have no vocation to this way.

How is that vocation recognized? Mainly by the ordinary ways. A life guided by prayer is presupposed. One couple finds the idea of contraceptives disgusting: that is a sound reason for not bringing them into the intimacies of married life. Another finds them destructive of the spontaneity of self-giving: the same follows. But yet another has no such feeling and on the contrary finds that to maintain abstinence is to create nervous disorder, or mutual alienation: and then the contrary follows. It is a matter for the careful exercise of conscience. And the great value of the Report and Resolutions is that they make this very clear.

This was only one of many problems which pointed to the need he had so successfully met in Manchester—for a body of reasonably educated, carefully trained, sympathetic women who would be competent to give advice on such matters in the private lives and homes of the people. His earliest known views on the position that women should fill in the life and work of the Church were given in a letter to a priest's wife, written in March 1916:

If there were no other ground for belief in a personal Devil (or devils) I should find enough in the way that, when a great movement gets under way, its strength is often sapped by another *good* movement. Personally I want (as at present advised) to see women ordained to the priesthood. But still more do I want to see both real advance towards the re-union of Christendom, and the general emancipation of women. To win admission to the priesthood now would put back the former and to moot it would put back the latter.

Temple maintained these two objections to the end. But there existed an Order for women in the Church which he used to the full and developed both in Manchester and York. The exact ecclesiastical status of a deaconess was not easy to define, and the issue had been to some extent confused by the title: Temple was at pains to insist that a deaconess is not a 'female deacon', but a 'woman minister'. He consulted many historians and several bishops, and became confirmed in his view that the ministry of deaconesses is an ordained ministry—of 'lives set apart in perpetuity and endowed with answering grace by the laying-on of hands and prayer in ordination'—but that in ordaining deaconesses he was not creating a fourth order of the historic threefold ministry of bishops, priests, and deacons. Many subsidiary questions—whether, for instance, deaconesses would rightly rank as members of the House of Clergy or the House of Laity if elected—remain to be answered, but Temple was chiefly concerned (as always) with the establishment of a principle, the details to stand over for settlement as occasion offered or demanded.

In all this side of his diocesan activities, especially in his continuous encouragement and support of the Diocesan Board for Women's Work—which (not without a struggle) he organized on the same lines as in Manchester—his chief helper was his wife. Perhaps it would be more accurate to say that he was her chief support in it, for the leadership was largely hers. Behind her lay the wide experience of all her efforts for moral welfare in Lancashire, and it was at once recognized that her heart was in the work. To help it forward she initiated the annual 'Women's

Offering' by the parishes in the diocese, which was made at a service held in York Minster and every year brought in a large and increasing sum. In this as in several other ways Mrs. Temple's work has lived, not least in all that she did for the church and village at Bishopthorpe. One friend, fully qualified to judge, has written—'Mrs. Temple was the best neighbour that Bishopthorpe could ever have had in an Archbishop's wife'.

XXVI

'Lambeth 1930'—Home Reunion

We should, I think, approach the question whether or not a particular scheme of union is acceptable with the conviction that the fundamental anomaly is that any two disciples of our Lord should not be in communion with one another. We are so used to this state of things that we seldom pause to appreciate its gravity. I would urge that we try to recover in some measure the horror of divisions among Christians which is evident in St. Paul. It does not follow that we shall at once agree to any scheme of union rather than perpetuate disunion, for, as I have said, we are trustees for an apprehension of truth which we have to bring into the treasury of the united Church. But our initial disposition will be towards effecting union if we can without disloyalty to truth, rather than towards so emphasizing our distinctive tradition as to make the accomplishment of union harder than it is bound in any case to be.

W. T., Presidential Address to the full Synod of the Convocation
of Canterbury, May 1943.

THE Lambeth Conference of 1920 has been widely held to be the most important since the series began in 1867. Two factors combined to give it this prominence: it appeared, generally, to bear more closely than any of its predecessors on the secular order, and its primary message was deliberately related to the world situation in the years that followed the Armistice of 1918. One section of the Report of its proceedings was entitled *An Appeal to all Christian People*; a strong plea for fellowship in unity was made to a distracted world and a divided Church, and steps were immediately and officially taken in response, by the Churches of Great Britain, towards healing the divisions of Christendom. Many obstacles blocked the way to home reunion, among which were two that required patience and goodwill for their removal— few members of the Established and Free Churches knew anything of one another's faith and worship, and by most of them any aspirations after unity were regarded with an almost cynical indifference. There might be, within a stone's throw of each other, in a town or village, a parish church and what used to be called a dissenting chapel, but of fellowship and understanding between them there was usually none. If ever the High Church servers at S. Gregory Thaumaturgus', who had received much 'definite Church teaching', contemplated the future state of the Saints in Lantern Yard, they could only hope, even in their most generous moments, that there might be something in certain 'uncovenanted mercies' (occasionally mentioned by the charitable Vicar) to mitigate the unpleasantness of their lot: the Saints in Lantern Yard, on the other hand, were almost ecstatically unanimous in being under no shadow of doubt that the entire congregation of S. Gregory's—with its 'goings-on' that were for a hissing and a reproach in Israel—would burn to all eternity in Hell. But this mattered less than the blind indifference of both to the shame and the disgrace of disunion. Each was perfectly happy in its own small corner of the Lord's vineyard—why disturb this equanimity with talks and negotiations that could only serve to confirm the contrast between two completely distinct conceptions of religion and worship?

A little higher in the scale of intelligence was the type of churchman who disliked extempore prayers and was convinced that 'what these dissenters want is not reunion but recognition', and nonconformists who saw the red light of a fixed liturgy, state-appointed bishops, and a theory of Apostolic Succession resting upon what they dismissed as unhistorical assumptions and unwarranted conclusions. But there were a few leaders on both sides, some of whom had already been influenced by the 'Faith and Order' outlook, who determined to come together, and in February 1920 (six months before the Lambeth Conference) they met at Mansfield College, Oxford. Few of them are now alive, but they included (on the Anglican side) T. A. Lacey, J. E. C. Welldon, Gough McCormick, Arthur Burroughs, A. J. Carlyle, Arthur Robinson, and Canon Guy Rogers: and among the Free Churchmen were such stalwarts as P. T. Forsyth, J. H. Jowett, J. H. Shakespeare, W. B. Selbie, P. Carnegie Simpson, and Dr. Scott Lidgett. Temple, who was one of the youngest of the party, wrote to his wife:

William Temple

The Queen's College, Oxford.
January 8, 1920.

... We have conferred from 9.30–1.0; from 2.15 to 4.0; from 4.30 till 7.0; from 8.15 till 10.45. I have just got back a little after 11.0. Welldon queered the pitch with some very clumsy resolutions. We shall improve on them; but everything now turns on the question whether general interchange of pulpits is to be advocated *provided that* the principle of episcopacy for the future is absolutely accepted, or whether these two are to be advocated concurrently but independently. The former I can agree to; the latter is (I think) impossible. ... Lacey has been most emphatic all day that Nonconformist Ministers are 'ordained ministers of Christ' and therefore there must be no question of their Ordination by us but of their seeking the supply of what we think defective in the mode of their Ordination.

Temple's speech on 'Relations with Nonconformists at Home' was described by the *Church Times* as 'a notable utterance; and in a matter where there is much wild speaking and foggy thinking Canon Temple's words will do more than anything else to clear the air and help matters forward'. The Resolutions of this gathering (which concerned the nature of the Church, the Ministry, and the Sacraments) and the explanatory memorandum that accompanied them are too long for quotation—the same ground was to be covered again and again in succeeding years—but the mere holding of such a meeting made it easier for something on the same lines to be inaugurated by Christian leaders as soon as the message of the Lambeth Conference had spread through the Churches. The 'Appeal' had been cordially welcomed by many prominent Free Churchmen—Dr. Gillie compared it with 'a warm breath of spring in a rather chilly atmosphere'—and in response to a formal invitation from Lambeth a long series of meetings began (the like of which had not been seen since the Savoy Conference of 1661) of Anglican representatives appointed by the Archbishops and Free Church representatives appointed by the Federal Council of Evangelical Free Churches. For six years these conversations

456

continued, when it was decided to discontinue them for a time, partly in order that the Lambeth Conference of 1930 might be consulted on some of the major issues that had emerged. One of these went to the heart of the deliberations; it dealt with the spiritual efficacy and authority of Free Church Ministries. To this section of the Report the Anglican representatives, who included both Archbishops (Davidson and Lang), nine bishops, and W. H. Frere (later Bishop of Truro), contributed a special memorandum in which the following words occur:

> ... It seems to us to be in accordance with the Lambeth Appeal to say, as we are prepared to say, that the ministries which we have in view in this memorandum, ministries which imply a sincere intention to preach Christ's Word and administer the Sacraments as Christ has ordained, and to which authority so to do has been solemnly given by the Church concerned, are real ministries of Christ's Word and Sacraments in the Universal Church.

'Inevitably', Temple said, these words 'made a great impression', the strongest being made on the Free Church delegates to the conversations when the words were first read to them. What more could any Free Church minister ask than this? But did the Anglican representatives realize the full implications of the phrase —'real ministries of Christ's Word and Sacraments in the Universal Church'? If they did, then (said Carnegie Simpson) it was 'the most notable thing which Lambeth has said to any non-episcopal Church since the time of, say, Bancroft or Laud'. He warned the Anglican delegates that it was a phrase which would be much quoted and used by Free Churchmen in the future. Let them reconsider it if they wanted to. Did they really mean it? The answer was—Yes; but with the reservation made in the words immediately following: 'Yet ministries, even when so regarded, may be in varying degrees irregular or defective.' The word 'irregular' could not but lead to protests from Free Churchmen. There was something distasteful to them in the use of it, almost a suggestion of inferiority—so might a 'regular' colonel have spoken of the old 'volunteers'. Temple had often used it. The

William Temple

only unfortunate phrase of his that was remembered by an audience of Free Church ministers in Manchester was his description of them as the 'irregular troops of the Church', and as late as June 1943, Dr. Scott Lidgett, in thanking Temple for a copy of his Presidential Address to the full Synod of the Convocation of Canterbury on 25 May 1943, wrote:

> Your Grace speaks of 'irregular' ministries; and on your principles you are entitled to do so, using the adjective in its strict sense. Yet its use upsets Free Churchmen, and I wish that it could be avoided.

Temple replied:

> You realise of course that one has to choose one's terminology with special reference to particular audiences, and I think we are at present in that stage of the business where it will be impossible to rally Anglican waverers unless some phrases are used which are bound to be unwelcome to Free Churchmen, for I think it is the phrase more than the substance of my meaning that causes distress on the Free Church side. Everything for us is 'irregular' which does not fall under the rule given in the Preface to the Ordinal: the only question is whether one uses the *word* 'irregular' or not. I quite understand the dislike of the word, but I felt obliged to use it. . . .

On the same occasion he wrote to the President of the Methodist Conference, the Rev. W. J. Noble, who complained that the word was 'wounding and untrue':

> By 'irregular', of course, I mean falling outside the rule, and the rule is given in the preface to the ordinal in our prayer books. I regard it as the most colourless word imaginable. On the other hand, I know that other people regard it as suggestive of rather strong colour, and consequently the use of it does arouse feelings.

Whatever the qualification might mean, the findings of the Anglican representatives on Free Church ministries had given new life to the reunion movement, and it was in an atmosphere of hopeful expectancy that the seventh Lambeth Conference opened in July 1930. A century ago, except for the bishops in America, there were less than a dozen Anglican bishops outside the British Isles; in 1930 there were 400, of whom more than 200 walked in procession on 6 July in their Convocation robes down Cannon Street, and passed in double file through the west door of S. Paul's. Randall Davidson was to have preached, but he had died a few months before and Temple took his place. After a moving reference to the passing of the old Archbishop, Temple preached a memorable sermon on the Majesty of God, which ended on a note of triumphant assurance:

> While we deliberate, He reigns; when we decide wisely, He reigns; when we decide foolishly, He reigns; when we serve Him in humble loyalty, He reigns; when we serve Him self-assertively, He reigns; when we rebel and seek to withhold our service, He reigns—the Alpha and the Omega, which is, and which was, and which is to come, the Almighty.

The Conference was divided up into committees, and the Free Church delegates were received by the Committee on Unity, composed of seventy-three bishops, of which Temple was chairman. Whether or not the verdict of the Anglican representatives on Free Church ministries was even mentioned in the Committee, there is no hint in the Report or the Resolutions that it came before the full Conference. After a reference to the Orthodox Churches of the East and the Church in South India, the Synodical Letter continues:

> Though in . . . our relations with the non-Episcopal Churches of our various countries no such memorable advance can be recorded . . . it was with renewed hope of progress that the Conference decided to invite these non-Episcopal Churches to enter into full conference with us once more.

This was seriously to misjudge the situation. In the Free Church view an advance of quite immeasurable importance had been made: had not a body of responsible and representative Anglicans, including the two Archbishops, after deliberations which had extended over six years, made a declaration which almost startled the Free Church delegates by its novelty—that certain Free Church ministries were 'real ministries of Christ's Word and Sacraments in the

459

Universal Church'? And now, at the end of their discussions, they were asked—'to enter into full conference once more'! It was all too clear that 'someone had blundered'. Even if the time of the Conference was heavily mortgaged to the Orthodox Churches and South India, Free Churchmen had a right to expect more sympathetic treatment. Exactly where the responsibility lay may be disputed. Some have assigned it to the President of the Conference, the Archbishop of Canterbury, who had taken a leading part in the meetings of the delegates, and knew well the importance attached by Free Churchmen to the statement; but Lang's opinion was that Temple, as Chairman of the Committee on Unity, was at fault in his treatment of the Free Church delegates and in not making more of their visit in his Report to the full Conference. If this were so, Temple made what amends were in his power at the first meeting of the Anglican and Free Church representatives after the Conference. In spite of the disapproval of many Free Churchmen the 'Lambeth Conversations' were resumed, and Temple made a full explanation and a generous apology—he also offered to publish it, but this was courteously declined—which removed many misunderstandings and enabled the discussions to be continued in a free and friendly atmosphere. The apology might not have been accepted so willingly from a bishop who had not won the confidence and respect of the Free Church delegates as fully as Temple.

But what more could be gained by the new Lambeth Conversations than had been achieved by the old? All that could be said had been said so often that the delegates were weary of wrangling on the exact meaning of words like 'validity' and 'authority'— along that road no advance was possible. At last it was seen that (in Temple's words) 'discussion is only fruitful when it is concentrated on some definite proposal', and that 'there can be but little valuable discussion of re-union in England until a scheme is suggested'. In 1938, therefore, there was published an *Outline of a Reunion Scheme* for the Church of England and the Evangelical Free Churches which described 'the kind of Church in which the Churches represented at the Conference might find themselves united without loss of what is specially valuable in their distinctive traditions'. This was one of the essentials on which Temple insisted. At the root of the suspicions that one Church had of uniting with another lay the fear that it might be 'absorbed' or be asked to surrender much and receive little, and he knew that nothing would allay those suspicions except a clear assurance that in the united Church what each valued most in its own Communion would be preserved. The *Outline* received little attention outside those circles in which there was already some interest in Christian reunion, but in 1943 it came prominently before the Church when Temple delivered his address to the full Synod of the Convocation of Canterbury on 'Christian Unity and Church Reunion'—details of which will be best left till the South India Church scheme is considered.

No comment on reunion between the Anglican and Free Churches would be complete without a recognition of all that has been accomplished and some tribute to the leaders on both sides. Mention has already been made of the older men: among those who were prominent in taking up and carrying forward their work were the Bishops of Coventry (Haigh) and Lichfield (Woods), Dr. James Reid, and Dr. Hugh Martin. Few developments in the history of British Christianity during the last generation have been more striking than the improved relations between Anglicans and Free Churchmen. For this a large measure of credit is due to the men who, through all disappointments and setbacks, continued —in a spirit of frankness, perseverance, and hope—their common study of the issues involved, and lived to see that spirit gradually, if slowly, spreading among the rank and file of Christian congregations.

Conversations were also opened with the Church of Scotland, which agreed to 'enter into unrestricted conference' with the Church of England. Temple, who was chairman of the Anglican delegates, wrote hopefully to his wife:

> Lollards Tower,
> Lambeth Palace, S.E. 1.
> April 29, 1932.
>
> ... The talks with the Church of Scotland went very well this morning, though of course we were only considering how to

propose the problem. Cosmo offered to commend the invitation to confer to the General Assembly and the Scots leapt at it, so he will go on May 27 and I go on May 29, so that for the first time the Assembly will be addressed by both Archbishops in one session. I offered to postpone my visit for a year, but they wouldn't have it.

Eighteen months later he writes—the second letter suggests that one at least of the graces of Christian 'Life and Work' had survived even the ceaseless claims of 'Faith and Order'!—

> Edinburgh,
> November 24, 1933.
>
> ... All is going very well, there is no news to tell. We have conferred all day and now there is a pause before dinner—after which we go on again. But we are reaching a large measure of agreement both about what to do and what to leave over at present.

> Edinburgh,
> November 26, 1933.
>
> ... I set off at 9.45 this morning for Holy Trinity Church— about a mile away (not quite). There is a steepish hill near that Church, and just above the bottom of it I overtook a small boy, about 14, pushing up a heavy milk cart. He had to walk on his toes and lie nearly flat to make the wretched thing budge. So I gave him my umbrella to carry instead and pushed for about 120 yards—with the result that I arrived in the Church on a cold frosty morning gasping and blowing and sweating as if I were emerging from the wood below High Stile. No doubt the verger thought I had got up late and had to run. Now I am just off to preach at S. Mary's Cathedral. Lionel [Smith] is as nice as ever.

Unfortunately, the conversations came to an abrupt end. To the great distress of the Scottish delegates Dr. Archibald Fleming came up from London and, in a fiery speech, swayed the General Assembly of the Church of Scotland into passing a wrecking resolution which made further 'unrestricted' conference impossible. The conversations have remained in abeyance.

In these as in all negotiations for reunion the Anglican representatives were hampered by one recurring difficulty. There were matters of Church Order and doctrine on which opinion within their own Communion was divided, and the Free Church delegates were fully awake to the fact that these were often the very points on which precision of statement was most desirable if agreement of any value were to be reached. No less important was it that they could feel assured that the Anglicans spoke not for this or that school of thought but for the whole Church of England. There were other reasons why some clear statement of Anglican doctrine was desirable—fears had been openly expressed that the inclusiveness of *Ecclesia Anglicana* which some regarded as its glory might some day prove its downfall—and in 1935 the report of a Doctrinal Commission which had been sitting for some years was being eagerly awaited. The history of the Commission goes back to the last week of 1922, when it was appointed by the Archbishops of Canterbury and York (Davidson and Lang) with the following terms of reference:

> To consider the nature and grounds of Christian doctrine with a view to demonstrating the extent of existing agreement within the Church of England, and with a view to investigating how far it is possible to remove or diminish existing differences.

The request for the appointment of a Commission came to Lambeth from the Bishop of Oxford (Burge): he had already been approached by Dr. (now Sir) Will Spens and others who were gravely concerned about the wide differences of doctrinal belief then exhibited in the National Church. Davidson did not care about the idea—why could not those who wished to make their voices heard come together and publish a book like *Lux Mundi* or *Foundations*? This was not a very helpful suggestion—Burge made the obvious retort that the contributors to those books had been more or less like-minded men, and the deliberate procedure of the proposed Commission would be to bring together round a table men with admittedly divergent views—but the Archbishop was standing on surer ground when he confessed to some astonishment that he should be asked to appoint a Commission of comparatively young men, who would be charged with the duty of producing an 'unambiguous statement' which they would wish to see regarded as an expression of the Church's official teaching! Much correspondence followed. The idea of an Anglican *Summa* was dropped; twenty-five members representing the three main schools of thought in the Church were nominated by the Archbishops, under the chairmanship of the Bishop of Oxford, whose place as chairman, on his death in 1925, was taken by Temple: Prebendary E. Rich (then Chaplain to the Bishop of Oxford) was the first Secretary, and among his successors was the Rev. Geoffrey Allen, now Anglican Bishop in Egypt. The Commission held its first meeting in September 1923, and on 8 April 1935 Temple writes to his brother:

> The Doctrinal Commission held its last [most recent] meeting at Balliol, and I was established in your old rooms, next door to my own. It all seemed very familiar. They have just hung in Hall, next to the copy of Herkomer's portrait of Father which Mother gave them, a 'sketch' of me by de Laszlo, which he did as a present to the College last October when he painted my portrait for the Church House.

The Report was received by the Archbishop of Canterbury at Lambeth in 1938. It dealt, in three sections, with The Doctrines of God and Redemption, The Church and Sacraments, and Eschatology. To paraphrase any section or paragraph of it is impossible: the writing is highly condensed, and the omission of a sentence, or even a phrase, in many paragraphs would destroy its balance. But a word may be added, in general, on the weakness and the strength of the Report.

It suffered, perhaps chiefly, from the long intervals between the meetings of the Commission and the fact that all the members were men who had prior claims on their time. Of this difficulty Sir Walter Moberly writes:

> Ecclesiastical Councils which have produced statements of permanent importance have generally consisted of theologians brought together for a year, five years, ten years, or whatever may be necessary, to do that job and nothing else. We were

Archbishop of York, October 1940

mostly busy men, able with difficulty to meet together as a whole four or five days once a year, and more informally in local groups possibly once or twice a year besides. In between meetings most of us were able to give little or no attention to the matters under discussion, so that year by year we were liable to waste some time travelling over ground previously traversed. This in itself accounts for a good deal of amateurishness.

The same defect appears in the general form of the Report. It was originally assumed that the conclusions would be produced in each section as a series of numbered propositions or articles of faith—which accounts for the terseness of the style in the earlier and more condensed sections. Later the conclusions are given almost in essay form, and the contrast between the two portions weakens the unity of the whole. Had not the members of the Commission been already sitting for fourteen years at their task, some effort might have been made to assimilate the two styles: but there was time to do no more than omit the numberings of the paragraphs in the earlier sections—which accounts for the disjointed and unfinished effect that is left on the readers' minds. Who exactly these readers were to be appears uncertain. It was written neither for the 'general public' nor 'primarily for the expert theologian'; and the number of those who 'have paid serious attention to the problems of religion' and 'have some acquaintance with theology' will never be large. On the issues between Catholic and Evangelical the Report is a good and constructive piece of work: on those between traditional and modernist it is less satisfactory. The most disappointed readers were those who had been wondering exactly what to believe on the authority of the Church of England, and more than once—on the very points about which they most needed the reassurance of certainty (such as miracles, the Virgin Birth of our Lord, and his physical Resurrection)—had to content themselves with the verdict that while 'It is felt by many that . . .', 'on the other hand . . . many feel', or while 'Many of us hold . . .', on the other hand 'there are some among us who hold . . .'. The general opinion of readers was on the same lines: while it was 'felt by many' that the Report

H h

displayed the irritating inconclusiveness of Anglican compromise, 'on the other hand many felt' that it was a triumph for toleration and for the comprehensiveness of the National Church. Toleration is always sure of its meed of adulation, even in the most tolerant ages, and on that most of the secular newspapers fastened. But here and there were persons or groups who remembered that, while it is the duty of good Christian men to 'tolerate the tolerable', that cliché means exactly nothing until it is decided at what point the tolerable passes the limits of toleration. A clergyman wrote from a parish in Norfolk to say that a group of laymen who had studied the Report had asked him to send to the Chairman of the Commission a copy of the resolution which they passed —'That, after reading the Report, they considered that a higher standard of honesty was expected among business men than among the clergy.' Temple replied:

April 1, 1938.

It seems to me that some of those whose feelings you reported are approaching what are always difficult questions, requiring a good deal of delicate handling, with what Dr. Sanday once spoke of as 'that kind of arrogance that goes with common sense'. If one sticks to the 'commonsense' attitude, of course it seems purely pedantic and sophistical to discuss the relation of poetic to historical truth, but no one can have done more than a trifle of philosophical thought without discovering that there is such a thing as poetic truth, that it is not the same as historical truth, and that the relating of the two is an extremely complicated matter.

Of course if the word honesty is to be interpreted as saying what you think when you have not taken the trouble to think much, it may be true that the average business man has a finer sense of it than the average ecclesiastic. But if honesty of mind means, as it ought, an effort to do justice to the various aspects of truth before responsibility is taken for expressing opinion, a different result may possibly be reached.

The reply is characteristic of Temple in this especially, that even the rudest communications were always answered—as this clearly was—with a chuckle rather than with a scowl or a snort.

As Chairman of the Commission Temple was in his right place. He did not hesitate, when he saw how the work was developing, to treat the terms of reference as no more binding than quite general instructions. He was the most representative Church of England man of all its members; though no Anglo-Catholic himself, he believed that the Report was one of the first important documents written by men of varying schools of thought which recognized that Anglo-Catholicism has a place, as of right, in the National Church. He drafted much of the text, was ready to do other men's work as well as his own—'Jack [Rawlinson, now Bishop of Derby] had not been able', he wrote to his wife in June 1935, 'to finish his draft, so when we broke up at 11.15 I got him to complete one part while I wrote another, and so got to bed at 12.45'—and was always prepared to revise or destroy his own scripts if others expressed doubts of their value. The Dean of Winchester remembers how 'Temple's patience, conciliatoriness, and humour in the chair were only matched by his regularity in Chapel and his vigour on the tennis court. (Eternally hopeful, he nearly always brought a tennis racket.)' To another member of the Commission, the Rev. C. J. Shebbeare, Professor Clement Webb remarked:

There are many things about this Commission which would have surprised your father and mine; but I don't think that anything would have surprised them more than to see it presided over by a bishop dressed in flannels.

The limits of toleration became a practical concern for Temple when, as Metropolitan of the Northern Province, he had to deal with what might have been an awkward administrative problem. On three Sundays in June 1933, Dr. L. P. Jacks, the well-known Unitarian leader, had accepted an invitation to give an address in Liverpool Cathedral at a 'special' (i.e. non-liturgical) service at 8.30 p.m.; and a few months later another Unitarian, the Rev. L. Redfern, was the preacher at the 11.0 a.m. Sunday service, on the occasion of a visit of the Judges of Assize to the cathedral. The incidents were widely noticed in the local Press, and many protests reached the Bishop of Liverpool and the two Archbishops, including a personal appeal to the Archbishop of Canterbury from Lord Halifax. Towards the end of December definite action was taken by Lord Hugh Cecil (now Lord Quickswood) who communicated both with the Bishop of Liverpool (David) and Temple (as Archbishop of the Northern Province). His letter to the Bishop contained a 'Petition' lodging formal complaint against the Dean, and asking him to issue a Commission of investigation under the Church Discipline Act of 1840: to Temple he appealed as Metropolitan to cite the Bishop of Liverpool before himself or the Episcopal Synod, or any other court that the Archbishop might consider competent to try the case. Dr. David, in his reply, drew a distinction between the occasions on which the sermons had been preached. Mr. Redfern had preached at a 'regular' Church Service, and this the Bishop had neither approved nor sanctioned: but he 'fully and gratefully' approved the invitation sent to Dr. Jacks: the services at which Dr. Jacks had preached were 'special' ones, and any such service 'is non-liturgical, and has regard not to Anglicans only but also to all who look to the Church of England for hospitality such as can best be offered not through her parish churches but through her cathedrals'. Dr. David added that the Dean had accepted his ruling on the Assize Sermon and had expressed his regret, and therefore—as he (the Bishop) could not agree with Lord Hugh Cecil that the Dean had 'encouraged men to hold heretical opinions'—no difference between himself and the Dean remained and he must decline to proceed against him.

Temple's reply was sent after he had consulted the Archbishop of Canterbury and the Vicar-General. Sir Lewis Dibdin—though he admitted that Temple had 'proposed a poser' to him—held that Lord Hugh Cecil had no power to compel the Archbishop to hear his case in a court. Temple accordingly wrote to Lord Hugh on 14 January that he would bring the matter before the Upper House of the Northern Convocation, which had already passed resolutions about the admission of ministers not episcopally ordained and members of Christian communions separated from the Church of England. These resolutions, he pointed out, had 'a bearing upon this question so intimate that respect for Convocation alone would have been sufficient to lead me to submit this matter to its authority'. Dr. David, unfortunately, was obliged to go abroad without delay under medical orders, and the matter could not come before the Upper House until June; but Temple decided to make a reference to the controversy at a meeting of the full Synod of the Northern Convocation on 25 January. It was essential, as the Archbishop of Canterbury had warned him, not to say a word that might seem to prejudice the particular issue on which the Upper House would have to make up its mind, and he confined himself to an urgent plea for the revision of the Church's laws and canons, and an emphatic statement on the need to adhere to the full Christian doctrine of the Incarnation as 'the foundation alike of our theology and of our worship'.

Before the Upper House met, Temple kept in close touch with the Bishop of Durham, who wrote of his concern lest any step might be taken which would 'hearten the mob of heresy-hunting fanatics who will exploit Hugh Cecil's quite reasonable protest'. Henson added a personal reminiscence:

You will easily understand that this Liverpool Controversy hits me harder than any other Bishop. I have been myself a 'storm centre' on this very point of the limits of orthodoxy, which the preaching of Unitarians in English Churches must needs raise: and, as you will not forget, I came into public collision first with Ingram and then with Gore by preaching in non-Anglican buildings, a practice which is nearly akin to that directly challenged in Liverpool. I am not conscious of having changed my opinions respecting the limits of theological liberty, or respecting the wisdom of a reasonably conditioned inter-change of pulpits, but it is not surprising that I should be *supposed* to have done so, when I have to 'change over' from the side of innovation to that of authoritative discipline. I went through the Lenten penance of reading again some of my writings, e.g. the *Open Letter to the Bishop of London* (June 7, 1904), and the Preface to *The Creed in the Pulpit* (July 13, 1912), and I do not find myself required to embark yet on the composition of my *Retractationes*! But, of course, time moves on, and raises ever novel issues. Men's minds are no longer exercised on the questions which stirred them 30 or even 20 years ago: and one does not grow mentally more elastic as one declines into old age.

The debate in the Upper House on 7 June was worthy—except for an unfortunate speech by the Bishop of Ripon (Burroughs)—of so important an occasion. The Bishop of Liverpool expressed his regret that Mr. Redfern had been asked to preach at one of the ordinary morning services of the cathedral, but defended the invitation extended to Dr. Jacks. He repeated that the services at which Dr. Jacks had preached were not 'Anglican Services', and quoted the opinion of a judge of the High Court that Unitarianism was 'admittedly a form of Christianity'. The Bishop of Durham then asked leave to alter the wording of the motion that stood in his name. He explained that the salient clause, which was the last one as printed on the agenda paper, might seem to some to cast an aspersion on the Bishop of Liverpool's loyalty to the faith of the Church, whereas his own single object was to affirm that the House would 'endure nothing that seemed to throw doubt on the cardinal verity of the Incarnation'. The clause, as amended, ran as follows:

> Accordingly, this House is of opinion that, in the exercise of discretion approved in 1922 with regard to invitations to preachers at special services, the bishop should not extend such invitations to any person who does not hold, or who belongs to a denomination which does not hold, the 'common Christian faith' in Jesus Christ as 'Very God of Very God, Who for us men and for our salvation came down from heaven and was made man'.

In his summing up, Temple emphasized the doctrinal issue by declaring that at the centre of the controversy lay the question—'With whom are we to unite in making a common front?' They could not unite with all who accepted a spiritual interpretation of the universe, and the point at which they ought to make their stand should be 'the doctrine of the full deity of Jesus Christ'.

The resolution was passed by twelve votes to none, and the same evening the Bishop of Liverpool wrote to Temple:

> Royal Station Hotel,
> York.
> 7 June, 1934.

My dear W.T.,

You and I had very difficult parts to play to-day. I wish I could think that I have handled mine in anything like the same spirit that you shewed. Nothing could have been fairer than your summing up. You will not expect me to agree with all of it, but I haven't often admired you more, and in what you said I have nothing to complain of. Durham has been very unfortunate in his Unitarian contacts. It was not necessary to wound them so by selecting the worst of their utterances and producing them as representative. I shall not answer him further, and in any references I may make to this business next week I shall avoid so far as possible all mention of the actual debate. But as I told you . . . I am publishing a pamphlet on the larger issue which I do not think ought to offend.

More than my usual gratitude to you and Mrs. Temple for Bishopthorpe!

> Yours ever,
> A. L.

Dr. David's gratitude to Temple was shared by all with whom the Archbishop had dealings throughout the controversy. He had taken trouble to discuss its details, fully and frequently, with all the protagonists; he was astute in assessing the significance of the personalities as well as the issues concerned, and his sympathetic understanding made it impossible for any trace of bitterness to be left when the debate was over. With the unfortunate sequel, which dragged its squalid length along for some months, we need be no more concerned than he was; he was ready to advise personally when his advice was asked, but was unwilling even to read of it in the newspapers unless he was deliberately requested by those engaged in it to do so. His action as Metropolitan ended when the following letters had passed between himself and Lord Hugh Cecil:

William Temple

21, Arlington Street,
S.W. 1.
June 10th, 1934.

My dear Archbishop,

Thank you for your letter. I need hardly tell you that I read the Resolution with great thankfulness and satisfaction. It completely fulfilled my wish for an authoritative declaration that no one who denied the deity of Christ should preach in church.

I gather that you do not think any other action is necessary in respect to my Petition considered as the beginning of an ecclesiastical suit. So far as relates to this particular case I desire nothing more. But in the interest of the discipline of the Church of England I am anxious not to be a party to setting a precedent which might confirm what I believe to be a thoroughly mistaken opinion, that a Metropolitan has no jurisdiction to hear and determine charges against his Suffragan Bishops. I conceive that the denial of the jurisdiction of the Metropolitans is purely an invention of Roman lawyers, anxious to exalt the authority of the Pope. And it is obvious that, though it is much to be hoped that no Bishop may ever commit any offence requiring deprivation, one cannot be certain that such a scandal might not arise. I incline to think that it would be better for me to write a formal letter withdrawing my Petition now that the Convocation of York has made a declaration that makes any further proceedings unnecessary. But I will not take that course if for any reason you think it would be inexpedient. I am however fearful that if the matter is merely allowed to drop in silence, it may seem that you have declined jurisdiction.

I remain,
Yours very sincerely,
HUGH CECIL.

12 June, 1934.

My dear Lord Hugh,

I should personally very much welcome a formal letter from you withdrawing your Petition.

It seemed to me wiser to deal with this matter as we have done rather than to institute a metropolitical visitation of any

472

kind, or constitute a trial before the Synod. There were two reasons for this. One was that to have adopted the other course would have created the maximum copy for the press, and I had hoped that we should be able to get a satisfactory decision in a fairly quiet manner, and I still hope that this has in fact occurred.

The other reason was that the Bishop of Liverpool claimed to be acting under a Resolution of Convocation and sincerely believed himself to be covered by the terms of it. Consequently any kind of judicial procedure would have been awkwardly complicated because the rule under which he was acting would itself have to be defined.

It therefore seemed to me best to let our procedure take the technical form of determining the meaning of our own Resolution. It was, of course, clear that in deciding as we did we expressed an opinion that his action was regrettable, and so far open to grave objection.

But I cordially agree with you that for the general purposes of the welfare of the Church there must be maintained a formal right of the Metropolitan, sitting with his comprovincials, to hear and determine charges against any one of them.

There ought also to be a means of dealing with the Metropolitan himself, but I am less sure whether these really exist!

Yours very sincerely,

WILLIAM EBOR:

Lord Hugh Cecil thereupon withdrew his Petition. The last sentence of Temple's letter raises an interesting constitutional point. There is now no judicial process for censuring an Anglican archbishop: a hint of the reason for this is given in Lord Hugh Cecil's letter. Before the Reformation such censures lay with the Pope; his powers in the matter were transferred to the King and were then made entirely unworkable by the prohibition of 1641 against delegating any prerogatives of the supremacy to Commissioners. But it may be supposed that, if it were desirable to deprive an archbishop, this would have to be done by Parliament, either by an impeachment or more probably by a Bill of Pains and Penalties introduced in the House of Lords, and perhaps petitioned for by Convocation.

473

XXVII

The New Primate of All England

Reading about Pitt and Napoleon has led me to say *Aut Caesar aut nullus* with great violence: and yet I suppose the probability is a life of mediocre ability, trivial usefulness, and a canonry at some country cathedral.

W.T., letter to H. Hardy, January 1901.

I need not try to express the sense of responsibility with which I am answering the letter telling me of your desire to submit my name to His Majesty in connexion with the vacancy soon to occur in the See of Canterbury. But it is clear that no man could be justified in refusing to undertake that office if those responsible for making the selection call upon him to do so. Accordingly, with a great sense of inadequacy for the needs, opportunities, and responsibilities of that See at the present time, I agree to the proposal with which you have honoured me.

W.T., letter to the Prime Minister, February 1942.

'I SHALL always be sorry', Sir Hugh Allen remarked a few months before his death, 'that I never saw Willie Temple after he had been appointed to Canterbury. How he would have laughed if I had told him that I drew him in the New College Senior Common Room sweep, but I fancied his chances so little that I sold half of him for sixpence and lost nineteen and six on the deal!' Many others besides the Heather Professor of Music in the University of Oxford doubted whether Temple would be translated to Canterbury. Of the chief reason for this he was well aware. He wrote on 27 January 1942 to his brother:

I shall be surprised if just at this moment the 'powers' select me for Canterbury. Some of my recent utterances have not been liked in political circles, and it would be thought by some that to choose me now is to endorse them. I don't deny I should like to be asked! But if I were, I should have to go; and I do not think I should like the job there as much as the job here. Anyhow—it's as it will be. (Confidentially)—yes, Cosmo does want me to follow him and has told me so quite plainly.

474

The New Primate of All England

But it was impossible to pass him over. It is safe to say that, under any system of election or appointment, by Church or State or both, the choice would have fallen on Temple. No other bishop possessed in equal measure his many qualifications—a temperament exactly adapted to varied human relationships, unusual stamina, immense powers of concentration, a conveniently mediating mind which was yet without smudges, exceptional lucidity in teaching and speaking, a deep devotional life, a wide knowledge of the history of Church and State, a great reputation among the continental and American Churches and in the Anglican Communion overseas, and a fund of learning on which he seemed at all times able to draw with accuracy and ease. He was the most enlightened bishop in the National Church. The word is aptly chosen by Bernard Shaw: 'To a man of my generation', he writes, 'an Archbishop of Temple's enlightenment was a realized impossibility. Nothing like him had happened since Whately [Archbishop of Dublin 1831–63, author of *Historic Doubts relative to Napoleon Buonaparte*], of whom there was an engraving in the parlour of my birthplace.'

The Man of Letters

In one aspect of this enlightenment, he was (as *The Times Literary Supplement* pointed out) the first Primate since Edward White Benson who could in the true sense be called a man of letters; and he never ceased, even in his busiest days, to add to his learning. Again this is the *mot juste*, for Temple 'learned'—quite automatically—everything he read. He had a photographic memory, inherited from his father, which enabled him to remember what a page of printed words looked like, and never to forget it. He first discovered that he had this gift when, at the age of sixteen, he had to write an essay on Shelley. He had no book in front of him and the essay included many quotations. When he compared these with the text, he found that in one line he had written 'mercy' for 'pity'—otherwise there was not a verbal mistake in any of the 240 lines he had quoted.

He read entirely through one eye. (A more observant nurse or governess would have noticed the screwing up of his eyes

475

whenever as a small boy he had looked into a bright light or at a distant object; and some years passed before the defect—a congenital cataract on the right eye—was attended to and he was given special glasses to wear. This led to at least one salutary result; 'he then saw what other people looked like', his brother recalls: 'he was never dapper, but he did begin to shave better—though this came later in life—and to arrange his tie a little more carefully.') Largely owing to this defect he always read slowly, and he read everything at the same pace, whether it was a novel or a philosophical treatise—'at the pace at which I can pronounce all the words separately, doing that pretty fast'. Yet the amount of reading he got through would have been prodigious for a much less busy man. Nothing came amiss to him, except mathematics, and most of physical science. The *Summa* of Aquinas he described as 'the most complete map ever drawn', and in his early thirties he once remarked that he was probably the only English clergyman who had read it through from beginning to end. Philosophy, theology, history, and sociology he devoured, biography above all, especially the lives of statesmen and other public men. He disliked what he called gaps in his knowledge, and every year, before his summer holiday, there would be packed some authoritative volumes on a period (it might be) of French, Polish, or Spanish history, along with books of theology and devotion, and a novel or two. He could read at any time, among any distractions. Canon Peter Green has this memory of one of the Blackpool missions:

Half way through one of the missions he offered to lend me Croce's *Philosophy of History* which he said he had brought to read in the train and had finished. But it seemed impossible that he could have read a great book of some 600 pages in the intervals of preaching the special daily sermons in S. John's, speaking each day on the sands at one or more stands and interviewing a constant stream of visitors of all sorts. So as I had plenty of leisure I read the book and then said to him: 'I do not believe it was translated from the Italian but from the German edition.' He replied: 'Yes, there is a bad example of that in the second chapter.' I tried him with another criticism and he quoted in full the passage I had in mind from a later chapter. I then said: 'But, good heavens, when you read a book do you learn it by heart?' He laughed and said: 'Oh, no. But I can generally remember the position on the page and can see it before me.'

He would have made a formidable opponent at blindfold chess!

He was fond of detective stories—'so long as the body comes in the first chapter'—and especially of books by John Buchan, Dorothy Sayers, Angela Thirkell, Ann Bridge, and (sometimes) J. B. Priestley; but with many novelists of his earlier days he felt less sympathy. In 1914 he writes to his mother from Repton about Arnold Bennett:

I have finished *The Old Wives' Tale.* Very fine: but the end is so dismal and drab. Of course there is an angle from which life looks like that—just a series of pleasures and sorrows and then a mere 'petering out': but it is a bad sign that nearly all good writers of the moment see things from just that angle.

In his presidential address to the English Association in 1939, he explained where and why he had found the deepest charm of English poetry—'In Shelley, Coleridge, Keats, and Browning (I give the names in my own order of discovery), in parts of Wordsworth, in Tennyson's lyrics, and, of course, in Shakespeare.' He added:

My catalogue dates me, I know; I belong in these matters to the Browning–Botticelli era; and indeed these are the names of my favourite poet and my favourite painter.

Four years later, one of his most stoutly held aesthetic convictions led to a sharp brush with the critics. In the course of delivering the first annual lecture of the National Book Council, he passed this judgement on *Tess of the D'Urbervilles*:

Although Tess may no doubt be rightly described on the title-page as a pure woman, the net result of the novel is to produce the impression that it does not matter whether she was or not; and that is much more disastrous than if she had been, quite frankly, an impure woman.

William Temple

This was to put the cat among the pigeons with a vengeance! Not only was he rebuked in a leading article in *The Times Literary Supplement*, but many wrote private letters to contend that no work of creative imagination should be judged in the light of morality or philosophy, but solely as a work of art. To one of these letters—from Samuel Courtauld—in which two charges which he had no difficulty in refuting were made against his treatment of the subject, Temple replied:

Of course you cannot know that I speak fairly frequently at Moral Welfare meetings connected with the Church and that on every occasion I denounce the dual standard. I do not think I have ever spoken on that subject without doing so. I also point out the fearful danger of pharisaism in this field and the need for a charity scarcely ever shewn towards women who have got into sexual error. Certainly my conscious mind is entirely free of all the influences which you think led to my judgment on Hardy's novel. What is in my unconscious mind I can't say, because no one ever knows what is there—or it would not be unconscious!

I think the point probably appears in the fact that you should cite Hardy's quotation of Gloucester's speech in *King Lear*. That is not an utterance by Shakespeare; it merely represents the frame of mind of Gloucester at that moment. In my chapter 'The Nature of Tragedy' in *Mens Creatrix*, I accept from A. C. Bradley and build upon the belief that great tragedy always creates the impression that nobility of character, whatever befalls it, is enormously worth while and therefore, in other words, that the universe is not indifferent to it but that it is near the heart of reality. But the novel *Tess* does at the end give me the impression, which I tried to express, that Tess had this noble quality and that to the universe at large it was of no consequence whether she had it or not. That is precisely the opposite impression from the one given to me by Shakespeare's tragedies; they always create a sense of a great purpose, which meets with outward frustration but inward vindication. Hardy's novel gives me the impression that the outward frustration cancels any inward vindication that there might be.

478

Of course we are here in the realm of purely personal impressions, but there are no concluding lines to any of Shakespeare's tragedies, or, I think, in the mouth of any of his noble characters, which leave the gloom unrelieved. In *King Lear*, for example, Kent's last words are a distinct pointer to another life, so that the fearful midnight gloom ends with the faintest glimmer of a possible dawn. Hamlet may end his life with the words 'The rest is silence'; Horatio immediately caps it with 'Flights of angels sing thee to thy rest'—and so on. But Hardy pulls down the curtain on the statement that the President of the Immortals had only been having a game and now it was finished. To me the difference is quite polar.

The artistic mastery in the writing of *Tess*, the skill with which the whole impression is worked up, is consummate; but the impression to produce which all this skill is lavished is one which I think it morally disastrous that any man should receive. It has nothing in the world to do with any censure of Tess herself; all my sympathies are with her; that is precisely what makes my fury at the last words of the novel so intense. I want to say something like: So men kicked Tess into the dustbin, but her soul had been with God throughout and is there now.

To one special favourite of his youth he remained loyal through his life. He had a sincere admiration for Bernard Shaw both as writer and thinker, and he snatched eagerly at any chance of seeing a Shaw play. His 'uproarious merriment' was once so embarrassing at a performance of *John Bull's Other Island* that R. H. Tawney, who was with him, began to 'wonder how long it would be before the management asked us to leave the theatre'. He came nearer to summary ejection when, as a young man, he went with some friends to a theatre in Athens. The play was *Medea*—not Euripides, but a translation in modern Greek of a French play on the story. The audience was very small. When Medea at a tragic moment advanced to the footlights and said in modern Greek pronunciation 'Phef! Phef!' (= φεῦ, φεῦ) Temple exploded in a roar of laughter. An attendant arrived and warned

479

William Temple

him that if it happened again he would be expelled from the building.

After seeing *Saint Joan*, Temple wrote an article on it in the *Pilgrim*. He sent a copy of the issue containing his critique to Bernard Shaw, who replied:

15 January 1925.

. . . I am so pleased with the *Pilgrim* article that I have not the faintest impulse to demur to it in any way. This is not so much the effect of your very generous estimate of my achievement in writing the play as of your grip of the fact that the Roman Catholic Church is the stronghold of Rationalism on earth, and has damned itself over and over again by committing the most horrible crimes (like the burning of Joan) simply as the final term of a syllogism. As between the priest who has a first-rate collection of arguments to lead you by a logical path to the bosom of the Church, and George Fox knocking you down with his 'I have experimental knowledge of God', I am for George all the time; and being myself fairly able to construct arguments to prove, as the witness in Dickens offered to, 'in a general way, *ennythink*', I judge the character of a man or a Church not by the reasons they find for things, but the things they find reasons for. . . .

P.S. By the way, *Methuselah* entirely repudiates the value of experience: its thesis is that our conduct and character are determined by our *expectation* of life, not by our experience. Old men are wicked because they say *Après moi le déluge*.

There were lighter moments in which during the evening he would read one of the *Winnie-the-Pooh* books, or ask for the week's *Punch* and turn at once to 'Smith Minor', which he delighted to read aloud. Temple's friends can picture the chuckle with which he wrote:

Lambeth Palace, S.E.
June 11, 1943.

My dear Smith Minor,

As I am one of those who wuold have worried a lot over your Deth, I am writing to say I hope you will long maintain

480

your vigour of mind, as recently illustrated by meditations upon goats and hedgehogs, and of body as exemplified in jumping on and falling off the other boy's biscycle. The only thing worse than your Deth wuold be that you shuold Grow Up. So please don't do that either.

Your constant reader—with or without brains—

WILLIAM CANTUAR:

A few days later, this reply reached Lambeth:

The Artchbischop of Canterbury.

Dear Artchbischop of Canterbury*

You cuold of nocked me down with a feather when I asked Green if he knew who Mr. Cantaur was, and, he knowing, he said it was you. Honestly I never thort that poeple like you read things by poeple like me, that is, if there are any others (poeple like me, Green says proberly not), thouh mind you, Sir, amoung the poeple who have written to me are, i.e.:

1. A Lord (honestly)
2. A Countess („)
3. Two very famous other authers.
4. A cricketer with an average of 47·08.
5. A German prisoner, who ones got to admit seamed nice, why not, if you don't think it wrong to say so.

The above, or rather on the other side, are only some, but I have never been written to before by an Artchbischop, and you have no idea what it makes one feel like, in fact, it put this poym into my head

This thort shuold bring good chear to all—
The Great can think about the small,

which is why I often think of small things like worms and ants, not that I am great, yet, lo! to them I might seam so.

I'll try not to grow up if you think not, thouh it may be difficult later on, still, I'll try not, honestly I cant say I really want to.

If this letter isnt the kind one ouht to write to an Artchbischop I hope you wont mind, but its the only sort I can think of, and so I will have to send it *pour mieux ou mauvaise*, as they say.

> Yours sinscerely, Sir,
> SMITH MINOR.

*Or however one shuold start, I'm not sure. S.M.

P.S. It's funny, but somehow your letter has made this rather quear Life seam less grim.

A few men of his generation possessed wider and more massive learning than Temple, but none knew better how to use and impart it. This facility of being able to draw on all his accumulated knowledge at a moment's notice he once accounted for by saying: 'I keep it all at the front of my mind instead of the back'—and there is an illuminating confession in the Preface to his Gifford Lectures: 'All my decisive thinking goes on behind the scenes; I seldom know when it takes place, and I never know the processes which I have followed.' Writing took little out of him, because all that was needed could be produced without effort; and this, added to his power of complete detachment, enabled him to do some of the best work of his life during odd moments of many days. Apologizing for his delay in answering a letter, he wrote in 1939: 'Life is rather hectic! And if I do get a clear half-hour I write the next bit of St. John instead of personal letters'; and frequently, late at night, he would say—'I must do half-an-hour at my St. John'—or 'at my Giffords'—'before I go to bed'; a very large part of his *Readings from St. John* was written in these 'clear half-hours'. He dictated none of his later books or articles, but wrote them in almost uncorrected manuscript; nor did he make notes before writing. If he were interrupted, he would be careful to break off in the middle of a sentence, so that he could come back to the manuscript hours or even days later and at once pick up the train of thought exactly where he had left off. A few days before the S.C.M. Quadrennial Conference in 1925 he writes to his wife's mother:

> I am working pretty hard. The lectures take about six hours each to write. I have finished the second. Then, most unfortunately, I have to give the opening address as Lord Cecil

has failed, and they want that written to-day if possible—which will take about three hours.

The Preacher and Teacher

For the same reason neither speaking nor preaching involved any physical or spiritual strain and, unlike his immediate predecessor at Lambeth, he felt no sense of restraint in preaching, but was as much at home in the pulpit as on a platform. 'People ask me', he once said, 'whether I am not wearing myself out with all this speaking. The truth is that what wears one out is not what one does but what one doesn't do.' To speak five times in one day cost him little more than to speak once, and fewer than five minutes were usually needed in which to decide on his subject. Once, after preaching a fine sermon in S. Mary's Cathedral, Edinburgh, he asked a friend (on their way out of church) whether it had been up to standard. His friend looked surprised at such an unusual question from him, but Temple explained that on his way up the pulpit steps he had noticed in the congregation an English bishop who had recently retired from his see; and, 'as he had been present some time before in another church where I preached the sermon I was just going to deliver, it seemed only fair to him to take some other subject; and I wondered whether the last-minute change had done any harm'. On another occasion, careful preparations had been made to receive him in a huge canteen at Woolwich Arsenal, and a great body of men had come to listen to him. Unfortunately he had forgotten what the subject of his address was to be and, a minute before the meeting began, he confessed this lapse to the Chief Superintendent of Ordnance Factories who was looking after him. The Chief Superintendent, who naturally regarded this either as clerical bluff or as the prelude to the delivery of a few unprepared generalities, raised his eyebrows and told Temple the title of the address he had promised. Temple then spoke for forty minutes without a single note, held his audience throughout, submitted at the end to a fire of questions, the answering of which gave him the keenest pleasure, and left with the men a memory of one of the greatest spiritual and intellectual treats they had ever enjoyed. Nor was this unusual. All platforms came alike to him; and to every audience he showed some part of his personality which made its special appeal. As Chairman of the Church Assembly 'he had' (wrote Lord Quickswood at the time of Temple's death) 'almost beyond parallel, quickness of apprehension and agility of mind. However novel the circumstance and unforeseen the occasion, his mind adjusted itself for effective use with an ease of precision which gave the impression of being effortless.' From the men in the Forces, the workers in the shipyards, the mechanics and the factory hands of the Midlands and the North, his sheer humanity earned him the tribute of being 'the people's Archbishop': 'I have spent', wrote a Leeds mechanic on hearing of Temple's death, 'the last twenty years of my working life in an engineering works, and can say with truth that in my experience of ordinary working folk no man, whether statesman, soldier, or prelate, was ever held in such esteem, so much trusted, and so much beloved as Archbishop Temple': and, broadcasting on 'Religion in the Eighth Army' in January 1944, a B.B.C. observer spoke of the effect produced on the soldiers' minds by 'the salaries of Anglican bishops—this, curiously enough, mixed with quite a lot of regard for one prelate in particular, the Archbishop of Canterbury, who seems to have caught the soldier's fancy, in spite of his income'. The sixth-form public schoolboy and the student, quick to mark his fundamental integrity, felt that Temple had made the Christian Faith an intellectually respectable thing and had set their feet in a large room. Of his visits to Eton Dr. Alington writes:

It need hardly be said that with young people he was expert. During his regular visits to Eton, there was always a gathering of boys of all kinds, plying him with questions (and meringues) and revelling in his answers: their views both of Archbishops and of the Christian faith received a very notable enlargement, which none of them are likely to forget. If he complained on one occasion that it made him feel exposed 'Like being shut up with a bee in a bathing-machine', there could be no doubt that he enjoyed the experience.

Social reformers who hailed him as the true successor of Maurice,

Westcott, and Scott Holland knew that they could rely on his well-instructed support. To the churchman he was the inspired teacher and interpreter of revealed truth. The debater and heckler found in him a formidable adversary who could 'think on his feet', whose charity and courtesy were as wide as his knowledge, who never attempted to defeat an opponent—it was enough to disarm him. As a speaker he lacked the bell-like voice and the finished art of Lang; nor had he any of the movements or mannerisms of the popular orator. With one hand in his pocket or holding a small half-sheet of notepaper with a few headings on it, and the other clutching the lapel of his coat or with its fingers resting lightly on the table in front of him, he stood motionless except for an occasional tilt of the head or the raising of a hand to adjust his glasses. The style of his oratory exactly satisfied the standard of one of the most fastidious men of letters: 'People think', Matthew Arnold once said, 'that I can teach them style. What stuff it all is! Have something to say, and say it as clearly as you can. That is the only secret of style.' This is precisely what Temple did, through both the written and the spoken word. Of some of his collected essays and addresses R. H. Tawney writes:

> They deserve, I think, more praise than they have received. They do not talk to a brief, or regurgitate the learning of the schools, but speak with the voice of firsthand experience and personal meditation. For all their delusive simplicity of style, they surprisingly often say the profound things which cause an attentive reader to exclaim: 'That is true, and I never thought of it before.'

To this it should be added that he possessed to an unusual degree those qualities by which an audience is moved and held—obvious authority, intense conviction, and a mastery of words which placed him among the most lucid teachers in Christendom.

The Churchman

At the heart of this teaching lay the full doctrine of the Church of England—catholic, evangelical, and reformed. It will already have been seen that there were several halting-places on Temple's

485

journey to that 'central' position where ultimately he stood firm; each of them is plainly marked, when once he has resolved his earliest confusions. In the letters written from Balliol to his mother and father he is so obviously thinking his way along and through, that inconsistencies abound in his first efforts to build up a system of belief which will discard what he considers to be of no spiritual value and conserve the essentials. But the foundations are clear—there must be 'the scientific outlook' and the Bible—and only 'Broad Churchmen' can be trusted to lay them securely. 'I can't see', he writes to his father in 1901, 'what is to save England from getting like France' except 'a great Broad Church movement'. But there is a condition; such a movement must draw its inspiration from the Scriptures. The next step can be foreseen: 'I can work up practically no interest in anything (except lawn tennis) but the *interpretation* of the Bible,' he writes in 1902. This must be both 'rational and practical'; the Scriptures are to be not only believed but applied, and herein lies the remedy for all social ills. The Church is not as yet seen to matter much, since 'where thinking men differ from the Church, it is as likely as not that the Church is wrong'. But by 1905 the emphasis has shifted. He is taking a holiday in Germany and attends a Sunday morning service in the cathedral at Schwerin. Here, surely, if anywhere, he will find the Bible treated with due and reverent intelligence. But the reverence seemed to him disproportionate. He writes to his mother:

There is practically no liturgy: a long sermon, and both that I have heard so far—last Sunday and to-day—have consisted very largely of repetitions of phrases from the Sermon on the Mount over and over again. I believe the explanation of German theology is the habit of standing while the Bible is read, and then only. It tends to a horrible and idolatrous worship of the text—sufficiently shewn in the appearance of people while it is being read—the result of which naturally is a fierce antipathy between the ordinary devout worshipper and the critic. In England happily we sit to listen to S. Paul just as we sit to listen to Scott Holland—and I really believe this habit has the effect of making us more tolerant of criticism: and of course the result of that toleration is a greater gentleness on the part of the critics, who are not protesting against current beliefs as well as criticising. Besides, this extreme reverence for the Bible is a form of idolatry, and a very bad form, as it idolises the one weapon by which idolatry can be destroyed. I want to preach to a Lutheran congregation on the text 'The letter killeth, but the spirit maketh alive'. If one has to choose between the sole authority of the Bible and the sole authority of the Church, in Heaven's name let us have the Church, which is alive, and, because *plainly* subject to error, is also capable of truth. And above all, let us be profoundly thankful that the Reformation in England was a political and not a religious movement, and consequently tied up the Church in definite statements less than anywhere else.

Thenceforward the Church holds the centre of the picture. Long talks with Sanday, for whom he had an affectionate respect, do not help much: he finds the professor's knowledge profound, and his conversation stimulating—'though how he ever makes up his mind I don't know'—and this was written in the year of his life when Temple was to feel most keenly the pressing need for his own decision. A further truth emerges. Shortly before his ordination he wrote to his mother:

It becomes plainer and plainer that the extreme High and the extreme Low are practically identical—and that their identity consists mainly in their being religious, whereas 'The great body of moderate opinion' (as *The Times* always calls it) is hopelessly infected with Moralism—I mean with the notion that a man is to aim primarily at being good, the love of God being a kind of sauce (ingredients unknown, and perhaps better not to ask) which may be added to that *pièce de résistance*. Unfortunately the resistence [*sic*] is so great that most folk only succeed in getting just as good as the determining influences of society generally make them, become quite satisfied with that, and tend to say of enthusiasts that if they do cast out a devil or so it is by Beelzebub: and we know what happens to people who say that! Religion is in all respects 'not of this world', and

487

of it one may say that there is safety in extremes and nowhere else. There!

This new development sadly displeased his Broad Church friends. Among them was Hastings Rashdall, to whom many years later he gratefully acknowledged his debt. 'I know', he wrote in 1923 (the year of Rashdall's death), 'that at a critical time of my life [your] influence, rooted in your combined love of truth and personal devotion to our Lord, was of supreme value.' Soon after Temple's ordination Rashdall said to him: 'I used to be afraid that you would be too much of a heretic to be ordained: now I am beginning to fear that you will end up in the Pusey House.' The words were spoken in jest; but it was, as Temple himself declared, to the first Principal of Pusey House that he largely owed those views of Christian doctrine which for the last thirty years of his life were to form the kernel of his religious beliefs. In his dedication of *Studies in the Spirit and Truth of Christianity* (1914) to Charles Gore, he describes him as one 'from whom I have learnt more than from any other now living of the spirit of Christianity, and to whom more than any other (despite great differences) I owe my degree of apprehension of its truth'. But what he ultimately accepted as the whole truth was not reached easily or all at once. He was able, it may be remembered, to assent to the fact of the Virgin Birth of our Lord before his ordination; some years later, while he was Rector of S. James's, Piccadilly, he experienced absolute certitude of its truth—at a second of time during a symphony concert at the Queen's Hall—and from that moment his recurrent doubts, whether or not it should be included in the Creed as an article of faith, were dispelled. His sympathy with the Tractarians grew through his life, though not without reservations—in July 1935 he wrote to his brother that the centenary celebrations of the Oxford Movement 'on balance have done, I think, more good than harm, which is exactly what I should say of the Movement itself' —and it was not until he was appointed Bishop of Manchester that he received sacramental absolution, for the first and only time in his life. He was not much interested in ceremonial, but he enjoyed it when it was well done and on a large scale, and he makes this defence of the use of a cope in a letter to his brother in 1925:

> I don't think a cope an ugly garment: on the contrary, for processions (its proper use) or for acts where the wearer is seated (as at Ordination or Confirmation) I think it is more dignified than any other garment I know. Also it is curiously effective in obliterating the sense of individuality in the wearer, which, for official acts, is to my mind a great advantage. . . . And on the whole, especially at such times as Ordination, one wants to claim continuity with the Church of the earlier time rather than to assert the independence secured at the Reformation.

We have travelled far from the 'Broad Church Movement' which was to save the Church of England, yet many of its essential tenets held a lasting place in Temple's convictions—especially the belief that on Christian truth alone could be based the high ethical standards from which both public and private morality seemed to be slipping away. Back, then, to the Ten Commandments—but 'they ought to be recited at Evensong if they are to be heard by the majority of people, and especially by people other than devout communicants, who probably need much more the positive teaching of the Summary'—and forward, also, to any new movement that sets the good life at the heart of its propaganda! For that reason, though he saw its limitations, Temple found it possible to commend the Buchmanite Movement. It did sometimes effect what it claimed to do, which was to change men's lives. But there were 'dangers of a serious kind' to which its disciples were exposed, chiefly

> the ignoring by members of the admitted limitations and consequent supposition that the Groups can be substituted for the Church. That, of course, is bad, because the Groups make no provision for worship in the sense of adoration, and the activity of the Groups is almost confined to what members can personally accomplish—so that if there is no religious interest beyond what the Groups cater for, the social reference of the

Gospel largely drops out. When I took that Mission in Oxford last year I came to the conclusion that the best folk in Oxford were those who had got into the Movement and had then got partially out again—not with any repudiation of it, but simply going on to a wider fellowship and outlook. For someone already active in the Church there would be no occasion to get out again because he would never be 'in' in the sense of having no vital religion outside.

But the great Broad Church Movement for which he had once hoped seemed to Temple to have degenerated either into the 'Religion without Dogma' of the popular newspapers, or the old-fashioned anti-sacramental modernism of Dr. Barnes. On the first of these he writes to a correspondent in 1942:

> You would hardly find any theologian now who supposes that Christian ethics can survive for half a century in detachment from Christian doctrine, and this is the very last moment when the Church itself can come forward with outlines of Christian ethics in the absence of the theological foundation which alone makes them really tenable. Our people have all grown up in a generally Christian atmosphere, and take it for granted that all people not actually perverted hold what are essentially Christian notions about human conduct. But this is not true, and we are confronting a widespread repudiation of the Christian standards of conduct in Germany, in certain respects in Russia, and to a considerable extent among our own folk, though it has only at present shewn itself at all widely in regard to the relation of the sexes.

And this to Dr. Barnes in January 1930:

> My dear Bishop,
>
> Thank you for sending me the copy of the *Birmingham Post* containing your address on the Progress of Modernism. It illustrates very well a feature of Modernist utterances that some of us find objectionable. By claiming as 'Modernist' a great deal which is held by all educated Christians, it implies that those who do not wish to be so described do not hold these views. For if Modernism is simply what you say here, there is

no need for (nor, I should say, excuse for) a 'Modern Church-man's Union'. Inge said that Modernists do not build their faith on miracles; hardly anybody does; if miracles are accepted, it is on the basis of a faith already and independently accepted. You say 'the story of the Virgin Birth cannot be used to prove the divinity of Christ'. Armitage Robinson said the same in his popular little book 'The Study of the Gospels' in about 1900. No one was surprised. He was saying what was already accepted among educated people. You say that ten years ago a religious teacher who accepted evolution was still suspect. Suspect to whom? Not to any ecclesiastical authority. When my Father announced and defended his acceptance of evolu-tion in his Brough Lectures in 1884 it provoked no serious amount of criticism. The general position of *Essays and Reviews* had really made a tumult twenty years before that; but the particular battle over evolution was already won by 1884. The real difference now is not in the attitude to modern knowledge, but in the attitude towards the admittedly necessary adjustments of tradition. Thus you say: 'The story of Adam and Eve is, of course, incompatible with modern knowledge, and the serious theologian sets it aside.' I should have said that the serious theologian never sets anything aside without asking what (if anything) of spiritual value has been faultily expressed here, and taking care to give it better expression. As soon as it is realized that the Garden of Eden is a myth, it is seen to be a very good myth, curiously congruous with evolution, be-cause the Fall is (in the myth itself) a 'fall upwards' seeing that by it the knowledge of good and evil was obtained. Similarly Genesis i, as soon as it is taken as a myth, is an overpoweringly good myth.

Of course the writers did not know it was a myth, no one ever did (or could) write a myth deliberately, because myth belongs to the stage when men had not learnt to distinguish between historic and poetic truth.

I regard Rashdall's book on the Atonement as a great achieve-ment, but essentially a bad piece of theology—because when he has decided that some Pauline or Augustinian computation is untenable he never stops to enquire why S. Paul or S. Augustine *wanted* to hold it, what spiritual value it had for them: he omits from his study the very thing that matters most. And that seems to me typical of very many Modernist utterances.

Personally I regret the existence of a special organization of Modernists. Modernism, as you yourself describe it, is an intellectual movement leavening the whole Church, and quite indispensable to its progress or even survival. But to separate out the people specially concerned with it weakens their leavening capacity, and stiffens others in resistance. Milner White and Wilfrid Knox will do more for wholesome Modernism by their reply to Vernon, and their defence of it in the last *Church Times*, than any number of Modernist utterances called by that name. These inevitably give the suggestion that to the speakers negations are of primary interest: which of course is not true.

Incidentally also I think it seriously unfair to imply (as you clearly do) that Transubstantiation involves a localized presence: no doubt, Roman and Anglo-Catholics often behave as if it did; but S. Thomas Aquinas is most explicit that it does not: *Corpus Christi non est in hoc sacramento sicut in loco.* I regard Transubstantiation as a quite impossible doctrine intellectually, and full of danger spiritually; but in its most authoritative exponent it avoids the particular evil that you find in it.

Yours ever,
WILLIAM EBOR:

This aspect of sacramental truth he emphasized in an address to the York Diocesan Conference. There were two dangers, he said, in the kind of reverence that some were inclined to pay to the Sacred Elements:

First that those who learn to rely on the help of Christ's sacramental Presence may find it more difficult to apprehend His Presence when there is no sacramental medium at hand; the second is that they may easily slip into some form of superstitious belief in an actually localized Presence of Christ which is not far from some of the evils of idolatry, and has already crossed the line between sacramentalism and magic. Catholic Theology has always kept on the right side of that line; but many of the current expressions of popular Catholic devotion lie on the wrong side of it. Thus, while I think it impossible to say with truth or justice that the practice of offering prayer in the presence of the Blessed Sacrament either rests upon or gives rise to false doctrine, yet I regard it as so closely attended with great spiritual dangers that I am convinced that the Church should not permit that practice to receive the sanction and encouragement of organized worship in which it forms a part.

All the more did he stress the sacrificial aspect of the Eucharist. The Holy Communion was indeed a meal of fellowship, but 'if this had been the essential note it would have been enough for our Lord to say "Do this in remembrance of Me", which it is not quite certain that He did say. There would have been no need for the tremendous and unquestioned words, "This is My Body; this is My Blood of the New Covenant".'

As he grew older, Temple's sympathy with the Catholic outlook increased. This was remarked by several of his non-Anglican friends in the Oecumenical Movement, and Reinhold Niebuhr has described a conversation he had with Temple on the last night of a visit to Canterbury in July 1943:

> I asked him to give the evening over to a discussion of the only matter upon which I felt any disagreement with him, that is on his ecumenical position. In the Convocation of Canterbury held several weeks previously he had argued for the interchange of pulpits, had opposed intercommunion, had declared that the ministry of other churches was 'owned by the Holy Spirit' but was nevertheless 'irregular'. I accused him of having a Catholic conception of both the Church and the Sacraments. I suggested that to have a really common Communion only after the Church was in fact organically one, and that upon the Anglican basis, was to deny the eschatological element in

493

the Sacrament as Protestantism conceived it: that we recognized the Sacrament as an 'earnest' of the Kingdom of God, of a unity beyond all chasms of nature and history which was and was not achieved in the Church, and which would be the more surely achieved if the Church did not claim too much for any actual realization. I told him that his conception of unity was irrelevant to the American ecumenical problem where we would have to win the strong sectarian influence in the Churches over to some conception of Order rather than any particular right Order. Temple countered my ideas vigorously and did not budge an inch. He declared that my or our conception represented a sanctification of present divisions and would retard unity. He insisted that his interest in Order was determined by his concern for the preservation of the full substance of the Church and that only the episcopal orders could guarantee that substance. I mentioned a few bishops who did not seem to me to have the 'full substance' of the Gospel in their preaching and asked him how their authority could guarantee the full substance of the Church. He countered by suggesting that in terms of general tendencies episcopal authority discouraged vagaries and heresies more than we were able in the non-episcopal Churches. I told him that I thought the Prayer-book had saved the Anglican Communion from rationalism and Pelagianism more than the Episcopacy had done.

The position that would have been assigned to him by most Anglicans was 'Central Churchmanship'. To some the phrase suggests a loose and almost Laodicean attitude to the essential verities of the Christian Faith. But this is to rob the words of their natural and more wholesome meaning; and if they imply a firm hold on the articles of the historic creeds, a conviction that what is best in each school of thought within the Church is worth conserving, and a refusal to believe that any one group or party within the Church of England, or indeed in the whole Catholic Church, enjoys a monopoly of truth, then it is a phrase which may well describe his position. If ever there was a full Church of England man, it was William Temple.

The Father-in-God

Some account has already been given of him as a bishop—of his diocesan conferences and ordination retreats, and of his sharing in the work and recreation of his clergy. But for many of them the most sacred memories are of private talks with the Archbishop. They received from him something which no other bishop had given them. Of all the articles of Temple's working faith, none was lived out more consistently than his conviction that the personality of every man and woman is sacred; and there was almost a reverence in the courtesy and consideration with which he received and treated any who came to him for help or advice. The least sensitive could not help noticing—especially in the last years of his life—the atmosphere of stillness and peace (which yet seemed charged with power) that pervaded Temple's room, the gentleness of his voice, and the quiet patience with which he sat motionless in his chair, listening with an attentive sympathy that invited frankness even from the most diffident. To that sympathy everyone who sought his counsel bore witness; but not all came away entirely satisfied. Some missed the probing analysis of a situation, the shrewd penetration through all details to the essential heart of a problem, that they had been accustomed to gain from Lang. 'I wanted the Archbishop', one of his clergy remarked after discussing for half an hour in Temple's study the possibility of a change of work, 'to tell me what was *right*. He almost seemed to advise me to do what I liked best.' The man felt that his spiritual leader had been less exacting with him than he would be with himself, which was probably true; for Temple believed that, generally speaking, 'a man does best the work he feels he wants to do', and he was too prone to assume in others the same stern training of the affections and the will which he himself had undergone through years of spiritual discipline, and the same consistently dedicated use of that 'liberty of the children of God' which not even an archbishop should presume to violate.

His sympathy was less marked in some of his routine letters. He would dictate or write between thirty and forty of these daily— which in itself demands a certain compactness of style—and often

by their very accuracy and lucidity they seemed to lack that warmth
of personal touch which clergy specially value in correspondence
with their bishop; sometimes a slight addition or alteration, which
would soften the tone and interpret him more fairly, was suggested
by his secretary and willingly adopted. There were also occasions
when he would write more hopefully than circumstances warranted to parish priests anxious to move, which led to disappointment when the hopes he had aroused could not be fulfilled.
But more often his letters showed the friendly courtesy that was
natural to him. After preaching at a church festival in one of his
parishes, he wrote this in his own hand on the night of his return
home at the end of an exacting day:

> Bishopthorpe,
> York.
> July 12, 1931.

My dear Canon Lowe,
 I am so truly sorry that I should have got into my car to-day
without properly saying Good-bye. I had meant to shake hands
after I was in it through the door, but the policeman shut the
door and my driver started, with no farewell or thanks expressed. Thank you so much for all you did to make my visit
to Otley so delightful.

Historic celebrations such as those at Otley (where the church
was keeping the 1,300th year of its foundation) gave Temple great
pleasure, and he invariably did justice both to himself and the
occasion. In more informal meetings he felt less at home. Ordinary
parochial gatherings seemed almost to immobilize him, except
when his wife was with him, when all would be well; her social
ease enabled her to do a little unobtrusive shepherding of the
Archbishop, without any apparent effort to manage him and his
movements, and to make sure that he was not monopolized by a
few of the company, or did not confine his attention to those who
most obviously interested him. In his sermons at the institution
of new incumbents he gave the impression of thinking more of
the message he had come to deliver than of the people to whom
he was giving it. Here it was difficult to follow his predecessor.

Lang was expert in using every available scrap of 'local colour' at such a service. His shrewd and kindly references to the old and the new incumbent, his topical allusions to the particular attractions and difficulties of a parish, and to the special contribution which a Christian congregation in a certain place could make to the church life of the diocese, all helped to bring home to simple people the place they held in the thoughts and ministrations of their father-in-God. Temple's addresses on such occasions would be largely theological, usually concerning the fragment of divine truth that was at the moment uppermost in his mind: 'but it was, I think,' writes one of his archdeacons, 'in keeping with the general tenor of his life—the subordination of himself, and of others with himself, to the truth which is in Christ Jesus'. It also manifested one of his outstanding gifts. Temple was a born teacher. He was one of the few among his Christian contemporaries who was never known to preach without teaching.

The privilege of being on his diocesan staff was highly valued by his suffragans and archdeacons: to work with one who was never 'hot and bothered', who could transform a staff meeting into a family gathering, who gave himself unremittingly alike to the largest and the smallest problems of administration, and with whose serene patience it was impossible not to be infected, was a constant joy. But there were difficulties. Knowing the full weight of the burdens he could shoulder, Temple was not adept at delegating to others work which he could do for himself. 'Very well, I can see to that quite easily', he would say as he gathered up the papers about some routine business discussed at a staff meeting, of which one of his archdeacons would gladly have relieved him. For the same reason he had no domestic chaplain at Bishopthorpe—with the help of an excellent secretary he knew he could manage without one, and it was essential to economize man-power in the diocese. This worked well enough so long as Temple was in charge, his mind was his minute-book and he could dispense with the written word; but it was not always easy for his assistants to gather up all the threads and to feel assured that no relevant factors in any situation were being left out of account. Some of his appointments, also, sadly perplexed his staff;

William Temple

they found him too inclined to be at the mercy of the last person who had his ear, and occasionally, when they were not agreed among themselves, there might be some playful manœuvring to secure the last word with him. That he sometimes failed in his judgement of men is to be admitted, but there is a background to this which must not be overlooked. It was said of Westcott that he could not see much difference between the intellectual standard of his ordination candidates and that of his examining chaplains, and this line of thought is at least suggestive. In Temple's olympian mind there seems to have been a lack of insight in assessing gradations of intellect on a lower level than his own. There were the obviously first-class men whose gifts he recognized and used, but below them was an 'omnibus' class in which the rest were jumbled together with little attempt to differentiate. Also in the background were his unworldly innocence and his determination to see the best in every man. Sincerity was what he first looked for in those who applied for ordination; and for him this was sometimes allowed to outweigh the seriousness of countervailing defects. Randall Davidson's remark, already quoted, cannot be left out of count—'The trouble with dear William is, he is so kind that he cannot say No'—nor is his faithful chauffeur's verdict irrelevant: 'You might go the length and breadth of Europe and not find another man like the Archbishop. There's only one thing he cannot do: he can't tick you off properly.'

The Man

Such—in lamentably bare outline—were the man of letters, the teacher, the churchman, and the bishop. But they were all combined in a single person; to explore this personality, and so to get to the heart of Temple himself, some endeavour must now be made. The difficulty of any such scrutiny was well described a few years ago by John Buchan (in a tribute paid to the memory of one of his own close friends) in two sentences: 'It is not easy to draw on a little canvas the man whose nature is large and central and human, without cranks or oddities. The very simplicity and wholesomeness of such souls defy an easy summary, for they are as spacious in their effect as daylight or summer.' Not a syllable

498

of this need be altered in the effort to describe Temple's genius. He was so comprehensive and representative a person, his character and attainments were all so much of a piece, that no particular gift or virtue seems to stand out obviously from the rest. But his disciples and critics have at least this judgement in common—that there was only one William Temple. The psycho-analyst would have found him an irritatingly unsatisfying subject. Here was one who had been in the limelight through most of his life, who had met on equal terms the most brilliant and the most influential of his contemporaries, whose hold on the hearts and minds of his countrymen grew steadily with his growth till it was unique in his generation. This was the public figure, the Primate of All England who could fill the Albert Hall at a few days' notice and was, beyond question, the greatest moral force in Britain. There was also the William Temple of private life—a genial, friendly, and apparently uncomplicated person, with no vestige of pomposity, vanity, or conceit, with no intolerances to shed or inhibitions to conceal, and without a single one of the fears and frustrations that have marred the personalities even of the greatest. But surely—the doubt might at first seem justified—this was a pose, the kind of pose which public men, trained in the art of impressing the multitude, are driven frequently to adopt? Yet, the more intimately his friends came to know Temple, the more absurd the suggestion seemed. They could find no trace in him of a dual personality; no mask was put on and off; the public and the private man were one and the same person. Nor was he a perpetual battle-ground of repressions and frustrated desires. He had an inner unity and harmony of soul which no discords of the world, the flesh, or the devil could break. He grew into a wholly integrated personality, at home and happy in a friendly universe— a little too friendly perhaps ('we have had', he writes on his brother's fiftieth birthday, 'a big share of the things most worth having, haven't we?') for was it not commonly and truly remarked that the note of tragedy was missing from Temple's life, that he had never been 'up against it'?

To write of his personal friendships is more difficult. By no conscious effort, but because it was natural for him to do so, he showed to each and all of those with whom he had relations the same tenderness, charity, and understanding, and so gathered a host of friends. Yet to many he remained oddly remote. While some would claim an intimacy with him which he himself might have hesitated to admit, to others he seemed either a man without close friends or one whom it was not easy to know. If an attempt be made to account for this apparent remoteness, two suggestions may be hazarded: one (which could be reinforced by the complaint sometimes made of the lack of emotion in his preaching) that the emotional side of his nature did not develop *pari passu* with his intellect—and here perhaps is the one slight complication in his personality—the other that his friends' views of human relationships were more restricted than his own. The almost intellectual affection he bestowed on all alike was so obviously sincere as to enlarge the hearts of any who came under his influence, but it did not satisfy the desire of those—and they are not a few—who wish to possess their friends. He held back from nobody what he could offer of himself, and all that each could gain from contact with him, each was entitled to have and to keep. But he himself remained inappropriable. The world of men was too wide, and the claims on his active sympathy too diverse, for any such embarrassing occupation of his whole personality as would have satisfied the more exacting of his friends.

From his complete integration some of the finest qualities derived, not least his absolute assurance. Sure of God and of God's universe as he was from the beginning, sure as he became of the basic principles of ethics—of the science of relationship with his fellows—he grew, as a result, to be sure of himself; and never was this quality more marked than at a time when a paralysing uncertainty was creeping over the nation. Some day the historian will portray in detail the unforgettable misery of that fourth decade of the twentieth century. He will recall the atmosphere of social, intellectual, spiritual, and emotional insecurity in which the hopeless fatalism of the people reflected faithfully the impotence of its leaders. But there will be evidence enough that a few still kept their heart and hope, and that one of those whose leadership never faltered, and who never lost his sense of direction, was William Temple. This sense of assurance was well described in two sentences written by Kierkegaard more than a century ago:

> The more profoundly a man has planned his life ethically, the less will he feel the need of talking every instant about duty, of being fearful every instant whether he has fulfilled it, of taking counsel every instant with others about what his duty is. When the ethical is rightly viewed, it makes the individual infinitely secure in himself.

This judgement is almost echoed by Lionel Smith, in looking back on his long friendship with Temple: 'I believe he must have learnt very young what some people never learn—that if you are sure of yourself, it does not matter whether or not you are sure of what you are going to meet round the corner.'

To move habitually in such an atmosphere is to live without fear. A more worldly-wise person, possessed of an intellectual eminence and gifts of leadership which marked him out for high office, would have been less ready to commit himself, more concerned to observe the direction of the wind before he set sail. Those who knew him only at the peak of his career need to be reminded that the political and economic commonplaces of to-day were considered almost anarchic when Temple first announced his social sympathies and his plans for incorporating them in the Statute Law of England: the young socialist don in the first years of the century was not a popular figure in the older universities. More subtle must have been the temptation in the early days of his fame to say no word that would lessen his chances of reaching the high goal of his desire; and the greater the natural ambition attributed to him, the more remarkable must be accounted his courage in subordinating it throughout his career to an unswerving honesty and a single-minded devotion to truth. But even this must have entailed less of a struggle to a man of his acute sympathy than to face the distress he could not help inflicting on honest and good men no less dedicated than himself to the service of the Church, who regarded almost with horror his political affiliations and the doctrines that flowed from them. Temple at least could claim that he had held his course; and this consistency has left his lifelong friends, as they stir their memories of him down the years, with a vivid sense of continuity. The remark of his Oxford tutor, that none of his pupils seemed to have changed so little as Temple, has already been quoted. This was true of great and small things alike. A letter written by him in 1894 is in much the same handwriting as one of fifty years later. His aesthetic and literary tastes were constant. When he was sixty he would chase with his spoon the dregs of sugar round the bottom of a coffee cup with the same deliberation as when he was sixteen. 'For five years', writes Lionel Smith, 'I must have spent several hours every day in school and out of school, and at meals, in his company or even next to him, yet . . . I do not think I ever heard anything acrimonious or unkind said by him or in his presence'; the only time some of his friends saw tears standing in the Archbishop's eyes was when an uncharitable remark had been made in his presence about another person.

From the more common weaknesses of the man who is sure of himself Temple was wholly free: he had none of the blustering self-assertion that marks the superficial self-confidence of the bully and the worldling. Many who knew him well, if they were asked in which of the Christian virtues he came nearest to his own ideal, would reply without hesitation—in his humility. To achieve it cost him a struggle, yet he seems to have known all his life that the victory would be worth the effort. Few of the letters he wrote while still at Rugby are more revealing than one in which he replies to a friendly rebuke from Harry Hardy. The occasion was trivial enough, when Temple's use of scriptural language in ordinary conversation had offended some of his more rigidly pious school-fellows:

. . . I do not think that this habit has at all diminished my reverence, but if all that you say is true, it is far worse than that. . . . That it could ever cause anybody to offend I had never dreamt, and of course I see now that it can and should have seen it before. Will you complete your benefit by adding your prayers to mine that my good resolutions may not be broken till they are transformed into habit? . . . Having read this effusion, I am afraid you will think that I am parading all my virtues to extenuate one fault: That is not at all my intention. I feel really humble; a strange feeling for incarnate conceit!

The struggle was continued at Oxford. Some of his contemporaries remember occasions when he was rough, almost rude, in his manners; and the bluntness of his father's speech, which unconsciously he may have imitated, sounded less pleasing in the mouth of a rather dogmatic undergraduate than in that of an aged ecclesiastic who had the reputation of being something of a 'character'. But gradually, and with a deliberate striving, the rough edges were smoothed down, the self-assertion was sublimated into simple reliance on the grace of God, till it was given to him to manifest—through the years of his greatest influence—the truth of that most misunderstood and least appreciated of the Beatitudes, that the meek shall inherit the earth. Here, however, all depends on definition; and Temple helped to rescue a noble word from the ignoble use it has suffered at many hands. As early as 1924, in *Christ in His Church*, he describes the essence of the virtue it was his hope to achieve:

Humility means that you feel yourself, as a distinct person, out of count, and give your whole mind and thought to the object towards which they are directed, to God Himself in worship and to the fulfilment of His will in Christian love; and humility, in that sense, is quite plainly a source of effectiveness. The humility which consists in being a great deal occupied about yourself, and saying you are of little worth, is not Christian humility. It is one form of self-occupation, and a very poor and futile one at that; but real humility makes for effectiveness because it delivers a man from anxiety, and we all know that in all undertakings, from the smallest to the greatest, the chief source of feebleness is anxiety. . . . But there is nothing big enough to hold a man's soul in detachment from the centre of himself through all the occupations of life except the majesty of God and His love; and it is in worship, worship given to

God because He is God, that man will most learn the secret of real humility.

This is almost a pen-picture of Temple himself, and two highlights stand out from it. 'The chief source of feebleness is anxiety.' It was impossible to disturb his serenity; 'again and again', the Archbishop of York recalls, 'after troublesome meetings I found Temple quiet and unruffled.' The ordinary friction in the life of a busy archbishop—the solution of tiresome administrative problems, the choice between conflicting claims of essential duties, the making of drastic alterations in his time-table owing to some important incident in Church or State, the frequent need for swift decision in speech or action, the attention owed to individuals who sought his help in increasing numbers—none of these disturbed the calm deliberation with which the day's duties were carried out. Least of all was a moment wasted in vain regrets over any speech or work that may have fallen below his own high standard; this partly explains why at times he seemed almost deliberately unaware of the opposition he aroused. 'Are you not', a Rugby master had asked him in discussing one of his essays, 'a little out of your depth here?' 'Perhaps, Sir,' was the confident reply, 'but I can swim'—and so he did. Against whatever tides he had to battle, he would usually breast the waves with a cheerful courage and land high and dry, little the worse for his buffeting. But there is another way of keeping one's head above water: one can float—and sometimes Temple was content to float. This refusal to be drawn irritated his opponents. More than once, after he had made a speech containing some disputable statements, the critics would fasten on these, perhaps pointing out some inconsistency with previous utterances, and challenging him in the columns of *The Times*; and Temple's usual retort would be a request that they would do him the favour of reading his whole speech verbatim when it came to be printed. There was a strength in his refusal always to keep his ear close to the ground for the voice of the 'average man', or to weaken the positive straightforwardness of his appeal by anticipating the strictures of his opponents; but it led to occasional failures to assess not so much the volume as the value or authority of the opposition he incurred. To most of this he was indifferent: he had said what he had to say; with what others might think of one or another of his particular pronouncements he was little concerned. This was due in part to the way in which his mind worked. It was less like a razor than a massive and powerful engine revolving with a regular and sustained rhythm, more fitted to deal with large issues than small disputes, more deeply concerned with dominant principles than with the casuistry incidental to some passing controversy, adapted rather to the dictation of strategy than to the planning of tactical details. There is also much truth in an intuition of the Swedish Bishop Brilioth, whose penetration into Temple's character was acute: 'This gift of overlooking difficulties seems often to be a part of the genius of leadership.' But fundamentally more decisive than these was his obedience to the very letter of the apostolic precept—'In *nothing* be anxious'.

The other word that stands out from our quotation is 'detachment'. To some of the minor pleasures that for many lessen the austerity and the friction of life Temple had been for a long time —to two of them all his life—a stranger. From the day when he began seriously to keep his gout in check, he forwent the pleasures of the table which had once attracted him. He was a non-smoker and a teetotaller. His father, who had never smoked, had drunk wine well into middle life, but from the day he began his temperance crusade he had given it up for the sake of example; the most decisive influence, however, on Temple's practice was that of his mother, who was almost fanatical in her belief in total abstinence. Later in life he grew increasingly convinced that strong drink was a grave social danger. In the second World War, as Chairman both of the Central Council for Health Education and of the British Social Hygiene Council, he had consultations with the Ministry of Health on the possibility of a No Treating order, or at least a No Treating campaign. There was general agreement at the Ministry that a reduction of drinking among young people would help materially in the control of venereal disease; but the decision lay with the Home Office, and nothing was done. He was careful, in all that he said or did, to explain that he was bringing no general charge of drunkenness against the men and women in the Forces: 'The major harm', he wrote, 'comes from that inhibition of the faculties of self-criticism and self-control which occurs long before anything that could rightly be called drunkenness.'

Never can he have been more thankful for this gift of detachment than when the time came round for his annual holiday. He allowed himself few other relaxations in the course of the year. Occasionally he dined as a member of Grillion's, and of 'The Club', and in November 1929 a Balliol dinner was given to the two Archbishops, Lang and Temple, with Grey (of Fallodon), as Visitor of the College, in the chair. There is mention, too, in a letter to his brother, of a day's rest at Bishopthorpe:

June 24, 1941.
We have kept our Silver Wedding here to-day in great restfulness; we are both tired, so having kept the day clear we slept nearly all the afternoon in the garden.

The heavier cares of office were shed when he started on his summer holiday, though the few weeks were never wholly free from work: 'Letters', he wrote one summer before starting off, in the *York Diocesan Gazette*, 'will be answered, but not welcomed' — a courteous hint which his correspondents were slow to take; he records one morning the arrival of sixty-two letters, but even they were not allowed to mar the enjoyment of his freedom. So long as his work allowed he crossed the Channel. He delighted, while still at Queen's, to take one or two undergraduates to Florence, stand them in front of some picture in the Pitti, and tell them to remain there for half an hour in that 'active repose of contemplation' recommended in the Gifford Lectures which his pupils found so much harder to achieve than their tutor. Assisi, the Italian Lakes, Oberammergau, The Hague and Haarlem, the countryside of Brittany (soon after his appointment to York, when 800 letters had to be acknowledged)—all had special memories for him and his wife, and they were no less happy at Aix where he went more than once to be treated for gout. But it was to four districts of

England—the Isle of Wight, the Lakes, the valley of the Kennet, and the Quantocks—that they were most devotedly attached. At Totland Bay—where they spent seven successive holidays with their close friends Mrs. Duff and her two daughters—in intervals between bathing, lawn-tennis, and walking on the Downs, he did his best to become a golfer, but with indifferent success. The one benefit he derived from his gout is described in an undated letter to his brother:

> Yesterday morning I awoke with mild gout in the left knee, and proceeded to do my best half-round—53 for nine holes—and as I took 9, 7, and 10 for the last three you will observe that I played the first six rather well. I expect the bad left knee made me put my weight on the right leg in a wholesome manner.

He had loved the Lakes from childhood: the name of every track, and of almost every crag and beck, was well known to him; and his companions—Repton boys, Queen's pupils, and his own contemporaries—will not forget the sense of utter freedom and the boyish zest with which he led their expeditions by day and their games at night, for nobody knew better how to get every hour's enjoyment out of a holiday. They remember the old Norfolk jacket—so weathered by time and use that its original colour might have been any shade from grey to green—with sandwiches sticking out of one pocket and maps from another; the open-necked shirt, the plus-fours, and on occasions a hat which defied description, accidentally but extensively perforated in the crown. They recall him forging slowly up a stony track on Scarth Gap or Easedale, lying flat to drink from a hill-stream, consulting a map to verify the name of some small crag, perhaps to make sure of avoiding a bog; then—as the party turned for home—leaping down a steep fell-track, with knees bent to lessen the jarring of his weight, flourishing his stick, and at the bottom turning round with streaming and glowing face—like Mr. Pickwick on the slide at Dingley Dell—to watch the more sober descent of his friends; nor can they forget the appetite he brought to the tremendous farm-house teas of bread and butter, cream, bilberry jam, and apple pasty, which were the crown of the day's outing. Of one such day Sir William Fyfe writes:

In the spring of 1929 I spent a week with Temple, Harry Tawney, and Geoffrey Bell (Headmaster of Highgate School and one of Temple's head-boys at Repton) at a delightful house near the head of Buttermere, which a Manchester admirer had lent to the newly appointed Archbishop of York. William knew the Lakes intimately and was a stalwart and steady walker. Having more to carry he progressed more slowly than the rest of us. One hot morning Tawney, Bell, and I, having reached the summit of Great Gable, watched William climbing steadily upwards and 'larding the lean earth' as he came. When he reached the rock on which we were sitting, he sat heavily down, wiped his brow and exclaimed: 'Thank God, I do *not* believe in the resurrection of the *flesh*!'

Soon after they were married, Temple and his wife took the Manor Cottage at Ramsbury, in Wiltshire, where they were near his old friends, Dr. and Mrs. Cyril Alington. It was a small thatched house near the Kennet, standing in a wonderful setting between a mile of grass ('The Race-Course') on one side and a slope of beech woods on the other. Here they could entertain their friends, join in expeditions and lawn-tennis with the Alingtons, and walk in Savernake Forest. How this house had to be given up has already been told.

But it was at Lower Weacombe, near the village of Bicknoller —half-way between Taunton and Minehead—that he and his wife found their most peaceful holiday home. Every August, from 1933 to the year of his death, they spent some weeks here in the home of the Misses Hooper. Nothing was left undone for their comfort. There was an attractive covered-in balcony (where it was possible to sit in almost all weathers) which, with a garden shaded by an apple tree, exactly met their needs: and the height of luxury for Temple was to put aside his letters till later in the day, and directly after breakfast take out a deckchair in which he could read under the apple tree. Professor Grensted recalls a chance meeting at Bicknoller:

It was by pure accident that I found Temple there on a summer holiday, and neither I nor any of my family will easily forget the expedition which we all made together to Cleeve Abbey, the hilarious attempts to preserve his incognito in the tea-room, and the complete freedom with which (I think that Mrs. Temple was a little shocked) he discussed the problem of how to grow suitably corpulent with a small boy who had opened a conversation by asking how much he weighed!

The books to be read, the walks to be taken, the bus connexions to be made, were all discussed for months beforehand. At Weacombe alone in the later years he and his wife knew the close and uninterrupted companionship which elsewhere they could never hope to enjoy and in which, for a few weeks every year, they found welcome recompense for the restricted intimacy of their workaday living.

Another sign of the detachment which grew upon him was that he came to sit more and more loosely to party politics. As far back as 1928, he had noted the danger that threatened British political life. In a sermon preached for the I.C.F. at Holy Trinity, Sloane Street, in October of that year, he said:

> What we need desperately in our country is to cultivate independence of mind and fellowship of spirit, and what we are developing through the present machinery of our political life, and developing very fast, is herd mentality with the spirit of pugnacity. You have got to try to invert that and teach people to feel together and to think for themselves, instead of thinking together and feeling for themselves. It is going to be done in the realization of the idea that we are all children of one family, and that our Father is the God of Love.

We have seen how and why he joined the Labour party, but he was disappointed in its parliamentary achievements, and the inconsistency of its policy in the Far East was the immediate reason why after seven years he gave up his membership of the party. But he continued to feel more sympathy with its general programme than with that of any other political group, though he was not always ready to give Labour leaders the active help they frequently sought and expected from him. On 20 October 1931 he writes to his wife:

> . . . It was quite a good meeting in the afternoon for the Port and Station work at Liverpool. Two telegrams came. The first from the *Daily Herald*: 'Shall be very much obliged if you could write 1,000 word article for the *Daily Herald* supporting Labour. Beseech you to do this if at all possible. Editor, *Daily Herald*.' The second was from Harold Laski: 'Very greatly hope you will counteract tragic effect of Canterbury pronouncement on Church's position in Labour movement by message to *Herald*. Harold Laski.'
>
> Laski amuses me. He dislikes the Church intensely, and his net is spread too visibly in the sight of the birds. I wired to the *D.H.*: 'Regret impossible and you would not wish to print what I should have to say.' The clerk at the Lime Street Station telegraph office grinned broadly at it.

Such incidents as this may have been in Temple's mind when he wrote to a correspondent, in January 1942, on the general relationship of the Church to the Labour party:

> I find the Labour Party generally has conspicuous difficulty in realizing that our first job is with the Gospel, and that we can only commit the Church as a whole to what indubitably follows from the Gospel. They see so clearly what seems to them both the justice and the expediency of the Labour Party programme that it seems to them we ought to support that straightway. In fact, they often want us to give up being specifically a Church, i.e. the Household of our Lord, and become a political party. They do not really want this when it is nakedly presented to them, but they often want a line of action which in fact involves this; and then they become more irritated with a person like myself who actually sympathizes and agrees with them in most of their programme than they do with open opponents, because they think we are hedging for some discreditable reason.

Increasingly he came to shrink from revolutionary movements, alike in theology, in the Church, and in the State. 'I often wonder,

sometimes with real torment of mind and soul,' he once wrote to
D. C. Somervell, 'whether I have not been turning my back on
the light.' There were times when he felt 'most violently drawn
to scrap all forms and traditions and merely launch out into the
deep'; and the persons who were connected with movements for
reform seemed to him much more zealous and attractive than
those who were chiefly concerned with reverencing tradition—
'but each time I come out confirmed in my own position'. In this
position there was some weakness which the more critical were
quick to note. To several of his friends, in speech and writing, he
expressed doubt whether, for instance, it was right for an archbishop of his day to live at Bishopthorpe—'but that', he always
added, 'is for the Church to decide'. This is a different conception of a leader's function from that which had moved him to
head Life and Liberty deputations to Lambeth, in order to plead
with the Archbishops that they should not wait to follow the
Church but should take the lead themselves; and it was remembered that Gore had not waited for any decision of 'the Church'
before he refused to live at Hartlebury Castle. So, too, the question of an established Church ceased to be a moral issue: it became
merely a matter of 'machinery', which must not be allowed to
distract the attention of the Church from the urgent task of
spreading its gospel.

These were the views which came to him with age and experience, but other influences on his development were at work—
among which was Lambeth Palace. The words are used of an
atmosphere rather than a domicile. In a sketch of the life and
character of Charles Gore, so excellent that it deserved wider
circulation than it had through the magazine of the Community
of the Resurrection, the Rev. E. K. Talbot, C.R., described a
moment in Gore's life when, on returning from a meeting at
Lambeth, he was seen to stop half-way across Lambeth Bridge and
turn round to shake his fist at the Palace—'I forget', Fr. Talbot
adds, 'what compromise had stirred his indignation'. But in that
building Gore had frequent converse with men perpetually
tempted to confuse principles with opportunism or expediency,
to adopt almost unconsciously the motto 'It will last my time',

to be satisfied if they could just keep the machine running, and— in the less pleasant interpretation of the phrase—to 'prolong the reign of the dead'. Gore was the only man who began his work on the Bench as a rebel, and remained a rebel to the end. There will be no general agreement on the extent to which, from the years which began at Manchester, Temple was influenced by this atmosphere. Any suggestion that it affected him in the more usual and vulgar ways can at once be rejected: from pride, worldliness, and pomposity he was as free on the last day of his ministry as on the first; his gaiters were nothing to him except 'the most comfortable leg-coverings I have ever worn'. And, if it cannot be disregarded as one of the factors that encouraged his gradual movement to the Right during his later years, it weighed less in the balance than another influence which was dominant. That was his complete absorption in what he was convinced was his mission. The wider his vision became and the more inclusive his ambitions for the Church, the more deliberately he avoided what he held to be distractions, however important they might be, and the less relevant seemed the worldly palliatives, or the details of Church reform, which loomed large in the eyes of lesser men. The peak of his evangelistic appeal is reached in the introduction to a book published in the year of his death, *The Church Looks Forward*. This may be taken as a summary of his last message:

Our need is a new integration of life: Religion, Art, Science, Politics, Education, Industry, Commerce, Finance—all these need to be brought into a unity as agents of a single purpose. That purpose can hardly be found in human aspirations; it must be the divine purpose. That divine purpose is presented to us in the Bible under the name of the Kingdom (Sovereignty) of God, or as the summing-up of all things in Christ, or as the coming-down out of heaven of the holy city, the New Jerusalem.

In all those descriptions two thoughts are prominent: the priority of God and universality of scope. Nothing is to be omitted; 'all things' are to be summed up in Christ, but it is in Christ that they are thus gathered into one. All nations are to walk in the light of the holy city, but it comes down out of heaven from God. The Kingdom of God is the goal of human history, but it is His Kingdom, not man's.

Such was the House of Life as Temple saw it, and into every part of it his abundant personality penetrated, spilling over, as it were, from one room to another, till there was no corner where he would not claim for the Gospel the right of entry and assert the indisputable priority of God. Here, too, was the Master of the House, *speciosus et amabilis*—to welcome, to consecrate, and to control—on whose guiding hand his hold never relaxed, so fully had the prayer been answered which he had asked the diocese to offer for him, when he was enthroned at Manchester. And here he lived that spiritual life which was his whole life. He was among the 'once-born' who, as he wrote, 'are capable of the deepest experience of all'. His spiritual life was not confined to fixed times or transient moods from the ecstasy of which he went out to face the hard realities of the world. For him earth was indeed 'cramm'd with heaven', and not only every 'common bush' but every true human activity, every art and craft, every task and pleasure, and every one of the least of Christ's brethren, was 'afire with God'. None of them was excluded from the orbit of his active energy because each of them had a place in his prayer. All those who worked closely with him saw this most clearly. His assistants in the university missions were left with many experiences of his spiritual insight and converting power: but as they think of Temple now they think chiefly of prayer—of his own prayer, of his concern for the prayers of others, and of his rating of prayer more highly than any other human activity. When Canon Eric Abbott, who was his assistant in the Dublin University mission, was appointed to the Wardenship of the Bishop's Hostel, Lincoln, Temple wrote: 'You will use it as a basis for what we need more than all else—to teach the clergy to be teachers of prayer;' and to more than one of those who were invited to conduct his ordinands' retreats he said: 'I am entirely convinced that prayer is the chief thing.'

This was to him the value of the long solitary drives in his car, as he went about the diocese: they gave time for preparation and opportunities for thought and prayer which no distractions were allowed to disturb. His chauffeur recalls a war-time evening in the black-out when the Archbishop came out of the vicarage at Thornaby-on-Tees at 5 p.m., and told him that he had just remembered an important meeting at the Yorkshire Club which he had promised to attend at 6 o'clock—and would Brindle please 'step on it' and get to York as soon as ever possible? The distance was sixty miles. There were moments during the drive that were far from pleasant—it normally takes an hour and a half to cover the distance in daylight when the roads are fairly clear—but at five minutes past six the car drew up at the door of the Club. For the whole hour Temple had not once moved or spoken, and as he left the car 'he said "That was very good, Walter", just as if it had been an ordinary run'. On these lonely drives through the dales of Yorkshire or the Kentish lanes, it was his habit to pray for each of the villages through which he passed, to concentrate his thoughts on his next engagement, and then to say the Lord's Prayer slowly for his intention: so he was at once and confidently ready to mount the platform or pulpit for which he was bound.

This meditative side of his nature was nourished by his strong affection for the Psalms. To a public school master who had asked his advice on the eight psalms which he would choose for divinity lessons, he wrote:

> Here is my order: 103, 23, 104, 107, 139 (but it falls off at the end), 126, 130, 51 (but I should put this first if it were not for the *dreadful* bathos of the last verse). But I am not sure if further meditation might not lead to one or two substitutes. And of course I am going by the Prayer-book version. The things I most want to work in are—84, especially verses 5–7, which is one of the most exquisite things in the world, though its beauty is mainly due to a mistranslation in 6; 90, a splendid piece of stoicism; 16, which is near the top of religious aspiration; 46, chiefly for the sake of the first words of v. 10 and for v. 6; 137, only it is spoilt by verses 7–9. In fact I want twelve places and then I can get in all my favourites.

You will see that in the Psalms I prefer the meditational ones to those of direct praise or of narrative, and the tender ones to the sturdy ones. But on reflection it seems absurd to leave 90 out of the first list, so it must go in, I think, instead of 130. In certain moods I should put it top. I suppose you know it is attributed to Moses. . . . And then I have left out 19! I think it must go in instead of 46.

The words with which the second paragraph of this letter opens throw a light upon the way in which much of his *Readings in St. John's Gospel* was written. It can now be seen why for Temple 'clear half-hours' were enough in which to record the thoughts evolved through many years of meditation. There was little need to dig either into commentaries or into the deeper regions of his own mind: he had only to transfer to paper what was in the forefront of his daily thinking—almost casual thinking, it might seem, so simply and naturally is the full meaning of the Fourth Gospel expounded, in words which more clearly than any other of his writings reveal his own intimate and meditative self. The same simplicity marked his celebration of the Holy Communion. Eyes, voice, and posture, all gave the impression of an almost childlike awe and reverence with which he approached the Holy Mysteries, and to this was added authority—the high authority of his office, the more impressive for being obviously unstudied.

Any but the most restrained comments would here be out of place—perhaps the nearest to the right word has been written by Sir Walter Moberly:

> I have had what was, I presume, the experience of all Temple's older friends. More and more there was added to the old affection and admiration something for which 'reverence' seems the only possible term. No one could make less claim for himself or take it more wholly for granted that he met you on equal terms. But his ever growing stature became such that, to look at him at all, one must look *up* at steeper and steeper angles.

The Prophet

Well, indeed, that this was so: for he was called, especially in the last few years of his life, to the most hazardous and exacting

515

vocation which any man may be summoned, in the providence of God, to fulfil. For what did it all mean—this ceaseless and deliberate progress from one platform and pulpit to another, this complete dedication to an ideal, this certitude in believing and assurance in uttering the word he felt bound to proclaim? It could mean only one thing—that Temple was a prophet. The decline of classical learning and the growth of popular superstition have combined to obscure the true sense of this splendid word: to many it suggests little more than a mixture of 'Templegate' and Pastor Russell. Yet that meaning—the power of foretelling either the result of a horse-race or the date of the world's end—is only the fourth of several definitions given in a standard dictionary. The first is the oldest and truest—'One who speaks for God . . . as the inspired revealer or interpreter of his will.'

Such pre-eminently was William Temple; and the man on whose shoulders the prophet's mantle has fallen lives and works thenceforth by the rules of his Order. His course is set. It is no longer for him to decide whether or not he shall speak; the compulsion upon him is irresistible. His is what Max Weber has called the 'charismatic quality', which includes the belief that 'it is the *duty* of those who have been called to a charismatic mission to recognize its quality and to act accordingly'. Twenty-seven centuries earlier, the first of the great Hebrew prophets had said the same thing in more picturesque language—'The lion hath roared, who will not fear? The Lord God hath spoken, who can but prophesy?' There is no silencing the prophet. Without fear or favour, without doubt or delay, with a disarming innocence and a conviction that is absolute, he will bid men hear the word of the Lord. This is what Temple did in London at a time when, for most of those who ever troubled to listen, the word of the Lord had for long been so carefully watered down or so discreetly filtered that they were unable to recognize the authentic voice of the prophet who stood among them. It was about as likely, for example, that the average City alderman would understand Temple as it was that the average City policeman would understand Ezekiel. To the pundits of Threadneedle and Throgmorton Streets, it must be presumed, it is given to know the mysteries of the City of London—though these have become a good deal less mysterious in the last few years—and Temple's attempt to unveil for their souls' health some of the mysteries of the City of God seemed an irrelevant impertinence. He spoke to them across seas of misunderstanding. It was not ill-will so much as a lack of insight that lay at the root of their mistrust; they passed him by almost as a museum-piece of pseudo-religious enthusiasm. He would willingly have suffered the scriptural fate of the unwelcome prophet when on 5 September 1944 he kept his last public engagement in London. Standing among the ruins of the bombed City, outside the Mansion House and opposite the church of S. Stephen Walbrook, he spoke at a lunch-hour service organized by two City rectors. Stones were certainly not what the modern trades-man would call 'in short supply' on that site and on that day—even the pulpit was made of them. But our City Fathers let them lie, and only succeeded in being a good deal 'on the north side of' gracious or even courteous to the Primate of All England.

So we must go farther and ask—What if your prophet happens also to be Archbishop of Canterbury? Did Temple ever think out an entirely consistent answer to this question? For thirty years he had said much more shocking things than he ever said while he was at Lambeth, but the world will find excuses for the youthful enthusiasms of the church reformer (even of the diocesan bishop) who is inclined to interpret with a disturbing literalism the Gospel he is commissioned to proclaim; and a casual charity can overlook, as no more than venial extravagances, the effusions of the provincial sciolist. But let such a man come to London, as head of the National Church—and a new situation arises, both for the Church and for himself. To thumb the guide-book of history for a precedent is useless: few prophets have sat in the chair of S. Augustine, and a study of Anselm's message and methods 850 years ago would be of little help in the twentieth century. In that century—as in many that preceded it—until the year 1942 the voice of the prophet had never been heard from that bleak study on Thames-side, when suddenly the emphasis of its authority began almost to burst on men's ears—and few had any idea how to react to it. If an Archbishop of Canterbury begins an important pronouncement with the words: 'It may not be entirely inconceivable to many (dare I say all?) men of good will that . . .' the parenthesis suggests the possibility of a loophole, by which the more timorous can evade the responsibility of commitment, or of that gentlemanly dissent which leaves each man's conscience inviolate and avoids all the unpleasantness of an open breach. But should the Lambeth trumpet sound the charge with the words 'Thus saith the Lord', decision becomes imperative. From each his own answer. Thomas Carlyle's reaction is the simplest and the most forthright: 'The prophet says, Thus saith the Lord. Yes, Sir, but what if it be not the Lord, but only you who take your own fancies for the word of the Lord?'

Few of Temple's critics were prepared to go as far as this. A vaguely superstitious respect for the Primate's office was enough to forbid so uncivil a retort; for if there were such a thing as the Word of the Lord, common sense suggested that the Archbishop of Canterbury would not be unfamiliar with its content. The more usual comment was either that the Word of the Lord was irrelevant to problems of economics and high finance and that ecclesiastical cobblers should stick to their last, or that the Archbishop must remember that he stood at the head of the National Church, which of necessity became involved in, perhaps even committed by, his public pronouncements. Temple's reply was to point to his reiterated statement that, whenever he expressed his social or economic convictions, he was speaking as a private citizen and not as Archbishop of Canterbury; and he emphasized this in a speech at Birmingham very soon after he realized that he had shown less than his usual wisdom at the Albert Hall. In any person not so transparently honest with the world and himself as Temple, such a defence would have been condemned as disingenuous, for he knew well enough—and it was a handicap to which he refers in his correspondence—that if there is one thing an Archbishop of Canterbury cannot do, it is to speak 'as a private citizen'. But in this matter he was the victim partly of his own temperament, and partly of tradition. He might have examined the joint stock banks, for instance, no less thoroughly than he had once investigated the whole problem of unemployment, with a similar band of experts making a comprehensive inquiry into the current system of banking and the morality of certain practices incidental to it. Had he done so, the result would almost certainly have been as illuminating and informative as *Men Without Work*—a social study of which the value was unquestioned because it had been produced with the aid of the best professional skill available. The authority of such a pronouncement would have done much to refute the contention that the Church must stand apart from worldly controversies and entanglements; for all but the hopelessly prejudiced would have seen how fantastic is the logic which suggests that a man may share and strengthen the common counsel of his fellow citizens until his moral and intellectual worth has raised him to the highest position in the Church, but from the day of his appointment to the Primacy he must 'thereafter for ever hold his peace'. Temple's ideal—and who can say whether, had he lived, he would not have realized it? —was not to bar the Primacy to men of charismatic gifts, but to have at Lambeth a prophet in close and constant touch with expert advisers, and so armed with a weapon of immense potential strength in a society lacking the moral guidance which a Christian leader should be specially fitted to give. At the 'Christian Frontier' lunches organized by Dr. Oldham—a Christian thinker and leader for whom Temple had an affectionate admiration—he was able to meet picked men and women of weight in their own professions, on whose sympathetic co-operation he could rely; but his constant temptation was to respond indiscriminately to the pleas of enthusiasts and to act and speak independently of the expert in matters where the expert's knowledge and judgement were essential. When all has been said, however, the truth will stand that by his public utterances he performed a noble service. He raised the moral atmosphere of the country and infused a new sense of vocation into the Church. Into ears dulled with the reverberating catchwords of the world he cried aloud the fact of God's Kingdom and His righteousness. He put the Church 'on the map', and broke the paralysing tradition that the most essential virtue in a Christian leader is prudence. He administered one salutary jolt after another—whether it was to the City of London, or the

Church of England, or the Government of the day, or any other organization wrapped in the comfort of complacency or dulled by moral torpor—and so helped to roll away the reproach (the words will bear a second quotation): 'It is not by its indiscretions, but by the obduracy of its discretions, that the Church has lost repute.'

Of the many questions raised in this chapter, the last—perhaps for those who most admired and trusted William Temple it should be the first—must not go unanswered. It was asked some years ago in *The Common Reader* by Virginia Woolf in her teasing sketch of William Thomson, a predecessor of Temple both as Fellow of Queen's and Archbishop of York. She tells of his Grace's life at Bishopthorpe: of the nine children in the nursery and the seven cows in the park; of the Archbishop's great ability —did he not wear a hat which was 'eight full'?—of his pedometer, his camera, and his clock-mending; of the soap which he bought for the Princess of Wales's visit; of the eighty letters answered before breakfast. . . . But—the essay ends—'is it easy, is it possible, for a good man to be an Archbishop?' If the question be asked of the Primate who forty years later sat in Thomson's seat, two answers may be given. One evening during the Oxford Mission, an undergraduate on his way back to college from the service at S. Mary's was heard to remark to a friend in a high-pitched voice: 'I can't say I think much of the Archbishop's philosophy, but he struck me as being what one might call a *good* man.' In the same week—on 16 February 1931—his old friend Cyril Bailey wrote:

I must just send a word—I won't say of gratitude—but of very deep thanksgiving. As I walked away on Sunday night with an undergraduate I know well, he said: 'It is wonderful to come away from a very great man and to feel that one has been listening not to him, but to God.' And that is just what I want to say.

This is the prophet's only and high reward, which he must pray for without ceasing—but will never dare to accept.

. . . There was also William Temple the thinker—and here let the philosopher speak.

XXVIII
The Philosopher
by
DOROTHY EMMET

We saw, as folk who desired to think like Christians, a little further into the meaning of our world than those who sought no illumination from that faith. We had to lead as many as we could to see life in that light of the knowledge of God, which we had ourselves received. We tried, so to speak, to make a map of the world as seen from the standpoint of Christian faith. In my own case the preparation for this enterprise was more philosophical than theological.

W. T., in *Theology*, November 1939.

THERE is a story that, in his second year as an undergraduate at Balliol, Temple read a paper to the newly constituted Jowett Society entitled 'The Book of Job, the Epistle to the Romans, and the Philosophy of Immanuel Kant: a comparison and a contrast'. The story may be apocryphal, but at any rate it may be taken as symbolic of the spirit in which Temple approached the study of philosophy. A pupil of Edward Caird, he was inspired to look on philosophy as the search for a unifying spiritual principle in terms of which he might achieve a synthesis of different, if not opposing, tendencies of thought. In Temple's Oxford days such a synthesis seemed to some almost within sight of achievement, and as late as 1924 in the Preface to *Christus Veritas* he described the dominant philosophical atmosphere as 'not materialist or atheist' but 'both spiritual and theistic'; and he believed that with a very slight touch to the intellectual balance the scales might incline in favour of an 'exposition of the Christian idea of God, life and the world, or, in other words, a Christocentric metaphysics'. It is symptomatic of Temple's sympathetic awareness of contemporary trends of thought that, looking back in 1939, he could quote this statement and note how irrelevant it would be to the intellectual situation of the present day. But as a young philosophical theologian he set out to offer his contemporaries a 'map of the world' in which all experience might be

521

interpreted in the light of the Christian doctrine of the Logos as a unifying principle. His zest for synthesis was reinforced by his gift for clarity of exposition and rotundity of statement.

As an undergraduate Temple was also evidently very much excited by the study of Kant. To begin with he seems to have taken his Kant as opening the door straight to idealist and theistic metaphysics. He writes (22 September 1901) to his brother: 'I am disposed to write you a brief treatise on phenomena and noumena', and proceeds to tell him how 'transcendentally, the Universe must be treated as one undivided whole, no part of it ever being considered by itself; and this as we see it has only a subjective existence'. He writes in similar enthusiasm to his father; and we have the Archbishop's shrewd and dry comment, 'Dear William, The young Kantian must be always on his guard lest he slip unconsciously into the religion of the Gypsies:

> Yea, God and man, the future and the past,
> Are but to them one chaos dark and vast;
> One gloomy present, one unchanged to-day,
> Stirred by no storm and brightened by no ray.'

And the old Archbishop reveals himself the sounder Kantian in advising his son to stop thinking about the nature of 'things-in-themselves', 'for Time and Space are a part of you and you cannot do without them.' This counsel may have been taken to heart. At any rate, a paper read to the Jowett Society and dated 1901 (though the date is queried in Temple's own hand) shows a sober appreciation of the limitations of 'Abstract Speculation'. He quotes a verse of Ecclesiastes as an epitome of Kant's philosophy: 'I have seen the travail which God hath given to the sons of men ... he hath set eternity in their hearts, yet so that man cannot find out the work that God hath done from the beginning even to the end.'

Nevertheless, up to the very last phase of Temple's philosophical work this cautious mood is recessive. In the papers written during his Oxford time the dominant temper is that of speculative idealism, reinforced by his studies in Plato. Thus in *The Province of Science* (a paper read to a College Society before he took

Greats) he starts from the assumption that the explanation of the world must be consonant with the demands of mind, and since mind is not only cognitive, but also moral and purposive, 'the explanation must ultimately be not logical only but moral also. ... The mind is not only logical, but also moral, and will not be content with an account of the world which does not demonstrate its morality.'

This was the position at which he had already arrived in his early years at Oxford, and it is the essential thesis of his first solid book, *Mens Creatrix*, published in 1917. He tells us in the Preface that the book was planned in 1908, when he was a junior philosophy don in Oxford, and 'at that time I had the presumption to believe that I was myself destined to be a philosopher'. Life had led him into other paths, and he offers *Mens Creatrix* as 'likely to be my only extensive essay in the sphere which I once hoped would be mine'. In spite of its clarity of style and exposition, *Mens Creatrix* is a curiously disjointed book. It bears the marks of having been largely dictated in odd half-hours (as he tells us was in fact the case). It passes quickly from one large topic to another: from idealist logic to discussions of art, tragedy, ethics, international and social politics, and Christian theology, without the ground gained at each stage being established sufficiently firmly to bear much searching criticism. (There is a long critical notice of the book by A. E. Taylor in *Mind*, N.S., 106.)

But it was not, as he then thought, destined to be his only extensive essay of the kind. In the middle of the even more exacting claims of an Archbishopric he was to achieve the Gifford Lectures, *Nature, Man and God*, and it will be by this work, rather than the earlier essays, that his philosophy will be judged. The Lectures do not merely show that, in spite of the swan song in *Mens Creatrix*, Temple had in fact been able to keep up his interest and reading in philosophy: they are also a carefully planned piece of work, and though we may feel that the argument has not been subjected to the constant scrutiny for which we look in a writer to whom philosophy has been a primary vocation, nevertheless the achievement proves that Temple's early love was too strong and persistent to be stifled by the demands of high office, and also that he must have had considerable power of doing sustained thinking in the intervals of other claims. That he could do so was partly, no doubt, due to his extraordinarily retentive memory, but also I suspect that he must have been the possessor of a singularly well-ordered and well-behaved subconscious mind, in which there was no waste of energy and which threw up not merely uncoordinated intuitions, but well-formulated ideas consonant with his conscious beliefs and purposes. Hence his writing gives us the impression that he is never thinking just with the top part of his mind, but reacting with the whole of a balanced and well-integrated personality. But we also get the impression that he is never very seriously puzzled.

The key to this unified thinking is undoubtedly to be found in Temple's single-minded faith in God. He always knew that this was his starting-point, and he also knew too much about metaphysics, a way of thinking whose standards are exacting and where proof is perhaps impossible, to represent this faith as the demonstrated conclusion of a philosophical argument. We know the type of book of apologetics which claims to start from scratch, without any presuppositions, and arrives by the last chapter at all the articles of the Christian Faith, leaving us with an uneasy feeling that there have been jumps somewhere. Temple's apologetics were not of that kind. He recognized that the real rub in the relation between philosophy and faith lies not so much in the compatibility or incompatibility of their conclusions as in the reconciliation of two very different attitudes of mind. For, as he wrote in the second chapter (in Part I) of the Gifford Lectures—the whole chapter contains a discerning statement of this problem—'the primary assurances of religion are the ultimate questions of philosophy'. How can one debate with critical impartiality the existence of a Being to whom one is utterly surrendered? So he was as unwilling to press critical philosophy into the service of being a handmaid to theology as he was to identify religious faith with certain debatable philosophical views.

He had already arrived at this way of seeing the difference of method when he wrote *Christus Veritas*. 'Theology', he wrote in the Preface to that work, 'accepts [its doctrines] from Religion, and shows them to be probable by exhibiting them as the springs of a conception of Reality which, when reached, commends itself as the most satisfying conception which is in fact available. The method of Theology is thus precarious, and is only justified by the result; in the result it is justified, and that on grounds acceptable to Philosophy. The method of Philosophy is secure, but its result comparatively barren. One day, perhaps, the two will perfectly coincide; but that day is not yet; both philosophers and theologians are concerned to hasten it, but meanwhile the motto of Theology must be *Credo ut intelligam*.' To which he adds in the second chapter of *Nature, Man and God* that both Philosophy and Theology should observe the motto of the Platonic justice: 'To mind one's own business. . . . But let no one think that this principle is as easy to practise as it is to enunciate.'

Temple therefore does not claim that his own conclusions are based simply on argument. He claims to present a *theological* philosophy, i.e. one which, starting from the presupposition of faith in God as holy and righteous Will, seeks to show that *if you have this faith*, the facts of experience can be made more intelligible in the light of it than in the light of any other world view. This is quite different from saying that this faith is reached inferentially from studying the facts of the world and experience. *Credo ut intelligam*. But Temple does not think this *Credo* need be a blind irrational leap. He sees it as supported by the convergence of three distinct lines of approach: (i) a general philosophical argument, (ii) religious experience, (iii) the testimony of Christian tradition. In the Gifford Lectures he is naturally concerned chiefly with the first.

The foundations of his philosophical argument had been laid down in *Mens Creatrix*. There Temple had given a description of the principles underlying mind's different interests and activities, logical, moral, and aesthetic, seeking to show how these can be integrated in a unifying principle. Working in this way, the mind following out 'the principles of its own procedure', we are led, Temple holds, to a view of the Absolute as a 'Commonwealth of Value', that is, a society of finite minds each finding its purpose in realizing the different facets of Value made possible by the informing order of the system as a whole. Such a metaphysics bears some resemblance to that of Bosanquet, to whom Temple often acknowledges his indebtedness. He tells us indeed that 'at one time my main concern was to discover what was my point of divergence from one who carried me so far with him'. The point of divergence came with Temple's theism. He did not fall into the trap of identifying this kind of metaphysical absolutism with the spiritual philosophy of Christian theism. Such an absolutism leads us in the end to an immanent and impersonal order, which is the logical ground of values realized in finite centres of experience. And at the time when he wrote *Mens Creatrix* Temple maintained: 'From the standpoint of the Will to Know we can demand no more. The intellect *working only upon the principles of its own procedure* will never lead to the Transcendent God of Religion, for its claims can be satisfied with less, and the further step is a leap in the dark such as Science may not take.' Nevertheless, though the bare claims of intellect need not and in Temple's view should not ask more than that the universe should be informed by a coherent order, we may want to go on and ask why such an order should exist at all. We may ask the more boldly if 'within the Whole as the intellect apprehends it there are elements favourable to an expansion of our conception though they cannot be said to demand it'. These elements are drawn from moral and aesthetic experience, where mind is purposive, and where the will to achieve Good is taken as a sufficient explanation of why anything should be brought about. 'Mind does accept as final an explanation in terms of Purpose and Will; for this (and, so far as our experience goes, this alone) combines efficient and final causation. "Why is this canvas covered with paint?" "Because I painted it." "Why did you do that?" "Because I hoped to create a thing of beauty for the delight of myself and others."' If, then, we can show grounds for saying that the world as a whole is the result of a purpose to achieve Good, that will be the kind of explanation which will satisfy our minds, whereas an immanent system of order might simply be an ultimate fact, to be accepted as such without further explanation. This becomes the dominant theme of the Gifford Lectures, where we find a much more elaborate working out of the contention that any explanation of the world which is to be satisfying to our minds must be in terms of a Purpose to which mind assents, together with 'the thought of a Mind which in a perfect intuition grasps that very process which as Will it is engaged in working out'. Such a metaphysics obviously has one root in the Platonic philosophy, always a dominant influence in the back of Temple's mind. (He has told us that the three continuously formative influences on his mind were Plato, S. John, and Robert Browning.) Plato tells us that in the last resort things happen because of the Idea of the Good. But with the emphasis on the purposive character of 'a Will to achieve Good' we pass beyond Platonism and over the dividing-line between metaphysical absolutism and Christian theism. Moreover, the contention in *Mens Creatrix* that in itself the intellect might be satisfied by coherent order is here dropped.

Does Temple assume too easily the unique explanatory value of the category of Purpose when it is applied not only to certain kinds of activity within the world, but to the world as a whole? And does he tend to assume that, if an explanation in terms of Purpose would satisfy our minds, then such an explanation there must be? In his earlier work he does often seem to be saying just this. But increasingly in his later work he puts forward the idea of a Divine Purpose for Good as a venture of faith, supported though not demonstrated by reason and experience. In *Nature, Man and God* in particular Temple shows much more readiness than in his early work to recognize that the fact that the intellect makes a demand is not in itself sufficient evidence that the universe is such as to satisfy that demand. His trend of thought is thus away from idealism towards a more empirical view of the emergence of mind in nature, which he calls 'dialectical realism'. But I doubt whether his conversion to 'realism' went very deep. He was trained in a different school, and owed little or nothing to the modern epistemological realisms. The name was obviously chosen with an eye to the Marxists. Their philosophy of 'dialectical materialism' has, Temple says, so strong an appeal to the minds of many of our contemporaries 'that only a Dialectic more comprehensive in its range of apprehension and more thorough in its appreciation of the inter-play of factors in the real world can overthrow it, or seriously modify it as a guide to action'. Temple's 'dialectical realism' describes the world as consisting of different levels, of which we can discern those we call Matter, Life, Mind, and Spirit. Each of these presupposes the levels lower than itself, and each finds its full actualization only when it is possessed or indwelt by the level above it. Such a way of looking at the world has obvious affinities with some aspects of the philosophies of Alexander and of Whitehead. When such very different lines of thought converge on a generalization of this kind, we can be the more confident in believing that something like it can stand.

It is implicit in this view that we can only believe in the supremacy of Spirit if we also believe in the reality of the Matter which it informs. Temple insists that this is sound Christian philosophy; he often observes that Christianity is the most materialist of all the great religions. Since, however, he contends that the process which gives rise to minds can only be explained if it is seen as itself the product of Mind, 'the Materialism of our empirical starting-point is balanced by the uncompromising Theism of our conclusion'. But whereas in his earlier statements 'explanation' was sought in the cognitive demands of Mind *qua* knowing subject, such an idealism is here repudiated, and the emphasis is laid on the *volitional* character of the Divine Mind as the ultimate explanatory factor within each situation. This belief in the Transcendent Will for Good as the final level of reality, all other levels existing ultimately as media for its expression, does of course distinguish Temple's view from that of Whitehead, to whom in certain other respects he acknowledges warm indebtedness. Whitehead leads us finally to the conception of a logical-aesthetic order, and Temple is, I think, justified in his criticism that much of the quasi-personalist language which Whitehead uses about this at the end of his *Process and Reality* goes beyond what is warranted by his own theory. Temple met Whitehead while on a visit to Harvard shortly after the publication of *Nature, Man and God*. They evidently met with great mutual appreciation, Whitehead greeting Temple with, 'Your reasons for disagreeing with me are precisely my reasons for disagreeing with you, so I take it we are really agreed.' Temple quoted this remark with obvious relish on his return.

Temple's argument for the supremacy of Purposive Mind in the universe is supported in part by his belief in the kinship of mind as we know it with reality. By 'kinship' he says he means 'an experience which has two aspects: first, that [mind] finds the counterpart of the principle of its own activities as for example the mathematical properties of mechanical combinations of forces or of aesthetic proportions; secondly, that with this discovery goes a feeling of being at home with the object.' A theism referring to such experience must obviously come to terms with the problem of evil. This he had grappled with in *Mens Creatrix*, and for all the idealism of that book, he refused from the start to represent evil as an apparent discord in a Whole which, if seen as a Whole, would be found to be harmonious. He presents evil as a real discord which is only justifiable when it has been overcome, and when greater resources of good have been called out to meet it. If this can happen, the past is not strictly unalterable, since the value of an act in the past may be altered by what is made of it by the resources of good. 'Fact' he refuses to divorce from 'Value'. The reality of anything, he says, must include its value as well as the mere fact of its occurrence. Thus, he says, in itself the Crucifixion was the worst possible event; in the light of its value for the world it was the best possible. Here we have the *O felix culpa!* argument, but handled soberly, and with an appreciation of tragedy. Evil, therefore, must be held not to be directly willed by God, but to fall within the Divine Purpose, both because it is an occasion for evoking greater resources of good, and because God produced in man a being who sins, not perhaps inevitably, but with an overwhelming degree of probability. Presumably God knew that this would be the case, and knew what He was about in so creating him. Here Temple gives us what has been described as a theory of a 'Fall upwards'. As a result of his emergence as a self-conscious individual, a man, if not necessarily yet with overwhelming probability, will see things from the centre of his own mind, and as related to his own good. Since such self-centred thinking and acting is characteristic of other men too, the world becomes cumulatively a maze of conflicts and cross-purposes. The only solution is that a man may be drawn away from his self-centredness to devotion to good other than his own apparent good. This cannot be completely achieved by his own efforts after disinterestedness. For, as S. Augustine pointed out, if we will to will the Good, there is already a conflict within our will, and we cannot be willing the Good with an undivided will. The solution of self-centredness can fully come, Temple says, only if there can be a revelation of Love sufficient to call out a man's whole response of devotion. Natural Theology can only point to this need, the satisfaction of which would answer its own problem; for the claim that the need has been met we must turn, he says, from Natural Theology to Revealed Religion.

The distinction between natural and revealed religion bore a generally accepted meaning when Lord Gifford drew up the terms of his lecture. It consisted in the distinction between arguments based on a general appeal to reason, and arguments based on appeals to formularies or the writings of Scripture as finally authoritative. Lord Gifford wrote: 'I wish the Lecturers to treat their subject as a strictly natural science . . . without reference to or reliance upon any supposed special, exceptional or so-called miraculous revelation.' Put in these terms, the distinction has seemed to most recent lecturers on the Gifford Trust unduly to narrow the scope of natural theology. They have, therefore, felt themselves called on to show in what sense the subject-matter and method of their discussions could properly be described as 'natural theology'. Perhaps the most ingenious attempt in this respect was Karl Barth's, in bringing his lectures under the wing of natural theology by saying that, to understand what it is, it is necessary to understand its antithesis. He therefore proposed to exhibit the antithesis of natural theology in a wholehearted exposition of the content of Reformation dogmatic theology.

Temple seems to interpret the limitations imposed by the Trust to mean that 'reliance on' any alleged revelation is excluded as *argument*, though not necessarily that 'reference to' its possibility, or even probability, is not open to examination. But I cannot help feeling that his anxiety continually to remind himself and his readers that he is lecturing on 'natural theology' has in some ways hampered him in the wholehearted carrying out of what he described in the Preface as his endeavour 'to provide a coherent articulation of an experience which has found some measure of co-ordination through adherence to certain principles'. It has also prevented him from holding consistently to the distinction which he had drawn between the methods of 'theological' and 'critical' philosophy. The difficulties I feel about his actual execution are exactly stated in a letter from Dr. Emil Brunner, found in Temple's own copy of *Nature, Man and God*. I am glad to quote (in translation) some sentences of Dr. Brunner's letter:

> Your conception of natural theology does not seem to me a consistent one. *On the one hand*, it approaches what I would call Christian Philosophy—thought which does indeed start from the Christian faith, but which is abstracted from it in the actual process of development and presentation; the Christian faith itself, however, determines the course of thought, performing, we might say, a regulative rather than a constructive function.

> *On the other hand*, it seems also intended as true natural theology, by which I mean a kind of thought which does not even allow the Christian faith a regulative influence on the thought process, but which comes down simply and solely on the side of that power of logical argument which is at anyone's disposal, and of the facts, which are accessible to anyone.

> *Thirdly*, you understand by natural theology thought which includes in its scope the facts of religion, and therefore also of Christianity as well, and which consequently, as embracing Christianity, seems to be striving towards a kind of synthesis of Christian faith with reason. So, for instance, your conception of religion is determined *a priori* by Christian faith, and is deduced from it; the same applies to your concepts of sin, love, personality, etc. This means, however, that in these passages your natural theology is natural only in appearance, whilst it

is in truth Christian. In the third and final part of your book, your expositions are substantially, even predominantly, nothing more nor less than Christian dogmatics, even though the difference in method is repeatedly stressed.

That Temple was never really clear about what he understood by natural theology is to be regretted the more in that he himself expresses a most valuable view of the nature of 'revealed theology'. He holds that the fatal mistake in much of Christian history has been to look on 'revelation' as though it were given in the form of *propositions*, to be held as 'revealed truths'. Rather we should speak of 'truths of revelation', that is to say, propositions which seek to express more or less adequately 'truths about revelation'. Revelation, he says, is to be found in the coincidence of divinely guided *events* with divinely enlightened appreciation. The propositions in which minds then seek to express and interpret their belief in the significance of such events are never themselves the matter of revelation. They are attempts to point to the underlying events in which those who formulated them believed that revelation had been given. There are, of course, still difficulties in this view. How is 'revelation' to be distinguished, if at all, from the prophetic consciousness? Claims to have received revelation are found in different religious traditions; is there any criterion by which they can be judged? If the vehicle of revelation is events, how do we relate their doctrinal interpretation to empirical attempts to determine what the actual historical events were? If Temple has not really answered these questions, neither has any other philosophical theologian to my knowledge. Nevertheless, his work has surely been of real help in breaking unequivocally with the conception that revelation is contained in a set of absolute propositions. He has put the view of 'revelation in events' with a clarity which has caused it to make its mark in contemporary theology. But if questioned, he would no doubt have been the first to say that he owed this way of looking at it to that great teacher Father Herbert Kelly, S.S.M., to whom he often acknowledged his general indebtedness. Father Kelly once put (in a letter to myself) the allied point concerning the difference between faith in propositions and faith in that to which they refer in his own characteristic way:

The holy *Bradshaw* teaches (p. 80) that 'the first train for Sebastopol starts from Newport (Mon.) at 4.55'. If I go to catch it, that is, so far, *faith in Bradshaw*, but that is secondary. My basic faith is in the *train* and the railway system to which I surrender myself that *these* (not *Bradshaw*) will carry me there. This is sound theology.

But when asked whether the criticism of 'revelation in propositions' was not part of his influence on Temple, Father Kelly says he gives the credit 'to the greater portion of Christian history'. He holds that the tendency to look on the sacred books as strings of authoritative statements only came in with the growth of legalistic interests in the Western Church. On this question I can only defer to the Church historian. (But I find that Temple has been challenged concerning his interpretation of S. Thomas's teaching on this very point by Father Victor White, O.P., in *Blackfriars* of March 1944, where Father White comments on a notable address on *Thomism and Modern Needs*, given by Temple to the Aquinas Society of London in October 1943, and printed in the same number.)

The question of the possibility of what is sometimes called 'particular', as distinguished from 'general', revelation is discussed by Temple with refreshing freedom from the conventional presuppositions often held by those who disbelieve as well as by those who believe in such revelations. It was a matter central to his earliest interests in philosophical theology. In the passage from which we have already quoted in the Preface to *Christus Veritas*, he had written of the dominant philosophy of his contemporaries at Oxford that 'the idea of God which it reaches is such as to preclude His ever doing anything in particular in any other sense than that in which He does everything in general'. Temple's own answer concerning the possibility of 'particular revelation', and the allied question of the possibility of miracles, follows from his taking seriously the idea of the Mind and Purpose of God as *personal*. To act always by unalterable rules is not, he says, characteristic of personal mind and wisdom; rather, it is characteristic of woodenness. The characteristic of personal mind and wisdom is to maintain its constancy of purpose by adapting its mode of activity as best may meet the situation set by circumstances as they arise. This sentence, as I have written it, is not perhaps the best way of expressing Temple's view. It is rather suggestive of British military strategy in the first years of the late war, in which the initiative seemed always to be with the other side, and we modified our plans in a brilliant series of strategic withdrawals, interspersed with occasional counter-attacks. Of course, Temple means that the initiative throughout lies with the Divine Purpose, but that it is manifested through a general or exceptional mode of activity as its wisdom may decree.

Hence the distinction of the natural and the miraculous is as such untenable. The religious man 'must not postulate reserves of energy or power which may break in upon the ordinary course of events from without but must recognize that the normal constancy of nature expresses the will of God no less truly than the occasional variation, and that the explanation of what he calls a miracle is exactly the same as the ultimate explanation of the most commonplace event'. Yet this does not mean that all events are equally revelatory of the divine character. Temple illustrates how this distinction might be conceived by analogy with the way in which a man's character may be revealed in some of his actions rather than in others: 'The attempt to interest a company by the story of how the great Duke of Wellington used to eat figs was a failure: "It turned out to be the ordinary way, quadrisection down the stalk and then four licks." There are, however, events which show that the Duke could react to circumstances by methods not at all familiar, such as the tactics of Salamanca or the carrying of Catholic Emancipation; and it is these which reveal the real man. ... So it may be with God Himself. The routine of nature manifests His Will; but there may come occasions where action of a special and specially characteristic quality is required and the action so taken may be in an especial degree revealing; such acts are commonly called miracles.'

I cannot myself see that, granted a strong belief such as

Temple's in the *personal* character of the Divine Purpose, there is anything with which anyone could quarrel in principle in such a view of miracles in so far as *ultimate* explanations are concerned. There remains, however, the problem that in appealing to 'miracle' the theologian challenges the scientist and historian, if he claims that *proximate* explanation cannot be found in other causes. Moreover, difficulties in accepting particular alleged miracles follow not so much from theological or philosophical principle as from critical questions concerning the historical evidence and the psychological atmosphere of the societies in which such miracles are said to have happened. Having regard to the prevalence among mankind of what Bergson calls *la fonction fabulatrice*, as illustrated by the growth of legend, such difficulties are very real. But this kind of empirical question was not, it seems, of primary interest to Temple. His interest lay rather in general questions concerning principle. His courageous handling in this instance shows how the whole meaning of the category of the 'miraculous' calls for thorough philosophical examination, which should be undertaken in conjunction with a re-examination of what is meant by 'laws of nature'. Temple would hardly have undertaken the latter part of this task. He shows very little interest in theories of natural science, and is content simply to refer to the 'scientific view of the world' as dominated by the conception of 'monotonous uniformity'. Nor, I think, had he very much interest in the empirical methods of natural science.

But Temple's human interests were wide and generous, and it is especially in their bearing on these that his philosophical writings stand as an impressive exposition of a reasonable faith. The key throughout is his firm belief in the Divine Purpose for Good, as realized in the relations of persons with the Absolute Person and with one another. His insight into what this should imply is the source of his carefully balanced discussions of practical ethics. The strength of these lies in the way in which he never loses sight of the fact that problems of ethics arise within a context of personal relationships. Their weakness, in my judgement, is that they tend to give too exclusively personalist an interpretation to moral obligations. Is it really true that all obligations are social obligations, and therefore that (as he writes in *Mens Creatrix*) 'The Atheistic Debauchee upon a Desert Island is not liable to moral censure'? (It is admitted that he may be called foolish.) Are there no intrinsic goods which we may have a duty to realize besides those found in personal relationships? Nor can I see that Temple's statement that that action is right which tends to increase the total volume of love can really serve as an ethical criterion. In *Nature, Man and God* this is put more soberly in terms of what may be described as an Ideal Utilitarianism. The right act is that which will promote most good on the whole ('Good' being ultimately described in terms of love and trust between persons). But it seems to me that in some of his occasional pronouncements on ethical questions during the last years, Temple showed that he saw that such a directly personalist ethics could be misleading, and in particular could fail to meet the problems set by the relations between organized groups, unless it could take up into itself a true appreciation of the nature of justice. Writing in the *Christian News-Letter* of 29 December 1943, on 'What Christians Stand for in the Secular World', he says: 'We need a clearer and deeper understanding of the difference between justice, human love and Christian charity. The last transcends both justice and human fellowship while it has contacts with each. Associations cannot love one another; a trade union cannot love an employers' federation, nor can one national State love another. The members of one may love the members of the other so far as opportunities of intercourse allow. That will help in negotiations; but it will not solve the problem of the relations between the two groups. Consequently, the relevance of Christianity in these spheres is quite different from what many Christians suppose it to be. Christian charity manifests itself in the temporal order as a supranatural discernment of, and adhesion to, *justice* in relation to the equilibrium of power. It is precisely fellowship or human love, with which too often Christian charity is mistakenly equated, that is *not* seriously relevant in that sphere.' I take it that Temple means that charity is like justice, in being a *universal* goodwill which sees each individual in his relations with others, 'without respect of persons', and can therefore take up into itself the impartial and impersonal elements in obligation. But it never forgets that justice is to be sought within an order which is a community of persons.

So we come back to Temple's earliest description of the way in which he saw the final reality of the world: the conception of a Society of Spirits as a Commonwealth of Value. But this is not now put forward as a description of the already existing composition of a metaphysical absolute; rather, it is seen as a dynamic process in the realization of which we can be caught up. This ethical religious faith was the aspect of his philosophy with which Temple was able to inspire people's imagination, and it was the secret of his moral leadership. It would surely stand even if a good deal of his systematic metaphysics were to be re-thought. The link may be found in his original view of evil, a view in which he had come to see a greater significance. If an event or action is to be held to consist in 'the whole difference it makes', the past is not strictly unalterable. The 'value' of the past is part of the 'reality' of the past, and that ultimately depends on what can be wrought out of it by the active power of good.

Temple himself recognized towards the end that a change of emphasis was taking place in his metaphysical outlook. He indicated it in an article in *Theology* (November 1939), and described it to me in a letter of 16 July 1942. Since this letter contains a most clear and succinct statement of the direction in which his mind was moving in the last years, I venture to quote from it at length:

> The particular modification (in my thinking) to which I am feeling driven is not substantial, though I think it is very important. It is a much clearer perception of what is worked out in the Gifford Lectures about process and value. What we must completely get away from is the notion that the world as it now exists is a rational whole; we must think of its unity not by the analogy of a picture, of which all the parts exist at once, but by the analogy of a drama where, if it is good enough, the full meaning of the first scene only becomes apparent with the final curtain; and we are in the middle of this. Consequently

537

the world as we see it is strictly unintelligible. We can only have faith that it will become intelligible when the divine purpose, which is the explanation of it, is accomplished.

Theologically, this is a greater emphasis on eschatology. Another way to put it is that the *Logos* is not to be conceived as a static principle of rational unity, but as an active force of moral judgment which calls upon us to be its fellow-workers and agents. So that we ourselves, by our moral endeavour, are positively bringing into existence that which alone renders rational and intelligible our experience of to-day—though of course our contribution to this is so small that for practical purposes the vital matter is rather assurance of what the Word of God is accomplishing than of any contribution we make; and anyhow we only contribute at all so far as the Word of God dominates us.

All this is really there in the Gifford Lectures, but I don't think the total presentation in that book or in *Christus Veritas* sufficiently gives this impression of a dynamic process and leaves too much that of a static system.

Thus, if it be claimed that a Christian philosophy 'makes sense' of the world, we should need to underline *makes*. We should not use the phrase to mean 'shows that as it stands the world *is* sense'. This may seem a long journey from the metaphysical ambitions of Temple's Oxford days. But the traveller's perception has surely gained in depth. Nor would it be true to represent this last phase as a surrender to Pragmatism. The light given to our minds may not give us a 'total explanation', or 'map of the world'; it may nevertheless help us to see in their true character certain features of the landscape through which we must pass. I should like to end by referring to a passage from the *Readings from St. John*, a book in which Temple takes us into his confidence in the personal religion within which his philosophy was enfolded. He is commenting on S. John 1. 5, 'The light shineth in the darkness, and the darkness did not absorb it': 'Imagine yourself standing on some headland in a dark night. At the foot of the headland is a lighthouse or beacon, not casting rays on every side, but throwing one bar of light through the darkness. It is some such image that St. John had before his mind. The divine light shines through the darkness of the world, cleaving it, but neither dispelling it nor quenched by it. . . . Take any moment of history and you find light piercing unillumined darkness—now with reference to one phase of the purpose of God, now another. The company of those who stand in the beam of the light by which the path of true progress for that time is discerned is always small. Remember Wilberforce and the early Abolitionists; remember the twelve Apostles and the company gathered round them. What is seen conspicuously in these two examples is always true; and as we think of the spiritual progress of the race this truth finds a fresh illustration. As we look forwards, we peer into darkness, and none can say with certainty what course the true progress of the future should follow. But as we look back, the truth is marked by beacon-lights, which are the lives of saints and pioneers; and these in their turn are not originators of light, but rather reflectors which give light to us, because themselves they are turned to the source of light. . . . To [St. John's] deep spiritual insight it is apparent that the redemption of man is part, even if the crowning part, of a greater thing—the redemption, or conquest, of the universe. Till that be accomplished the darkness abides, pierced but unillumined by the beam of divine light. And the one great question for everyone is whether he will "walk in darkness" or "walk in light".'

XXIX

The Christian Leader in War-time

But as the fact that we are right now does not obliterate our past sin, so our past sin in no way alters the fact that we are right now. No positive good can be done by force; that is true. But evil can be checked and held back by force, and it is precisely for this that we may be called upon to use it. If it be so, let us do it in calm but unshakable resolution, trying, in spite of all the agony, to bear no ill-will to those whom we must resist, seeking to inflict no more suffering than is inevitably involved in the resistance that we must offer, bearing with patient courage the suffering that comes to ourselves. And while we do our utmost to secure the triumph of right as it has been given us to see the right, let us steadily look beyond the conflict to the restoration of peace, and dedicate ourselves to the creation of a world-order which shall be fair to the generations yet unborn.

W.T., in a broadcast address, August 1939.

FROM the day of his first broadcast after the outbreak of war, on 3 October 1939, Temple became a national leader who through the five years that followed spoke for the conscience of Britain. The broadcast was, as even his keenest critics admitted, in every way a memorable utterance. After contrasting the spirit with which the country had entered the war of 1914—when 'what had to be done appeared as a painful and vexatious interruption of a manner of life which it was hoped that we might resume before long'—with the 'deep determination, accompanied by no sort of exhilaration, but by a profound sadness' in the hearts of his fellow countrymen in September 1939, he went on:

We enter the war as a dedicated nation; and it is this fact which has called forth the response of the younger generation in so marvellous a manner. . . . The prevailing conviction is that Nazi tyranny and oppression are destroying the traditional excellencies of European civilization and must be eliminated for the good of mankind. Over against the deified nation of the Nazis our people have taken their stand as a dedicated nation.

The address (which was later printed in *Thoughts in War-time*) was at once relayed throughout the Dominions, and when Temple took the chair at a National Society Conference on the next day

Sankey opened the proceedings by saying: 'Before even the Minutes are read, I want in the name of all here—and I believe of all Englishmen—to thank our chairman for his broadcast last night.'

At the outset Temple laid down for himself one standard—only for the *Christian* conscience could he or would he speak. At the end of five years his rule remained unbroken; in no single utterance can it be said that he allowed himself to sink below the high level of his own faith and practice. All the more for this reason he found himself called to vindicate the character of God and to justify the taking up of arms in the name of the Prince of Peace. He became involved in all the old questions he had answered a quarter of a century before from the pulpit of S. James's, Piccadilly; but now they were being asked not, as then, in a regretful whisper but with defiance and distress. From the mass of his letters, sermons, and speeches of five years, some extracts will show why, and how, as a Christian leader he believed that the Second World War should be waged.

Doubts and Scruples

Again, as in 1914, he proclaimed that the war was a 'divine judgment' and again, as then, men retorted that they could not believe in a god whose conception of punishment seemed to be so utterly disproportionate to the offence. Again Temple made the same answer, that so long as men could not dissociate their thinking from the tendency of the Hebrew mind to take no account of secondary causes, so long would they misunderstand the meaning of the words. Early in the war he wrote:

Apparently this language suggests to some people the notion that 'God sent the war'; and they refuse to believe this. Of course, they are quite right if they are rejecting the notion that God decided abruptly that Europe had become too bad to be borne with any longer, and by a momentary act of will let loose a war. But it is a terrible mistake to suppose that God's judgment is to be seen only in events which are due to His direct intervention.

Alike in the Old Testament and in the New we are taught to

541

trace God's judgment in the working-out of those laws of cause and effect in the moral world which are a part of creation as God has ordered it. As in the physical realm so in the moral realm, causes produce their effects. The law of gravitation does not control your will; you need not walk over the edge of the precipice; but if you do, you will fall to the bottom. So, too, you need not conduct your life on selfish principles; but if you do, you involve yourself and all others whom you affect in catastrophe. 'Whatsoever a man soweth, that shall he also reap.'

Now, when by the operation of the law of God calamity comes upon us as a consequence of our neglect or defiance of His will, it is evident that this is properly called the judgment of God.

Most of Temple's correspondents were less concerned with intellectual difficulties than with the practical obligations of a Christian citizen in war-time. Prominent among these were the pacifists—more numerous, better organized, and on the whole more intelligent, than in the first World War. Their outlook and Temple's were both so clearly defined that the difference could never be resolved. The pacifist syllogism (if it can be stated so baldly) ran—It is not right for a Christian to do anything that is contrary to the mind of Christ: War is, by the consent of all Christians, contrary to the mind of Christ: Therefore, it is not right for a Christian to take part in war. For Temple this was altogether too simple a reading of an extremely complex situation —had it not been said that 'Logic is the enemy of truth'? He replied that in a fallen world the rightness of most acts is relative: 'to kill is right, if at all, relatively and not absolutely; that is, it can only be right in special circumstances. But in those circumstances it is absolutely right.' He expanded this in a letter to a young friend in November 1939:

I am glad you thought my letter some use. When I say that in the circumstances killing is right, I am not denying that it is sinful; but we are in a position, as indeed we frequently are in other relations, where the choice is between two evils. Every available course is in this sense sinful that it belongs to an order of things which has departed from the rule of God, or in other words, you have moved from the absolute to the relative realm; and then the important principle comes in that relative terms are within their relations absolute. . . . So we are involved in an entanglement due to the sin of mankind, including our own, in which the best thing we can do is still a bad thing. None the less it is right to do it, because it is the best possible. And so we have got to do it and be penitent while we do it. That is the only hope I see of both resisting injustice and securing that justice comes out of it. Where the method of redemptive suffering is possible and the people concerned are capable of rising to it, it is no doubt the best of all; but there is no way that I can see in which we could redemptively suffer so as to change the heart of Germany and deliver Poles and Czechs; and if there is, our country is not yet anything like prepared to do it. So once again we have to do the best we can, being what we are, in the circumstances where we are—and then God be merciful to us sinners!

While disagreeing strongly with their outlook, Temple treated pacifists with unfailing consideration. Conscientious objectors knew that in the Archbishop they had a champion who would combat any attempt to restore the odious 'cat and mouse' treatment of them which had disfigured the administration in the first World War; Temple was involved in long and tedious correspondence over some of the cases, and occasionally his protests were effective. Moreover, he understood the pacifist point of view and declared openly that its adherents might be fulfilling a vocation to which God had called them by refusing to fight and so showing to the world their faith in the supremacy of love. This was recognized by a leading pacifist, the Archdeacon of Stoke:

I can say with certainty that although he was in my judgement the strongest theological opponent of pacifism he was tremendously loved and respected in pacifist circles; and no one welcomed his appointment at Lambeth with more enthusiasm than we did. For one thing we always felt that his criticisms were fair because he was careful to find out what we did believe before he began to criticize—which was by no means true of all our critics.

To another Temple wrote:

... Though you cannot advance the Kingdom of God by fighting you can prevent Christian civilization, or a civilization on the way to becoming Christian, from being destroyed and that is what we are now engaged in. If you look at the New Testament carefully there can be no doubt that there is a theology of the State as well as of the Church, and that it is our duty to do as citizens in support of the State things which it would be inappropriate to do as Churchmen in support of the Church and its cause. The soldiers are therefore quite right when they say that war is not Christianity, but they would be quite wrong if they went on to say that therefore Christians ought not to fight. The duty to fight is a civic duty which, if the cause is good, Christianity accepts and approves, but it is not a duty which has its origin in Christianity as such.

The most tiresome of his correspondents were of the 'kid-glove' school of warfare. Constant protests reached Temple against one particular form of fighting and bombing or another, and these outbursts were specially vigorous after the bombing of the Ruhr dams. The following letter—with more than a suggestion of Lincoln both in the matter and manner of it—was sent to one protester, after the Archbishop had had some correspondence with the Secretary of State for Air:

> Lambeth Palace,
> S.E. 1.
> 24th May 1943.

Dear Madam,

I am afraid this letter will not bring you any comfort. The decision whether or not to go to war or to support a country in war is a desperately serious one, but whichever way it is answered, the answer must be regarded as carrying with it the full consequence. If we answered 'No', we ought to have been naturally ready for the establishment of the Nazi régime, Gestapo and all the rest of it, in England rather than fight. If we

At a War-time Service at the British Thomson-Houston Company's works at Rugby, 14 June 1942

answer 'Yes', we must also be ready for what is required in order to defeat the enemy other than the infliction of useless suffering. I think there is no doubt that the bombing of the Ruhr dams was a perfectly legitimate act of war. There is a great deal to be said for refusing to fight, though I think myself that in this case it would be the shirking of duty. There is still more I think to be said for fighting in support of freedom and justice, but there is nothing whatever to be said for fighting ineffectively.

One would look in vain for some common formula in these letters: each was intensely personal. The sentiments might be the same, but Temple's expression of them varied with the particular needs—and, it seems, with the tone and temper—of his correspondents. A few of them were almost brusque:

I am grateful for your letter and enclosure. It leaves me quite in the dark what the psychological cure to the situation may be, but if the psychologists know of one, they certainly ought to produce it.

. . . It seems to me that in the phase the war has now reached [June 1942] to object to the blockade on the ground presumably of the suffering that it will cause is stark materialism. The issue at stake for the future of the world is something vastly bigger than this.

But most of his replies—especially those dealing with the consciences of young men—show the tenderness of Temple's humanity, tempered by a firm grasp of what he held to be Christian principles. He writes to an engine-driver on the L.N.E.R. whose son is in the R.A.F.:

If you would like to put me in touch with your son, I should be very glad to see if I could help him in any way. It is evident that a clean choice has to be made whether he thinks it can ever be right to fight or not. If it is right, as I believe, then it is also our duty to fight effectively. But the other is the big question: Can it for a Christian be right or compatible with his religion? If it is true that your son is really troubled about this and thought that I could help him, I should be most happy. Of course I take my start from the principle common to us both, that we must at all costs follow our Lord whatever that involves: His will is alone supreme.

Temple's anger was reserved for those who professed the Christian Faith and yet called for reprisals on Germany, especially when flying bombs began to be launched on England. An Anglican priest incurred this rebuke:

A correspondent has sent me your article 'It is Time for Reprisals', and I feel obliged to express to you the distress and consternation with which I read it. I think its argument quite false and its ethics quite deplorable. . . . The proposal that we should decree that for every civilian life taken here, we would take ten German civilian lives, represents just that descent to the enemy level which we must at all costs avoid if we are to be able to stand for any principles at all in the world of the future. I need not dwell upon this; you must be quite familiar with the point and must have decided to discount it—but I cannot think why!

Bereavement

No one with as many friends as Temple could hope to escape the grief of personal losses in the war. His natural sympathy was offered in full measure to the bereaved, to whom he did not shrink from opening his heart if their loss was also his own. He described as 'numbing' the blow he received on hearing of the death of Stanley Richardson, a young poet whom he came to know well in the early years of the war. To Richardson's mother he wrote:

. . . My affection for him, my admiration both for his gifts and for his single-mindedness, and my hopes for his achievement all steadily increased. He was here for a night exactly a week before his death, and I thought once again how much he had grown in character. Now the hopes—for this world—are cut short. But I dreaded war experience for him because the suffering of others was a torture to him. I can even, a little, give thanks that he is delivered from it. But there will be a big gap in my life till it ends. And for you the aching emptiness must be fearful. God bless you and help you to find in it a real fellowship with our Lord in His agony for us all.

And this, to the father of a naval chaplain who had gone down with his ship:

... The courage of your letter moves me very much. I have no children, but when I read what you say of your own great loss, I get a new understanding of the saying, 'God so loved the world that He gave His only Son'.

But Temple was careful never to allow his expression of sympathy to transgress the truth as he held it. He thought little of the earthly body when the breath had gone from it, or of the place where it had been laid after death. In one letter to his mother, after a visit to Canterbury, he tells her that he did not visit his father's grave in the Cloister Garth because he found himself in closer spiritual communion with him inside the cathedral than at the graveside. He knew that many of those who looked to him for help would be distressed at this attitude and was very gentle in leading them to a more spiritual view of death. The following letter (written during the first World War) shows how he was able to combine the sympathy he felt for a mother who had lost her son with loyalty to his own strongest beliefs:

August 11, 1915.

I feel a wish to write to you after yesterday's service. It is little enough that human words can bring in the way of comfort. And I feel specially unfitted, because I notice that you have, what I have not, a very strong sentiment for the body of any beloved one after the spirit has left it. I have never voluntarily looked at—far less touched—the body of one whom I had loved and who has died. And so I do not enter as some would do into the sorrow which I saw you felt in leaving the grave. A funeral for me is not a parting, but merely the only way open to us of showing honour and love. And I feel that this way of thinking and feeling saves much pain—as well as being, in my judgment, truer to the Christian faith.

Anyhow you will know where to seek comfort for the days that remain to us before we join our friends in the world beyond;

and you will turn your thoughts more and more to that fuller life of richer service, till the memory of this sad week is swallowed up in the joy of faith and the hope of re-union. And for us who have learnt from Christ, there is the perpetual reminder that to share the sorrows of others is the way to conquer our own. Thousands are full of suffering now; in praying for them, and serving them if opportunity comes, we find the alleviation of our unhappiness.

Few of the bereaved whom he knew appear to have sought to communicate (at spiritualistic séances and the like) with those whom they had lost; but in a letter written in 1942 Temple sets out his tentative conclusions on spiritualistic phenomena. It was written to a business man who had consulted the Archbishop (as 'a learned and discreet person') on the 'appearance' of his wife after her death and on some talk the two had had together. The writer was careful to add—'I have never dabbled in spiritualism, know very little about it, and don't like what I know.' Temple answered:

> Old Palace,
> Canterbury,
> Nov: 7, 1942.

I am deeply touched that you should consult me about this experience. I wish I felt more competent to help. I have always thought it a mistake to go into questions connected with spiritualism unless one could do it thoroughly; and for that I have had no time. But of course I have been interested and have reached some conclusions, which have, I regret to know, very inadequate bases. However, here they are:—

(1) I draw a sharp distinction between any experience which, like yours, is unsought, and anything resulting from resort to a medium or deliberate waiting for messages—e.g. by automatic writing; the latter so obviously makes opportunities for the subconscious mind to act;

(2) So far as I have considered psychical phenomena, I know nothing that would persuade me to accept so great a conclusion as survival of death if I did not believe it on other grounds; but

as I do believe it on other grounds I am strongly inclined to interpret some of the phenomena as actual communications;

(3) The evidence for appearances at the moment of death, or in a dream state at later times, of those who were very closely bound by love to the person concerned is stronger than for any other such communication.

With that background of thought I am led by the description of your own experience to believe that it was a perfectly real communion between you and your wife, in which she took the first step by 'coming' to you. It cannot be more than a 'probable' judgment; but the probability seems to me to lie on that side rather than on the side of hallucination. I think therefore that you should think it both possible and even probable that the experience was due to an external cause and that God did thus permit your wife to make known to you her love and (so far as that might be called for) her forgiveness.

But all this rests on (1) faith in God and His care for us, (2) consequent faith in our survival of death and continued fellowship. And this order of priority is very important both for the logic of the belief reached and for the spiritual outlook of anyone who holds it. I was glad to see your phrase about God's permission to your wife to help you, because that shews that the right order of priority is in your mind.

On this point there is no evidence that Temple altered his views during the last two years of his life.

The Armed Forces

But there was a wider field for his sympathy and labour than the hearts and consciences of individuals: as Archbishop of Canterbury he could not evade responsibility for the spiritual oversight of the fighting men, though the more direct supervision was exercised by the Chaplains' Department, with which he was in constant correspondence. He was not blind to certain difficulties in the chaplains' work. They all knew of his understanding regard for them and, of his many acts of thoughtfulness during the war, none was more deeply appreciated than the personal letter he sent in May 1944 to all chaplains in the 21st Army Group. But he received many complaints about the Chaplains' Department and became convinced that there was substance in some of them. In fairness to the Department he reminded himself (and others) of two determining factors in the situation: the first was that very few of the best and strongest of the clergy became army chaplains in peacetime—their thoughts turned more naturally, on ordination, to parish work and to the needs of large cities—so that, on the outbreak of a war and the entry of several hundred clergy into the Forces, some of the leaders in the Chaplains' Department were not men of the calibre to grapple with new and clamant problems of administration in which account had also to be taken of differences of outlook, spiritual sympathy, and pastoral gifts, among the new-comers: there was too much 'room at the top'. The second factor was that the Chaplains' Department was just one cog in an enormous machine, and—as Temple put it—the Army seemed to have 'imposed upon the Chaplains' Department administrative methods which are, one supposes, the best for its own purpose, but tend to be inappropriate in spiritual work. . . . If I want to give advice to a curate, I don't tell the suffragan bishop to tell the archdeacon to tell the rural dean to tell the vicar to tell the curate.' So he unburdened himself in a long letter to an influential friend— Was it true that if a chaplain lodged any complaint he was at once moved on somewhere else? Or that, when chaplains went on refresher courses, the time so spent was counted as part of their leave, while that of other officers who went on courses was not? Did his friend think that clergy preferred the Navy, as the Archbishop had heard, because naval chaplains had no official rank— several generals had told him how much they would like to see the chaplains without rank in the Army? And why could not static troops, e.g. on gun-sites, be under the spiritual care of the parish priest, which would save the chaplains' petrol and time and energy? And so on. . . . And then suddenly in January 1944 there popped up a body with the somewhat alarming title of 'The Interdenominational Advisory Committee on Army Chaplaincy Services'. It did not appear to have met since the outbreak of war, and Temple had never heard of it. Perhaps the Bishop of London would know something? He wrote to Dr. Fisher:

I never knew there was such a Committee. It seems to have doddered on since the last war, until the outbreak of this one, when it fell into complete coma; then suddenly it revived itself . . . in order to discuss the pay of Chaplains as compared with the pay of doctors in the R.A.M.C.! 'Oh Lord, how long?' as the Saints beneath the altar justly wailed!

Dr. Fisher knew no more than the Archbishop. But it did not matter much, as Temple had already decided that he must have some closer personal contact with the Chaplains' Department, and after threshing the matter out at several conferences he appointed Dr. Leslie Owen (who was then Bishop of Jarrow) to be the chief liaison officer between himself and the Services and to undertake the work of 'a kind of Provincial Suffragan' (with the title 'Bishop of Maidstone') in all matters relating to the Forces, which included dealing with the 2,500 men in the Services who had offered themselves for ordination. The arrangement worked well, but Temple wrote to more than one correspondent of his determination to hold a 'thorough enquiry' into the Chaplains' Department as soon after the war as possible.

Much nearer to his heart than this and other problems of administration was his personal touch with men in the Services. Whenever it was possible he delighted to go among them, and one of his visits to the Army deserves special mention for the light it throws on Temple's behaviour when he had committed what some regarded as an unfortunate oversight. In September 1943 he preached at a service held in S. Paul's Cathedral to commemorate the Battle of Britain. On the day after the service a General wrote from the Headquarters of Anti-Aircraft Command, to complain that no mention had been made of the fact that the Army had taken any part in the Battle—nor was the Army even mentioned in the prayers. Temple replied at once:

> Lambeth Palace, S.E. 1.
> 30th September 1943.
>
> My dear General,
>
> I must thank you for the manner in which you have called my attention to a very serious omission for which I should like

to express my deep regret so far as it concerns myself. It is true that in the Sermon I made no attempt to offer anything resembling a complete list of the groups and types who took part in the Battle of Britain. But it is quite plain that if any separate groups were mentioned at all, Anti-Aircraft Command should have been among them.

As regards the Prayers, I have no direct responsibility for I did not compile the Service nor was I consulted about it. It would be contrary to the use of S. Paul's to have held any such consultation. I do not suppose it is in the least worth while for you to mention my expression of regret in any quarter, but perhaps if anyone else were to comment on the omission you would inform them that I most fully acknowledge the fault that was committed and have expressed my deep sorrow that it was so.

The General replied that a letter 'couched in such generous terms' had made him 'feel very uncomfortable'. Could the Archbishop spare time one morning to visit some of the mixed gun-sites and searchlight-sites and lunch with him afterwards? On 1 December Temple paid his visit, had an interesting tour, and lunched at the Mess; and, before he left Stanmore, the Archbishop and the General had each made a new friend.

Nor did he neglect the men afloat. In September 1942 he accepted an invitation to visit the Home Fleet at Scapa. He was met at Thurso and taken across the Pentland Firth to the Orkneys in the destroyer H.M.S. *Eclipse*. The passage was a rough one in a bumpy sea, but every preparation had been made for his comfort, and he was left to lie down in the Commander's airy sea-cabin, which was equipped with a settee—and a basin. Commander E. Mack, R.N., takes up the story:

> After an hour we were in the calm water again between the Islands, so I sent down an officer to the Archbishop with a message that the worst was over and if he would like to come up and see the view it was quite pleasant on the bridge. There was considerable delay and my officer returned to say that after repeated knocking on the door of the cabin, he had walked in

and found no-one there; what should he do? This was rather alarming and we quickly telephoned the Wardroom, where his Chaplain was, to enquire if he had seen him, and also sent sailors along the deck to find out if anyone knew where he had gone, for a destroyer in a rough sea is rather a dangerous place for an elderly man. However, just as we were beginning to get anxious on the bridge a sailor, a relief look-out, arrived up and casually mentioned that the Archbishop was on the Messdeck with the Ship's Company and having a very good time.

It seemed that as soon as we had left him safely in my cabin and the rest of us had departed, he had slipped out and gone down to the Messdeck to see the men; his only anxiety had been to get rid of the various officers and Chaplains who were following him around. And down below in the crowded atmosphere and smell of dinner being prepared he had stayed throughout the trip. He appeared afterwards on the upper deck, still looking extremely well, surrounded by my men who were hugely delighted.

Just over a year later, when my ship was sunk in the Mediterranean with the loss of many of her crew, I was very touched to receive a letter of regret and sympathy from the Archbishop, and an invitation to me to see him if I could. This, unfortunately, I was never able to do.

Before the end of the month Temple received the following letter from the Commander-in-Chief of the Home Fleet:

My dear Archbishop,

Please forgive me for not having written before, but just after you left I got involved with the running of the Russian convoys. How extremely kind of you to send me a copy of your book. I am looking forward to studying it.

I can never tell you how deeply we all appreciated your undertaking the long journey to come and see us in the Home Fleet; my only regret is that service requirements prevented so many officers and men seeing and hearing you.

As I told you, it is my firm conviction that throughout the Service and on shore there is a deeper religious feeling and a greater longing to live a more Christian life than ever before in my lifetime. Your visit has been an inspiration and an encouragement to us all, and it is comforting to know that you will be there, with your wise counsel and great faith to lead and direct us when the even more difficult times come after this vile war is over.

Yours very sincerely,
JACK C. TOVEY.

Prayers and Services

The 'deeper religious feeling' of which the Admiral wrote was not confined to the Armed Forces. Thousands of men and women in civil life were undergoing the same experience, but the problem set to Primate and parish priest alike was how to link up this 'religious feeling' with the worship of the Church and 'buy up the opportunity' for the Kingdom of God. Were the parish clergy, Temple asked in his *Diocesan Gazette*, doing all they could to make the Church services relevant to the felt needs of the day? 'I hope', he wrote, 'that . . . care may be taken in the leading of the special prayers to shew that regard is paid to whatever may from time to time be uppermost in the hopes and anxieties of the people.' Again:

> If people come to Church with hearts filled with either anxiety or gratitude and find the service conducted without reference to the occasion of their feeling, they learn to think of the Church as something aloof and unsympathetic, and without any message for their needs. By meeting those needs we may lead people increasingly to make their requests known to God and to cast their care upon Him—a lesson which, once learnt, will be a permanent source of spiritual strength.

Among the commonest requests that reached the Archbishop were those for special days of public prayer, sometimes on the most trivial excuse. For more than one reason—unless such a day had been ordered by the King or there was some outstanding cause—Temple was reluctant to grant them with any frequency; but on occasions special services were put out by authority, which inevitably evoked criticisms of their form or content from church-people of varying types. One difficulty was felt very keenly by Temple himself—that of inserting prayers for victory. It distressed him all the more that neither his predecessor at Canterbury nor his successor at York was able to share his conviction. In February 1944 he wrote to the Archbishop of York:

I am afraid I distress you by the fact that the forms of prayer which I draw up do not contain direct prayers for victory. I have always felt that it is wiser to avoid this, and have publicly stated that it ought to be avoided. I am of course prepared to say, with the form in the Book of 1928, 'Grant us victory, *if it be Thy Will*'; but I am sure that clause ought to be added in such a case, even though it governs all our praying at all times.

But I have tried always to draw up prayers which do not range us over against any of our fellow-Christians in Germany or elsewhere, because it seems to me that the primary concern in prayer—and I mean 'primary' quite seriously—must be the approach to the Father of all men, with recognition that all His other children have the same right of approach, and that if we pray as our Lord taught us, we are never praying against each other, because we are always praying not that what we want shall be done, but that what God wants shall be done, and that we may be used for doing it. I regard this as really fundamental, and while it may lead one to be perhaps excessively sensitive about some kind of petition, I believe that sensitiveness is a pretty sound guide.

I am very much encouraged by knowing that on this point I am in agreement with Abraham Lincoln, who seems to me to have led his people in war more Christianly than pretty well anybody in history.

I was horrified when, in the exhortation inserted in one of the official forms, the words occurred: 'Do not hesitate to pray for victory'; that came out with a note to say that it was issued under the authority of the Archbishops of Canterbury and York, Cosmo having in fact telegraphed to say that there wasn't time to let me see the form and he was assuming my agreement!

But apart from that there has not, I think, been a direct and unqualified prayer for victory officially issued, and I do not see how I can be associated with the issue of one. I think the maintenance of the spiritual fellowship of all Christians is for the Church a concern that takes precedence even of the military defeat of Nazi-ism.

I thought perhaps I had better try to open up my mind to you about all this.

Dr. Garbett replied:

I quite understand your views about prayer for victory, though I do not agree with them. I am afraid I have often told people not to hesitate to pray for victory, and I regularly pray for it myself. But in view of what you say I should not think of pressing for any alteration in the prayer which you have drawn up, and I accept it most gladly.

Broadcasting and the Press

Many churches were thronged with worshippers for these special services; but there was a wider audience within the range of Temple's voice. He was an admirable broadcaster, with a natural and effortless delivery well suited to the microphone, and he became convinced that by broadcasting he could make his greatest personal contribution to the nation's war effort. Through this medium the Primate's voice reached every land, and the B.B.C. were not backward in calling on him. He was Chairman of the Central Council for Broadcast Adult Education, and Chairman of the General Advisory Council from its first meeting early in 1935 till he had to resign, from pressure of other work, in the spring of 1937. One of his most noteworthy feats on the air was achieved on 'D-Day'—6 June 1944. On the evening of that day the King broadcast an appeal to the nation, and solemnly called his people to prayer. With his genius for touching the imagination of listeners, Dr. James Welch (the Director of Religious Broadcasts) felt that nothing except a religious service could follow such an appeal, but this involved dislocating the B.B.C.'s evening programme, collecting a choir, drawing up a service—and securing somebody to give the address. The Archbishop was in London. He was due to take the chair in the afternoon at what he described as 'a rather critical meeting' of the Governing Body of Rugby School, and not until he started out for this meeting was he told of the service. From the Governors' meeting he went straight to the House of Lords, to speak on the Second Reading of the Education Bill. From there he drove to S. Martin's-in-the-Fields where he was due to lecture between eight and nine o'clock, and was then taken in a B.B.C. car to their studio in Maida Vale. Two days later he wrote of the service:

I think Dr. Welch and his colleagues deserve great credit for the Service. Dr. Welch had drawn it up. I composed one Prayer (the Prayer for the Homes of the Soldiers) during the singing of one of the Hymns and inserted this at the last moment. I had only been told of this Service as I started for the Rugby Governing Body meeting, so my own Address had to consist in part of something I had recorded for broadcast to America and in part of sentences either composed during the singing of another Hymn or composed in the moment of delivery! I had had no moment till then in which I could possibly make a continuous script. It is therefore a great relief to me to know that the Service was really effective. Dr. Welch had hustled the regular singers of the B.B.C. from Bedford up to London and the Voluntary B.B.C. Chorus was brought across in buses to the Maida Vale Studio from the Albert Hall, where they had already been singing from 7 to 9 at the Commemoration Concert in memory of the composer Delius, so that they had put themselves to much personal inconvenience to take their part, but they were evidently most happy to do it and really put their hearts into the singing.

It was typical of the Archbishop to describe in so matter-of-fact a way his own part in the service. Yet his impromptu sermon seemed to those who heard it a model of what a broadcast address should be. The King was pleased to express his appreciation, and one listener, after hearing both the King's appeal and the service which followed, wrote: 'That seventy-five minutes was more memorable than anything we have listened to since the Coronation.'

From almost every European country messages reached Temple thanking him for his broadcast addresses and prayers; and he kept as close contact as he could, throughout the war, with the leaders of other Churches on the Continent, though it was little enough he could do to help them or their people. When the Greek Metropolitans wrote a piteous appeal begging the Archbishop to save their nation from the atrocities being committed by the Germans and Italians, Temple could offer no immediate hope of release from their agony—'nothing will give security against such atrocities except the completion of the allied victory'—nor could he give any other reassurance to the Patriarch of Rumania who wrote to protest against the allied bombing of his country. He corresponded regularly with some of his friends in the Oecumenical Movement and only a few weeks before his death sent a cordial greeting to Pastor M. Boegner, in which he spoke of 'the new day dawning for France'. A similar letter was sent to the Cardinal Archbishops of Malines and Rheims: the French Cardinal wrote, in a moving reply, of the peace to which they were looking forward, founded *sur le droit naturel qui vient de Dieu.* There was also evidence that many of his broadcasts were heard in Germany. On Pastor Niemöller's birthday in January 1943 Temple preached at the Lutheran Church in London, and thanked God that 'the one effective centre of resistance to Nazi oppression in Germany had been the Christian Church'; and, like other good Europeans of repute, he was constantly watching for a chance of reaching those sections of the German people which had little sympathy with the Nazi régime and little stomach for the war.

The 'Lansdowne Letter'

The origin of one of his most keenly debated efforts in this direction is told in a letter to his wife:

Lollards Tower,
Lambeth Palace, S.E. 1.
November 28, 1939.

. . . Sir Arthur Salter came to dinner and was very interesting

The Christian Leader in War-time

about many things, including the proposal that I should try to get a letter into to-morrow's *Daily Telegraph* recalling Lord Lansdowne's letter of November 29, 1917, pointing out the contrast in the situations and repeating his plea. Kurt Hahn joined us at 9.30, and Arnold Forster (whom I had not known to be in London) came in this morning—and we got a letter prepared and despatched.

The *Daily Telegraph* published the letter on 4 December. Temple's object was to suggest 'prior conditions the fulfilment of which must be assured before an armistice can be concluded', and he gave reasons why he thought the time a suitable one for publishing them:

I am aware, of course, that such proposals have no chance of being accepted by the Nazi Government. That is no reason for not putting them forward: for when Hitler answers No, very many Germans may answer Yes in their hearts; and then, after some grave military disappointment—we can hardly hope for any change before that happens—there may be a real response from the Germany which is silenced now. . . . We must not underestimate the difficulties in the way of such a change of heart. After all that has happened the response may be long delayed. But we may well refuse to credit the claim of Goebbels that there is not now, and never will be, a Germany for which Hitler cannot speak.

The *Daily Telegraph*, in a leading article, took Temple to task for his reading of history on an important point, and was supported by a peer and an Anglican dean. But the Archbishop knew his documents better than his critics and quoted in reply the so-called 'Clemenceau Letter' of 16 June 1919—which had been drafted by Philip Kerr (later Lord Lothian). The 'miserable wriggle', as one of Temple's correspondents called it, of the leader-writer was in sharp contrast with the unqualified withdrawal of the peer and the dean. Nothing could have been more frank than Lytton's second letter to the paper:

Perusal of all the relevant documents to which my attention has been called leaves no doubt in my mind that the Archbishop of

559

York was right in saying that peace was offered to the Germans on the basis of the Fourteen Points (as qualified by President Wilson's letter of Nov. 5) and that I was wrong in describing this as 'an historic fallacy'.

But a red herring had been drawn across the trail, the scent was never properly picked up again, and the most important part of the letter, which dealt with third-party judgement and the limitation of state-sovereignty, received little attention. A further effort was made in February 1940, when the Primate of Norway invited four leaders of British Christianity—the Rev. W. Paton (Presbyterian), the Rev. Henry Carter (Methodist), the Bishop of Chichester, and the Archbishop of York—to meet leaders of the Scandinavian Church; and the text was issued to the Press of a note describing the agreement of the group that, if certain 'points were secured', it would be right for Britain to enter into negotiations with Germany.

More notice was taken when a year later there appeared on the middle page of *The Times* a letter under the headings—'Foundations of Peace—A Christian Basis—Agreement among the Churches'. It was signed by the two Anglican Archbishops, the Roman Catholic Archbishop of Westminster (Cardinal Hinsley), and the Rev. Walter Armstrong, Moderator of the Free Church Council; the signatories expressed their acceptance of the Pope's 'Five Peace Points' and added to these the five standards 'by which economic situations and proposals may be tested'. They dealt with inequality in wealth, education, the family, daily work, and the use of the resources of the earth 'as God's gift to the whole human race'. The appeal had a wide circulation: the five standards were felt to 'put the snapper on the whip' of the Pope's points, and it was noteworthy that the signatories spoke for all the Churches in England. There was also an internationally minded group—Henry Brinton's 'platoon', as the Archbishop called it—with which he was associated; and the Peace Aims Group, which was built up by William Paton, did effective work in bringing together the 'Points' and the Atlantic Charter and calling for a world outlook on the problems of peace. But no organization

Evacuees at Bishopthorpe

Canterbury on the morning after the raid, 1 June 1942, with Mrs. Temple

made a stronger appeal to Temple than the Committee for Christian Reconstruction in Europe, which was inaugurated by the British Council of Churches to strengthen Church life in Europe by the training of clergy, the building of temporary churches in the bombed areas, and the provision of Bibles and Christian literature. He regarded this as 'an immensely important enterprise; it is', he wrote to Lord Grey, who was chairman of the Central Board of Finance of the Church of England, 'something more than merely raising money to meet a need: it is an expression of the fellowship of the Churches in their service of God and man.' Three days before his death he wrote to Dr. Garbett:

> I may add that if the Church Assembly turns it down, I shall run the thing for all I am worth myself! No doubt it is important to avoid any direct collision between this and our appeal for our own needs; but I am quite sure that it is a case like that of the missionary claim and we shall tend to gain more for the Church at home by shewing that we care for the Church in Europe and throughout the world than if we concentrate on home needs only.

And so, had he lived, he would have done, for the amount of work he was prepared to undertake was incredible. The natural anxiety of his wife and friends increased with each new burden he laid on himself—surely there must be a breaking-point, even for William Temple!—why, at least, could he not be more selective in choosing persons and causes for his active patronage? And was there not a danger of debasing the currency if he continued to sign letters to the Press on what seemed the slightest provocation? At last one of his friends made a timely protest. In 1943 a letter was prepared towards the end of Lent, which was to appear in *The Times* on the Monday in Holy Week. It was signed by leading Anglicans, Roman Catholics, and Free Churchmen, and by the Pastors of many Continental Churches in London. Temple asked Dr. Garbett's advice about signing it, and received this reply:

> I certainly would suggest that you should not sign this statement . . . it really has nothing in it beyond the statement that the world is in anguish now and there will be no improvement

until we all become Christians. This is all very true, but is it really worth while for the leaders of religion to sign this kind of document? It only tends to cheapen their signatures to really important declarations. So I should certainly advise 'No'!

But Temple's name duly appeared at the head of the signatories.

Works of Mercy

There could, however, be no question of an Archbishop's duty where works of mercy were concerned, though it would not have been surprising if, with all the claims made on his bodily and mental strength, Temple had relegated to a secondary place in his life the more personal and specifically Christian duties of a minister of the Gospel. Yet he gave himself untiringly to these works throughout the war, though few of his efforts left him with so little sense of achievement or so scanty a return for his labours. In his attempts to alleviate the famine in countries occupied by the enemy, to secure justice and discriminating treatment for refugees, and to save some at least of the Jews in Europe, he had to bear what was to him the greatest agony—that of knowing that millions of his fellow men were being starved, tortured, or murdered while he was almost powerless to rescue or succour them. Yet his courage and persistence never flagged. If he took up the case of an individual, he refused to drop it until an absolutely immutable decision had been reached; he began, for instance, making inquiries about one interned German pastor in whom he was interested in the second month of the war, and in 1942 he was still corresponding about him. In organizing famine relief (in which the Bishop of Chichester took a courageous and leading part) he was perpetually searching his own heart and seeking expert advice on how to solve the problem which the Foreign Secretary posed to him in one of the many letters that passed between them—'how to mitigate the sufferings of the Belgian and other allied peoples without helping the enemy'—and he spared no effort on behalf of the Jews. But it was uphill work. The story of one attempt after another is the same. There would be information from individuals or societies or a paragraph in a newspaper, telling of some fresh horror or giving heartrending statistics of disease and mortality. Correspond-

ence with the Prime Minister, the Foreign Secretary, or the Home
Secretary would follow and the well-known official phrases would
recur in the Government replies—the matter is being 'looked into',
'actively examined', or 'considered with regard to international
relations'—after which there would be a pause of some weeks,
when the next step had to be taken. This might be the sending
of an influentially signed letter to *The Times*, an address to Members of Parliament at a private gathering in the House, a public
meeting in the Albert Hall ('I have had some difficulty', Temple
wrote to the Bishop of Chichester in July 1942, 'in resisting the
demand for public agitation'), an appeal in the House of Lords,
a broadcast to European Christians—one specially noteworthy
appeal was addressed to Christians in Hungary—or a deputation
to one of the Ministers of State: and all the while Temple would
be in constant correspondence with the leaders of the Roman
Catholic and Free Churches. Whenever a deputation to a Minister
was received by Mr. Eden or Mr. Richard Law its members knew
that their case would be heard with consideration and their pleas
answered with courtesy and reasoned arguments, but it was not
always so—at the beginning of December 1942 Temple wrote to
Mr. Eden: 'In face of what is happening the kind of arguments
addressed to a recent deputation by the Home Secretary [Herbert
Morrison] seemed so trifling as to be almost profane'—while at
the best it was cold comfort that the deputations took away with
them. And all the time he ran the risk of misunderstanding or
abuse. There was need for considerable restraint on occasions
when Temple felt bound to protest against some action or inaction
of the Government or the Service chiefs, and when he alone could
decide whether the protest should be made through some public
pronouncement or letter to the Press, or whether he should personally and privately approach the authorities. One general reason
why care had to be exercised was given to a correspondent:

... Do not imagine that if nothing is said publicly nothing is
being said at all. As a general rule in dealing with a Government
it is of great importance to avoid putting the Ministers of the
Crown on the defence. They then commit themselves to deci-

sions from which they might have been dislodged if the approach had been made more privately. No doubt there is a proper occasion for both methods. But if what we are concerned about is what happens rather than a satisfaction of our feelings there must be a good deal of use made of the method of private approach, which of course does involve that the public knows nothing about it.

This difficulty was illustrated and emphasized when in October 1942 some of our prisoners were shackled by the Germans. Feeling ran high in the country. The demand for reprisals was as insistent as were the appeals to the Government not to lower our standards by shackling German prisoners in England, and letters poured into Lambeth pleading that the Archbishop should make some public statement. Temple had a difficult decision to take. He had received personal letters in answer to his own both from the Prime Minister and Sir Stafford Cripps, saying that the Government were doing all in their power, and giving reasons why their own efforts would be made more difficult by the issue of any public appeal from the Church. At the same time he knew that the Roman Catholic Archbishop of Westminster had written a letter to *The Times* which he was on the point of sending, and Temple was naturally anxious that the National Church should not seem to be behindhand in upholding publicly the principles of the Christian ethic. The Upper House of Canterbury Convocation had already met and had passed a resolution, in private session, affirming its 'abhorrence of all reprisals against prisoners of war by whomsoever taken', but stating that it felt itself 'precluded through negotiations now proceeding from engaging at this moment in public debate on the subject'. The Archbishop of Westminster behaved with great consideration for Temple and held up his letter day after day, till at last the Government were able to announce that their negotiations had proved successful. Temple was inclined, when all was over, to publish the resolution of Convocation, but he was checked by the wise dissent of the Bishop of Winchester—even though the result was that the Church stood convicted of cowardice in the eyes of many thousand earnest Christians—and the resolution was buried in the Chronicles of Convocation. The incident provided a partial response to the question why the Church did not 'do something'—a phrase Temple particularly disliked. 'Oh dear!' he exclaimed once on opening a letter, 'here's somebody else who wants to know why the Church of England "does not do something". I wish the man would say what he really means, which is—"Why does not the Archbishop of Canterbury write what *I* think in a letter to *The Times*?" '

Even at times of what seemed the least excusable procrastination Temple never wrote or spoke unjustly of the Government. In June 1943 he writes to Miss Pye, the Hon. Secretary of Dr. Bell's Famine Relief Committee:

> There is no doubt about Lord [——]'s personal sympathy, but some of the points he mentions he asked me to keep secret and their very real importance gives greatly increased difficulties. That is no reason why we should not maintain our pressure. Unless the Government is able to state the grounds of its non-action, it cannot resent pressure from a public whose sympathies are deeply stirred. But we ought to exhort with the recognition that there is genuine good will on the Government side. Some of the expressions used in Resolutions passed in different parts of the country are entirely non-appreciative of this, and have worked out in substance as quite unjust.

None the less the Government pressed their questions—Was the Archbishop quite convinced that this or that committee of displaced Europeans in Britain was not a pro-Nazi or Communist cell in disguise? Had his Grace considered the possibility of an anti-Semitic outbreak in England which might follow on some special favour being shown to Jews? (A few newspapers were not backward in publishing the names of any black-market offenders who might be Jews.) And was there not a danger of giving Hitler an excuse for further barbarities if he could point to British acts of charity and tell his people that the Jews were now seen to be the friends of Britain and therefore the enemies of the Fatherland?

By the beginning of 1943 it was clear that no word spoken in

England or anywhere else could make Hitler's treatment of the
Jews more diabolical than it was, and on 23 March Temple moved
in the House of Lords:

> That, in view of the massacres and starvation of Jews and
> others in enemy and enemy-occupied countries, this House
> desires to assure His Majesty's Government of its fullest sup-
> port for immediate measures, on the largest and most generous
> scale compatible with the requirements of military operations
> and security, for providing help and temporary asylum to per-
> sons in danger of massacre who are able to leave enemy and
> enemy-occupied countries.

After quoting figures of the massacres and torture of the Jews
'before which the imagination recoils', Temple made several suggestions for Government action and pleaded especially that, in
view of the magnitude of the problem, 'there should be appointed
someone of high standing, either from within the Government or,
if not that, from the Civil Service, to make it his first concern'.
The speech moved the House deeply, especially by the passionate
sincerity of its closing sentences:

> My chief protest is against procrastination of any kind. . . .
> The Jews are being slaughtered at the rate of tens of thousands
> a day on many days, but there is a proposal for a preliminary
> exploration to be made with a view to referring the whole
> matter after that to the Inter-Governmental Committee on
> Refugees. My Lords, let us at least urge that when that Con-
> ference meets it should meet not only for exploration but for
> decision. We know that what we can do is small compared with
> the magnitude of the problem, but we cannot rest so long as
> there is any sense among us that we are not doing all that might
> be done. We have discussed the matter on the footing that we
> are not responsible for this great evil, that the burden lies on
> others, but it is always true that the obligations of decent men
> are decided for them by contingencies which they did not them-
> selves create and very largely by the action of wicked men. The
> priest and the Levite in the parable were not in the least respon-

566

sible for the traveller's wounds as he lay there by the roadside, and no doubt they had many other pressing things to attend to, but they stand as the picture of those who are condemned for neglecting the opportunity of showing mercy. We at this moment have upon us a tremendous responsibility. We stand at the bar of history, of humanity, and of God.

The horrors culminated in the Buchenwald massacres of 1944, but Temple's active intervention never ceased. He remained unshaken in his conviction that, whether or not a word from him would be effective at any given moment, 'it ought to be said for the sake of the principles of justice itself, and I shall continue the advocacy which I have endeavoured to offer hitherto.' It is not to be wondered at that a statement issued by the World Jewish Congress on Temple's death contained these words:

. . . Lamented by the Christian world, the premature death of Dr. Temple will be particularly mourned by the Jewish people whose champion he was. His maintained interest in the welfare of our much persecuted brethren was not rooted, as is the case with many theologians, in an attitude of sanctimonious pity. He approached the overwhelming problem of the destiny of the Jews in a mood more positive, more comprehensive, more liberal, and, above all, more human. His interest in Jews was not a by-product of his sacred duties. . . . Profoundly conscious of the physical suffering of the Jews, and acutely sensitive to its spiritual significance, he was at all times ready to make every contribution to the alleviation of the great tragedy that had befallen a great people.

Of the countless tributes offered to Temple's memory on his death, none was more justly earned than this, nor was any more generously paid. Whatever duties imposed by the war the Archbishop may have neglected (and it is hard to point to any) during those exacting five years when mind, body, and spirit were kept without remission at their tightest stretch, one injunction given when he had knelt to receive his consecration was never forgotten —'Be to the flock of Christ a shepherd . . . hold up the weak. . . .

William Temple

Bind up the broken.' . . . But one day the war would be over. There was a new world to be built and a new social order to be created—how different from their prototypes none could foretell, though hopes and fears abounded—and here again William Temple stepped into his appointed place.

XXX

Education Act, 1944—The Albert Hall

The need of the world now is not more liberty for the exercise of men's various faculties, but some purpose in life which may give significance and harmony to the enjoyment of that liberty. In other words, the supreme task to which we are called is the reconstruction of the unity of life upon the basis of the revelation of God in Christ, not by the old method of compelling those who differed from Christian truth, as the Church understood it, to profess acceptance of it, but by the method of permeating with the spirit of the Gospel all the activities and even the desires of men. This is not a task for a few men or a few years. It calls for a general movement of thought and dedication in the whole body of the Church for a period not to be estimated in advance.

W. T., First Presidential Address to York Diocesan Conference,
June 1929.

Of course I completely agree with you that the whole business of applying Christian principles to social questions is secondary to the fundamental truths of the Gospel, and to present the matter in any other way would seem to me to be complete apostasy.

W. T., letter to the Rev. Egerton Swann, March 1943.

ON the outbreak of war there began in Britain a social movement which was to prove at once a portent and a stimulus. Thousands of women and children were removed to safety from crowded cities and centres of war industry which were likely targets for the enemy's bombers, and the interest of those who received them in the more sheltered parts of the country centred largely on the children. Many of these came from homes where their parents, often at great sacrifice, had striven to bring them up to be decent and God-fearing men and women: they soon shook down in their new environment on terms with their hosts, most of whom welcomed the opportunity of this form of war-service. But there were others whose arrival in the English country-side was greeted with pity and disgust. Who were these boys and girls —half-fed, half-clothed, less than half-taught, complete strangers to the most elementary social discipline and the ordinary decencies of a civilized home? Only one answer was possible. They were the products of the free institutions of which Britons are bidden to think with pride; they were partakers of that family life which good Christians have assumed to be the foundation of society. They were also 'the citizens of to-morrow'—could their condition possibly be due, in part at least, to the fact that so few responsible persons had thought of them as the children of to-day? Anyhow, one duty was clear: even the vaguest altruist felt that something ought to be done about it; the more precise fastened on the word Education, and the cry was taken up throughout the country.

In every respect the time was exactly ripe for a thorough over-haul of the nation's schools. Employers and heads of commercial firms, the authorities responsible for recruiting in the Services, and not least the parents, were at one in deploring the mental and spiritual equipment with which thousands of boys and girls were every year sent out into the world. No less timely was the changed attitude of the Churches. They had wrecked the Birrell Bill through their disagreements, and there was now grave public concern lest denominational differences should once more impede a settlement. But the Churches also had learned their lesson—it was remarked by the cynics how pleasant it was to see the Churches now as much interested in the welfare of the children as they used to be in the success of their own propaganda—never were Anglicans and Free Churchmen working in closer harmony than at the outbreak of the second World War (Copec and the Lambeth Appeal of 1920 were beginning to bear fruit), and the widespread decline of religion in the national life suggested a serious weakness in the religious teaching of the schools. Two persons, moreover, who would be deeply concerned in any reformation were exactly suited to the rôles for which they had been cast. The President of the Board of Education was R. A. Butler, a man of strenuous purpose, unwearying patience, and outstanding diplomatic skill; and the new Archbishop of Canterbury was one to whom the cause of education was not only a lifelong interest but a genuine passion. His interest was partly inherited, for Temple's father had been deeply involved in the Act of 1870 and spoke for the last time in the House of Lords on the Act of 1902. The subject of Temple's own first speech in public, as well as of his first speech in Convocation (in February 1918, on the Fisher Bill), was education; his experience of adult education was profound; and he knew the history of the successive parliamentary enactments as well as he understood the machinery for putting them into effect. Everything pointed to the moment as one at which a great advance was both desirable and practicable. 'If all the main partners', wrote the President of the Board of Education to Temple in November 1942, 'do not solve this question together on this occasion—however patient we may have to be—I rather wonder who will find a way out ever.' 'The time for a settlement', urged *The Times*, 'is now or never.'

Temple's own position was entirely realist. A major social development of the preceding half-century had been the passing of directive power—in education as in other departments of the national life—from the hands of the Church to those of the State; and this process was bound to continue. To turn a blind eye to it, or to expect that it would ever be reversed, was useless—what was the right attitude of the Church in the face of it? 'Our main business', the Archbishop stated at his first diocesan conference at Canterbury in July 1942, 'is, not surely to be fighting a rearguard action in perpetual retreat till we are driven off the field by the competition of the resources of the State, but to take care that we are interpenetrating with our influence all that the State itself is doing.' To effect this, there must be a clearer conviction of what is meant by religious education. When he opened his campaign with his first speech to the National Society, he insisted that

education is only adequate and worthy when it is itself religious. ... There is no possibility of neutrality.... To be neutral concerning God is the same thing as to ignore Him. ... If the children are brought up to have an understanding of life in which, in fact, there is no reference to God, you cannot correct the effect of that by speaking about God for a certain period of the day. Therefore our ideal for the children of our country is the ideal for truly religious education.

He defended the dual system which many education experts deplored; 'there is no doubt', he wrote to his wife in February 1944, after a W.E.A. Conference, 'that most of these people detest the dual system—and the Church schools'. Temple approved of it partly because he saw great value in its 'duality': his ideal for the schools was a variety of types with a considerable measure of individual autonomy. He ended by declaring that the system must remain, and that there must be no wholesale surrender of Church schools. Some surprise was expressed that he had made no reference to the condition of many school buildings—399 on the Board's black list of 700 were Church of England schools—but he had been careful to remember the particular audience he was addressing: 'I was doing', he wrote to Canon Tatlow, 'a rather elaborate egg-dance, and some of the eggs are such as it is most important not to break, because the smell would be awful!'

The interim Report of the National Society (which was now the Church's Central Committee for Religious Education) was accepted by the Church Assembly in November 1942, though there was some opposition both from those who followed the Bishop of Chichester in his advocacy of a modified form of the Scottish system, and from the Bishop of Oxford's group, which Temple regarded as 'largely detached from reality'. He wrote to the President of the Board:

> I have felt all through that what the Bishop of Oxford and his friends have been urging might have been the right policy to adopt in the middle of the last century when the whole thing was starting, and consequently also in 1870, but in 1870 it was already too late.

The President agreed: some sections of the nation still regarded the Cowper-Temple clause as 'the ark of the covenant', and 'to attempt any reversal of our long established religious education ... would be ... liable to wreck all hope of comprehensive educational legislation in our time'.

In July 1943, when the White Paper on Educational Reconstruction was published, the more conservative of the Archbishop's critics were still a little uncertain where he stood. They were not left long in doubt—there was no egg-dancing when he spoke clearly and candidly to his diocesan conference on 25 October. The White Paper presented 'a glorious opportunity'. He accepted its policy and was not prepared to risk that policy as a whole for the sake of the few modifications he would like to see made in detail. He mentioned the justifiable grievance of Nonconformists in the single-school areas; and after expressing surprise at the lack of enthusiasm shown by churchpeople at the Government's offer to find 50 per cent. of the cost of readjusting and maintaining the Church schools—had anybody made the suggestion even ten years earlier, 'it would have been regarded as merely visionary'— he ended with this warning:

> Above all let us not give the impression that our concern as churchpeople is only with the adjustment of the dual system: we ought as Christians to be concerned about the whole of educational progress. I am quite sure that the raising of the school age will of itself do more to make permanent the religious influence of the school than anything that can be done with directly denominational purpose.

Six months were allowed for the country to study the White Paper, after which, within a few days of Christmas, the Bill was published. It was inevitably a compromise: to attempt to strike a detailed balance of loss and gain to the Church would here be irrelevant, nor indeed is it possible, for the final reckoning will be spread out over many years. No responsible body was prepared to accept the Bill without slight or important reservations; but public opinion was overwhelmingly in its favour, and this was specially true of the section dealing with adult education. On this a strong lead was given by a conference at Oxford, with Temple in the chair and Sir William (now Lord) Beveridge and Sir Richard Livingstone taking part, which urged, among other things, that local authorities should be pressed to give prominence to this part of the national task in their schemes; and at the time of his death Temple was busy in helping to create a central organization for securing co-operation between all the bodies interested in adult education.

In the Church Assembly the procedure was unusual. When the debate was over, Temple sent an account of it to Lang, whose skill in reading Parliamentary Bills and relating the smallest sub-section to the whole design Temple had already found invaluable:

The debate in the Assembly was satisfactory. Rees presented the case for his impossible amendment in an admirable speech and I am very glad that it should have been well stated in the Assembly and received with very close attention. Henry Brooke, who is our chief watch-dog in the House of Commons, spoke quite admirably in reply and carried the Assembly completely with him. He made the suggestion that we should not vote on Rees' Motion on the ground that it would be a misfortune that it should be either carried or rejected which is I think true, but that in place of carrying the Resolution we should determine to send to Butler a transcript of the whole debate. Consequently the previous question was carried by a huge majority and then the decision to send the transcript was carried unanimously. I hope Butler will read Rees' speech carefully. It was the best statement I have heard or seen of that case. I think it completely ignores large numbers of relevant facts, more particularly the outlook of the teachers, but as it is widely held it is important that it should be understood. I am very glad that this result was reached without my intervening from the Chair though of course I was ready to do so if I thought that there was any doubt about the decision we should reach and that I could influence the matter.

The warning about the teachers was needed. For years they had repeated their battle-cry of 'No Tests for Teachers'—'the teaching profession', Temple wrote to a friend, 'represents the intelligentsia of the last generation more than any other section of society'—and they saw the thin end of the wedge in the compulsory period for an act of worship laid down in the Bill. Temple was not the first educationist who must have been sorely tempted to call the N.U.T. bluff, and he wrote in another letter:

> On the whole and very much on a balance I am inclined to think it is best to leave the Clause in the Bill and trust that it will be administered with tact and gentleness. Of course it is quite true that for prayers to be taken in a perfunctory or hypocritical way can only do harm. On the other hand, the majority of people try to do well what they do at all and there will be a

considerable number who are led to include prayers because of the Statutory requirement who would otherwise let them slide. I think teachers are a little liable to ignore the fact that while it is objectionable to force the teachers to conduct prayers against their consciences it is also objectionable to force the children to omit prayers for the sake of the teachers' consciences.

At the same time Temple did all in his power to conciliate the teachers and was warmly applauded when he delivered the first of what an educational journal called 'inspirational lectures' to 600 London teachers in the County Hall on 'Education, Citizenship, and Religion'. He was also generous in finding time to address other than Church audiences on behalf of the Bill. R. H. Tawney recalls:

> The last large public gathering at which I heard Temple speak was a conference of representatives of Labour and educational organizations, with Sir Walter [now Lord] Citrine in the chair, to demand the passage of the Bill at an early date. He was greatly overburdened at the time and, as usual, arrived late. He spoke simply, avoiding technical details, and making no attempt to give the impression of special knowledge. The effect of his speech on the audience was due to his transparent sincerity and to the fervour of moral conviction with which he spoke: it was, I think, profound.

Among the critics were those who objected to raising the age of leaving school, but here Temple was adamant—'it is the most essential element of the Bill'. So strongly did he feel about this that he once said, in conversation with a friend: 'I am putting this very crudely, but I believe that our Lord is much more interested in raising the school-leaving age to sixteen than in acquiring an agreed Religious Syllabus.'

There remained the Nonconformists; and no account of the passing of the 1944 Act would be complete without some tribute to their effective co-operation. The lines on which their leaders and Temple worked together are described by the Archbishop in this letter to the Moderator of the Free Church Federal Council, Dr. R. D. Whitehorn:

. . . I am very glad that *The Times* has after all printed your letter, though with some delay. I am sure it will be useful. The best hope for anything like a peaceful settlement is that people like you and me should temperately advance our special concerns and not leave the whole field open to the people who want to raise a hullabaloo, while at the same time being determined to avoid getting drawn into really heated controversy. It is only right that the concern on the different sides should be expressed; then the Board and Parliament know what is being felt and can act in the light of that knowledge. But I am sure it will be most disastrous to raise that kind of controversy which might lead to the withdrawal of the Bill, partly because the main reforms in the Bill are so urgently needed, partly because it would vastly increase the prospect of a purely secular solution.

The Nonconformists' chief grievance was that in many villages their children were compelled to attend Church of England schools. The President of the Board left the handling of this controversy to the Churches, and efforts were made to reach some form of compromise; two meetings were held over which Temple presided, but all to no purpose—and the grievance remains. But the Bill contained so much of national value that Free Churchmen felt impelled to support it; they worked cordially with Temple in the preliminary stages, and it was a joint Anglican and Free Church committee which worked out 'The Archbishops' Five Points' (though neither Archbishop was a member of it). There was one unique feature in the reception of a deputation which waited on the President of the Board to press for the inclusion of these points in the Bill. He asked Lang, who led the deputation, to close the meeting with prayer. Could the Archbishop help contrasting this incident with the atmosphere in which the bitter struggle over the Birrell Bill had been waged in 1906?

Temple's speech on the Bill was one of the best he ever made in the House of Lords. During his early years as a member he gave the impression of not being quite in tune with what Randall Davidson called 'that very mixed assembly'. One of his personal friends in the Upper House suggests a possible reason for this:

BE WARNED, SINNER! TURN TO HIGHER THINGS!

HERE, SIR, DON'T YOU KNOW YOU'RE ON PRIVATE PROPERTY?

The Social Reformer

(From the *Evening Standard*, November 1942 and April 1943)

I always felt that this was entirely due to some psychological nervousness or antipathy on *his* part, and was not due to any inherent hostility on the part of the House of Lords. The House of Lords, like the House of Commons, takes no account, in judging a man, of whether they agree with his views or not. No doubt nine-tenths of the House violently disagreed with his political views, but I think this affected him much more than it affected them. I always regretted that he did not speak more often than he did, but from the time he became Archbishop his speeches were more frequent, and I think it is true to say that he gained the ear of the House increasingly. Certainly the House both liked and respected him, and increasingly appreciated the great weight of thought behind his words. His speeches on the Education Bill were notably successful and he spoke with great authority.

Nowhere was the improvement in the general atmosphere more noticeable than during the discussion in the House of Commons. In the two-day debate nearly twenty out of thirty-one speeches were largely concerned with the religious issue; no more than twenty votes could be mustered for an amendment against the compulsory period for an act of corporate worship; not one member rose to plead for a secularist solution; and Harold Laski was left to draw what comfort he could from the singular conclusion that by favouring the compulsory act of worship in the schools the Churches were 'in truth announcing that they have exhausted their religious vitality, and desire to be no more than a minor arm of the State's police power'.

For this successful issue much credit is due to two men—to the President of the Board, who combined an impartially generous treatment of all claimants for his consideration with unswerving loyalty to his department, and to the Primate whose understanding sympathy and charity towards those who differed from him were never allowed to obscure the principles which he believed to underlie a just and lasting settlement. But both the protagonists were aware that the Act existed, as yet, only on paper; both were particularly anxious that the local education authorities should seize the opportunity to make the fullest provision possible for the continued education of young people whose schooldays were behind them; and of all the national causes that miss Temple's leadership and inspiration to-day, in none is his loss more keenly felt than in the cause of adult education.

But what was to be the object of it all? When the top rung of the educational ladder set up under the Act was reached, what would the climber have gained? He would be equipped, was Temple's hope, for Christian citizenship and for taking up the further duties that it involved. To widen that sense of citizenship and to christianize it had been the burden of what he had said and taught for thirty years; but now that he sat in S. Augustine's chair, what, it was being asked, would his teaching be? Would he go back or forth on words already spoken? On 26 September 1942 the answer was given in the Albert Hall. Did Temple foresee the storm he was to arouse when he took the chair in a crowded hall on that day?

It was a strong platform. The other speakers were the Archbishop of York, the Bishop of Bristol, Sir Stafford Cripps, and Miss Knight-Bruce, and they all spoke well, though Temple's speech was no more outstanding than many others he had made on the same subject. He affirmed, as he had frequently done, the right and the duty of the Church to 'declare its judgment upon social facts and social movements and to lay down principles which should govern the order of society'; Christians were 'the trustees of a revelation who go out into the world calling men to accept and follow it'. Justice was more important than comfort, and the 'profit motive' should never be allowed to predominate. ('There is no harm', he admitted, 'in the profit motive as such'; only when it comes first in the determination of economic and industrial activity is it to be condemned.) After giving one or two illustrations of his main contention, Temple pleaded for a return to dependence upon the grace of God and to the fellowship of the Eucharist, in which the whole of life is consecrated by worship.

There was, however, a section of his speech which attracted wide notice:

In my judgment at least—I don't claim that it is worth much, but I want to offer it you—in my judgment at least it should now be regarded as improper for any private person or corporation to issue new credit; as it was in the Middle Ages for any private person or corporation to mint actual money, for the two are equivalent. And so I should like, I confess, to see the banks limited in their lending power to sums equivalent to that which depositors have entrusted to them, and all new credit to be issued by some public authority.

He then paid a graceful tribute to the 'singular integrity, ability, and public spirit' of British bankers.

For any detailed examination of Temple's views on banking and credit, the reader is asked to look elsewhere than in this book. All the issues he raised are highly technical, some are still topical and controversial, and most of them are as yet unresolved. But comment is demanded, and it may be confined to three points. First, Temple was assuredly speaking only a little ahead of the event, and was rightly interpreting the underlying trends of thought which characterized a period now already beginning to seem distant, though it is only a few years back. Second, in his technical arguments and his use of technical terms there can be little doubt that he went astray. (This becomes even clearer from the many subsequent letters that passed between him and his friends and correspondents among the bankers.) And third, in one speech after another during the last years of his life he insisted that his audiences were not to take his incursions into banking and other fields as anything but pegs on which he was hanging his own personal views—the opening sentence of his speech quoted above makes this luminously clear—they afforded 'illustrations' of the principles on which a Christian social order could be founded. He was not one of the many critics of the banking system who advertise their opinions because (or rather, as if) they understand banking. He felt entitled to commend his views because he understood something else, which mattered more than all the banks in the world. 'The joke about financial questions, generally speaking,' one banking expert wrote to him, 'is that nobody knows the

technical answers to them. If somebody will start giving the moral
answers, we may get somewhere.' No words could describe more
exactly the purpose on which Temple's efforts were concentrated.
This is not to shirk the question which was asked as frequently by
his supporters as by his critics in the last years, whether the Archbishop of Canterbury can possibly speak as a private individual—
the point has already been discussed in a previous chapter (p. 517).

The fluttering in the City dovecotes had hardly subsided before
Temple received an invitation to address a meeting of the Bank
Officers' Guild. It seems uncertain what enquiries he made before
accepting it—the Guild was the most 'Left' of all the bank clerks'
organizations—but he wrote in reply:

> I am very much concerned about the character of this meeting.
> It may be that you have asked me more especially because I have
> made some reference to the banking system and the issue of
> credit in some recent speeches. I want it to be clear that I should
> not dream of speaking to a meeting of your Guild directly on
> those subjects; but I should like to speak about the Christian
> view of the right relationship between Finance, Production,
> and Consumption, which may carry with it some implications
> for banking. But I should not be speaking directly upon
> banking.

The Guild accepted this offer, and Temple addressed its members in February 1943. It is difficult to acquit him of a strategic
blunder in choosing as a forum the one body known to be extremely critical of banking as then carried on—which meant the
bankers. Some weeks later, after the salutary experience of being
'entirely outraged' by the unscrupulous use made of his name by
a group of cranks, he made this revealing admission to a friend:

> I think it likely that I have paid too little consideration to the
> question in what company I may have been placing myself from
> time to time and what use would be made by that company not
> so much of what I said as of the fact that I had said it to them
> at all. My inclination has been to expound what I think to be
> the truth to anybody who has asked me and is willing to listen,
> and I do not deny that I find it difficult to bring in as a further

consideration the question whether or not my doing this may advertize the people whom I seek to instruct. Obviously that results merely from one's office and in no way from one's self.

The reactions to the Albert Hall meeting were world-wide. In Temple's own postbag there were a few of the usual letters relating personal experiences of which the relevance was not at once obvious—such as that of a gentleman who had known no peace till he had mastered the measurements of the Great Pyramid, a study on which the Archbishop should immediately embark if he hoped to be among those present at the gathering-in of the elect. There was also a double-edged compliment from an attorney in Nebraska who had read Temple's speech 'to the broad effect that current world economic ideologies are at fault in the property setup. That far you are exactly right. Your remedy', he unfortunately added, 'I think is wholly wrong.' But the large majority were serious and enthusiastically favourable, and the writers of a hundred and fifty letters received by Sir Stafford Cripps were, with negligible exceptions, profoundly grateful for the lead which the Archbishop and the Lord Privy Seal had given. In the Press notice was taken in almost every quarter of the globe. *The Times* published a selection of letters on several consecutive days; hardly a newspaper or magazine failed to comment; and the general opinion was one of intense relief and satisfaction that the Archbishop had, as Robert Lynd wrote, 'taken the only step possible to a modern Christian leader in demanding that politics and economics should be christianized'. The 'general conclusion' of the *Spectator* probably expressed as nearly as possible the majority verdict. This was that

> support for Dr. Temple and his Albert Hall speech far outweighs the criticism it has evoked. The effect of the controversy, indeed, is to impress on many people who had overlooked it that the new Primate is a man of great knowledge and brilliant intellect, as well as of abundant moral courage. . . . It is not by its indiscretions, but by the obduracy of its discretions, that the Church has lost repute, in so far as it has lost it, in the last twenty years.

Temple, on his main contention, stood his ground. When one of the first financial experts in the City told the Archbishop that he had been trying all his life to think out what money is and had not discovered it, Temple retorted that this was the reason why he wanted everybody to start thinking about it, so great was the power of money and of those who control it, and so grave was the consequent social danger of ignorance. He had issued his challenge, he had stirred many consciences, he had provoked wide attention, to such an extent that some men of affairs began to wonder whether they were as sure of their premisses as they had thought: and 'after all,' as one City man remarked at the close of an argument, 'Throgmorton Street may be amused at the Archbishop's mistakes, but no honest churchman could ever be amused at the mistakes of Throgmorton Street'.

The campaign was at once taken out by the I.C.F. into the provinces. In every city visited by the Archbishop the same tale was to be told—of the largest halls filled to capacity and overflow meetings packed, of audiences keyed up to a rare expectancy and never disappointed, and of an increased hopefulness for some resurgence of social idealism within the Church. But frequent complaints reached Lambeth of the 'political' tone of the Archbishop's speeches, and of the lack of any adequate reference in them to religion. Temple's reply was twofold. First, so far from the 'fundamental truths of the Gospel' being neglected, they were being preached with striking results in the 'Religion and Life' weeks organized by the British Council of Churches in many parts of England, and this evangelistic enterprise must be included in the reckoning alongside the meetings held specially to advocate the 'application of Christian principles to social questions'. Second, it was not altogether surprising that most of his correspondents should have a distorted conception of the purport of these meetings—the truth being that (however faithfully the reporters did their work) by the time the sub-editors in the newspaper offices had done theirs, those parts of his speeches in which God and His Kingdom were mentioned were almost always excised. At last he was moved to protest, in the following personal letter to the editor of *The Times*:

September 4, 1944.

Do you think it would be possible to give to your subordinates who do the necessary cutting of reports for publication a suggestion that any sentence in a sermon or address of mine which contains the name of God is less, and not more, appropriate for excision on that account? You very kindly included a rather full outline of those parts of my broadcast sermon which might just as well have been uttered by a heathen, but you omitted the whole point of the sermon, which was that if these obligations are to be fulfilled or these hopes realized, we must win from God both the strength and the direction that we need. Forgive my reiteration of my perpetual grouse—or *toujours perdrix!*

The Editor replied at once:

I can only offer my heartfelt apologies and promise amendment for the future. At the same time the enclosed cutting will show you the form in which your address appeared in the larger part of Monday's issue. Under the pressure of incoming news some misguided hand took the line of least resistance and removed the final paragraph, which quite clearly was essential to the whole. I hope that you will not have further cause to complain.

Temple did not always receive such courtesy at the hands of the Press, especially when charges were brought against the Church of owning 'slum property' and of harbouring brothels on its estates. The chief target for these attacks was the Ecclesiastical Commission. On the first of two main charges the Commissioners' reply was ultimately accepted as complete. It was that there did exist on the Commissioners' urban estates houses which had become out of date, or were overcrowded or otherwise unsatisfactory; that, as structures deteriorated and standards rose, this was at any given time inevitable; that rehabilitation or replacement was continually being carried out, wherever the Commissioners could get control; that the few properties remaining to be dealt with on their estates were houses outside their control because still outstanding on long lease; and that they were co-operating to their utmost with the housing authorities, whose statutory powers enabled them to deal effectively with such difficulties as the Commissioners could not overcome.

The second attack was concerned with the existence of sporadic prostitution in one part of a large estate at Paddington. This estate had come to the Commissioners in 1870 subject to a perpetual lease (converted under general statute in 1925 to a lease on the same terms for a firm 2,000 years) which had been granted at the end of the eighteenth century at the ground rent not of a fixed sum but of a share in the lessees' profits. Here the answer of the Commissioners was inevitably less direct. Briefly, it was that the evil referred to did exist on the estate; that neither the management nor the houses were at fault but temporary occupying tenants, birds of passage, often remote sub-tenants of under-lessees of the lessees of the Commissioners; that the Commissioners, so far from drawing money from the misused properties, spent far more than any ground rent attributable to them on preventive measures; that the burden of effective discovery and proof required further powers, and that the powers they had tried to secure had been refused to them. To the question why, if houses were unfit or were being used for immoral purposes, the Commissioners did not at once clean their hands by selling them, the answer was made that to do so would be an evasion of responsibility. It would aggravate the very evil which the Commissioners were combating, and they ought not to take this easy way of escape. But the cry was taken up in the less reputable sections of the Press, and Temple protested to two of the most offensive. He lamented to more than one correspondent the inadequacy of the Church's system of dealing with the Press and the difficulty of giving it the thorough overhaul it needed; but he also felt that he was personally involved. He studied all the available evidence, not merely to assess dispassionately the weight of the arguments on each side, but also to consider whether any obligation might lie upon himself. As Archbishop he was Chairman of the Commissioners, and as a member of the House of Lords he had the right to ventilate the subject in Parliament. After an impartial review of the whole field he was left in no doubt that, as the law stood, the Commissioners were doing all they could. There was, however, one action which he himself could take; he could argue authoritatively the moral case for removing such disabilities. He could try to wrest from the Government the promise of freedom for the Commissioners (or any other landlord) to intervene in the management of their property where conscience and morality, or an unequivocal refusal to grant such powers, justified it. When his mind was made up, he informed the Secretary of the Commission of his intention, but he feared that (as he had been told) the time was inappropriate for such an approach, for the war was occupying the whole attention of the Government. He wrote to Lady Cripps on 27 March 1944:

I am hoping before long to take some action which would partly meet the reference to what is . . . described quite erroneously as Church Ownership of Slums. . . . The reference is usually to the Ecclesiastical Commission, about whom you probably know it is quite untrue, but I despair of getting ordinary folk to appreciate the difference between a ground landlord who has no control whatever over the property on the land after he has let it, and the landlords of house property: and it would seem to be shirking responsibility to give up the ground rents, because if you retain them you have control of the property when the lease falls in, and can put things right, whereas if you sell it, or even give it away, you have no means of securing that the evil is remedied at all.

He also asked the Secretary of the Ecclesiastical Commission to let him know whenever the right moment came, in order that he might fulfil the promise to which he had committed himself. But in the seven months between the letter to Lady Cripps and his death the opportunity never occurred.

XXXI

The Church of South India—Lambeth and Canterbury—Theologians Old and Young

I know, of course, that in the tradition of Christendom Churches have been either in communion with one another or not; full communion and excommunication have been the only alternatives. I am always suspicious of the dilemma in connection with spiritual realities. It is almost inevitable that its crude dichotomy should do violence to the complex delicacy of spiritual relationships. We are dealing with a situation in which great Christian traditions have grown up in varying degrees of detachment from the Catholic tradition. It does not seem to me possible to speak of some of the communions inheriting those traditions either as fully qualified or as totally unqualified to be called Churches. They seem to me to be Branches in the Vine in which some strands—notably the Apostolic Ministry—have been severed, but in which others—especially the use of the Scriptures and of the Sacraments—remain, so that the sap or life of the Vine truly flows in those Branches, and certainly none can deny that they bring forth fruit. . . . No large alienated group, so far as I can recollect, has been won back by the method of anathema and ex-communication. A new method is called for and the novelty of the South India Scheme may be regarded as one of its merits. The parties to the negotiations in India are attempting what is, so far as I know, an unprecedented enterprise; it is at least possible that unprecedented expedients may be legitimate and appropriate.

W. T., to the Upper House of Canterbury Convocation,
January 1944.

THE most serious church controversy in which Temple was engaged during his Primacy arose from a proposed Scheme of Union between four dioceses of the Anglican Church of India, Burma, and Ceylon, and certain non-episcopal Churches in India. The origin of the Scheme is to be traced back to May 1919, when thirty-two men of various church affiliations met at Tranquebar, of whom all but two were Indians. The Indians had recently held a joint evangelistic mission, the happy fellowship of which encouraged them to consider whether some more permanent co-operation could not be attempted through a union of the Churches for which they severally spoke. The motive was, in the first place, evangelistic and pastoral (in his address on 'Chris-

tian Unity and Church Reunion' delivered to the Convocation of
Canterbury in full Synod on 25 May 1943, in which he referred
to the South India Scheme 'by way of illustration only', Temple
declared that 'pastoral urgency is a main factor in the whole
situation'); and a further pressing need was to strengthen the
sense of Christian fellowship for which Indian converts felt a deep
longing, placed as they were in the environment of an overpoweringly hostile world. The internal disputes of the Churches were
unintelligible to them, and even if they had not been they would
have appeared irrelevant, 'so great is the difference' (as a Brahmin
convert of North India explained) 'between a man who worships
Jesus Christ and a man who worships a cow'. The thirty-two
men drew up a scheme which was in substance the one eventually
agreed to by the three Churches that decided to go forward with
the venture. These were the Anglican Church of India, Burma,
and Ceylon (as regards its four dioceses in South India); the
South India Provincial Synod of the Methodist Church; and the
South India United Church, which was itself a union of Presby-
terians, Congregationalists, and other Missions. Together they
were to form the Church of South India, on the fourfold basis of
the Scriptures, the historic Creeds, the two Sacraments of Baptism
and Holy Communion, and the historic Episcopate.

Few members of the home Church were more interested in the
Scheme than Temple when it first emerged in 1919. His sympathy with it was enhanced by the fact that the setting, the background, of the Scheme differed totally from anything in England,
and therefore made more possible of fulfilment one of his lifelong
dreams—the union of the best in both the Catholic and Protestant
traditions within the bounds of a single Church. He first had
some responsibility for the progress of the Scheme at the Lambeth
Conference of 1930, when he was chairman of the Committee on
Unity (see p. 459) and drafted its Report, much of which deals
directly with the South India Scheme. It was, of course, well
understood that the Lambeth Conference had no constitutional
authority to accept or reject the South Indian proposals. Lambeth Conferences are entitled to consider and offer advice on any
subject, but have no executive or administrative functions. The

responsibility for any action in connexion with the South India Scheme—in so far as Anglicans were concerned in it—rested with the Church of India, Burma, and Ceylon. The Lambeth Conference of 1930, however, considered carefully the report of its Committee, and among the points agreed by the whole Conference were these:

That the Church which will result from the union will not be a Province of the Anglican Communion but will be a Province of the Universal Church;

That the Church of South India after the union will at once enjoy a restricted communion with Churches of the Anglican Communion; and

That the whole Scheme is one of union for the purpose of attaining ultimate and complete unity.

On the widest view the last of these three points was the most important. The Scheme was entirely new. Several other plans for bringing Churches together had been canvassed or proposed, but every one of them aimed at attaining unity before union. A precisely reversed process was outlined in the South India Scheme; it aimed at union for the purpose of gradually attaining unity; it was to mark the initiation, not the consummation, of union. Much of the opposition to it appeared to be founded on the assumption that all the issues on which the uniting Churches were disagreed would have been settled once and for all, as if by some irrevocable agreement, in the Scheme itself. Nothing could have been further from the minds of those responsible for it, and this was emphasized in the Report of the Lambeth Conference:

We observe as a novel feature in the South Indian Scheme, that a complete agreement between the uniting Churches on certain points of doctrine and practice is not expected to be reached before the inauguration of the union; but the promoters of the Scheme believe that unity will be reached gradually and more securely by the interaction of the different elements of the united Church upon one another. It is only when the unification resulting from that interaction is complete that a final judgment can be pronounced on the effect of the present proposals.

Thus there were to be both a short-term and a long-term policy, and this conception can be illustrated from two statements in the Scheme about the Ministry in the United Church. All the ordained ministers of the uniting Churches, working in it at the date of union, who assented to the Basis of Union and accepted the Constitution of the Church, were to be accepted as ministers of the Word and Sacraments in it; but 'it is the intention and expectation', stated the Constitution, 'that eventually every minister exercising a permanent ministry in it would be an episcopally ordained minister': the initial state of the Church of South India is thus to be an interim state and is acknowledged to be designed to grow into a specific unity. The same view was taken by the Lambeth Conference of the restricted communion suggested in the period immediately following the union: it was accepted in the clear light of a hope that ultimately it would develop and lead into unrestricted intercommunion.

In India the Joint Committee of the uniting Churches continued their work in the years after the Lambeth Conference of 1930, and certain changes were introduced into the Scheme in 1936 and 1941 on which the opinion of the Consultative Committee of the Conference was asked—and was given two years after the changes had been made. In 1938 its response was favourable, and in 1943—although criticism was not lacking of one or two of the changes—it decided that on the whole there was no reason for modifying the reply given five years earlier.

It must not be concluded, from this skeleton outline of the history of the Scheme, that all went smoothly for Temple and its other supporters. Apart from his personal correspondence, which included not only letters to and from those with whom he took counsel but also private letters to critics and waverers, there was definite opposition which was shown in two ways—by a deputation he received at Lambeth on 26 January 1943, and by the action of the Superiors of certain Anglican Religious Communities. The deputation was introduced by Lord Quickswood: among the members were Dr. Rocksborough Smith (formerly Bishop of Algoma), Professor N. P. Williams, Canons Demant and Hood, the Rev. E. K. Talbot, C.R., Mr. T. S. Eliot, and Lord Sankey.

Lord Quickswood stated that the Scheme offered no security of orthodoxy; its treatment of the Ministry and the Sacraments was unsatisfactory; it would introduce schism into the Anglican Communion; and the religion latent in the Scheme was what might be called 'undenominational'. Sankey deprecated the treatment of episcopacy and the lack of a Book of Common Prayer in the proposed Church, and Canon Demant criticized the Scheme as being an example of an indigenous local expression of Christianity, to which many equally dangerous parallels could be found in the history of the Church. Dr. Edwin James Palmer (formerly Bishop of Bombay) replied to the points that had been raised, and after a few questions had been asked and answered Temple gave a short history of the procedure that he had thought fit to adopt, spoke of the very great 'urge towards unity' (largely on pastoral grounds) that was now manifest in South India, and emphasized his own duty to withhold decisive judgement till he had had an opportunity of reviewing all the opinions set before him. His most serious charge against the deputation was expressed a few weeks later in a letter to the Rev. W. B. O'Brien, of the Society of S. John the Evangelist:

> I had hoped that the deputation which came here would have analysed the Scheme from the standpoint of its members more thoroughly than it did. There was much said about the evil of compromising the Church, there was much less said in support of the contention that the Scheme in fact does this. . . . It is apparent from some of the letters which I have received that the writers have not studied the Scheme, just as it was apparent in the course of the deputation that one at least of the speakers had not read the Resolutions of the Lambeth Conference concerning it, for he expressed anxieties with regard to the position that would arise in England itself, which those Resolutions quite expressly precluded.

He stressed this point after a conference held at Canterbury in February 1944, in a letter addressed to all who took part in it:

> I am wondering how many of [X]'s friends have read the

Scheme. Of course it has not been easy to get copies in England. And if one had seen only Fr. O'Brien's account of it, or some others which have been sent to me, the matter would not seem open to doubt. But I should maintain that these are gravely misleading. What surprised me was to discover that [X] himself had not noticed that this is the point where views diverge. He told me he started from the supposition that the Scheme betrays the principle of the Apostolic Ministry and therefore could not explain how I could both affirm that principle and accept the Scheme. I had hoped that both my speeches in Convocation had made clear the fact that I can accept the Scheme precisely because it does, among other things, impart the Apostolic Ministry to bodies of Christians hitherto deprived of it. And I was attacked in *The Times* by Hensley Henson for saying exactly this. The fact that they do not receive it as such does not greatly trouble me. I have bestowed it on many young men who did not accept it as such; most of them knew later what they had received, and valued it.

Far more serious, of course, is the question of schism. . . . This whole thought of seceding on the grounds stated by [Y] shocks me profoundly—morally and spiritually. His main ground was lack of assurance concerning the faith of the United Church arising from the failure to include Creeds in its public worship. This seems to me inevitably to pre-suppose the major premiss that we should not be in communion with persons or bodies unless we have a guarantee that they hold the full Christian faith; whereas to me it is axiomatic that we should seek to be in communion with all persons or bodies claiming that they hold the full Christian faith unless we have ground for assurance that they do not. Anything else seems to me startlingly discordant with the ethos of the New Testament. . . .

I have wondered if the position which I have described as 'to me axiomatic' would seem to be illustrative of procedure on 'minimal' lines. I do not think it should. I want Anglicans to go into any Union proclaiming the Catholic tradition of Faith and Order and offering it to others. And I want those others to come in proclaiming their own principles. Of course, if they actually *repudiate* the Catholic tradition union is impossible; and if their principles are positively incompatible with it, union is impossible. But non-acceptance is quite different from repudiation.

In one of my Convocation speeches I said that many of our troubles seemed to me to be the drawing of negative conclusions from positive premises. In this debate I seem to detect the frequent recourse to a kindred fallacy, the confusion of contradictories with contraries (Sorry! 'Once a don, always a don.' But one must think as one can and not another way). By this fallacy non-acceptance is treated as repudiation. Thus it seemed to be assumed that, of course, everyone would say the Creed if he could; if he does not, it must be because he does not believe what it contains. But, as the Bishop of Derby said, there are Christian traditions according to which the whole content of the Creed is accepted but the credal form is objected to as coming between the soul and the Word of God. I believe that is a mistake, and that through association with Creed-saying congregations those who at present hold this view will learn the value of the public recitation of the Creeds and will largely adopt the practice. But as the perversion of a purely Scriptural theology is anarchy or vagueness—against which we rightly urge the value of the recitation of the Creeds—so the perversion of the Catholic tradition is mechanization, against which some sects have sought to guard by the avoidance of some at least of its traditional forms. The coming together of two such streams of tradition may well be advantageous to both. But each must appreciate the real ground on which the other is valued—and this surely is the essence of the 'maximalist' approach.

The opposition of the Superiors was carefully organized under the auspices of the Church Union. Their 'Open Letter' to the Archbishop of Canterbury declared that the Church of India, Burma, and Ceylon would be 'condoning an Act of Schism' if it approved of four of its dioceses being included in the Scheme; and the letter ended by declaring that 'many hundreds, we might say thousands, of loyal clergy, with strong lay support', if they were driven to choose between 'their conscience and their present ecclesiastical allegiance', would receive 'not only sympathy but aid in re-establishing a body which could claim with justice to be the legitimate heir of the authentic principles of our Church of England'. This threat was too much even for Temple. The Open Letter had been sent to him before publication, with a request for a reply that might be published with it. He answered that he would gladly meet the Superiors at a Round Table Conference if they withdrew their threat of secession. They remained obdurate, even after a private interview with Temple at Lambeth, and refused to withdraw it. The Archbishop therefore declined to write the reply for which they had hoped. An answer was, however, printed in a pamphlet by Dr. Palmer, in which the Bishop dealt with the charge of schism and pointed out the many errors and inaccuracies of which the Superiors had been guilty. Temple's own reply was in fact given when he addressed the Upper House of Convocation after the answer to the Metropolitan of India had been finally settled. To discuss in detail the disagreement between him and his opponents on the exact meaning of one 'Church' being 'in communion' with another would involve, to begin with, two long essays on the correct interpretation of the words ἐκκλησία and κοινωνία. Here little more can be done than to emphasize the main point of contention. The opposition knew only two possibilities—either one Church was in communion with another, or it was out of communion with it. Having said this, they went on to assume what they wished to prove, that the word 'communion' was equivalent to 'full communion', which implies 'complete interchangeability of ministers and complete mutual admissibility to Communion'. Temple might have retorted that in certain details the relationship between the Roman Church and those Churches which Romans call 'Oriental' and we call 'Uniat' does not bear out the assumption; but he was content to reply (in the quotation at the head of this chapter) that the 'crude dichotomy' of the dilemma did 'violence to the complex delicacy of spiritual relationships': in other words, he had come to the conclusion (adopted by the Lambeth Conference of 1930) that the

Q q

dilemma was inapplicable to the proposed South India Scheme, which was admittedly an attempt to devise new measures for dealing with a wholly new set of circumstances.

Temple had already stated in Convocation that he might be asked certain questions by the Metropolitan of India, and in October 1943 he announced that he had received them: they had been sent to all Anglican Metropolitans. He consulted the Upper House, who, while they determined to keep the decision in their own hands, sought the counsel of the Lower House. Full consideration was given by the Lower House to the draft reply, and several suggestions were made which led to alterations in it before the Upper House gave their final advice to the Archbishop. Thus the reply, which was finally settled in January 1944, expressed the common mind of the bishops and had behind it the general agreement of the Lower House. It was concerned with two questions. Temple's answer to the first was that the Church of England would not break off communion with the Church of India, Burma, and Ceylon if that Church decided that four of its dioceses (Madras, Travancore, Tinnevelly, and Dornakal) were allowed to unite with the negotiating Churches according to the latest edition of the Scheme. His reply to the second—whether the Church of England would refuse to be in communion with the Church of South India—was of some length, and ended with the statement that 'there would not at this stage be unrestricted intercommunion between the Church of South India and this Province, but there would be such intercommunion between clergy and laity of the united Church and those of the Province as I have stated'. In January 1945 the General Council of the Church of India, Burma, and Ceylon accepted the Scheme in its final form.

One ominous conclusion was drawn by not a few from Temple's last utterances on the South India Scheme; but before it is stated two facts should be emphasized. First, it is difficult to exaggerate the strength of the suspicion with which—in this particular matter—he was regarded in certain quarters, where the soundness of almost any pronouncement of his on reunion would be *prima facie* questioned; and, second, he tended, from the first day that the Scheme came before the home Church, to leave things open and to hope, rather than to work strongly for precision. But it was contended that on one or two points he had not made his own meaning, or the full implications of the Scheme, entirely clear, especially on the exact nature of the 'intercommunion' of which he had spoken; and his successor at Lambeth took the opportunity of making a statement in the full Synod of Canterbury Convocation on 15 May 1945. In a masterly survey Dr. Fisher placed Temple's words in their true setting, and expressed his own conviction of the intention underlying any sentences that might be open to misunderstanding. But what did it mean, that Temple—of all teachers and expositors the most lucid —should have suffered this lapse from complete clarity? Only one answer was possible, and it was the answer his friends dreaded most. Ever since his enthronement he had borne an incredibly and increasingly heavy load of work. In the same period through which he had been engaged in the intricate correspondence and interviews demanded by the South India Church Scheme and in meeting a strong and determined opposition, he had never slackened his hold on the problems and duties imposed on him by the war or the legislature such as those described in the last two chapters, or on the day-to-day tasks of a diocesan and a metropolitan—and it was clear that already the strain was beginning to tell. 'Few in the long succession since S. Augustine', Mr. Winston Churchill had written when he told Temple of his intention to recommend him to the King for the Primacy, 'have received the succession to Canterbury at a time when the burden of the Primacy was heavier.' This was the bare truth. Of his two last addresses to Convocation on South India a lifelong friend has written: 'They seem to be genuine William, but it is a tired William who is writing, and the arrangement is not so clear and logical as usual. But they have the importance of being his last word on the subject.'

When the history of the Church of South India comes to be written at full length, it may be Temple's first word rather than his last which the Church will have cause most gratefully to remember. His patient charity towards critics of the Scheme never failed, and he was at pains to procure the best advice on matters of ecclesiastical precedent and other details in which he was not particularly interested, so that no weapon might be lacking in his armoury. But it was at the Lambeth Conference of 1930 that he saw his vision of the possibility of breaking through the close-spun web of separated traditions in which the home Churches had become entangled through the course of history: and to his skill in drafting and presenting the Report to the assembled bishops—a Report read and heeded by Church leaders the world over—is largely due the dispersal of what serious opposition there might have been to the Scheme at that critical moment in its history. It cannot be that this decisive contribution was forgotten when on 27 September 1947 the first corporate union was effected between episcopal and non-episcopal Churches by the solemn inauguration of the Church of South India in the cathedral church of Madras.

It is now time to gather up a few of the threads that went to make the pattern of the life at Lambeth and Canterbury. When Temple and his wife first stood in the wreck of his London home, his thoughts must have turned sadly to the Lambeth Palace of his youth with its wide corridors and spacious rooms, in which open house had been kept for his Rugby and Oxford friends. Part of the roof of Wren's library had been burnt away, 2,000 books were now ashes, and 3,000 more were jumbled together in a sodden heap on the floor. Piles of smashed furniture and pictures torn by the blast lay in a litter of broken glass and rubble, the great drawing-room was a mere gaping hole, and the chapel was open to the sky. It was not easy to see the Palace as his future home; but his wife's ingenuity triumphed. They made their dining and sleeping quarters on the ground floor which, though they had no spare room, provided enough space for the chaplain (the Rev. Ian White-Thomson), Miss Sinker, and their two selves. There were studies and offices on the first floor, and a temporary chapel of singular beauty designed by Mr. Cachemaille Day. Their devoted friend and gardener, Jasper Wright, and his wife had already moved from Bishopthorpe, Francis Woodward (Temple's head gardener at Repton) and his wife remained in charge of the Morton's Tower gateway, and Mrs. Berry, who had been house-keeper at Lollards' Tower for nine years, kept house for them, with a parlourmaid to help her. With this staff their life began, in a house where there had once been between twenty and thirty on the domestic staff alone.

At Canterbury the problem of living was easier. Whenever it was possible Temple spent from Friday evening to Monday or Tuesday morning (except for one week-end a year at Croydon) at the Old Palace, and these days were the happiest of his life as Primate. Here everything spoke to him of his father—the house which Frederick Temple was the first Archbishop to restore to its use as the Primate's home, the primatial cross he held as he gave his first Blessing after the enthronement on S. George's Day 1942, which his father had so often handled, the cathedral itself, and in it the monument to the old Archbishop which was now hidden by sandbags. (It had long distressed him that a blunder had been made of the inscription on it, which was due to the obstinacy of Dean Wace. Many years before he had written about it to his brother:

> Bishopscourt,
> Manchester.
> June 13th, 1924.

The enclosed has come from Caroe and I had meant in any case to consult you about the subject. The last sentence in the inscription on Father's monument at Canterbury was ruined by Wace. Armitage Robinson had drafted it 'Born under the fourth George, he crowned and blessed the seventh Edward', which gives the dates with a little literary point. Wace would not allow George IV to be mentioned because he was 'a very wicked man'. Armitage Robinson replied, 'So was Pontius Pilate'. That settled it, and Wace re-wrote the sentence, 'He lived through the reigns of William IV and Victoria and crowned Edward VII'. This of course is supremely pointless; many people lived through those two reigns. It does not even get the dates right, by leaving out 'George IV', and is altogether absurd.)

597

He was content to leave most of the diocesan administration to his staff, and here he was well served. The Archdeacons of Canterbury (T. K. Sopwith, followed by Alec Sargent, who had been a chaplain at Lambeth), Maidstone (Julian Bickersteth, formerly Headmaster of Felsted), and Croydon (H. W. Bradfield, now Bishop of Bath and Wells), and the Bishops of Dover (Alfred Rose) and Croydon (Maurice Harland, now Bishop of Lincoln), lifted much of the work from the Archbishop's shoulders, but he took as many Confirmations as possible in the Kentish towns and villages, and drank deep of his boyhood memories of their charm. Much of the peace he had hoped to find in his week-end home, however, was shattered when the bombing of Canterbury began within a few days of their moving into the Old Palace. Soon after the midnight of 31 May 1942 he and his wife were startled out of their sleep by the wailing of 'Tugboat Annie', as the hooter was called; flares began to drop, and bombs fell before they had reached their hide-out under the great oak staircase, where for two hours they sat helpless, fearing that each bomb might have struck the cathedral, especially one which was found to have destroyed the Library. Before long it seemed as if half Canterbury was blazing. Burgate Street (which forms one end of the Precincts) was alight from end to end, and the small household of the Old Palace used their stirrup-pumps on the house next door to theirs—Temple's sight was too bad and his movements too slow for him to be of much active help, but he went backwards and forwards with cups of tea. The full horror of the raid was not revealed to him till the next morning when he walked through the streets with his wife before he left for London; almost every one of the painters, cleaners, and others at work on the Old Palace had lost some member of his family, or some part of (if not all) his possessions. During the next week Temple had to spend several nights in London, much as it distressed him to be away from the danger and from his wife. But whenever he was in Canterbury he and his wife lunched in a restaurant, mixing with the people and giving them confidence by his own unruffled calm, and at the end of the following week he led a short service 'for the renewed dedication of our City to the Service of God and of thankfulness for the spirit of its people in the recent time of trouble'. The cathedral was packed to the doors. Some of those present still think of it as the most impressive service he ever took: it would have been terribly easy to dramatize the situation, but the Archbishop spoke and prayed with his usual and simple sincerity. By this time the people had taken him to their hearts: he and his wife became in truth citizens of Canterbury, a title which he fully earned by the leading part he played with his friend Charles Lefevre, the Mayor, when the plans for rebuilding their city came to be set on foot.

It would be idle to attempt to catalogue the Archbishop's activities during the short years of his Primacy. All kinds of international association and gathering claimed his support. In the House of Lords he was present and spoke whenever the subject of the debate (such as that on Family Allowances) seemed to him of first-rate importance; and in this part of his work especially he was able to rely on the help of the Archbishop of York. No men could have worked better in double harness than the two Primates. Twenty years—first as curate, and for ten years as vicar—in the large parish of Portsea had left Dr. Garbett with more than a superficial knowledge of the problems of the poor. His exceptional skill in administration and his mature judgement were the invaluable complements of Temple's prophetic gifts and his desire for vigorous and immediate action; and whenever the Archbishop of York spoke in the House of Lords on the housing of the workers, the Peers knew that they were listening to one who had made a close study of his subject. Though not always approving entirely of Temple's methods, Dr. Garbett shared to the full his enthusiasm for social welfare, and they stood side by side on many platforms during the 'Religion and Life' weeks. While sparing all the time he could for such efforts, Temple remained true to old affiliations like the Bermondsey Mission and the W.E.A.; and societies or organizations—such as Town and Country Planning and Youth Hostels—which looked ahead to the world after the war, were sure of his active help. There was one exception. On 24 June 1942 he writes to a correspondent who had asked for his sympathy with a new sodality:

... I have no doubt there are many people to whom the sort of ceremony that you describe would have an attraction. Of course there are others whom they intensely alienate. Most of my acquaintances would much sooner shoot themselves than call themselves 'Knights of St. George'. I believe that if anything is to go very widely in England it must have a rather colourless title. I remember one friend of mine remarking to me that Sir Oswald Mosley might at one time have made a big thing of his movement if he had dressed his supporters in Norfolk jackets, grey flannel trousers, and a rather inconspicuous tie that would be recognized by those who really knew its meaning. I think there was much wisdom in that. If however you find a backing for your idea you would certainly be right to go ahead with it in the interest of those to whom it appeals. We want to mobilize all the idealism we can in the days before us.

In this mobilization Temple himself was perpetually busy. Each September he presided over a conference at the Old Palace on the Church and the post-war World, to which he invited many men prominent in the life of the county—among those who attended one was Minister of Health and another became President of the Master Builders' Federation—and none came away, if he had stayed for the Archbishop's summing up, without some new conception of the implications of the Gospel for the coming generation. Another special interest was the Church Training Colleges for Teachers. In them, and not in the school buildings, he saw the Church's most valuable assets and its greatest potential hold on the training of Christian citizens, and he spent a whole week-end in consultation with Sir Walter Moberly, Canon Cockin (now Bishop of Bristol), Dr. J. W. Welch, and others on the future of the colleges.

But at the centre of his heart and mind lay the Eternal Gospel, and the commission to impart it to his fellow-men—and here the grave and growing danger was unmistakeable. He was well aware that a new missionary force had arisen in the world, and that a rival philosophy of life was being assiduously preached and practised in every continent. Communism, he said at a meeting of the York Diocesan Conference in the summer of 1933, 'is undoubtedly the most serious menace which has threatened the Christian Faith in the civilised world for some hundreds of years'. He was never attracted to it either as an economic system or a philosophy or a religion—'it is', he contended, 'all these three things'—for he could have little sympathy with a system that cut at the root of his most dearly cherished beliefs by denying 'the metaphysical worth of the individual', and by encouraging that 'shockingly false psychology' which assumed that men and women could and should be taught the lessons of freedom by the methods of servitude. All the more to be emphasized, therefore, was his conception of the Church's first and paramount duty. A few years before he came to Canterbury he had written these words:

The plain fact is that in the missionary enterprise we are ministering to the heart of the world's need, and satisfying the world's age-long quest. Nothing else in the same way touches all contemporary problems alike of practical life and theoretical enquiry. This is the field in which—whether our work is theoretically at home or abroad—we may most effectually serve both God and man.

As soon, therefore, as he was settled at Lambeth, he made arrangements to hold regular informal conferences with experts who kept him in touch with the bafflingly diverse needs of every section of the mission field, and one of his deepest concerns was the project for a College of the Anglican Communion which it was his hope to see founded at Canterbury. At home the task of evangelism was a different and, in some ways, a harder one. Here was no going out in hope to a people who had never heard the name of Christ, no glad response to a gospel which seemed to meet the deepest human needs, no romantic conquests of heathendom in far-off lands with the Church daily giving thanks for what Newman called 'the joyous swing of her advance'; but a dour struggle for the souls of a people who had given up the belief of their fathers, and the degeneration of whose ethics—in spite

William Temple

of Thomas Huxley's prophecy that, whatever happened to Christian theology, Christian morality would always be strong enough to hold its own—had exactly kept step with the decline of their faith. And were the clergy of the Church of England interpreting the Gospel in words and terms that would wake any echo in the hearts, and evoke any response from the wills, of the new generation? To these young people conceptions such as 'atonement' and 'redemption' as commonly treated in the pulpit were unintelligible. Through no fault of their own they had been denied such cultural training as that which an ancient university could offer, with its background of Christian history and tradition and the continued witness of its Theological Faculty, college chaplains, and chapel services. What was there in common between those who found long ago that *Lux Mundi* or *Foundations* answered at least some of the questions they were asking, and these new devotees of the cinema, the dance-halls, and the communal lawn-tennis courts? And—for this would be the greatest disaster—were the few preachers who could attract the notice of the younger men and women offering them the full Christian Faith or just so much of it as needed little mental or spiritual effort either to declare or to assimilate? When, therefore, in the year of his death, he was asked by the Church Assembly to appoint an Evangelistic Commission to survey the whole field, Temple's aim was to secure that the answering of these questions should not be left in the hands of the Old Guard, with whose outlook he and others were already familiar, but with men and women who could approach the problems of evangelism with the outlook of those whom it was hoped to evangelize: 'the only service the Commission can really offer', he wrote to one of its younger members, 'is to make some suggestions which are novel, and anything novel will seem to some people revolutionary.'

While the Commission was sitting (its Report was not published till after Temple's death) he kept in close touch with three means of evangelization—two of which he felt were being almost entirely neglected—the theatre, the cinema, and the B.B.C. With the work of the religious department at Broadcasting House he was entirely satisfied: 'it is', he wrote, 'very conscious of its

602

responsibility and taking most effective steps to meet it'; but its programmes were heard by only a comparatively few listeners, and it was more important that those who listened to the Brains Trust broadcasts should hear the Christian answers to some of their questions than that the already converted should hear a good broadcast address on Sunday evening. Temple had some inconclusive correspondence with the Joint Directors-General of the B.B.C.; one of them replied that 'the Brains Trust is designed essentially as a light-hearted entertainment programme', to which Temple retorted that 'though the answers are light-heartedly given they are often seriously accepted', and after he had heard again from the other Joint Director-General, he closed the correspondence with this letter:

> I am very grateful for your letter. I perfectly understand how the present situation with regard to the Brains Trust arose and I see the difficulty of handling it in a way that would to a person like me be completely satisfactory. [——] is of course definitely hostile to the notion of a Divine Revelation of any specific kind: [——] has lately become a Theist but is still by no means a Christian in doctrine, and these two have taken an extremely prominent part all through. You cannot help many questions arising which involve answers that carry Christian or anti-Christian implications. I certainly should not dream of suggesting that the denominations should appoint representatives. If you asked me for suggestions and I sent six names at least three of them would be non-Anglican. But I still think that so long as there is a likelihood of questions like—What is the difference between a man and a monkey?—being put to the Brains Trust, there ought to be someone there who would give the specifically Christian answer along with the various people who would give answers of another kind.

As President of the Christian Cinema and Religious Film Society, Temple gave his full support to the making and producing of good religious films. He had little leisure for going to the cinema himself and before 1937 he had only seen two films in his life. But he understood as well as any the chief problem with which the Society was faced. Most other arts had been religious in the first place and had afterwards expanded into secular forms; the cinema began in a secular form and it was the Church's duty, so to speak, to christen it. This would not be done merely by occasionally showing films based on some Bible story, but by illustrating the expansion of the Christian Church in the world, and showing the progress of the Gospel and the methods of the evangelists in the regions that had come under their influence. He realized the handicaps, such as the lack of capital and the difficulties of technique, and urged upon all those responsible for religious films that the technical side of the work must be of the highest order if they were to take their place by the side of the best secular output. One result of a conference held at Lambeth in July 1943 was the establishment by the S.P.C.K., at Temple's request, of a Film Department for the Church of England; and he consented to take part in two films—one of them, depicting Canterbury Cathedral and the Kentish country-side, being shown at thousands of picture-houses.

The theatre, on the other hand, was linked to the Church by a long tradition, and to strengthen the bond between the two was his constant endeavour. On the initiative of Martin Browne (whose Pilgrim Players had set themselves the same task) a few actors and producers met at Lambeth in May 1943, and an informal group was formed to obtain, if possible, plays from leading writers and to interest other producers and actors, while the Pilgrim Players continued to build up a public that would be ready to welcome the plays as they were put on.

In such ways Temple fostered the means that lay to his hand for the evangelization of England. But there was a more fundamental difficulty to which he had to address himself. What exactly was the 'evangel'? What truths were they that lay at the heart of the Church's Gospel, truths which the theologians ought to be continuously analysing and expounding, so that they might be proclaimed Sunday by Sunday from the pulpits of the National Church? The less thoughtful of the Church's leaders saw no reason for the question; it was difficult for them even to understand its meaning. Familiar throughout their lives with the Scheme of Salvation handed down by their fathers, mentally inelastic and undisturbed by the successive shocks of two World Wars, unaware of the new and strong currents of religious belief that were flowing over the continent of Europe, they were woefully 'at ease in Zion'. But Temple had been watching closely for some years the growth of a new trend of thought within the Church, and long before he came to Lambeth he had said to a friend: 'I do not think I understand what some of our younger theologians are trying to get at, and I am quite certain that they do not understand me.' This was a state in which he could not rest, and during the last years of his life he set himself, with some of his like-minded contemporaries, to find out exactly what it was that separated them in thought from the younger theologians and, if there was a chasm, to attempt to bridge it. His own position can hardly be understood unless two factors are taken fully into account—the foundation on which the structure of his theological thought had been built up, and the environment in which his most formative years had been passed. Here let Bishop Brilioth again be called in witness. After expressing the doubt he occasionally felt 'whether Temple's extraordinary ability did not carry with it a certain lack of depth in his thinking, whether he did not in certain cases give way to the temptation to gloss over difficulties with a happy formula', he goes on:

Of his theological work I am not competent to judge. It would be of great interest if his philosophical ideas could be analysed in connexion with his sociological and devotional writings. Perhaps he appeared too theological for the philosophers and too philosophical for the theologians. An enquiry into his social ethics from a Lutheran point of view would probably shew that the common criticism against Anglo-Saxon theology as founded on a superficial conception of the Kingdom of God cannot be applied to him. *But it could perhaps be maintained that the philosophical categories which he handled so skilfully did not further a really thorough-going analysis of fundamental theological principles.*

Temple would not have resented the suggestion in the words here italicized. He made no profession to be a 'very well-read man' in theology, and denied that there was any 'weight of learning behind' his books comparable with that behind the work of Dr. Kenneth Kirk or the late Professor A. E. Taylor. On the effect of his philosophical training on his theology, he wrote to Dom Gregory Dix in 1939:

> So far as [my work in the field of theology] has had an influence, I think it was due to the fact that I was a philosopher, by profession at least, before I seriously turned to theology, and I was able to build bridges across which people could travel, from the outlook common in universities and such places from 1910 to 1920 or even 1930, to a Christo-centric view of the world. That is what *Mens Creatrix* and *Christus Veritas* are all about. I don't think it was a blind alley, because I do think it led to Christ. The trouble with it now is not where it leads to, but where it starts from; and this is a point at which nowadays an increasing number do not stand, though some still do.

It is difficult to portray, except for those who once breathed it, the atmosphere 'common in universities and such places' forty years ago. Liberalism was triumphant—as in politics so in theology, both in method and outlook. There was not only a widespread belief in the power of truth to prevail on its own merits in an atmosphere of free discussion, but associated with it there was also the type of religious outlook to which Dr. Sanday had given the name of 'reduced Christianity'. Moreover men were living in what was, to all appearances, a stable world. A vague acceptance of Christian principles—if not too meticulously analysed—could be generally assumed, and Christian standards of conduct had not yet been widely disowned; but, side by side with this ineffective remnant of a great religious tradition, there was a growing belief in almost automatic progress which made any talk of Redemption appear irrelevant. The dominant philosophy of those days, though 'theistic and spiritual'—Temple wrote in an article which, by way of flying a kite, he contributed to *Theology* in November 1939—left 'no room for a specific Incarnation', and it was in the theology of the Incarnation that the Christo-centric metaphysics for which he was searching (see Chapter XXVIII) was to be found. But by the time (October 1937) he signed the Preface to *Doctrine in the Church of England* the war-clouds were gathering, and with prophetic instinct he wrote:

A theology of Redemption (though, of course, Redemption has its great place in the former [*sc.* a theology of the Incarnation]) tends rather to sound the prophetic note; it is more ready to admit that much in this evil world is irrational and strictly unintelligible; and it looks to the coming of the Kingdom as a necessary preliminary to the full comprehension of much that now is. If the security of the nineteenth century, already shattered in Europe, finally crumbles away in our own country, we shall be pressed more and more towards a theology of Redemption. In this we shall be coming closer to the New Testament.

This pressure was felt increasingly towards the end of his life, but his words written earlier had remained, and much that had contributed to their origin and their context—Christian standards, liberalism, security, a 'Christian map of the world', Christianity as a clue to some universal synthesis, and so on—meant nothing to men reaching manhood first under the constant threat, and then among the horrible realities, of war. To the younger generation what they could see of the universe did not make sense. The tension between the Love of God in which they were bidden to believe and the experiences of life was very severe, and the burden that lay on them was to grapple with what appeared to many an inescapable dualism between God and the world. Yet God had spoken. And the 'younger movement in theology', wrote the Rev. E. L. Mascall (*Theology*, December 1939) in answer to Temple,

is concerned not so much with trying to prove by the methods of contemporary secular thought that the Christian religion can make out a good case for itself as with taking the Faith as something revealed by God in Christ and examining how it can be applied to the problems of the present-day world.

The significant conclusion is reached that

whereas it is usually the old who are theologically conservative and the young who are inclined to kick over the traces of orthodoxy, to-day . . . the older men are to a greater or lesser degree liberals, while the younger are demanding a return to dogma.

Here, then, the younger theologians saw their hope. Repelled by the humanistic liberal-individualist idiom of thought which they traced in the pre-war theologians, they pleaded for a return to that dogmatic theology which they held to be one of the great legacies of the Middle Ages to the Church, and to a view of the Bible as the inspired word of God which it was the theologian's first duty not to criticize but to interpret. Nor, they contended, need this interpretation necessarily follow the lines of continental Protestantism, for it would find expression in Catholic rather than in neo-Calvinistic and neo-Lutheran terms. In this at least they were sure of Temple's sympathy. He was no Barthian. He was concerned to insist strongly that the Creator can be known from the creation; and he mistrusted Barth's assertion of the irrelevancy of natural theology—'How, in the face of *that*,' he once asked a friend with whom he was walking, as he stopped in the street and pointed to a cat washing its face, 'can they deny the existence of natural theology?' But, on the main contribution which the younger theologians could make to theological thought, and of the help he could personally give them, he wrote while still at Bishopthorpe:

I doubt if I can now *lead* them; perhaps I might do a little in steering them. . . . But is it really the function of an Archbishop to be a theological leader? If so, my predecessors both before and after the Reformation were a sorry lot; and Canterbury—not much better. After St. Anselm, who? Perhaps Bradwardine, Cranmer, and *before he was Archbishop* my father. And the Popes are no better.

But even if the younger generation of theologians had, as Temple said, 'to find its own starting-point and build its own bridges', at least he could meet them and learn more specifically of their outlook across the conference table; and a small party, representing both older and younger, was invited to spend the last three days of January 1940 at Breadsall Mount. The Bishop of Derby (Rawlinson), one of the acutest theologians among Temple's contemporaries, was their host, and the Bishop of Coventry (Haigh, now Bishop of Winchester) added weight to the counsels of the older group: the younger were represented by the Rev. Michael Bruce, Canon V. A. Demant, Dom Gregory Dix, and the Rev. E. L. Mascall. The divergence of outlook was found to be considerable. All were agreed that the discussions had been immensely worth while: but an impression was left on the minds of the bishops that the younger leaders were in danger, in their reaction from liberalism as describing a particular set of not very satisfactory opinions, of too hastily repudiating liberalism in the sense of a method of free inquiry. This found expression in a letter Temple wrote to his wife during a fuller conference which was held in April of the same year:

> College of the Ascension,
> Selly Oak.
> April 9, 1940.

. . . This Conference is extraordinarily interesting and worth while. It very quickly ceased to be older *v.* younger and turned into a general discussion of fundamentals. A good many of us feel that the neo-Thomist group in their eagerness to re-assert the truth and authority of the Bible are ignoring the lesson of the 19th century and becoming involved in a position which is either obscurantist or humbug. E.g. one of them, when pressed, after saying that the Bible is true both in whole and in part, said its truth might consist in the 'true statement of a false position'! But there are several most hopeful spokesmen of sane catholicism and sane evangelicalism.

A third effort was made when Temple invited the original group, a little enlarged, to Canterbury in February 1944. Here there was a sense of tension that had not been felt before: the proposed scheme for the Church of South India dominated the proceedings, words such as 'schism' and 'secession' passed from mouth to mouth, and the cleavage between the two groups was unmistakable. But much was gained through these conferences. To the younger theologians they brought contact with one who had succeeded in understanding them, who was not only interested in their views but also grateful to those who expressed them, and who was ready to meet the frankest of criticism with honesty and good will. Some of the younger group had come, feeling that they disagreed so fundamentally with Temple that they would be unable to say what they really thought. They soon found that his attitude towards them not only made complete candour possible, but even demanded it. The strongest impression—that of Temple's forbearance and humility—was common to them all. They knew, writes one of them,

> that we had been meeting with a man of prayer and a saint. That realization overshadowed everything else. It was not his great intellect, or his astonishing gift of understanding, or the wideness of the theological rift, that made the deepest impression, but the fact of his holiness.

The effect of the conferences on Temple—strongly as he maintained his own position—can be deduced more from his private correspondence with those who took part in them than from any of his public utterances, though some have traced their influence in his notable Supplement to the *Christian News-Letter* of 29 December 1943—'What Christians stand for in the Secular World'.

It was his intention, had he lived, to carry the conferences farther. For a time, it seemed, the 'Christian map of the world' must be rolled up; but as he laid it aside there were no idle regrets, no pessimism in his summary of the task immediately ahead—nothing but an inspired determination and a patience that waited upon God:

> We must dig the foundations deeper than we did in pre-war years, or in the inter-war years when we developed our pre-war

thoughts. And we must be content with less imposing structures. One day theology will take up again its larger and serener task and offer to a new Christendom its Christian map of life, its Christo-centric metaphysic. But that day can hardly dawn while any who are now already concerned with theology are still alive. The task that claims our labour now is far less alluring to one of my own temperament and upbringing, yet there can be no doubt that in theology as in life we shall be rather enriched than impoverished, even though we are concerned to light beacons in the darkness rather than to illuminate the world, if we are more completely dominated in thought and aspiration by the redeeming acts of God in Jesus Christ.

XXXII
Last Days

I wish Cranmer had not urged us to pray against 'sudden death'. He meant 'death for which we are unprepared'—the Latin is *ab improvisa morte*. Let one be always prepared and then go suddenly for the sake of one's self and all one's belongings.

> W. T., letter to his brother, February 1939.

. . . To be happy to the end, and then to fall asleep here and wake there, is just what one might have prayed for.

> W. T., letter to Lady Frederick Cavendish on his
> mother's death, April 1915.

AMONG the addresses which Temple gave to the Manchester Diocesan Conference, one of the most warmly received was on 'The Ministry of Healing'. It was delivered in 1924 at a time when the subject was being widely discussed, as the Bishop of Bradford (Perowne) had recently conducted a mission of healing in his own diocese which had been extensively but unfortunately advertised in some of the popular newspapers. Temple expressed his gratitude to the Bishop for taking the mission and so affording some guidance to all who might be responsible for such efforts in the future; but he gave a number of reasons why he could not personally 'take any formal part' in a mission of healing. The incident was used chiefly as a peg on which to hang his own views concerning the relation between body and spirit in sickness and in health, as he saw it in the light of the method and mind of Christ. These views he impressed upon the Guild of Health, a pioneering body with which for many years he was associated, and later upon The Churches' Council of Healing, which was founded with his guidance in 1944; its aims were to act as a co-ordinating centre for all healing movements that rested on a Christian basis, to promote co-operation between doctors and ministers of religion, and to bring the work of healing into closer relation with the regular work of the Churches.

On two points he felt no doubt. 'You cannot', he said to his diocesan conference, 'read the Gospels and cut out the ministry

612

of healing without tearing them to ribbons', and 'you cannot draw a sharp line between what is physical and what is mental. The two merge into each other in most baffling ways.' Nor was 'spiritual' healing to be identified with that which M. Coué was then practising at Nancy and elsewhere; though himself a Christian man, M. Coué made no use either of his own or his patients' religion in effecting his cures. True spiritual healing was only possible through religious faith, and therefore for those only to whom health was 'strictly incidental' and in whose lives faith in God was 'uppermost'. Many in the audience who knew Temple well must have felt that throughout the address he was telling of his personal experiences, and in one passage he so exactly expresses his own spiritual achievement that it deserves to be quoted at length:

We all know instances of really saintly people who are suffering constantly from physical disabilities that bring them great pain. . . . Once you have reached [the] point of real supremacy over your body, it is at least possible that the spiritual power may be increased by its constant exercise against something physical which to others would seem to be weakening and even debilitating. . . . The causes of health, as the causes of sickness, are very many, but among the forces which will tend to keep us in health will be a faith which is extended to a real expectation of God's goodness in every department of our being. That will bring us either actual health or a greater power of triumphing over ill-health, and either of these is a great blessing. Moreover, when we triumph in the way that I have described over ill-health, the result is, in fact, that our health is somewhat better than if we were merely lying passive in the grip of our disease, because owing to the exaltation of mind there is a real access of vitality which tends to combat the disease itself. The way in which, as I think, faith chiefly promotes health is precisely by the creation of peace of mind beyond what can be reached in any other way, and especially beyond what can be reached by those who have much to distract them, whether in their circumstances or in their bodily condition.

No words could better describe Temple's own triumph in his lifelong struggle against the discomfort and the crippling pains of gout.

His first attack came when he was two years old, and he was suffering from the last when he died. There seems to be no particular medical reason why he should have been numbered among its victims—though in defiance of popular theory the disease does appear to assail teetotallers with no less virulence than topers—but it has been suggested that men of genius are more likely to be tormented by it than others. In one volume of his fascinating autobiography Osbert Sitwell has written:

> Of this illness, mysterious in its origin and manifestation, the late Dr. Havelock Ellis wrote that 'it occurs so often, in such extreme forms, and in men of such preeminent intellectual ability, that it is impossible not to regard it as having a real association with such ability', and again that it would be impossible to 'match the group of gouty men of genius, for varied and preeminent intellectual ability, by any combination of non-gouty individuals on our list'.

Temple was specially liable to be attacked when he was tired or when the strain of work was unusually great—while he was a Fellow of Queen's he wrote to his mother that a bout from which he was suffering was due to 'ordinary end-of-terminess'—and in a letter to his brother in 1942 he mentions that 'it often comes with snow'. But only by reading a continuous series of letters, such as those which he wrote to his brother, is it possible to realize how seldom he could hope to be completely immune. In one after another the subject recurs. The following are typical; they are taken from the years 1925 to 1928, and they cover part of the period when he went abroad to take a cure:

Chine House,
Totland Bay,
I.W.
August 19, 1925.

We got down here on August 7, and I promptly succumbed to the worst attack of gout that I have had. It went on developing for four days. Now it really is going off, and in a special sort of boot, actually sold as a 'gout-boot', I got up Headon Hill yesterday, walking like Agag. As this house is at that end of the green-walk it is, of course, only a step to the top; but it marks a stage.

Those who don't have gout might say—'Then, if you had to keep still, you had nothing better to do than to write letters, so you might have written to your big brother before now'. But those who do have it would not say that . . . while the foot was worst, I could hardly steer my pen. Pitt, who knew all about gout except its 'causes, prevention, and cure', would have fully sympathised with his correspondent who wrote in a postscript—'Please excuse my bad hand-writing, but I have a sharp attack of gout in the foot'.

(Temple was not amused once to hear this sentence from Dundas's letter to Pitt quoted, by a priest who was taking his ordinands' Retreat, as an excellent instance of an 'irrelevant' excuse.)

Hotel Beau Site,
Aix les Bains.
April 30, 1926.

I told you that I was being ordered to take a cure. Accordingly we came here arriving on April 21. On the way I developed an attack, and it became very acute. They would not start the general cure till it subsided. So a precious 9 days out of the time allotted have been wasted. By abandoning a visit to Oxford planned for Whitsuntide I can squeeze in 6 more days than had been intended, and so (I hope) get the benefit of the plan. I really *must* get on top of this gout somehow.

Windsor Castle.
April 23, 1927.

The gout which began on Easter Day became quite serious and is by no means gone yet. I can hobble, but can only go up or down stairs one step at a time. But it is on the go, and may be quite gone in about two days' time. It is rather a disappointment that I have not been able to keep clear for the whole year from one Aix cure till the next. But I am going back there starting on May 2, and ought therefore to have a good spell free after that.

> Bishopscourt,
> Manchester.
> Feb. 5, 1928.

Never before have I had two attacks of gout in a month. But it has just happened. I trust I am getting free now. But having got into a shoe for the first time on Jan. 25 (after three weeks), I had to go back to bed on Feb. 2.

So, year after year, the tale is the same; stronger as he became in spirit, he never lost heart, but it was an unequal struggle. There were periods in the last years of varying length during which he suffered no attack, but as he grew older he could not hope for the buoyant resilience with which after each bout he had once returned to his work. New tasks came to his hand, and he saw none among the old ones that could be surrendered, until by the spring of 1944 it was clear that he was carrying a load of work beyond the power of any man to bear. Early in March he wrote to his brother that he was 'a bit tired' with 'a mild headache every evening', and on the 17th he and his wife escaped for a short break to Grasmere. One day he was fit enough for them to reach the top of Helvellyn: he was overjoyed to be trudging again up the fell tracks and lying on the grass or sitting on a rock, and looking out on the familiar hills and valleys; but there was now none of the leaping downhill he had once enjoyed, and it saddened him to find how much more slowly he had to pick his way down the tracks. In spite of this long climb, which brought on an attack of gout, he came back to London refreshed for the hardest summer's work he had yet faced, and though his time-table was far too heavy he managed somehow to fulfil his engagements. 'Religion and Life' meetings still claimed much of his time. On 4 May he had a busy afternoon and evening at Swansea. He returned to London in time for a meeting on the morning of the following day, and by the afternoon he was in Bournemouth. Here, the Bishop of Winchester writes, he was met by the Vicar of Bournemouth, Prebendary Boyd, and taken up to his vicarage for a cup of tea. At 6.20, before addressing an immense gathering in the Pavilion on 'The Cross', and on a hot evening, he declined an invitation to be driven in a car and walked by himself (more than a mile). On his arrival at the Pavilion there were 2,500 people inside, and fully 1,500 outside who could not get in. I had to meet the Archbishop and ask him to walk some way to S. Peter's Church and speak to as many of the 1,500 as could be got there, for a few minutes. This he readily consented to do. Half an hour later he came back to the immense meeting in the Pavilion and he spoke to them for a full hour, again without a note, on 'The Cross'— the finest address that I ever heard him give and I think in many ways the finest I have ever heard anyone give. On returning after all this to the Vicarage for supper he appeared both then and afterwards as fresh in mind and body as if he had done nothing at all all day.

Of this address Temple wrote to his wife:

It was on 'The Cross' and I am sure that the introduction of a purely religious theme for one evening is a thing we must encourage elsewhere. They have had the usual programme otherwise: that is, Religion in Home, School, Industry and Commerce, the World of Nations, and the World-wide Church. But that programme takes for granted what religion *is*. There was a very remarkable atmosphere. I took it on the plan of the Oxford Mission—an exposition, a hymn, an application.

It had always been difficult to persuade him to relax between his engagements: the Bishop of Winchester remembers another day —at Coventry, a few years earlier—when between 4 p.m. and 10 o'clock Temple spoke at three meetings and attended a reception. There was an interval of fifty minutes in the six hours, and this he filled (as his too frequent custom was when he was away from home) by writing letters in his own hand: 'as I went to pick him up at 6.50', the Bishop writes, 'he was just licking up the envelope of the fourteenth letter.' On another occasion he went down by night to Plymouth, spoke six times on the next day, and returned by the night train to London.

He was never entirely free from gout as the pace quickened during his last summer. June and July were always exacting: 'I *must* leave more time', he had written to his brother in 1943, 'in future years for routine and the unexpected calls. They are far more numerous than at York', and this year an overwhelming number of persons and causes, committees and conferences, lectures and addresses, claimed every moment that could be spared from his normal duties. The pressure was intense, and the strain was increased by the part he had to play in the passage of the Education Bill through Parliament—and by the flying bombs. As a rule these passed over Canterbury without doing damage, though east Kent and 'Bomb Alley' suffered considerably as they were brought down, and one Sunday evening a bomb fell not far from a village church between Ashford and Maidstone while he was preaching. In Croydon—that small ecclesiastical island that still remains in the Canterbury diocese—the destruction was widespread; and he found time on July 11 to drive down with his wife and chaplain and meet his suffragan, the Bishop of Croydon. Together they made a tour of the parishes, on one of the most trying evenings the town had endured. As they left the church in the first of the eleven parishes he visited, there was a loud explosion about half a mile away on the opposite side of the main road. 'Which way do we go now?' Temple asked. 'This,' replied the Bishop, pointing to the column of dust which was just beginning to subside. Temple's ironic laughter rang out as they started on their way, and there were several more crashes before he left the district—but the clergy and the people of Croydon felt that they knew their diocesan the better for his having shared their danger on that day. The bracing effect of his cheerful confidence had been felt on a similar occasion three years earlier by Professor Julian Huxley, who writes:

My last recollection of him is exceedingly vivid. The P.E.P. group was to meet for lunch one fine day in 1941, and Temple was to attend. That morning, however, witnessed one of the worst daylight raids which central London ever experienced. I was the only one of our group to reach Queen Anne's Gate, and found the staff huddled in the not particularly safe shelter of the basement. After a quarter of an hour, during which the elements of a snack lunch were provided, Temple appeared, his arrival heralded down the basement stairs by characteristic gusts of laughter. I don't think that we got much further that day in the definition of war aims, but I do know that Temple's presence acted as a vivifying tonic on every human being present in that by no means agreeable situation, from the youngest typist up to the research director.

Nor was there much peace at Lambeth. On no night was it possible to look forward to undisturbed rest, and Temple took to sleeping on a sofa in the ground-floor passage of the palace, where there was a domed roof which had so far stood up to shock and blast since the beginning of the war. On 26 July he wrote to the Archbishop of York:

I hope you were not alarmed by the telegram lately sent? The flying bombs have been falling rather near here lately: there was one at the end of the garden which broke all our windows on that side of the house, and some others; then there was one in the bombed part of St. Thomas' Hospital which did a little damage but nothing very serious; there was one in Lambeth Walk, just behind the railway embankment, which broke a few more on the other side of the house; but last Friday morning there was one just across Lambeth Road, beside but not on Lambeth Bridge House, which blew in all the windows facing that way as well as a good many others, and shook down several ceilings; it blasted the back door clean off its hinges on to the ground and it jammed the front door and the big gates in Morton's Tower so that they would not open (that is still true of the big gates).

There was some alarm that rumours might get round, because the thing was rather bad, suggesting that it was desperate. Nobody to do with us was hurt, though one man was killed in the garage across the road where the bomb actually fell. Of course it all causes much inconvenience, but for us nothing worse than that, so far, and this hideous house stands like the Rock of Gibraltar!

Temple might have added with truth that when the last of these bombs fell he had finished shaving and was just getting ready for his bath. He scrambled out into the passage, and a second later a good part of the ceiling collapsed.

At last the time came for their summer holiday. Before the end of July he and his wife were back at Weacombe where they were out of the danger area, and in an atmosphere of unbroken peace and quiet happiness they took up the old routine. Again they walked and ate their sandwiches on the top of the Quantock moors looking across the Bristol Channel to Wales, and sat under the apple tree, or on wet days on the verandah, with their books; again each Sunday they walked through the village lanes to the early Communion Service and to Evensong. Once more there was time for intimate talk; and this year it turned much on their plans for the future. Some day, they both supposed, he would retire: 'You must not leave it too late,' his wife urged, 'we must have time to settle down and enjoy ourselves.' 'Yes,' Temple replied, 'and I must give up in time to let Geoffrey [Dr. Fisher, his successor in the Primacy] have his whack.' Then, after a moment of thought, he added: 'I think I shall write a book about the Holy Spirit. I have always wanted to have a try at that.' On his other subjects he had little to add to the volumes already published: 'I have written all I have to write', he told Bishop Brilioth, who stayed with him at Canterbury during 1942, 'on philosophy or sociology.' The book of which the Churches stand in sore need was never written, nor was the more romantic vision of the young Fellow of Queen's to be fully realized: 'I would like', he had once said when the talk had turned on personal ambitions, 'to be Archbishop of Canterbury, and after that Archbishop of Pekin.'

On the last of their outings a crowded omnibus passed them, and they failed to get the lift which would have shortened the walk by a full three miles. The next morning Temple complained of gout in the knee. He returned to London in some pain, which had increased by the time he went down to Luton to broadcast for the Day of National Prayer. A special message of welcome had already been written to him by the Secretary of the local Trades Council, and the B.B.C. sent a comfortable car to bring him to Luton on the evening of Saturday, 2 September, when he recorded in the parish church a service which was broadcast in several transmissions on the following day. With the help of a stick he climbed into the pulpit—many listeners noticed the clatter of the stick as it fell down the pulpit stairs during the broadcast— after which there was a delay of more than half an hour. Owing to a severe storm thirteen telephone lines were down, and while they were being repaired Temple had to remain standing with the whole of his weight on one leg. Dr. Welch, then Director of Religious Broadcasts, recalls this incident:

His patience and good humour, despite the frustrating delays and the great pain he was suffering, were unforgettable. When I went up to the pulpit to offer our abject apologies, and before I could open my mouth, he said: 'I am so sorry, Welch, that the engineers are having all this trouble, I know how anxious and bothered they must be.'

It had been arranged for him to preach on the Sunday morning at the main broadcast service of the Day of Prayer, and as he was going to bed Dr. Welch asked him whether he would like also to celebrate the Holy Communion: 'I don't think I ought to,' he replied, 'as I can't kneel, and it might upset the people if I had to remain standing through the Service.' This objection was over-ruled, and he celebrated the Sacred Mysteries for the last time at the altar of Luton Parish Church.

On 5 September, after an open-air service in the City (see p. 517), he went to Pleshey, in Essex, to share a Retreat with some of the clergy in his diocese. He was obviously unfit to go, but insisted that he must join them. When, halfway through the Retreat, it was suggested that he might be taken home he merely replied 'I need this Retreat', and stayed to the end, sitting a good deal in his bedroom where it was easier to be in a position that relieved the pain. The Retreat House, he said at breakfast on the last morning, had 'the right quality of peace'; and he himself left, the Warden wrote, 'in the minds of those who saw him at Pleshey an unforgettable impression of serenity and unbroken recollection'. He motored down to Canterbury on the Friday and dealt with some correspondence in the evening, but by the time he went to bed the gout had flared up and developed into one of the worst attacks he ever had, and several engagements were at once cancelled. On 16 and 17 September there was a small conference—a 'diocesan Malvern'—in the Old Palace, at which he took the chair without apparent effort, while aeroplanes with gliders attached to them roared overhead on their way to the airborne landings at Arnhem. He was determined also to be present at a Synod of his clergy which he had planned some months before, and on 18 September ('by dint of heavy drugging', as he wrote to the Archbishop of York) he was able to be taken into the cathedral to give his Charge: 'I think it probably set me back a lot, but if so I still think it was worth it.' Three days later he confessed to his brother (in a dictated and typed letter) that the gout had 'returned before it was quite gone in prodigious violence, and I have now got acute gout in both knees, which, as you can imagine, is quite immobilizing'.

In the middle of October he wrote to Lang a description of the service at which he delivered his Charge:

> My entry was not really very Papal! I was not carried in at the tail of the procession fully vested; but ten minutes before the service began I was taken in by four St. John Ambulance men in uniform with only a cassock, in a carrying chair. They deposited me on the platform of the Throne and got me upright. Ian helped me into an alb and stole. I then got into the Throne, in which we had put a high chair, and he then put the cope on me. But it did mean standing a lot on the one leg which was still wholesome, and no doubt it was largely a result of this that what had been the good knee went bad. Since then both have been completely out of action.

The address, which was given after the Eucharist and lasted

about fifty minutes, was in part an exposition of Ephesians iii.
14–21, in part an appeal for the right reception to be given to the
men and women of the Forces on their return to civil life; and
through it all there sounded the pastoral note: 'It was', wrote the
Archdeacon of Croydon, 'the most impressive of all his addresses
which I heard. Looking back it seems as if he was handing on to
us his mission and his task.' But the strain had been too great,
and when the Archdeacon saw him on the next day he knew for
the first time that Temple was seriously ill. He now seemed more
subdued, and less inclined to conversation even with those whose
company he normally enjoyed—but the last of the engagements
he had resolved to keep before leaving Canterbury was yet to
come. From 21 to 23 September he saw the ordination candidates
one by one in his bedroom, and then called them all to sit round
him while he delivered his Charge to them from his bed. This was
his last ministerial act, and it is doubtful whether he would have
chosen any other.

Plans had been made, on the doctor's advice, to take him on
2 October to Westgate, where it was hoped that the change of
air might help to reduce the gouty inflammation in his legs; but
he was not well enough to make the move till the following day.
He was taken from his bedroom to the ambulance in a carrying-
sheet—'I'm sorry I am so heavy', he said to his bearers on the way
downstairs—and arrived at the Rowena Hotel, where everything
was done to make him comfortable, apparently not much the
worse for the journey. But it was clear that recovery would be
gradual, and on 14 October a notice appeared in the Press that the
Archbishop was obliged to cancel all his engagements up to the
end of November—which brought a kindly letter of sympathy
from the Roman Catholic Archbishop of Westminster. For the
next three weeks he was kept as quiet as possible; twice the Rev.
W. E. M. Williams, Vicar of S. Saviour's, Westgate, celebrated
the Holy Communion in his room, and on Temple's sixty-third
birthday, 15 October, the Vicar and his churchwardens came to
offer the present of a cheque for £63, from the people of their
parish—a gift which deeply moved him. His chaplain and
secretary came over in turn from Canterbury to help him deal

William Temple

with any affairs that were still left in his hands, and on 22 October he was visited by two American bishops, Dr. Oldham of Albany and Dr. Hobson of Southern Ohio. They found him weak, but alert in mind and full of plans for the World Council of Churches and the next Lambeth Conference. The Bishop of Albany had been entrusted to deliver this letter from the President of the United States:

> The White House,
> Washington.
> September 19, 1944.

My dear Archbishop,

The mission which my old friend Bishop Oldham, in whose diocese I have long worshipped, is undertaking gives me an opportunity to send you a brief word of greeting.

In these victorious days and in the times to come we need, more than ever before, that spiritual strength which is essential to a just and enduring peace. The Church is indeed fortunate to have at this critical time a leader of your strength and understanding.

With warm personal regards and best wishes for success.

> Very sincerely yours,
> FRANKLIN D. ROOSEVELT.

On the 23rd he sent a hopeful message to his diocese, but in a letter to Lang he told how it was not the gout that his doctors chiefly feared:

... Though I have sat up for a few hours with my legs on a rest for two or three days, I have really been in bed ever since. The change of air helped a bit, but progress was still so absurdly slow that we got the specialist down from London, who promptly said that the gout was being kept alive by a quite independent infection, which must be tackled first. I wanted to issue a notice that I was suffering from sub-acute strepto-coccal infection, but some people thought that would be unduly alarming. What the origin of this infection is, they are trying to find out. ...

On the following day he wrote a similar letter to the King's

624

*On the way to his Enthronement at Canterbury on 23 April 1942,
preceded by his Chaplain, the Rev. Ian White-Thomson*

Private Secretary, and by the first post on Thursday the 26th came a cheering note from London to say that they were 'on the track of the bug' responsible for the infection. He read *The Times* as usual after breakfast and the Sister who attended him had come in to make his bed, when suddenly he said: 'I feel very faint.' His wife could see from the expression on his face that this was no ordinary fainting attack and hurried away to get help, returning quickly with a heart specialist who happened to be staying in the hotel, and who at once did what he could in the short time that remained. 'Are you in great pain?' he asked, to which Temple replied: 'No, but I can't breathe'—and a few moments later, painlessly and peacefully, he died.

All had been as he would have wished. He had often commended the use of the prayer from the Burial Office of the Prayer Book: 'Suffer us not, at our last hour, for any pains of death, to fall from thee', and had hoped to be spared the test of a long and painful illness. From this he was saved. His body was taken to Canterbury, where it was received at the west door of the cathedral by members of the Foundation and escorted, with the singing of the *Miserere*, to the Chapel of Our Lady in the crypt. Here it lay in state before the altar, while continuous watch was kept for twenty-four hours, during which thousands—with a notable proportion of men and women in the Services—came to honour his memory and to thank God for his life. On the Eve of All Saints a large crowd gathered and waited in the drenching rain to be admitted to the funeral service. How many could help contrasting the clear April sunshine of that S. George's Day two and a half years before—when the cathedral was bright with spring flowers, and when all who waited for the Kingdom of God were exulting in the joy of promise as the new Primate was borne to his enthronement by the hopes and prayers of Christendom— with these leaden October skies and the wail of the *De Profundis*? Yet this was not the dominant note of the service. The sense of desolation passed into thanksgiving and triumph as the congregation joined in the hymn 'The strife is o'er, the battle done', and Bach's Choral Prelude 'Hark! A voice saith, all are mortal', which was played on the organ as the body was carried out through the choir, foreshowed the tranquil bliss of the Celestial City:

> O what peace and joy hast thou!
> Lo! The sun is rising now,
> And the breaking day I see
> That shall never end for me.

Of this he had no doubt. 'There is nothing in the world', he had said to his wife as they talked one day of the life after death, 'of which I feel so certain: I have no idea what it will be like, and I think I am glad that I have not, as I am sure it would be wrong.' Twenty-five years earlier he had written, in a letter to D. C. Somervell, of immortality:

> I remember once saying to Bertie Russell: 'I believe in it far more than the evidence warrants'. He said: 'And I *dis*-believe far more'. For myself, I do cling to it immensely. I do not mean that I want it for myself as mere continuance, but I want it for my understanding of life. . . . Also, just for myself I hope I may somewhere get further in ὁμοιῶσις τῷ Θεῷ. And moreover 'God is Love' appears to me nonsense in view of the world He has made, if there is no other. I state this as 'Confession', and not as argument.

It had been Temple's wish that his body should be cremated, and when this had been done the ashes were brought back from Charing by the Bishop of Dover and the Archdeacon of Croydon: they remained in the Old Palace chapel until the next morning, when Dr. Fisher (then Bishop of London) celebrated the Holy Communion in the presence of the Old Palace household and a few friends. On All Souls' Day the cathedral was again filled for the Memorial Service, and through the Eucharist there rang the same note of triumphant praise. The ashes were committed to the earth in the Cloister Garth next to the grave of his father—again as he wished—and there, while the world mourned, they were content to

> Leave him—still loftier than the world suspects
> Living and dying.

Many had feared that the Archbishop was gravely ill, but few thought of gout as a disease that ended fatally and there was a confident hope that, though the bout was more prolonged and more serious than usual, he would recover from it as he had from earlier attacks. But it soon became known that the immediate cause was not gout but a blood-clot and that he died, with little warning, of pulmonary embolism. The suddenness of the news caused a shock beyond description. A man who had lived at the heart of public life for more than half a century said that he could recall only two incidents that had had a comparable effect—the postponement of the Coronation of King Edward VII and the loss of Lord Kitchener in H.M.S. *Hampshire*. Among the first cables to reach England was this, to the King from President Roosevelt:

> I am deeply grieved to learn of the death of the Archbishop of Canterbury. He was rightly considered a good friend of the United States, and his efforts to promote Anglo-American understanding and co-operation were unceasing. As an ardent advocate of international co-operation based on Christian principles he exercised profound influence throughout the world. The American people join me in extending this expression of sympathy.

From Pretoria Field-Marshal Smuts cabled:

> A great man has passed. Church, nation, and the world, have suffered an irreparable loss.

And the Provost of Queen's, his old colleague and friend R. H. Hodgkin, wrote that Temple's sudden death 'seemed to shake the western world as if one of its pillars had been removed', and that the college had lost the most distinguished of its Fellows since 1341.

In each of these messages there is a single word by which some measure can be taken of what passed from the earth with Temple's death. Many primates have ruled the Church with vigour and distinction, one or two have helped to determine the course of its history, and a few have wielded an appreciable influence over one section or another of the life of England. But of none except Temple, since the Reformation, can it be said that the *world* was the poorer for his passing. The weight of his moral authority was equalled only by that of Franklin Roosevelt: its extent was unique. Cables and letters of sympathy with his widow poured into Canterbury from the world's centres of influence—universities (from America to China), embassies and ministries (especially of those countries for whose rights he had so arduously contended), teachers, Trades Councils, statesmen, mayors, men of letters, and Church leaders in every continent. And to a much larger part of 'the world'—that is, to the common man—his death was the loss of a champion and a friend. 'His memory', wrote J. S. Middleton on behalf of the National Executive of the Labour Party, 'will be cherished in countless homes, and will remain a great inspiration in countless hearts.' At the memorial service in Sheffield Cathedral 'I found myself sitting', wrote a northern industrialist, 'behind an engine-driver and close to a cutler who I knew must have asked for time off at his own expense to attend'. A North London parson was only one of a thousand ministers of religion who might have written this:

> I am a plain working parson and I know nothing about theories of Church and State. But what I do know is that working people in my parish are saying that for the first time in their lives there has been an Archbishop interested in their problems and their difficulties.

In a Japanese prison-camp in Singapore 'thousands of men'— in the words of one of them—'British, Australians, and Dutch, spoke with love and affection of one whom they had never seen', and 'the whole camp drooped with the shock'. Two thousand labourers in the sugar industry on the Island of St. Kitts sent a cable, as they were 'assembled on eve of crop', which was signed by their Archdeacon and the President and Secretary of their union, deploring the loss of 'a champion of justice and righteousness'. A schoolboy of fourteen, who had had tea with Temple at Canterbury on the last day he came downstairs for it, wrote home telling of his grief at the news—'this is the first time in my life that any one has died whom I know really well'. 'When his sudden death was announced', writes Lord Selborne, 'there was not a Peer who did not feel that the House of Lords had been greatly impoverished'; and in a dressing-room of a London theatre her old dresser murmured to Dame Sybil Thorndike: 'The poor man has lost a friend.'

To the Churches the blow was shattering. 'None of his predecessors', was the verdict of his friend and lifelong critic Hensley Henson, 'appealed to so large a proportion of the Christian Society throughout the world, and none will be more sincerely and affectionately remembered': 'Surely', wrote Mrs. Arnold Rowntree, 'there never was a servant of the Church who "belonged to" different denominations and classes as he did.' But it was his own Church that felt the shock most severely. Leadership such as his had not been given in living memory; the results of it, in enthusiasm and confidence, were being felt in every department of the Church's life; and high hopes were cherished that the impetus might be even greater during the last years of his rule. Much of this has been written by Canon Spencer Leeson, Chairman of the Secondary Section of the National Society, in describing a meeting which was being held at the offices of the Society a few hours after Temple's death:

There was a general feeling among us all that with him at Lambeth we should always get encouragement and drive, and never be encountered by the kind of caution that puts obstacles in every path. An example of this came on the day of his death; at four in the afternoon we had just finished a long and difficult bit of work, and we all of us said to each other that the thing to do was to go to the Archbishop and ask him to put it through—it would mean a very large-scale evangelistic appeal as applied to education, something in the form of a pastoral letter. We knew all the difficulties about joint pastoral letters, but we were confident that he would overcome them and that something would be done. At that very moment the news of his death came—and I do not think I have ever seen ten men so broken down as we were then; as if by instinct we all pushed our papers away and fell on our knees, and the Bishop of Willesden said the best prayer he could think of in the stress of the moment. This account is not in any particular exaggerated, as the Bishop could tell you. We felt in a sense that we had to start all over again—it was like the loss of a father.

And so the tale could be extended, till once more the question presses: How was it that one who felt uncomfortable in the company of strangers, who lacked the gift of natural contact with men and women, of talking easily to them of their own small concerns and trivial tastes, succeeded in carrying the Church into many hearts and corners where it was unknown or despised before, and was able so to touch the imagination of the common man as to earn the title of 'The People's Archbishop'? The answer must lie in the fact of Temple's great humanity, founded as it was on his love of God and fortified by massive knowledge, absolute simplicity, and a sincerity that was beyond question. He was, in the words of Professor H. G. Wood, 'an essentially honest and true leader'. He cared about people and he understood their problems—and they knew that he cared and understood. In all the matters that struck deep to the roots of their living—health and housing, education and industry—they had watched him for forty years as he stood in the forefront of the battle on their behalf, never wavering or afraid, never playing down to them or up to others of whose good opinion a smaller man would not have dared to risk the loss. Besides this—to quote the Rev. Ian White-Thomson, the domestic chaplain who served him with devotion from his first days at Lambeth to the end—there was

> his own geniality and simplicity of bearing, his ready smile, his cheerful greetings to them, his deep humility, and, as he travelled by bus or train, his entire unself-consciousness of manner. Here was someone they understood, someone with real dignity but no airs, someone who walked about amongst them as one of themselves.

Let the last memory be that of one well versed in men and affairs, who had enjoyed his friendship since the days when they were undergraduates together at Balliol, and was brought in close personal touch with him towards the end of Temple's life. Lord Beveridge writes:

I have one last recollection of him coming down near the end of the war to address the Oxford Union. He gave a magnificent address but some of the other speeches were tragic in their flippancy, and unworthy of his presence. This illustrates the loss that the world has suffered through having William Temple no longer with us. We are only gradually beginning to realize that in some ways the greatest evil of war is spiritual even more than material, in rousing evil passions and sanctifying them under the name of patriotism, in breeding materialism, cynicism, and disillusion. Against that William Temple seemed to many of us the ideal destined leader. He was greater than his great office. His loss to the world in its untimeliness is second only to the loss of Franklin Roosevelt.

Which of these and a hundred other eulogies, we may wonder, does Temple remember most gladly? First, perhaps, the President's: 'gratifying' he would have called it, and his eye would have twinkled. For the rest, our fancy may picture him lingering here and there over some word the more precious for its telling not of his personal and particular triumphs, his manifestly great achievements, or his immense influence—but of that common touch which bound him to the multitude in the primal fellowship of human-kind. So it will be with his friends. Their thoughts of him may range far and sink deep, as they look back on whatever of life it was their joy to share with him; but not a few, nor these the most trivial, of their happiest memories will be quickened by the simple tribute of a Cumberland dalesman, who, when he heard of Temple's passing, shook his head and muttered sadly: 'He was a very *jolly* man.'

SOME EVENTS IN
WILLIAM TEMPLE'S LIFE

The following record does not give a complete list of his writings, or of his journeys to the continent of Europe for the Oecumenical Movement.

1881 Born 15 October, in the Bishop's Palace at Exeter: second son of Frederick Temple and Beatrice, daughter of the Rt. Hon. W. S. S. Lascelles.

1891 Colet Court Preparatory School, Hammersmith.

1894 Confirmed, June.
Rugby School, September.

1895 Scholar of Rugby.

1900 Balliol College: Exhibitioner.

1902 First Class, Classical Moderations.
Archbishop Frederick Temple died; (born 1821).

1904 President of the Oxford Union.
First Class, Literae Humaniores.
B.A.
Robert Browning: An Essay.   ⎫ Printed for private
The Province of Science: An Essay. ⎭ circulation.
Fellow and Lecturer of Queen's College, Oxford.

1905 Joined the Workers' Educational Association. President 1908–24; President of the North-Western Section 1924–9.
Visited Germany: Berlin, Jena.

1906 Ellerton Theological Essay Prize: honourably mentioned.
Revisited Germany.
First public speech: Church Congress, Barrow-in-Furness.

1907 M.A.
Lay member of Oxford Diocesan Conference.

1908 Made Deacon by Archbishop of Canterbury (Randall Davidson).

1909 Ordained Priest by Archbishop of Canterbury.
Student Christian Movement Conference at Matlock.

1910 Hon. Chaplain to Archbishop of Canterbury.
The Faith and Modern Thought: Addresses to the London Inter-collegiate Christian Union.
Edinburgh Conference.

632

Visited Australia for the S.C.M.
Headmaster of Repton.

1911 *The Nature of Personality*: Six lectures in Oxford.

1912 *The Kingdom of God*: Lectures for the Cambridge Christian Evidence Society.

Two essays in *Foundations: A Statement of Christian Belief in terms of Modern Thought*, by Seven Oxford Men.

1913 *Repton School Sermons: Studies in the Religion of the Incarnation*: Sermons preached in the school chapel during his first two years as headmaster.

1914 Rector of S. James's, Piccadilly, London.
Studies in the Spirit and Truth of Christianity: University and School sermons.
Edited *Papers for War-time*.

1915 Hon. Chaplain to the King.
His mother died, 2 April; (born 1845).
Visited U.S.A.
Church and Nation: Bishop Paddock Lectures delivered at the General Theological Seminary, New York.
Editor of the *Challenge* until 1918.
The Collegium.

1916 Married Frances Anson, 24 June.
Plato and Christianity: University Extension Lectures in Oxford.
One of the Secretaries of the National Mission of Repentance and Hope.
Report of the Archbishops' Commission on Church and State, of which he was the youngest member.

1917 Proctor in Convocation.
Issues of Faith: Lent lectures.
Mens Creatrix: An Essay.
First Chairman of the Secondary Schools Examination Council.
Presided at the meeting on 16 July in the Queen's Hall, London, to launch the Life and Liberty Movement.
Resigned Rectory of S. James's, Piccadilly.
Competition: one of the five collaborators in this Collegium book.

1918 D.Litt., Oxon. In the 26 years which followed he received 12 degrees from 11 universities, including 2 from Oxford and 1 from Cambridge. The Cambridge Doctorate of Divinity, in

1933, was the first honorary degree of D.D. given by the University under its new statutes.
Life and Liberty Campaign.

1919 Canon of Westminster.
Visited the Forces in France.
The Enabling Act passed.

1920 *Fellowship with God*: Sermons in Westminster Abbey and elsewhere.
Edited the *Pilgrim* until 1927.
Chairman of Universities Relief Committee.

1921 Bishop of Manchester: consecrated 25 January in York Minster, enthroned 15 February.
Life of Bishop Percival.
The Universality of Christ: Addresses to the S.C.M.
His first mission on Blackpool sands; he took part in the mission annually while Bishop of Manchester.

1923 A member of the Archbishops' Commission on Christian Doctrine: first meeting, September. Chairman in 1925, on the death of Dr. Burge. On 1 October, 1937, he signed the Report, which was published in 1938.

1924 *Christus Veritas*: An Essay.
Chairman of the Interdenominational Conference on Politics, Economics, and Citizenship (Copec), Birmingham.

1925 Took his seat in the House of Lords.
Hon. Fellow of Queen's College, Oxford: later (as Archbishop of York) Visitor.
Christ in His Church: Charge at his Primary Visitation of the Diocese of Manchester in 1924.
Christ's Revelation of God: Three lectures to an S.C.M. Conference in Manchester.

1926 *Personal Religion and the Life of Fellowship*, in the Bishop of London's Lent Book Series.
General Strike: Coal stoppage.

1927 *Essays in Christian Politics and Kindred Subjects*: Articles from the *Pilgrim* and addresses to the Manchester Diocesan Conference.
Lausanne Conference on Faith and Order.

Some Events in William Temple's Life

1928 Jerusalem Missionary Conference.
Christianity and the State: Henry Scott Holland Memorial Lectures.

1929 Enthroned Archbishop of York, 10 January.
Chairman of the Central Council for Broadcast Adult Education.
Chairman of the Continuation Committee of Faith and Order.
Sworn a member of the Privy Council.

1930 His first Lambeth Conference: Chairman of the Committee on Christian Unity.
'Lambeth Conversations'.

1931 *Thoughts on Some Problems of the Day*: the Charge at his Primary Visitation of the Diocese of York.
Oxford University Mission: the most notable of several missions to universities. The addresses were published (from a shorthand writer's report) in
Christian Faith and Life, of which the eleventh impression appeared in 1945.

1932 Opening sermon at the Disarmament Conference, Geneva, 6 March.

1934 *Nature, Man and God*: Gifford Lectures at Glasgow. The first lecture was delivered on 21 November 1932 and the last on 2 March 1934.
The Ethics of Penal Action: The Clarke Hall Fellowship Lecture.

1935 *Christianity as an Historical Religion*: The Charles Gore Memorial Lecture.
Second visit to the United States, for the International Convention of the Student Volunteer Movement at Indianapolis, December.
Chairman of the B.B.C. General Advisory Council.

1936 *The Preacher's Theme To-day*: Four lectures at the College of Preachers, Washington.
The Church and its Teaching To-day: The William Belden Noble Lectures at Harvard.
Christianity in Thought and Practice: The Moody Lectures in the University of Chicago.

1937 Oxford Conference on Church, Community, and State.
Chairman of the Edinburgh Conference: Faith and Order.
President of the Library Association.
Chairman of the Governing Body of Rugby School.

1938 Holy Week services in Athens.
Consecrated S. George's Cathedral, Cairo.
Chairman of the Committee which produced the Report,
Men without Work.
Doctrine in the Church of England (see 1923).

1939 *Readings in St. John's Gospel* (First Series).
Letter to the Daily Telegraph (the 'Lansdowne Letter').
Amsterdam World Youth Conference.

1940 *Readings in St. John's Gospel* (Second Series).
Thoughts in War Time: Religious, political, and theological addresses and articles.
The Hope of a New World: Talks and sermons.

1941 Malvern Conference, 7–10 January.
Citizen and Churchman, in the Archbishop of York's Lent Book Series.
'Religion and Life' weeks begin.
Chairman of York Council for War-time Service.

1942 *Christianity and Social Order*: a Penguin Special.
Palm Sunday to Easter: Broadcast addresses during Holy Week and Easter.
Enthroned Archbishop of Canterbury, 23 April.
Albert Hall, 26 September. Addressed other meetings in the campaign 'The Church Looks Forward', with the Archbishop of York, in several large cities.
Freedom of the City of York, 30 October.

1943 Freedom of the City of Exeter, 1 May.
Church Assembly Commission on Evangelism.
Social Witness and Evangelism: The Beckly Lecture, 13 July.
Thomism and Modern Needs: Lecture to the Aquinas Society, 19 October.
What Christians Stand for in the Secular World: Supplement to the *Christian News-Letter*, 29 December.

1944 *The Church Looks Forward*: Sermons and speeches of his first eighteen months as Archbishop of Canterbury.
Reply to the Metropolitan of India on the South India Church Scheme, and address to Convocation on 'Problems of Unity', January.

Some Events in William Temple's Life

Addresses at many 'Religion and Life' meetings in the spring
and early summer.

Broadcast from Luton Parish Church, 3 September.

Diocesan Synod in Canterbury Cathedral, 18 September.

Died at Westgate, 26 October.

Funeral in Canterbury Cathedral, 31 October.

Memorial Service in Canterbury Cathedral, 2 November.

PORTRAITS OF WILLIAM TEMPLE

1. *By* J. WATSON NICHOL, 1915. Subscribed for by Old Reptonians, parents, and masters. The Audit Room, The Old Priory, Repton.

2. *By* J. WATSON NICHOL, 1915; a copy of the above. Given to W.T. by the Old Reptonian Society. The Library, Queen's College, Oxford.

3. *By* T. C. DUGDALE, 1929. Given to W.T. and his wife by 'friends and fellow-workers in the dioceses of Manchester and Blackburn'. Lambeth Palace.

4. *By* T. C. DUGDALE, 1929. Given by the same donors to the Manchester Art Gallery.

5. *By* PHILIP DE LASZLO, 1934. Painted by direction of the Council of the Corporation of the Church House. Church House, Westminster.

6. *A study by* PHILIP DE LASZLO, 1934. Given by the artist to Balliol College. Balliol Hall, next to the Herkomer portrait of Frederick Temple.

7. *By* OSWALD BIRLEY, 1942. A parting present from the clergy and laity of the diocese of York. Bishopthorpe.

ACKNOWLEDGEMENTS

I T would be less than generous to leave unrecorded the debt I owe to many who have helped me in the making of this book— to Mrs. William Temple first, for honouring me with the invitation to write it; for the letters from her husband that I have reproduced, as well as for others I have not had space to quote which have thrown for me a strong light on the Archbishop's character and outlook; no less for the accounts which she wrote of various events in her husband's life and freely placed at my disposal, and for the more personal help and intimate counsel which none but she could have given. To the Archbishop's brother, Col. F. C. Temple, C.I.E., I am particularly grateful for his friendly confidence in entrusting to me about seven hundred of his brother's letters to him, with full permission to use them as I wished. 'Those relations', wrote Samuel Johnson, 'are commonly of most value in which the writer tells his own story'; and the extent to which I took advantage of Col. Temple's generosity will be seen in every chapter of the book.

Much of the hesitation I felt in undertaking the task was put away when Miss Dorothy Howell-Thomas, who was the Archbishop's secretary at the time of his death, consented to give her whole time for six months to collecting, sorting, and arranging the mass of material available to the biographer: in every one of the countless boxes and files which she filled with letters and papers I found evidence of her industry and sound judgement, and without her unselfish co-operation the work would have been impossible. Nor can I forget the untiring patience with which Mr. A. Hodkinson, Lay Vicar of Lichfield Cathedral and Secretary of Lichfield Theological College, attacked the exasperating task of reading my handwriting and reproducing it in legible form, or the timely assistance of Miss Lily Wood, who was my first secretary thirty-five years ago and returned to my help by typing the whole book and preparing it for the publishers.

All the chapters have been read (either in proof or typescript) by Mrs. Temple, the Archbishop of York, the Bishop of

Chichester, Sir Walter Moberly, Col. Temple, and Mr. R. H. Tawney. Not one of these is to be held responsible for any of my views or statements; but I dread to think how many inaccuracies would have appeared in the text if I had not been able to profit by their numerous criticisms and corrections. My friends Mr. Hubert Dobell and Canon J. E. W. Wallis (Chancellor of Lichfield Cathedral) have kindly read all the proof-sheets; and I also owe to them several suggestions for clearing up the inconsistencies and ambiguities which they detected. I began to make a list of Temple's many friends, not only in this country but also on the continent of Europe and in the United States of America, whom I wished to thank for reminiscences of their intercourse with him and for their illuminating assessments of the Archbishop's views and achievements; but the catalogue grew to such an inordinate length that I had to give it up, and I must ask them to accept this 'omnibus' word of most sincere thanks. I cannot, however, do so without mentioning three persons whose particular knowledge I have been privileged to share—the Rev. Eric Fenn, whose willingness to let me draw on his familiarity with the Oecumenical Movement, in all its ramifications, saved me from the despair of ever being able to present an account of Temple's work for it in a concise and intelligible form; my old friend the Bishop of Derby, whose insight into Temple's theological development is probably unequalled among their contemporaries; and the Archbishop of Canterbury, of whose affection for his predecessor I took almost shameless advantage. Though I have harried him frequently during the last two years, his Grace has withheld nothing from me that could bring me to a better understanding of periods and incidents in Temple's life, and I cannot be too grateful for the tolerant courtesy with which he has met my importunate questionings.

It remains to offer public acknowledgement of the use I have made of Dr. George Bell's *Life of Randall Davidson*, that inexhaustible quarry from which the most persistent digger will never fail to extract accurate and detailed information on the period of church history which it covers; of the prolonged consideration shown to me by my colleagues the Residentiary

Canons of Lichfield Cathedral, who have magnanimously overlooked my necessarily frequent absences and absorption in the
work; and, lastly, of the ready help I have received from my
publishers. They have borne with my inexperience and the delays
caused by pressure of other work (as well as by several bouts of
ill health) with the utmost patience and sympathy, and to their
accurate and cultured staff I owe the avoidance of many of the
pitfalls that lie in wait for the elderly amateur who is suddenly
called upon to write a book. Of none of my dealings and doings
in the past three years shall I retain happier memories than of
my association with the Oxford University Press.

F. A. I.

INDEX

645

Index

Index

Index

652

Index

Index

Church's, alleged immoral use of, 583–5.
Prospect for Christendom, 434.
Protestant Party (in C. of E.), 181, 189, 217, 287, 351; outlook, tradition, 587, 608.
Psalms, the, W. T. on, 514–15.
Punch, 480–2.
Pusey House, Oxford, 89, 488.
Pym, T. W., Chaplain of Balliol College, Oxford, 1932–8, 377.
Pythagoras, 145.

Quantocks, the (Somerset), 375, 507, 620.
Queen's College, Oxford, 50, 60–72, 87, 96, 122, 126, 131, 133, 371, 456.
— — Musical Society, 67.
— Hall, London, 29, 30, 67, 220, 227, 228, 230–3, 234, 239, 346.
Quick, Professor Oliver C., 395.
Quickswood, Lord: *see* Cecil, Lord Hugh.

Rachmaninoff, music of, 30, 63.
Ramsbury (Wilts.), 270, 294, 508.
Rashdall, Hastings, 155, 488, 491–2.
Rawlinson, A. E. J., Bishop of Derby 1936– , 163, 467, 592, 609, 640.
Real Presence, doctrine of the, 492–3.
Reckitt, Maurice, 430, 434.
Record, the, 181.
Redemption, theology of, 607.
Redfern, L., 467–8, 470.
Redman, E., 170.
Rees, A. H., 574.
Reformation, the, 100, 181, 296, 330, 354, 485, 487, 489.
Refugees in Britain, 197, 565–6.
Reid, James, 461.
Reiss, Richard L., 339.
Religion and Life Movement, 312, 423, 582, 599, 616–17.
Religious communities, 589.
Representative Church Council, origin of, 234; relation to 'Life and Liberty', 229, 234–6, 357; meeting (1917), 244–5, 247, 248; (1918), 256, 257–61; and Enabling Act, 273.
Reprisals, question of (Second World War), 546.
Repton School, 135–6; W. T. appointed Headmaster, 77, 132–5, 147, 310; his work there, 16, 136–54,

157, 161, 201, 249, 261; links with, 3, 202, 371.
Reservation of the Sacrament, 189, 348–9, 353, 357, 493.
Revelation, Book of, 44, 174, 313–14, 315, 316.
— philosophy of, 532–3.
Rheims, Archbishop (Marmottin) of, 558.
Rhondda, unemployment in, 442.
Ribbentrop, Joachim von, 384.
Rich, Prebendary E., 464.
Richardson, Stanley, 546.
Ridgeway, F. E., Bishop of Salisbury 1911–21, 208.
Ripon, Bishops of: *see* Burroughs; Strong.
Robinson, Arthur, 455.
— J. Armitage, Dean of Westminster 1902–11, Wells 1911–33, 110–12, 116, 118, 120, 140, 491, 597.
Rochdale (Lancs.), 364.
Roey, Cardinal van, *see* Malines.
Rogers, Canon Guy, 455.
Roman Catholic Church, Roman Catholics, 106, 162, 311, 323, 351, 390, 418–24, 492, 563, 593.
Rome, in Second World War, 422.
Roosevelt, President Franklin D., 624, 627, 628, 631.
Rose, Alfred, Bishop of Dover 1935– , 598, 626.
Rotherham (Yorks.), 57.
Rowntree, B. Seebohm, 338, 340, 341, 342.
— Mrs. Arnold, 629.
Royal Commission on the Coalmining Industry (1919–26), 336, 337–8, 342, 343.
Royden (*afterwards* Royden-Shaw), Maude, 184, 232, 236–7.
Rugby Club (Notting Dale, London), 32, 34, 42.
— School, 132, 151, 224, 230; Frederick Temple's Headmastership, 2, 12; W. T. at (1894–1900), 4–5, 11, 12–36, 51, 72, 96, 269; his opinion of, 13–15; links with, 12–13, 60–1, 133, 135, 138, 152, 309–11, 557.
Ruhr Dams, bombing of the (1943), 544–5.
Rumania, Church in, 558.
Ruskin, J., 27, 86.

Index

Index

Temple, William (*contd.*):
375; ordination (1908), 96–123, 488; visits Australia and Ceylon (1910), 128–31, 392; Headmaster of Repton (1910–14), 77, 86, 128, 131–54, 155, 157, 158, 161, 177, 249, 261, 507; Rector of S. James's, Piccadilly (1914–17), 167–79 (cf. 180–238 *passim*), 243, 488; edits the *Challenge* (1915–18), 180–96, 198, 218, 249, 255, 311, 323; Chaplain to the King (1915), 261–2; visits U.S.A. (1915): Bishop Paddock Lecturer at New York, 178, 239; his marriage (1916), 197–203; work in National Mission (1916), 13, 88, 190, 191, 198, 202, 203–19; in Life and Liberty movement (1917–20), 170, 189, 193, 196, 217, 220–61 *passim*, 266–70, 272, 274–5, 361, 511; Proctor in Convocation (1917–20), 217–18, 239, 570; offered various posts, 261–3; Canon of Westminster (1919–20), 263–72, 322, 334; edits the *Pilgrim* (1920–7), 315, 316, 322–3, 445, 480; takes part in discussions with Free Church leaders (1920–38), 455–61.

Becomes Bishop of Manchester (1921), 282–95, 488, 513; his episcopate, 30, 84, 176, 296–359, 400, 489, 512, 597, 612–13, 614–16; leaves Manchester, 360–2, 364, 367, 508; his episcopate recalled, 365, 372, 373, 392, 451; chairman of Government Committee on Adult Education (1921–2), 293–4; President of North-western Section of W.E.A. (1924–9), and continues his work for it later, 311, 359, 370, 571, 599; member of Archbishops' Commission on Doctrine in the C. of E. (1925–37), Chairman 1927–37, 320, 370, 464–7; President of 'Copec' (1924), 328, 333–6; his action during the Coal Stoppage (1926), 336–44; his part in Prayer Book revision (1927–8), 347–59; at Lausanne Conference on Faith and Order (1927), 400–2, and serves on its Continuation Committee, 402–6; visits Palestine for Jerusalem Conference (1928), 392–8.

Becomes Archbishop of York (1929), 359–60, 363–4; his archiepiscopate, 57, 67, 138, 154, 176, 195, 202, 318, 359, 363–86, 452–3, 490–3, 495–8, 504, 506, 523, 601, 608, *and see* Chapters XXIII–XXVI *passim*; Chairman of Lambeth Conference Committee on Unity 1930, 459–60; conducts Mission to the University of Oxford (1931) and several subsequent missions to universities, 134–5, 377–80; preaches at Disarmament Conference (1932), 375–7; initiates enquiry into unemployment (1933), 441–3; revisits U.S.A., and lectures at Indianapolis, Washington, Harvard, Chicago, &c. (1935–6), 380–1; at Oxford Conference on Church Community and State (1937), 410–11; Chairman of Edinburgh Conference on Faith and Order (1937), 406–8; Chairman of Provisional Committee of World Council of Churches (1938–42), 411–13; first President of British Council of Churches (1942), 413–15; Convener and Chairman of Malvern Conference (1941), 429–34.

Becomes Archbishop of Canterbury (1942), 474–5; his archiepiscopate, 95, 173, 176, 400, 424, 458, 493–4, 495, 499, 504, 571–611, 616–23; work in preparation for Education Act, 1944, 557, 571–8; Chairman of Albert Hall meeting (1942) and takes part in campaign 'The Church Looks Forward', and 'Religion and Life' weeks, 578–83.

Last days and death (1945), 616–27; tributes to him, 627–31.

See also subjects such as Banking, 'Copec', Death Penalty, Economics, Education Acts, Pacifism, Student Christian Movement, War, Women in the Church, &c., *and pp.* 632–7.

His personal qualities, &c.: *see* Chapter XXVII, cf. 35–6, 43, 57, 58, 63–5, 417, 610, 618–19, 621, 629–31; his mental powers, 52–3, 476–7, 482–3; his theological development, 485–90, 605–11; as teacher, preacher, philosopher, and

660

Index

University College, Durham, 261-3.
— Extension Movement, 74, 76, 191.
Utrecht Conference (1938), 382, 388, 408, 411, 417.

Vaisey, Mr. Justice, 420.
Vassall, H., 137, 138, 141.
Vatican, the, 412, 419, 424.
Vaughan, W. W., Master of Wellington 1910-21, Headmaster of Rugby 1921-31, 149.
Venereal diseases, compulsory treatment of, 449-50.
Venice, W. T. visits, 381.
Versailles, Treaty of, 376.
Vestments, W. T. and, 249-50, 489.
Victoria Park (London), W. T. speaks in, 43.
Virgil, 16, 52, 53, 310.
Virgin Birth, doctrine of the, and W. T.'s ordination, 106, 109, 111, 112, 113, 115-16, 120; and *Foundations*, 157, 163; and Doctrinal Report, 465; W. T.'s mature views, 488, 491.
Vodden, H., Bishop of Hull 1934- , 373.

Wace, Henry, Dean of Canterbury 1903-24, 319, 597.
Waggett, P. N. (S.S.J.E.), 162.
Wagner, music of, 67-8.
Wakefield, Bishops of: *see* Eden; Seaton.
Wales, Church in, 172; *see also* South Wales.
Walker, E. M., Provost of Queen's College, Oxford, 1930-3, 122.
— Dr. Jane, 184.
Walpole, Sir Hugh, *Wintersmoon*, 393.
War, First World (1914-18), and W. T.'s career, 88, 193-4, 218, 266-9; his teaching on, 171-5, 177-9, 185-8, 192, 319, 541, 547; and National Mission, 204-7, 210, 222; and 'Life and Liberty', 222, 229-30; referred to, 299, 381, 408, 428; War Guilt question, 376.
— Second World (1939-45), W. T. and, 179, 385-6, 540-7, 549-68, 595, 596-7, 598-9, 618-20, 621, 622; the Vatican and, 421-3; and social reconstruction, 428, 429, 569, 585; referred to, 212, 412, 413, 425, 628.

Warman, F. S. G., Bishop of Manchester 1929-47, 317.
Washington, W. T. at, 380.
Watts-Ditchfield, J. E., Bishop of Chelmsford 1914-23, 189.
Weacombe, Lower (Somerset), 508-9, 620.
Webb, Professor C. C. J., 467.
— Sidney (Lord Passfield), 226.
Weinel, Heinrich, 69.
Welch, James, 556-7, 600, 621.
Welldon, J. E. C., 455.
Wells, H. G., 50, 186, 220, 259.
Wendt, H. H., 69, 70, 71.
Wesley, John, 100.
— S. S., 289.
West, Sir F., 362.
Westcott, B. F., Bishop of Durham 1890-1901, 337, 485, 498.
— F., Bishop of Calcutta and Metropolitan of India 1919-45, 593, 594.
Westgate (Kent), 623.
Westminster Abbey, 31-2, 130, 375; W. T. and Canonry, 149, 150, 261-2; as Canon (1919-20), 264-79, 282, 310.
Westminster Gazette, the, 89.
Wey, Dr., 395-6.
Whalley Abbey, 300, 302.
Whately, R., Archbishop of Dublin 1831-63, 475.
Whitby, Bishops of: *see* Woollcombe; Hubbard.
White, Fr. Victor (O.P.), 421, 533.
White-Thomson, Ian, 596, 622, 623, 630.
Whitehead, A. N., 528-9.
Whitehorn, R. D., 575.
Whitelaw, R., 16, 17, 22, 28, 135.
Wilberforce, William, 539.
Wild, H. L., Bishop of Newcastle 1915-27, 261.
Wilde, Oscar, 50.
Williams, Garfield, Dean of Manchester 1931- , 396.
— H. H., Bishop of Carlisle 1920-46, 291, 292.
— Professor N. P., 589.
— W. E. M., 623.
Wilson, H. A., Bishop of Chelmsford, 1929- , xii.
— James M., Headmaster of Clifton 1879-90, 149.

PRINTED IN
GREAT BRITAIN
AT THE
UNIVERSITY PRESS
OXFORD
BY
CHARLES BATEY
PRINTER
TO THE
UNIVERSITY